TORTS
in Ireland

EOIN QUILL

GILL & MACMILLAN

Gill & Macmillan Ltd
Goldenbridge
Dublin 8
with associated companies throughout the world
www.gillmacmillan. ie

© Eoin Quill 1999

0 7171 2832 6

Index compiled by Julitta Clancy
Print origination by
Carrigboy Typesetting Services, County Cork
Printed by
ColourBooks Ltd, Dublin

A catalogue record is available for this book from the British Library.

1   3   5   4   2

Contents

Contents

Contents

Contents

Preface

This is the first book I have written and my first acknowledgment must be to those who afforded me the education which enabled me to write it. Foremost among them is my family, whose support simply cannot be summed up. For my legal education and my academic career, I must thank the members of the law faculty at UCC during the 1980s, particularly the late professor J.F. (Seán) O'Connor, Dr Gerard Quinn and Pat Horgan.

Thanks must also be expressed to a number of others, whose support was invaluable during the years spent writing the book: to Catherine and Emma, for putting up with my stranger than usual behaviour and absences from home; to the law department at the University of Limerick (particularly Ray Friel, Paul McCutcheon, Henry Ellis and Mary O'Brien); to John Brennan and Ray Friel (again) for reminding me, in times when I ran into difficulty with aspects of the book, that since I meant nothing in the greater scheme of things, I should not worry about such difficulties and should just get on with it.

A general thank you also goes to everyone at Gill & Macmillan for converting my efforts into such a presentable text. A significant debt of gratitude is owed to those who waded through drafts of the material, with suggestions for improvement. Their input has made the finished text significantly better than the drafts. Any remaining flaws are purely my responsibility. The text sets out the law of torts, as I understand it, as of December 1998. Unfortunately, some of the 1998 cases could not be given the degree of attention they deserve and could only be noted briefly. Perhaps the future will afford me an opportunity to give them more detailed consideration.

EOIN QUILL
March 1999

Table of Cases

Table of Cases

Table of Statutes

Table Of Statutory Instruments

Table of Articles of the Constitution

Table of Conventions

Table of EC/EU Legislation

Introduction

What are Torts?

The law of torts embraces a collection of distinct causes of action, concerned with a variety of interests. Much of the subject is concerned with compensation claims, where the plaintiff is seeking financial recompense for damage which has been brought about by the defendant's wrongdoing. The damage may involve personal injury, damage to property, interference with economic interests or interference with other personal rights, such as reputation or privacy. The subject cannot, however, be equated with the concept of accident compensation, despite the significant level of overlap between the two areas. In many instances tort claims are used to support claims for other remedies, such as injunctions, which are not designed to compensate, but rather seek to prevent damage occurring or to compel the defendant to undo a wrong. Furthermore, accident compensation is sometimes achieved through branches of the law, other than torts, such as social welfare or contract law.

Tort claims are used in respect of harm caused by motor accidents, occupational injuries, professional malpractice, false statements, deliberate violence and many other types of behaviour which carry a risk of damage to others. It is the primary method provided by the common law for resolving private disputes concerning interference with civil rights. The subject eludes precise definition, as there are insufficient common features linking the various issues embraced by it, but one can discern its domain by examining some general features of the subject and contrasting it with other legal subjects.

At one time strong opinions were voiced on whether it was appropriate to describe the subject as 'tort' or 'torts', the former being preferred by those who saw the subject as a coherent body of law and the latter by those who saw it as a fragmented collection of discrete matters. Either term may be considered to be appropriate, since the subject has established a degree of common ground between the various causes of action which distinguish it from other branches of law, while retaining many of the distinctions between the individual types of action. The choice of term is a matter of personal preference and may be compared to the use of the terms 'body' and 'bodies'. A crowd of people may be seen as a collection of bodies or as a single body of persons; conversely, a single individual may be seen as a body or as a collection of bodies (focusing on the myriad individual components of which the person is comprised).

1

Functions of the Law of Torts

The law of torts, like so many branches of the common law, has developed gradually, over several centuries. It serves multiple purposes and has been influenced by many different and often conflicting sets of values. The law attempts to provide an impartial set of rules for resolving private disputes over claims of improper interference with individual rights.

Providing Remedies for Wrongs

The word tort is derived (via French) from the Latin *tortum*, which means wrong. This is not particularly helpful, however, as many legal wrongs fall outside the domain of tort law. Tortious wrongs fall into the sphere of private, rather than public, law. Private law embraces those branches of law which are predominantly concerned with relations between private persons (including corporate entities), such as contract, property and family law. Public law embraces those branches of law which are predominantly concerned with the functioning of the state (including relations between private persons and the state), such as criminal, constitutional, administrative and public international law. This division is somewhat fluid and there is some overlap between public and private law within the various branches mentioned. Furthermore, private law wrongs are not exclusively governed by the law of torts; they also include matters governed by other branches of the law, such as contract and trusts. Consequently, the domain of the law of torts is not easy to describe, but a useful start can be made by looking briefly at the ways in which it determines whether conduct amounts to a 'wrong'.

Wrongfulness is measured by different standards in the law of torts, each with its own area of application. The bulk of the individual actions require some element of fault on the defendant's part, before the conduct is categorised as a wrong. There are, however, a few situations where no fault is required; these are referred to as cases of strict liability, where the defendant's action is classified as a wrong simply because it has an adverse effect on the plaintiff. Strict liability has only a limited sphere of application at common law, most notably where a defendant is involved in a highly hazardous activity, such as the production or storage of toxic or flammable substances. There are also instances of strict liability created by the legislature, particularly in respect of defective products and some types of occupational injury.

Fault is measured by different standards for the various torts. The most common standard for establishing wrongfulness is negligence, measured as a failure to do as a reasonable person would have done in the circumstances. This standard is not subjective, i.e. the law does not equate negligence with personal carelessness amounting to a moral failure; rather, an objective measure, based on prevailing social standards, is used. For some torts even negligence is not a sufficient degree of fault to establish a wrong. Intentional wrongdoing is required in respect of some torts. Intent is also determined objectively and people are presumed to intend the probable consequences of their actions. In a small number of situations, wrongfulness is measured by a standard of recklessness, which lies somewhere between negligence and intent.

The choice of standard depends on the type of risk generated by the defendant. While the appropriate standard is well settled for most of the various types of tort action, the issue is still the subject of intense academic and social debate. Some people are convinced that legal wrongdoing is too easily established and hinders economic development, while others feel that the present legal standards provide insufficient protection to victims whose rights have been interfered with. There is no demonstrably correct measure of wrongfulness; everyone must form his own view and the law will only command respect where it reflects the views of a sufficiently wide cross-section of society.

The primary function of tort law is to determine whether a wrong has occurred and, if so, to provide a remedy. The dominant form of remedy is an award of damages, but the equitable remedy of an injunction is of growing importance as a means of dealing with tortious conduct. Other remedies are occasionally employed (such as orders for the recovery of property), but instances of these are rare.

Compensation and Vindication

The vast majority of tort actions take place after harm has been suffered and, consequently, most claims for redress are claims for compensation. The appropriate amount of compensation involves an assessment of both the harm suffered by the plaintiff and the extent to which the defendant's wrong is deemed to be responsible for bringing about that harm. All losses are not necessarily compensated; the law only compensates for those losses which are deemed to be the result of a wrong. Losses which are the result of 'pure' accidents (i.e. where there has been no wrong), or where the source of a wrong cannot be traced, will go uncompensated by the law of torts.[1] Furthermore, the level of compensation for torts will be reduced if the injured person has contributed to the injury by his own wrongful conduct.

Since most tort claims arise after harm has occurred, the immediate function of an award of compensation in a successful case is to vindicate the rights of the plaintiff, i.e. to provide a valuation of the rights interfered with, demonstrating their worth and providing some substitute for their loss, and indicating that the interference was wrong. Vindication of rights is an issue which is also of relevance to defendants; if a court rules that the defendant has not committed any wrong, then the legitimacy of the defendant's conduct is

---

1 Some of these losses may be compensated for by other methods, such as social welfare payments or the compensation scheme for accidents caused by uninsured or untraceable motorists, run by the Motor Insurers Bureau.

confirmed. In most instances vindication will be partial rather than total; for successful plaintiffs compensation may be less than complete recovery for all adverse effects and money may be a poor substitute for the loss caused (particularly in cases of serious personal injury); vindication may fall short for either party because legal responsibility and personal fault are divorced in modern tort law, so the outcome of cases may not correlate directly with the social acceptability of the defendant's behaviour.

Compensation and vindication, therefore, are of considerable importance, but neither is completely achieved. Each must yield to other facets of the law and the pragmatic limits of what any legal system can achieve. Full satisfaction of all social goals is impossible in present society, but modern tort law gives considerable priority to these two particular goals and attempts to reflect their importance in society as a whole.

Deterrence and Protection

A secondary function of tort remedies is to deter future wrongs. The ruling that particular conduct is wrongful, and leads to the granting of a particular remedy against the wrongdoer, may carry effects beyond providing vindication for the successful plaintiff. It may also serve as a warning to the defendant and to others that this type of conduct will not be tolerated and may clarify, for future occasions, the limits of acceptable behaviour. As with crime and punishment, the deterrent effect of tort law is difficult to gauge. There are many factors which will have a significant bearing on whether the outcome of a case has any real deterrent effect. Public awareness of the ruling is of critical importance: if others are unaware of the outcome of the case, then no lessons will be learned. Willingness to modify behaviour and fulfil legal obligations is another critical factor. Deterrence is more likely in well organised areas of activity, such as professions, than in diffuse activities, such as driving. Professional bodies are likely to take cognisance of judicial decisions in respect of professional practice and modify codes of practice in order to fulfil their obligations; conversely, individual motorists are unlikely to keep abreast of motor accident litigation in a bid to update their driving habits.

Deterrence cannot be relied on as a means of preventing future harm and preventive strategies largely fall outside the realms of tort law. Other mechanisms, such as public information campaigns or administrative authorities (public health or occupational safety inspectors, for example), are better able to bring about a reduction in the volume of accidents. The law of torts does, however, provide a protective role in limited instances. Some torts may be remedied by injunction, allowing a plaintiff to prevent further harm (in some instances an injunction may be sought before any harm has yet occurred). Prevention forms only an ancillary part of tort law as a whole and is not a central objective. In limited instances, however, it does take centre stage (mainly in cases where injunctions are granted).

Corrective Justice and Distributive Justice

There is a popular perception that law and justice go hand in hand, but this is not always the case in practice. Justice often has to yield to pragmatism, in order that the legal system remains functional. Nonetheless, the law must make some effort to strive for justice, if it is to command any respect in society. The problem with the search for justice in tort law is that there are differing conceptions of justice and even theoretical coherence can be elusive.

Tort law is predominantly concerned with corrective justice, i.e. it seeks to rectify wrongs. The paradigm tort case involves the injured plaintiff seeking compensation from the wrongdoer who has caused the injury. The object is to right the wrong, transferring the harmful effect from the plaintiff to the defendant, by translating the injury into a remedy (usually a sum of money to be paid over as damages). Only that portion of the injury which was caused by the wrong is transferred to the defendant, and it is the combination of wrongfulness and causing of harm which makes the correction just.

This paradigm situation presents a very individual process, with a one to one contest between the victim and the wrongdoer. One might then expect that justice between the parties would involve a straightforward contest between the individual interests of the two parties, so that the result reached should appear fair to both. This is not always the case, however. Tort rules usually involve a third dimension, in addition to the interests of the opposing parties – the public interest. Legal rules are not generally confined to considering what is a fair solution between the individuals before the court, but are overlaid with a consideration of whether it would be good for society in general to apply that solution to others in similar circumstances. The result is that a solution that appears fair as between the litigants can be rejected because of its broader social implications. Viewed in reverse, a solution which appears unfair can be justified on grounds of its social implications. Thus, even in a standard tort dispute, the ideal of corrective justice contains a conflict between individual and collective justice.

A more fundamental question is whether corrective justice is the appropriate objective to have. Should the law concern itself exclusively with righting wrongs in this individualised format? The main competing objective is distributive justice, which is concerned with dispersing the cost of harm as broadly as possible in society. Under this approach the injured plaintiff is granted a remedy against a person, other than the immediate wrongdoer, who is in a position to offset the costs involved by passing them on to others.

The best example of this is making an employer responsible for injuries inflicted by employees. If the victim sues the employee who caused the harm, a result based on corrective justice is theoretically possible, but the defendant worker may not have the necessary resources to pay. The result is that the plaintiff recovers little or nothing and in practice has not received justice. If the employer is made responsible (without having committed any wrong), the plaintiff stands a better chance of receiving compensation and the employer can recoup the costs by including them in the pricing of goods or services and accident costs are thereby dispersed into society. The practical operation of this process is generally modified through the use of liability insurance. The employer insures against the risk of being held liable for an employee's conduct; the insurance company, in turn, spreads the cost of accident compensation through the pricing of premiums for all of their customers and employers recoup insurance costs through the pricing of goods or services. Corrective justice is absent (or at least significantly diluted) in this solution, but the objectives of tort law can be better attained. First, the victim stands a greater chance of recovery (though it is still not guaranteed), satisfying the remedial function. Since a wrong on the part of the employee still has to be established, the role of tort in identifying wrongs remains present. Deterrence can also result, since the employer is likely to be in a position to influence working practices, so as to reduce the likelihood of further injuries. Also, the defendant is not unduly prejudiced, as the cost can be recouped.

Distributive justice, through employer liability and through the widespread availability of insurance, is a significant feature of tort law in practice. The rules of tort, however, are still predominantly formulated in terms of corrective justice. The tension between these two notions is apparent in many aspects of the subject and forms a central part in the critical appraisal of the law.

Torts and Other Legal Categories

Legal categories in the common law are imprecise and there is often a degree of overlap between the various branches into which the law is divided. Nonetheless, some progress towards an understanding of the law can be made by drawing some rough divisions, provided one does not treat the classification process too rigidly. The law of torts forms part of private law, which concerns the rights and duties between persons, as opposed to public law, which concerns the relations between people and government. In particular, it forms part of the law of civil obligations, which is usually regarded as consisting of contract, torts and restitution (though one might also include other equitable obligations, such as those related to trusts).

Tort and Contract

The classical distinction between contractual and tortious obligations, in vogue in the nineteenth and early twentieth centuries, was that contractual obligations were voluntarily created and defined by the mutual assent of the parties, whereas tortious obligations were imposed by law. This is no longer a satisfactory distinction (if it ever really was), since many contractual obligations are implied by law, irrespective of the wishes of the parties and voluntariness plays a significant role in defining the extent of many tortious obligations.

The central distinction is that contractual relations must involve some form of bargain between the parties; in other words, there must be an agreement between the parties involving an element of exchange (each must receive something in return for his commitment to the transaction). This element of bargaining, or mutual exchange, is not essential to tortious obligations. Tortious obligations arise because the conduct of the defendant poses a risk to the interests of the plaintiff; there need not be any reciprocal obligation on the plaintiff. Also, obligations in tort may be owed to strangers as well as persons in close relationships (a motorist must be equally careful not to injure a passing stranger or a passenger in his vehicle; a doctor volunteering to treat a stranger owes the same duty to the stranger as to a paying patient). The existence of some particular relationship (such as those arising out of contracts or trusts) may or may not be present, but this will only be one of a number of relevant factors to be considered in determining whether a tortious obligation exists.

The object of contract law is to promote the performance of bargains and, in cases of breach, to compensate the innocent party for loss of expected benefits, i.e. to give the plaintiff what was bargained for (or its financial equivalent). The objective of tort is to compensate for harm to existing rights or interests, rather than to fulfil disappointed expectations. There is some blurring of this general distinction in some situations. A party to a contract may recover compensation for injuries resulting from a breach of contract, which will involve compensation for harm to existing rights or interests, and a party in a tort action may recover some compensation for lost expectations. The distinction is useful, nonetheless, because these situations are exceptional; the predominant function of tort is not the fulfilling of expectations generated by bargains and compensating injuries is not the predominant function of contract.

There is a considerable degree of overlap between contract and tort and a sharp distinction is not maintained between them in modern common law. The two branches of the law are intersecting sets of obligations; there is a limited amount of common ground, where both branches are applicable to the same situation, but each branch also has a considerable independent domain, free of the other and with different objectives.

Tort and Restitution

Restitution is concerned with remedying unjust enrichment. The defendant is obliged to forfeit some advantage unfairly received. Tort and restitution approach private rights and obligations from opposite directions. In tort, the plaintiff has suffered a wrong, though the defendant need not have derived any benefit from the commission of the wrong; in restitution, the defendant has unjustly gained a benefit, though the plaintiff may not have been wronged.

There are possible situations of overlap, where there is a wrong committed by the defendant against the plaintiff and the defendant unfairly benefits from the wrong. Even here, however, there are differences between the two branches of law. Tort focuses on repairing the harm to the plaintiff, while restitution focuses on removing the unjust enrichment from the defendant. The harm to the plaintiff and the benefit to the defendant will not match each other exactly, thus each branch of the law will measure the obligations differently. Take, for example, a situation where a defendant wrongfully obtains information from the plaintiff and exploits it to make a profit in trading with third parties. The wrong to the plaintiff may be measured as the price that should have been paid for the information (e.g. royalties), whereas the benefit to the defendant is the profit from the ensuing transactions.

Tort and Criminal Law

There is a considerable degree of overlap in the factual situations governed by tort and criminal law, since the criminal law is the public law on wrongs. There are a number of differences in the manner in which public and private law deal with wrongs. Whereas tort law is concerned with the interests of the parties, tinged with aspects of broader public interest, the criminal law is predominantly concerned with public interest. This change in focus produces differing objectives for the two subjects, leading to both substantive and procedural differences.

Take a simple case, where one person has deliberately beaten another, causing significant injuries. Both a tort action and a criminal prosecution may ensue. The tort action is brought by the injured party against the wrongdoer (the state is not a party; its only involvement is through the fact that the judge is a public official); the criminal prosecution is brought by the state against the wrongdoer (the injured person is not a party to the proceedings, but may be involved as a witness). The remedy in the tort action will be an award of damages, payable by the wrongdoer to the victim and measured in an amount to reflect the degree of harm caused to the victim. The criminal sanction will be a fine (payable to the state) or imprisonment or both and will be measured in an amount reflecting the wrongfulness of the conduct.

There are a number of other significant differences between criminal law and tort. One is the degree of proof required to establish that a wrong has, in fact, occurred. The criminal law requires proof beyond a reasonable doubt, as a high degree of certainty is needed to justify the intervention of the powerful state apparatus against an individual. The civil standard of proof is lower, requiring a party to show a better than 50 per cent likelihood of truth in order to establish an allegation, so the more credible party carries the day (this standard is described as 'the balance of probabilities'). Furthermore, the determination of what actually constitutes a wrong differs between the two areas of law. A civil wrong only occurs when the conduct of one person impinges

8

on the rights or interests of another. Conduct creating a risk of harm is not normally an actionable wrong and pre-emptive civil proceedings, to prevent completion of the wrong, are exceedingly rare. In criminal law, however, the public interest in preventing harm is such that conduct which poses a risk to others is deemed wrongful in itself, prior to the occurrence of any harm to others. So, to drive at excessive speed or while intoxicated is a crime, even though nobody has been harmed; the same conduct only becomes a tort if the wrongful conduct results in injury to another person. The converse is also true; some conduct causes interference with the rights of others amounting to an actionable tort, but does not sufficiently concern the public interest to be branded as a crime. Many accidentally inflicted injuries would fall into this latter category.

This simple sketch shows that, although there is some common ground between tort and criminal law, each has different methods for dealing with the situations where there is overlap; also each has independent areas of operation, which do not concern the other.

About this Text

A few words should be said about the manner in which the law of torts is approached in this text. It is primarily addressed to the needs of undergraduate law students, though it should also be of use to students of other disciplines, such as business, who have an interest in a general awareness of the law on civil wrongs and to legal practitioners (by providing a fresh perspective). Because of its primary focus, it may appear overly technical in places to non-lawyers and lacking in detail to experienced practitioners.

Style

The text focuses on substantive rules of law and not procedure; in other words, it deals with the constituent ingredients of torts and not the mechanics of the procedure for processing claims. The dominant approach is descriptive of the legal rules and some of the social values reflected in those rules. A secondary aspect of the style is to provide an introduction to both legal reasoning, as it operates in the law of torts, and critical appraisal of this area of law. The descriptive approach is used in order to generate an understanding of the principal rules of the subject, on which readers can build their own understanding and appraisal of the law. The object is to provide the reader with sufficient skills to navigate the subject independently.

The main body of legal principles and underlying values of torts are distilled from the case law, statutes and leading academic commentaries. The focus is on Irish law, but material from other jurisdictions (predominantly common law) is also included. The comparative material is used, in some cases, for the purposes of identifying alternative approaches to issues; in other situations it is used to deal with matters which have not yet arisen in Irish law.

Given the size of the jurisdiction, there are many aspects of the subject which have not been authoritatively resolved in Ireland. Traditionally, English law has been the dominant external influence on the development of Irish law, but some significant divergence is now visible in the law of torts. Irish courts have consciously developed distinct principles, reflecting different values from our neighbours in some aspects of the subject. There is also an increasing knowledge of other legal systems, both in judicial decisions and in academic writings, and improved global communication makes material more accessible. The text draws on material from the United States, Canada, Australia and New Zealand to a significant degree. The comparative material is not intended to provide a comprehensive, up to date picture of torts in these jurisdictions, but merely provides a selection of materials whose persuasive value may be of benefit in furthering an understanding of the subject. One of the principal American sources drawn upon is the American Law Institute's *Second Restatement of the Law of Torts*, which is only of persuasive value even in the American jurisdictions.

The coverage of legal reasoning is necessarily abridged, in order to keep the size of the text within manageable bounds. The presentation of principles is a summarised account of the main rules of the law of torts, with consideration given to their potential application in novel situations. The reasoning process is sketched and the reader should turn to the referred sources for a more expansive treatment. There is no substitute for extensive reading of detailed legal argument to discern the reasoning process of the law and a textbook can only provide a general flavour of it.

Critical appraisal of the law is an important part of a legal education. This text identifies, in a very rudimentary fashion, some of the principal social values underpinning the legal rules and briefly mentions different critiques of the rules and some suggestions for reform. This provides students with a foundation from which to build their own critical appraisal; they have a synopsis of both the rules and the values which they attempt to reflect. Furthermore, detailed appraisal of the law is available to the reader by pursuing the references provided (the text provides a wide variety, giving the major competing views). Ultimately, critical appraisal is something one must develop for oneself; while the views of others can help to provide some ideas and perspectives, each of us has to form his own opinion and make his own value judgments.

The principles, values and appraisal presented in the text are not intended to reflect an entirely personal view. A neutral stance is attempted, though inevitably coloured in part by personal views – the selection of materials and the form of presentation necessarily entail some personal element. This text is designed to convey the core legal principles and values with the meaning generally accepted in the legal community and selects the main views from different schools of thought in disputed areas. It is an introduction, a rudimentary road map, from which an understanding and appraisal of tort law can begin; it is not the end of the road, but the preparation to allow one to set out.

The selection of material is focused on modern material to a large extent, though references also include many classic authorities and commentaries. In some areas there is a lack of modern cases and commentaries; the treatment of these is necessarily focused on older material, but the text does attempt to show the continuing relevance of these aspects of the law. The emphasis on modern material is not intended to denigrate classical tort scholarship and jurisprudence; it is designed for the purpose of introducing readers to the present state of the law and of legal thought.

Layout

The particular elements peculiar to each distinct tort are covered first (Part I), in order to demonstrate the disparate nature of the subject. This gives a feel for the substance of the subject in all its various guises, before moving to the general issues relevant to tort law as a whole, straddling each of the different actions (Part II). The coverage of the constituent elements of the actions includes issues raised by both sides, in order to give a rounded picture of what each tort embraces. To entirely segregate the elements raised by a plaintiff from issues raised by the defence would be misleading. The interaction between both sides of the dispute forms an important part of an understanding of the subject. Consequently, the list of elements for each of the torts includes one item ('lack of defence') which is not, strictly speaking, an element of the action. The rules are set out on the normal model of a tort action, with the plaintiff as the victim (or alleged victim) and the defendant as the wrongdoer (or alleged wrongdoer). In practice this will not always be the case; the dispute may arise, for example, by way of a counterclaim, where the defendant is actually the victim.

The first segment (Section A of Part I) deals with rather wide ranging torts, described in this text as 'umbrella' torts. This description is used because each action covers a wide variety of conduct and protects different interests, gathered together by a common factor. The first of these torts is negligence, where the behavioural standard applied by the law is the common thread linking the different situations covered by the tort. The action can be used to deal with situations as diverse as a traffic accident, a will drawn up by a solicitor which fails to confer a benefit intended by the testator, or defective workmanship in the construction of a building. The linking factor is that the defendant's conduct in each case unreasonably inflicts a loss on the plaintiff. The coverage of negligence is divided into a chapter on general principles (Chapter 1) and a chapter on their application to selected situations (Chapter 2). The coverage is considerably shorter than that found in leading texts; there are two reasons for this. First, many of the issues traditionally discussed in respect of negligence involve liability issues, which are relevant to all tort actions; consequently, they are left to the section on general issues in this text (Part II) and are only briefly noted in the negligence chapters. Secondly, many of the issues raised in discussions of negligence are repetitive, involving a repackaging of arguments from one context to another. This text focuses on a representative sample of the key issues, rather than an extended exposition of the myriad variations of their application. Students will, consequently, have to engage in supplementary reading of the sources referred to in the text, in order to gain a more detailed picture of the issues raised.

The other umbrella type action involves statutory duties, where it is the source of the obligation which provides the common thread (Chapter 3). As with negligence, a variety of fact situations are covered, including defective products, occupiers' duties towards entrants onto premises and employers' obligations in respect of safety in the workplace. Here there is no common behavioural standard; the link between the different situations is that the obligations are based on legislative measures. The chapter provides a representative sample of statutory obligations, rather than exhaustive coverage.

The second segment (Section B of Part I) covers the various torts, each with its own area of application and distinct interests, such as defamation, which seeks to balance the rights to reputation and free speech, and the trespass torts, which protect persons and property (both land and goods) from specific types of violation. It contains seven chapters (Chapters 4–10), each of which groups together actions with some common aspects. The coverage focuses on the main types of action, with a sketch of some of the others. The list of actions covered is not exhaustive, but covers enough of the subject to give the reader an understanding of the bulk of its terrain and the skills to navigate the remainder.

Next is the general section, covering issues common to all actions (Part II). It begins with two chapters dealing with miscellaneous liability issues (Chapters 11 and 12). These provide detailed discussion of several matters which have only been raised in outline during the discussion of the constituent elements of the various actions. The earlier chapters discuss the obligations imposed on defendants, whereas these chapters deal with important elements in converting a general obligation into a concrete claim for a remedy, such as causation of harm, proof, defences and time limits for bringing claims. There are then two chapters on participants. One deals with special rules relevant to particular parties, such as children, mental incompetents, diplomats and so forth (Chapter 13); the other deals with defendants who are responsible for wrongs committed by others, such as an employer's responsibility for employees (Chapter 14). The final chapter (Chapter 15) deals with remedies; the dominant focus is on damages, but other remedies, such as injunctions, are sketched also.

Finally, there is an afterword, which briefly seeks to integrate tort with the rest of the legal system. It emphasises the potential for reform and critical appraisal. Once readers have gained a knowledge of the principles of tort, they are in a position to evaluate both individual aspects of the law (which should be ongoing, throughout the reading of the text) and more importantly, the body of law as a whole.

PART I

Causes of Action

Section A: Umbrella Torts

CHAPTER ONE

Negligence: General Principles

Introduction

The tort of negligence is the most extensively used form of tortious action in modern legal practice; for this reason alone it would be a natural starting point for the study of torts. Its usefulness as a starting point is enhanced by the expansive range of situations contained within its scope, which will help to give a clearer idea of what a tort entails. The tort is not confined to the protection of any one particular interest or the regulation of any one particular activity; rather it affects many interests and activities – such as professional misconduct, motor accidents, occupational injuries, defective construction, the manufacture and supply of dangerous products and so on – leading to personal injury, physical damage to property or financial loss. The only connecting factor is the behavioural standard on which the action is based – a failure, on the defendant's part, to exercise the level of care which the law deems to be due to the plaintiff. The level of care required is expressed as 'reasonable care in the circumstances', though knowing how to decide which circumstances are relevant in a given instance and how to evaluate what is reasonable involve skills best acquired through reading cases and detailed commentaries such as journal articles and major treatises. A general textbook cannot hope to impart such skills comprehensively, but it is hoped that this text will provide a sufficient introduction at a macro level to equip students for the further pursuit of these skills.

Negligence only emerged as a specific cause of action gradually over the course of the nineteenth and early twentieth centuries; it evolved from a number of diverse forms of action which were dependent on proof of negligent behaviour, but there was no single form of action carrying the title 'negligence'.[1] The tort is unusual in a common law system because it is based on a broad general principle – that members of society owe an obligation to others not to injure them carelessly – from which the outcome in specific cases

---

1 For a discussion of the emergence of negligence as a separate tort see Winfield, 'The History of Negligence in Torts' (1924) 42 LQR 184; and Baker, *An Introduction to English Legal History*, 3rd ed. (London: Butterworths, 1990) at chapter 22.

is derived, rather than beginning with specific rules from individual precedents. Thus, the reasoning process used in its development differed from that normally encountered in the common law, a fact which can generate difficulties for experienced lawyers and students alike. In modern cases there has been something of a return to a more traditional common law approach, drawing on the authority of specific analogous cases.

The method in which the elements of the tort are presented here is designed to introduce the principal issues to students and differs significantly in style from the approach used by practitioners or the judiciary and even from that used by other academic writers. In judgments, for example, the several elements of the tort will often be mixed together in a discussion without any attempt to disentangle them. The difference in approach taken in this text, however, reflects the difference in objectives between an academic writer and a practitioner. A lawyer representing a client may be primarily concerned with obtaining a successful outcome for the client, while a judge is more likely to be focused on finding the correct resolution of the dispute presented by the parties. Academic works may have a variety of purposes; some will attempt a comprehensive statement of the law on a chosen topic, others a critical analysis of the law (perhaps with proposals for reform), still others an exploration of the relationship between various aspects of law or between law and other disciplines, such as politics, sociology or economics. This book aims to provide a statement of the main principles of tort law (not a comprehensive statement), while the structure is designed to show some of the ways in which those legal rules can be grouped for analysis.

This chapter attempts to give students the principal tools for understanding the tort of negligence by identifying the major principles on which it is based and an analytical framework through which these principles can be classified for the purpose of evaluating them. The next chapter then builds upon this foundation by looking at the refinement of the general principles into more specific rules in particular situations. Students should also look to other books and judgments on the subject to find alternative analytical frameworks, but should note that as there is no single coherent methodology designed for the analysis of negligence, reading different authors and judgments can generate a certain degree of confusion. One should not, however, be discouraged unduly by this confusion, as it is something that is faced by anyone attempting to understand this tort.

Requisite elements

1. Duty of care
2. Breach of duty
3. Damage
4. Causation
5. Lack of defence

This chapter concentrates on the first three elements, while giving an outline sketch of the last two, which are covered later. The principal reason for leaving causation and defences until later is that the issues involved are not peculiar to negligence actions, but are common to most torts.

Duty of Care

The legal liability of a defendant to a plaintiff is based on the defendant's failure to fulfil a responsibility, recognised by law, of which the plaintiff is the intended beneficiary. The first step in determining the existence of a legally recognised responsibility is the concept of an obligation or duty; this concept reflects the idea that the defendant is expected to behave in a certain way and liability can only arise if the defendant has failed to do so.[2] In the tort of negligence the term used is 'duty of care', reflecting the notion that the defendant is expected to take precautions against injuring the plaintiff. The concepts of 'duty' and 'liability' should not be confused, as duty is only one of the requisite elements for establishing liability.[3] A simple example will serve to demonstrate this distinction.

Example

Three motorists (M1, M2 and M3) were approaching a pedestrian crossing at which a pedestrian (P) was attempting to cross the road. M1 and M2 were approaching from the same direction at 100 kph, while M3 was approaching from the opposite direction at 50 kph. M3 stopped before reaching the crossing and P safely crossed the lane M3 was travelling on. M1 drove through the crossing, without attempting to stop, but did not injure P. M2 attempted to stop, but lost control of the vehicle and collided with both P and M3's vehicle, causing extensive personal injuries to P and M3 and destroying M3's vehicle.

In this case all three motorists owe a duty to P and to the other motorists to drive in a manner which does not put them at risk of injury (we need not concern ourselves here with the precise formulation of the duty owed). M3 has discharged his duty by driving with the appropriate degree of care, as his driving did not put the others at risk. M1 failed to discharge his duty, as he put

---

2   There is a long standing divergence of opinion on the nature of legal obligations. One view is that obligations only exist to the extent that there is a remedy for their non-observance; another is that the obligation includes a choice to comply with the law or pay for non-compliance as an alternative; a third view is that legal obligations have a value apart from the availability or effectiveness of the remedies provided for breach. The use of the term obligation in this chapter is based on the third view.

3   See *Restatement, Second, Torts,* St Paul, Minn.: American Law Institute, 1965, 1977, 1979, §§4 and 5 for a discussion of the distinction between duty and liability.

P (at least) at serious risk; however, M1 is not liable for any of the injuries/ damage outlined as he did not cause any injury/damage. M2 has breached his duty and thereby caused damage and will be liable, provided the appropriate steps are taken by the injured parties to recover their losses. Thus all three motorists carry a legal duty; two of them breached that duty, but only one is liable for the injuries sustained. It should be noted that the driving of M1 and M2 could also give rise to criminal prosecution, but that is a separate issue from tortious liability.

Modern tort law uses a general formulation of the duty concept for the tort of negligence. An early attempt was made to introduce this approach by Brett MR in the Court of Appeal in *Heaven v Pender*,[4] where he stated that:

> Actionable negligence consists in the neglect of the use of ordinary care or skill towards a person to whom the defendant owes the duty of observing ordinary care and skill, by which neglect the plaintiff has suffered injury to his person or property.[5]

He went on to describe when such a duty would be owed by saying that:

> . . . whenever one person is by circumstances placed in such a position with regard to another that anyone of ordinary sense who did think would at once recognise that, if he did not use ordinary care and skill in his own conduct with regard to those circumstances, he would cause danger of injury to the person or property of the other, a duty arises to use ordinary care and skill to avoid such danger.[6]

However, the majority (Cotton and Bowen LJJ) refused to accept the broad principle set out in the second quotation above;[7] nevertheless, it was later cited with approval by Lord Esher MR and Smith LJ in the Court of Appeal in *Le Lievre v Gould*.[8]

In 1881 the American jurist, Oliver Wendell Holmes (later to be a renowned judge of the US Supreme Court), put forward a general theory of liability in trespass and negligence, based on the view that the crucial element was a failure to act as a prudent man would have acted.[9] According to this view,

---

4   (1883) 11 QBD 503; [1881–5] All ER Rep 35 (Brett MR later became Lord Esher). For an earlier example of such a general formulation of liability in negligence see Baker, *op. cit.* at pp. 468–9 citing a practitioners' manual dating from the latter half of the eighteenth century.
5   *Ibid.* at p. 507; p. 38.
6   *Ibid.* at p. 509; p. 39.
7   *Ibid.* at p. 516; p. 43.
8   [1893] 1 QB 491 (Lord Esher MR and Brett MR being the same person).
9   Chapter III of *The Common Law*, originally published in 1881 by Little, Brown & Company; reprinted in 1963 by Harvard University Press.

statutory provisions and cases setting particular standards of conduct for specific situations involved the adaptation of this general concept to a concrete form appropriate to the situation under consideration. Though never stated in a precise formula, it is clear from reading the argument of Holmes that the concept involved was substantially the same as that expressed by Brett MR. The principle is formulated in the American Law Institute's *Restatement* as an obligation aimed at the 'protection of others against unreasonable risk of harm',[10] which is substantially similar in scope.

The establishment of the general principle in English law had to wait until the House of Lords decision in *Donoghue v Stevenson*.[11] Lord Atkin's formulation of the 'neighbour principle' is probably the most famous and respected formulation of the general concept of the duty of care.

> You must take reasonable care to avoid acts or omissions which you can reasonably foresee would be likely to injure your neighbour. Who then, in law, is my neighbour? The answer seems to be persons who are so closely and directly affected by my act that I ought reasonably to have them in contemplation as being so affected when I am directing my mind to the acts or omissions which are called in question.[12]

The first reported approval of this approach in Ireland was by Gavan Duffy J in the High Court in *Kirby v Burke & Holloway*,[13] relying on both Holmes and *Donoghue v Stevenson*. Since then the tort has developed, in Ireland, to a point where it is currently the most litigated tort (at superior court level at least) and the dominant form of action for accident compensation.

The general concept of the obligation contains a number of elements. First of all, there must be 'proximity' between the parties, i.e. a close connection; this may be a closeness in distance, time, relationship or some other connecting factor. Secondly, there must be 'reasonable foreseeability', i.e. the injury must be a consequence which a reasonable person would anticipate as a possible result of the defendant's conduct (the use of the reasonable person indicates that the analysis should be objective rather than subjective, i.e. based on the general standards of the community and not the individual perspective of the defendant). Proximity may also involve an objective analysis, because proximity is not just a question of existing fact, capable of scientific measurement. It also involves value judgments as to the degree of closeness which is required to create a legal obligation. These value judgments may be based on objective

---

10 *Restatement, Second, Torts*, §282.
11 [1932] AC 562; [1932] All ER Rep 1.
12 *Ibid.* at p. 580; p. 11.
13 [1944] IR 207; Gavan Duffy J, at p. 215, indicates that *Donoghue v Stevenson* alone would not have been a sufficiently convincing authority, but the neighbour principle was accepted in light of the fact that it conformed to the views expressed by Holmes.

standards, but need not be. If the two requirements of proximity and reasonable foresight are satisfied, then a duty of care is owed by the defendant to the plaintiff. This means that the defendant is under a legal obligation to take precautions against foreseeable risks to the plaintiff. Proximity and reasonable foreseeability, therefore, are central to establishing the existence of a duty of care. The next step in the process is to consider the standard of care placed on the defendant by this obligation. The defendant's conduct must be tested against an objective social standard – 'reasonable care'. The standard of care is used to determine whether there has been a breach of duty by the defendant. Thus, questions as to what is reasonable affect the examination of cases in relation to determining both the existence of a duty of care and the appropriate behaviour which the law demands of the defendant in order to fulfil the duty.

The general concept is translated into concrete form in individual cases by a reasoning process which attempts to decide the specific content of the terms 'proximity', 'reasonable foreseeability' and 'reasonable care' for the facts in dispute. For instance, in the earlier hypothetical case of the motorists and the pedestrian, a court might formulate M2's duty in the following manner:

Example

M2 owed a duty to P to drive in a manner which would not place P at risk of personal injury and owed M3 a duty to drive in a manner which would not place M3 at risk of personal injury or damage to his vehicle.

This formulation is specific to the manner in which damage was caused, but should not be treated as the only duty applicable to driving a vehicle. Driving may also give rise to liability to onlookers or members of P's and M3's family for psychological injury arising from the impact of the accident on them.[14] A decision based on the narrow formulation given above may establish no more than the fact that driving at 100 kph when approaching a pedestrian crossing constitutes the tort of negligence when it leads to personal injury or vehicular damage but may remain silent on broader aspects of the duty (as opposed to liability) applicable to driving. It is common for judgments to be framed in such narrow terms, even to the extent that where there is no liability the judgment may speak in terms of there being no duty owed to the plaintiff. Such narrow statements are probably better regarded as findings of fact rather than binding legal principles and so have little precedential value. The approach demonstrated in this example also blurs the distinction between establishing the existence of a duty and establishing a breach of that duty. This is a common feature of judgments in negligence cases; however, the two issues involve distinct elements of the cause of action and will be considered separately.

---

14   The duty in respect of negligently inflicted psychological damage is considered later in this chapter.

There is a tendency, in both academic writing and judicial pronouncements, to speak of the neighbour principle as a 'test' for negligence. The frailty of this approach is that it presents the principle in a manner akin to a mathematical formula, capable of providing a single correct answer in each case. In fact, in many instances, negligence cases raise complex questions of public policy which require value judgments to determine which competing interest should attract greater protection under the law. Before looking more closely at this issue we should first look at three major refinements of the neighbour principle, which have been treated as tests for determining the existence of a duty of care. Two of these were enunciated in the House of Lords, the third in the High Court of Australia and subsequently approved by the House of Lords.

The first is best expressed by Lord Wilberforce in *Anns v Merton London Borough Council*[15] (described subsequently as the two stage test), when he proposed the following approach to the duty of care issue:

> . . . the position has now been reached that in order to establish that a duty of care arises in a particular situation, it is not necessary to bring the facts of that situation within those of previous situations where a duty of care has been held to exist. Rather the question has to be approached in two stages. First one has to ask whether, as between the alleged wrongdoer and the person who has suffered damage, there is a sufficient relationship of proximity or neighbourhood such that, in the reasonable contemplation of the former, carelessness on his part may be likely to cause damage to the latter, in which case a prima facie duty of care arises. Secondly, if the first question is answered affirmatively, it is necessary to consider whether there are any considerations which ought to negative, or to reduce or limit the scope of, the duty or the class of person to whom it is owed or the damages to which a breach of it may give rise . . .[16]

This indicates that proximity and reasonable foreseeability create a case for the defendant to answer, while policy factors may be used to deny the existence of an obligation or to curtail its scope. This approach disguises the fact that the concepts of proximity and reasonable foreseeability involve questions of policy, since both involve value judgments as to whether it is appropriate to impose a duty. Thus, while the approach may seem pro-plaintiff, it really states that courts must balance the competing factors to determine whether a duty exists and, if so, to map out its content. This then is no more of a 'test' than the neighbour principle, as it does not identify what the relevant considerations are or what weight is to be attached to them. Lord Wilberforce's judgment does,

---

15   [1978] AC 728; [1977] 2 WLR 1024; [1977] 2 All ER 492. The approach had arisen earlier in *Home Office v Dorset Yacht Co. Ltd* [1970] AC 1004; [1970] 2 WLR 1140; [1970] 2 All ER 294. ·

16   *Ibid.* at p. 751; p. 1032; p. 498.

however, clarify our understanding of negligence cases because it acknowledges the practice known as 'judicial legislation' – the making of new law by judges – and indicates that the basis of such law making is the furtherance of important elements of public policy. Whether one supports or objects to this practice, a study of negligence cases should leave little doubt that it exists.

The second refinement is perhaps best summarised by Jones:

> The formal requirements that it now appears must be satisfied before a duty of care is held to exist are:
> (a) foreseeability of the damage;
> (b) a sufficiently 'proximate' relationship between the parties; and
> (c) even where (a) and (b) are satisfied it must be 'just and reasonable' to impose such a duty . . .[17]

This approach is virtually identical to the two stage approach, but is couched in more neutral language which removes the pro-plaintiff slant. 'Judicial legislating' is clearly endorsed by requiring the implementation of the courts' perception of justice in negligence cases. It should be noted that despite the apparent similarity between the three formulations of 'duty of care', the first two have been associated, in English law, with the expansion of the tort of negligence to embrace new situations, while the third has been associated with its recent contraction. This shows how subtle changes in judicial language can indicate significant shifts in attitude and may be regarded as one of the more perplexing aspects of a common law structure, since these subtle shifts may be detected by experienced lawyers, while being missed by students, lay people or lawyers from a civil law background. Detecting such shifts may be described as a 'feel' for the law and represents something of an intuitive appreciation of the law, which defies concrete expression.

The third approach, which may be described as the incremental approach, involves a more explicit constraint upon the development of liability in negligence. This approach requires the development of negligence liability in

---

17 Jones, *Textbook on Torts*, 5th ed. (London: Blackstone, 1996) at p. 30; judicial expressions of this approach can be found in *Smith v Eric S. Bush* [1990] 1 AC 831; [1989] 2 WLR 790; [1989] 2 All ER 514, per Lord Griffiths at p. 865; p. 816; p. 536 (HL) and *Caparo Industries plc v Dickman* [1990] 2 AC 605; [1990] 2 WLR 358; [1990] 1 All ER 568, per Lord Bridge at pp. 617–18; p. 365; p. 574 (HL). Lord Bridge went on to say, however, that the 'concepts of proximity and fairness . . . are not susceptible of any such precise definition as would be necessary to give them utility as practical tests . . .' The 'just and reasonable' formula was in evidence for some years prior to this particular formulation of the duty of care concept, see *Governors of the Peabody Donation Fund v Sir Lindsay Parkinson & Co.* [1985] AC 210; [1984] 3 WLR 953; [1984] 3 All ER 529, per Lord Keith at p. 241; p. 960; p. 534 (with whom the other four members of the court agreed) (HL).

novel situations by analogy to existing categories of cases. While this seems sensible enough, a rigorous application would effectively deny the existence of any general principle as a foundation for negligence liability: there would only be distinct categories of cases where a duty of care exists. While analogy to existing cases is a useful tool for examining new situations, exalting it to being the only mechanism for doing so would considerably reduce the flexibility of the tort and constrain its development. The incremental approach was postulated by Brennan J in *Sutherland Shire Council v Heyman*[18] and endorsed by members of the House of Lords on a number of occasions.[19] The Irish Supreme Court has expressly rejected the incremental approach in *Ward v McMaster*,[20] expressing a preference for a more general approach and the maintenance of flexibility.

The development of negligence in Ireland since *Kirby v Burke & Holloway* has been greatly influenced by English law on the subject. Although Gavan Duffy J, in *Kirby*, relied more on the American jurist, Holmes, than *Donoghue v Stevenson*, subsequent development shows little evidence of reliance on American material. The most significant divergence between Irish and English law on this subject has been the reluctance of the Irish courts, since the mid 1980s, to follow the English courts in contracting the scope of the tort. In relation to the general formulation of the duty principle, the superior courts in Ireland have not sought to refine the concept beyond the constituent elements of proximity, foreseeability and public policy.[21] This is borne out in the

---

18 (1985) 60 ALR 1.
19 See for example the judgment of the Privy Council in *Yuen Kun-yeu v AG of Hong Kong* [1988] AC 175; [1987] 3 WLR 776; [1987] 2 All ER 705, delivered by Lord Keith; Lord Bridge and Lord Roskill in *Caparo Industries plc v Dickman* [1990] 2 AC 605; [1990] 2 WLR 358; [1990] 1 All ER 568; Lord Keith in *Murphy v Brentwood District Council* [1991] 1 AC 378; [1990] 3 WLR 414; [1990] 2 All ER 908 (with whom the other six members of the House agreed); see also Howarth, *Textbook on Tort* (London: Butterworths, 1995) at pp. 26–32, on the resistance to generality in English law.
20 [1988] IR 337; [1989] ILRM 400, at p. 347; p. 407 per McCarthy J, with whom Finlay CJ and Walsh and Griffin JJ agreed. The incremental approach has not found support generally in the High Court of Australia, despite the efforts of Brennan J; see Trindade & Cane, *The Law of Torts in Australia*, 2nd ed. (Melbourne: Oxford University Press, 1993), pp. 328–9; for detailed analysis of incremental development see Dolding & Mullender, 'Tort Law, Incrementalism and the House of Lords' (1996) 47 NILQ 12.
21 The two stage approach and the 'just and reasonable' formula are occasionally referred to, but they are not used for changing the general trend in negligence decisions. For some examples of the approach taken in Ireland see *Ward v McMaster* [1988] IR 337; [1989] ILRM 400; *Sweeney v Duggan* [1991] 2 IR 274 (HC); unrep. SC, 14 February 1997; *John C. Doherty Timber Ltd v Drogheda Harbour Commissioners* [1993] 1 IR 315; [1993] ILRM 401, discussed in Byrne & Binchy, *Annual Review of Irish Law 1992* at pp. 552–3; *Gorey v Gorey* unrep.

judgment of Costello P, in *HMW v Ireland*:[22]

> The view of the Irish courts has been that *Anns* was a 'confirmation' of the long established principles of the law of tort contained in *Donoghue v Stevenson* and was not (as some commentators in England seem to consider) a major innovation in the law of tort.

Another instructive judicial comment on the nature of the various approaches to the question of duty is that of Cooke P:

> A broad two-stage approach or any other approach is only a framework, a more or less methodical way of tackling a problem. How it is formulated should not matter in the end. Ultimately the exercise can only be a balancing one and the important object is that all relevant factors be weighed. There is no escape from the truth that, whatever formula be used, the outcome in a grey area case has to be determined by judicial judgment. Formulae can help to organise thinking but they cannot provide answers.[23]

The primary consequence of having a general conception of the duty of care concept is that the boundaries of the tort of negligence are somewhat fluid, allowing courts to extend its scope when faced with new situations or to contract its scope when it is seen to lead to injustice.[24] The existence of a duty has been established for many of the more frequent situations which give rise to accidental injury; consequently, modern cases usually address the question of whether a duty exists in problem areas, such as misstatement, economic loss, psychological injury or the review of existing authorities. The refinements on the neighbour principle highlight the fact that the basis for expanding or contracting the boundaries of the tort of negligence is the judicial consideration of public policy, which allows the law to develop with changing views of what is just. Students should consider for themselves the advantages and disadvantages of such an approach after studying the development of the tort in more detail.

HC, 10 June 1993 at p. 12; *Convery v Dublin County Council* [1996] 3 IR 156, per Keane J; *McShane Wholesale Fruit & Vegetables Ltd v Johnston Haulage Co. Ltd* [1997] 1 ILRM 86 at p. 88; see also Byrne & Binchy, *Annual Review of Irish Law 1991*, pp. 386–7; 1990, pp. 510–13.

22 [1997] 2 IR 142; see also Gaughran, 'Tort, Public Policy and the Protection of Constitutional Rights' (1998) 16 ILT 88.

23 *Mortensen v Laing* [1992] 2 NZLR 282; see also Trindade & Cane, *op. cit.* at pp. 330–1.

24 See Byrne & McCutcheon, *The Irish Legal System*, 3rd ed. (Dublin: Butterworths, 1996) at chapter 12 on the operation of the doctrine of precedent and the judicial capacity for developing the law; see also Manchester et al., *Exploring the Law* (London: Sweet & Maxwell, 1996) at chapter 1; Zander, *The Law Making Process*, 4th ed. (London: Butterworths, 1994) at chapter 7.

Classification of Conduct

Negligence cases have developed two major distinctions in the classification of defendants' conduct – that between acts and omissions and that between physical conduct and statements. The application of the neighbour principle to omissions and statements involves some adaptation of the requirements for a duty of care to the specific context of the conduct in question. This adaptation tends to set the two areas apart from 'ordinary' negligence cases and gives rise to a cautious approach to the imposition of a duty of care.

Acts and Omissions

In principle, acts and omissions are easily distinguished – acts involve positive steps on the defendant's part which pose a risk to the plaintiff, while omissions involve a danger to the plaintiff which the defendant could avert but has not done so. Imposing a duty for acts involves no more than requiring people to consider others when acting, while imposing a duty in respect of omissions requires people to intervene to protect others. The latter (often referred to as an affirmative duty) is a greater constraint upon the defendant's personal liberty and common law jurisdictions have been cautious in imposing such constraints. The distinction is amply demonstrated by the approach adopted in the American Law Institute's *Second Restatement of the Law of Torts*:

§284. Negligent Conduct; Act or Failure to Act

Negligent conduct may be either:
(a) an act which the actor as a reasonable man should recognize as involving an unreasonable risk of causing an invasion of an interest of another, or
(b) a failure to do an act which is necessary for the protection or assistance of another and which the actor is under a duty to do.

Later sections instance the manner in which affirmative duties are imposed.[25] This clearly indicates that the general duty of care formula should be applied to acts, while more constrained principles should apply to omissions. This is significantly different from saying that the same formulation of duty applies to both acts and omissions, but allowing the fact that conduct was omissive to be one of the circumstances to be taken into account.

On closer examination, the dividing line between acts and omissions is less clear, as there is a considerable amount of conduct which involves both; e.g. in the earlier example of the motoring incident, M2's conduct can be classified as a positive act (driving) or an omission (failing to apply the brakes in time). In

---

25   §§314–324A.

a situation like this it is clear that a duty should arise and the defendant should be liable for the injuries caused and that the distinction between act and omission is irrelevant to the core issue of assigning responsibility. However, in more difficult cases, the distinction in the classification of conduct can become crucial to the outcome of a case.[26] It is clearly an issue of public policy as to whether one should be under a duty to act where an omission leaves others at risk. There are a number of situations where such positive duties have been imposed, for example motorists may be under a duty to exercise control over their passengers,[27] prison authorities to control prisoners[28] or occupiers to maintain their property in a safe condition.[29] The circumstances in which an affirmative duty to act for the protection of others arises (at least in Irish and English law) may be classified, in general terms, in four categories:[30]

  (i) where the relationship between plaintiff and defendant is such that the defendant is to be treated as responsible for the plaintiff's protection against the injury in question, e.g. parent and child, childminder and child;
 (ii) where the relationship between the defendant and the wrongdoer is such that the defendant should have interceded for the plaintiff's protection, e.g. motorist's duty to control passengers so that they do not cause injury to other road users;
(iii) where the defendant has created the danger – the duty here would be to take precautionary measures to prevent foreseeable injuries (this would be appropriate where the actual creation of the initial risk was not negligent in itself);
(iv) where the defendant has knowledge of a danger emanating from property under his control, e.g. an occupier's duty in respect of the occupied property or a motorist's duty in respect of the roadworthiness of a vehicle.

Some brief examples will serve to demonstrate the operation of this classification structure. The first category is where the relationship between the plaintiff and defendant gives rise to a duty to protect. This has been considered in two

---

26 See, for example, *Smith v Littlewoods* [1987] AC 241; [1987] 2 WLR 480; [1987] 1 All ER 710.
27 *Curley v Mannion* [1965] IR 543.
28 *Home Office v Dorset Yacht Co. Ltd* [1970] AC 1004; [1970] 2 WLR 1140; [1970] 2 All ER 294; *Muldoon v Ireland* [1988] ILRM 367; *Bates v Minister for Justice* unrep. SC, 4 March 1998.
29 *McNamara v ESB* [1975] IR 1; *Foley v Musgrave* unrep. SC, 20 December 1985; *Mullen v Quinnsworth (No. 1)* [1990] 1 IR 59; *Clancy v Commissioners of Public Works* [1991] ILRM 567; [1992] 2 IR 449; *O'Toole v Dublin Corporation* unrep. HC, 18 February 1994; see chapters 2 and 3 *infra*.
30 Adapted from the judgment of Lord Goff in *Smith v Littlewoods* [1987] AC 241; [1987] 2 WLR 480 [1987]; 1 All ER 710, at pp. 272–7; pp. 503–7; pp. 730–2; §§314–324A of the *Restatement, Second, Torts* provide a more detailed classification.

recent Supreme Court decisions – *McMahon v Dublin Corporation*[31] and *McKenna v Best Travel.*[32] In *McMahon*, the plaintiff seriously injured his fingers when swinging from a rope attached to a clothes-line pole. The incident occurred at a complex of flats, owned by the defendant corporation, in which the plaintiff resided. The Supreme Court held that the relationship between the parties was not sufficiently proximate to impose a duty on the defendant to make itself aware of the activities of children and to warn them against the dangers of such activities. O'Flaherty J, delivering the judgment of the court, noted, *obiter*, that any such duty to protect children lay with their parents. In *McKenna*, the Supreme Court held that a travel company owed a duty of care to warn its client of dangers at her destination. The plaintiff booked a holiday to Cyprus; the first defendant was the tour operator and the second defendant was the travel agent, through whom the holiday was booked. Both defendants were aware that the plaintiff intended to take a mini cruise from Cyprus to Israel and Egypt (she wished to book this in advance in Dublin, but this was not possible). During the course of this cruise, the plaintiff was injured as a result of civil unrest in Bethlehem. Barron J outlined the defendants' duty as follows:

> Although the ultimate responsibility for the safety of the tourists must lie with the tour operator, the travel agent must also familiarise itself with the conditions likely to be met by such person. Although the mini cruise was not booked through the second defendant, it was aware that the plaintiff and her sister intended to travel on it. In these circumstances, its duty was the same as if the tour had been booked through it.
>
> The duty of care in tort arises from the proximity created by the contractual relationship. The duty of care extends to all matters concerning the safety, well-being and comfort of the tourists which by the nature of the relationship between the tourists and those providing the service would or should be known to the latter but not to the former. The standard of knowledge to be attributed to the tourists is that of someone who having decided to go on holiday to a particular country, or area or place within that country, might be expected to have gained from advertisements or news items relating thereto. The standard of knowledge to be attributed to someone in the travel industry is that of the person on the spot providing the service.[33]

On the facts the defendants were found not to be liable, as they had no special knowledge of risk and, therefore, were not required to give a warning in this instance. The general principle is that a duty will be imposed in respect of

---

31 Unrep. SC, 29 June 1998; Irish Times Law Report, 7 September 1998; see also the *dictum* of Saville LJ in *Marc Rich & Co. AG v Bishop Rock Marine Co. Ltd and Others* [1994] 1 WLR 1071; [1994] 3 All ER 686; at p. 1077; p. 692.

32 Unrep. SC, 18 November 1988.

33 *Ibid.* at pp. 4–5 of the judgment.

specialist knowledge, which the travel company ought to possess. It is also clear that the duty is directly linked to the relationship between the parties; consequently, a duty to warn the public as a whole would not be imposed on travel companies.

The second category of case deals with injuries caused to the plaintiff by a third person under the defendant's control. In *Curley v Mannion*,[34] for example, a child opened the door of a parked car, knocking the plaintiff from her bicycle. The defendant driver was seated in the driver's seat of the car at the time and the Supreme Court held that he owed a duty to the plaintiff to exercise reasonable care in controlling the child.[35] Similarly, in *Carmarthenshire County Council v Lewis*,[36] a duty was imposed on a local authority to exercise proper supervision of young children in a school under its control. In this case a four year old child was temporarily left unsupervised and ran out of the school onto the road, causing a truck driver to swerve and crash.[37]

The third category places an affirmative duty on persons whose prior conduct has generated the risk. An example of such a situation would be where a producer releases a product on the market without being negligent, but subsequently discovers a defect or danger, as occurred in *Rivtow Marine Ltd v Washington Iron Works*.[38] In this instance the initial acts of the producer, in manufacturing the product and releasing it on the market, are not negligent. However, once a defect is subsequently discovered, a duty to warn customers arises. The producer's conduct in creating the risk generates the affirmative duty. The inference from the present state of the law is that the discovery of a defect in some other producer's product would not give rise to such a duty, though the author is aware of no direct authority on the issue.

The final category is where the defendant is in control of property from which the danger emanates. *Curley v Mannion* also provides some guidance on this issue. The duty of control imposed by the Supreme Court was expressed to be part of the general duty owed by motorists to other road users, arising out of the control of the vehicle.[39] The implication from this is that other affirmative duties may also be imposed on motorists, such as a duty to maintain their vehicles in a reasonable state of repair. In the case of dangers arising from the condition of

---

34 [1965] IR 543.
35 The case was referred back to the High Court to determine whether, in fact, the defendant had been in breach of his duty.
36 [1955] AC 549; [1955] 2 WLR 517; [1955] 1 All ER 565.
37 The driver was killed and his widow succeeded in an action against the local authority.
38 [1974] SCR 1189; (1973) 40 DLR (3d) 530; this issue is considered further in chapter 2 *infra*, in the discussion of products liability
39 [1965] IR 543, per Ó Dálaigh CJ at p. 546; per Walsh J at p. 549. The judgments make it clear that the duty to control a person and the duty to control the vehicle are distinct; the overlap between them in this instance is incidental.

buildings and land, there are distinct statutory principles applicable to injuries to entrants.[40] Where buildings and land are a source of danger to neighbours and passers-by, torts other than negligence may also be applicable.[41]

The distinction between acts and omissions is perhaps overstated by both academic writers and the judiciary, as most instances of pure omissions would fail to give rise to liability due to a lack of causation. Liability only arises where a breach of duty causes damage, and if there is no causal connection between the omission and the damage, the question of duty becomes irrelevant. Conversely, if there is no affirmative duty of care, the question of causation becomes irrelevant. The distinction between reasoning based on the question of duty and that based on causation is not merely semantic, because use of the former approach can affect the general nature of the duty concept in the legal system.[42] The courts have generally preferred to deal with the issue as an aspect of duty, rather than causation. Affirmative duties of care will be briefly reconsidered later, in chapter 14, where they will be contrasted with other forms of responsibility.

Physical Conduct and Statements

The effects of statements are, as a general rule, more difficult to establish and to control than those of physical conduct, at least in the context of financial losses – it is easy to envisage statements made to one person being passed on to others and being acted on in a variety of ways.[43] Thus, foreseeability is a poor mechanism for controlling duty, as the range of foreseeable consequences is almost limitless. As a result, the approach to negligent statements, causing financial loss, has developed in a manner significantly different from that to physical activity. Prior to the House of Lords decision in *Hedley Byrne & Co. Ltd v Heller & Partners Ltd*[44] the generally accepted position in respect of negligent statements causing economic loss was that a duty of care only arose

---

40 These are considered in chapter 3 *infra*.
41 Other relevant torts would be public nuisance, private nuisance (considered in chapter 5 *infra*) and the rule in *Rylands v Fletcher* (considered in chapter 6 *infra*).
42 For detailed examination of omissions in tort see Markesinis, 'Negligence, Nuisance and Affirmative Duties of Action' (1989) 105 LQR 104; Howarth, 'My Brother's Keeper? Liability for Acts of Third Parties' (1994) 14 LS 88; Haberfield, '*Lowns v Woods* and the Duty to Rescue' (1998) 6 Tort L Rev 56; Honoré, 'Are Omissions Less Culpable?' in Cane & Stapleton (eds), *Essays for Patrick Atiyah* (Oxford: Clarendon Press, 1991); Howarth, *op. cit.* at pp. 171 *et seq.*; for a general consideration of the analysis of omissions through causation see Frankel, 'Criminal Omissions: A Legal Microcosm' (1965) 11 Wayne L Rev 367; Epstein, 'A Theory of Strict Liability' (1973) 2 J of LS 151; Leavens, 'A Causation Approach to Criminal Omissions' (1988) 76 Calif. L Rev 547.
43 See the comments of Lord Pearce in *Hedley Byrne & Co. Ltd v Heller & Partners Ltd* [1964] AC 465; [1963] 3 WLR 101; [1963] 3 All ER 575, at p. 534; p. 150; pp. 613–14.
44 [1964] AC 465; [1963] 3 WLR 101; [1963] 3 All ER 575.

where there was a fiduciary relationship between the parties or where the statement constituted a term of a contract between them.[45] In the *Hedley Byrne* case it was established,[46] in English law, that a duty exists where there is a 'special relationship' between the parties and the maker of the statement can foresee the recipient's reliance on the statement, though the defendant bank escaped liability because their statement incorporated an express disclaimer. Thus, in order to establish liability in respect of statements, the plaintiff must show reliance on the statement, that the reliance was both foreseeable and reasonable, and that there was a special relationship between the parties. The 'special relationship' requirement reflects the need for proximity, while the reliance requirements cover causation and reasonable foreseeability. Reasonable foreseeability is relevant both to the duty issue and to the issue of remoteness of damage. Remoteness is considered separately and foreseeability in respect of duty does not raise any special problems in misstatement cases.

The crucial question is: what degree of relationship qualifies as 'special'? In *Hedley Byrne* the plaintiff company requested a credit reference, through their bankers, from the defendant bank in respect of one of the bank's clients. The purpose of the request was to determine the viability of a proposed commercial transaction between the plaintiff company and the defendant's client. This constitutes a sufficiently proximate relationship, but what of other aspects of banking? As a general rule, a bank owes no duty of care to the payee of a cheque,[47] but where the bank voluntarily proceeds to offer an explanation of its conduct, it may owe a duty in relation to representations arising from that explanation, as occurred in *TE Potterton Ltd v Northern Bank Ltd*.[48] In this case, the plaintiff company had received a cheque from a customer, drawn on an account with the defendant bank. The cheque was presented for payment, but the bank refused to pay, as the drawer's overdraft facility was insufficient to meet the total liabilities on this and other cheques presented at approximately the same time. A straightforward dishonour of the cheque would have alerted the plaintiff to the insecure financial position of the drawer, but the bank returned the cheque marked 'Refer to Drawer Present Again Alteration req's drawer's conf.' (requires drawer's confirmation); this was an apparent reference to the fact that one of the words was written in block letters, while the rest were in ordinary script.

---

45 *Candler v Crane, Christmas & Co.* [1951] 2 KB 164; [1951] 1 All ER 426; a majority decision of the Court of Appeal, Denning LJ dissenting. The dissenting judgment describes a duty of care substantially similar to the duty developed in *Hedley Byrne*.

46 Relying on a *dictim* of Lord Dunedin in *Nocton v Lord Ashburton* [1914] AC 932; [1914–15] All ER Rep 45, at p. 964; p. 58.

47 *Dublin Port & Docks Board v Bank of Ireland* [1976] IR 118, at p. 141 per Kenny J; *TE Potterton Ltd v Northern Bank Ltd* [1993] 1 IR 414, at p. 419 per O'Hanlon J.

48 [1993] 1 IR 414.

O'Hanlon J held that the explanation offered by the bank constituted a misrepresentation that there was only a technical difficulty in clearing the cheque, rather than a difficulty with the drawer's funds. In making this representation, the bank owed a duty of care to the plaintiff, as there was a significant risk of financial loss to the plaintiff if there was any delay in seeking proper payment from the drawer of the cheque.

The *Hedley Byrne* principle was approved in Ireland, shortly after the original decision, by the President of the High Court, Davitt P, in *Securities Trust Ltd v Hugh Moore & Alexander Ltd*,[49] where the relationship between a limited company and its shareholders was considered to be sufficiently close to give rise to a duty in respect of documents concerning the shareholders' rights; it was also indicated that no duty was owed to persons with a beneficial interest in the shares, unless their interest was known to the defendant. The range of circumstances in which a duty may be owed has developed significantly over the years, though the courts still tend to look for close factual analogies to previous cases in misstatement cases.[50]

Hedley Byrne has also been considered in a line of cases concerned with representations to purchasers of property by auctioneers and other sellers' agents. In *Bank of Ireland v Smith*,[51] Kenny J stated *obiter* that the relationship between auctioneer and purchaser was not, of itself, sufficiently proximate in respect of statements concerning the property being auctioned; an auctioneer would not be expected to anticipate that all statements made in respect of the property might be relied upon. In subsequent cases, however, a number of particular statements by auctioneers have been held to give rise to a duty. In *McAnarney v Hanrahan*,[52] an auctioneer informed a prospective purchaser of leasehold premises that the freehold could be purchased for approximately £3,000. In fact, the auctioneer had made no enquiries of the freehold owner as to the likely price. After the purchase of the leasehold the landlord sought

---

49 [1964] IR 417.

50 The development of liability in respect of negligent misstatement in Ireland is traced by Donnelly, 'Recent Developments in the Tort of Negligent Misstatement' (1996) 14 ILT 123.

51 [1966] IR 646, at pp. 659–60.

52 [1993] 3 IR 492; [1994] 1 ILRM 210; see also *Stafford v Keane, Mahoney, Smith* [1980] ILRM 53, action failed as Doyle J found that no representation had actually been made and, even if it had, the plaintiff was not the intended recipient; *Donnellan v Dungoyne* [1995] 1 ILRM 388, an optimistic press release and a brochure portraying a shopping centre in a good light were held to be acceptable sales techniques by the letting agent and were not treated as actionable misrepresentations; however, a firm forecast that all, or nearly all, the units would be let and trading by a specific date in the near future was sufficient to give rise to a duty of care; *McCullagh v P.B. Gunne plc*, unrep. HC, 17 January 1997; Irish Times Law Report, 28 April 1997, auctioneer assisting purchasers in obtaining finance held to owe them a duty of care.

£40,000 for the purchase of the freehold, but eventually accepted £30,000. Costello J held that the volunteering of specific information, of clear significance to the value of the leasehold interest, gave rise to a duty on the auctioneer towards the purchaser.

A more unusual example of a duty in respect of a misstatement is *Meates v AG*,[53] a New Zealand case, in which it was held that the state could be liable for statements made to business investors by a government minister, provided the necessary proximity, foreseeability and reliance could be shown to exist. More recently, the House of Lords has held that a former employer, giving a reference to a prospective employer of a former employee, owes a duty to the former employee, even though he is not the recipient of the reference, but its subject.[54] From these examples one can discern that it is more than the physical nexus between the parties that is relevant – one must also consider the surrounding circumstances, particularly the subject matter and objective of the statement, and the state of knowledge of the maker of the statement.

Cases in recent years have shown a high degree of judicial caution in respect of claims for negligent misstatement causing economic loss and the decisions have generated a degree of confusion as they often fail to distinguish clearly between the several elements of liability. The most celebrated case on this issue is *Caparo Industries plc v Dickman*.[55] The plaintiff invested in a company on the basis of, *inter alia*, accounts prepared by the defendants in their capacity as auditors of the company in question. The plaintiff alleged that the accounts were inaccurate and that this was due to the defendants' negligence and that it caused a loss to the plaintiff.

The House of Lords held that there was no duty of care owed by the defendants to the plaintiff; the rationale for this finding, however, was expressed in terms of a general approach to misstatements. The views expressed by the court involve a restrictive interpretation of the criteria in *Hedley Byrne*. The special relationship requirement was construed as requiring the defendant to have knowledge of the plaintiff either as an individual or as a member of an identifiable class of persons, while the foreseeability criterion was construed as requiring that the purpose of making the statement was connected with a specific transaction or type of transaction.[56] The disadvantage of such an approach is that it generates a further obstacle to all plaintiffs in actions based on negligent statements. There may have been valid reasons for excluding liability on the facts of the case, but to reformulate the entire duty concept seems an overzealous method for doing so.

---

53 [1983] NZLR 308.
54 *Spring v Guardian Assurance plc* [1995] 2 AC 296; [1994] 3 WLR 354; [1994] 3 All ER 129; noted by Allen (1995) 58 MLR 553.
55 [1990] 2 AC 605; [1990] 2 WLR 358; [1990] 1 All ER 568; noted by Martin (1990) 53 MLR 824; see also McBride & Hughes, '*Hedley Byrne* in the House of Lords: An Interpretation' (1995) 15 LS 376.
56 See in particular the judgment of Lords Bridge and Oliver.

A similar reformulation of the duty concept was evident in Ireland some years previously in Carroll J's judgment in *McSweeney v Bourke*.[57] The defendant gave financial advice to a group of companies which included, as one of a number of options for rescuing the group's financial state, the possibility of investment by existing shareholders. The plaintiffs invested more money in the group pursuant to that advice and sued the defendant for losses suffered through that course of action.

The judgment appears to indicate that where there is a duty to a client there may be an additional duty to third parties, but that once the primary duty to the client is discharged no liability to third parties could be established.[58] This would make the duty to third parties ancillary to and dependent on the primary duty (i.e. a form of piggy-back duty). While it may be that different degrees of precaution may need to be exercised in respect of the different parties affected by one's conduct, surely each party is owed a separate duty and the discharge of a duty towards one person should not be regarded as dispositive of the duty towards another.[59] On the facts outlined in the judgment, the decision to deny liability appears to be correct; however, the legal basis offered in justification is dangerously confusing.

A more orthodox application of the *Hedley Byrne* principle can be found in Lardner J's judgment in *Kelly v Haughey Boland & Co.*,[60] though the case turns principally on the plaintiffs' inability to establish sufficient facts to support their claim. The defendant accountants prepared audited accounts for a company over a number of years, and these were used by the plaintiffs in the course of a take-over of the company. The auditing process was improperly conducted, as the auditor failed to make adequate checks on the stock taking procedure, thereby departing from up to date professional practice. The plaintiffs incurred significant losses in running the company and sued the defendants on the grounds that the audited accounts presented an inaccurate picture of the company's financial condition.

Lardner J held that the defendants did owe the plaintiffs a duty of care, both in respect of accounts drawn up when they had specific knowledge of a take-over bid and for previous accounts where the company's financial state was such that a take-over was a reasonably foreseeable possibility.[61] Despite the existence of a duty and negligence in the performance of the audit, the plain-

---

57 Unrep. HC, 24 November 1980.
58 The judgment is ambiguous on the issue and could be interpreted as merely finding, on the particular facts, that any duty owed to the plaintiffs was discharged by the exercise of reasonable care in respect of the companies.
59 The linking of a duty between primary and secondary victims has been rejected by the Supreme Court in the context of rescuers, *Phillips v Durgan* [1991] ILRM 321.
60 [1989] ILRM 373.
61 *Ibid.* at p. 387.

tiffs failed to prove that the accounts gave a misleading picture of the company's financial condition; consequently there was no misstatement.[62] The accounts were not misleading because the errors were minor. Thus, the actual state of the company's finances and the position indicated by the accounts were substantially the same.

The contrast between *Caparo* and *Kelly* demonstrates two significant differences between the law in Ireland and England. The first difference relates specifically to the duty owed by auditors to potential investors, which will be considered in the following chapter in the discussion of professional negligence. In brief, the position in Ireland is that a general duty to potential investors is recognised, whereas in England a duty arises only in narrowly defined circumstances. The second, more general point of distinction is that the Irish approach to misstatement, as a whole, is more flexible than the English approach. The Irish approach retains the general criteria of special relationship, reasonable foreseeability of reliance, and other policy considerations. The English approach involves a constrained interpretation of special relationship and reasonable foreseeability and an underlying concern with the 'floodgates' policy argument.[63] This means that English authorities must be treated with caution, since the Irish courts may impose a duty of care in a wider range of circumstances.

A final point worth noting on the topic of negligently made statements is that in *Hedley Byrne* voluntary assumption of responsibility was regarded as the proper basis for the duty owed in respect of statements; this has been repeated in many subsequent judgments, including some Irish decisions.[64] This is, however, misleading, as it gives the impression that the existence of a duty is a matter of the subjective choice of the defendant to accept one. This is not so; the question of whether a duty exists is one for the courts to determine and the defendant's wishes on the matter can be only one of several competing factors and should not be dispositive of the issue of itself.[65] The only truly voluntary aspect is that the defendant chooses whether to make the statement or

---

62   *Ibid.* at p. 399.
63   The Irish judges are generally less impressed than their English counterparts with the floodgates argument; see, for example, Costello J in *HMW v Ireland* [1997] 2 IR 142 at p. 160, who describes the floodgates argument as being 'of doubtful validity' (the statement was not, however, made in the context of misstatement).
64   Carroll J, in *McSweeney v Bourke*, at p. 18 of the judgment, speaks of the defendant not undertaking any separate duty towards the plaintiffs; see also *TE Potterton Ltd v Northern Bank Ltd* [1993] 1 IR 414, at pp. 423–4 per O'Hanlon J; *McAnarney v Hanrahan* [1994] 1 ILRM 210, at p. 214 per Costello J; *Kennedy v AIB* unrep. SC, 29 October 1996, per Hamilton CJ at pp. 49–50 of his judgment.
65   This has been recognised in a number of judgments; see Ormrod LJ in *Esso Petroleum Co. Ltd v Mardon* [1976] QB 801; [1976] 2 WLR 583; [1976] 2 All ER 5, at pp. 827–8; p. 602; p. 22; Lord Griffiths in *Smith v Eric S. Bush* [1990] 1 AC 831 [1989] 2 WLR 790; [1989] 2 All ER 514, at p. 862; p. 813; p. 534; Lord Roskill in *Caparo Industries Ltd v Dickman* [1990] 2 AC 605; [1990] 2 WLR

not, much as a motorist chooses to drive or a manufacturer chooses to market products. In these latter situations we speak of the duty on the motorist or manufacturer as one imposed by law; similarly, the duty in respect of statements should be regarded as an imposed one. Prior to making a statement, one has a choice either to make the statement or to refrain from doing so. If one chooses to make a statement, there is a further choice either to include a disclaimer of responsibility or to make the statement without such qualification. The cases show that where the maker of a statement is possessed of particular skill or expertise, on which the recipient is dependent, then the making of a statement, without disclaimer, constitutes an assumption of responsibility.[66]

Policy Issues

Judicial decisions often involve making choices on matters of public policy. The rationale underlying legal rules reflects some social value or other and the promotion of one value may require another competing value to be overridden, or at least lowered in ranking.[67] The role of policy in respect of the duty of care can be either to determine whether any duty is owed at all or, alternatively, as part of the determination of the extent of the duty owed. A wide variety of policy factors can influence the duty concept and there will often be several competing factors raised in a case. The approaches taken in respect of omissions and statements are based on policy choices which are sufficiently clearly established as to be treated as matters of legal principle and the question of the fundamental merits of the distinctions rarely arises. Other policy issues vary in the strength of their position in the law and there are still many areas of uncertainty, where policy arguments can flourish. At this point, the discussion is designed to introduce the type of policy issues that can arise, not to determine the weight to attach to them. The list of policy factors is not exhaustive, but is a representative sample of the type of factors typically met in negligence cases.

358; [1990] 1 All ER 568, at p. 628; p. 375; p. 582; the issue is analysed in some depth by Cane, 'The Basis of Tortious Liability' in Cane & Stapleton (eds) *op. cit.*
66 See *Tulsk Co-operative Livestock Mart Ltd v Ulster Bank Ltd* unrep. HC, 13 May 1983; *TE Potterton Ltd v Northern Bank Ltd* [1993] 1 IR 414; *McAnarney v Hanrahan* [1994] 1 ILRM 210.
67 The role of policy in judicial decision has been the subject of extensive debate and analysis; see Griffith, *The Politics of the Judiciary*, 4th ed. (London: Fontana Press, 1991) at chapters 8 and 9; Bell, 'Conceptions of Public Policy' in Cane & Stapleton (eds) *op. cit.*; Stone, *Precedent and Law* (Sydney: Butterworths, 1985); specifically on the role of policy in negligence see Bell, *Policy Arguments in Judicial Decisions* (Oxford: Clarendon Press, 1983) at chapter 3; Howarth, *op. cit.* at chapter 5; Jones, *op. cit.* at §2.1.4.

Public Expectations and Reliance

A wide variety of services provided by public and private agencies and individuals generate certain reasonable public expectations as to the standard of their provision. These expectations would add weight to an argument for the imposition of a duty in respect of the performance of those services. Examples of issues affected by such expectations would be professional competence, manufacturing quality and accountability of public bodies. In addition to the issue of expectations, there is also usually an imbalance of power between the parties; the professional or manufacturer has special skills on which others are dependent, leading them to place their trust in the expert. A counterbalancing factor would be the notion that the legal standard in respect of the provision of services should not be so high as to hamper the services. Thus, for example, public dependence on medical services leads us to expect that there is a duty on doctors not to injure patients, but the need for such services also requires that the level of duty should not be so high as to discourage doctors from accepting patients.[68] This issue is expanded upon in the next chapter, where the application of general principles to particular situations is dealt with. In some situations the inhibiting effect of legal obligations may be so great that the courts will refuse to impose any duty; the advocate's immunity, discussed below, is an example.

Self-responsibility

This issue arises in a number of aspects of tort law and consideration of the injured party's role in respect of injuries sustained can be found in topics such as contributory negligence, assumption of risk and causation (discussed later). These topics deal with self-responsibility, where one has been partly responsible for causing one's own injuries, in addition to a breach of duty by another person.

Occasionally self-responsibility can arise in respect of the preliminary question of whether a duty is owed to the plaintiff, i.e. should the defendant owe any duty to the plaintiff, or is the situation one where the plaintiff should accept responsibility for himself, as a matter of principle, independent of any consideration of the causation aspect of the injury suffered? Should fire-fighters bear the risk of injury by fire or smoke, since this is an inherent risk in the type of work they are paid to do? A similar question may arise in respect of other dangerous occupations, such as soldiers and police officers. The issue also arises in respect of owners of property, since ownership carries responsibilities as well as rights. There may be certain types of risk against which the owner may be expected to protect, without assistance from others who are in a position to do so. A clear example of this can be seen in *John C. Doherty*

---

68 See *Dunne v National Maternity Hospital* [1989] IR 91; [1989] ILRM 735, per Finlay CJ at p. 110; p. 746.

Timber Ltd v Drogheda Harbour Commissioners.[69] The plaintiff had been given permission to leave a cargo of timber on a quay in a port for which the defendants were the statutory authority. The quay was also a public thorough-fare; no security personnel were engaged to protect goods left there and the plaintiff's goods were severely damaged when set on fire by children.

Flood J held that the plaintiff company should, as the owner of the goods, bear responsibility for the loss suffered, as the risk could be foreseen by them as easily as it could by the defendants. In the absence of a bailment, the plain-tiff's self-responsibility negatived any possible duty owed by the defendants. Bailment arises when the owner of goods entrusts them to the care of another person on a temporary basis and is governed by specialised rules of property law. Merely leaving one's goods on the property of another person is not sufficient to create a bailment.

Self-responsibility has also arisen in other situations. Cases concerning dangerous sports, for example, have produced some decisions indicating that participants must take a greater share of responsibility in respect of the risk of accidental injury than non-participants. In *McComiskey v McDermott*,[70] the Supreme Court held that a rally driver's duty of care towards his navigator was less than that of road user to road user, while in the American case of *Cincinnati Bengals v Hackbart*,[71] concerning an injury incurred during a professional football game, the federal appeal court opined that negligence principles could not be applicable as unreasonable risk of personal injury was an inherent element in the game; thus, once one chooses to participate, one has to accept responsibility for oneself in respect of accidental injuries.[72]

It has upon occasion been suggested that rescuers should accept responsi-bility for their own safety, at least where they are professionals and are being paid for taking risks, but the recent Supreme Court decision in *Phillips v Durgan*[73] indicates that there is a duty of care owed to rescuers. If a person negligently creates a situation which involves a reasonably foreseeable possi-bility of a rescue attempt, then a duty of care is owed to the rescuer, as well as

---

69   [1993] 1 IR 315.
70   [1974] IR 75.
71   (1979) 444 US 931.
72   Tortious liability would attach to reckless or wilful injury; *Condon v Basi* [1985] 1 WLR 866; [1985] 2 All ER 453; *Elliott v Saunders* unrep. QB, 10 June 1994; see also *Marshall v Osmond* [1982] 2 All ER 610, where Milmo J held that the duty of police officers to joyriders was less than that owed to other road users; contrast the view of the Court of Appeal [1983] 2 All ER 225.
73   [1991] ILRM 321; relying on the House of Lords decision in *Ogwo v Taylor* [1988] AC 431; [1987] 3 WLR 1145; [1987] 3 All ER 961, where a fire-fighter was held to be entitled to sue the person that started the fire; for further discussion on rescue see Byrne & Binchy, *Annual Review of Irish Law 1990* at pp. 493–500; O'Dell, 'Danger Invites Rescue' (1992) 14 DULJ 65.

the party initially imperilled. Similarly, soldiers are entitled to sue in respect of injuries resulting from the negligence of their superiors.[74] The fact that they are paid to engage in dangerous conduct does not mean that they are expected to accept all responsibility for injuries sustained through their employment. The particular nature of their employment does, however, give rise to special considerations in respect of the standard of care owed to them, which will be considered later. The duty owed to soldiers has recently given rise to public controversy, as a result of a large number of claims filed by soldiers in respect of damaged hearing.[75] The cases to date have not, however, led to any extensive consideration of duty and no novel principles on the existence of a duty have arisen.[76]

Responsibility for Others

Examples of this have already been met in the discussion of the distinction between acts and omissions. Two distinct issues arise here. The first is the extent to which a special relationship gives rise to a duty towards the other party; the other is the extent to which such a relationship leads to a transfer of responsibility, such that one person is made responsible for the conduct of the other. It should be noted, for example, that the law does not make parents responsible for the torts of their children, but does impose a duty to protect them. An employer, on the other hand, is often responsible to third parties for employees' tortious conduct and also owes a duty of care towards employees.[77]

Public Interest

Justice between the litigants is not the only matter of concern to the courts in addressing questions of duty: the broader implications for the community are often considered also. A typical example of this is known as the 'floodgates' argument – that if liability is imposed on this defendant it will herald a flood of claims which either will swamp the courts with unmeritorious claims or will bring economic disaster for people in the defendant's circumstances. Thus, a plaintiff's claim may be rejected on the basis that claims of this type would

---

74 *Ryan v Ireland* [1989] IR 177; discussed in Byrne & Binchy, *Annual Review of Irish Law 1989* at pp. 410–18; *Gardiner v Minister for Defence* unrep. HC, 13 March 1998.

75 In *Gardiner v Minister for Defence, supra,* Johnson J noted that 1,488 cases had been dealt with prior to that case; 1,405 were settled, without admission of liability; 51 were withdrawn or dismissed; 32 led to awards in favour of the plaintiffs. In *Greene v Minister for Defence* unrep. HC, 3 June 1998, Lavan J, at pp. 9–10, notes that 11,500 claims had been issued and the number was increasing at a rate of approximately 100 per week.

76 These cases will be considered further in relevant parts of this text.

77 These issues are explored further in chapter 14 *infra*.

lead to a growth in undesirable claims. This issue is raised later in respect of claims for economic loss and psychological damage, where the argument has been at its most prevalent.

A narrower public interest argument can be seen in *Marc Rich & Co. AG v Bishop Rock Marine Co. Ltd and Others*.[78] The third defendant, a maritime classification society, employed a surveyor to examine a ship which had developed a crack in its hull. He negligently advised that it could continue on its journey after temporary repairs were carried out. The repairs failed *en route* and the ship and cargo were lost. The plaintiff cargo owners recovered a portion of their loss from the ship owners under standard maritime arrangements. They claimed the balance of their loss from the defendants.

The House of Lords held, *inter alia*, that it would be contrary to public policy to impose a duty of care on the defendant society, as it was an independent, non-profit making organisation, whose sole purpose was ensuring safety at sea (thereby relieving state agencies of the need to conduct such work at public expense). The imposition of a duty would add both additional expense and complexity to the resolution of maritime cases and this was unnecessary, since existing contractual and insurance arrangements could provide the plaintiffs with adequate protection.[79] Here we can see the possible prejudice to a public service being used as a policy consideration. This policy issue, coupled with the fact that denial of a duty would not unduly prejudice the victim (who would still have recourse to alternative means of compensation), outweighed the fact that there was sufficient proximity between the parties for the imposition of a duty.

The Integrity of Other Legal Rules

Respect for existing principles of law can provide a policy constraint on the development of a duty of care, an example of which is graphically illustrated by *Leigh & Sillavan Ltd v Aliakmon Shipping Co. Ltd*.[80] In this case the plaintiffs suffered economic loss as a result of damage to a cargo they had agreed to buy,

---

78 [1996] 1 AC 211; [1995] 3 WLR 227; [1995] 3 All ER 307; noted by Feng (1996) 112 LQR 209; Mullender (1996) 4 Tort L Rev 9.

79 *Ibid.* at p. 241; pp. 251–2; pp. 331–2 per Lord Steyn, delivering the majority judgment. Standard shipping rules would have provided limited compensation, but Lord Steyn noted that the disparity between the actual loss suffered and the standard level of compensation could have been insured against. This is unusual, as courts normally disregard the availability of insurance when determining the existence of a duty of care.

80 [1986] AC 785; [1986] 2 WLR 902; [1986] 2 All ER 145; this issue was also raised in *Marc Rich & Co. AG v Bishop Rock Marine Co. Ltd and Others* [1996] AC 211; [1995] 3 WLR 227; [1995] 3 All ER 307; *McCann v Brinks Allied Ltd* [1997] 1 ILRM 461; *Madden v Irish Turf Club* [1997] 2 ILRM 148; *Trevor Ivory Ltd v Anderson* [1992] 2 NZLR 517; analysed by Borrowdale (1998) JBL 96.

the damage having been caused by the defendants. Clearly the situation was capable of being treated as coming within negligence principles – damage to property causing loss to someone with an immediate economic interest in the damaged property. But the situation was also one which conformed to an established principle, derived from the law of bailment, that only a proprietary interest would suffice to give *locus standi* in respect of damage to property. In the instant case the House of Lords ultimately chose to follow the latter and refused to extend the duty of care so as to encompass a buyer's economic interest. While the merits of the actual decision are debatable, it cannot be doubted that, as a matter of principle, courts have the right to deny the existence of a duty in order to pursue an existing line of authority, from another branch of the law, affecting the relations between the parties.

The proper boundary between contract and tort has been the subject of vigorous debate in both judicial decisions and academic writing. Regard for the integrity of contractual principles is sometimes raised as a ground for rejecting the development of the duty of care in negligence.[81] This issue came before the Supreme Court in *Kennedy and Others v AIB*.[82] The plaintiffs sued in both contact and tort in respect of the defendants' failure to advance money in respect of certain property transactions. Both actions failed in the High Court,[83] and the appeal to the Supreme Court was principally focused on the question of whether a duty was owed in tort and, if so, what was its extent? The essence of the plaintiffs' claim was that the defendant financial institutions, who had a contractual relationship with the plaintiffs, owed a duty either to advance the money sought or to inform them in advance that the money would not be forthcoming and to disclose the reasons for this (including the contents of an independent report that had been prepared for the defendants). The Supreme Court held that the existence of a contractual relationship between the parties gave rise to a sufficient degree of proximity to give rise to a concurrent duty in tort in respect of the proper performance of contractual obligations; however, the duty in tort was not more extensive than the contractual obligation.[84] In other words, the plaintiffs had a choice as to which

---

81 See Burrows, 'Contract, Tort and Restitution – A Satisfactory Division or Not?' (1983) 99 LQR 217; Holyoak, 'Tort and Contract After *Junior Books*' (1983) 99 LQR 591; Markesinis, 'An Expanding Tort Law – The Price of a Rigid Contract Law' (1987) 103 LQR 354; Fleming, 'Tort in a Contractual Matrix' (1995) 3 Tort L Rev 12; Cooke & Oughton, *The Common Law of Obligations*, 2nd ed. (London: Butterworths, 1993) at pp. 52–6; Somers, 'Contractual Barriers to the Existence of a Duty of Care' (1997) 2 Bar Rev 174.

82 Unrep. SC, 29 October 1996.

83 Unrep. HC, 18 May 1995, before Murphy J.

84 Unrep. SC, 29 October 1996, per Hamilton CJ at pp. 41–9, citing the following in support of this proposition: *Halsbury's Laws of England*, 4th ed. Vol. 3(1) §149; *Tai Hing Cotton Mill Ltd v Lieu Chong Hing Bank Ltd* [1986] 1 AC 80; [1986] 3 WLR 317; [1985] 3 All ER 947; *Henderson v Merrett Syndicates Ltd* [1995] 2 AC

form of action would be pursued, but this could not affect the content of the legal obligation. Hamilton CJ summarised the law as follows:

> The cases clearly establish that when parties are in a contractual relationship their mutual obligations arise from their contract and are to be found expressly or by necessary implication in the terms thereof and that obligations in tort which may arise from such contractual relationship can not be greater than those to be found expressly or by necessary implication in their contract.[85]

The Chief Justice went on to state that an additional undertaking of responsibility, under the *Hedley Byrne* principle, could give rise to a more extensive duty, independent of contract, but there was no evidence of such an undertaking in this particular case.[86] Consequently, once it was found that there was no breach of contract, there was no breach of any duty of care in tort.

Administration of Justice

Individual justice occasionally has to give way to the consideration of the proper administration of justice. This provides, for example, the basis of the advocate's immunity from liability in negligence.[87] At first sight one might think that a client's dependence on the advocate would justify the imposition of a duty, but actions by clients could undermine the administration of justice in two ways. First, holding advocates to an enforceable obligation towards clients would give losing clients a second opportunity to argue their case, undermining the finality of the original decision. Secondly, the advocate's input into the original trial may be tainted by a concern to insulate himself from a professional negligence suit by the client. Furthermore, the advocate has certain public duties, which distinguish him from other professionals. Costello P, in *HMW v Ireland*,[88] reiterating the views of Lord Reid in *Rondel v Worsley*, explained the immunity as follows:

> Lord Reid pointed out that every counsel has a duty to his client to act fearlessly in his interests but that as an officer of the court concerned in the

---

145; [1994] 3 WLR 761; [1994] 3 All ER 506; *National Bank of Greece SA v Pinos Shipping Company (No. 3)* [1988] 2 Lloyd's Rep 126.

85 *Ibid.* at p. 49.

86 *Ibid.* at pp. 49–50.

87 See *Rondel v Worsley* [1969] AC 191; [1967] 3 WLR 1666; [1967] 3 All ER 993; *Saif Ali v Sydney Mitchell & Co.* [1980] AC 198; [1978] 3 WLR 849; [1978] 3 All ER 1033; *Giannarelli v Wraith* (1988) 165 CLR 543; Carswell, 'Professional Negligence – The Sword of Damocles' (1997) 48 NILQ 197, at pp. 199–201, is critical of the immunity.

88 [1997] 2 IR 142 at pp. 158–9; the immunity was applied in respect of the Attorney General in this case.

administration of justice he has an overriding duty to that court, to the standards of his profession and to the public. A barrister must not mislead the court, nor cast aspersions on the other party for which there was no basis in the information in his possession, must not withhold authorities or documents which may tell against his client but which the law or the standards of his profession require him to produce. Because the barrister is required to put his public duty before the apparent interest of his client the public interest requires that on the grounds of public policy the barrister's immunity from suit be maintained.

The concern with the promotion of unfettered participation in the administration of justice and the existence of a public duty also applies to the participation of judges.[89] Witnesses are also able to claim an immunity; the level of public duty applicable to witnesses may differ from that of advocates and judges, but concern for free and unfettered participation justifies such an immunity.[90]

Advocacy at District Court level is usually conducted by solicitors, while in the Circuit Court and the superior courts, it is usually conducted by barristers. The immunity applies to the actual presentation of the case in court and to necessary preparatory work. It does not apply to non-advocacy work, such as giving advice on the legal implications of proposed transactions or the preparation of reports for clients' consideration.

Breach of Duty

Breach of duty involves two distinct issues; the first is the legal question as to the precise content of the duty of care and the second is the factual question as to whether the defendant has discharged the duty. The earlier discussion of duty was general in nature, but we now must look more specifically at the substance of the duty of care, i.e. what does the law expect from the defendant? The division here between the existence and content of the duty is necessary in order to identify the several elements that make up the concept of 'duty', but is not always engaged in by the judiciary or practitioners. On reading negligence cases one will often find both existence and scope of duty considered together as one issue, or, at least, discussed together without any significant attempt to separate them; furthermore, the 'scope' of the duty can involve multiple issues, such as the type of harm embraced by the duty, the type of conduct under scrutiny and the behavioural standard required to fulfil the duty. In those instances where there is separate discussion of the scope and content of the duty, the term usually employed to deal with the level of precaution required of the defendant is the 'standard of care'.

---

89 *Ibid.; Deighan v Ireland* [1995] 2 IR 56.
90 *Fagan v Burgess* unrep. HC, 25 March 1998.

42

Standard of Care

In general terms the law requires that reasonable care be taken to avoid injury to those to whom a duty is owed – 'reasonableness' being the crucial issue. The standard of behaviour demanded by the law is objective in nature. This means that persons who owe a duty are expected to live up to a general standard of behaviour, without regard to their individual ability to attain or exceed the standard. Thus, a motorist will be judged by the standard of the reasonable motorist, though his own personal competence may be greater or less than the norm. The law will, however, have regard to the circumstances and this may lead to some regard being had to an individual's limitations or abilities – a child will be held to a standard that can reasonably be expected of a child of his age and development; a person who holds himself out as having specialist skills in respect of the conduct under scrutiny will be held to the standard of the reasonable specialist. The standard is, nonetheless, objective in nature, as a solicitor, for example, would be judged on the standard of a reasonable solicitor irrespective of whether he was recently qualified or a seasoned practitioner. In respect of the allowance made by the law for a person's limitations, Holmes observes:

> There are exceptions to the principle that every man is presumed to possess ordinary capacity to avoid harm to his neighbors . . . When a man has a distinct defect of such a nature that all can recognize it as making certain precautions impossible, he will not be held answerable for not taking them.[91]

It may, of course, be negligent to engage in conduct when one knows of one's lack of abilities in respect of the proper performance of the task. In addition, it may be noted that no allowance will be made for limitations where the defendant has misled the plaintiff by concealing his lack of abilities, as where a person pretends to be an expert when he is, in fact, totally unqualified in the relevant field.

Some general factors can be identified as having a bearing on the level of behaviour expected in any given situation and an examination of these factors and their effects will help to clarify the manner in which the law operates. Before doing so, however, it must be pointed out that one factor which should not affect the issue is hindsight – it is always easier to be critical of others when one has the benefit of hindsight. What the law requires is that a person act in a manner that is reasonable at the time of acting, not what one would consider to be reasonable after seeing the result of the defendant's conduct.[92]

---

91 *Op. cit.* at p. 109.
92 For judicial comments on the danger of hindsight see Denning LJ in *Roe v Minister of Health* [1954] 2 QB 66; [1954] 2 WLR 915; [1954] 2 All ER 131, at p. 83; p. 923; p. 137; Kingsmill Moore J in *Daniels v Heskin* [1954] IR 73, at pp. 85–7.

Magnitude of the Risk

The nature of the risk generated by the conduct in question will have a significant bearing on the level of behaviour expected of the defendant in order to discharge the standard of care, though it will not be the only relevant consideration. The relationship between risk and the behavioural standard is directly proportional, i.e. as the magnitude of the risk increases, so does the level of precaution required of the defendant by the law. In other words, the interpretation of what is reasonable in the circumstances varies with the level of risk. Conduct which would be regarded as reasonable in a low risk situation may be regarded as unreasonable in a high risk situation. The magnitude of the risk can be affected by two distinct issues; the first is the likelihood of injury occurring, and the second is the extent of the threatened harm.[93] The same type of conduct can give rise to differing levels of risk, depending on the surrounding circumstances.

First consider varying levels of probability – driving a car in a busy urban area in the middle of the day gives rise to a greater risk of injury to others than driving at the same speed on a motorway at the same time, or driving in the same urban area at 4 a.m.; consequently, the degree of care required will vary such that conduct discharging the obligation to exercise reasonable care in one instance will not suffice in another. There have been a number of decisions where the courts have indicated that the low probability of injury occurring can justify a finding that the defendant's conduct has not fallen below the requisite standard.[94] Some risks may be so unlikely that they would not be regarded as foreseeable, but others might be foreseeable yet not have to be guarded against – the standard is one of *reasonable* care, not one of absolute care. It must also be borne in mind that some risks may be highly unlikely to materialise and yet need to be guarded against. Take, for example, a motorist overtaking another vehicle; if he overtakes when approaching a bend in a remote area with little traffic, the chances of meeting oncoming traffic may be extremely slight, but the risk is sufficiently real that the driver would be regarded as falling below the required standard of behaviour. The leading Irish authority in respect of the relevance of the likelihood of harm occurring is *Kelly v Governors of St Laurence's Hospital*,[95] where Walsh J explained in some detail the legal principle for assessing behaviour under the concept of 'standard of care'. The following extract gives the main thrust of this explanation:

---

93 See *Restatement, Second, Torts* §293.
94 *Blyth v Birmingham Waterworks Co.* (1856) 11 Ex 781; *Healy v Bray Urban District Council* [1962–3] Ir Jur Rep 9; *O'Gorman v Ritz (Clonmel) Ltd* [1947] Ir Jur Rep 35; *Bolton v Stone* [1951] AC 850; [1951] 1 All ER 1078; *O'Keeffe v Irish Motor Inns Ltd* [1978] IR 85.
95 [1988] IR 402; [1989] ILRM 437.

The duty the defendants owed to the plaintiff was to take reasonable care to avoid permitting him to be exposed to injury which a reasonable person ought to foresee. . . . In my view, it would not be correct to tell the jury that they must be satisfied that what has to be foreseen is a probability of injury . . . Undoubtedly the standard of care which might reasonably be expected may be sufficient if it is commensurate with the degree of possibility, but that is different from saying that no standard of care is expected until the possibility reaches such a high degree as to be classified as a probability.[96]

Henchy J addressed the issue concisely:

In my view the essential question is whether the risk of injury or damage complained of was such that a reasonably careful person in the position of the defendant would have taken the precaution suggested by the plaintiff.[97]

The second element of magnitude of risk is the extent or seriousness of the threatened injury. One of the most famous examples of this is *Paris v Stepney Borough Council*,[98] where the plaintiff, having only one good eye, was blinded by an injury to that eye. The House of Lords, overruling the Court of Appeal, held that the level of precaution expected of the defendants in respect of the plaintiff was higher than that in respect of persons with normal vision. A recent Irish example on this point can be found in *Fitzsimons v Bord Telecom Éireann and the ESB*.[99] In this case the plaintiff's husband was killed when attempting to move a fallen telephone cable, which had come in contact with an overhead power line. Barron J, relying on the judgment of Walsh J in *Kelly v St Laurence's Hospital*, held that, once there is a foreseeable possibility of harm, the standard of care expected from those owing a duty must be commensurate to the risk involved in order to be considered reasonable. As the risk here included the possibility of someone being killed, the behaviour required to discharge the standard of reasonable care was set at a high level and, although the manner in which the incident occurred was somewhat improbable, liability was imposed on both defendants. It would seem that liability would not have been imposed had there been only a risk of slight injury. Both of these cases show that the nature and extent of the injury which may result from the impugned conduct can have a significant impact on determining the

---

96 *Ibid.* at p. 410; p. 444; Hederman J agreed with Walsh J's judgment, while McCarthy J adopted Walsh J's views on this issue only (at p. 417; p. 451). Under section 1 of the Courts Act 1988 juries are no longer to be used in most personal injuries cases, but Walsh J's statement still expresses the legal principle which a trial court should use in determining the appropriate level of behaviour for the discharge of the duty of care.

97 *Ibid.* at p. 415; p. 448.

98 [1951] AC 367; [1951] 1 All ER 42.

99 [1991] 1 IR 536; [1991] ILRM 276.

standard of behaviour that will satisfy the test of reasonableness. It is also worth noting that the seriousness or gravity of harm issue can be specific to the plaintiff, as in *Paris*, or general to all those affected by the impugned conduct, as in *Fitzsimons*.

Social Utility of Conduct

Where the defendant's conduct is serving a useful social purpose this fact may serve to lower the standard of behaviour which is required to discharge the duty, so that obvious dangers, which would ordinarily have to be guarded against, need not be addressed by the defendant.[100] A classic example of this may be seen in *Whooley v Dublin Corporation*.[101] The plaintiff was injured when she stepped in an open fire hydrant box, which had been opened by an unauthorised person. The allegation against the defendant was that it had been negligent in using a box, the design of which permitted easy access, thus facilitating unauthorised interference by third parties. The purpose of having the box easily accessible was to avoid delay in dealing with fires. McLoughlin J determined that it was not possible to satisfy the social purpose of facilitating the fire service and protect the public against malicious interference; consequently, he concluded that the defendant was not negligent in failing to protect the plaintiff through the use of a more secure box.

Marshall v Osmond[102] also provides a useful example of the relevance of the utility of the defendant's conduct in determining the appropriate standard of care. In this case the English Court of Appeal held that where a police officer caused an injury through his driving, the fact that he was in pursuit of joyriders was relevant in determining the level of behaviour required. In this case the police officer's driving was held not to be negligent, though similar driving by a civilian for his own pleasure would, undoubtedly, be classed as negligent.[103]

---

100 See *Restatement, Second, Torts* §292.
101 [1961] IR 60; see also *Superquinn Ltd v Bray Urban District Council and Others* unrep. HC, 18 February 1998, at p. 65 of the judgment, Laffoy J held that local authorities and the contractors they engage are entitled to a degree of latitude in assessing the reasonableness of their conduct in carrying out necessary public works.
102 [1983] QB 1034; [1983] 3 WLR 13; [1983] 2 All ER 225.
103 See also *Gaynor v Allen* [1959] 2 QB 403; [1959] 3 WLR 221; [1959] 2 All ER 644; and *Johnstone v Woolmer and Others* (1977) 16 ACLR 6. Both of these cases emphasise that the duty on police officers, driving in the course of their duties, is to exercise reasonable care in the circumstances. The social utility of the conduct is a relevant circumstance and thus affects the level of behaviour required. The issue was considered in Ireland in *Strick v Tracey* unrep. HC, 10 June 1993, considered in chapter 2 *infra* in the discussion of road accidents.

Burden of Prevention

In some instances the burden of avoiding or reducing the risk can be balanced against the magnitude of the risk in deciding whether the impugned conduct was reasonable. For example, if nobody drove motor vehicles, people and property would not be damaged by them; however, the burden of a total withdrawal from the use of such vehicles would be socially and economically undesirable, and, consequently, the act of driving is not considered to be negligent in all cases. In this example the cost of preventing all injuries is considered to be higher than the benefit to be gained by such prevention and the standard of behaviour is not set at such a high level as to require a discontinuance of the use of automobiles. The cost–benefit analysis also works in reverse – where the risk is of great magnitude and the cost of avoidance is low, a failure to incur the avoidance cost is likely to be regarded as a breach of the standard of reasonable care. Economic analysis of negligence cases, using the law as a tool for the promotion of economic efficiency, has been more prominent in American jurisprudence than in other common law jurisdictions and even there it is by no means the dominant method of approach.[104] Cost–benefit analysis has a recognised role in the setting of behavioural standards outside of America, though it is less developed. In Ireland, along with many other jurisdictions, the courts will be slow to reduce the behavioural standard where the finances of the defendant are unable to meet the cost of avoiding the risk (if one cannot avoid the risk then, perhaps, one should not engage in the activity). In many situations, where the cost of avoidance is high, insurance may be available to offset the cost to the defendant of his liability to the plaintiff. When the reverse cost–benefit situation applies, the courts in Ireland are more willing to use the economic analysis as a ground for finding the defendant to be in breach of duty.

The cost–benefit approach suffers from three major deficiencies: first, economic values are not the only ones which a society may wish to pursue, particularly when the risk includes serious personal injuries; secondly, evidence of the relevant economic factors may be difficult to obtain, leaving the merits of the issue to be determined more instinctively; finally, the decision makers (whether judge or jury) may not be equipped to properly evaluate the evidence which is available, so that a fair result might not be obtained even where the necessary evidence is available.

Policy Issues

The role of policy has been raised earlier in explaining the duty concept. These factors can serve different purposes; some will be used solely to determine whether any duty exists, as in the case of the advocate's immunity, while

---

104 See Landes & Posner, *The Economic Structure of Tort Law* (Cambridge, Mass.: Harvard University Press, 1987).

others will be used to determine the standard of behaviour appropriate to the relationship between the parties, as in the balance between public expectation and reliance and the need not to hamper the provision of a public service. There is no specific formula for determining the correct weight to attach to each relevant policy factor; rather it is a value judgment to be made by the court, drawing on previous cases for guidance.

Hay v O'Grady[105] provides an unusual example of a policy issue being invoked to determine whether a duty had been breached. The plaintiff was injured by a psychiatric patient, who had been released from a psychiatric institution into community based residential care. Lynch J, in the High Court, took cognisance of government policy, which advocated greater use of community care,[106] in holding that the defendants owed no duty to the plaintiff in respect of patients' behaviour:

> This scheme, as I said, is a very good scheme and, I think, it accords with state policy that those fit for community living should not, as far as is possible, be locked away in large institutions for the rest of their lives. It is inevitable that there would be some failure with these clients who are referred to these homes. This does not mean that they should abandon the scheme, because it is a good scheme, nor does it mean that if an individual falls from grace, so to speak, because of some tantrum or other and [*sic*] that he or she must immediately be treated as forfeiting the benefit which has been offered to him, without giving him the opportunity to be retrained.[107]

Special Circumstances

A variety of special circumstances can affect the setting of the appropriate level of behaviour. We have already noted that the performance of tasks requiring special skills involves the standard of the reasonable specialist, rather than a reasonable lay person. Just as the profession of expertise can have the effect of raising the level of behaviour required, other factors can have the opposite effect. In *McComiskey v McDermott*,[108] for example, the plaintiff, the navigator of a rally car driven by the defendant, was injured during the course of a rally. The Supreme Court held that the standard should be that of the reasonable rally driver and that this was lower than the standard applicable to normal road use. These situations involve taking consideration of the nature of the activity in which the parties are engaged. While this involves a subjective element in

---

105 [1992] 1 IR 210.
106 The emergence of the community care policy followed the review of psychiatric services published in 1984: *The Psychiatric Services – Planning for the Future* (Dublin: Stationery Office, 1984).
107 [1992] 1 IR 210 at p. 215 (quoted by McCarthy J, delivering the Supreme Court decision).
108 [1974] IR 75.

the setting of the appropriate level of behaviour, the degree of subjectivity is slight and its exclusion would run counter to prevalent notions of fairness.

There are other cases where the subjective element is even greater, as in *McKevitt v Ireland*[109] and *Kelly v St Laurence's Hospital*.[110] In the former case negligence was alleged against the police in respect of their care of the plaintiff following his arrest. The Supreme Court held that the police officers' knowledge of the plaintiff's drunkenness, and the consequent increase in the likelihood of his causing damage to himself or others, was a relevant factor to be used in determining the appropriate level of behaviour to be expected of them. In the latter case the plaintiff was in hospital for the purpose of determining the cause of certain aspects of his behaviour, which were abnormal. The Supreme Court found the defendant hospital's knowledge to be relevant to determining the appropriate level of behaviour to be expected in caring for the plaintiff. In these cases the subjective element appears greater, involving consideration of the defendants' actual knowledge of the plaintiffs' conditions. However, in the absence of actual knowledge, a defendant could still be found to be in breach of his duty where he ought to have known of the plaintiff's condition. In this latter scenario the subjective element relates to the plaintiff's condition, but since it is the defendant's conduct which is the subject of scrutiny there is no compromise of the objective nature of the examination.

Another example arose in *Ryan v Ireland*,[111] where the Supreme Court held that the application of the standard of care to the duty owed to soldiers would have to take account of the nature of the work. The position was set out by Finlay CJ as follows:

> In broadest terms the duty can be stated to be to take such care for the safety of the plaintiff as is reasonable in all the circumstances of their relationship and the activity in which they were engaged. Quite clearly those circumstances in this case are unusual for they are the circumstances of military service in which the carrying out of the task allotted to the forces concerned could involve an unavoidable risk of death or serious injury. In such situations considerations of standards of care drawn from the experience of the workplace may be of little assistance. There could, I think, be no objective in a master and servant relationship which would justify exposing the servant to risk of serious injury or death other than the saving of life itself. In the execution of military service exposing a soldier to such risk may often be justified by the nature of the task committed to the forces concerned. Furthermore, there can, in relation to armed conflict, be many situations where those in authority must make swift decisions in effect in the agony of the moment. Mere proof of error in such decisions would not of itself establish negligence. Importance may be attached, I am satisfied, in

---

109 [1987] ILRM 541.
110 [1988] IR 402; [1989] ILRM 437.
111 [1989] IR 177.

regard to alleged negligence in a military situation, to the question as to whether the role of the soldier at the time of the alleged negligence is one of attack or defence, or, to put the matter another way, whether he is engaged actively in armed operations or is only passively engaged in them.[112]

It should be noted that the cases involving claims for hearing damage caused to soldiers have involved the use of weapons in training and so are more comparable to ordinary workplace cases.[113] Other forms of employment which may give rise to special considerations are policing and fire-fighting.[114]

Statutory Provisions

Apart from those statutory provisions which are directly enforceable, under the principles considered in chapter 3, the courts can sometimes derive guidance from legislative provisions in setting the standard of care. Provisions whose primary purpose is for administrative or criminal regulation may be useful in assessing a defendant's behaviour; examples such as road traffic regulations, occupational safety regulations and building regulations are considered in chapter 2.

Proof of Breach

After determining the extent of the duty owed by the defendant to the plaintiff the next step is to examine the events that led to injury in order to determine whether the defendant discharged his duty. At this point an outline discussion will suffice (more detailed discussion will be deferred to Part II of the book dealing with general issues, as matters of proof are relevant to all torts).

Where elements of fact are in dispute the Irish legal system normally requires the asserting party to prove his assertion. This obligation to support allegations made is called the 'burden of proof' (sometimes referred to as the 'onus of proof'). In order for this obligation to be successfully discharged the evidence must be such as to satisfy the requisite legal standard. In civil cases the standard of proof is called the 'balance of probabilities'; this means that the allegation must be shown to be more likely to be true than not. Until relatively recently tort actions in Ireland were tried by judge and jury. The judge would instruct the jury on the legal principles applicable to the case, while the jury would determine the facts and apply the legal principles to those facts. Section

---

112 *Ibid.* at pp. 183–4.
113 See, for example, *Gardiner v Minister for Defence* unrep. HC, 13 March 1998; *Greene v Minister for Defence* unrep. HC, 3 June 1998; *Whiteley v Minister for Defence* [1997] 2 ILRM 416.
114 Claims by police officers are covered by the Garda Síochána (Compensation) Acts 1941 and 1945. The position of fire-fighters was considered in *Heeney v Dublin Corporation* unrep. HC, 16 May 1991, discussed in chapter 2 *infra*.

6 of the Courts Act 1971 abolished the use of juries in civil cases in the Circuit Court and section 1 of the Courts Act 1988 abolished the use of juries for most personal injuries litigation in the High Court, so now the judge also decides the factual issues.

There is one special evidential tool of particular assistance to plaintiffs in negligence cases – *res ipsa loquitur*, which literally means the thing speaks for itself. The phrase is used to describe the situation where the fact of the plaintiff's injury is tendered as evidence of the defendant's negligence. Thus, instead of proving that the defendant acted in a particular manner and that this fell below the requisite standard of care, the plaintiff would seek to have negligence inferred from the fact that the injury was suffered at all. This particular form of proof, by way of an inference drawn from circumstantial evidence, has proved quite controversial and there is tremendous diversity of thought in respect of the precise parameters of its operation and effect. A more detailed discussion is contained in chapter 12 of this textbook.

Damage and Causation

Even where breach of a recognised duty has been established liability will not necessarily attach to the plaintiff; failure to conform to the required standard of behaviour does not, of itself, give rise to a cause of action for negligence. To be actionable, the breach of duty must be the cause of compensable harm to the plaintiff. The causal connection must be sufficiently proximate to be legally recognised as grounding liability and the damage suffered must be of a type for which recovery is permitted. 'Remoteness' is the term used for the legal mechanism which determines the extent of liability – if the damage suffered is regarded as being too remote, its recovery will not be permitted. The particular nuances of causation and remoteness as controlling mechanisms in respect of liability in torts in general will be dealt with in chapter 11. The tort of negligence has, however, developed its own peculiar classification of damage which should be considered at this point because it has a significant impact on the general nature of the duty of care concept – the duty is to take reasonable care to avoid foreseeable injury and the classification of a plaintiff's losses governs the concept of 'injury'. If the damage is not an injury that the law requires the defendant to guard against, then no breach of duty arises by causing that loss. The analysis of damage in negligence cases may be roughly classified as follows:

(i) physical damage to the person or property of the plaintiff;
(ii) economic damage – which may be consequential to physical damage or independent of such damage;
(iii) psychological damage.

Although damage to property is a form of economic damage it is one which is conceptually different and has traditionally been classed by reference to its physical aspect. A simple example may serve to demonstrate the difference between the different types of interference with property and economic interests, i.e. physical damage to property, consequential economic loss and non-consequential or 'pure' economic loss.

Example

D drove his car negligently and crashed into P1's van, causing extensive damage to it. As a result P1 lost the profits of that day of business and incurred the cost of hiring a van for three weeks, while the damaged van was undergoing repair. P2 was driving behind P1 and, although his car was not damaged in the incident, the resulting traffic jam caused him a fifteen minute delay. As a result of the delay P2 was late for a business meeting and his lateness caused the other party to withdraw from the transaction.

The damage to P1's van is physical, valued by reference to the cost of repair; P1's loss of profit and the cost of hiring a van are consequential economic losses; P2's loss of the value of the transaction is a pure economic loss. It is worth noting that physical damage to property is confined to damage to the plaintiff's tangible property – as intangibles cannot be physically damaged – and the plaintiff's interest must exist independently of the tortious relationship which led to the damage. Thus, where the plaintiff acquires defective goods, damage to the goods themselves does not come within the category of physical damage to goods; rather it is treated as a pure economic loss. Another simple example should serve to explain this issue.

Example

P bought a truck from M, a motor dealer. The body of the truck was manufactured and fitted by D, a specialist in truck bodies. The hinges on the back doors were too weak to support the weight of the doors and the first time P used the truck, the doors fell off and P's goods inside fell out and were extensively damaged.

Here the damage to the goods is physical damage to property, but the damage to the doors is pure economic loss. The latter damage represents no diminution of P's prior physical property, but involves the diminution of P's investment in the truck. This distinction is extremely artificial, given that both types of damage represent a loss to P by way of the expenditure needed to make good the loss. Nevertheless, the two losses fall into different categories and the principles applicable to each may not be identical, leaving a possibility that one could be recoverable and the other not. Likewise, if a person acquires property as a result of negligent advice from an expert, such as a surveyor, auctioneer or financial institution, any defects in the condition of the property will be classed as pure economic loss.

Liability in negligence has traditionally encompassed physical damage and consequential economic loss, but has had greater difficulty accommodating pure economic loss and psychological damage. Authorities on these latter issues have often imposed supplementary criteria to constrain the meaning of proximity and foreseeability in determining the existence of a duty. Consequently, these issues have become linked to discussions of duty rather than factors related to the nature of liability. One example, which we have already met, is the requirement of a 'voluntary assumption of responsibility' in respect of negligent misstatements, leading to economic loss. This makes the duty of care narrower than it might otherwise be. If one looks at the cases involving banks, for example, a duty of care towards third parties has only been imposed in limited circumstances and a general obligation to persons who rely on a bank's skill and expertise has not developed. Further examples of such supplementary criteria will be considered in respect of economic loss and psychological damage. It should also be noted, by way of contrast, that in respect of physical injury the proximity concept is generally subsumed within the concept of 'reasonable foreseeability'; thus, where physical injury to the plaintiff's person or property is a reasonably foreseeable consequence of the defendant's conduct, a duty will normally be held to exist, without a separate inquiry into the degree of proximity between the parties.

Economic Loss

Consequential economic loss is recoverable in all cases provided that it does not fall foul of the principles relating to remoteness of damage. There are two distinct approaches to the recovery of pure economic loss discernible from the available case law. One is a restrictive approach which treats pure economic loss as falling outside the *Donoghue v Stevenson* principle and arising only in exceptional categories of cases; the other treats the issue under the neighbour principle, subject to the same general principles as physical damage.[115]

The restrictive approach allows for recovery only where the loss is a direct result of the defendant's conduct and the plaintiff is the immediate victim, such as loss resulting from a misstatement, or where there is an exceptionally high degree of proximity between the parties. This approach would deny recovery for indirect loss, such as where the defendant injured a third party and the plaintiff suffered economic loss as a knock-on effect of the third

---

115 The development of this dichotomy is traced by Dwyer, 'Negligence and Economic Loss' in Cane & Stapleton (eds), *op. cit.*; for an extensive treatment of pure economic loss see Feldusen, *Economic Negligence*, 2nd ed. (Toronto: Carswell, 1989).

party's loss. The House of Lords decision in *Leigh & Sillavan Ltd v Aliakmon Shipping Co. Ltd*[116] demonstrates the operation of this approach. The plaintiff had contracted for the purchase of goods which were damaged in transit by the defendant's negligence. At the time of damage the plaintiff company had no proprietary interest in the goods, though they had a financial interest because they carried the risk in respect of damage to the goods. The plaintiff was unable to recover as the House of Lords held, in addition to the policy ground discussed earlier, that the duty owed in respect of damage to property was confined to persons with a proprietary interest and those suffering pure economic loss could only recover where there was a high degree of proximity, akin to a contractual relationship, between them and the defendant.

The consequence of this decision is that the person with the proprietary interest suffers no loss (as the buyer still has to pay) and the person who actually suffers loss is outside the range of persons to whom the duty is owed. The restrictive approach to pure economic loss was applied in the Irish High Court, by O'Keeffe P, in *Irish Paper Sacks Ltd v John Sisk & Son (Dublin) Ltd.*[117]

The principal reason for judicial reluctance to allow the recovery of pure economic loss is that the scope of liability is difficult to contain, raising the judicially unpalatable prospect of liability for 'an indeterminate amount for an indeterminate time to an indeterminate class'[118] – this is the notorious floodgates concept in its economic guise. The issue is succinctly, if somewhat cautiously, stated by Lord Pearce in *Hedley Byrne*:

> How wide the sphere of the duty of care in negligence is to be laid depends ultimately on the courts' assessment of the demands of society for protection from the carelessness of others. Economic protection has lagged behind protection in physical matters where there is injury to person and property. It may be that the size and the width of the range of possible claims has acted as a deterrent to extension of economic protection.[119]

---

116 [1986] AC 785; [1986] 2 WLR 902; [1986] 2 All ER 145; see also *Weller v Foot and Mouth Disease Research Institute* [1966] 1 QB 569; [1965] 3 WLR 1082; [1965] 3 All ER 560, where the defendants negligently caused an outbreak of foot and mouth disease, causing the plaintiff auctioneers economic loss by disrupting their business in livestock sales, due to the closure of local marts; recovery denied by Widgery J; *Spartan Steel & Alloys v Martin & Co.* [1973] 1 QB 27; [1972] 3 WLR 502; [1972] 3 All ER 557, where the defendant company negligently damaged an electricity cable, cutting off the supply to the plaintiff's premises; a claim for loss of trading profits for the period between disruption and restoration of supply was rejected by the Court of Appeal.

117 Unrep. HC, 18 May 1972, the facts of which were substantially similar to those in *Spartan Steel & Alloys v Martin & Co., supra.*

118 Per Cardozo CJ in *Ultramares Corporation v Touche Niven and Co.* 255 NY 170 (1931).

119 [1964] AC 465; [1963] 3 WLR 101; [1963] 3 All ER 575, at pp. 536–7; p. 152; p. 615.

The other prominent policy argument in the economic loss cases relates to the integrity of the rules of contract; many judges and commentators have expressed the view that the law of contract is the appropriate mechanism for determining the economic interests raised by the cases and that tort law should not be developed in a manner which would hamper the operation of contractual principles. This latter argument survives even in some of the cases taking a broader approach to economic loss.

The alternative approach to pure economic loss is broader and treats this category of damage as falling under the same principles as physical damage, i.e. if there is sufficient proximity between the parties and the damage is a reasonably foreseeable consequence of the defendant's conduct, then the defendant is under a duty to exercise reasonable care to avoid that consequence. Under this approach the problem of containing the extent of the defendant's liability becomes a question of determining a cut-off point for the defendant's legal responsibility for the practical consequences of his conduct and this is a 'remoteness' issue. Lord Wilberforce in *Anns v Merton London Borough Council*[120] stated that the 'damages recoverable include all those which foreseeably arise from the breach'. Perhaps the most famous judicial endorsement of the broad approach is that of Lord Roskill in *Junior Books v Veitchi*,[121] which describes the distinction between economic loss and physical loss as 'somewhat artificial' and indicates that the distinction should not be employed to delineate the general issue of a defendant's obligation to a plaintiff. In addition the judgment is critical of the policy basis for the distinction: 'The history of the development of the law in the last fifty years shows that the fears aroused by the "floodgates" argument have been unfounded.'[122]

Costello J endorsed the extension of the scope of the duty concept in *Ward v McMaster*[123] and recovery for pure economic loss appears to be more readily available in the High Court since then.[124] More recently, Flood J held that economic loss was recoverable on the same general principles as personal injury and physical damage to property – proximity, reasonable foreseeability and considerations of public policy – and such claims could not be distinguished as a class.[125] Thus, it would seem that in Irish law there is no

---

120 [1978] AC 728; [1977] 2 WLR 1024; [1977] 2 All ER 492, at p. 759; p. 1039; p. 505.
121 [1983] AC 520; [1982] 3 WLR 477; [1982] 3 All ER 201.
122 *Ibid.* at p. 545; p. 494; p. 213.
123 [1985] IR 29 at p. 44.
124 See for example *O'Connor v First National* [1991] ILRM 208 and *Bedford v Lane* unrep. HC, 22 November 1991.
125 *McShane Wholesale Fruit & Vegetables Ltd v Johnston Haulage Co. Ltd* [1997] 1 ILRM 86; analysed in Byrne & Binchy, *Annual Review of Irish Law 1996* at pp. 573–4; the matter came up as a preliminary issue, before embarking on a trial in respect of economic loss arising out of a loss of electrical power in the plaintiff's premises, caused by a fire on the defendant's premises.

general objection to claims for pure economic loss and policy arguments against such claims must focus on more detailed considerations than the mere nature of the loss or size of potential claims. It should be noted, however, that in the context of misstatements, Irish law does apply a modified approach to pure economic loss. As we have already seen, the *Hedley Byrne* approach, based on a 'special relationship' and an 'undertaking of responsibility', is employed and not the more restrictive *Caparo* approach applied in England. The approach to some examples of economic loss, such as a solicitor's duty to the intended beneficiary of a will (considered in chapter 2), utilises a combination of the standard approach to duty and the 'undertaking of responsibility' approach from *Hedley Byrne*.

The principal difference between the two approaches is that the restrictive approach imposes a duty only where there is an exceptionally high degree of proximity between the parties, such as that required under the *Caparo* decision in respect of misstatements. In recent English cases this approach has been used to reduce the scope of established duties in respect of defective buildings, thereby reducing the ability of buyers to recover the cost of such defects through the tort system. In *D. & F. Estates v Church Commissioners for England and Wales*,[126] the House of Lords used the restrictive approach to economic loss to curtail the development of builders' duty of care to purchasers; this case, in turn, was instrumental in the subsequent retraction of local authorities' duty in *Murphy v Brentwood District Council*.[127] Fleming points out that England stands alone in its approach to the exclusion of claims for pure economic loss.[128] The *Murphy* decision has recently been rejected by the Canadian Supreme Court in *Canadian National Railway Co. v Norsk Pacific Steamship Co.*,[129] where the railway company recovered, from the defendants, the economic loss suffered when the defendants negligently damaged a bridge owned by a third party, but extensively used by the railway company. This case confirms earlier development of liability for pure economic loss in Canada.[130] The Australian[131]

126 [1989] AC 177; [1988] 3 WLR 368; [1988] 2 All ER 992.
127 [1991] 1 AC 378; [1990] 3 WLR 414; [1990] 2 All ER 908. Both of these decisions are considered in chapter 2 *infra*.
128 Fleming, 'Economic Loss in Canada' (1993) 1 Tort L Rev 68.
129 [1992] 1 SCR 1021; 91 DLR (4th) 289; comment by Waddams (1994) 2 Tort L Rev 116; Fleming, *loc. cit.*; in this case even the dissenting judgment rejected the approach taken in Murphy. See also *Winnipeg Condominium Corporation No. 36 v Bird Construction Co. Ltd* (1995) 121 DLR (4th) 193.
130 The most notable decisions are *Rivtow Marine v Washington Iron Works* [1974] SCR 1189; (1973) 40 DLR (3d) 530; and *City of Kamloops v Nielson* [1984] 2 SCR 2; (1984) 10 DLR (4th) 641.
131 *Caltex Oil (Australia) Pty Ltd v The Dredge 'Willemsted'* (1976) 136 CLR 529; see Hogg, 'Relational Loss, the Exclusionary Rule and the High Court of Australia' (1995) 3 Tort L Rev 26; see also *Bryan v Maloney* (1995) 182 CLR 609.

and New Zealand[132] courts have also displayed a greater willingness than the English courts to permit recovery under this head of loss. Both Fleming and Fridman are critical of the lack of clarity in the reasoning behind the more liberal approach to pure economic loss:

> Although the courts have recognised that there may be a duty of care to avoid producing pure economic loss, they have not as yet formulated any settled definitive basis for distinguishing those cases when such a duty arises from those when it does not. There seems to be no guiding principles on which a proper resolution of the issue can be founded, save the broad general and vague notions of foreseeability, proximity, assumption of responsibility, directness and remoteness, whichever be the most relevant or appropriate in the particular circumstances.[133]

Doubtless many law students will support these sentiments on reading the available case law and commentaries on this topic.[134] As a final word on this issue, it should be noted that the *Second Restatement of the Law of Torts* provides no special provisions related to economic loss, but §281(a) does require that 'the interest invaded is protected against unintentional invasion'.

Psychological Damage

Psychological damage refers to injury to one's mental state and, though the term may not be the most scientifically accurate, it is more descriptive of the phenomenon under consideration than the term regularly employed by lawyers – nervous shock. When such damage is consequential to personal injury it is, like consequential economic loss, readily recoverable in common law jurisdictions.[135]

---

132 *South Pacific Manufacturing Co. Ltd v New Zealand Consultants & Investigations Ltd* [1992] 2 NZLR 282, though a duty was denied, a broader approach to duty was taken than that used by the English courts; see also *Invercargill City Council v Hamlin* [1996] AC 624; [1996] 2 WLR 367; [1996] 1 All ER 756 (Privy Council, on appeal from New Zealand); reactions to *Murphy* are considered further in chapter 2, in the treatment of duties in respect of construction.

133 Fridman, *The Law of Torts in Canada* (Toronto: Carswell, 1989), vol. 1 at p. 285; see Fleming, *loc. cit.*

134 For commentary see, for example, Vaggelas, 'Proximity, Economic Loss and the High Court of Australia' (1997) 5 Tort L Rev 127; Markesinis, 'Compensation for Negligently Inflicted Pure Economic Loss: Some Canadian Views' (1993) 109 LQR 5; Stapleton, 'Duty of Care and Economic Loss: A Wider Agenda' (1991) 107 LQR 249; Huxley, 'Economic Loss in Negligence – The 1989 Cases' (1990) 53 MLR 369; Cane, 'Economic Loss in Tort: Is the Pendulum Out of Control?' (1989) 52 MLR 200. A wide range of discussion can be found in the major textbooks on tort also.

135 See chapter 15 *infra* under quantum of damages. An example would be where an individual undergoes a personality disorder as a consequence of physical injuries which have been negligently inflicted such as in *Meah v McCreamer (No. 2)*

Mental suffering by way of grief is compensable under the Civil Liability Act 1961 where family members can recover a limited amount in the event of a victim's death through tortious conduct.[136] This action is derivative in nature, springing from an original tort against the immediate victim, without necessarily involving any tort against the relatives. Mental injury, unaccompanied by physical injury to the person, may also be the subject of a negligence action, involving a direct duty of care between the plaintiff and defendant. These type of actions involve plaintiffs who have been traumatised by major accidents, without being physically injured in the incident. The trauma may induce a physical injury (e.g. a heart attack, brought on by a shock) or may lead to a psychological injury (e.g. post traumatic stress disorder, depression or some other form of mental illness). A number of specialised principles have developed in respect of such claims, and the focus of the debate has been the duty of care.

Judicial reluctance in respect of non-consequential psychological damage was traditionally based on three concerns, viz:

  (i) the possibility of false claims being made;
 (ii) the difficulty of assessing the level of damage; and
(iii) the risk of an undue level of litigation (i.e. 'floodgates').[137]

Developments in medical science have greatly improved our understanding of mental illness, such that the risk of fraudulent claims has greatly diminished. In turn the judicial concern on this issue has dwindled greatly during the course of the twentieth century and is now probably no greater than the risk of fraud in any other type of tort claim.[138] Problems with the assessment of damages arise in many tort cases and the issue has also dissipated as a ground for judicial reluctance to deal with claims of mental injury. The third concern, over the scope of claims, has remained a concern and forms the focus of attention in cases on this issue.

Early Irish authorities indicated that liability would attach to negligent conduct where the plaintiff was put in fear of physical injury, but injury was suffered through the operation of 'fright' rather than physical impact. In *Byrne*

[1986] 1 All ER 943; see also *McCarthy v Murphy* unrep. HC, 10 February 1998; Irish Times Law Report, 6 April 1998.

136 This is considered separately in chapter 13 *infra* in the discussion of relatives as parties to an action.

137 See the judgment of Lord Wensleydale in *Lynch v Knight* (1861) 9 HLC 577; 11 ER 854; and the Privy Council opinion in *Victoria Railway Commissioners v Coultas* (1888) 13 App Cas 222.

138 For an outline of the illnesses suffered by the plaintiffs in many of the leading cases over the past century see Kelly, 'Post Traumatic Stress Disorder: A Recognisable Psychiatric Illness (Part I)' (1998) 16 ILT 10.

v Southern & Western Railway Co.,[139] the defendant's train negligently collided with a building which was occupied by the plaintiff at the time of the collision. Although there was no physical impact with the plaintiff, the effect of the mental impact led to a deterioration of his health and the Court of Appeal upheld the trial court's verdict in favour of the plaintiff. In *Bell v Great Northern Railway Co.*,[140] the plaintiff was a passenger in a train carriage which became detached and careered backwards down a hill. Again there was a lack of physical impact causing injury, but the plaintiff's mental health suffered and recovery was permitted by the Exchequer Division. These cases were cited with approval in the English Court of Appeal by Kennedy J at the turn of the century.[141] The consequence of these decisions is that where fear of physical injury induces physical damage or a medically recognised psychiatric disturbance, the plaintiff's suffering comes within the ambit of 'injury' in the legal sense and this injury is within the realm of a duty of care. This much is not particularly exceptional and would hardly merit special consideration within a general introduction to negligence. In fact, the first injury is physical – the psychological aspect relates to causation (if the injury is brought about by mental rather than physical contact is the defendant's conduct a legal cause of the injury?) – while the second is a medically identifiable personal injury, caused to a person within the recognised scope of duty.

The real difficulty relates to situations where the psychological suffering is sustained by someone who was at no point subject to any likelihood of being physically injured by the defendant's careless conduct. This would cover, *inter alia*, witnesses to an accident; rescuers of accident victims; medical personnel treating victims; friends and family of victims coming to visit them in hospital. Through the course of this century common law jurisdictions have slowly developed the law relating to the duty of care owed by a defendant in respect of psychological damage caused by his conduct.[142]

The first step beyond cases of fear of injury to oneself was to accept that parents fearing for the safety of their children would be owed a duty, provided they perceived the injury or near miss with their own unaided senses.[143] It was

---

139 Unrep. CA, February 1884.
140 26 LR (Ir) 428 (Ex. Div., 1890).
141 *Dulieu v White & Sons* [1901] 2 KB 669; [1900–3] All ER Rep 353.
142 For extensive treatment see Mullany & Handford, *Tort Liability for Psychiatric Damage* (Sydney: The Law Book Company, 1993); Napier & Wheat, *Recovering Damages for Psychiatric Injury* (London: Blackstone Press, 1995).
143 *Hambrook v Stokes Bros* [1925] 1 KB 141; [1924] All ER Rep 110, where a woman saw an unattended lorry rolling downhill towards her children, who were just out of sight; the caution of the courts in dealing with such claims can be seen in *King v Phillips* [1953] 1 QB 429; [1953] 1 All ER 617, where the plaintiff's claim was distinguished from that in *Hambrook* on the grounds that she was further away from the incident and, consequently, it was less foreseeable that she would be traumatised.

subsequently accepted that bystanders, unrelated to the immediate victims, were owed a duty if they witnessed an accident, provided that the accident was sufficiently serious.[144] It would have to be such that one could reasonably foresee that it could shock a person of reasonable fortitude. The next step was the acceptance that witnessing the immediate aftermath of a serious accident could be sufficient to bring a person within the scope of the duty owed by the defendant. Both relatives and rescuers have been held to come within the scope of duty in such cases.[145] One major difficulty faced in recent years is the determination of the boundaries of 'immediate aftermath' – how far removed from the incident must one get before the situation is no longer immediate? A second problem is deciding whether particular witnesses to the aftermath are foreseeable. Spouses, parents and rescuers are owed a duty, but what of siblings, friends or strangers, who come upon the aftermath?

In addressing these problems, the critical issue is whether the legal test for a duty between plaintiff and defendant is the ordinary test for negligence or whether there are additional criteria (it would seem that the nature of the damage is no longer a matter of doubt – the plaintiff must suffer a recognised form of mental disorder[146]). The epitome of the conflict on this issue is the House of Lords decision in *McLoughlin v O'Brian*.[147] The plaintiff suffered severe psychological injuries as a result of seeing the injuries suffered by her husband and children. The defendant's negligent driving had caused the injuries to the plaintiff's family, though she herself was not present at the accident but came to the hospital shortly after.

The House of Lords unanimously held for the plaintiff, but there was disagreement as to the principles applicable to such claims. Lords Bridge and Scarman held that the normal negligence principles were appropriate, with

---

144 *Dooley v Cammell Laird & Co. Ltd* [1951] 1 Lloyd's Rep 271, workman witnessed an accident involving his colleagues.

145 *Boardman v Sanderson* [1964] 1 WLR 1317, father of the victim heard accident and saw the immediate aftermath; *Hinz v Berry* [1970] 2 QB 40; [1970] 2 WLR 687; [1970] 1 All ER 1074, wife and mother of the victims of a car crash heard the accident and saw the aftermath; *Chadwick v British Transport Commission* [1967] 1 WLR 912; [1967] 2 All ER 945, volunteer rescuer after a rail crash; *Mount Isa Mines Ltd v Pusey* (1970) 125 CLR 383, co-worker heard an explosion and went to the aid of a severely burned victim. For the development of the duty towards persons other than those at risk of physical injury, see also Kelly, 'Post Traumatic Stress Disorder: A Recognisable Psychiatric Illness (Part II)' (1998) 16 ILT 26; for consideration of the concept of 'immediate aftermath', see Kelly, 'Post Traumatic Stress Disorder: A Recognisable Psychiatric Illness (Part III)' (1998) 16 ILT 39, at p. 40.

146 See Mullany & Handford, *op. cit.*, chapter 2; though see pp. 18–21 for cases awarding damages for injury to the mind not amounting to a recognised psychiatric disorder.

147 [1983] AC 410; [1982] 2 WLR 982; [1982] 2 All ER 298; see also Teff, 'Liability for Negligently Inflicted Nervous Shock' (1983) 99 LQR 100.

factors such as the plaintiff's relationship to the victims and the circumstances surrounding her perception of the incident being relevant to answering whether actionable negligence had been established. Lords Wilberforce and Edmund-Davies took a different view and suggested that additional rules relating to these factors, based on policy grounds, should apply to such cases. This latter view would involve the development of specific rules as to matters such as the degree of relationship required for a duty to be owed and the manner in which the victims' injuries were perceived (seeing or hearing the accident, coming upon the scene afterwards etc.). This would then require a plaintiff to establish proximity, foreseeability and other elements, e.g. sufficient relationship to the victim, direct perception of the accident or its immediate aftermath. A similar difference of opinion was evident in the decision of the High Court of Australia in *Jaensch v Coffey*.[148] Brennan J preferred a reasonable foreseeability approach, while Gibbs CJ and Deane J held that proximity was also relevant (though their approach was not as stringent as that of Lord Wilberforce).

Initially Lord Bridge's approach was dominant; the Court of Appeal in *Attia v British Gas*,[149] dealing with a preliminary issue, held that the plaintiff could maintain a case, having been traumatised by witnessing her house burning down due to the defendant's negligence. In *Hevican v Ruane*,[150] the plaintiff, the father of a deceased accident victim, was held to be within the scope of the duty, where he identified his son's body in the mortuary. The plaintiff in *Ravenscroft v Rederiaktiebølaget Transatlantic*[151] was informed of her son's death, but did not otherwise perceive the incident, yet she was considered to be a foreseeable victim by the trial judge. This latter decision was overturned by the Court of Appeal, in light of a subsequent change of approach by the House of Lords.[152] Kelly describes the latter two cases as following a 'chain of causation' argument.[153] The plaintiffs were outside the scope of the immediate aftermath; the plaintiff in *Ravenscroft* had no direct perception of the event, while the perception by the plaintiff in *Hevican* was not comparable to that of the plaintiff in *McLoughlin*. Nonetheless, each link in the chain of causation, from the defendant's negligence to the plaintiff's injury, was reasonably foreseeable. The chain in *Hevican* was as follows: first the defendant's negligence led to the death of the plaintiff's son; then the plaintiff was informed of this by a school friend of the son; then the death was confirmed at a nearby police station; then the plaintiff saw his son's body at the hospital; and, finally, the plaintiff suffered a continuing sense of loss. In *Ravenscroft*, the chain

148 (1984) 54 ALR 417; 155 CLR 549.
149 [1988] QB 304; [1987] 3 WLR 1101; [1987] 3 All ER 455.
150 [1991] 3 All ER 65.
151 [1991] 3 All ER 73.
152 [1992] 2 All ER 470, this is a note recording the judgment, rather than a full report.
153 Kelly, (Part III) *loc. cit.* at pp. 40–2.

began with the crushing of the plaintiff's son on the defendant's ship; then the news of the death was communicated to her, by her husband, at the hospital; and, finally, her imagination of the suffering her son must have gone through.

Lord Wilberforce's approach has subsequently gained supremacy in English law in aftermath cases. The turning point was the House of Lords decision in *Alcock v Chief Constable of South Yorkshire*,[154] involving a number of claims by relatives of the victims of the Hillsborough football stadium disaster (in which ninety-five people died and several hundred were injured due to overcrowding). The decision clarified the requirements that would have to be met in respect of the various factors raised by Lord Wilberforce. On the question of the relationship between the plaintiff and the immediate victim, it was held that spouse and parent–child relationships gave rise to a rebuttable presumption of a sufficiently close tie to be within the scope of duty. Other family members or friends would have to adduce evidence of a close tie of love and affection with the immediate victim. With respect to proximity in time and space, identification of a body at the morgue some eight to nine hours after the event was held to be too remote. The means of perception would have to be direct perception of the event or its immediate aftermath; third party communication is insufficient and media broadcasts are insufficient, unless the suffering of a recognisable individual is depicted.[155] The psychological impact must be a 'shock' (i.e. the sudden perception of trauma/horror), not a gradual onset over a prolonged period.[156] This approach rolls back the expansion of the parameters of the duty which had taken place since *McLoughlin* and affirms Lord Wilberforce's view that the facts in *McLoughlin* are close to the outer margins of duty.

The subsequent Piper Alpha disaster, involving an explosion on an oil rig, gave a further opportunity to the English courts to review the law in this area and the Court of Appeal decision in *McFarlane v E.E. Caledonia Ltd*[157] provides a useful summary. English law now distinguishes between primary and secondary 'nervous shock' victims. Primary victims are defined as participants in the original accident, embracing those in the actual area of danger, those that

---

154 [1992] 1 AC 310; [1991] 3 WLR 1057; [1991] 4 All ER 907; noted by Lynch (1992) 108 LQR 367.

155 For a radically different approach to perception see Mullany, 'Recovery for Psychiatric Injury by Report: Another Small Step Forward' (1996) 4 Tort L Rev 96.

156 This element is trenchantly criticised by Teff, 'The Requirement of "Sudden Shock" in Liability for Negligently Inflicted Psychiatric Damage' (1996) 4 Tort L Rev 44; see also *Walker v Northumberland County Council* [1995] 1 All ER 737; noted by Dolding & Mullender (1996) 59 MLR 296, gradual onset through pressure of work held to be recoverable (plaintiff was a primary victim).

157 [1996] 1 AC 155; [1995] 1 WLR 366; [1994] 2 All ER 1; noted by Feng (1995) 111 LQR 48; see also *Hegarty v E.E. Caledonia Ltd* [1996] 1 Lloyd's Rep 413.

reasonably believe themselves to be in danger and rescuers.[158] Secondary victims are non-participants, i.e. witnesses, with no fear for their own safety, and those coming to the aftermath. The duty to participants suffering psychiatric harm is based on reasonable foreseeability of injury, while the duty to non-participants suffering psychiatric harm is based on foreseeability and proximity, using the *Alcock* criteria. The plaintiff, who witnessed the disaster from a support vessel some distance away, failed to recover, as he was a secondary victim, lacking a sufficient relationship to the immediate victims.

A somewhat curious result of the approach taken by the English courts is that, while family and friends of those killed and injured in the Hillsborough disaster failed in *Alcock*, a number of police officers were successful in *Frost v Chief Constable of South Yorkshire*,[159] because, as rescuers, they were not subject to the more restrictive criteria applicable to non-participants. The English approach has been subjected to extensive academic analysis and criticism.[160]

The issue came before the High Court in Ireland for the first time in almost a century in *Mullally v Bus Éireann*.[161] The facts were substantially similar to those in *McLoughlin* and the plaintiff in this case did perceive the immediate aftermath of the injury to her family. Having been informed that her husband and children had been involved in a bus crash, she had to visit two separate hospitals in order to find all of the injured family members; furthermore, the scale of the accident was so great that the administrative system at one of the hospitals had difficulty in coping and the plaintiff had to walk through the wards, looking at all the victims, in order to locate one of her sons. The injuries to all of the family members were serious and presented a distressing sight. Not surprisingly, the defendant bus company, whose driver negligently caused the accident, was held to owe a duty of care to the plaintiff. Denham J

---

158 The Court of Appeal in *Hunter v British Coal Corp. and Another* [1998] 2 All ER 97; [1998] 3 WLR 685 held that 'participant' includes a person who, due to the defendant's negligence, reasonably believed himself to be involuntarily involved in causing the death of another. The plaintiff in the instant case failed, however, as his injury was found to have resulted from an irrational reaction to the news of the death of a colleague and, therefore, was not a foreseeable consequence of the defendants' negligence.

159 [1997] 1 All ER 540, noted by Teff (1997) 5 Tort L Rev 184; Mullany & Handford (1997) 113 LQR 410.

160 Oughton & Lowry, 'Liability to Bystanders for Negligently Inflicted Psychiatric Harm' (1995) 46 NILQ 18; Dunford & Pickford, 'Nervous Shock: Another Opportunity Missed to Clarify the Law' (1997) 48 NILQ 364; Hilson, 'Nervous Shock and the Categorisation of Victims' (1998) 6 Tort L Rev 37; Burrows, 'Liability for Psychiatric Illness: Where Should the Line be Drawn?' (1995) 3 Tort L Rev 220 (comment on the 1995 Law Commission Consultation Paper No. 137); Sprince, 'Negligently Inflicted Psychiatric Damage – A Medical Diagnosis and Prognosis' (1998) 18 LS 59.

161 [1992] ILRM 722.

preferred the approach adopted by Lord Bridge, using standard negligence principles, with foreseeability as the dominant issue. Denham J employed the chain of causation approach, rather than relying exclusively on the immediate aftermath approach.[162]

A laudable aspect of the judgment is the degree of focus given to addressing the nature of the injury. The plaintiff was found to be suffering from post traumatic stress disorder, which was held to be a psychiatric disease. This was held to be a compensable injury for which liability in negligence could attach. In order to establish whether the plaintiff was suffering from a recognised illness, Denham J used medical evidence to establish the criteria for post traumatic stress disorder and then applied those to the facts as found from the evidence. It is worth noting that the evidence as to the plaintiff's condition was not exclusively medical; Denham J also relied on evidence given by the plaintiff, friends and family as to the plaintiff's personality before and after the accident. The criteria applicable to post traumatic stress disorder were identified as:

  (i) exposure to a recognisable stress or trauma outside the range of usual human experience, which would evoke significant symptoms of distress in almost anyone;

 (ii) re-experiencing of the trauma through intrusive memories, nightmares or flashbacks or intensification of symptoms through exposure to situations resembling or symbolising the event;

(iii) avoidance of stimuli related to the trauma or numbing of general responsiveness indicated by avoidance of thoughts or feelings, or of situations associated with the trauma, amnesia for important aspects of the trauma, diminished interest in activities, feelings of estrangement from others, constricted effect, sense of foreshortened future;

 (iv) increased arousal indicated by sleep disturbance, anger outbursts, difficulty concentrating, hyper vigilance, exaggerated startle response, psychological reactivity to situations resembling or symbolising the trauma;

 (v) duration of disturbance, at least one month.[163]

The Supreme Court in *Kelly v Hennessy*[164] has adopted an in-between position, reflecting aspects of both approaches. It has shifted the focus towards proximity for aftermath cases, but has rejected the concept of specific policy constraints to the extent adopted in England. Hamilton CJ set out six principles to determine whether a plaintiff, suffering psychological harm, comes within the defendant's duty of care:

---

162 *Ibid.* at p. 731; see also Kelly, (Part III) *loc. cit.* at p. 42.
163 *Ibid.* at pp. 728–9.
164 [1995] 3 IR 253; [1996] 1 ILRM 321.

(i)   the plaintiff must suffer a recognised psychiatric illness;

(ii) the illness must arise by way of 'shock';[165]

(iii) it must be foreseeable that the initial event could cause psychiatric injury: foreseeability of general personal injury is not enough;[166]

(iv) the illness must result from the perception of actual injury, or a risk of injury to oneself or another person;[167]

(v)   if harm results from perception of the aftermath, there must be a close personal relationship between primary victim and plaintiff;[168]

(vi) there are no public policy limits on recovery where the plaintiff establishes sufficient proximity and foreseeability by fulfilling the above conditions.

Notably, Denham J moved from her High Court position in *Mullally* and used proximity, rather than reasonable foreseeability, to deal with questions on the necessary degree of relationship, time and space.

While it is difficult to predict the precise impact of this decision, some general comments may be made on its implications. The sixth principle, the lack of policy constraints, strongly indicates that the courts are willing to engage in incremental development of the duty in novel situations. Consequently, witnesses, such as those in the Piper Alpha cases, and family members perceiving the aftermath in circumstances similar to the Hillsborough claimants would appear to have arguable cases, if such situations occurred in Ireland. Secondly, the fact that only one of the six principles is directly addressed to aftermath situations suggests that the other principles are of general application to all psychiatric damage claims.

The first principle, that the injury must amount to a medically recognised psychiatric illness, is not new; this point was comprehensively dealt with in *Mullally* and is well established in other jurisdictions.[169] The second principle,

---

165 Relying on the judgment of Brennan J in *Jaensch v Coffey* (1984) 54 ALR 417; 155 CLR 549.

166 This is contrary to the English position, reached in *Page v Smith* [1996] AC 155; [1995] 2 WLR 644; [1995] 2 All ER 736, noted (1995) 145 NLJ 723; Trindade (1996) 112 LQR 22; Thomson (1996) 112 LQR 383, where foreseeability of personal injury was held to be sufficient. The plaintiff in this instance, however, was a primary victim, exposed to a risk of physical harm.

167 This would preclude claims such as that in *Attia v British Gas* [1988] QB 304; [1987] 3 WLR 1101; [1987] 3 All ER 455.

168 This precludes claims by strangers perceiving only the aftermath; the position with respect to rescuers is not dealt with, though the earlier decision in *Phillips v Durgan* [1991] ILRM 321 would suggest that rescuers would come within the scope of the duty.

169 See, in particular, Lord Bridge in *McLoughlin v O'Brian* [1983] AC 410; [1982] 2 WLR 982; [1982] 2 All ER 298; Lord Oliver in *Alcock v Chief Constable of South Yorkshire* [1992] 1 AC 310; [1991] 3 WLR 1057; [1991] 4 All ER 907; Brennan J in *Jaensch v Coffey* (1984) 54 ALR 417; 155 CLR 549.

that the injury must be shock induced, suggests that cases such as *Hevican* may not succeed, since part of the chain of causation of harm was the plaintiff's continuing sense of loss. Other cases excluded by this rule would be a spouse who is worn down by caring for an injured husband or wife, or a parent who is distraught at the conduct of a brain damaged child, even if the spouse or parent suffers a medically recognised psychiatric illness as a result.[170] The third principle, that psychiatric injury be foreseeable, indicates that the initial incident must be one which is sufficiently distressing that the shock of its perception would be enough to induce a psychiatric illness in a person of normal fortitude. This will depend heavily on the factual circumstances. In all the successful aftermath cases, for example, the plaintiffs witnessed extremely distressing sights. Although they were some distance away from the actual scene of the accident, the physical conditions were such as to be attributable to the original incident. In *Mullally*, the accident was so bad that the scene at one of the hospitals made it look 'like a hospital out of a war film, like a field hospital'[171] and the plaintiff's family members had suffered extensive injuries, presenting an extremely distressing sight. The fourth principle, the perception of personal injury or risk thereof, places no definitive limits on the means of perception, but suggests that witnessing the event or aftermath is required. In *Kelly v Hennessy*, the facts, as found by Lavan J in the High Court,[172] were that the plaintiff immediately went into shock and became ill on being informed, over the telephone, of the injuries to her husband and daughters; that she was ill during the journey to the hospital; and that she witnessed distressing scenes at the hospital. In the Supreme Court both judgments expressly refer to the fact that the plaintiff witnessed the scene at the hospital.[173] It must, therefore, be doubted whether a claim such as *Ravenscroft* would succeed in Ireland, since it was based exclusively on being informed of the horrific accident.[174]

---

170 These examples were given by Brennan J in *Jaensch v Coffey* (1984) 54 ALR 417; 155 CLR 549 and it was on this judgment that the Supreme Court relied in *Kelly v Hennessy*. Contrast *Walker v Northumberland County Council* [1995] 1 All ER 737 (stress induced illness, resulting from the plaintiff's employment).

171 [1992] ILRM 722, at p. 724. The other cases in which plaintiffs succeeded in respect of aftermath claims also involved extensive injuries to close family members: *Kelly v Hennessy* (husband and daughter permanently brain damaged; another daughter seriously injured); *Jaensch v Coffey* (husband seriously injured); *McLoughlin v O'Brian* (one child killed; husband and two other children seriously injured).

172 [1993] ILRM 530.

173 [1995] 3 IR 253; [1996] 1 ILRM 321, at p. 259; p. 326 per Hamilton CJ; p. 274; p. 340 per Denham J; contrast the approach of Lavan J in the High Court [1993] ILRM 530, at p. 533. He held that the injury was caused by the communication of the incident over the telephone and that this was aggravated by what the plaintiff saw at the hospital.

174 The plaintiff in such a case would, however, be able to receive limited compensation through a fatal injuries claim; see chapter 13 *infra*.

One other issue of note which has been left unresolved is the position of rescuers. The Supreme Court held that in aftermath cases there must be a close personal relationship between the primary and secondary victims, if a duty is to be imposed in respect of the secondary victim. This was stated, however, in the context of a person coming to the hospital to see the primary victims. The words of a judgment are not to be read and interpreted as though they were statutory provisions; consequently, one cannot infer that rescuers are excluded because they do not have a 'personal' relationship with the primary victim. Given the fact that the Irish courts have shown a greater degree of flexibility than their English counterparts, it is unlikely that they would reject a claim by a rescuer. This is particularly so in light of the fact that claims by rescuers are well established in other jurisdictions.[175]

To conclude on the issue of damage for the moment, the broader views of recovery for pure economic loss and non-consequential psychological damage require the use of the same legal principles as other negligence cases. If that were the only view on the matter then the foregoing discussion would have been entirely unnecessary. However, there is a significant body of opinion which holds that these two types of damage require the employment of special rules, in order to determine whether there is a duty to avoid such damage. In Ireland the present position is that economic loss is not subject to special principles, but psychological damage is.

Defences

Detailed discussion of defences is deferred to chapter 12 of this text, but a brief sketch at this point may assist in putting some perspective on the material covered. Liability can only attach where the plaintiff has established the requisite elements of a cause of action and the defendant has no available defence. Thus, while the plaintiff, in general, bears the burden of establishing duty, breach, damage and causation, and the defendant bears the burden of establishing a defence, the winning of a case by a plaintiff requires both the establishment of the first four elements and the absence of a defence. A tactic regularly employed in negligence actions is to dispute the existence of some or other of the requisite elements, such as denying that any duty was owed or arguing that the duty was discharged or that the breach did not cause the injuries in question. Clearly a lack of duty or breach will fully relieve the defendant, but arguments based on causation or remoteness can provide either partial or complete protection, depending on the circumstances. For example, it may be found that a defendant breached a duty, causing damage, but that

---

175 See *Chadwick v British Transport Commission* [1967] 1 WLR 912; [1967] 2 All ER 945; *Mount Isa Mines Ltd v Pusey* (1970) 125 CLR 383; *Frost v Chief Constable of South Yorkshire* [1997] 1 All ER 540.

some of the consequences for which the plaintiff seeks compensation are too remote; thus the defendant is only partially responsible for the consequences.

A defendant may of course argue that the plaintiff was negligent and, therefore, should be regarded as wholly or partially responsible for his own injuries. The causal principle known as *novus actus interveniens* may be used to argue that the plaintiff's behaviour was such as to be regarded as the sole legal cause of his injuries, while the defence of contributory negligence, if successful, will lead to an apportionment of responsibility between the parties.

Another defence would be to argue that the plaintiff had legally accepted the risk in relation to the conduct in question, thereby freeing the defendant of any responsibility. This would arise, for example, where a commercial contract allocates specific risks to each of the parties, requiring them to obtain insurance against the risks allocated to them.

Finally, it may be noted that a defendant may obtain protection by way of procedural restraints on litigation. While this may seem less glamorous than the other options, it is nonetheless effective when successfully invoked. Examples of such restraints would include statutory limitation periods (which preclude initiating action after a specified period has elapsed); diplomatic immunity; and judicial discretion to dismiss claims (which would include the ability to dismiss a plaintiff's claim because of inordinate delay in proceeding with the case).

CHAPTER TWO

Negligence: Specific Applications

Introduction

In the previous chapter the general aspects of a negligence action were outlined and we saw that the principal factors are proximity, foreseeability and reasonableness, each of which involves the making of value judgments on issues of social policy. This chapter focuses on more concrete aspects of how these factors have developed into specific applications to certain everyday activities. The chapter begins with *Donoghue v Stevenson*[1] itself and considers how the principle of a manufacturer's duty to consumers developed into broader principles of product liability. Then the discussion moves on to consider the effect of the neighbour principle on some areas where negligence based principles had begun to develop prior to *Donoghue v Stevenson* – employer's duty to employees, road accidents and professional conduct. The latter part of the chapter then goes on to consider the expansion of the neighbour principle into new terrain, focusing on the construction of buildings and the activities of public authorities. The selected examples reflect the principal sources of case law on negligently inflicted injuries and the running order is designed to give some feel for the way in which negligence principles have evolved historically, moving from the less contentious applications of the neighbour principle through to the outer margins of its current application.

Dangerous Products

Injuries arising from the negligent use of goods were a source of liability long before *Donoghue v Stevenson*, but liability in tort for providing someone with a dangerous product was extremely limited, mostly confined to intentional wrongdoing.[2] *Donoghue* began the development of a general obligation, based on reasonable care, to ensure that goods were not dangerous as a result of being defective, or inherently dangerous. The case created an obligation on manufacturers, independent of contract, to take precautions against injuries resulting from the ordinary, non-negligent, use of goods.[3] The common law principles considered here are not the only provisions governing product liability; the statutory action under the Liability for Defective Products

---

1 [1932] AC 562; [1932] All ER Rep 1.
2 See Heuston and Buckley, *Salmond & Heuston on the Law of Torts*, 21st ed. (London: Sweet & Maxwell, 1996) at §12.3 for the historical development of liability for dangerous products.
3 In America the development of a more generalised duty in respect of defective or inherently dangerous products began slightly earlier, see *McPherson v Buick Motor Co.* (1916) 217 NYS 382; 111 NE 1050.

Act 1991 (considered in the next chapter) and contractual principles are also relevant.

The dispute itself came before the House of Lords as a preliminary question as to whether the facts asserted by the pursuer constituted a good cause of action. Those facts (which were never actually proven) were that the pursuer suffered shock and a bout of gastro-enteritis, after consuming a portion of a bottle of ginger beer, before discovering the decomposed remains of a snail in the bottle. The remains could not have been discovered prior to being poured out, as the bottle was opaque. The ginger beer had been manufactured by the defendant and sold to a retailer, who in turn sold it to a customer, who then gave it to the pursuer. The central issue was whether the absence of any contractual relationship between the victim and the manufacturer prevented her from recovering compensation. Distinguishing apparent authorities to the contrary, the House of Lords held that a duty of care in tort was owed by the manufacturer to the ultimate consumer.

Apart from the general implications of the decision, considered previously, the ruling sparked an extensive development of liability in respect of the production and distribution of dangerous goods. The common law on defective products has now been supplemented by the introduction of a statutory cause of action, but the present discussion is confined to the common law action.[4]

Duty Situations

The narrowest interpretation of the duty established in *Donoghue v Stevenson*, and *Kirby v Burke & Holloway*[5] in Ireland, is that it applied to manufacturers of food products, for the protection of ultimate consumers. The principle rapidly developed to impose duties on other people in the distribution process, embracing a wide range of products and protecting persons other than consumers.

The expansion has led to the imposition of a duty on persons, such as assemblers, installers and repairers of products. In *Power v Bedford Motor Co. and Harris Bros Ltd*,[6] for example, the first defendant was held to owe a duty to the driver of a car (a subsequent purchaser) in respect of repair work which it carried out on the steering. The second defendant was also held liable to the plaintiff for the negligent failure to discover the defect during the course of subsequent maintenance work on the car. Suppliers have also been held to be subject to a duty in certain instances. In *Keegan v Owens*,[7] the defendant supplied swing

---

4   The statutory action is considered in chapter 3 *infra*.
5   [1944] IR 207.
6   [1959] IR 391; see also *Brown v Cotterill* (1934) 51 TLR 21 (a mason erecting a tombstone held to owe a duty to exercise reasonable care as to the stability of the stone); *Malfroot v Noxal Ltd* (1935) 51 TLR 551 (defendant held to owe a duty in respect of the fitting of a side-car); *Herschtal v Stewart & Ardern Ltd* [1940] 1 KB 155; [1939] 4 All ER 123 (duty of repairer of motor car to driver).
7   [1953] IR 267; see also *Andrews v Hopkinson* [1957] 1 QB 229; [1956] 3 WLR 732; [1956] 3 All ER 422 (garage selling a second hand car owed a duty to inspect

boats to a carnival and was held to be under a duty to keep them properly maintained. Here the plaintiff was injured when stopping one of the boats by hand. The nut fixing the boat to one of the swinging bars was secured by a wire nail, instead of a split pin, and the nail caught on the plaintiff's hand. The Supreme Court held that there was sufficient evidence of negligence to be capable of supporting a verdict in favour of the plaintiff and, consequently, the High Court dismissal of the plaintiff's action was overturned and a retrial ordered.

The principal connecting factor between the categories of person who have been subjected to the duty is that they have control over both the condition of the product and its release into circulation (or continuation in circulation in the case of repairers and suppliers of used goods). They usually also possess special skill or expertise with respect to the product, and those who do not (such as suppliers) have superior knowledge to the plaintiff in respect of the condition of the product. The defendants are also almost invariably commercial entities, profiting from their involvement in the circulation of products. The development of the law reflects a policy choice that commercial entities must accept some responsibility for the cost of injuries resulting from their activities and that the public are entitled to expect a certain level of safety in respect of commercially marketed goods.[8]

The 'ultimate consumer' concept in *Donoghue* and *Kirby* includes any user of the product, such as the driver of a car or even a passenger.[9] The scope of the duty has expanded to embrace other persons in physical proximity to the product, such as persons in the chain of distribution or passers-by. In *Keegan v Owens*, the plaintiff was a voluntary assistant, helping with the operation of the swing boats, and not a user or customer. He was owed a duty, as the defendant supplier had provided insufficient staff to operate the swing boats and could, therefore, have anticipated the presence of an assistant provided by the carnival organisers.[10] In

---

or warn buyer of the lack of inspection); *Watson v Buckley, Osborne, Garrett & Co. Ltd* [1940] 1 All ER 174 (wholesalers of a hair dye, obtained from an unusual source, owed consumers a duty to test the safety of the product, because they advertised it as being safe); *Restatement, Second, Torts* §§405–408 on donors, lenders and lessors of chattels.

8   For detailed analysis of the underlying policy issues in product liability, including modern developments towards strict liability, see Stapleton, *Product Liability* (London: Butterworths, 1994) at Part 2, dealing with both economic and justice based theories of liability.

9   In both *Power v Bedford* and *Andrews v Hopkinson* the plaintiff was the driver of the car; in *Power* it was stated *obiter* that passengers would be owed a duty also, per Lavery J [1959] IR 391, at p. 411; see also *Restatement, Second, Torts* §388, comment a; §395, comments h and i.

10 See also *Barnett v H. & J. Packer & Co. Ltd* [1940] 3 All ER 575, the plaintiff was a confectioner, placing sweets on display, when he was pricked by a piece of wire protruding from a sweet, causing blood poisoning which interfered with his grip for a considerable period of time. The sweets were manufactured by the defendant and purchased by the plaintiff through a middleman. It is worth noting

Brown v Cotterill,[11] the plaintiff was a child who, while visiting a grave, was injured by a tombstone which fell due to negligent erection. This plaintiff was clearly not a consumer or user of the product, but it is not difficult to see why the court would regard her as coming within the scope of the mason's duty.

Subject Matter of Duty

The duty is applicable to all sorts of dangerous products and a comprehensive list of subject matter is neither possible nor desirable, but a brief glance at a few examples provides a general indication of the breadth of this field of duty. The cases already considered involved contaminated food products, unroadworthy vehicles, carnival equipment and even a gravestone. The duty has also been applied in respect of items such as clothing causing skin complaints,[12] or manufactured with flammable materials,[13] pharmaceuticals with dangerous side-effects[14] and lifts.[15]

Products can be dangerous for a variety of reasons, but the dangers can be grouped into three general categories, any one of which will be sufficient to give rise to a duty of care – design defects, quality of workmanship and inherent dangers.[16] At the design stage there is a duty to consider safety aspects of the product, such as the provision of suitable guard mechanisms for moving parts. Safe designs may become dangerous products by deficient production, so the duty of care includes reasonable quality control. The second category of dangers also extends to the quality of maintenance, repair and installation, though the duty will fall on different people at various stages in the circulation of the product. The third category deals with products that have been designed and made in as safe a manner as possible, but carry inevitable risks. In the case

that the defence did not contest the existence of the duty, but argued (unsuccessfully) that there had been no negligence.

11 (1934) 51 TLR 21; see also *Lambert v Lewis* [1982] AC 225; [1981] 2 WLR 713; [1981] 1 All ER 1185, manufacturer of a towing hitch owed a duty to passing motorists, hit by a runaway trailer which detached from a vehicle due to a design defect in the hitch.

12 *Grant v Australian Knitting Mills Ltd* [1936] AC 85; [1935] All ER Rep 209 (underpants, containing excessive sulphite, causing dermatitis).

13 *O'Byrne v Gloucester* unrep. SC, 3 November 1988 (brushed cotton skirt, lacking warning in respect of flammable properties); *Duffy v Rooney and Dunnes Stores (Dundalk) Ltd* unrep. HC, 23 June 1997; Irish Times Law Report, 8 September 1997 (child's coat lacking warning in respect of flammable properties; liability denied on grounds of a lack of causation); affirmed on appeal, unrep. SC, 23 April 1998.

14 *Best v Wellcome Foundation Ltd* [1993] 3 IR 421; [1992] ILRM 609 (whooping cough vaccine causing brain damage).

15 *Haseldine v Daw & Son Ltd* [1941] 2 KB 343; [1941] 3 All ER 156 (negligent repair of lift in block of flats causing injury to lawful user).

16 See Newdick, 'Strict Liability for Defective Drugs in the Pharmaceutical Industry' (1985) 101 LQR 405, at pp. 409–10.

of such products there may be a duty to provide information to assist in the safe use of them and perhaps even a duty to consider the wisdom of allowing them into circulation at all.

The law relating to dangerous products has, to date, applied to physical damage to persons, or to property other than the product itself. It has not extended to quality defects in the product itself, which are still generally treated in the law of torts as non-recoverable pure economic loss.[17] Statutory consumer protection does, however, provide non-commercial buyers with extensive contractual protection, while commercial buyers can only be deprived of contractual redress where a fair exclusion clause has been incorporated in the contract of sale.[18]

Standard of Care in Products Cases

The standard of care in products cases has thrown up some illuminating applications of the general principles, outlined in chapter 1. Pharmaceuticals causing adverse side-effects raise fundamental questions as to the appropriate balance between social utility and magnitude of risk. Here the law is required to judge the degree of risk to which individuals may be exposed in the development of medicinal products, which will ultimately benefit society as a whole.[19] A balance must also be struck between the benefit to the individual and the risk posed. It may be fair, for example, to expect an individual to accept minor impairment as a side-effect of a life saving drug, while the same level of impairment would be seen as unacceptable in a drug designed to offset the effects of influenza.[20]

Cases involving flammable materials in clothing provide examples of balancing risk against the burden of prevention. The risk of personal injury may be statistically slight, but the level of harm is particularly serious in those cases where the risk does materialise. By contrast, the burden on the manufacturer to include a warning label, so as to allow consumers to take precautions in the use of the product, is low. Therefore, the balance tends to indicate that

---

17 Cf. *Junior Books Ltd v Veitchi Co. Ltd* [1983] AC 520; [1982] 3 WLR 477; [1982] 3 All ER 201. Such loss may be recoverable if there is an unusually high degree of proximity between the parties.

18 Sale of Goods Act 1893 and Sale of Goods and Supply of Services Act 1980.

19 See Newdick, *loc. cit.* at pp. 406–7, pointing out that there is no definitive scale on which such matters can be weighed and that value judgments by experts tend to provide the answers in practice; see also *Best v Wellcome Foundation Ltd* [1993] 3 IR 421; [1992] ILRM 609, in particular, Finlay CJ at pp. 462–3, where he indicates that compliance with mandatory or minimal requirements of a national regulatory authority will not suffice in cases of serious side-effects; Stapleton, *op. cit.* at pp. 43–4.

20 See Newdick, *loc. cit.* at p. 415, who presents the issue in terms of cost to the patient of the benefit obtained – people should accept reasonable costs (side-effects) of treatment. This reflects an element of self-responsibility on the patient's part.

the standard of reasonable care mandates the provision of a warning.[21] The absence of such warnings might seem to provide indisputable examples of negligence, but they would not have been so forty or fifty years ago, when product liability was in its infancy in Ireland. The change reflects the increased level of awareness in society of product safety and increased expectations on the provision of information in respect of the content and properties of consumer products. So, although the general legal principles have not changed, their application to concrete facts has.

In general, products cases require consideration of a variety of factual issues, which must be slotted into the appropriate points of principle, in order to be judged so as to produce a specific result. Courts will examine matters such as the level of safety testing conducted by a manufacturer; the quality control methods employed in the production process; the practices of competitors; the clarity and suitability of instructions and warnings provided in respect of the product; the uses to which the product could be expected to be put; the cost of making the product safer; and the value of the product.

One aspect of the standard of care which has undergone a principled change in approach is the relevance of intermediate examination. In the early cases it was not regarded as negligent to allow a dangerous product into circulation, if the danger could reasonably be discovered by way of intermediate examination, either by the buyer or by a middleman in the chain of distribution.[22] Under section 34(2)(f) of the Civil Liability Act 1961, the possibility of such discovery is to be treated as evidence on the issue of whether it was negligent to release the product in a dangerous condition, but it is no longer conclusive. Thus, a manufacturer may still be treated as having breached a duty of care towards the ultimate consumer, even if the defect ought to have been discovered prior to harm occurring.

A final point to note is that the duty of care is of a continuing nature, so manufacturers may be expected to provide warnings in respect of risks discovered after the product has been put into circulation in order to discharge the duty.[23] Furthermore, if the risk is sufficiently serious, they may even be expected to recall the product.

---

21 See *O'Byrne v Gloucester* unrep. SC, 3 November 1988, per Finlay CJ at p. 9 of his judgment.

22 Lord Atkin's formulation of the duty in *Donoghue v Stevenson* [1932] AC 562; [1932] All ER Rep 1, at p. 599; p. 20, included a requirement that there was 'no reasonable possibility of intermediate examination'; see also *Buckner v Ashby & Horner Ltd* [1941] 1 KB 321.

23 *Hobbs (Farms) v Baxenden Chemical Co.* [1992] 1 Lloyd's Rep 54; *Rivtow Marine Ltd v Washington Iron Works* (1973) 40 DLR (3d) 530.

Employers' Duty to Employees

The owner of a business owes obligations to a variety of persons affected by the manner in which the business is conducted. If the business is involved in the manufacture or distribution of products, then the duties related to dangerous products will be applicable; if the business involves the delivery of professional services, then professional negligence principles will apply; as an occupier or owner of property, the business will be subject to duties in respect of maintenance of the property. There is also a considerable body of law concerned with the employer's liability *qua* employer, i.e. the responsibilities arising out of the existence of the employment relationship. The employer's responsibility for the torts of workers, committed in the performance of their work, comprises a significant portion of the law in this field. Detailed consideration of this issue is deferred until chapter 14, however, as the principles apply to all types of tort actions and are not confined to negligence cases. The present discussion is confined to the obligations owed to employees, in respect of hazards within the workplace. Employers may also owe a duty of care to former employees in limited instances, unrelated to occupational safety, such as the provision of references.[24]

It was accepted, prior to *Donoghue v Stevenson*, that employers owed a personal duty to employees to exercise reasonable care for their safety in the course of their work.[25] Initially, however, the doctrine of common employment seriously restricted the level of protection afforded to workers, as it excluded claims for injuries caused by co-workers, even though the co-worker was performing an activity on the employer's behalf. This doctrine was abolished in Ireland by section 1 of the Law Reform (Personal Injuries) Act 1958. Occupational safety is now subject to a significant level of statutory regulation, but negligence actions are still frequent.[26] Whether an individual is classified as an employee is dependent on specialised rules considered later, in the treatment of vicarious liability.[27]

---

24 *Spring v Guardian Assurance* [1995] 2 AC 296; [1994] 3 WLR 354; [1994] 3 All ER 129; noted by Allen (1995) 58 MLR 553. This situation requires a delicate balance to be set by the courts on two fronts – one between the duty to the former employee and the duty towards the prospective employer and the other between the torts of negligence and defamation. In *Sweeney v Duggan* [1997] 2 ILRM 211 the Supreme Court held that an employer does not owe a duty to warn an employee of the lack of a policy of liability insurance in respect of any claims the employee may have against the employer.
25 *Smith v Charles Baker & Sons* [1891] AC 325; [1891–4] All ER Rep 69; the duty was considered as an implied obligation in the contract of employment in some cases, but it is now generally accepted that there is a concurrent tortious duty.
26 Statutory obligations are considered in chapter 3 *infra*; accident costs are also partially met under social welfare legislation.
27 Chapter 14 *infra*; the same principles are used to define an 'employee' for the purpose of determining both an employer's duty towards the worker and the employer's

Employers' Standard of Care

The duty of reasonable care for the safety of employees tends to be sub-divided into four aspects: place of work, system of work, equipment and competence of co-workers. There is an element of overlap between these issues in many cases, but the sub-division provides a useful method of breaking down issues for analysis. One must always bear in mind, however, that it is not a rigid structure which must be followed in all situations.

Place of Work

An employer must take reasonable steps to ensure that employees have a safe place to work in. This obligation concerns the physical environment in which work takes place, such as the suitability of buildings for the work being carried on, the condition of floors and doorways, the quality of light, air and so on.[28] The obligation is not confined to the safety of places directly under the employer's control, but can extend to other places where the employee is required to go in the performance of work. *Dunne v Honeywell Control Systems Ltd and Virginia Milk Products Ltd*[29] provides an appropriate example. The plaintiff was employed by the first defendant, as a service technician. He was injured in a fall when descending a ladder, after repairing equipment at the second defendant's premises. The ladder was found to be dangerous for a variety of reasons, including the fact that it posed a problem for a worker to carry a tool-case up and down.

The first defendant, although having no control over the second defendant's premises, was found to have been in breach of duty, as no warning was given to the plaintiff of the risk of carrying the tool-case on the ladder. Barron J held

---

responsibility for the worker's conduct affecting third parties – *Dunne v Honeywell Control Systems Ltd and Virginia Milk Products Ltd* [1991] ILRM 595; Byrne & Binchy, *Annual Review of Irish Law 1990* at pp. 502–3, are critical of this approach. They suggest that the two areas raise different policy issues, requiring different criteria.

28 *Kielthy v Ascon Ltd* [1970] IR 122 (one of the modes of access to the employer's premises was unsafe); *Gallagher v Mogul of Ireland Ltd* [1975] IR 204 (roof of a mine collapsed, due to inadequate provision of support); *Daly v GPA Ltd* unrep. HC, 13 February 1998 (plaintiff walked through a glass panel which was not sufficiently noticeable); see also McMahon & Binchy, *The Irish Law of Torts*, 2nd ed. (Dublin: Butterworths, 1989) at pp. 323–4.

29 [1991] ILRM 595; see also *Hanratty v Drogheda Web Offset Printers Ltd* unrep. SC, 2 June 1994 (*ex tempore*), discussed in Byrne & Binchy, *Annual Review of Irish Law 1994* at p. 444, plaintiff injured when descending from equipment which his employers had supplied to another company. The plaintiff had been demonstrating the operation of the equipment to the new owners. The case also provides an example of overlap between 'place of work' and 'system of work'.

that the duty in respect of the provision of a safe place of work included an obligation to inspect places to where an employee would be sent.[30]

Courts are reluctant to impose an exacting standard in respect of premises not owned by employers, but which employees are required to visit. Apart from practical limitations, there may be important policy considerations to be taken into consideration, as was demonstrated in *Mulcare v Southern Health Board*.[31] The plaintiff worked for the defendant, providing home help to elderly patients. She injured her ankle on an uneven floor in a patient's house and alleged negligence on the defendant's part in failing to examine the house in advance. She had previously visited the house on a number of occasions over a seven year period, without injury.

The claim was rejected on the grounds that the house was not sufficiently unsafe as to require the defendant to take action for the plaintiff's protection. The case raises an issue as to the balance between the social utility in providing the home help service and the risk to employees; it also raises a public policy issue on interference with property rights. The only practical measures open to the defendant would be either to insist that the patient carry out repairs or to withdraw the service. Clearly such an exercise of power by a public authority over an infirm individual would be a matter of considerable public disquiet. Given the low level of risk involved on the facts, Murphy J declined to interpret the standard of reasonable care as requiring such a drastic approach.[32] However, in cases of more serious risk the employee's safety may be a more pressing concern than the patient's property rights, though the precise dividing line will be difficult to draw.

System of Work

The provision of a safe system of work includes adequate training and supervision, as well as a suitable method of operation for the employee's work.[33] A safe method of operation requires the exercise of care both in design and in implementation or operation of working practices.

---

30 *Ibid.* at p. 601; the fact that the maintenance contract was one involving ongoing relations between the parties, with regular visits to the second defendant's premises, was also an influential factor. This case also involved a question of negligence in respect of the provision of suitable equipment; the plaintiff had previously used a satchel for his tools (which could be carried over his shoulder), but this was replaced by a case (which had to be held by hand) to improve the corporate image.

31 [1988] ILRM 689; see also *Wilson v Tyneside Window Cleaning Co.* [1958] 2 QB 110; [1958] 2 WLR 900; [1958] 2 All ER 265.

32 [1991] ILRM 595 at p. 692; see also McMahon & Binchy, *op. cit.* at p. 325.

33 For training see *Muldoon v Brittas Plastics Ltd* unrep. HC, 18 March 1993 (claim failed as training would have made no difference, since the employee was aware of the particular risk which training would have identified); for supervision see *Hough v Irish Base Metals Ltd* unrep. SC, 8 December 1967; see also McMahon &

The design of a suitable system of work has been considered in a number of recent cases. In *Heeney v Dublin Corporation*,[34] the plaintiff's husband, a fire-fighter, died as a result of injuries sustained while fighting a fire without suitable breathing apparatus. Apart from the question of providing equipment, two matters related to the system of work were raised. Barron J held that the defendant was negligent in failing to give instructions that fire-fighters without breathing apparatus should not enter burning buildings, but should wait for the arrival of suitably equipped colleagues.[35] Furthermore, the failure to implement a Labour Court recommendation on the provision of appropriate medical examinations, to assess the suitability of fire-fighters for their tasks, was also held to be negligent.[36] In *Barry v Nitrigin Éireann Teo.*,[37] the plaintiff was supplied with protective earmuffs, but the internal communication system required him to remove them, while still in the noisy area, in order to maintain necessary contact with other parts of the workplace and this was held to be an unsuitable system of work.

Perhaps the most noteworthy decision on systems of work is that of Egan J, for the Supreme Court, in *Walsh v Securicor (Ireland) Ltd.*[38] The plaintiff was driving a security van for the defendants, transporting cash between Cork and Cobh, and was injured when ambushed by armed raiders. Although a police escort was provided on the run, it was held that the failure to vary the timing of the delivery (which was at the same time every week for the previous seven years) amounted to negligence, even though the variation would have required the agreement of the employer's customers. The fact that the police escort significantly reduced the risk of robbery and injury, coupled with the long history of safe delivery, was insufficient to discharge the duty of care. Egan J held that '[e]very precaution must be taken in a high risk operation' and 'it was unwise to retain a clockwork precision'.[39] The term 'every precaution' perhaps overstates the requirement of reasonable care, but the forceful expression demonstrates that

---

Binchy, *op. cit.* at pp. 329–32 for a review of the range of cases on the provision of a safe system of work; see also *Mullen v Vernal Investments Ltd* unrep. HC, 15 December 1995, analysed in Byrne & Binchy, *Annual Review of Irish Law 1995* at pp. 490–2; statutory provisions may also be relevant in respect of training, see *Dunleavy v Glen Abbey Ltd* [1992] ILRM 1.

34 Unrep. HC, 16 May 1991; noted in Byrne & Binchy, *Annual Review of Irish Law 1991* at pp. 398–9.

35 *Ibid.* at p. 7.

36 *Ibid.* at p. 8; the failure had partially resulted from trade union objections to aspects of the package of proposed changes and Barron J noted that both sides had allowed financial considerations to overshadow the safety aspects of the situation.

37 [1994] 2 ILRM 522, at p. 524 per Costello J.

38 [1993] 2 IR 507; see also *McCann and Cummins v Brinks Allied Ltd* unrep. HC, 12 May 1995 (too great a distance between the parking point for the security van and the bank door). The judgment contains a useful discussion of the balance between burden of prevention and magnitude of risk, at pp. 8–9 per Morris J.

39 *Ibid.* at p. 510.

the courts demand an exacting standard of behaviour in cases of serious risk and that safety standards have increased in practical terms over recent years.[40]

McDermid v Nash Dredging & Reclamation Co.[41] provides an example of failure to operate the system of work properly. The plaintiff was untying hawsers connecting a tug boat to a dredger; the system of work required the captain of the tug to wait until the plaintiff knocked twice on the wheelhouse door, before starting off (in order to ensure that the plaintiff was clear of the hawsers). The plaintiff was seriously injured when the captain took off without waiting for the knocks, resulting in the plaintiff being dragged into the sea as the ropes tangled around his leg. The failure to implement a suitably designed system of work constituted a breach of the employer's duty of care for the plaintiff's safety.

Equipment

The employer's obligation in respect of equipment requires the provision of suitable equipment and its maintenance in a proper condition. Cases range from simple failure to provide cheap protective equipment for a clearly apparent risk,[42] to more complex questions about the introduction of new, and often expensive, technology. *Heeney v Dublin Corporation*, for example, involved the failure to provide breathing apparatus to fire-fighters. The introduction of new equipment, and the training of workers in its proper use, could not be expected to occur instantly. However, in the instant case the defendant had begun introducing the equipment some eight years prior to the incident in question and its provision to the particular branch of the fire brigade had been authorised two years before the incident. Thus, the failure to provide the equipment was held to be negligent.[43] The obligation here is not confined specifically to safety equipment, but extends to all equipment which presents a foreseeable and avoidable hazard. *Deegan v Langan*,[44] for example, involved the provision of poor quality nails to a carpenter.

Equipment which is initially suitable may become dangerous due to inadequate maintenance. Thus, the employer's duty extends to taking reasonable measures to repair or replace deficient equipment. The defendant in *Burke v*

---

40 See Byrne & Binchy, *Annual Review of Irish Law 1993* at pp. 541–3, contrasting this and other recent cases with earlier decisions on occupational safety.

41 [1987] AC 906; [1987] 3 WLR 212; [1987] 2 All ER 878.

42 For example *Kennedy v Hughes Dairy Ltd* [1989] ILRM 117 (failure to supply gauntlet to worker handling crates of glass); *Barry v Nitrigin Éireann Teo.* [1994] 2 ILRM 522 (the particular type of goggles and earmuffs provided to the plaintiff were incompatible, as the goggles pushed out the earmuffs slightly, thereby reducing their effectiveness); *Gardiner v Minister for Defence* unrep. HC, 13 March 1998 (army failed to supply protective equipment in respect of risk to hearing from exposure to excessive noise).

43 Unrep. HC, 16 May 1991 at pp. 5–7, the delay in supply resulted from delays in the provision of training.

44 [1966] IR 373.

John Paul & Co. Ltd[45] was found to be negligent where a blunt blade on cutting equipment caused the plaintiff to suffer a hernia, due to the exertion of additional force. A further ground of negligence in *Barry v Nitrigin Éireann Teo.* stemmed from the fact that the effectiveness of the earmuffs, supplied to the plaintiff, deteriorated due to a deficiency in the spring mechanism which kept them in place. In this latter instance the neglect lies in the failure to remedy the deficiency; the initial selection of the earmuffs need not necessarily have been negligent, as the deficiency may not have been discoverable.

Competent Co-workers

The employer's duty to exercise reasonable care to provide competent staff is of reduced significance since the abolition of the doctrine of common employment. Because an injured worker can now recover compensation from the employer for the tortious conduct of fellow employees, there is less need to resort to attempts to establish a breach of care by the employer. The employer's direct duty (as opposed to vicarious responsibility) is still relevant in some cases; for example, an incompetent employee may cause an accident without being negligent. The employer's duty in this area principally relates to the selection of the workforce. Matters such as qualifications and experience must be properly considered when engaging a person to work in a position which carries the potential to put others at risk.[46] The employer's obligation also extends to the monitoring of performance through supervision and, perhaps, discipline.[47] This latter aspect of the obligation overlaps with the provision of a reasonably safe system of work, again showing that the analytical classification is not to be considered rigidly.

Road Accidents

Road accidents have given rise to a very small proportion of the reported cases on negligence in recent years.[48] There are, however, a large number of unreported cases. The application of general negligence principles to most road accidents is

---

45 [1967] IR 277.
46 *Black v Fife Coal Co. Ltd* [1912] AC 149 (hiring of a colliery manager, without experience in relation to carbon monoxide, which was a known hazard at the pit, held to be negligent).
47 *Hudson v Ridge Manufacturing Co.* [1957] 2 QB 348; [1957] 2 WLR 948; [1957] 2 All ER 229 (continued employment of a man involved continuously in horseplay amounted to negligence in the provision of suitable co-workers; the man was repeatedly reprimanded over a four year period, but no further action had been taken by the employer); *Hough v Irish Base Metals Ltd* unrep. SC, 8 December 1967 (prank not reasonably capable of detection and of recent origin; no failure in duty to supervise and, presumably, no reason to doubt the suitability of the workers involved).
48 There is a considerable volume of case law prior to the 1970s; see McMahon & Binchy, *op. cit.* at chapter 15.

unproblematic and so does not give rise to many novel points of principle in respect of the duty and standard of care. The cases often involve important points of principle on matters such as causation, contributory negligence, the quantification of damages and the like, rather than duty and standard of care.[49] The duty of care owed by road users is to exercise reasonable care towards those sufficiently proximate to be foreseeably affected by their actions. This will principally mean other road users in their vicinity, but to a lesser extent it will include others, such as the owners of property adjacent to the road and relatives of accident victims, or rescuers, suffering psychological harm. The duty in respect of psychological harm is one of the few examples of road users' duty to give rise to significant disputes and has been considered already in the previous chapter.

Standard of Care on the Road

The determination of the level of precautions that a road user should take in any given circumstance is largely dependent on factual matters. In most instances the rules of the road and a modicum of common sense will give a sufficient indication of what is reasonable. The application of general negligence principles to road accidents provides little in the way of additional legal principles, specifically adapted to the context of road use. The cases mainly demonstrate straightforward applications of the various factors discussed in chapter 1 in respect of the standard of care.

Thus, for example, situations of increased risk of harm demand a corresponding increase in the degree of caution that a motorist must exercise. Motorists approaching buses with disembarking passengers will be expected to anticipate the risk of children running out suddenly from behind the bus. Reasonable care demands that the driver significantly reduce his speed to a level where the car can be brought to a halt and, perhaps, sound the horn in order to alert children to the car's presence.[50] Other situations of increased risk will also give rise to a duty to take appropriate added precautions.[51]

---

49 One area where the duty of care in respect of road accidents has been vigorously debated is in respect of psychological damage, see chapter 1 *supra*. Important cases involving road accidents are also considered in respect of matters such as contributory negligence (chapter 12 *infra*) and the quantum of damages (chapter 15 *infra*).

50 See, for example, *Mulcahy v Lynch and Butler* unrep. SC, 25 March 1993; Irish Times Law Report, 12 July 1993 (plaintiff driving at between 5 and 10 mph approaching a school bus held negligent for not sounding her horn); *Connolly v Bus Éireann and Others* unrep. HC, 29 January 1996 (continuing at the legal maximum speed when approaching a school bus held to be negligent).

51 See, for example, *Moore v Fullerton* [1991] ILRM 29 (truck driving at 12–14 mph approaching another lorry on a busy market day held not to be negligent in respect of injury to a child running out on the road suddenly); *Van Keep v Surface Dressing Contractors Ltd* unrep. HC, 11 June 1993 (truck driver negligent in failing to observe a cyclist between the truck and the kerb, when making a left turn); *Buckley v Maloney and Gore* unrep. SC, 2 July 1996 (*ex tempore*); Irish

The social utility of a driver's purpose, such as an emergency vehicle in a rescue situation or a police officer in pursuit of an escaping offender, will afford the driver a greater degree of latitude than ordinary driving situations.[52] In such instances the driver is not immune from liability in negligence, but the social utility of the driver's actions will permit the creation of a greater level of risk to others than would normally be tolerated. *Strick v Tracey*[53] provides an excellent example of the limits of this proposition. A police car was escorting a yellow Civil Defence fire tender to a fire at a school. The police car entered a busy intersection, controlled by traffic lights, against the lights and stopped in the midst of the intersection. The fire tender, which had been a considerable distance behind the police car, did likewise. Both emergency vehicles were using flashing lights and sirens. Mrs Tracey approached the intersection from the right of the emergency vehicles, with the traffic lights in her favour. She saw the police car break the lights and noticed the yellow vehicle approaching the lights from her left, but, believing the danger to have passed, continued into the intersection and collided with the fire tender.

Although emergency vehicles are entitled to a degree of latitude in determining negligence, O'Hanlon J held that all three drivers in this case had been negligent to some extent. The driver of the police car was negligent in allowing too great a gap to develop between the police car and the fire tender and in not taking steps to halt traffic at the intersection.[54] The driver of the fire tender was negligent, as he had a good view of approaching traffic and should have been more cautious when proceeding against the traffic lights.[55] Mrs Tracey was negligent in assuming the emergency had passed, particularly as she had noticed the approach of the fire tender.[56]

The burden of prevention on motorists is usually slight, as they will often merely be required to slow down or keep a greater look out, thereby marginally increasing the length of their journey. Vehicle owners will also be expected to incur reasonable costs in maintaining vehicles; if one chooses to put a vehicle on the road, then the cost of making it relatively safe cannot be avoided. The need to incorporate new safety devices is more problematic, but

---

Times Law Report, 26 August 1996 (driver of a low loader held negligent for not reducing speed and failing to give a sufficiently wide clearance when passing a cyclist travelling in the same direction); *Byrne v CPI Ltd* unrep. HC, 3 February 1993 (truck driver crossing a footpath, to enter a premises, negligent in failing to observe a teenage pedestrian on his way to school).

52 *Marshall v Osmond* [1983] QB 1034; [1983] 3 WLR 13; [1983] 2 All ER 225, considered in chapter 1 *supra; Daborn v Bath Tramways Motor Co. Ltd* [1946] 2 All ER 353; *Watt v Hertfordshire County Council* [1954] 1 WLR 835; [1954] 2 All ER 368.

53 Unrep. HC, 10 June 1993.

54 *Ibid.* at p. 8.

55 *Ibid.* at p. 7; he had a 'clear, unobstructed view for a long distance back to his right . . .'

56 *Ibid.*

it is possible that the owner of a vehicle could be held negligent for failing to incur a small expense installing a safety device which would significantly reduce the magnitude of risk.[57]

The case law demonstrates that the courts are quite demanding in the behaviour required of drivers to meet the legal standard, though they are occasionally satisfied that serious accidents can occur despite the exercise of reasonable care.[58] Lavan J, in *O'Brien v Parker*,[59] accepted in principle that a driver will not be in breach of duty if he loses control over the vehicle due to the sudden and unforeseeable onset of a disabling medical condition. In the instant case, though, the driver was found to have had sufficient advance warning and so ought to have stopped driving.

Professional Conduct

The relationship between professional persons and their clients is often contractual. This raises an initial question of policy as to whether any tortious duty arises; clearly, there is proximity between the parties and it is reasonably foreseeable that a failure by the professional person to exercise care can result in damage to the client, but if the relationship is contractual, would the law of contract suffice to govern the obligations? Leading decisions on this issue in a number of jurisdictions, including Ireland, have resolved it in favour of the imposition of concurrent liability in contract and tort, allowing injured clients to choose the type of action to proceed with.[60] Bearing in mind that the relationship between professional person and client need not be contractual, as the service may be provided gratuitously,[61] or paid for by a third party, the concurrent liability rule ensures that the obligations imposed by law are broadly the same for all clients.[62]

---

57 See the *dictum* of Budd J in *Byrne v CPI Ltd* unrep. HC, 3 February 1993 at p. 5 in respect of the fitting of an additional mirror on heavy vehicles to reach a blind spot, minimising the risk of injuring pedestrians and cyclists.

58 Contrast *Migiliore v Gerard* (1987) 42 DLR. 4th 619 (Ontario HC) (driver found not to have breached a duty towards his children in failing to have them wear seat belts; it was only a momentary lapse in judgment) with *Galaske v Stauffer* (1994) 112 DLR. 4th 109 (Canadian SC) (driver held liable for not ensuring his eight year old son was wearing a seat belt); contrast *Mulcahy v Lynch and Butler* unrep. SC, 25 March 1993; Irish Times Law Report, 12 July 1993 with *Moore v Fullerton* [1991] ILRM 29 and *Byrne v CPI Ltd* unrep. HC, 3 February 1993.

59 [1997] 2 ILRM 170.

60 The Irish Supreme Court resolved this issue in *Finlay v Murtagh* [1979] IR 249; other notable decisions on this topic include *Midland Bank Trust Co. Ltd v Hett, Stubbs & Kemp* [1979] Ch 384; [1978] 3 WLR 167; [1978] 3 All ER 571 (Ch D) and *Central Trust v Rafuse* [1987] LRC (Comm.) 492 (Canadian SC).

61 For example, free legal aid or public health services.

62 The range of affairs covered by the professional duty has been considered in a number of cases; a solicitor's duty applies to the legal implications of the facts

Professional conduct may also affect persons other than clients and the operation of the doctrine of privity of contract will, in most instances, preclude any contractual nexus between the parties. Where a contractual relationship does not exist, the injured party will be exclusively reliant on tortious principles.

Problems arising in respect of professional duties can be categorised as being of two types:

(i)   to whom is the duty owed? and
(ii) what standard of behaviour is required to discharge that duty?

The examination of these issues involves striking a balance between two principal policy factors. The first is the need to address the expectations that our society has in respect of the provision of professional services; the second is to ensure that the standard is not so high that it would hinder the provision of services.

Professional Duty

In relation to the first question set out above, it is well settled in the common law world that a duty of care is owed to clients (with the notable exception of the advocate's immunity[63]); however there is little agreement beyond this as to the class of persons to whom a professional person owes a duty. One of the more enlightened observations on the subject is that of Jackson & Powell:

> There are no general principles governing the liability of professional persons as a class (distinct from other groups) to third parties. There are 'pockets of law' relating to specific areas of professional liability . . . It is to such pockets of law that the courts and the practitioner should have recourse in the first instance. However, in the novel situations which will inevitably arise from time-to-time, it is submitted that the general principles [of negligence] . . . will guide the courts in determining the existence and scope of any duty of care.[64]

---

presented by the client, not the legal aspects of all the client's affairs, see *McMullen v Farrell* [1993] 1 IR 123; [1992] ILRM 776 (HC); unrep. SC, 9 February 1994; a doctor engaged by an employer, an insurance company or a health board to examine a person for the purposes of providing a report in respect of a proposed course of conduct may owe a more limited duty to the patient than the patient's regular doctor, see *X v Bedfordshire County Council; M v Newham London Borough Council* [1995] 2 AC 633; [1995] 3 WLR 152; [1995] 3 All ER 353.

63 See *Rondel v Worsley* [1969] 1 AC 191; [1967] 3 WLR 1666; [1967] 3 All ER 993; *Saif Ali v Mitchell & Co.* [1980] AC 198; [1978] 3 WLR 849; [1978] 3 All ER 1033; *H.M.W. v Ireland* [1997] 2 IR 142. Considered in Chapter One, *supra*.

64 Jackson & Powell, *Professional Negligence*, 3rd ed. (London: Sweet & Maxwell, 1992) at p. 37.

One of the more likely situations where a duty is likely to arise in respect of a third party is by way of negligent misstatement, which will be governed by the principles enunciated in *Hedley Byrne & Co. Ltd v Heller & Partners Ltd*[65] (or, in England, the reformulation set out in *Caparo Industries Ltd v Dickman*[66]). Thus, the legal principles applicable to professionals are the same as those applicable to other defendants in respect of statements and advice relied on by parties other than clients. The most significant 'pockets of law' have developed in respect of lawyers, doctors and auditors.

Solicitors' Duty to Third Parties

The principal third party duty affecting solicitors is that owed to the intended beneficiaries of their work for a client. Cases in a number of jurisdictions have held that a solicitor drawing up a will has a duty of care to the intended beneficiaries.[67] In the leading Irish decision on the subject, *Wall v Hegarty*,[68] the plaintiff recovered the legal costs incurred in defending an action in which the will was contested, as well as the loss incurred by way of the failure to receive the intended benefit under the will. The duty owed in this situation differs from *Hedley Byrne* type liability in that there is no requirement of reliance on the plaintiff's part and the duty covers actions rather than statements. The duty has not found universal approval, having been rejected in Scotland[69] and the Australian State of Victoria.[70] The main policy reason favouring the imposition of the duty is to fulfil public expectations with respect to their dependence on the proper performance of such functions.[71]

It was held, in *Clarke v Bruce Lance & Co.*,[72] that the solicitor's duty to the beneficiary is confined to the drawing up of the will and does not extend to

---

65 [1964] AC 465; [1963] 3 WLR 101; [1963] 3 All ER 575.

66 [1990] 2 AC 605; [1990] 2 WLR 358; [1990] 1 All ER 568.

67 *Ross v Caunters* [1980] Ch 297; [1979] 3 WLR 605; [1979] 3 All ER 580; *White v Jones* [1995] 2 AC 207; [1995] 2 WLR 187; [1995] 1 All ER 691; *Wall v Hegarty* [1980] ILRM 124; *Whittingham v Crease & Co.* (1979) 88 DLR (3d) 353; *Gartside v Sheffield Young & Ellis* [1983] NZLR 37; *R.F. Hill & Associates v Van Erp* (1997) 71 ALJR 478; Brady, 'Solicitor's Duty of Care in the Drafting of Wills' (1995) 46 NILQ 434.

68 [1980] ILRM 124.

69 *Weir v J.M. Hodge & Son* [1990] SLT 266.

70 *Seale v Perry* [1982] VR 193; the Supreme Court of Western Australia chose to impose the duty in *Watts v Public Trustee for Western Australia* [1980] WAR 97; the High Court of Australia imposed the duty in *R.F. Hill & Associates v Van Erp* (1997) 71 ALJR 478.

71 This is particularly strong in the case of wills, since the client will have died and be unable to rectify the situation. The principle may also be explained as involving a voluntary assumption of responsibility by the solicitor, as is the case with misstatement; see Yeo, 'Rethinking Proximity: A Paper Tiger' (1997) 5 Tort L Rev 174.

72 [1988] 1 WLR 881; [1988] 1 All ER 364.

other transactions affecting the value of the assets the beneficiary is to receive. In this case the defendants, a firm of solicitors, drew up a will, which was properly executed, in 1973. One of the provisions of the will was that the plaintiff was to receive a service station, owned by the testator. Shortly after the will was drawn up, the testator leased the station to a third party. In 1979 the testator entered into an agreement, varying the lease by giving the tenant an option to buy out the property for a fixed price and the option could be exercised only after the death of the testator or his wife, whichever was later. The defendants also acted for the testator in this subsequent transaction. The plaintiff argued that the defendants owed him a duty of care to advise the testator that the transaction was improvident (since the fixed price could be significantly lower than the actual value of the property, as the right might not be exercised until several years after the agreement was made). The Court of Appeal rejected the plaintiff's claim, holding that the plaintiff had no entitlement to have the value of a potential benefit preserved during the testator's lifetime. The testator was free to dispose of the property, diminish its value or change his will at any time. The imposition of the duty sought by the plaintiff could require the solicitors to interfere with the legitimate exercise of their client's rights, potentially leading to a conflict of interest with the duty to the client. The Court of Appeal also identified a second distinction between this situation and the improper drafting of a will. In this type of case the testator's estate would be able to bring an action against the solicitors if they were negligent and that negligence led to a reduction in the value of the estate; whereas, in the case of an invalid will, the value of the estate is not diminished, though the testator's wishes in respect of its distribution are defeated. Thus, since a remedy is available to the estate in the case of the devaluing of assets, there is no need for a distinct remedy for the beneficiary against the solicitors.

It is possible that the duty to beneficiaries is not confined to wills but would include other acts for the benefit of third parties, such as the setting up of a trust, though there is a dearth of case law on the subject.[73] One decision of note on the matter is *Hemmens v Wilson Browne*.[74] Here a client instructed the defendants to draft a document giving the plaintiff a right to call on the client to pay her £110,000. The document drafted gave the plaintiff no enforceable right and when she asked for the money the promisor refused to pay.[75] Judge Moseley QC (sitting as a judge of the High Court) held that although there was sufficient proximity between the defendant solicitors and the plaintiff, and loss to the plaintiff was reasonably foreseeable, it would not be fair, just or reasonable to impose a duty. The reason was that, since the client was still

---

73 See Jackson & Powell, *op. cit.* at pp. 318–26 for a full discussion of the duty.

74 [1994] 2 FLR 101; [1994] 2 WLR 323; [1993] 4 All ER 826.

75 The document was not a contract, as there was no consideration; it was not a deed, as it was not under seal; and it was not a trust, as there was no identifiable fund which could form the subject of a trust.

alive and fully competent, he was in a position to rectify the error if he saw fit; furthermore, he could refuse to pay for the inadequate drafting of the original document and sue the solicitors for breach of contract for any losses incurred in completing the gift. It was accepted that a duty could be imposed if, for any reason, the client was unable to complete the transaction. A second argument advanced by the plaintiff was under negligent misrepresentation, as one of the defendant solicitors informed her that the document was 'akin to a trust'. This argument was rejected because the solicitor had made it clear that he was acting for the promisor only and that the plaintiff should obtain independent legal advice. Although the formulation of the duty of care in this case (the tripartite approach, identified in the previous chapter, i.e. proximity, reasonable foreseeability and whether it is fair, just or reasonable to impose a duty) is not generally employed by the Irish courts, the case is, nonetheless, instructive as it does highlight potential restrictions on the solicitor's duty to beneficiaries of *inter vivos* transactions.

There have been miscellaneous cases imposing a duty on solicitors in respect of third parties based on unusual fact situations, though there is no single unifying principle which can readily explain all such cases.[76] One such case is *Al-Kandari v J.R. Brown & Co.*[77] The defendant solicitors were acting for the plaintiff's husband in matrimonial proceedings against her. They agreed to hold the husband's passport, in order to prevent the possibility of his removing the children from the jurisdiction. They forwarded the passport to the Kuwaiti embassy, who in turn allowed the passport to fall into the husband's hands and he absconded with the children. The defendants neglected to inform the plaintiff of the fact that they had parted with the passport. The plaintiff sued the defendants for negligently facilitating the wrongful removal of her children, leading to personal injury to her (both physical and emotional) and economic loss in attempting to recover her children. The Court of Appeal held that a solicitor would not normally owe a duty towards the opposing party in contested litigation, but a duty could be owed in exceptional circumstances. In this case a duty was imposed on the basis that there had been a voluntary assumption of responsibility by the defendants (akin to misstatement cases).[78]

A solicitor's duty to a third party was explained in general terms by the Supreme Court in *Doran v Delaney*.[79] Keane J adopted the following passage from Lord Jauncey in *Midland Bank plc v Cameron, Thom, Peterkin & Duncans*:[80]

---

76 See Jackson & Powell, *op. cit.* at pp. 326–32 for examples of such cases.
77 [1988] QB 655; [1988] 2 WLR 671; [1988] 1 All ER 833.
78 See also *National Home Loans Corp. plc v Giffen, Couch & Archer* [1997] 3 All ER 808, solicitor acting for both sides in the conveyance of property.
79 [1998] 2 ILRM 1.
80 [1988] SLT 611 at p. 616.

In my opinion four factors are relevant to a determination of the question whether in a particular case a solicitor, while acting for a client, also owed a duty of care to a third party:

(1) The solicitor must assume responsibility for advice or information furnished to the third party;

(2) The solicitor must let it be known to the third party expressly or impliedly that he claims, by reason of his calling, to have the requisite skill or knowledge to give the advice or furnish the information;

(3) The third party must have relied on that information as a matter for which the solicitor has assumed responsibility;

(4) The solicitor must have been aware that the third party was likely so to rely.

The Supreme Court found such a duty to apply in respect of an answer to one of the requisitions in respect of the sale of property. The requisition from the purchaser was as follows: 'Is there any litigation pending or threatened in relation to the property or any part of it or has any adverse claim thereto been made by any person?'[81] The solicitor was aware that there had been a dispute over the title and asked her client about it. He replied that it had been sorted out, but she never sought to ascertain the terms of the alleged settlement. In reply to the requisition, the solicitor stated 'Vendor says none.' In fact, the dispute had not been resolved and, as a result, the purchaser had to sell on the property at a loss. The particular response was found to be a matter which came within the above criteria, though not all responses to requisitions would give rise to a duty. Although the response was truthful in a literal sense, the Supreme Court held that it conveyed the impression that the solicitor had no reason to doubt the truth of the vendor's assertion.

Doctors' Duty to Third Parties

In relation to doctors, two distinct categories of cases give rise to the bulk of the debate on third party duties. The first involves conception, pregnancy and birth, giving rise to the possibility of actions either by the child or by the spouse (or other partner) of the patient. The available case law indicates that a duty is owed to a foetus by a doctor treating a pregnant woman.[82] If the child is born alive, but incapacitated due to the doctor's negligence, then the child may maintain an action. No action appears to be available if the doctor fails to

---

81 This is a standard requisition (No. 13.8).

82 The leading Irish case involving a claim by a child in respect of pre-natal injury, *Dunne v National Maternity Hospital* [1989] IR 91; [1989] ILRM 735, appears to have proceeded without any dispute as to the existence of such a duty – see pp. 105–6; pp. 741–3 for the principal grounds of appeal; *Burton v Islington Health Authority* [1993] QB 204; [1992] 3 WLR 637; [1992] 3 All ER 833; see also the Congenital Disabilities (Civil Liability) Act 1976, which governs actions in England in respect of births after 22 July 1976.

discover an untreatable deficiency in the foetus during pregnancy, as the doctor's failing does not present any risk to the foetus. In other jurisdictions it has been argued that discovery of the defect would have allowed the woman to avail of the option of a therapeutic abortion, but this is not an available option in Ireland, thus neither the parents nor the child can claim that the birth itself is a form of harm.

A duty may also extend to children not yet conceived at the time of treatment, though both judges and commentators acknowledge a degree of conceptual difficulty with the imposition of a duty towards a person not yet in existence at the time of the conduct complained of.[83] The factual circumstances on which such a claim could be based would require negligent care of the mother, prior to conception, in such a way as to create a risk of harm to the foetus subsequently conceived. The administration of dangerous drugs or inadequate advice in relation to the risk of contracting an illness, such as rubella, during pregnancy might give rise to such a claim.[84]

Injuries to children may also bring increased economic costs to parents, so the husband may have a claim for economic loss arising out of negligent diagnosis, advice or treatment of his wife before or during pregnancy. Furthermore, a failed sterilisation operation, leading to unwanted pregnancy, may give rise to claims for economic loss in relation to the costs of pre and post natal care and the cost of raising the child.[85]

The second category of cases involves situations where the patient's condition presents a danger to third parties. Typically this would arise where the patient is suffering from a mental illness or a communicable disease, though there are surprisingly few available cases on the subject and no clear guidance as to how to resolve the question of whether a duty of care exists.[86] Perhaps the most unusual example of danger to a third party is the case of *Urbanski v Patel*,[87] where a

---

83 See Kennedy & Grubb, *Medical Law – Text with Materials*, 2nd ed. (London: Butterworths, 1994) at pp. 927–47 for extracts from and discussion of the leading cases in common law jurisdictions; see also the Congenital Disabilities (Civil Liability) Act 1976 .

84 See White, *Medical Negligence Actions* (Dublin: Oak Tree Press, 1996) at §14.2.06.

85 *Emeh v Kensington and Chelsea and Westminster Area Health Authority* [1985] QB 1012; [1985] 2 WLR 233; [1984] 3 All ER 1044; *Thake v Morris* [1986] QB 644; [1986] 1 All ER 497; Symmons, 'Policy Factors in Actions for Wrongful Birth' (1987) 50 MLR 269; Donnelly, 'The Injury of Parenthood: The Tort of Wrongful Conception' (1997) 48 NILQ 10; see also *Veivers v Connolly* [1995] 2 Qd R 326; noted by Devereux (1996) 4 Tort L Rev 107.

86 For the main cases and a discussion of the issues raised by them see Jones, *Medical Negligence* (London: Sweet & Maxwell, 1991) pp. 45–55; Kennedy & Grubb, *op. cit.* at pp. 663–71. The principal difficulty with the imposition of such a duty is the impact that it would have on doctor–patient confidentiality.

87 (1978) 84 DLR (3d) 650; noted by Robertson (1980) 96 LQR 19; for further cases and comment see Kennedy & Grubb, *op. cit.* at pp. 1141–4.

doctor negligently removed a patient's only kidney and was held to owe a duty to her father, who eventually donated one of his kidneys for a transplant operation. In terms of proximity and foreseeability this case is certainly at the outer margins of the tort of negligence and is comparable to the cases of psychological damage discussed in the preceding chapter.

Auditors' and Accountants' Duty to Third Parties

We have already seen that the Irish and English courts have diverged in their approach to negligent misstatement. The impact of this is particularly significant in the context of an auditor's duty in the preparation of accounts for a company. The English position, under *Caparo Industries Ltd v Dickman*,[88] is that a plaintiff, relying on the accounts, must be known to the auditor, either individually or as a member of a limited class of persons, and the transaction entered into must be of a type known by the auditor to be within the plaintiff's contemplation.

In *Caparo* the auditors prepared and certified a public limited company's accounts and the plaintiffs, existing shareholders, made a successful take-over bid, relying on the accounts in fixing the price of their offer. They claimed that the accounts were misleading and caused them to pay substantially more than the company was worth. The House of Lords held that no duty was owed. Potential investors, as a whole, was held to be too broad a class of persons to be owed a duty and, although existing shareholders was a sufficiently limited class of persons, the transaction (the purchase of shares) was not of an appropriate type to come within any duty that might be owed. The purpose of the accounts was to allow the shareholders to exercise their powers of control over the company, not to form the basis of decisions on the buying or selling of shares. Thus, in England, the mere preparation and certification of accounts will not generate a duty in respect of investment decisions, taken in reliance on those accounts. A duty may, however, be owed where an auditor or accountant is asked to prepare accounts for the express purpose of facilitating negotiations for a take-over,[89] or where the auditor or accountant confirms the contents of the accounts in response to direct questions from a prospective investor.[90]

The Irish position, as set out by Lardner J in *Kelly v Haughey Boland & Co.*,[91] is that a general duty towards potential investors is owed, once the financial

---

88 [1990] 2 AC 605; [1990] 2 WLR 358; [1990] 1 All ER 568.

89 It was accepted by the Court of Appeal, on a preliminary application, that the buyer would have an arguable case in such circumstances in *Morgan Crucible Co. plc v Hill Samuel Bank Ltd* [1991] Ch 295; [1991] 2 WLR 655; [1991] 1 All ER 142.

90 This was accepted by May J in *ADT v Binder Hamlyn* unrep. QB, December 1995; the principle was also considered in *James McNaughton Papers Group Ltd v Hicks Anderson & Co.* [1991] 2 QB 113; [1991] 2 WLR 641; [1991] 1 All ER 134, but the plaintiffs failed to establish that the statement was intended to verify the contents of the draft accounts shown to the plaintiffs.

91 [1989] ILRM 373.

position disclosed in the audited accounts is such as to make the company susceptible to a take-over bid. Subsequent decisions in respect of negligent misstatement causing economic loss have continued to utilise the *Hedley Byrne* formulation and the Irish judiciary have shown no inclination to use the more constrained approach in *Caparo*.[92] Similarly, in relation to pure economic loss in general, the Irish courts have continued to use a general approach based on proximity, reasonable foreseeability and other policy considerations, without any attempt to constrain the ambit of these concepts.[93] This means that auditors and accountants in Ireland are exposed to a broader obligation than their English counterparts. In order to avoid liability they will have to rely on more specific grounds than a 'floodgates' argument. It may be that, in particular circumstances, they can show, for example, that reliance was unreasonable (e.g. because the plaintiff had access to independent advice), or that the plaintiff was not misled (as occurred in *Kelly v Haughey Boland*), or that there was no breach of duty.

Professional Standard of Care

The available case law on professional duty has produced a number of guidelines that assist in giving more specific content to the concept of 'reasonable care' for the purposes of assessing the standard of care in respect of professionals and addressing the issue of whether a duty has been discharged.[94] At the outset of this excursion into the case law, students should know that there is a divergence of views on the significance of such cases. One view is that each case involves an adaptation of the general standard to the unique circumstances of the case before the court; thus, each formulation of the scope of the duty owed by the particular defendant to the particular plaintiff is an issue of fact rather than of law. The contrary view is that cases must have some value as precedents; therefore, each formulation of the scope of a duty is relevant to the resolution of cases arising out of similar fact situations.[95] Fortunately, students need not resolve this conflict in order to proceed, but may assume for the present that the courts, in deciding the cases discussed

---

92 *McAnarney v Hanrahan* [1993] 3 IR 492; [1994] 1 ILRM 210; *Donnellan v Dungoyne* [1995] 1 ILRM 388; *McCullagh v P.B. Gunne plc* unrep. HC, 17 January 1997; Irish Times Law Report, 28 April 1997.

93 *McShane Wholesale Fruit & Vegetables Ltd v Johnston Haulage Co. Ltd* [1997] 1 ILRM 86.

94 The application of the standard to the doctor–patient relationship is subjected to an extensive and thought provoking analysis by Teff, *Reasonable Care* (Oxford: Clarendon Press, 1994); the book is critical of the dominance of professional paternalism in English law and looks at a number of other models of measuring professional practice and highlights a variety of underlying values in setting legal standards.

95 For further discussion see Brazier, *Street on Torts*, 9th ed. (London: Butterworths, 1993) at pp. 222–5; Jones, *op. cit.* at p. 112; White, *op. cit.* at §7.3.01.

below, intended to provide some guidance for future cases without necessarily intending the guidelines to be a rigid set of rules of law.

Now we turn our attention to the standard of care in cases alleging professional negligence. First let us consider the importance of standard practices within the professions. While such practices can assist with establishing the appropriate level of care, they do not provide a definitive measure of the legal standard required for the discharge of a duty of care. There is good reason to resist using standard practices as a measure of the legal standard of care. The principal reason is that standards are set by the professionals themselves, while the responsibility for determining the legal standard rests with the judiciary (or the legislature, should it choose to intervene). A corollary of this is that there may be factors which the professions have not considered but which the judiciary feel ought to be relevant, or the respective bodies may differ as to the weight to be attached to the relevant considerations. As the professionals have a particular interest in the setting of the appropriate standard, the proper balance of public policy issues is better served by independent determination of standards. In most instances, however, the professional standards are likely to have developed with due consideration for the interests of affected parties and will, in practice, coincide with the legal standard.[96]

The Supreme Court in *Roche v Peilow*[97] unanimously held that where a standard practice was subject to an inherent defect, which would be apparent to any qualified person giving consideration to the matter, following the standard practice would not discharge the duty owed. The circumstances in which the matter arose were as follows. The defendants were acting as solicitors for the plaintiffs in respect of a transaction under which the plaintiffs contracted with a construction firm for the lease of a site and the construction of a house thereon. The site was part of a portion of land which the construction company used to secure a debt and this charge was registered in the Companies Office. Standard conveyancing practice was to search the Companies Office for registered charges immediately prior to execution of the conveyance. Searches were not conducted at an earlier point, even though clients might have to incur considerable expenditure prior to execution (as was the case with the plaintiffs). The purpose of the practice was to avoid increasing costs through the conduct of additional searches. The plaintiffs were not warned by the defendants as to the risk of loss

---

96 For a detailed discussion of the relationship between professional standards and the legal standard of care see Jackson & Powell, *op. cit.* at p. 39 (judicial function); pp. 123–8 (architects); pp. 213–16 (surveyors); pp. 336–9 (solicitors); pp. 468–76 (doctors); pp. 656–9 (accountants); Kennedy & Grubb, *op. cit.* at pp. 449–62; White, *op. cit.* at §§7.3.09–9.3.10 and §§8.2.09–8.2.13.

97 [1985] IR 232; the principle is reiterated in *Dunne v National Maternity Hospital* [1989] IR 91; [1989] ILRM 735, at p. 109; p. 745 per Finlay CJ; see also the advice of the Privy Council in *Edward Wong Finance Co. Ltd v Johnson, Stokes & Master* [1984] AC 296.

arising by way of a third party claim in respect of title to the site, leaving them unaware of, and unprotected against, such risk.

The Supreme Court held that the defendants had been negligent in not conducting a search before the plaintiffs paid out any money, or alternatively, for not making them aware that they were at risk of losing the money.

The converse of this proposition also holds true, i.e. a deviation from standard practice does not necessarily indicate a failure to exercise due care. In fact, where the earlier proposition is applicable, a deviation is required in order to discharge the duty of care. In situations where the deviation is not based on an obvious flaw in the standard procedure it would have to be justified. A defendant who has departed from standard practice would probably have to show that the course of conduct taken posed no greater risk to the plaintiff than the standard procedure. It should be kept in mind that the development of professional practice, designed to keep pace with changing social needs, must begin with a deviation from existing practice. Thus, many current professional practices have their origins in deviations from established practices. The role of the tort of negligence in respect of such developments is to ensure that reasonable consideration and protection is given to the interests of those affected by the conduct.

In many instances more than one practice may be approved and followed within a profession. This is particularly so in the case of medical procedures. In such instances the danger of assessing conduct with hindsight is heightened.[98] The Supreme Court judgment in *Dunne v National Maternity Hospital*[99] indicates that the selection of any one of the practices will discharge the duty owed, provided there was no apparent flaw in the practice selected. Thus, it is not open to the courts to substitute their opinion for that of the professional as to which course of action should have been selected from the alternatives; once the alternatives each involve a satisfactory level of care for the interests of the affected parties, the selection ought to be a matter of discretion within the control of the professional person who has been called upon to exercise his specialist skills.

There will also be occasions where there is no common practice in relation to the subject matter of a dispute. In such cases one must revert to general principles and apply them in light of the policy issues identified earlier in respect of professional conduct.[100]

---

98 The danger of being wise after the event is a frequent risk in all types of negligence action and is not confined to medical negligence cases. For judicial recognition of the risk see particularly Denning J in *Roe v Minister of Health* [1954] 2 QB 66; Kingsmill Moore J in *Daniels v Heskin* [1954] IR 73; Carroll J in *McSweeney v Bourke* unrep. HC, 24 November 1980.

99 [1989] IR 91; [1989] ILRM 735; see also *Daniels v Heskin* [1954] IR 73; Finlay CJ in *Murphy v Greene* [1990] 2 IR 566 at p. 577; *Bolton v Blackrock Clinic Ltd* unrep. SC, 23 January 1997; Jones, *op. cit.* at pp. 61–71; Kennedy & Grubb, *op. cit.* at pp. 450–2.

100 See, for example, the judgment of Barrington J in *Desmond v Brophy* [1985] IR 449.

Types of Conduct

All aspects of professional conduct are subject to the duty and standard of care, save a refusal to take on a client in the first instance (and even such a refusal may be a breach of duty in some instances[101]). In cases of alleged medical negligence there is no difference in principle between the standard applicable to diagnosis and that applicable to treatment.[102] Since treatment is dependent on the preceding diagnosis, it is appropriate that the legal standard applicable to them should be of the same nature. In addition to the duty to exercise reasonable care in diagnosis and treatment, medical practitioners may also be subject to a duty to warn patients of inherent risks in a proposed course of treatment where there is a serious risk.[103] This will be considered separately below, as it gives rise to some special considerations. It is clear from the cases that all of a doctor's conduct is subject to a duty of care, whether it involves advice or physical acts and whether it is by way of omission or commission.

The same may be said in respect of other professionals, as is amply demonstrated by the available jurisprudence on solicitors' negligence. In *Roche v Peilow*,[104] the negligent conduct could be classified as a failure to act or warn and could be regarded as a pure omission. The solicitor allowed a client to proceed with a transaction, without taking steps to protect the client's interests. It was held that the solicitor should have either taken the appropriate precaution to protect the client or warned of the danger of proceeding without it. *Desmond v Brophy*[105] involved the passing on of a client's money without taking precautions to ensure its return in the event of the collapse of the transaction. This was not a pure omission, as it involved positive conduct on the solicitor's part in forwarding the money. *McMullen v Farrell*[106] provides an example of negligent advice without any active conduct; two firms of solicitors, engaged by the plaintiff, failed to inform him that the landlord could not unreasonably withhold consent to a change of use of leasehold property. It was held that a solicitor's duty of care would not be discharged simply by following a client's instructions, but would require consideration of the legal

---

101 In some instances a doctor may be in breach of duty where a person presents himself for treatment and the doctor refuses to accept him; see Kennedy & Grubb, *op. cit.* at pp. 78–80.

102 See the Supreme Court decisions in *Dunne v National Maternity Hospital* [1989] IR 91; [1989] ILRM 735 and *Reeves v Carthy & O'Kelly* [1984] IR 348.

103 See White, *op. cit.* at §§9.3.01–9.4.03; Healy, 'Failure of Doctors to Communicate Risks to Patients at the Pre-treatment Stage: A Case of Negligence or Medical Negligence?' (1995) 13 ILT 196; Trindade, 'Disclosure of Risks in Proposed Medical Treatment' (1993) 109 LQR 352.

104 [1985] IR 232.

105 [1985] IR 499.

106 [1993] 1 IR 123; [1992] ILRM 776 (HC); unrep. SC, 9 February 1994 (reversing in part on grounds of causation).

implications of the facts brought to the solicitor's attention.[107] Furthermore, if the solicitor's opinion differs from the client's instructions, 'he must advise his client on his views and all reasonable approaches to the problem'.[108]

Informed Consent to Medical Treatment

An issue which has generated a significant amount of dispute and debate is the degree of information that a doctor must disclose to a patient when obtaining consent to medical treatment. If there is a serious risk attached to the proposed course of treatment, must the doctor disclose this fact? As we have already seen, in chapter 1, the seriousness of the risk may be due to its probability of occurrence or the gravity of the consequences – both factors need not be present. The Supreme Court addressed this issue in *Walsh v Family Planning Services Ltd*,[109] where the plaintiff suffered a rare but serious injury following a vasectomy operation, though the operation itself was performed with due care. The Supreme Court upheld the finding of McKenzie J that the doctor had given a sufficient warning and, consequently, had discharged the duty owed. What is of importance for present purposes is the fact that the Supreme Court indicated that there was a duty to warn in respect of the risk in this case.

Furthermore, Finlay CJ stated that the duty to warn would arise once there was a real risk of injury in respect of elective surgery, but that the situation may be different in respect of essential surgery.[110] If we pause for a moment to consider the purpose of a duty of care, the significance of this proposition should become apparent. The imposition of a duty of care in respect of negligent conduct is designed to reduce the risk of foreseeable injury to those likely to be affected by the conduct. In the case of elective surgery a warning will indicate to the patient the risk involved in the surgery and allow the patient to determine for himself whether the objective of the surgery is worth the risk. There is no 'risk' attached to not having the surgery, so the imposition of a duty to warn seems to be the correct result of the application of negligence principles once the risk arising from the surgery is a significant one, since the warning allows the risk to be considered by the patient. In the case of essential surgery, however, the possibility of the patient refusing the surgery is itself a risk, since it will permit an existing illness to go untreated, or at least less effectively treated than is possible. This gives rise to the possibility that giving a warning could increase the risk to the patient, which might lead a court to hold that the giving of the warning was a breach of duty. Thus, there may be valid reasons for treating the two situations differently. A strong contrary

---

107 *Ibid.* at p. 792 per Barron J (HC).
108 *Ibid.* at p. 793 per Barron J (HC).
109 [1992] 1 IR 496.
110 *Ibid.* at p. 510.

viewpoint is that since the patient is the one at risk it should ultimately fall to the patient to decide which risk to undertake.

The distinction between elective and essential surgery, suggested by Finlay CJ in *Walsh*, was applied by the Supreme Court in *Bolton v Blackrock Clinic Ltd*.[111] The plaintiff was referred to the defendants in respect of bronchial problems. The initial operation proposed carried a risk of further harm to the plaintiff (restenosis), which, if it materialised, would require a second and more serious operation (pneumonectomy). The initial operation was performed, with the plaintiff's consent, but the adverse effect (restenosis) ensued and, consequently, the second operation then had to be performed (and the plaintiff again gave her consent). This latter surgery carried a slight risk of damage to the laryngeal nerve, which, unfortunately, materialised in this case. The plaintiff accepted that both operations were performed with due care and skill; the cause of complaint related to the information given to her in respect of the associated risks.

The plaintiff alleged that her consent to the first operation was not an informed one, because the doctors had not carried out sufficient tests before advising that she undergo the surgery and had not given a sufficient warning in respect of the risk of restenosis. The scope of the obligation was set out by Hamilton CJ:

> The surgery was undoubtedly elective surgery in the sense that it was a matter for the Appellant to decide whether or not she would undergo such an operation and to give or withhold her consent thereto.
>
> Before obtaining such consent there was a clear obligation on [the surgeon] to
> (1) satisfy himself as to the necessity for the operation;
> (2) explain to the Appellant the necessity for the operation and the consequences of failing to have the operation;
> (3) explain to the Appellant the nature of the operation, and
> (4) inform the Appellant of any possible harmful consequence arising from the operation.[112]

The Supreme Court upheld the trial judge's findings that a sufficient warning was given; the plaintiff was informed that there was a 1 per cent risk of death and a 5 per cent risk of restenosis, and that a pneumonectomy would be required if restenosis occurred. The trial judge's finding that sufficient tests had been carried out was also upheld. Thus, the doctors were found to have discharged their duty in respect to both diagnosis and advice. In relation to the second operation, the plaintiff's complaint was that she was not informed that there was a $1/2$–1 per cent risk of laryngeal nerve damage. The Supreme Court

---

111 Unrep. SC, 23 January 1997.
112 *Ibid*. at p. 13 of the judgment.

upheld the trial judge's ruling that, although the risk was not disclosed, there was no breach of the duty to adequately inform the plaintiff as to the nature and effect of the operation. This was justified on the basis that the second operation was necessary and the risk was slight.[113]

It is significant to note that the interpretation of elective surgery by Hamilton CJ is significantly different from that sketched in the discussion of *Walsh v Family Planning Services.* In *Walsh*, the plaintiff was healthy and the surgery was a matter of choice of lifestyle, rather than treatment of an illness. In *Bolton*, the initial surgery was for the treatment of serious illness. The latter decision narrows the scope of necessary surgery to cases where there is no viable alternative. This places an extensive duty on doctors to disclose risks and reflects a strong regard for patient autonomy by confining therapeutic privilege (the doctor's ability to withhold information, out of concern for the patient's best interests) to a narrow range of cases.

The Supreme Court in *Walsh* was divided in respect of the appropriate standard of care to be applied, once a duty to warn arose. Finlay CJ indicated that the principles identified in *Dunne* were the appropriate ones and that the standard in respect of the duty to warn was, in principle, the same as that applicable to diagnosis and treatment.[114] O'Flaherty J rejected the applicability to the duty to warn of the principles in *Dunne* with respect to following established practice.[115] Citing the decision of the Supreme Court of Canada in *Reibl v Hughes*,[116] he expressed a preference for 'established principles of negligence' in setting the standard of care. The difference between the two views may be more apparent than real, as the principles in *Dunne* simply provide more specific detail as to the meaning of the general principles in respect of a doctor's duty. It may be the case, however, that O'Flaherty J meant that the specific formulation used in respect of diagnosis and treatment is not appropriate in respect of the duty to warn. In *Bolton*, the Supreme Court preferred Finlay CJ's view and applied the *Dunne* principles.[117] It should be noted that there is some divergence in common law jurisdictions in respect of the appropriate method for measuring the standard of care in respect of a doctor's duty to warn, with views ranging from medical paternalism to a standard based on the reasonable patient.[118]

---

113 *Ibid.* at p. 44 of the judgment; Geoghegan J, in the High Court, had stated that he did 'not think that every conceivable contingency has to be explained to a patient'.

114 [1992] 1 IR 496, at p. 510.

115 *Ibid.* at p. 535. Hederman J concurred at p. 513.

116 (1980) 114 DLR (3d) 1.

117 Unrep. SC, 23 January 1997, at pp. 7–12 of Hamilton CJ's judgment.

118 For the range of views on this subject see McMahon & Binchy, *op. cit.* at pp. 268–9; Jones, *op. cit.* at pp 234–47; Jackson & Powell, *op. cit.* at pp. 515–26; Kennedy & Grubb, *op. cit.* at pp. 172–200; Teff, *op. cit.* It would seem that the conflict in respect of the correct approach is peculiar to medical cases and there is no equivalent debate in respect of other professions.

English law favours the former,[119] while the US,[120] Canada[121] and Australia[122] have all opted for the latter.

This issue will be revisited in chapter 4 in relation to trespass to the person. A final point to consider for present purposes in relation to this divergence is that the latter approach could take the issue of advising patients outside the realm of the tort of negligence entirely, as it could impose a strict duty to disclose risks. Negligence principles require doctors to act as the reasonable doctor would, not as the reasonable patient would.

Construction and Maintenance of Real Property

Injuries incurred through the defective condition of buildings and land give rise to a number of issues concerning the scope of the tort of negligence and there is a substantial body of jurisprudence on the subject (so much so that a number of jurisdictions now have specialised journals devoted to construction law). From the title of this section it can be seen that the first division of the topic is to separate issues related to construction from those related to maintenance. These in turn can be further sub-divided – construction issues include an examination of the duties owed by a number of people in the construction process, *inter alia*, builders, local authorities, surveyors and architects; the range of persons to whom such duties are owed also produces fertile ground for debate. Maintenance issues include the duties of both occupiers and owners and also a consideration of the range of persons affected.

Duties in Respect of Construction

A variety of persons are involved in the construction of buildings, such as architects, developers, builders (including sub-contractors) and, in some cases, local authorities. Furthermore, the sale of the finished buildings usually involves others, such as financial institutions, surveyors and valuers. Many of these will be subject to duties under principles which have been given separate treatment in this text and do not need detailed reiteration at this point. Architects and surveyors, for example, will be subject to professional negligence principles and the rules on negligent misstatement. Local authorities will be subject to the principles governing the imposition of obligations on public authorities, considered later in this chapter. Financial institutions will be

---

119 *Bolam v Friern Hospital Management Committee* [1957] 1 WLR 582; *Chatterton v Gerson* [1981] QB 432; [1980] 3 WLR 1003; [1981] 1 All ER 257; *Hills v Potter* [1984] 1 WLR 641; [1983] 3 All ER 716; *Sidaway v Board of Governors of the Bethlem Royal Hospital* [1985] AC 871; [1985] 2 WLR 480; [1985] 1 All ER 643.
120 *Canterbury v Spence* (1972) 464 F 2d 772 (DC Cir); see also Prosser et al., *Prosser & Keeton on Torts*, 5th ed. (St Paul, Minn.: West, 1984) at pp. 189–93.
121 *Hopp v Lepp* (1980) 112 DLR (3d) 67; *Reibl v Hughes* (1980) 114 DLR (3d) 1.
122 *Rogers v Whitaker* (1992) 67 ALJR 47.

subject to the rules on negligent misstatement.[123] The key area of difficulty in the development of the law is whether builders owe a duty of care to purchasers, occupants or visitors and it is this issue which provides the focus for the present discussion. The liability of local authorities is also of critical importance, but is considered separately, because the applicable principles are not confined to defective buildings cases.

Builders' Duty

The relationship between builders and purchasers of buildings remained outside the scope of the tort of negligence for a considerable period in the post *Donoghue v Stevenson* era. Where the builder was engaged by the owner of land, the relationship was seen as being governed exclusively by contract, with no tortious duty of care in respect of the condition of the finished building. Speculative builders, building on their own land and selling or leasing out the completed development, were given the benefit of the immunity granted to all vendors and lessors of real property.[124] This immunity was a surviving aspect of the *caveat emptor* principle, which had dominated sales relationships in classical contract law, but had been ousted from sale of goods contracts.[125] The knock-on effect of these rules was that subsequent purchasers were not owed any duty by the builder, and nor were others such as entrants or passers-by.

The turning point in respect of builders' duty was the decision of the Northern Ireland Court of Appeal in *Gallagher v N. McDowell Ltd*.[126] In this case the plaintiff was the wife of the tenant of a house, which had been built by the defendant building contractors for the Northern Ireland Housing Trust. She was injured shortly after moving into the house, due to the defendant's negligence in the installation of a deficient floorboard. The court held that the builder's position was analogous to the manufacturer of a product and that a distinction based merely on the fact that the product was realty, rather than a

---

123 *O'Connor v First National Building Society* [1991] ILRM 208.
124 For the history of builders' immunities in tort and their eventual demise see Mahon & Binchy, *op. cit.* at p. 232–47; Law Reform Commission, *The Law Relating to the Liability of Builders, Vendors and Lessors for the Quality and Fitness of Premises* (LRC Working Paper No. 1–1977); Law Reform Commission, *Report on Defective Premises* (LRC 3–1982); Binchy, 'Builders, Defective Buildings and Public Authorities' (1986) 4 ILT 76; *Ward v McMaster* [1985] IR 29; [1986] ILRM 43, at pp. 36–42; pp. 49–53 per Costello J.
125 The Sale of Goods Act 1893 was one of the key developments in displacing the principle in the sale of personal property; modern developments in respect of unfair and unconscionable contracts have further displaced the remnants of *caveat emptor* from contract law.
126 [1961] NI 26.

chattel, was not justified.[127] In consequence, the defendant was found to be liable for the plaintiff's injury.

The analogy to manufacturers was extended to speculative builders in England by *dicta* of the Court of Appeal, in *Dutton v Bognor Regis Urban District Council*,[128] and the House of Lords, in *Anns v Merton London Borough Council*.[129] Both cases were expressly concerned with the liability of local authorities, but it was felt that it would be anomalous if the local authority could be liable as the enforcement agency for building regulations, while the builder directly responsible for the deficiency could escape liability. The decisions indicated that the builder's duty would be to avoid latent defects, which posed an imminent danger to persons or property. This approach was applied in Ireland in *Colgan v Connolly Construction Co. (Ireland) Ltd.*[130] The plaintiff was the second owner of a house built by the defendant company and was claiming for the cost of repairing various construction defects. Mahon J found the defendant liable for the cost of repairing dangerous defects, describing the duty as follows:

> The builder's breach was . . . of the common law duty of care recognised by the principle in *Donoghue v Stevenson*. I think that it is a duty to take care to avoid defects in the product which may cause personal injury or damage to property but the product itself has not been regarded as falling within the scope of the duty. The obligation of the builder or manufacturer in regard to the quality of his product is, in my view, something which ought to rest in contract only.[131]

These decisions did incorporate one significant extension to the *Donoghue v Stevenson* principle by allowing recovery of the financial cost of repairing dangerous defects.[132] Manufacturers, repairers and so forth, in product cases, have only been held liable for personal injuries or damage to property other than the product, but not for the cost of remedying the defect. There is no clear explanation in the cases why this extension was provided. In principle, however, it can be justified, as the cost of repair to the owner of the property is foreseeable; furthermore, the duty is not unduly uncertain in scope, since it is only owed to a limited class of persons. Also, there is no compelling policy reason why builders should be relieved of the consequences of their neglect on the fortuitous ground that their breach of duty has been discovered before it has caused any physical injury or damage.

---

127 *Ibid.* at p. 38; the decision was confined to builders contracted to build on another person's land and did not extend to speculative builders.
128 [1972] 1 QB 373; [1972] 2 WLR 299; [1972] 1 All ER 462.
129 [1978] AC 728; [1977] 2 WLR 1024; [1977] 2 All ER 492.
130 [1980] ILRM 33.
131 *Ibid.* at p. 37.
132 *Ibid.* at p. 36.

The House of Lords extended the scope of the duty to incorporate non-dangerous defects in *Junior Books Ltd v Veitchi Co. Ltd.*[133] Here the defenders were specialist sub-contractors, nominated by the pursuers' architects to install a floor in the pursuers' factory, prior to the installation of equipment. Due to defective workmanship the floor began to crack. Although there was no immediate danger of injury to persons or property, the House of Lords held that the pursuers' were entitled to recover the cost of having a new floor installed.[134] This decision was followed in Ireland in *Ward v McMaster and Louth County Council.*[135] In this case the defendant had built a bungalow for himself and subsequently sold it on to the plaintiff. Later, the plaintiff discovered several defects in the house; there were serious structural defects and also several non-dangerous defects in respect of the quality of materials and workmanship. Costello J, relying on the judgment of Lord Roskill in *Junior Books*, stated that:

> . . . the duty of care which the defendant owed to a purchaser of the bungalow which he built was one relating to hidden defects not discoverable by the type of examination which he could expect his purchaser to make before occupying the house. But the duty was not confined to avoiding foreseeable harm to persons or property other than the bungalow itself . . . but extended to a duty to avoid causing the purchaser consequential financial loss arising from hidden defects in the bungalow itself . . .[136]

This extension of the scope of the builder's duty was based on the foreseeability of the damage and the absence of any compelling policy reason to deny the duty. The justice of imposing this responsibility on builders (and others, such as local authorities) is succinctly stated by Cooke:

> . . . prima facie, he who puts into the community an apparently sound and durable structure, intended for use in all probability by a succession of persons, should be expected to take reasonable care that it is reasonably fit for that use and does not mislead. He is not merely exercising his freedom as a citizen to pursue his own ends. He is constructing, exploiting or sanctioning something for the use of others. Unless compelling grounds to the contrary can be made out, and subject to reasonable limitations as to time or otherwise, the natural consequences of failure to take due care should be accepted.[137]

---

133 [1983] AC 520; [1982] 3 WLR 477; [1982] 3 All ER 201.
134 In the long term, replacement would work out cheaper than continuous repair.
135 [1985] IR 29; [1986] ILRM 43.
136 *Ibid.* at p. 44; p. 55; the *Junior Books* decision was, in turn, based on Lord Wilberforce's two stage approach in *Anns*.
137 Cooke, 'An Impossible Distinction' (1991) 107 LQR 46, at p. 70, grounding his view on ethical rather than economic argument. The article is an extrajudicial opinion from the President of the New Zealand Court of Appeal.

The House of Lords subsequently re-evaluated the duties owed by builders and local authorities in respect of dangerous buildings. In the seminal decisions on the issue, *D. & F. Estates Ltd v Church Commissioners for England and Wales*[138] and *Murphy v Brentwood District Council*,[139] the House of Lords held that the economic loss of repairing defects is outside the scope of the duty of care, unless there is an unusually high degree of proximity between the parties. In fact the House of Lords went so far as to overrule *Anns* in *Murphy*; *Junior Books*, however, was regarded as being correctly decided, because of the high degree of proximity disclosed in the particular facts of the case. The builder's duty in England is now comparable to a manufacturer's duty in respect of a defective product.

Other jurisdictions have refused to follow *D. & F. Estates* and *Murphy* and continue to apply the builder's duty in respect of economic loss.[140] The Privy Council, in *Invercargill City Council v Hamlin*,[141] has accepted that the difference of approach is justified on the basis of differences in policy considerations, such as public expectations and community standards, between the jurisdictions. Differences of opinion persist between the various jurisdictions as to the scope of the duty owed. The Supreme Court of Canada, in *Winnipeg Condominium Corporation No. 36 v Bird Construction Co. Ltd*,[142] confined the duty to dangerous defects, including the cost of repairing such defects before any physical harm had occurred. The scope of the duty in Canada, therefore, is the same as in *Anns* and *Connolly*. The New Zealand Court of Appeal, in *Invercargill City Council v Hamlin*,[143] and the High Court of Australia, in *Bryan v Maloney*,[144] both held the duty to extend to any defects which would diminish the value of the building. This clearly includes

---

138 [1989] AC 177; [1988] 3 WLR 368; [1988] 2 All ER 992; analysed by Wallace, 'Negligence and Defective Buildings: Confusion Confounded?' (1989) 105 LQR 46.

139 [1991] 1 AC 378; [1990] 3 WLR 414; [1990] 2 All ER 908; analysed by Wallace, '*Anns* Beyond Repair' (1991) 107 LQR 228.

140 *Bryan v Maloney* (1995) 182 CLR 609 (Australia), measuring the loss in terms of diminished value, rather than cost of repair; noted by Wallace (1995) 3 Tort L Rev 231; *Zumpano v Montagnese* (1997) Aust Torts Rep 81–406, noted by Wallace (1997) 5 Tort L Rev 152; Martin (1996) 59 MLR 116; *Winnipeg Condominium Corporation No. 36 v Bird Construction Co. Ltd* (1995) 121 DLR (4th) 193 (Canada), noted by Palmer (1993) 3 Tort L Rev 240; Hoyano (1995) 58 MLR 887; see also Stychin, 'Dangerous Liaisons: New Developments in the Law of Defective Premises' (1996) 16 LS 387.

141 [1996] AC 624; [1996] 2 WLR 367; [1996] 1 All ER 756 (appeal from New Zealand), noted by Wallace (1996) 112 LQR 369; Todd (1996) 4 Tort L Rev 91; *Invercargill* is analysed in more depth by Wallace, 'No Somersault After *Murphy*: New Zealand Follows Canada' (1995) 111 LQR 285.

142 (1995) 121 DLR (4th) 193.

143 [1994] 3 NZLR 513; approved by the Privy Council [1996] AC 624; [1996] 2 WLR 367; [1996] 1 All ER 756.

144 (1995) 182 CLR 609.

dangerous defects, but also extends to non-dangerous defects, provided that they are sufficiently significant to affect the value of the property. Thus, minor defects are not embraced by the duty in those jurisdictions, but serious defects are included irrespective of whether they are dangerous or non-dangerous. This is closer to the position in *Junior Books* and *Ward*. The distinction between the treatment of buildings and products can be justified on two grounds. First, the risk to the purchaser is generally of a different magnitude and, consequently, it may be argued that there is a greater need for protection against economic loss.[145] Secondly and perhaps more importantly, legislative intervention in respect of the sale of goods has provided extensive protection to purchasers of products, removing the need to reconsider the scope of the duty in tort. Thus, the development of the protection of purchasers of buildings may be seen as part of the natural progression of the tort of negligence over the decades following *Donoghue v Stevenson* and as a reflection of changing attitudes towards the underlying policy issues.

Standard of Care for Builders

We have already seen that section 34(2)(f) of the Civil Liability Act 1961 provides that the possibility of discovering defects is treated as an evidential issue in products cases and not as a bar to recovery. Mahon J, in *Colgan*, applied this provision to the builder's duty,[146] though this appears to treat the analogy between products and buildings too literally. The sub-section was not considered in *Ward*, as the plaintiff's reliance on the examination conducted on behalf of the local authority was justified in the circumstances. The definition of the duty by Costello J, quoted above, however, suggests that there is no breach of duty by the builder, if the purchaser ought to have discovered the defect prior to purchasing the property.

The decision in *Ward* also demonstrates that the appropriate standard is that of the reasonable builder, even where the builder possesses no appropriate training or expertise. This is an application of the objective approach to the standard of care, considered in chapter 1. Once persons engage in a specialised activity, they effectively hold themselves out as having competence in that field of activity and must meet the standard of the specialist, without any allowance for their lack of expertise.[147]

The Building Regulations 1997[148] provide technical standards for construction work. While these regulations do not generate binding civil obligations,[149]

---

145 The purchase of some products, such as ships or aircraft, would raise comparable risks to buildings cases. One could argue that the manufacturer's duty in such cases should also extend to quality defects in the product.
146 [1980] ILRM 33, at p. 36.
147 See also *Sunderland v McGreavy* [1987] IR 372, at pp. 381–2 per Lardner J.
148 SI 497/1997.
149 S. 21 of the Building Control Act 1990.

they may provide some general guidance as to the reasonableness of measures taken by builders.[150] A minor and inadvertent deviation from the regulations, for example, is unlikely to be considered to be negligent, whereas a deliberate disregard of safety standards, in order to reduce costs and increase profit, is almost certainly going to be treated as a breach of the duty of care.

Duties in Respect of Maintenance

Owners and occupiers of property are subject to obligations to keep it from being a source of danger to others. The obligations towards the occupants of neighbouring property are governed by specific torts, such as private nuisance and the principle in *Rylands v Fletcher*, in addition to negligence. Passers-by may also have recourse to specific torts, such as public nuisance, in addition to negligence. The application of the general principles of negligence, discussed in chapter 1, to maintenance of premises does not give rise to any additional policy features of note. Where the injury results from active interference with the condition of the property, then plainly the actor will owe a duty of care to persons foreseeably affected by his conduct. Where the injury results from the failure to repair, then the general principles relating to omissions should be invoked to determine the appropriate defendant.[151]

The tort of negligence is not generally applicable to entrants to the property, where the injury arises from the condition of the property itself; the obligations towards entrants are governed by statute.[152] The employer's duty in respect of the condition of the workplace is an exception and the tort of negligence remains applicable to occupational injuries.[153]

Public Authorities' Duties

It is well established that public authorities can, in some circumstances, be liable for breach of mandatory statutory obligations. It is also well established that the exercise of discretionary powers and functions can give rise to a duty of care under the tort of negligence.[154] This area has grown in importance in recent years and has raised some key policy issues in the development of negligence as a tort.

---

150 On the propriety of using regulations as evidence of negligence, where there is no enforceable duty, see *Askin v Knox* [1989] 1 NZLR 252.

151 The principles in respect of affirmative duty will also be relevant in other instances, for example where the plaintiff seeks to sue a landlord for failing to prevent a tenant from putting the premises in a dangerous condition.

152 The Occupiers' Liability Act 1995, considered in chapter 3 *infra*.

153 Additional statutory obligations are outlined in chapter 3 *infra*.

154 See Craig, 'Negligence in the Exercise of a Statutory Power' (1978) 94 LQR 428; Todd, 'The Negligence Liability of Public Authorities: Divergence in the Common Law'(1986) 102 LQR 370; Todd, 'Public Authorities' Liability: The New Zealand Dimension' (1987) 103 LQR 26; Arrowsmith, *Civil Liability and Public Authorities* (London: Earlsgate Press, 1992) at chapter 6; Sopinka, 'The

The general requirements for establishing a duty of care have been adapted to the specific context of the exercise of statutory powers, by the Supreme Court in *Siney v Dublin Corporation*:[155]

(i)   the nature of the statutory function and the circumstances of the case must be such that there is a sufficient degree of proximity between the parties;
(ii) there must be reasonable reliance by the plaintiff on the public authority.

Costello J elaborated on this approach in *Ward v McMaster and Louth County Council* and his views were implicitly endorsed by the Supreme Court in upholding his decision:[156]

a)   When deciding whether a local authority exercising statutory functions is under a common law duty of care the court must firstly ascertain whether a relationship of proximity existed between the parties such that in the reasonable contemplation of the authority carelessness on their part might cause loss. But all the circumstances of the case must in addition be considered, including the power under which the authority is acting. Of particular significance in this connection is the purpose for which the statutory powers were conferred and whether or not the plaintiff is within the class of persons which the statute was designed to assist.

b)   It is material in all cases for the court in reaching its decision on the existence and scope of the alleged duty to consider whether it is just and reasonable that a common law duty of care as alleged should in all the circumstances exist.[157]

Nature of the Function

The central issue for courts in considering the imposition of a duty of care is the nature of the function being exercised. Some functions are well suited to the imposition of a duty, while others are not. In the early development of this area of negligence law a distinction was drawn between 'policy' decisions and 'operational' activities. The former were seen as discretionary choices between competing claims in the determination of priorities on matters of public interest and, so, unsuited to negligence actions;[158] the latter were considered to be

Liability of Public Authorities: Drawing the Line' (1993) 1 Tort L Rev 123; Brodie, 'Public Authorities – Negligence Actions – Control Devices' (1998) 18 LS 1; Hogan & Morgan, *Administrative Law in Ireland*, 3rd ed. (Dublin: Round Hall Sweet & Maxwell, 1998) at pp. 829 *et seq.*; *Ward v McMaster and Louth County Council* [1985] IR 29; [1986] ILRM 43, at pp. 45–9; pp. 56–9; liability for breach of mandatory duties is considered in chapter 3 *infra*.
155 [1980] IR 400; O'Higgins CJ at p. 414; Henchy J at p. 422.
156 [1988] IR 337.
157 [1985] IR 29; [1986] ILRM 43, at pp. 49–50; pp. 59–60.
158 An action for misfeasance in public office would be available in cases of public officials acting *mala fides*; see McMahon & Binchy, *op. cit.* at pp. 345 *et seq.*;

practical activities conducted in the implementation of policy and suited to private action. This form of distinction provides some general guidance, but can be difficult to operate in practice and has fallen out of favour in recent years.[159]

The key policy issue relates to the separation of powers. The judicial function should not extend to political decision making on resource allocation between competing public interests. However, all public activities involve some degree of resource allocation and all decisions imposing liability will have an impact on public funds. Thus, the dividing line between justiciable and non-justiciable issues is difficult to draw.[160] The separation of powers argument weighs more heavily against the imposition of obligations on central government than lesser public authorities, but even central government can be held liable where its actions are comparable to those of a private corporation.[161]

The approach applied in modern English authorities is to take each case on its individual merits, comparing the function in question to others which have previously been ruled upon. The imposition of a duty is seen as 'a question of an intensely pragmatic character, well suited for gradual development but requiring most careful analysis . . . in line with the incremental approach to the development of the tort of negligence'.[162] While Irish courts do not favour incrementalism to the same extent as their English counterparts, they do display a similar caution in respect of the duties of public bodies. The case by case approach probably reflects a more precise, if less coherent, method of analysis than any general classification of functions.

Kneebone, 'Misfeasance in a Public Office After Mengel's Case: A "Special" Tort No More?' (1996) 4 Tort L Rev 111; there are some important decisions on the dividing line between negligence and misfeasance, *Pine Valley Developments v Minister for the Environment* [1987] IR 23; [1987] ILRM 747, at pp. 35–7; pp. 757–8 per Finlay CJ; at p. 40; p. 761 per Henchy J (re planning functions); *McMahon v Ireland* [1988] ILRM 610 (re Registrar of Friendly Societies); *CW Shipping Co. Ltd v Limerick Harbour Commissioners* [1989] ILRM 416, at pp. 425–6 per O'Hanlon J (re Harbours Act 1946); *O'Donnell v Dún Laoghaire Corporation* [1991] 1 ILRM 300, at pp. 319–20 per Costello J (re functions as a sanitary authority).

159 See Arrowsmith, *op. cit.*; Jones, *Textbook on Torts*, 5th ed. (London: Blackstone, 1996) at §2.2.3.2.

160 Feldthusen, 'Failure to Confer Discretionary Public Benefits' (1997) 5 Tort L Rev 17 argues for a complete immunity in respect of discretionary powers. A further difficulty is that, even where judicial intervention is justified, a question arises as to whether the public law remedy of judicial review or the private law remedy of damages is the more appropriate means of doing so.

161 Such as representations intended to be relied on by individuals entering into commercial transactions, considered briefly in chapter 1 *supra*; on state liability generally, see chapter 13 *infra*.

162 *Lonrho plc v Tebbitt* [1992] 4 All ER 280, at p. 287 per Dillon LJ; see also *Rowling v Takaro Properties Ltd* [1988] AC 473; [1988] 2 WLR 418; [1988] 1 All ER 163.

Defective Housing Cases

Turning to the details of some of the cases provides some indication of the division between actionable and immune functions. The plaintiff in *Siney* suffered damage to his health as a result of dampness, caused by inadequate ventilation, in a flat supplied by the defendants under powers conferred on them by the Housing Act 1966. The Supreme Court held that once the defendants chose to operate their powers as a housing authority, to provide housing for persons unable to make provision for themselves, they owed a duty to exercise reasonable care to ensure that the house was fit for habitation.[163] The defendants were held to be negligent in failing to carry out a simple test in respect of the humidity in the flat, prior to allotting it to the plaintiff and his family. The court made it clear that not every aspect of housing functions would be amenable to such actions,[164] but the power in question here displayed the necessary characteristics to generate a common law duty of care. The power was protective in nature; the plaintiff was a member of the class of persons intended to benefit; the plaintiff was in a vulnerable position, dependent on the local authority for protection; and the danger was significant.

The duty in respect of fitness for habitation was held to be a continuing duty, rather than a once-off obligation at the time of letting, in *Burke v Dublin Corporation*.[165] The case concerned the installation of a solid fuel heating system. It was found that there was no negligence in the initial selection and installation of the system, but the Supreme Court held that the defendants could be liable in negligence for retaining the system after it had been discovered to be a danger to the health of occupants. It was also held that the duty in respect of fitness for habitation would extend to a tenant purchaser, buying out the premises which had been provided to them under the 1966 Act.[166]

Ward was concerned with a local authority providing finance for the purchase of a property, also under powers conferred by the 1966 Act. The loan was provided by the defendant council, after having the house inspected by an auctioneer (not a surveyor or engineer) and the plaintiff was charged an administrative fee of £10 with respect to the valuation. These facts, and the fact that the plaintiff had limited means, led to the finding that the council could anticipate that the plaintiff would rely on their examination of the property. A duty was imposed on the council in respect of the foreseeable risk of financial loss to the plaintiff if the house was deficient in quality.[167] The

---

163 [1980] IR 400, at pp. 414–15 per O'Higgins CJ; p. 421 per Henchy J.
164 *Ibid.* at p. 412; mandatory duties under the Act were held not to be amenable to enforcement by way of a tort action.
165 [1991] 1 IR 341, at p. 356 per Finlay CJ.
166 *Ibid.* at p. 351; the court was dealing with an implied warranty in contract, rather than a tortious duty; given the concurrent nature of the contractual and tortious obligations in housing cases, it seems likely that the tortious duty may also extend to purchasers.
167 [1985] IR 29; [1986] ILRM 43, at pp. 51–3; pp. 61–2.

function here was also protective in nature, providing finance for those unable to arrange private finance and ensuring that the property was of sufficient value to justify the amount paid; the plaintiff was a member of the class of intended beneficiaries; as with *Siney*, the plaintiff was in a position of dependency; and the risk was significant. The failure to have the house examined by a more qualified person was held to be negligent.

A duty of care has also been held to apply to the provision of a loan for home improvements to a tenant purchaser in *Howard v Dublin Corporation*.[168] This case involved the same type of heating system as *Burke*, but the dispute in *Howard* was over the economic loss resulting from the unsuitability of the system. On the facts it was found that the defendant corporation had not been negligent, but it was accepted that the power gave rise to a duty on similar grounds to the previous housing cases. It was also noted, *obiter*, that the duty to tenant purchasers would be more restricted than the duty to tenants, due to the difference in their circumstances (the former being less dependent than the latter).

Planning functions have been held not to give rise to a duty of care, as they are for the general public good, rather than for the protection of vulnerable groups in society. In *Sunderland v Louth County Council*[169] the plaintiff bought a house which turned out to be susceptible to flooding and claimed, *inter alia*, that the local authority had been negligent in granting planning permission. Lardner J held that there was insufficient proximity between the parties because 'the purposes for which these powers were conferred are quite different and distinct from and did not comprehend the subject matter of the plaintiff's complaints which more properly fall within the appropriate area of building regulations'.[170] The Supreme Court upheld this finding and found that planning functions were not designed primarily for the protection of future occupants.

Irish law is similar to other common law jurisdictions, with the notable exception of England, in the extent to which it imposes obligations on local authorities in respect of functions associated with the construction and provision of housing.[171] Apart from functions under housing legislation, local authorities may be susceptible to private law duties arising out of functions as building authorities under the Building Control Act 1990.[172]

---

168 Unrep. HC, 31 July 1996; analysed in Byrne & Binchy, *Annual Review of Irish Law 1996* at pp. 574–6.
169 [1987] IR 372 (HC); [1990] ILRM 658 (SC); analysed in Byrne & Binchy, *Annual Review of Irish Law 1990* at pp. 545 *et seq.*
170 [1987] IR 372, at p. 390.
171 See the discussion of builders' duty above; English courts have retained the local authorities' liability in respect of personal injuries, see *Targett v Torfaen Borough Council* [1992] 3 All ER 27.
172 See the Building Control Regulations 1997 (SI 496/1997) (governing administrative functions); Building Regulations 1997 (SI 497/1997) (providing technical specifications and standards).

Other Situations

There are numerous other examples of the consideration of private law duties in respect of public functions. A local authority owes a duty of reasonable care in respect of its functions as a road authority, under the Local Government Act 1925, provided the claim is concerned with misfeasance, rather than nonfeasance.[173] Nonfeasance involves cases of pure omission, where the authority fails to take measures to construct or repair; it has traditionally been immune from liability and this view has been confirmed by the Supreme Court decision in *Convery v Dublin County Council*.[174] Misfeasance involves a failure to exercise care after the authority has involved itself in an activity.[175] The provision and repair of roads appear to be significantly different from housing functions at first sight. The road authority function is not as obviously protective in nature and could be regarded as a matter of more general public interest, akin to planning. However, the functions of a road authority involve a significant element of safety and the degree of proximity to road users may be fairly considered to be greater than that between a planning authority and subsequent purchasers of property. The closeness of comparison and the fine distinctions involved here demonstrate the difficulty in anticipating how various functions are likely to be classified by the courts.

Regulatory authorities in the financial services sector have tended to be regarded as not owing a duty of care to potential investors. In cases from various jurisdictions, claims by new investors that regulatory authorities were responsible for negligently allowing institutions to trade in an improper fashion have failed.[176] The broad rationale behind the decisions is the floodgates argument that the regulatory authorities should not owe a duty to such a broad and indeterminate class as potential investors. A narrower ground in support of the rejection of a duty is that it may conflict with the interests of existing investors. Since regulatory authorities have limited power and the main sanction at their disposal is to preclude an institution from trading, the exercise of this power for the protection of potential investors may prejudice

---

173 *Weir v Dún Laoghaire Corporation* [1983] IR 242; [1984] ILRM 113, negligent construction of a road by a private contractor, authorised by the defendant corporation, causing the plaintiff to trip; considered further in chapter 14 *infra; Rowe v Bus Éireann and Wicklow County Council* unrep. HC, 3 March 1994, inadequate signs put up by the local authority after creating an unusual risk when conducting repairs; see also *Stovin v Wise* [1996] AC 923; [1996] 3 WLR 388; [1996] 3 All ER 801; noted by Convery (1997) 60 MLR 559.

174 [1996] 3 IR 153; this decision also casts serious doubt on whether *Weir v Dún Laoghaire Corporation* was correctly decided, as the conduct of the contractors should not have been treated as having been authorised by the corporation.

175 See McMahon & Binchy, *op. cit.* at pp. 477 *et seq.; The State (Sheehan) v Government of Ireland* [1987] IR 550; [1988] ILRM 437.

176 *Yuen Kun-yeu v AG of Hong Kong* [1988] AC 175; [1987] 3 WLR 776; [1987] 2 All ER 705; *Davis v Radcliff* [1990] 1 WLR 821; [1990] 2 All ER 536; [1989] LRC Comm 495 (Isle of Man); *McMahon v Ireland* [1988] ILRM 610.

the interests of existing investors; thus, the imposition of a duty of care could place regulatory authorities in an impossible position.

Other areas where disputes have arisen over private law duties in respect of public functions include the prosecution of criminal cases,[177] child care,[178] policing,[179] the prison service,[180] rescue services[181] and airport security.[182] Each function requires careful analysis, in order to determine whether a duty or immunity is appropriate to the public authority exercising it.[183]

---

177 *HMW v Ireland* [1997] 2 IR 142, where Costello P refused to impose a private law duty of care on the Attorney General, towards the victims of crime, in respect of the performance of functions under the Extradition Acts 1965–87. He also noted that such a duty could not be applied to either the Attorney General or the Director of Public Prosecutions in respect of the prosecution of crimes generally. He held that the imposition of such a duty could generate a conflict of interest between that duty and the proper performance of the prosecutor's public functions. See also *Elguzouli Daf v Commissioner of Police of the Metropolis* [1995] QB 335; [1995] 2 WLR 173; [1995] 1 All ER 833.

178 *X (a minor) v Bedfordshire County Council* [1995] 2 AC 633; [1995] 3 WLR 152; [1995] 3 All ER 353; noted (1995) 145 NLJ 993; Cane (1996) 112 LQR 22 (no duty of care on a local authority with respect to child protection functions, but vicarious liability for professional negligence by a member of staff could arise); *T (a minor) v Surrey County Council* [1990] 4 All ER 577 (local authority liable for negligent misstatement in respect of the suitability of a child minder); see also *Barrett v Enfield London Borough Council* [1997] 3 All ER 171; *H v Black* (1995) Aust Torts Rep 81–340; noted by McGlone (1996) 4 Tort L Rev 18.

179 *Hill v Chief Constable of West Yorkshire* [1989] AC 53; [1988] 2 WLR 1049; [1988] 2 All ER 238 (no general duty of care owed by the police to the general public with respect to the investigation of crime; a duty may arise in particular circumstances, such as the negligent control and supervision of an arrested person, who escapes and causes harm to a third party); see also *Elguzouli Daf v Commissioner of Police of the Metropolis* [1995] QB 335; [1995] 2 WLR 173; [1995] 1 All ER 833.

180 *Home Office v Dorset Yacht Co. Ltd* [1970] AC 1004; [1970] 2 WLR 1140; [1970] 2 All ER 294 (no duty in respect of decisions as to the appropriate form of placement for prisoners, such as the allocation of community service rather than custodial placement; a duty may arise in respect of control and supervision); see also *Muldoon v Ireland* [1988] ILRM 367; *Kavanagh v Governor of Arbour Hill Prison* unrep. HC, 22 April 1993; *Boyd and Boyd v Ireland* unrep. HC, 13 May 1993.

181 *OLL Ltd v Secretary of State for Transport* [1997] 3 All ER 897 (coastguard held not to owe a duty of care towards a person requiring rescue).

182 *Air India Flight 182 Disaster Claimants v Air India et al.* (1987) 44 DLR 4th 317 (adopts the same approach as the police and prison authority cases; no general duty to the public, but a duty related to specific aspects of behaviour in the performance of functions may be imposed for the protection of a limited class of persons).

183 For further examples see *Par Holdings Ltd v City of St John's* (1995) 127 DLR (4th) 749 (diver engaged by municipality causing flooding by sudden removal of obstruction in drain; municipality liable for failing to give proper instructions to diver); *Gordonna Ltd v City of St John's* (1986) 30 DLR 4th 720 (action against city for alleged breach of obligation to supply water to inhabitants).

CHAPTER THREE

Statutory Duties

Introduction

Statutory provisions provide a rich source of legal rights and obligations, some of which may give rise to tortious liability when they are breached. Like negligence, statutory provisions affect a diverse range of interests, relationships and conduct, but, unlike negligence, they do not have a single behavioural standard for the discharge of the obligations created. The only unifying element in respect of tortious liability for breach of statutory duties is the source of defendants' obligation towards the plaintiffs – a statutory provision. Not all statutory obligations can be enforced through an action in tort; the availability of an action can be determined in one of three ways, viz.:

  (i) there may be a statutory scheme of liability in which all the elements of the tort action are contained in the statute, such as the Liability for Defective Products Act 1991 and the Occupiers' Liability Act 1995;

 (ii) there may be a specific section in the statute expressly governing actionability, such as section 60 of the Safety, Health and Welfare at Work Act 1989;

(iii) where there is no express provision in a statute governing the availability of a civil action to enforce the obligations contained therein, it is a matter of judicial interpretation of the statute to determine whether such an action is available.

An action under the first of these three options is described as a statutory tort, while the second and third involve the common law action for breach of statutory duty. We will begin with the common law action; then deal with particular issues related to express provisions on actionability; and, finally, the schemes of liability in relation to defective products and occupiers of property will close the chapter.

Before dealing with these issues a brief note should be made of the approach taken in the American and Canadian courts, which embraces statutory provisions within the framework of the tort of negligence rather than using a separate tort of breach of statutory duty. Statutory provisions are used to determine the level of behaviour required of the defendant in order to discharge the duty of reasonable care.

Breach of Statutory Duty

This is a common law action because, although the obligation on the defendant (or the right of the plaintiff) originates in a statutory provision, the principles governing civil liability for breach of the obligation are determined by judicial decisions, based on precedent. The degree of regard to the provisions of the legislation varies from case to case.

Requisite elements

1. An actionable duty
2. Breach of duty
3. Damage
4. Causation
5. Lack of defence

Actionable Duty

Unlike many negligence cases, the existence of the obligation on the defendant is not normally in doubt in respect of statutory obligations;[1] the contentious issue is whether the obligation can be enforced by way of a tort action. Matters would be greatly simplified if statutes made express provision in respect of civil liability for breach of the duties they contained, a point eloquently made by Lord ᴖu Parcq half a century ago:

> To a person unversed in the science, or art, of legislation it may well seem strange that Parliament has not by now made it a rule to state explicitly what its intention is in a matter which is often of no little importance, instead of leaving it to the courts to discover, by careful examination and analysis of what is expressly said, what that intention may be supposed probably to be. There are, no doubt, reasons which inhibit the legislature from revealing its intention in plain words. I do not know, and must not speculate, what those reasons may be. I trust, however, that it will not be thought impertinent, in any sense of that word, to suggest respectfully that those who are responsible for framing legislation might consider whether the traditional practice, which obscures, if it does not conceal, the intention which Parliament has, or must be presumed to have, might not safely be abandoned.[2]

---

1 There are cases where there may be doubt as to whether a particular statutory obligation is applicable to the facts of the case, particularly where the statutory obligation carries flexible prerequisite characteristics; see, for example, *Dunleavy v Glen Abbey Ltd* [1992] ILRM 1 where the plaintiff was injured when manually lifting a load following the breakdown of a fork-lift truck. Barron J held that occasional breakdowns in the truck, leaving the plaintiff to move loads manually, were sufficient to bring into effect a duty to provide adequate training in respect of manual lifting techniques.

2 *Cutler v Wandsworth Stadium Ltd* [1949] AC 398; [1949] 1 All ER 544, at p. 410; p. 549; see also Thornton, *Legislative Drafting*, 3rd ed. (London: Butterworths, 1987) at pp. 248–50 on provisions in respect of civil liability; and at p. 114, where it is suggested that the initial instructions given to the draftsman should include the means by which the principal objects of the statute are to be achieved.

Unfortunately the provision of express guidance is still lacking in many instances, leaving the courts with the difficult task of interpreting provisions invoked by plaintiffs, in order to determine whether those provisions were intended to create actionable duties. The difficulty of this task is compounded by the lack of coherence and consistency in the available case law with respect to the development of principles of interpretation, a lack so great as to lead Lord Denning MR to say:

> The dividing line between the pro-cases and the contra-cases is so blurred and ill-defined that you might as well toss a coin to decide it. I decline to indulge in such a game of chance. To my mind, we should seek for other ways to do 'therein what to justice shall appertain'.[3]

The solution he offered was that a right of action should be available in cases where the plaintiff's 'private rights and interests are specially affected by the breach'.[4] The orthodox position, however, is that the issue is to be determined by the use of established criteria to determine the intent of the legislature.[5] The law in Ireland and England is substantially similar on this issue at present,[6] though the Irish cases provide little discussion of principle. The factors taken into account in reaching decisions, however, are broadly similar to those used in English decisions up to the 1980s. More recent developments in English law have yet to be considered in the Irish courts. One notable variation on the subject in Ireland is the possible use of constitutional argument by plaintiffs to support their claims.[7]

There are two types of provision that give rise to difficulty. One is where the legislation creating the obligation provides some mode of enforcement, such as a criminal sanction for breach, but does not deal with civil liability. The second is where no means of enforcement of any kind are expressly provided. The general rule governing the first situation is that enunciated by Lord Tenterden CJ in *Doe d, Bishop of Rochester v Bridges*:[8] '. . . where an Act creates an obligation, and enforces the performance in a specified manner,

---

3 *Ex parte Island Records Ltd* [1978] Ch 122; [1978] 3 All ER 824, at pp. 134–5; p. 829.
4 *Ibid.* at p. 139; p. 830.
5 For a more extensive discussion of the techniques of statutory interpretation see Byrne & McCutcheon, *The Irish Legal System*, 3rd ed. (Dublin: Butterworths, 1996) at chapter 14; Manchester et al., *Exploring the Law* (London: Sweet & Maxwell, 1996) at chapters 2 and 3.
6 See McMahon & Binchy, *The Irish Law of Torts*, 2nd ed. (Dublin: Butterworths, 1989) at chapter 21.
7 The relevance of constitutional principles was considered by the High Court in *Parsons v Kavanagh* [1990] ILRM 560, per O'Hanlon J and is discussed later in this chapter and again in chapter 9 *infra*.
8 (1831) 1 B & Ad 847; [1824–34] All ER Rep 167.

we take it to be a general rule that performance cannot be enforced in any other manner . . .'[9] Exceptions to this rule developed over time and Lord Diplock, in *Lonrho Ltd v Shell Petroleum Co. Ltd and Others*,[10] summarised the position by stating that there are two categories of exception:

(i) where the provision is designed for the protection or benefit of a particular class of persons and a member of that class is injured as a result of the breach; or

(ii) where the provision generates a public right, but the plaintiff has suffered particular injury over and above the type of harm suffered by the public generally.

These are no more than general guides as to the categories of cases where actions have been permitted and are not to be regarded as definitive criteria. Thus, where a case falls under one of the two headings it is still open to the court to hold that the statutory provision in question is not actionable in tort. This point is made patently clear by Lord Jauncey in *Hague v Deputy Governor of Parkhurst Prison, Weldon v Home Office*,[11] when he stated that:

> . . . it must always be a matter for consideration whether the legislature intended that private law rights of action should be conferred upon individuals in respect of breaches of the relevant statutory provision. The fact that a particular provision was intended to protect certain individuals is not of itself sufficient to confer private law rights of action upon them, something more is required to show that the legislation intended such conferment.[12]

In fact, the courts have used a variety of factors to determine whether a tort action should be available and have not confined themselves to those outlined by Lord Diplock. Such factors include the purpose of the legislation as a whole (as distinct from the purpose of the particular provision), the adequacy of other remedies and public policy considerations. These will be discussed in more detail presently.

The 'general rule' clearly reflects a literal interpretation of statutory provisions, confining the enforcement of legislative provisions to the means expressly authorised by the legislature. The exceptions involve an acknowledgment that legislative provisions cannot always be satisfactorily implemented by a literal interpretation, but on occasion require the courts to have regard to the purpose and intent of the legislation (thus the whole may be greater than the sum of its individual parts). The cases demonstrate that there are a variety of factors

---

9 *Ibid.* at p. 859; p. 170.
10 [1982] AC 173; [1981] 3 WLR 33; [1981] 2 All ER 456.
11 [1992] 1 AC 58; [1991] 3 WLR 340; [1991] 3 All ER 733.
12 *Ibid.* at pp. 170–1; p. 359; p. 750.

which may be taken into account in determining the legislative intent and no listing of such factors should be regarded as complete, given the level of ingenuity and creativity shown by the judiciary in dealing with claims for breach of statutory duty.

With respect to the second situation, where the statute has failed to provide any remedy, it is useful to begin by returning to Lord Tenterden CJ in *Doe d, Bishop of Rochester v Bridges*: 'If an obligation is created, but no mode of enforcing its performance is ordained, the common law may, in general, find a mode suited to the particular nature of the case.'[13] This epitomises the view that where there is a right there must be a remedy. This does not mean, however, that a right to damages is necessarily available. Other remedies, such as injunctions or public law remedies, such as mandamus,[14] may provide sufficient means of enforcement.

In general, the type of factors taken into account in determining whether an action for damages is available are the same as those mentioned above in relation to provisions where criminal sanctions have been provided. Early Irish authority on the subject, *M'Daid v Milford Rural District Council*,[15] suggests that, for an action to be available, the plaintiff must be a member of a class that the provision was designed to benefit and have suffered harm over and above that suffered by the other members of that class.[16] This appears, at first sight, to conflict with Lord Diplock's later formulation in *Lonrho* as it requires both elements to be present. If one takes a broader perspective and considers the Irish decision, not as a definitive statement of the only situation where an action is available, but as part of a wider principle that either criterion is insufficient on its own, then the case can be seen as compatible with modern English authorities. As we have already seen, Lord Diplock's two categories are only broadly descriptive of the situations where duties have been treated as actionable and each will need additional elements. Similarly the decision in Ireland in *M'Daid v Milford Rural District Council* may be regarded as indicating that benefit of a class is an insufficient criterion to ground an action, but when accompanied by additional factors, such as suffering particular harm, there will be sufficient reason to make an action for damages available.

All the statements of principle so far are rather vague, so we must consider their application to the facts of the cases in order to get a clearer picture of the significance of the principles in practice.

---

13 (1831) 1 B & Ad 847; [1824–34] All ER Rep 167, at p. 859; p. 170; see also *Restatement, Second, Torts* §874A.

14 Mandamus is an order compelling the performance of a public duty, obtained through judicial review proceedings. It is only available against public officials and public bodies (such as the police, local authorities and government ministers); see Hogan & Morgan, *Administrative Law in Ireland*, 3rd ed. (Dublin: Round Hall Sweet & Maxwell, 1998) at chapter 13 for detailed consideration of the public law remedies.

15 [1919] 2 IR 1.

16 *Ibid.* per Ronan LJ at pp. 21–2 and Molony LJ at p. 27 (CA).

Benefit of a Particular Class

There appears to be general acceptance in common law jurisdictions that industrial safety legislation gives rise to a right of action to those workers that the legislation was designed to protect.[17] In *Doherty v Bowaters Irish Wallboard Mills Ltd*[18] for example, section 34(1)(a) of the Factories Act 1955, concerning the condition of lifting tackle, was held to be actionable at the suit of an employee who was injured when the hook of a crane broke and dropped the load that was being carried, causing extensive personal injuries. Similarly in *Gallagher v Mogul of Ireland Ltd*[19] the plaintiff's employer was held liable for a breach of a statutory duty which included an obligation of '. . . supporting the roof and sides of every . . . working place as may be necessary for keeping [the place] secure',[20] when the plaintiff was injured by a fall of rock from the roof of the mine he was working in.

Careful examination of provisions is required, however, to determine the extent of the class covered, as the Supreme Court decisions in *Daly v Greybridge Co-operative Creamery Ltd*[21] and *Roche v P. Kelly & Co. Ltd*[22] demonstrate. Both were concerned with the provisions of the Factories Act 1955, and it was held that only persons working for the benefit of the employer who was subject to the statutory duty were intended to benefit, but that this class could include persons not directly employed by him. Walsh J stated the position as follows: '. . . the object of the Act is to protect only those persons who, broadly speaking, are employed in the factory premises at the work in which the factory is engaged or at work incidental to it'.[23] The plaintiff in the former case was a lawful visitor to the premises of the defendant, but not engaged in any work for the defendant's benefit and, consequently, fell outside the protected class; whereas in the latter case the plaintiff, although not an employee of the defendant, was engaged in work for the benefit of the company and was within the protected class.

The introduction of the Safety, Health and Welfare at Work Act 1989 has radically overhauled industrial safety law in Ireland and will be considered later

---

17 See McMahon & Binchy, *op. cit.* at p. 377; Rogers, *Winfield & Jolowicz on Tort*, 14th ed. (London: Sweet & Maxwell, 1994) at p. 189; Brazier, *Street on Torts*, 9th ed. (London: Butterworths, 1993) at p. 400; Trindade & Cane, *The Law of Torts in Australia*, 2nd ed. (Melbourne: Oxford University Press, 1993) at p. 663. The position in America and Canada differs due to the incorporation of statutory duties in the tort of negligence; nonetheless industrial safety features prominently as a source of actionable duties in those jurisdictions also; see Prosser et al., *Prosser & Keeton on Torts*, 5th ed. (St Paul, Minn.: West, 1984) at p. 224.

18 [1968] IR 277.

19 [1975] IR 204.

20 S. 49(1) of the Mines and Quarries Act 1965.

21 [1964] IR 497.

22 [1969] IR 100.

23 *Daly v Greybridge Co-operative Creamery Ltd* [1964] IR 497, per Walsh J at p. 502 (Ó Dálaigh CJ and Haugh J concurring).

in this chapter. While industrial safety cases are dominant in terms of successful actions for breach of statutory duty, the courts have occasionally held other types of statutory obligation to be actionable. In *Moyne v Londonderry Port & Harbour Commissioners*,[24] for example, the High Court held that the defendants' duty to maintain a docks and pier at a specific harbour was owed to the people living and working in the vicinity of the harbour rather than to the public as a whole, and that an action for damages was available to members of the class suffering damage as a result of a breach of the duty.[25]

Plaintiffs Suffering Particular Harm

Damage is an essential ingredient of the action for breach of statutory duty; however, it may also be necessary to show that the harm suffered by a plaintiff differs from that suffered by other members of the class of persons intended to benefit from the legislative provision. Plaintiffs falling within a protected class who have suffered harm which is no different from that suffered by the class as a whole are unlikely to succeed in an action for breach of statutory duty. In *M'Daid v Milford Rural District Council*[26] the defendants allocated a cottage to a person not falling within the class of persons to whom they owed a statutory duty in respect of such allocation. The plaintiff was a member of the class to whom the duty was owed, but, since only one person could be allocated the cottage, the plaintiff's disadvantage was no different from that of any other member of the class and his claim for damages was rejected by the Court of Appeal. In other words, all members of the class of persons eligible for allocation were equally disadvantaged by the allocation and the plaintiff did not suffer any particular harm which would distinguish him from the others.

It is debatable whether the reverse proposition holds true – that plaintiffs suffering particular harm who are not members of a class of persons intended to benefit from the legislative provision can recover damages. In a number of cases plaintiffs have suffered particular harm, but have failed to recover damages either because they were not members of the protected class, as in *Daly v Greybridge Co-operative Creamery Ltd*, or because the legislation was designed for the benefit of the general public, and not for the protection of a particular class of persons, as in *Atkinson v Newcastle & Gateshead Waterworks Co.*[27]

The phrasing of Lord Diplock's judgment in *Lonrho* seems to indicate that plaintiffs suffering particular harm may succeed, even in the absence of being

---

24 [1986] IR 299.
25 The duty in question arose under s. 33 of the Harbours, Docks, and Piers Clauses Act 1847 in conjunction with a number of provisions under the Londonderry Port and Harbour Acts 1854, 1874 and 1882.
26 [1919] 2 IR 1.
27 (1877) 2 Ex D 441; in this case the defendants breached a duty to maintain water pressure in pipes for supplying the city, thereby precluding the timely extinguishing of a fire in the plaintiff's property. The Court of Appeal held that the duty was not actionable in tort.

members of a protected class, though in practice examples of such cases are difficult to find. *Ex parte Island Records Ltd*[28] involved an application for an *Anton Piller* order[29] by performers and record companies in respect of unauthorised reproductions of their performances. Clearly the performers were within the class of protected persons, but the companies were, arguably, outside the protected class. The solution offered by the Court of Appeal, that breach of duty would be actionable where a plaintiff's private rights had been interfered with, was independent of the protected class criterion, but this approach was expressly rejected in *Lonrho*.[30] In *Parsons v Kavanagh*,[31] the plaintiff, a licensed operator of bus services, obtained an injunction against an unlicensed operator in respect of a breach of the Road Transport Acts 1932 and 1933, despite the fact that the Acts were construed as being for the benefit of the public and not a limited class to which the plaintiff belonged. This decision was, however, dependent on the fact that the right which the plaintiff was claiming interference with was an established constitutional right.[32] This aspect clearly strengthened the case for allowing the application; what is less clear is whether breach of statutory duty is an appropriate procedural vehicle for the vindication of constitutional rights. The alternative approach would be to regard constitutional rights claims as separate and independent of the tort of breach of statutory duty. The relationship between constitutional rights and the law of torts is discussed later,[33] but it is submitted that the vindication of such rights through existing tort actions is the better approach and, consequently, that an action for breach of statutory duty ought to be available where necessary for such vindication. The decision in *Parsons* was subsequently endorsed by the Supreme Court in *Lovett v Gogan*,[34] a case involving a similar factual situation.

Island Records, Parsons and *Lovett* involved applications for equitable remedies, rather than actions for damages, and so may be distinguished from other breach of statutory duty cases, but they do demonstrate that there is some scope for private law action for the enforcement of statutory obligations by plaintiffs unable to establish membership of a protected class. On balance the courts have shown a reluctance to allow private actions solely on the basis of the suffering of particular harm by the plaintiff.

---

28 [1978] Ch 122; [1978] 3 All ER 824.
29 This order is a specialised form of injunction to prevent the removal or destruction of evidence, see chapter 15 *infra*.
30 [1981] 2 All ER 456, at p. 463; no opinion was given as to whether a record company outside a protected class could succeed were they to proceed alone, without having the performers as co-plaintiffs.
31 [1990] ILRM 560.
32 *Ibid.* at pp. 565–6; the right in question was the right to earn a living by lawful means.
33 Chapter 9 *infra*.
34 [1995] 3 IR 132; [1995] 1 ILRM 12.

General Statutory Context

In deciding whether a statutory obligation creates a private right of action, courts will often consider the general objectives of the statute as a whole and not merely the objectives of the particular section of the statute in which the obligation is contained. In some instances this has the effect of strengthening a plaintiff's case by establishing that the statute as a whole has a protective purpose, in addition to the particular protection contained in the provision at issue. This is particularly evident in the industrial safety cases.[35] Resort to the general statutory context can also be used for the contrary purpose of counter-acting the protective language of the particular provision. The English case of *Hague v Deputy Governor of Parkhurst Prison*[36] is illustrative of the point. The plaintiff's case was grounded on the breach of regulations introduced under section 47 of the Prison Act 1952 in relation to the segregation of prisoners. Although the regulations included measures for the protection of prisoners' interests, the House of Lords held that the overall purpose of the Act and the regulations was to provide for the proper administration of prisons and not to provide any particular protection to prisoners.

Dicta from the Supreme Court in *O'Conghaile v Wallace and Others*,[37] in contrast, indicate that prisoners in Ireland would be entitled to damages for breach of a provision for their benefit. Fitzgibbon J stated that:

> . . . if it had been proved that the Governor denied to the plaintiff while in custody treatment or privileges to which he was entitled by statute or statutory rules and regulations, I think that the plaintiff would have been entitled to damages . . .[38]

In some instances the examination of context may go beyond the statute and extend to the common law prior to the introduction of the statute,[39] international treaties which have provided the impetus for the legislation in question[40] or provisions of European Community law.[41]

---

35 A typical example of this approach can be found in *Daly v Greybridge Co-operative Creamery Ltd* [1964] IR 497.
36 [1991] 3 All ER 733; [1993] 1 LRC 659.
37 [1938] IR 526.
38 *Ibid.* at p. 535; see also Murnahan J at p. 570 and Meredith J at p. 577 and p. 579.
39 See McMahon & Binchy, *op. cit.* at p. 381
40 See, for example, *Merlin v British Nuclear Fuels plc* [1990] 3 All ER 711 where Gatehouse J resorted to the provisions of Art. I(k)(i) of the Convention on Civil Liability for Nuclear Damage 1963 in order to determine the meaning of 'damage' for the purposes of s. 7 of the Nuclear Installations Act 1965.
41 On the requirement of member states to interpret national law in accordance with Community law see *Von Colson v Land Nordrhein-Westfalen* (case 14/83); [1984] ECR 1891; [1986] 2 CMLR 430; *Harz v Deutsche Tradex GmbH* (case 79/83); [1984] ECR 1921; [1986] 2 CMLR 430; *Marleasing SA v La Commercial*

General policy considerations may also be relevant in considering the broad context of legislative provisions. Courts rarely overtly identify policy issues which influence their decisions as to whether particular obligations are actionable, though it can hardly be doubted that such considerations exist and play an important role in adjudication. Again they may either strengthen or defeat a plaintiff's case.

Other Remedies

The availability and suitability of alternative remedies can be particularly influential in actions for breach of statutory duty. The inadequacy of criminal penalties has occasionally been used as a ground for allowing a tort action.[42] Confining enforcement to criminal sanctions would deprive the duty of any practical content where breach of duty could lead, at most, to a token sanction.

Where public bodies are subject to statutory duties, public law remedies may be available for the enforcement of the obligations, particularly an order of mandamus requiring the performance of the duty.[43] If such remedies provide adequate protection for persons injured or disadvantaged by a breach of duty, then private law remedies are likely to be denied.[44]

In the case of private persons subject to statutory duties the public law remedies will not be available for the enforcement of the obligations; however, the courts may consider the adequacy of equitable remedies when determining whether an action for damages should lie for breach of such duties. Injunctions may provide an adequate means of enforcement in some instances and are particularly appropriate for preventive purposes, allowing an applicant to seek to have a risk offset prior to the occurrence of harm.

Internacional de Alimentación SA (case C–106/89); [1990] ECR I–4135; [1992] 1 CMLR 305.

42 See McMahon & Binchy, *op. cit.* at pp. 380–1; the point is noted *obiter* by O'Hanlon J in *Parsons v Kavanagh* [1990] ILRM 560, at p. 567; the adequacy of alternative remedies may provide grounds for rejecting a claim, see *ILSI v Carroll* [1995] 3 IR 145; [1996] 2 ILRM 95, at p. 175; p. 105, per Blayney J for the Supreme Court, holding that disciplinary proceedings would be more appropriate in respect of s. 59 of the Solicitors Act 1954; *O'Connor v Williams* [1996] 2 ILRM 382, at p. 386, per Barron J on the suitability of criminal prosecution in respect of breaches of the Road Traffic (Public Service Vehicles) Regulations 1963 and the Road Traffic (Public Service Vehicles) (Amendment) Regulations 1983.

43 See Hogan & Morgan, *op. cit.* at chapter 13 for a full discussion of remedies against public bodies.

44 *Calveley v Chief Constable of Merseyside* [1989] AC 1228; [1989] 2 WLR 624; [1989] 1 All ER 1025; see also *Siney v Dublin Corporation* [1980] IR 400, at p. 412 per O'Higgins CJ, holding that the ministerial power of enforcement under s. 111 of the Housing Act 1966 was sufficient in respect of mandatory duties imposed on housing authorities.

Breach of Duty

Statutory duties are not subject to a single behavioural standard; the scope or extent of each obligation is dependent on the interpretation of the relevant statutory provisions. Some statutory provisions give rise to strict liability, where the exercise of reasonable care, or even the greatest possible care, will not suffice to discharge the duty. A duty is likely to be regarded as strict where it is phrased in an imperative form and the statute does not provide any restriction, such as a defence or express conditions for fulfilling the duty.[45] Other duties may only require the exercise of reasonable care in the circumstances, in which case they will have the same effect as a duty of care in the tort of negligence.[46] A third possibility is that the statute may involve a strict standard offset by special defences, as was the case in *Gallagher v Mogul of Ireland Ltd*,[47] which we have already considered in the context of the plaintiff's membership of a protected class. The imperative language of section 49(1) of the Mines and Quarries Act 1965 was offset by the fact that section 137 of the Act excused defendants where fulfilling the duty was impractical. The Supreme Court held that the exercise of reasonable care by the defendants was not sufficient to establish impracticability for the purposes of the defence because section 137 was 'not conditioned by considerations of either reasonableness or foresight'.[48]

The American approach to statutory obligations has produced two different views on the question of the standard of care. One view is that statutory provisions should be treated as a definitive interpretation of the standard of care and that a breach of statute necessarily constitutes negligence. The alternative view is that statutory provisions are to be regarded as relevant factors, to be weighed amongst the other considerations in determining negligence. Under the second approach a breach of statute would constitute evidence of negligence to be considered alongside other evidence. The *Second Restatement* suggests that the first approach should apply where there is an unexcused violation of a statutory provision which has been adopted as the standard of conduct required for the exercise of reasonable care[49] and a provision should be adopted when its purpose is:

---

45 See for example *Doherty v Bowater Irish Wallboard Mills Ltd* [1968] IR 277; s. 34(1)(a) of the Factories Act 1955 provided *inter alia* that certain equipment '. . . shall not be used unless it is of good construction, sound material, adequate strength and free from patent defect'. The Supreme Court held that the defendant was liable once the equipment proved deficient, despite the absence of fault, as the imperative nature of the provision was not qualified in any way by any other provision in the Act.

46 Many of the obligations related to occupational safety are of this type, particularly those contained in regulations under the Safety, Health and Welfare at Work Act 1989, considered later in this chapter.

47 [1975] IR 204.

48 *Ibid.* per Walsh J, at p. 209 (Budd and Griffin JJ concurring).

49 *Restatement, Second, Torts* §288B(1); excused violations are defined in §288A(2).

(a) to protect a class of persons which includes the one whose interest is invaded, and

(b) to protect the particular interest which is invaded, and

(c) to protect that interest against the kind of harm which has resulted, and

(d) to protect that interest against the particular hazard from which the harm results.[50]

The second approach should be used in respect of unexcused violation of a provision which has not been adopted as the appropriate standard of conduct.[51] The practical effect of these provisions would mean that compensation is available under roughly the same criteria as it is in Ireland and England. The principal difference would be in the form of pleading used for such an action.

The Canadian courts have favoured the use of the second of the American approaches in respect of all statutory obligations. The crucial decision giving rise to the incorporation of statutory obligations within the tort of negligence was *R. in right of Canada v Saskatchewan Wheat Pool*,[52] in which the Canadian Supreme Court rejected the use of the first American approach, preferring the flexibility of the second.[53] The major advantage of this approach is that it avoids the complexities attendant on determining the actionability of statutory obligations and places the evaluation of the defendant's conduct within a well established and coherent, if somewhat fluid, structure.

Damage and Causation

The action for breach of statutory duty requires proof of damage (in the case of an action for damages) or risk of damage (in the case of an application for an injunction). There is a further requirement that the damage suffered or threatened must be of a type that the statutory provision was designed to avert. The most celebrated case demonstrating the effect of this requirement is *Gorris v Scott*.[54] The plaintiff's sheep were being transported on the defendant's ship. The defendant failed to fulfil a statutory obligation to provide pens for the sheep and they were washed overboard during the course of the voyage. The provision of pens would have precluded the sheep from being lost, but it was held that the plaintiff's loss was not recoverable because the statutory obligation was designed to prevent the spread of disease, rather than to protect the security of the animals whilst in transit. Similarly in *Merlin v British Nuclear Fuels plc*[55]

---

50 *Ibid.* §286.

51 *Ibid.* §288B(2); see also §288 on criteria for refusing to adopt a provision as the standard of conduct.

52 (1983) 143 DLR (3d) 9.

53 See generally Fridman, *The Law of Torts in Canada* (Toronto: Carswell, 1989), vol. 2 at pp. 92–7.

54 (1874) LR 9 Exch 125.

55 [1990] 3 All ER 711; for further examples see Fridman, *op. cit.* vol. 2 at pp. 88–9.

Gatehouse J held that economic loss, by way of devaluation of the plaintiff's house, was not a type of damage included in section 7 of the Nuclear Installations Act 1965. Thus the plaintiff failed to recover compensation in respect of increased radiation levels resulting from emissions from the defendant's premises in breach of the Act.

By analogy it may be assumed that legislation dealing with personal safety, such as industrial safety legislation, would not extend to property damage or pure economic loss. Thus, if a breach of an obligation by an employer in respect of the maintenance of equipment led to damage to an employee's car parked nearby or led to a temporary closure of the business with a consequent loss of wages to employees, these losses would not be recoverable by an action for breach of statutory duty.

In common with other tort claims for compensation for damage suffered, the plaintiff in an action for breach of statutory duty must show that the breach of duty was a cause of the damage suffered and that the damage for which compensation is claimed is not too remote a consequence of that breach. Causation and remoteness are discussed later as part of the general issues affecting tortious liability.[56]

Defences

In some instances statutes may provide special defences in respect of the obligations they create or may restrict the application of general defences. We have already considered an example of a special defence, namely section 137 of the Mines and Quarries Act 1965, which was considered in *Gallagher v Mogul of Ireland Ltd*. An example of the second type of provision is section 60(4) of the Safety, Health and Welfare at Work Act 1989, which precludes the use of exemption clauses to restrict civil liability arising out of regulations under the Act, unless those regulations specifically permit the use of such clauses. This provision prevents defendants from availing of the defence of waiver that would ordinarily be applicable to tort actions.[57] Thus, in actions for breach of statutory duty, careful consideration must be given to the statute in order to determine whether there are any such special provisions affecting the liability of parties who breach their obligations.

Courts are more reluctant to admit the defence of contributory negligence in respect of breach of statutory duties, particularly in respect of occupational safety legislation. It has been suggested that the reason for this modification of the defence is because full application of the defence would diminish the effectiveness of the underlying protective policies in the relevant legislation.[58]

---

56 Chapter 11 *infra*.
57 See chapter 12 *infra* for consideration of waiver as a defence.
58 Byrne & Binchy, *Annual Review of Irish Law 1991* at pp. 408–9; McMahon & Binchy, *op. cit.* at pp. 392–5.

Therefore, although the defence is available, the defendant would have to establish a greater degree of fault on the plaintiff's part than would be the case in a negligence action, if he is to succeed in reducing the damages payable.

Express Provisions

The legislature does, on occasion, make express provision permitting or precluding civil action for damages in respect of injuries resulting from a breach of particular statutory duties. In such cases the need to consider the actionability of the obligation is avoided, but otherwise the foregoing discussion of breach of statutory duty will be applicable. The most significant sphere of liability is that of occupational injuries. The Safety, Health and Welfare at Work Act 1989 introduced a comprehensive framework to regulate occupational safety, going far beyond the sectoral approach previously taken. In the past safety legislation was piecemeal, with some areas of employment, such as factories, heavily regulated, while others, such as schools, were devoid of statutory regulation on safety. The regulatory framework under the 1989 Act serves the dual function of updating occupational safety law in compliance with Ireland's obligations under European Community law and establishing a more coherent structure for dealing with dangers arising from places of work.

Part II of the 1989 Act creates general duties applicable to all places of work, requiring the exercise of reasonable care by a wide variety of persons, including employers, employees, self-employed persons, designers and manufacturers of work equipment and designers and constructors of places of work, in respect of risks to health and safety. The Act makes detailed provision for enforcement through administrative agencies and criminal sanctions, but also expressly deals with civil liability in respect of the duties established in the Act.

Section 60(1)(a) provides that the general duties contained in sections 6–11 do not confer any right to civil action by aggrieved persons. However, section 60(2) provides that breach of duties imposed by regulations made in accordance with the Act will be actionable where damage is caused, unless the regulations provide otherwise.[59] The most significant set of regulations to date is the Safety, Health and Welfare at Work (General Application) Regulations 1993.[60] This statutory instrument is made up of ten parts providing detailed regulations in respect of a variety of occupational safety issues including the physical condition of the workplace, work equipment, personal protective

---

59 S. 28 governs the ministerial power to introduce regulations for the purpose of giving effect to the provisions of the Act. The fourth schedule to the Act provides a non-exhaustive list of the type of issues in respect of which the minister may make regulations. The list runs to thirty-seven numbered paragraphs covering a wide range of issues, giving some idea of the vast scope of the potential of regulations as a source of actionable duties.

60 SI 44/1993.

equipment, the handling of loads and the provision of first aid in the workplace. A detailed discussion of the wide range of duties arising under the regulations is beyond the scope of this text, but a few general observations are worth noting.[61] The first point to note is that the regulations do not exclude civil liability; thus injuries resulting from breach of the regulations will be actionable. Secondly, the regulations apply to virtually all workplaces[62] and so extend to situations not previously embraced by occupational safety legislation. Thirdly, the provisions are not exclusively for the protection of employees, but may in some circumstances extend to persons such as customers, suppliers and neighbours. Fourthly, the regulations do not revoke prior legislative provisions with which they overlap; thus, in some instances, a plaintiff may have a right of action at common law, under older legislation such as the Factories Act 1955 and under the regime provided by the 1989 Act and regulations thereunder. The influence of older legislation will diminish over time, since it is being gradually repealed as the 1989 Act is implemented.[63] Apart from the general regulations, there are several other sets of regulations, governing particular risks, which give rise to enforceable obligations.[64]

Damage in the context of the 1989 Act would probably be confined to personal injury and would exclude property damage or pure economic loss, since greater personal safety is the principal objective of the legislation, as evidenced

---

61 There are sixty-three regulations and twelve schedules in the General Application Regulations. For extensive discussion see White, *Civil Liability for Industrial Accidents* (Dublin: Oak Tree Press, 1994); Byrne & Binchy, 'The Extension of the Scope of Breach of Statutory Duty for Accidents at Work (Parts I and II)' (1995) 13 ILT 8 and 28.

62 There are limited exceptions excluding certain aspects of employment from the scope of the legislation. Regulation 3 of the 1993 regulations provides that the regulations are only partially applicable to the Defence Forces ('active operations', 'operational duties at sea', 'operations in Aid of the Civil Power' and training in respect of these three situations are excluded). The Workplace Regulations in Part III of the 1993 regulations apply primarily to indoor workplaces. Outdoor workplaces are subject to Part III, but places such as vehicles, construction sites, mines and woodlands are expressly excluded. S. 28(6) provides the minister with the power to exempt 'any specified class of activity or any specified class of person or place of work' from the statutory obligations where he is satisfied that the obligations are 'unnecessary or impracticable'.

63 The Safety, Health and Welfare at Work (Repeals and Revocations) Order 1995 (SI 357/1995), for example, contains an extensive list of repeals; s. 4 of the Act provides the foundation for all repeals under the new regime.

64 These include the Safety, Health and Welfare at Work (Biological Agents) Regulations 1994 (SI 146/1994); Safety, Health and Welfare at Work (Chemical Agents) Regulations 1994 (SI 445/1994); Safety, Health and Welfare at Work (Pregnant Employees Etc.) Regulations 1994 (SI 446/1994); Safety, Health and Welfare at Work (Signs) Regulations 1995 (SI 132/1995); Safety, Health and Welfare at Work (Construction) Regulations 1995 (SI 138/1995); and the Safety, Health and Welfare at Work (Extractive Industries) Regulations 1997 (SI 467/1997).

in the title of the Act.[65] The standards of care for the particular duties will largely depend on the wording of the particular provisions in question. The general duties in the Act itself require the exercise of such care as is 'reasonably practicable' and the obligations in the regulations generally reflect this flexible standard, using terms such as 'appropriate', 'sufficient', 'suitable', or 'necessary' to describe the measures to be taken on safety issues, though some of the regulations use imperative language mandating a specific state of affairs.[66]

Agencies engaged in the administration and enforcement of the legislation are provided with immunity against claims for damages for breach of the duties imposed on them by the Act.[67] Civil liability will thus only arise in respect of employers and persons in control of workplaces and not in respect of public bodies charged with the supervision of the occupational safety regime.

Other examples of express statutory provision for civil liability include section 7 of the Data Protection Act 1988 and section 21 of the Control of Dogs Act 1986.[68] Section 7 of the 1988 Act provides that the obligations on data controllers and data processors under the Act give rise to a duty of care in tort, which is owed to the data subject.[69] A data controller is defined as 'a person who, either alone or with others, controls the contents and use of personal data'; while a data processor is 'a person who processes personal data on behalf of a data controller' excluding employees acting in the course of employment.[70] This duty applies to persons compiling and controlling the use of information and is owed to the people on whom the information is compiled. The type of information to which the duty applies is termed 'personal data', defined as 'data relating to a living individual who can be identified either from the data or from the data in

---

65 The definition of damage in s. 60(5) states that it '*includes* death of or personal injury to any person' (emphasis added). Whether this necessarily excludes any other type of damage is open to debate. Since the emphasis throughout the Act is on personal safety it is likely that compensation claims will only be available in respect of such injuries. Personal injury embraces both mental and physical impairment – s. 2(1).

66 For example §12(1) of the second schedule (providing specific details in respect of Regulation 17) states that: 'Traffic routes to emergency exits and the exits themselves shall be kept clear at all times.' Similarly, §6(1) of the third schedule (also related to Regulation 17) states that: 'Swing doors and gates shall be transparent or have see-through panels.' Such provisions may be justified within a framework based on reasonable care on the basis that anything less than strict compliance in relation to these particular risks should be regarded as unreasonable. One should not conclude that it is generally open to the minister to introduce strict liability measures in relation to all matters within the ambit of the statute.

67 S. 61.

68 The Control of Dogs Act 1986 is considered briefly in chapter 10 *infra*; for further examples of express provisions in respect of civil liability see McMahon & Binchy, *op. cit.* at p. 375; see also s. 45(3) of the Freedom of Information Act 1997.

69 The obligations on data controllers and processors are specified in s. 2.

70 S. 1(1).

conjunction with other information in the possession of the data controller'.[71] The duty does not include recipients of the information, who may have suffered loss as a result of reliance on the information; any duty to such parties would have to be based on common law principles, such as negligent misrepresentation, deceit or breach of contract. In contrast to the provision in respect of controllers and processors, there is no provision made in the Act for civil action against the Data Protection Commissioner for breach of any of the duties imposed on the commissioner. The inference to be drawn is that an action for breach of statutory duty should not be available in respect of these duties.

Express provision may also be made for the exclusion of civil liability in respect of statutory duties, an example of which is section 13(2) of the Postal and Telecommunications Act 1983:

> Nothing in *section 12* or this section shall be construed as imposing on the company, either directly or indirectly, any form of duty or liability enforceable by proceedings before any court to which it would not otherwise be subject.

The sections in question set out the general objects and duties of the postal company established under the Act to take over the running of the national postal service. The section clearly precludes an action for breach of statutory duty based on any obligations generated by the sections. Section 15(2) provides the same protection to the telecommunications company established under the Act. The Act contains a number of other express provisions against civil liability for breaches of particular duties.[72]

Section 21 of the Building Control Act 1990 provides another example:

> A person shall not be entitled to bring any civil proceedings pursuant to this Act by reason only of the contravention of any provision of this Act, or of any order or regulation made thereunder.

This precludes the bringing of an action solely based on breach of obligations contained in the Act, but does not exclude consideration of the statute in the context of an action based on a common law obligation. Thus, for example, in a negligence or nuisance action the courts may take cognisance of obligations under the Act as one of the relevant factors in determining liability. The relevance of the Act in negligence actions was discussed briefly earlier.[73]

---

71 *Ibid.*
72 S. 64, s. 105; for these and further examples of express provisions excluding civil liability see McMahon & Binchy, *op. cit.* at p. 375; see also s. 14 of the Litter Pollution Act 1997, which provides local authorities and the police with immunity in respect of their duties under the Act; s. 45 of the Freedom of Information Act 1997, which provides public bodies and the Information Commissioner with immunity in respect of a number of duties contained in the Act.
73 Chapter 2 *supra.*

Statutory Torts

Statutory schemes establishing rights and obligations in respect of a particular type of activity or enterprise form a well established part of modern legal systems. Typical examples of activities regulated in this fashion would include intellectual property, such as copyright or patents, and employment. Although some aspects of these schemes would have similarities with tort actions, they are generally dealt with as part of their own specialised branches of law. Legislatures do occasionally enact schemes of liability which are specifically designed to modify the law of torts. Such schemes differ from the statutory material considered above in the level of detail provided in respect of the obligations generated. The two principal schemes in Ireland concern product liability and occupiers' liability. The product liability scheme operates in addition to the existing common law principles in respect of products, while the occupiers' liability scheme replaces most of the common law provisions in its area.

Liability for Defective Products

Civil obligations in respect of products arise under contract, the tort of negligence and the scheme of liability in the Liability for Defective Products Act 1991. Contractual protection for consumers is significant, but is confined to parties who have contractual relations in connection with the product. Tortious actions fill a void by providing relief for persons who either do not have the benefit of a contractual relationship (such as the recipient of a gift) or cannot obtain satisfactory redress through the law of contract (as would be the case if the seller of goods was gone out of business). The scope of the tort of negligence in respect of defective products has already been examined[74] and the statutory action now falls for consideration.

The Liability for Defective Products Act 1991, which came into effect on 16 December 1991,[75] was enacted in order to comply with Ireland's obligation to implement Council Directive 85/347/EEC on product liability. The recitals to the Directive state its purpose to be the harmonisation of member states' laws on product liability, the need for which is based on, *inter alia*, distortion of competition, impediments to the movement of goods and divergent protection of consumers caused by differences in member states' product liability laws.[76] The following discussion will focus on the Irish legislation, though there is a residual possibility of actions based on the Directive due to the delay in introducing the implementing legislation, which ought to have been in force by 30 July 1988.[77]

---

74 *Ibid.*
75 Liability for Defective Products Act 1991 (Commencement) Order 1991 (SI 316/1991).
76 The background to the Directive is traced in Stapleton, *Product Liability* (London: Butterworths, 1994) at chapter 3.
77 Article 19 of the Directive; see Robinson, 'Could the Product Liability Directive be Directly Effective in Ireland Without Implementing Legislation?' in Schuster

Scope of the Act

The Act applies to all moveables, excluding unprocessed primary agricultural produce,[78] which were put into circulation within the European Community after the commencement of the Act.[79] Once primary agricultural produce is put through any form of industrial process which could cause a defect, it becomes a product for the purpose of the legislation.[80] Raw materials and component parts incorporated into other products or into immoveables are included in the definition of 'product' in section 1.

Products cease to be covered by the Act once the limitation period has expired, which is not, in itself, unusual. The unusual feature of the limitation period under this Act, however, is the provision for the extinguishing of any right of action which has not already been initiated ten years after the product has been put into circulation by the producer, if that right of action has not already terminated under the standard limitation period.[81] Thus, products are prone to the initiation of litigation under the Act for a maximum period of ten years from the date they are put into circulation.

The cause of action established by the Act operates in addition to the existing causes of action in respect of defective products, leaving the injured party with a choice as to the type of action to pursue.[82] This leaves the victim with a choice of actions – a negligence action, a contractual action (where the injured party has a contractual relationship with someone responsible for the defect and the injury constitutes a breach of that contract) or an action under the 1991 Act – and there is no provision in the Act precluding the claimant

---

(ed.), *Product Liability: Papers from the ICEL Conference, March 1989* (Dublin: ICEL, 1989).

78 'Primary agricultural products' are defined in s. 1 as 'products of the soil, of stock-farming and of fisheries and game'.

79 The definition of 'product' in s. 1 includes electricity as a product in respect of damage caused by a failure in generation; s. 13 excludes from the ambit of the legislation any product circulated within a member state prior to commencement; see Stapleton, *op. cit.* at pp. 303–14 for an analysis of the definition of products under the Directive.

80 S. 1; the exclusion of unprocessed primary agricultural produce is based on a power to derogate under Art. 15(1)(a) of the directive; the Commission has recently proposed the deletion of this derogation, so that unprocessed primary agricultural produce would be subject to the scheme of liability; see the draft Directive in OJ C 337/no. 12; for further explanation of the background and reasons for the proposal see COM(97) 478 final. Only four member states have included unprocessed primary agricultural produce within the ambit of liability, Luxembourg, Finland, Sweden and Greece; see the Commission's first report on the Directive, COM(95) 617 final.

81 S. 7(2); the standard period of limitation under s. 7(1) is three years from the later of the following: (i) the date of accrual of the cause of action, or (ii) the date the plaintiff did, or ought reasonably to have, become aware of the damage, defect and identity of the producer. This issue is considered further in chapter 12 *infra*.

82 S. 11.

from pleading more than one cause of action. Additionally, section 10 prohibits the exclusion of liability, thereby providing some opportunity for redress in cases where other forms of action might be precluded as a result of the plaintiff having waived the right of action.

Elements

The cause of action is stated with stark simplicity in section 2(1): 'The producer shall be liable in damages in tort for damage caused wholly or partly by a defect in his product.' Each of the constituent elements – producer, damage, defect and product – is defined in the Act. We have already seen what is meant by 'product', so let us turn our attention to the remaining elements.

'Producer' is widely defined and not only encompasses the most obvious candidates – those who manufacture (or produce) finished products, component parts or raw materials and processors of agricultural produce – but also includes importers and suppliers in certain instances and persons holding themselves out as producers.[83] Importers are regarded as producers where they bring the product into the European Community, from without, for the purpose of supply in the course of a business. This is a significant extension of the concept of producer and should ease the jurisdictional problems that would be encountered by a person injured by such a product. Responsibility is placed upon the commercial entity that introduces the product into the Community, which would normally be in a better position than an individual consumer to protect itself against the impact of a defect in the product.[84]

A supplier can be regarded as the producer where the following four criteria are satisfied:

(i) the identity of the producer cannot be discovered by reasonable steps;
(ii) the injured party requests the supplier to identify the producer;
(iii) that request is made within a reasonable time of the occurrence of damage (while the injured party is unable to identify the producer); and
(iv) the supplier fails to supply the information (or the identity of his own supplier) within a reasonable time of receipt of the request.[85]

The effect of this rather cumbersome provision is that the injured person is not prejudiced by difficulties in identifying the producer. If identification difficulties do arise, the injured party is entitled to seek the producer's identity

---

83 S. 2(2); where two or more people are responsible under the Act for the same damage, s. 8 provides that they are to be treated as concurrent wrongdoers (on which, see chapter 13 *infra*).
84 The importer should be able to obtain protection either through the contract by which the product was obtained or through an insurance contract.
85 S. 2(3).

through any supplier that can be identified and the supplier will be treated as the producer in the event of non-compliance with such a request for assistance. This ensures that an injured person has access to redress, while suppliers are not unduly prejudiced given that they can discharge their responsibility by disclosing their source of supply if they themselves are unaware of the producer's identity.

The third group embraced by the extended definition of producer are those holding themselves out as such. A person may be regarded as holding himself out to be the producer by engaging in conduct such as putting a trade mark on the product or using some distinguishing feature of his business in connection with the product.[86] Although the Act specifies the type of conduct which *may* give rise to a finding of holding out, it does not clearly specify when it *will* do so. There are a number of possible standards of proof which could be applied to determining whether conduct amounts to holding oneself out as the producer. One is that any conduct within the specified range would be treated *prima facie* as holding out, leaving the alleged producer the opportunity of introducing contrary evidence. On this standard a retailer putting a trade mark on a product might avoid being treated as a producer by including additional information indicating that some other entity had manufactured the product. Another possibility would be that conduct within the specified range should necessarily be treated as holding out, without affording the defendant the opportunity to rebut the inference. This would be an extreme interpretation and would be unnecessarily harsh in cases where it was clear that the goods were independently manufactured. A third possibility would be to require the plaintiff to show that in addition to the specified conduct there was a real likelihood that the effect of this conduct would be to induce the belief that the defendant was the producer. This test seems the fairest and most plausible interpretation, but it is not free from ambiguity as it gives rise to further possibilities as to the standard that should be applied to establishing the likelihood of the effect of the conduct. With regard to this last point, an objective test, based on the effect on a reasonable customer, would seem appropriate and would allow potential defendants to anticipate the implications of their conduct in advance.

'Damage' includes death, physical or mental impairment and certain types of property damage.[87] It is not clear from either the Act or the Directive whether compensation for personal injury includes compensation for pain and suffering, or whether it is confined to medical costs and consequential economic loss.[88] A

---

86 S. 2(2)(d) identifies the range of conduct which may form the basis of holding out as 'putting his name, trade mark or other distinguishing feature on the product or using his name or any such mark or feature in relation to the product'.

87 S. 1 provides definitions of the types of damage covered; see also Stapleton, *op. cit.* at pp. 275–80.

88 See McMahon & Binchy, *op. cit.* at pp. 193–4 for possible interpretations of the Directive. The wording used in the 1991 Act does not make the position any clearer.

plaintiff can only claim for loss in respect of property damage where the damaged property was not the product itself, was of a type normally intended for private use and was primarily so used by the injured person. Quality defects in products are, therefore, outside the scope of the Act. The exclusion of cases where the damaged item was not used for private purposes, or not intended for such use, emphasises that the focus of the legislation is to benefit consumers. Thus, commercial entities that are more capable of protecting themselves cannot claim for property damage under the Act. The ability to recover for property damage is further restricted by the imposition of a threshold which must be exceeded before such damage is recoverable. At present property damage less than IR£350 is not recoverable and, where damage exceeds this threshold, only the excess is recoverable.[89] The threshold may be varied by ministerial order.[90]

A product is 'defective' where 'it fails to provide the safety which a person is entitled to expect, taking all the circumstances into account'.[91] This is a novel feature of the legislation, in that it defines the concept of deficiency from the perspective of consumer expectation, whereas the tort of negligence focuses on the ability of the producer to foresee dangers arising from the product and to take measures to alleviate such dangers. In practice these two perspectives may lead to the same result in many instances, but the shift in focus certainly appears to be pro-plaintiff, making the consumer's expectations the central point of concern, rather than one of a number of competing considerations in determining whether the product is defective. The Act further provides that the relevant circumstances include:

(a) the presentation of the product,
(b) the use to which it could reasonably be expected that the product would be put, and
(c) the time when the product was put into circulation.[92]

The subsequent introduction of a better product does not necessarily make a product defective;[93] thus the definition in terms of consumer expectation is not designed to hamper product development by leaving open the argument that improvements make older products defective by raising consumer expectations.

---

89 S. 3(1); Art. 16 of the Directive also provided member states with a discretion to impose a financial ceiling on liability, but only Portugal, Germany and Spain have availed of this option, see COM(95) 617 final. The ceiling relates to the total liability of a producer in respect of a particular type of defective item, rather than to individual claims.
90 S. 3(2) and (3).
91 S. 5(1); see Stapleton, *op. cit.* at chapter 10.
92 *Ibid.*
93 S. 5(2).

The measurement of consumer expectations is expressly linked to the time of circulation of the product, and the mere occurrence of subsequent improvements is expressly precluded as a basis for holding a product to be defective.

Section 4 provides that the onus of proof in respect of the damage, the defect and the causal relationship between them rests on the injured person. The onus in relation to establishing that the item which caused the damage was a product and that the defendant was the producer is not expressly dealt with in the Act, though ordinary principles of proof would suggest that the onus would lie with the plaintiff.[94] It is likely that these latter two issues would be non-contentious in most cases governed by the Act, but significant opportunities for dispute exist in relation to, *inter alia*, allegations that a defendant has held himself out as a producer or has processed primary agricultural produce. The effect of section 4 is that the cause of action is *prima facie* one of strict liability and the onus rests with the defendant to establish any of the appropriate defences that may be applicable to the case. Indeed the recitals to the directive expressly indicate that the basis of liability is intended to be strict, rather than fault based: '. . . liability without fault on the part of the producer is the sole means of adequately solving the problem . . . of a fair apportionment of the risks inherent in modern technological production'.[95] The practical implications of strict liability are partially offset by the range of defences available. In addition, product liability in negligence is, in many cases, stricter in practice than the theory and phrasing of the legal principles would suggest. The principal reasons for this are the availability of the *res ipsa loquitur* principle to assist the plaintiff in proving negligence[96] and the willingness of courts to make a finding of negligence when faced with a seriously injured plaintiff and a well funded or well insured defendant.[97]

Defences

Section 6 sets out six separate defences, any of which, if established by the producer, would completely exclude liability. In addition, contributory negligence provides a partial defence under which a producer's liability may be reduced where the injury suffered was, in part, caused by the negligence of the plaintiff (or

---

94 See chapter 12 *infra*.
95 Recital 2 of the Directive.
96 On which see chapter 12 *infra*.
97 For a comparison of liability in negligence and under the statutory scheme see Schuster, 'Product Liability Litigation in the 1990s' in Schuster (ed.), *op. cit.*, (comparison with the provisions of the Directive); Cane, *Atiyah's Accidents, Compensation and the Law*, 5th ed. (London: Butterworths, 1993) at pp. 88–90 (comparison with the equivalent English legislation, the Consumer Protection Act 1987). For general consideration of English product liability law see Clark, *Product Liability* (London: Sweet & Maxwell, 1989).

some person for whose conduct the plaintiff is deemed responsible).[98] Further-more, where damage is caused partly by a defect in a product and partly by the conduct of a third party (neither the producer nor the injured person) the liability of the producer to the injured person is not diminished, but the producer may seek a contribution from the third party under the provisions of Part III of the Civil Liability Act 1961.[99] As mentioned previously, section 10 of the Act precludes the use of exclusion clauses to curb a producer's liability; therefore, the defences under section 6 or the absence of one of the elements of the cause of action provide the only means by which liability can be completely averted.

The most significant defence is the so-called 'development risks' defence, which relieves the producer of liability where 'the state of scientific and technical knowledge at the time when he put the product into circulation was not such as to enable the existence of the defect to be discovered'.[100] The scope of this defence was recently considered by the Court of Justice in *EC Commission v UK*.[101] The relevant state of knowledge is not confined to established practices within the particular industrial sector in which the producer operates; rather, it is based on scientific information generally, 'including the most advanced level of such knowledge', provided that the knowledge was 'accessible at the time when the product in question was put into circulation'.[102] This means that manufacturers are to be judged on the basis of the best available standards and practices.

---

98 S. 9(2) makes the contributory negligence provisions of the Civil Liability Act 1961 applicable to actions under the 1991 Act. Apportionment under the 1961 Act is based on fault and s. 9(2) provides that for the purposes of contributory negligence the defect is to be treated as being due to the fault of persons liable under the 1991 Act. The purpose of the provision appears to be to avoid the possibility of having damages reduced to a nominal amount because of the absence of culpability on the part of the producer. The complicated format of the provision is an inevitable consequence of mixing the fault based apportionment mechanism with a strict liability tort; see chapter 12 *infra* on contributory negligence.

99 S. 9(1); see chapter 13 *infra* on the right to contribution in respect of concurrent wrongdoers.

100 S. 6(e); Newdick, 'Strict Liability for Defective Drugs in the Pharmaceutical Industry' (1985) 101 LQR 405 argues that this defence may entirely undermine the strict nature of the liability. The defence was an optional aspect of the Directive, but only Luxembourg and Finland excluded it from their implementing legislation; Spain excluded it in respect of medicines and food for human consumption, but included the defence for other products, see COM(95) 617 final.

101 Case C–300/95; [1997] 3 CMLR 923; the Commission alleged that the UK had failed to properly implement the Directive. Although the wording of the defence in the relevant legislation differed from that of the Directive, the Court of Justice was not convinced that there was any substantial difference in effect. A crucial factor in reaching this decision was that the national courts had not yet provided an interpretation of the legislation.

102 *Ibid.* at §§26–29 of the judgment; see also §20 of the opinion of the Advocate General.

The existence of this defence is an acknowledgment of the fact that the ability to develop products often outstrips our capacity to appreciate the risks associated with them. Thus, product development inevitably involves an element of risk and such risks were deemed to be inappropriate subjects for the strict form of liability contained in section 2. Persons injured as a result of the materialisation of such risks must use some other tort to ground their action. Negligence is the most likely candidate, leaving the courts to determine whether the release of the product, prior to the development of scientific knowledge in respect of the attached risks, fell below the requisite standard. It is paradoxical that a negligence action may be available when an action under the Act would not. An example would be the development of an experimental drug. If the best scientific knowledge available could not discern any risk, then a defence under section 6 would be available in respect of a statutory action; however, a court might accept that the release of the drug was negligent, on the basis that it is reasonable to expect the manufacturer to develop new scientific knowledge.

The statutory action makes no provision for a continuing duty to provide warnings, or even recall products, in respect of dangers which become discoverable after the product has been put into circulation. Persons suffering injury or damage in such cases will have to rely on common law provisions.

Two of the defences are designed for the protection of producers who did not cause the defect. If the defect was not present when the product was put into circulation by the producer, but came into being at some later point, then the producer is not liable under the Act.[103] In order to establish this defence the producer would have to show, as a matter of probability, either the absence of the defect at the time of circulation or a subsequent independent cause of the defect. Clearly the producer will be in a stronger position if an outside source can be shown to be the cause of the defect, but the probable absence of the defect at the time the product was put into circulation is sufficient to establish the defence. The extent of the quality control measures employed by the producer is likely to be an important feature in establishing this defence, along with matters such as the producer's production practices and safety record. Latent defects appearing some time after the product was put into circulation, but developing from normal use of the product, ought to be regarded as existing at the time the product was put into circulation. Thus, where a product fails after an unduly short period in normal usage, the failure should be properly regarded as resulting from defective production, rather than from its treatment while in circulation.[104]

---

103 S. 6(b).
104 So, if the brakes in a car work perfectly for a short period after the car is sold, but fail inexplicably after six months of average driving, the fact that the brakes worked properly when the car was sent out by the manufacturer should not be sufficient to establish that they were not defective at that time. If the potential for failure in the product exists, but does not materialise for some considerable time, the product is defective and is, in fact, more dangerous than a product which does

The producer of a raw material or component part is relieved of responsibility for defects in the finished product if such defect can be attributed to either the design of the product or the instructions given by the manufacturer of the finished product.[105] This defence relieves the producer of the raw material or component of liability on the basis that the flaw in the finished product results from the manner in which the raw material or component was used rather than the manner in which it was produced and the misuse is not caused by the producer of the raw material or component.

Two further defences are available to producers who are not responsible for commercial circulation of the product. The first covers producers who have not put the product into circulation at all.[106] This would clearly apply to situations where the product was stolen and distributed by the thief, but would also appear to cover damage caused while the product is still in the producer's possession, such as an injury to an employee or visitor in the producer's factory. Such persons would have to look to other causes of action as a source of a remedy for their losses. The second circulation defence covers producers who were neither producing or distributing in the course of business nor distributing the product for sale or other economic purpose.[107] It is not clear whether the two aspects of the defence are to be read conjunctively or disjunctively, though the phrasing of the section appears to favour the former interpretation. If both aspects must be satisfied then a producer selling for charitable purposes, but not acting in the course of a business, would not fulfil the requirements of the defence. Similarly, a commercial manufacturer giving a gift of a product for social rather than economic purposes might not be able to establish the defence if the goods were of a type manufactured and sold in the ordinary course of business.

The final defence available under section 6 is where the defect arises due to compliance with requirements of national or Community law.[108] It seems fair to producers to relieve them of liability where the defect arises from legally mandated conduct, rather than purely voluntary conduct. At first glance it may appear unlikely that legislators would mandate the production of defective products; however, it is possible that such a situation could arise. Technical requirements are often imposed on manufacturers and are usually based on the technical information available at the time. Over time deficiencies may be discovered in the technical requirements, but law reform may be slow to follow

---

not work at all. In many cases the production deficiency may be easily identifiable, but there are likely to be cases where the source of deficiency cannot be identified and in such cases the injured party will be assisted by placing the burden of proof on the producer to establish the absence of the defect at the time of circulation.
105 S. 6(f).
106 S. 6(a).
107 S. 6(c).
108 S. 6(d); see the EC (General Product Safety) Regulations 1997 (SI 197/1997).

or may not follow at all. In such cases the producer could fall foul of the criminal law by departing from the technical specifications, but could be producing an unsafe product by following them. The availability of a defence, at least in respect of a strict liability claim, would seem reasonable in such circumstances.

Comment

The type of liability introduced by the Act is not truly strict, given the range of defences available, yet it departs from negligence with regard to the evaluation of vital issues such as the constitution of a defect. The most significant development under the Act is the extended definition of producer, particularly with the imposition of responsibility on importers. The other notable feature is that the scope of the development risks defence carries the potential for more extensive liability for producers than the tort of negligence. The principal difference between the statutory regime and negligence in respect of development risks is that the former only excuses producers where technology could not discover the defect, whereas the latter may excuse the producer where the technology was available, provided it was reasonable not to utilise the available technology.

In contrast to the Irish (and European) approach to product liability, the American courts have developed strict liability for personal injury and property damage caused by dangerous products through an evolution of the common law.[109] This liability is truly strict in that it is not encumbered by the variety of defences present under the Act. This approach may prove instructive if the present state of the law fails to develop to the satisfaction of injured consumers. Given that the Act does not greatly advance the level of protection afforded to consumers and has so far failed to play any noticeable part in product liability litigation, such a failure is a very real possibility.

Occupiers' Liability

The Occupiers' Liability Act 1995 came into effect on 17 July 1995[110] and introduced a scheme of liability governing the relationship between occupiers of property and entrants to that property. The Act was introduced following a review of the existing law by the Law Reform Commission,[111] and for the most part follows the recommendations made by the commission.[112] The

---

109 See Prosser & Keeton, *op. cit.* at §§98–100; *Restatement, Second, Torts* §402A.
110 S. 9(2); the Act is analysed by Hall, 'The Occupiers' Liability Act, 1995: Modification of Occupiers' Duty to Entrants' (1995) 89 LSI Gaz 189; McMahon, 'Occupiers' Liability Act, 1995' (1995) 89 LSI Gaz 353; Byrne & Binchy, *Annual Review of Irish Law 1995* at pp. 493–518.
111 *Consultation Paper on Occupiers' Liability* (Dublin: Law Reform Commission, 1993).
112 *Report on Occupiers' Liability* (Dublin: Law Reform Commission, 1994).

impetus for this reform process stemmed principally from concerns arising out of recreational use of agricultural land. Farmers were concerned over the level of insurance costs in respect of potential liability to users of their lands, such as people engaged in shooting, fishing, hill walking and other such activities, while recreational users were concerned that they either would be denied access to farmers' lands or would have to meet the insurance costs themselves.[113] The common law had been in a transitional phase over approximately twenty-five years prior to the introduction of the Act and appeared to be on the threshold of assimilating the subject into the tort of negligence.[114] The earlier common law position involved special duties in respect of static conditions on the land, based on the relationship between the occupier and entrant. The Act uses a similar format, though the classification differs significantly from that used at common law.[115] The Hotel Proprietors Act 1963 and the Safety, Health and Welfare at Work Act 1989 provide additional measures in respect of particular occupiers, which may extend beyond the obligations in the 1995 Act in some instances.

Scope of the Act

The Act replaces the common law rules governing the 'duties, liabilities and rights which heretofore attached to occupiers' in respect of dangers to entrants due to the condition of the occupied property,[116] provided that the cause of action accrued after the commencement of the Act.[117] The effect on purely common law principles is, plainly, that they are no longer applicable. Provisions which are purely statutory are unaffected; but what of provisions involving a mixture of statutory provisions and common law? The action for breach of statutory duty, in cases where the statute makes no express provision for civil liability, involves a duty imposed by statute, but liability attaches by virtue of the common law. It is arguable that liability under such a provision should be regarded as replaced by

---

113 See chapter 1 of the LRC, *Consultation Paper, op. cit.*, for a discussion of the background to the legislation.

114 See particularly the Supreme Court judgments in *Purtill v Athlone Urban District Council* [1968] IR 205; *McNamara v ESB* [1975] IR 1; *Foley v Musgrave Cash & Carry Ltd* unrep. SC, 20 December 1985; *Mullen v Quinnsworth (No. 1)* [1990] 1 IR 59; *Smith v CIÉ* [1991] 1 IR 314; the High Court decision in *Cowan v Freaghile* [1991] 1 IR 389; and the judgment of McCarthy J in the Supreme Court in *Rooney v Connelly* [1987] ILRM 768. The assimilation of occupiers' liability into the tort of negligence also occurred in Australia in *Australian Safeways Stores Pty Ltd v Zaluzna* (1987) 162 CLR 479.

115 See McMahon & Binchy, *op. cit.* at chapter 12 and the LRC, *Consultation Paper, op. cit.* at chapter 2 for a detailed discussion of the older law.

116 S. 2(1).

117 S. 2(2); so, if the alleged tort was completed prior to the implementation of the 1995 Act, it falls to be considered under the common law principles; see, for example, *Duffy v Carnabane Holdings Ltd* [1996] 2 ILRM 86; *Thomas v Leitrim County Council* [1998] 2 ILRM 74.

the 1995 Act; thus the original statutory duty would survive, but an action for damages would no longer be available for its breach. The converse argument is that the action for breach of statutory duty is based on the presumed intent of the legislature, and while common law principles apply to 'discovering' the intention, the source of liability is the statute itself. This would preserve the action for breach of the duty and, it is submitted, should be preferred. An example of such a duty is section 16 of the National Monuments Act 1930, which was held to be actionable in *Clancy v Commissioners of Public Works in Ireland*.[118] This provision is partly catered for in the 1995 Act, as entrants entering free of charge to monuments covered by the section are classed as recreational users and are consequently owed a restricted duty. Whether the duty owed to fee paying entrants should be regarded as falling under the 1930 or the 1995 Act is uncertain, though the scope of the duty would be the same under each provision.

The definition of 'occupier' is based on control over the state of the premises and the dangers arising out of such state, and there may be more than one occupier, with the duty of each being related to their degree of control.[119] An occupier, in some instances, may also be a member of a particular class of persons on whom the law has placed special obligations and these are not affected by the Act. The Act specifically lists some examples, such as employers' duties towards employees and duties imposed under a contract of bailment or of carriage for reward,[120] but the list is not exhaustive. Thus, the Act is designed to regulate the obligations in respect of occupation only and is not intended to inhibit duties arising in respect of other characteristics of the occupier.

The definition of 'premises' is rather wide and includes land, water, fixed or moveable structures and means of transport.[121] The duties under the Act relate to dangers 'due to the state of the premises'.[122] This mirrors the common law distinction between 'static conditions' (to which special principles applied) and 'active operations' (which were subject to a duty of care under the tort of negligence).[123] The distinction between the two situations could be problematic in some cases; for example, should equipment such as machinery or materials be classified as part of the state of the premises or as a part of active operations?

Despite the abolition of common law provisions within the sphere embraced by the Act, there is still some scope for the courts to impose obligations on

---

118 [1991] ILRM 567; discussed in the LRC, *Consultation Paper, op. cit.* at pp. 33–4; Byrne & Binchy, *Annual Review of Irish Law 1991* at pp. 396–8.

119 S. 1(1); in England control has been given a broad interpretation; in *Harris v Birkenhead Corporation* [1976] 1 WLR 279; [1976] 1 All ER 341, a local authority was held to have sufficient control to be an occupier where it had served a notice, asserting its right of entry, in the course of compulsory purchase of a premises, even though it had not taken actual possession.

120 S. 8(b).

121 S. 1(1).

122 *Ibid.*

123 See McMahon & Binchy, *op. cit.* at pp. 209–10.

occupiers at common law by using a refined classification of situations. One route would be to hold the defendant to be a member of a class subject to a special duty, a route previously used to circumvent the common law principles on occupiers' liability. In *Purtill v Athlone Urban District Council*[124] the plaintiff was injured when exploding a detonator, which he had taken from the defendants' abattoir. The defendants argued that the plaintiff was a trespasser and therefore not owed any duty of reasonable care by them as occupiers. In the Supreme Court, however, it was held that they did owe such a duty, not as occupiers, but as custodians of dangerous chattels.[125] A second possible route would be to classify the danger as part of the defendant's activities, rather than as part of the static conditions. This would be a feasible option in respect of injuries resulting from equipment used by an occupier. Such an approach could be regarded as undermining the effectiveness of the legislation and so contrary to the legislative intent; alternatively it could be construed as a legitimate, albeit narrow, construction of the true scope of the Act.

Duties

The Act imposes a 'common duty of care', akin to the duty in negligence, on occupiers in respect of visitors. The extent of this duty is 'to take such care as is reasonable in the circumstances . . . to ensure that a visitor to the premises does not suffer injury or damage by reason of any danger existing thereon'.[126] Any of the following categories of entrant will be a 'visitor':

   (i) an entrant as of right;
  (ii) an entrant by virtue of a contractual provision (excluding recreational users);
 (iii) an entrant present at the invitation or with the permission of the occupier (excluding recreational users);
  (iv) a member of the occupier's family;
   (v) an entrant at the express invitation of a member of the occupier's family;
  (vi) an entrant for social purposes connected with the occupier or a family member.[127]

This effectively means that lawful entrants, other than those defined as recreational users, are visitors, whether their visit is for social or commercial purposes and the occupier owes them a duty of reasonable care to ensure that the premises are in a safe state.

---

124 [1968] IR 205.
125 *Ibid.* per Walsh J at p. 211 (Ó Dálaigh CJ and Budd J concurring).
126 S. 3.
127 S. 1(1).

Recreational users and trespassers are owed a more restricted duty than visitors. The occupier owes them a duty not to intentionally injure them or damage their property and not to act with reckless disregard for their person or property.[128] Recreational users are entrants whose purpose is to engage in recreational activity, excluding members of the occupier's family, entrants at the express invitation of the occupier or a member of the occupier's family, or entrants whose recreational activity is in connection with the occupier or a member of the occupier's family. They may have entered with or without permission, and they may be charged a reasonable amount in respect of the cost of providing parking facilities.[129] The distinction between recreational users and social visitors appears to be that social visitors are persons whose presence is desired by the occupier (or the occupier's family), whereas recreational users are those whose presence is tolerated. Trespassers are entrants who are neither visitors nor recreational users. Thus, they are entrants who lack any form of authority to be on the premises and whose purposes are other than the conduct of recreational activity.

There is an additional duty on occupiers in respect of structures, other than an entry structure such as a stile or gate, provided primarily for recreational users. The duty is 'to take reasonable care to maintain the structure in a safe condition'.[130] This duty would embrace structures such as dressing rooms in public sports grounds and playground equipment. It is essential that the structure is primarily for recreational users, so public access and a predominantly outdoor aspect to entrants' activities will be required.

These duties may be modified in accordance with the provisions set out in section 5. They may be extended simply by express agreement or by notice given by the occupier, but the duty towards recreational users and trespassers may not be restricted or excluded, while the duty to visitors may be restricted or excluded subject to certain conditions. Any express agreement purporting to restrict or exclude the duty towards visitors must be reasonable[131] and is not binding on strangers to a contract in which it is contained.[132] Any notice pur-

---

128 S. 4(1); Professor McMahon trenchantly criticised the proposal for such a reduced duty by the Law Reform Commission (*Consultation Paper, op. cit.* at pp. 92–100). His criticism and the LRC response are contained in the LRC *Report, op. cit.* at pp. 7–9. S. 8(a) preserves the common law rules on the defence of persons or property so that intentional harm within the parameters of that defence does not constitute an actionable breach of duty under the 1995 Act.

129 S. 1(1); recreational activity is defined so as to include open air activities, such as sport or nature study, 'exploring caves and visiting sites and buildings of historical, architectural, traditional, artistic, archaeological or scientific importance'.

130 S. 4(4).

131 S. 5(2)(b)(i).

132 S. 6(1); this provision applies even if the contract requires the occupier to admit the stranger to the premises, though it would be open to the occupier to seek an indemnity from the other party to the contract.

porting to restrict or exclude liability must be reasonable and reasonable steps must be taken to bring it to the attention of the visitor.[133] The modification or exclusion of the duty owed to visitors may not permit the occupier to intentionally or recklessly cause injury or damage to a visitor.[134]

Hotel proprietors are subject to the duties set out in the Hotel Proprietors Act 1963. In most instances these will be coextensive with the duties in the 1995 Act, but there may be situations where the duties under the former Act are more extensive than those under the latter. The hotel proprietor's duty in respect of the personal safety of guests is 'to take reasonable care of the person of the guest and to ensure that, for the personal use by the guest, the premises are as safe as reasonable care and skill can make them'.[135] It appears that the latter part of this provision would make a hotel proprietor responsible for the negligence of independent contractors.[136] Under the 1995 Act an occupier is only liable for the negligence of independent contractors where he knows or ought to know of the negligence[137] or where the work involved a non-delegable duty on the occupier.[138] In relation to property damage, a hotel proprietor is strictly liable for damage to property received from guests for whom sleeping accommodation is engaged,[139] though there is a £100 limit in the absence of fault.[140] The limit does not apply to damage to cars or property deposited by guests expressly for safe custody.[141]

Standards of Care

The duty to visitors under section 3 of the 1995 Act incorporates a standard of reasonable care and expressly includes two particular factors as relevant to determining what is reasonable in the circumstances. The first is the level of care that visitors can be expected to take in respect of their own safety.[142] The

---

133 S. 5(2)(b); s. 5(2)(c) provides that prominent display of the notice at the normal entrance is presumed to constitute reasonable notice, though this presumption is rebuttable.

134 S. 5(3).

135 S. 4(1) of the 1963 Act; s. 4(2) states that this duty is independent of any duty owed by the proprietor as an occupier. See also *Duggan v Armstrong* [1993] ILRM 222; analysed by Byrne & Binchy, *Annual Review of Irish Law 1992* at pp. 588–91.

136 McMahon & Binchy, *op. cit.* at p. 215; LRC, *Consultation Paper, op. cit.* pp. 7–8.

137 S. 7.

138 S. 8(c).

139 S. 6 of the 1963 Act.

140 S. 7 of the 1963 Act.

141 *Ibid.*

142 In *Staples v West Dorset District Council* (1995) 93 LGR 536 the defendant council was relieved of liability where the plaintiff fell in wet and obviously slippery conditions; see also *Simms v Leigh Rugby Football Club Ltd* [1969] 2 All ER 923, at p. 927 per Wrangham J on willing participation in a sport where the

second concerns visitors in the company of others and the level of supervision and control which those other persons can be expected to exercise over the visitors. The express inclusion of these factors does not in any way constrain the courts in determining what is relevant, but does serve to keep to the forefront of attention the relevance of self-responsibility and the duty of control which may be imposed in some cases. Self-responsibility may be a more significant factor in respect of adult visitors than child visitors, while the duty of control will be particularly relevant in cases involving supervised groups, such as school tours. It seems possible that such factors could lead to a complete shift of responsibility to the visitor or supervisor in some cases, rather than a sharing of responsibility with the occupier.

In relation to the duties towards recreational users and trespassers under section 4, there is no definition of intentional injury or damage, though an objective standard would be more consistent with the use of the term in tort law generally. This would embrace situations where such injury or damage is the natural and probable consequence of the state of the premises, where such state results from the voluntary action of the occupier; this would clearly cover the setting of traps, but would also extend to the creation of risks whereby injury was inevitable, though not subjectively intended by the occupier.

A non-exhaustive list of nine relevant factors is provided in respect of reckless disregard, though all relevant circumstances are to be taken into account.[143] The listed factors are:

   (i) whether the occupier knew, or had reasonable grounds for believing, that a danger existed on the premises;

  (ii) whether the occupier knew, or had reasonable grounds for believing, that the person or the property was, or was likely to be, on the premises;

 (iii) whether the occupier knew, or had reasonable grounds for believing, that the person or the property was, or was likely to be, in the vicinity of the danger;

 (iv) whether the danger was one against which the occupier should provide protection;

  (v) the burden of eliminating the danger or providing protection against it;

 (vi) the character of the premises (such as a tradition of open access);

(vii) the conduct of the entrant and the level of care that could reasonably be expected of entrants in relation to their own safety;

---

physical conditions meet the standards set by the governing authority for that sport; *Roles v Nathan* [1963] 1 WLR 1117; [1963] 2 All ER 908, where a warning provided by an expert, hired by the occupier, was sufficient to allow the entrants to avoid the risk of harm; occupier's duty held to be discharged; no liability for injury resulting from entrants' failure to heed the warning.

143 S. 4(2); the provisions in respect of intention and recklessness are equally applicable to cases involving a reduced duty towards visitors, see s. 5(3) and (4).

(viii) the nature of any warnings given by any person in respect of the danger;
  (ix) the level of supervision by persons accompanying the entrant that could be expected.

This lengthy list is somewhat unhelpful, in that it gives no indication as to the relative weight of its component parts. All the listed factors would be equally relevant to a negligence enquiry, but clearly the balance between them must differ from negligence based evaluations where the standard is one of reckless disregard. Quite what is required to breach this standard is not clear. The Law Reform Commission recommended gross negligence as a standard.[144] The express use of the term reckless disregard by the legislature may have been intended as a departure from the recommendation or may be simply an alternate phrase intended to have the same content as the recommendation. It will ultimately fall to the courts to decide the precise parameters of the standard.

Developments in the old law were principally driven by cases involving injury to children and the courts found a variety of ways to facilitate such claims. Both the Law Reform Commission and the legislature have vacillated on whether to make special provision in respect of child trespassers/recreational users.[145] The enacted legislation has not made any such special provision; nonetheless, the courts may be more willing to classify an occupier's conduct as reckless disregard in respect of child entrants than adults. Despite the significant reformulation of the law contained in the Act, the net outcome in many cases may be no different from what would have occurred under the tort of negligence or the older system of duties. The primary change may well be one of perception rather than substance, as the application of the reasonable care standard was unlikely to lead to the degree of liability feared by those who lobbied for this legislation.

A brief examination of some of the leading cases preceding the Act will serve to demonstrate the similarity of outcome between the common law and the statutory provisions. In *McNamara v ESB*,[146] the defendant was held liable for injuries suffered by an eleven year old boy, who was electrocuted in an electricity sub-station. The station was located in a residential suburb and the defendant was aware that the fence was in a poor state of repair and that children were in the habit of climbing the fence to play in the sub-station. The defendant failed to repair the fence over a prolonged period, but did have warning signs on the fence. It seems likely that, if such circumstances were to

---

144 LRC, *Consultation Paper, op. cit.* at pp. 97–9; LRC, *Report, op. cit.* at pp. 9–10 and 13.

145 LRC, *Consultation Paper, op. cit.* at p. 94 recommended special provision in respect of children; LRC, *Report, op. cit.* at p. 24 retracts that recommendation; s. 4(3) and (4) of the Occupier's Liability Bill 1994, as initiated, made special provisions in respect of children and mentally handicapped trespassers/recreational users, but these sub-sections were dropped and do not appear in the final legislation enacted.

146 [1975] IR 1.

arise in the future, a court would be inclined to hold the defendant to be in breach of the standard of reckless disregard. Factors of particular importance would be the location of the danger, the magnitude of the risk and the defendant's knowledge of the presence of children, who might neither comprehend nor heed the warning signs. By contrast, in *Keane v ESB*,[147] the defendant was found not to have breached the duty of reasonable care. Again the case concerned an eleven year old trespasser in an electricity sub-station. This time, however, the sub-station was in a rural location, not usually frequented by children and was surrounded by fencing. The fencing consisted of a 5 foot 9 inch chain-link wire fence with three strands of barbed wire on top, bringing the total height to 6 foot 9 inches. It is probable that the result would be the same under the statutory rules, as it is difficult to see how the defendant's conduct could be regarded as reckless disregard. Finally, the decision in *Smith v CIÉ*[148] is worth noting. The defendant failed to repair a damaged wall alongside its railway track and local residents crossed the track as a shortcut to some shops. The plaintiff, an adult, was injured when he was struck by a train, while he was in the process of chasing a youth. The youth had been riding the plaintiff's horse without permission and the plaintiff's intention was to beat him up. The plaintiff saw the approaching train, but persisted in his pursuit of the youth across the uneven terrain, fell and was struck by the train. The Supreme Court held that the defendant could not reasonably have foreseen that the plaintiff would have behaved in this way and that, in the circumstances, there was no breach of the duty of care. Under the statutory provisions the same result would ensue, as the courts are expressly entitled to have regard to the degree of care that the entrant could be expected to provide for himself.

Injury or Damage

Injury is used to refer to harm to the person of the entrant and 'includes loss of life, any disease or any impairment of physical or mental condition'.[149] This definition embraces fatal accidents, physical personal injuries and psychological harm. As there is no further elaboration on these terms it may be taken that they are to have the same meaning as they are given elsewhere in the law of torts. Damage is used to refer to harm other than personal injury and 'includes loss of property and injury to an animal'.[150] Property is given an extended definition and includes property 'in the possession or under the control of the entrant while . . . on the premises',[151] though that property may be owned by another person. This allows entrants to recover for damage

---

147 [1981] IR 44.
148 [1991] 1 IR 314; see also *O'Keeffe v Irish Motor Inns Ltd* [1978] IR 85.
149 S. 1(1).
150 *Ibid.*
151 *Ibid.*

caused to property they brought with them, thereby enabling them to compensate the owner of that property for the loss incurred. The Act is silent on whether an entrant can recover for pure economic loss, but since it is not specifically excluded and the definition of damage is not exhaustive, such loss should be recoverable in suitable circumstances. Such a possibility could arise where a vendor of goods, licensed to trade on the occupier's premises, suffers a loss of profit due to a negligently created hazard driving other entrants away; for example, a food vendor in a sports ground might suffer a loss of business if a section of a stand collapsed and the crowd were to flee the danger, leading to the abandonment of the event in question.

Existing common law principles will apply to issues such as causation, remoteness and quantum of damage. In relation to defences the only special features are those contained in section 8, referred to previously, which restrict the availability and scope of exclusion clauses and preserve the common law rules on defence of persons or property.

Section B: Specific Torts

CHAPTER FOUR

Trespass

Introduction

Trespass is made up of a number of distinct torts: battery, assault, false imprisonment, trespass to land and trespass to chattels. Battery involves unlawful personal contact, ranging from an undesired touch to serious personal violence. Assault is the threat of battery, such as the throwing of a missile or the brandishing of a weapon (no actual contact is required). False imprisonment is the unlawful deprivation of personal liberty. Trespass to land deals with various conduct which interferes with land (including buildings), such as unauthorised entry or engaging in unlawful activity after lawfully entering property. Trespass to chattels deals with certain types of interference with personal property, such as borrowing goods without permission or wrongful seizure of goods.

A brief treatment of the historical origins and development of trespass is first necessary, because the rules of trespass are still largely determined by ancient principles, which have not been extensively reconsidered in Ireland.

The origins of tort law lie in trespass, which provided the earliest examples of private actions for interference with basic civil rights, dating back to at least the twelfth century, though it was not until the thirteenth century that such actions became relatively common.[1] The early common law provided damages for trespass to one's person, land or chattels, but the common law courts (the king's courts) initially only dealt with cases where there was use of 'force and arms, contrary to the king's peace' (*vi et armis, contra pacem regis*). This meant that the early common law was primarily confined to dealing with forceful interference, posing a threat to public order. Less serious interferences were left to local justice, which was not a properly developed legal structure and had a forty shilling limit on the value of claims that could be entertained.[2] The *vi et armis* requirement was gradually relaxed and fell out of use in the latter half of the fourteenth century. This led to the emergence of a new species of action, which came to be known as an action on the case (so called because the plaintiff had to make out a special case to show that the impugned conduct

---

1 See Baker, *An Introduction to English Legal History*, 3rd ed. (London: Butterworths, 1990) at pp. 71–3.
2 *Ibid.* at p. 27 and p. 72.

was wrongful), from which much of the modern law of tort developed.[3] Trespass survived the development of the law of tort and trespass actions remain in respect of particular types of interference with the person, land, buildings or chattels of another. There was, and still is, considerable overlap between trespass and other tort actions, but from the eighteenth century onwards it became customary to use trespass to deal with wilful conduct directly causing harm and to use actions on the case to deal with accidental injuries and indirect harm.[4] The real legal distinction was between forcible and non-forcible interference, but the pragmatic distinction used in the eighteenth century became established as the accepted legal rule through sustained usage over a lengthy period of time. As a result, actions on the case came to dominate fields such as road accidents and industrial injuries in the nineteenth century and negligence, which developed from case, has continued as the dominant type of action in the twentieth century.

Modern usage tends to focus on trespass as an intentional tort, concerned with deliberate interference with the rights of another, with other torts such as negligence and nuisance being used for accidental interference. While this distinction is not strictly accurate it does give an indication of the practical usage of the different torts. Negligence, nuisance and other torts derived from the action on the case are predominantly used in the pursuit of compensation for personal injury and damage to property. Over the past century trespass has generally been used in respect of technical infringements of rights, rather than in cases of serious harm. Trespass is beginning to re-emerge in practice in a variety of situations, such as the use of force and detention of persons by private security personnel and the lawfulness of medical procedures on incapacitated persons or ill-informed patients.

We must turn now to deal with the content of trespass in modern law. In doing so the text departs somewhat from the style employed in other chapters; rather than looking at the constituent elements of each of the trespass torts, we will look first at the common features which apply to all of the different trespass actions and then we will look at the distinguishing features of each type of trespass. Defences will be discussed in some detail at the end of the chapter, as the understanding of the substantive content of the trespass torts is inextricably linked with the role of the defences and the scope of each tort can only be properly appreciated by looking at the operation of certain defences in the particular context of trespass.

---

3 *Ibid.* at pp. 73–5, pp. 456–9 (development of negligence), pp. 480–3 (development of nuisance), pp. 497 *et seq.* (development of defamation).

4 *Ibid.* at pp. 464–7. See also Cooke & Oughton, *The Common Law of Obligations*, 2nd ed. (London: Butterworths, 1993) at pp. 11–14. The most significant decisions offering this distinction are *Reynolds v Clarke* (1725) B & M 357; *Scott v Shepherd* [1558–1774] All ER Rep 295; (1773) 2 Wm Bl 892; 3 Wils 403; 96 ER 525; *Leame v Bray* (1803) 3 East 593; 102 ER 724; and *Williams v Holland* (1833) 10 Bing 112.

General Characteristics

1. Voluntary conduct
2. Direct impact
3. Intention or negligence
4. Burden of proof
5. Actionable *per se*

Voluntary Conduct

The fundamental requirement for a trespass action is that the defendant's conduct, which immediately causes the interference with the plaintiff, be voluntary.[5] Thus, if X pushes Y and causes him to collide with Z or to fall onto Z's land, Y cannot be said to trespass against Z, though X may. Surrounding circumstances might show Y to have been negligent in bringing about the situation, so that a negligence action might be available, but the involuntary nature of the contact with Z or Z's land precludes the use of trespass against Y. This requirement is not particularly unusual, as all torts will involve some voluntary conduct; what differs in trespass is that voluntariness relates to the immediate act generating the contact, whereas other torts may be committed where the immediate contact is involuntary, but results from a risk generated by earlier voluntary conduct. Involuntary contact giving rise to tortious liability could arise where the defendant negligently drives too close to the plaintiff and his car is hit by another motorist, forcing him into contact with the plaintiff; or where the defendant has created a danger which is subject to strict liability and involuntarily causes the materialisation of the risk, such as by falling onto the plaintiff's property while carrying a poisonous substance.

Conduct may be involuntary even where the actor is conscious of what he is doing and even where the conduct is deliberate, as in *Scott v Shepherd*[6] where it was held that persons throwing a lighted firework were acting involuntarily because they were acting in self-defence following the initial wrongdoer's initiation of the process. The person who instigated the process by lighting and throwing the firework into a busy marketplace was held responsible for the injury ultimately caused, but the intermediate parties, who flung the firework further afield, were not regarded as being responsible. In the case of the last

---

5 This point was established as far back as 1616, where the point was made *obiter* in *Weaver v Ward* (1616) B & M 331; Hob 134; Moore KB 864, which is quoted by McMahon & Binchy, *The Irish Law of Torts*, 2nd ed. (Dublin: Butterworths, 1989), at p. 400; further discussion of the case can be found in Baker, *op. cit.* at p. 458. The point was confirmed in a number of cases in the latter part of the nineteenth century, including *Holmes v Mather* (1875) LR 10; Ex 261; and *Stanley v Powell* [1891] 1 QB 86.

6 [1558–1774] All ER Rep 295; (1773) 2 Wm Bl 892; 3 Wils 403; 96 ER 525. This case is discussed later in relation to causation in chapter 11 *infra*.

person to throw the item this means that, although he deliberately threw the item and the immediate result was personal injury to the plaintiff, he did not commit a trespass because his conduct was involuntary. By analogy to this case, it would seem that a person acting under duress would not be acting voluntarily. So one probably would not commit any trespass if one were to break into a premises, steal some goods or beat up a person while acting under instruction from a gunman. But authority predating *Scott v Shepherd* held that duress was not a defence to trespass.[7] There is a dearth of modern authority on the subject, but it is submitted that the approach in *Scott v Shepherd* is to be preferred, at least where the duress involves serious personal violence and the trespass does not involve personal injury. This issue will be revisited in the discussion on defences at the end of this chapter.

Direct Impact

Each of the particular types of trespass requires the defendant's conduct to have a particular effect on the plaintiff; battery requires contact with the person, assault requires apprehension of such contact, false imprisonment requires confinement, trespass to land requires contact with the land and trespass to chattels requires contact with personal property. The term 'impact' is used here rather than 'contact', because assault and false imprisonment do not require any actual contact.

As noted earlier, from the early eighteenth century one of the principal distinctions between trespass and case was the use of directness and this distinction evolved into established legal doctrine.[8] Trespass is only available if the impact on the plaintiff or the plaintiff's property is the immediate result of the defendant's voluntary conduct. If the impact is an indirect consequence then some other tort, such as negligence or nuisance, must be used. However the action on the case, and therefore its offspring, is not confined to indirect impact, but may also be available in cases of direct impact. The result is that the plaintiff has a choice between trespass and other types of action if the impact is direct, but trespass is not available if the impact is indirect. In America the position is very different, as directness is not a necessary ingredient; in respect of trespass to the person by way of assault or battery the crucial requirement is that the impact must be harmful or offensive,[9] while in other types of trespass the requirement is that the impact on the plaintiff must be intended.[10]

---

7 *Gilbert v Stone* (1647) Aleyn 35.
8 Modern examples of the importance of directness include *McDonagh v West of Ireland Fisheries Ltd* unrep. HC, 19 December 1986 (trespass to chattels); and *Mann v Saulnier* (1959) 19 DLR (2d) 130 (trespass to land).
9 *Restatement, Second, Torts* §13 (battery) and §21 (assault).
10 *Ibid.* §35 (false imprisonment), §158 (land) and §217 (chattels).

The meaning of directness is somewhat vague, given that in *Scott v Shepherd* the defendant's lighting and throwing of the firework, which was subsequently thrown further by two intermediaries, was treated as the direct cause of the injury. Clearly liability should attach to the defendant, but was trespass the correct form of action for the imposition of liability? It is certainly arguable that the actions of the intermediaries made the defendant's throwing of the thing an indirect cause; an alternative approach is to consider the injury to flow directly from the lighting and exploding of the firework, with the throwing being an ancillary factor by which the plaintiff was selected as the victim. On this construction, lighting, exploding and injury can be seen as directly connected, though the reasoning seems somewhat strained. The majority decision in the case seems to have regarded the intermediaries' conduct as an inevitable result of the defendant's conduct and so the impact on the plaintiff was regarded as a sufficiently immediate result to be treated as direct.[11]

Furthermore, the use of an instrument, wielded by the defendant, does not make the contact indirect. Thus, where a person hits another with a club or uses a truck to deliberately ram into a car with somebody inside, an action for battery will be available; where a person throws rubbish onto another person's land, an action for trespass to land will be available; where a burglar fires a bullet through a television or an antique vase, an action for trespass to chattels will be available.

The English courts have moved away from the use of directness as a distinguishing feature of trespass; the majority of the Court of Appeal in *Letang v Cooper*[12] preferred to distinguish trespass from negligence on the basis of intent and this distinction has been followed in England in a number of cases, particularly in relation to allegations of medical malpractice.[13] Directness remains as a distinguishing feature of trespass in some jurisdictions, including Ireland, despite its dubious historical origins, though there is very little direct judicial authority on the matter since *Letang v Cooper*.[14]

---

11 See also *Esso Petroleum Ltd v Southport Corporation* [1955] 3 All ER 864; [1956] AC 218; [1956] 2 WLR 81, reversing [1954] 2 QB 182 for differing views on whether the jettisoning of oil at sea, where the tide would carry it to the shore, was sufficiently direct to constitute trespass.

12 [1965] 1 QB 232; [1964] 2 WLR 642; [1964] 2 All ER 929. Though some commentators suggest that directness is still a requisite element, see Heuston & Buckley, *Salmond & Heuston on the Law of Torts*, 21st ed. (London: Sweet & Maxwell, 1996), at pp. 5–6; Brazier, *Street on Torts*, 9th ed. (London: Butterworths, 1993) at p. 27; and Rogers, *Winfield & Jolowicz on Tort*, 14th ed. (London: Sweet & Maxwell, 1994) at p. 58.

13 See *infra* in the discussion of informed consent.

14 *Cook v Lewis* [1951] SCR 830 (Canada); *Williams v Milotin* (1957) CLR 465; [1957] ALR 1145 (Australia). Some Australian state courts have considered the issue since *Letang v Cooper* was decided and have disagreed with the reasoning in that case, expressing support for directness as a criterion quite apart from the obligation to follow the High Court of Australia's decision in *Williams v Milotin*, see Balkin & Davis, *Law of Torts*, (Sydney: Butterworths, 1991), at pp. 25–6;

The continuing use of directness does pose some difficulties in respect of situations, such as the setting of traps.[15] Certainly some forms of intentional harm can give rise to doubts as to the directness of the impact on the injured party, though the conduct is clearly wrongful. In such cases the legal issue to be determined is how to frame the action in tort. A residual role for the action on the case provides an alternative approach to dropping the directness requirement from trespass actions. This possibility will be discussed later.[16]

Intention or Negligence

The defendant must either intend or be negligent as to the impact of the impugned conduct on the plaintiff's person or property. The concept of intention is not exclusively subjective; as with other areas of law, one may be held to have intended consequences that were never desired. Certainly, if it can be shown that a person subjectively intended the consequences of a voluntary action, then trespass will lie no matter how improbable it was that such consequences would result. If, on the other hand, the consequences were not desired by the actor, they will still be regarded as intended if the actor knew that such consequences would be the probable result of the action.[17] This approach to the legal standard of behaviour involves a mixture of subjective and objective elements, thereby making it difficult to predict the effect of its application in any given instance. The preservation of the jury in High Court cases of intentional trespass to the person means that the decision as to whether the impugned conduct is to be treated as wrongful will be decided by lay persons rather than judges in such cases.[18] The abolition of the jury in civil cases in the Circuit Court, coupled with

---

Trindade & Cane, *The Law of Torts in Australia*, 2nd ed. (Melbourne: Oxford University Press, 1993), devote an entire chapter to negligent trespass, based on direct impact (chapter 8). But New Zealand has also discarded directness as a distinguishing feature of trespass in *Beals v Hayward* [1960] NZLR 131.

15 See Street, *op. cit.* at p. 30, giving the examples of poisoning and passing on an infectious disease as possibly involving indirect contact and suggesting that they would constitute actionable torts, though not trespass. Similarly, the setting of traps may lead indirectly to property damage rather than personal injury and should also be regarded as actionable. Computer viruses present a significant potential source of such indirect infliction of harm and at a much more serious level than routine practical jokes.

16 Chapter 10 *infra*.

17 Extensive discussion of intention is something of a rarity in the law of torts and the precise parameters of the concept are uncertain; for further discussion and sources see McMahon & Binchy, *op. cit.* at pp. 400–1; Winfield & Jolowicz, *op. cit.* at pp. 48–9; Street, *op. cit.* at pp. 20–1; Prosser et al., *Prosser & Keeton on Torts*, 5th ed. (St Paul, Minn.: West 1984), at §35; Stanton, *The Modern Law of Tort* (London: Sweet & Maxwell, 1989), at p. 24; Trindade & Cane, *op. cit.* at pp. 30 *et seq.*; Finnis, 'Intention in Tort Law' in Owen (ed.), *The Philosophical Foundations of Tort Law* (Oxford: Clarendon Press, 1995).

18 S. 1(3) of the Courts Act 1988.

the increase in the jurisdiction of that court, means that few cases will actually be decided by juries.[19] This has reduced the extent to which lay people are involved in the assessment of wrongdoing. Whether this is desirable depends on one's view of prevailing social values and one's view of the role of the judiciary in setting standards (as judicial determination is currently the primary alternative option that our legal system offers).

It should be noted at the outset that the defendant's intent or negligence need not extend to harm resulting from the impact. Consider the following scenarios:

Example

X locks Y into a room as a practical joke, intending to release him shortly afterwards. The lock jams and X cannot release Y. X gets help from Z, who eventually releases Y some hours later. The delay causes Y financial loss because it prevents him from completing a business transaction.

D clears a plot of ground adjacent to his house in the mistaken belief that it is his land and that the vegetation growing there consisted exclusively of weeds and wild plants. In fact the land belongs to P and the vegetation which D removed was a selection of expensive exotic plants that P had planted while D was away on holidays.

In both of these cases the initial impact is intentional, but the harmful effect is entirely unintended and may not involve any negligence. X intended to confine Y, but the duration of the detention and the resultant financial loss were not intended. The extended and unintended consequences were, however, the direct result of an intentional impact and so Y could recover damages in respect of both of these matters in an action for false imprisonment. In the latter case D's contact with P's land and the plants thereon was deliberate, even though he intended no harm to P, and so P would be entitled to damages for trespass to his land.

In actions for trespass to the person, the defendant's intent or negligence must be as to impact on a person. If the conduct was not intended to impact on anybody, such as a person pointing a gun in a mirror and uttering threats at a fictional victim, but unexpectedly affects somebody, such as an unanticipated visitor who wrongly perceives himself to be the subject of the threat, then no action will lie. Another example would be a person locking up a building and inadvertently locking someone inside. If the person locking the building exercised reasonable care to ensure that the building was empty, no action for false imprisonment will lie, even though the intentional locking of the exits has directly resulted in the confinement of the other person. In this case the

---

19 S. 6 of the Courts Act 1971.

locking of the exits is deliberate, but the impact on the other party is neither intended nor the result of any negligence.

What is the position where impact on somebody is intended, but the impact is on a person other than that intended by the defendant? There are a number of ways that this may happen; one would be where D deliberately hits a person in the belief that it is X, but it turns out to be P; another would be where X intends to hit Y, but misses and hits Z. In the first situation trespass clearly occurs because D intends contact with the person that contact is made with. His error as to the identity of that person was the motive or reason for the contact, but this is an ancillary matter and does not diminish the intent in respect of the contact. In the latter situation X's contact with Z is not intentional (unless his attempt to hit Y was such that contact with Z was a probable consequence), but may be negligent. If there is negligence, again there is no difficulty, as there is voluntary conduct leading directly and negligently to contact with Z. Where there is no negligence, as where Z's presence could not have been foreseen, the position is uncertain. In criminal law the concept of transferred intent may be used to make X responsible for the impact on Z, but in a civil action the function of the law is not identical, though some similarities exist. While it may be appropriate for the state to sanction deliberate malevolence, it is less certain that the inadvertent contact with the victim should give rise to a claim for compensation based on trespass.[20] The law in this area is not settled, but it is submitted that transferred intent should not be used in civil actions. A consistent approach to intent and negligence in trespass to the person would indicate that no action should lie because the contact with the victim was neither intended nor negligent.

In trespass to land and trespass to chattels, the intention or negligence must be in respect of contact with the property in question; there is no need to establish any intention or negligence with regard to the effect that contact will have on the plaintiff. Consequently, a defendant's mistaken belief in his entitlement to enter onto land or to take possession of goods will not be sufficient to excuse the interference, even though the defendant may have no grounds to suspect any impact, good or bad, on the plaintiff.

Burden of Proof

In trespass cases the plaintiff bears the burden of establishing that the defendant's conduct directly caused the objectionable impact and, once this is successfully done, the defendant bears the burden of establishing that impact was neither

---

20 Though see *Livingstone v Minister of Defence* [1984] NI 356 (CA); on transferred intent in criminal law see Clarkson & Keating, *Criminal Law: Text and Materials*, 3rd ed. (London: Sweet & Maxwell, 1994) at pp. 250–2; *AG's Reference (No. 3 of 1994)* [1996] QB 581; [1996] 2 WLR 412; [1996] 2 All ER 10; noted by Seneviratne (1996) 59 MLR 884.

intentional nor the result of negligence on the defendant's part.[21] Trespass is unlike other torts in requiring the defendant to disprove one of the central elements, but in practice the distinction does not make a great difference because both sides will generally introduce evidence on the issue and parties rarely rest their case on the opponent's inability to discharge the burden of proof. A more detailed discussion of proof is deferred until later and may be found amongst the general issues in Part II of the text.[22]

Trespass committed on the highway differs from other trespass actions and requires the plaintiff to establish intention or negligence on the defendant's part, but in practice negligence, not trespass, is used to litigate road accidents. In England the principle applied in respect of trespass on the highway has been extended to a general rule for trespass actions, so that the burden of proof in respect of intention or negligence ordinarily rests with the plaintiff.[23] The traditional rule survives in a number of jurisdictions.[24]

Actionable per se

Trespass actions protect fundamental civil liberties such as autonomy, security and dignity in respect of one's person and property and the significance of such rights is duly recognised by the fact that trespass actions do not require proof of damage. Lord Reid's comment in respect of personal liberty and autonomy also carries some force in respect of other forms of trespass:

> We have too often seen freedom disappear in other countries not only by coups d'état but by gradual erosion; and it is often the first step that counts. So it would be unwise to make even minor concessions.[25]

---

21 See *Stanley v Powell* [1891] 1 QB 86 and Baker, *op. cit.* at pp. 458–9 in respect of trespass to the person. *O'Conghaile v Wallace* [1938] IR 526, per Meredith J, *obiter*, at p. 573 in respect of trespass to chattels. This was a dissenting judgment, but the dissent did not relate to this point and in fact there is some oblique support for the proposition from one of the judges in the majority, Murnaghan J, at p. 569; see also *ESB v Hastings & Co. Ltd* [1965] Ir Jur Rep 51. *Petrie v Owners of SS Rostrevor* [1898] 2 IR 556, per Holmes LJ, in respect of trespass to land, using the older formulation, requiring the defendant to show that the impact was an 'inevitable accident'.

22 Proof is discussed in chapter 12 *infra*.

23 *Fowler v Lanning* [1959] 1 QB 426; [1959] 2 WLR 241; [1959] 1 All ER 290. Though the case specifically concerned trespass to the person, the reasoning would seem equally applicable to trespass to land or chattels. Followed in New Zealand in *Beals v Hayward* [1960] NZLR 131.

24 *McHale v Watson* (1964) 111 CLR 384 (Australia); Fridman, *The Law of Torts in Canada*, (Toronto: Carswell 1989), vol. 1 at p. 6 and pp. 51–2 cites a number of Canadian authorities on this point.

25 *S v McC* [1972] AC 24; [1970] 3 WLR 366; [1970] 3 All ER 107, at p. 43; p. 374; p. 111.

It is well established that damage is not a necessary ingredient in respect of trespass to the person or to land;[26] the point is undecided in respect of trespass to chattels, but the reasoning behind the principle is equally valid in respect of chattels.[27] Of course, proof of damage would increase the level of compensation awarded to a successful plaintiff, though it should not be assumed that a lack of damage will necessarily mean that compensation will be of a token nature. The insult to dignity, privacy or autonomy involved in some instances of trespass will give rise to significant levels of compensation and, in some cases, the award may include exemplary damages to punish the defendant for the manner in which the tort was committed.[28] Trespass to the person, for example, has led to awards of several thousand pounds in some instances, despite the absence of any physical or financial damage to the plaintiff. Furthermore, a plaintiff may seek an injunction rather than damages as a remedy, particularly in cases of continuing trespass to land.

Defences

An unusual feature of trespass (and defamation) is that much of the substance of the torts is defined by the defences rather than the substantive elements, or constituent ingredients, of the torts. While most torts can be understood by their substantive elements and defences can be seen as excuses for the harm done, this is not the case with trespass. The elements of trespass define virtually all direct contact with another person's body or property as unlawful unless excused; thus, the key distinction between lawful and unlawful contact is the scope of the excuses afforded by law. Even the most ardent supporters of individualism would not advocate a view of social relations which outlawed all direct contact with another person or his property. It is worth observing that the language of the law is contrary to historical reality and real life experience. People ordinarily regard conduct as lawful unless legally prohibited, whereas the language of the law in trespass categorises conduct as unlawful unless legally justified. This gives the misleading impression of law as the source of social relations, rather than as a regulatory or justificatory device for existing social relations. This usurpation of power by the law is not confined to trespass, but is evident in a number of areas, most notably in the development of collective activities such as companies and trade unions. Despite the philosophical impropriety of this approach, it is sufficiently well established in

---

26 *Ashby v White* (1703) 2 Ld Raym 938; *Russell v Moore* (1881) 8 LR (Ir) 318, per Fitzgibbon LJ, at p. 351 (trespass to land); *Cole v Turner* (1704) 6 Mod Rep 149; 90 ER 958; *Collins v Wilcock* [1984] 1 WLR 1172; [1984] 3 All ER 374, per Goff LJ at p. 1178; p. 378 (trespass to the person).

27 Academic opinion generally favours this view; there is a succinct review of the issue in McMahon & Binchy, *op. cit.* at pp. 523–4. There is some Canadian authority supporting the proposition, see Fridman, *op. cit.* vol. 1 at p. 2.

28 See chapter 15 *infra* on the assessment of damages.

legal discourse to be adopted for the purposes of exposition. The following discussion will first briefly identify the salient features of the various types of trespass action and then move on to consider the defences which determine the scope of the torts more precisely.

Trespass to the Person

There are three separate trespass actions designed to deal with personal harm, namely battery, assault and false imprisonment. They provide relief in respect of interference with certain basic civil liberties and predate modern constitutional jurisprudence on such matters by several centuries. In this text the primary focus will be on the common law, rather than the constitutional aspects of the rights embraced by these torts.

There is a lack of Irish case law in this area; consequently, much of the statement of legal principle which follows is necessarily tentative and there are a number of openings for development. The lack of litigation might lead one to conclude that the area is of little importance, but this would be misleading. There are various reasons why actions for trespass to the person are rare. One is that in many situations the wrongdoing is so obviously unlawful that there is no need for litigation to resolve the issue; another is that as society develops, the recognition of the importance of personal autonomy and freedom from interference with one's person leads to a reduction in the incidence of resort to personal violence for the resolution of differences; a third is that the person responsible for the trespass may not be worth pursuing. Despite lack of usage, these torts are of vital importance in giving recognition to the high social value attached to the rights protected and in providing the public with the reassurance that legal remedies are available, if required, to redress interference with those rights; though such remedies may be impractical in some cases.[29] It should also be noted that there has been something of a revival of trespass internationally in recent times in a number of fields, particularly medical malpractice, sports injuries and abuse of power by police and private security firms.

Battery

The tort of battery governs wrongful physical contact with the person. It is defined by Street as:

> any act of the defendant which directly and either intentionally or negligently causes some physical contact with the person of the plaintiff without the plaintiff's consent.[30]

---

29 Street, *op. cit.* provides a useful account of the continuing relevance of trespass at pp. 21–3; see also Winfield & Jolowicz, *op. cit.* at pp. 57–8.

30 Street, *op. cit.* at p. 24.

This definition is useful, but slightly inaccurate as it suggests consent is always necessary for personal contact to be lawful. While the existence or absence of consent is the most common criterion for determining the lawfulness of personal contact in cases of alleged battery, there are limited situations where non-consensual contact is legitimised by other means, such as arrest procedures. It would be more accurate if the words 'or other lawful authority' were added to the end of the above quotation. Stanton uses the phrase 'impermissible touching' to describe the tort.[31]

The essence of the tort is personal contact; thus, personal invasion without contact, such as taking photographs of a person or recording a person's telephone conversations, does not constitute battery. In such instances the invasion of privacy may be an actionable breach of constitutional rights, but it is not trespass.[32] The contact does not have to be dangerous or malicious, though trivial invasions are unlikely to lead to litigation. It is also widely accepted that a certain amount of contact in public places, such as jostling in a crowd or a tap on the shoulder to attract attention, does not amount to action-able battery. While this latter principle is satisfactory, legal justification for it has proved curiously elusive. Implied consent or necessity may be offered as explanations, but both are somewhat lacking as complete justifications. Implied consent is unsatisfactory because it is doubtful that even an express withdrawal of consent could render a defendant liable for battery in respect of harmless and inevitable contact in a crowd; and necessity is unsatisfactory because a certain amount of jostling could be avoided with the exercise of greater care, but the level of attention that it would require people to take to avoid contact with others would be unwarranted. Robert Goff LJ suggests that there is a general exception to the broad definition of battery based on 'the exigencies of everyday life . . . embracing all physical contact which is generally acceptable in the ordinary conduct of daily life'.[33]

A potential area of difficulty arises in respect of practical jokes. Here the person engaging in the prank may mean no harm, but if there is direct inten-tional contact there may be a battery. The English Court of Appeal, in *Wilson v Pringle*,[34] held that such a contact would only amount to a battery if it was 'hostile'. Hostility, in this context, has been given an esoteric meaning, involving the defendant understanding that the conduct is objectionable.[35] This meaning is similar to the American requirement that the contact must be 'offensive', which is satisfied where 'it offends a reasonable sense of personal

---

31 *Op. cit.* at p. 179.
32 *Kaye v Robertson* (1991) 18 FSR 62 (non-availability of trespass); invasion of privacy is considered in the context of interference with constitutional rights in chapter 9 *infra*.
33 *Collins v Wilcock* [1984] 1 WLR 1172; [1984] 3 All ER 374, at p. 1177; p. 378.
34 [1987] QB 237; [1986] 3 WLR 1; [1986] 2 All ER 440.
35 Street, *op. cit.* at p. 24; McMahon & Binchy, *op. cit.* at p. 404.

dignity'.[36] A subsequent *dictum* in the Court of Appeal doubted the suitability of the term 'hostile', in any sense, to define battery.[37] In the absence of the development of special principles to exclude practical jokes, the traditional principles would indicate that the prankster would be liable for battery in cases of direct infliction of harm.[38]

Battery will also be available where the contact exceeds the authority on which it is based. This would arise if excessive force was used in cases where a lesser degree of force would have been permitted. Examples include *Corcoran v W. & R. Jacob & Co. Ltd*,[39] where a security guard lunged at a worker, in excess of a contractual entitlement to search him, and *Dowman v Ireland*,[40] where a police officer used unnecessary force in effecting an arrest. Consent, lawful authority and excess of authority will be considered further in the discussion of defences, below.

Assault

Contrary to popular perception, assault does not involve any physical contact with the plaintiff, but rather applies to situations where a person is placed in apprehension of personal contact. It is defined by Street as:

> any act of the defendant which directly and either intentionally or negligently causes the plaintiff immediately to apprehend a contact with his person.[41]

The essential feature of this tort is the mental impact on the plaintiff, who must perceive the likelihood of imminent battery. This belief must be reasonable, in light of all the circumstances, and is not dependent on the defendant's actual intention or ability to implement the threatened contact. Thus, a person who employs threats or intimidating gestures without any intention of implementing the threatened harm commits an assault, unless the intention not to pursue the threat is reasonably apparent.[42] Consequently, the use of an imitation firearm would amount to an assault, if the plaintiff reasonably believed it to be

---

36 *Restatement, Second, Torts* §19.
37 *F v West Berkshire Health Authority* [1989] 2 All ER 545, per Lord Goff at p. 564.
38 *Wilkinson v Downton* [1897] 2 QB; 66 LJQB 493; [1895–9] All ER Rep 267 provides authority for the imposition of liability in respect of a practical joke leading intentionally to psychological harm. This case will be considered in more detail in chapter 10 *infra* under actions on the case.
39 [1945] IR 446.
40 [1986] ILRM 111.
41 Street, *op. cit.* at p. 28.
42 *R. v St George* (1840) 9 C & P 483; 173 ER 921, per Burke B at p. 493; p. 926; *Tuberville v Savage* (1669) 1 Mod 3; 86 ER 684, provides an example where words spoken by the defendant indicated an intention not to harm the plaintiff. However, in *Thomas v NUM* [1986] Ch 20; [1985] 2 WLR 1081; [1985] 2 All ER 1, it was held by Scott J, at p. 62; p. 1106; p. 20, that the defendant would have to

real; likewise, if the defendant wielded a remote control and a suitcase accompanied by a claim that the case contained a bomb, which was about to be detonated, a claim for assault would lie.

There is no assault where a defendant intends to harm the plaintiff, but the plaintiff is entirely unaware of the risk of harm. Thus, if a person lays an ambush for another, but is foiled before the intended victim arrives on the scene, there is no assault; similarly, if a person secretly puts poison in another person's food, drink or medicine, but that other does not consume it (because of a change of mind or because it falls on the floor, for instance), again there is no assault.

False Imprisonment

This tort is defined by Street as:

> any act of the defendant which directly and either intentionally or negligently causes the confinement of the plaintiff within an area delimited by the defendant.[43]

An alternate formulation is provided by Robert Goff LJ in *Collins v Wilcock*,[44] defining the tort as 'the unlawful imposition of constraint on another's freedom of movement from a particular place'.

Street's definition is more precise, as it indicates that the defendant must determine the scope of the confinement. Thus, a person who starts a process in motion, which leads directly to imprisonment, is not responsible for that imprisonment if there is an intermediate party exercising independent discretion. Therefore, a person providing information to the police, on foot of which the plaintiff is arrested, is not normally responsible for the imprisonment.[45] Where the intermediary does not exercise any discretion, the instigator of the detention will be responsible for it.[46]

The confinement must be total, so blocking a person's path and forcing him to take an alternate route is insufficient.[47] In cases where a person is detained,

---

have the capacity to carry the threat into effect (citing Dias (ed.), *Clerk & Lindsell on Torts*, 15th ed. (London: Sweet & Maxwell, 1982), at §14.10). It is submitted that the tort is complete if the plaintiff reasonably believes that the defendant has the capacity to implement the threat.

43 Street, *op. cit.* at p. 31.

44 [1984] 1 WLR 1172; [1984] 3 All ER 374, at p. 1177; p. 378.

45 *Davidson v Chief Constable of North Wales* [1994] 2 All ER 597. An action for abuse of process may be available where the instigator acts in bad faith, see Winfield & Jolowicz, *op. cit.* at p. 73, Salmond & Heuston, *op. cit.* at §7.3.

46 *Austin v Dowling* (1870) LR 5 CP 354. In *Martin v Watson* [1996] AC 74; [1995] 3 WLR 318; [1995] 3 All ER 559 (a malicious prosecution action) it was held that where the complainant has exclusive knowledge of the relevant facts, the police may not be in a position to exercise independent discretion.

47 *Bird v Jones* (1845) 7 QB 742, constraint not sufficient, as the plaintiff could have crossed the road; *Balmain New Ferry Co. Ltd v Robertson* (1906) 4 CLR 379,

but has an available means of escape, the preferred view seems to be that there is imprisonment if the means of escape was unduly dangerous or if the plaintiff could not reasonably have been aware of the means of escape.[48]

The method of constraint need not take any particular form, so it is not confined to locking a person into a room or building. A psychological constraint, such as an instruction by a security guard to submit to a search, may suffice.[49] Atkin LJ stated that 'any restraint within defined bounds which is a restraint in fact may be an imprisonment'.[50] Overt surveillance of a person by the police does not constitute a sufficient confinement, despite the fact that it inhibits the suspect's exercise of the right to freedom of movement.[51] Such surveillance may, however, constitute an invasion of privacy, requiring justification in order to avoid liability for breach of constitutional rights.[52] Failure to release a person, on expiry of a lawful right to confine, can constitute a sufficient means of confinement. Older authorities suggest that an employer may refuse to facilitate a worker leaving his place of work prematurely, though active steps to detain the worker may be regarded as excessive.[53] Changes in industrial practice and a shift in the legal balancing of the respective rights of workers and employers in the interim must cast some doubt on the continuing validity of these decisions.

Even prisoners lawfully in jail possess residual liberty capable of supporting an action for false imprisonment. In *Gildea v Hipwell*,[54] the Supreme Court held that transferring a prisoner to a prison other than that authorised by the

---

Griffiths CJ suggested confinement was not total as Robertson could have swam away.

48 *Sayers v Harlow Urban District Council* [1958] 1 WLR 623; [1958] 2 All ER 342; *Burton v Davies* [1953] St R Qd 26; McMahon & Binchy, *op. cit.* at p. 410; Street, *op. cit.* at p. 32; Winfield & Jolowicz, *op. cit.* at p. 66; Salmond & Heuston, *op. cit.* at p. 130; Stanton, *op. cit.* at p. 424; Jones, *Textbook on Torts*, 5th ed. (London: Blackstone, 1996), at p. 325; Balkin & Davis, *op. cit.* at p. 54; Fleming, *The Law of Torts*, 8th ed. (London: Law Book Co., 1993), at p. 28.

49 See *Phillips v Great Northern Railway Co. Ltd* (1903) 4 NIJR 154; the plaintiff's claim failed, as there was no evidence that her will had been dominated by the defendant's employee. The availability of an action, based on psychological restraint, is supported in principle by the judgment.

50 *Meering v Grahame-White Aviation Co. Ltd* (1919) 122 LT 44, at p. 54; see also *Dullaghan v Hillen & King* [1957] Ir Jur Rep 10, at p. 15 per Judge Fawsitt; *Bird v Jones* (1845) 7 QB 742; McMahon & Binchy, *op. cit.* at p. 411; Salmond & Heuston, *op. cit.* at §7.2; Street, *op. cit.* at pp. 32–3.

51 *The People (DPP) v Pringle* (1981) 2 Frewen 57; *Kane v Governor of Mountjoy Prison* [1988] IR 757; [1988] ILRM 724, but note the judgments of McCarthy and Hederman JJ, dissenting on this issue.

52 *Kane v Governor of Mountjoy Prison* [1988] IR 757; [1988] ILRM 724.

53 *Herd v Weardale Steel & Coke Co. Ltd* [1915] AC 67; *Burns v Johnston* [1916] 2 IR 445; [1917] 2 IR 137.

54 [1942] IR 489; constitutional issues also arise in respect of the manner of detention, see Kelly, *The Irish Constitution*, 3rd ed. (Dublin: Butterworths, 1994) at pp. 820 *et seq.*

court order under which he was detained constituted false imprisonment. In England a prisoner has no such residual liberty against the prison authorities,[55] but would appear to be entitled to claim false imprisonment against fellow prisoners or prison personnel acting outside of instructions from the prison warden, if they were to detain the prisoner in a confined area within the prison.[56]

Consciousness of confinement does not appear to be a requisite element of the tort, though the level of compensation would be less for a person who was not conscious of the confinement.[57]

Trespass to Land

This tort protects against direct interference with land, including buildings. The possessor of buildings and land is afforded protection against various forms of encroachment. There are two principal features to be considered at this point. First, who is entitled to bring an action and, second, what types of interference amount to trespass? A third issue to be considered is that trespass to land is sometimes a continuing wrong, capable of supporting multiple actions between the same parties.

Who May Sue?

Trespass to land is primarily concerned with interference with possession, rather than ownership. The possession of the land by the plaintiff need not even be lawful in order to maintain an action in cases where the defendant has no better entitlement to the land. This point is clearly evidenced by the judgment of Holmes LJ in *Petrie v Owners of SS Rostrevor*,[58] where the plaintiff had sought to commercially exploit an area of foreshore as an oyster bed, to which he had no legitimate entitlement, and the defendants' vessel had run aground, damaging the oysters in the process of freeing it: 'Petrie, by placing the oysters on the foreshore has become possessed of it *de facto*, and is consequently in legal possession as against all the world except its true owner.'[59] The defendants were not liable, as they were lawful users with authority derived from the owners of the foreshore. It is clear, however, that an action based on bare possession can

---

55 *Hague v Deputy Governor of Parkhurst Prison* [1992] 1 AC 58; [1991] 3 WLR 340; [1991] 3 All ER 733; [1993] 1 LRC 659.
56 *Ibid.* per Lord Bridge at p. 164; p. 353; pp. 744–5; pp. 671–2 (Lord Ackner concurring).
57 *Dullaghan v Hillen & King* [1957] Ir Jur Rep 10; *Meering v Grahame-White Aviation Co. Ltd* (1919) 122 LT 44, at pp. 53–4; *Murray v Ministry of Defence* [1988] 1 WLR 692. The decision in *Herring v Boyle* (1834) 1 Cr M & R 377 was to the contrary, but the House of Lords in *Murray* endorsed *Meering*. In American law there must be either consciousness of confinement or harm to the plaintiff – *Restatement, Second, Torts* §35 and §42.
58 [1898] 2 IR 556.
59 *Ibid.* at p. 584.

be maintained against a defendant with no lawful authority; thus, there is no general freedom to interfere with unlawful possession of property. The case also demonstrates that placing of goods on property can be a sufficient taking of possession, though not against lawful users or owners.[60]

Lawful occupants may maintain an action against the owners of the property where the owners exceed their lawful authority, as in *Whelan v Madigan*[61] and *Woodhouse v Newry Navigation Co.*[62] In *Whelan* a landlord was held to have committed trespasses against tenants by damaging property, including doors and letter boxes, while in *Woodhouse* the owners of a waterway were similarly held liable for dumping waste from their dredging operations on property lawfully occupied by the plaintiff. Detailed consideration of the respective rights of owners and occupiers constitutes a specialised area of law in its own right and readers should consult works on property law for further details.[63]

Possession may be established by showing occupation or use of the property by the plaintiff,[64] but this will be insufficient where the defendant has a superior lawful right[65] or where the possession is not sufficiently exclusive. For example, a lodger or hotel guest does not have sufficient possession of the occupied room to maintain an action for trespass.[66] The proprietors, however, can maintain an action, despite the fact that they are not the ones actually using the rooms. Such a position is clearly acceptable, as the proprietors retain control over the use of the rooms and have access to them. From this one can see that actual occupation or use of every part of the property is not necessary, but some sort of authority over the property will be necessary.

Holders of legal interests in property, such as an owner out of possession or the holder of an easement or profit, may maintain an action in trespass where the defendant's conduct interferes with their proprietary interest.[67] This will generally

---

60 Such possession may ultimately entitle the occupier to claim legal title by way of adverse possession.
61 [1978] ILRM 136.
62 [1898] 1 IR 161.
63 See generally Wylie, *Irish Land Law*, 3rd ed. (Dublin: Butterworths, 1997); Lyall, *Land Law in Ireland* (Dublin: Oak Tree Press, 1994); Coughlan, *Property Law*, 2nd ed. (Dublin: Gill & Macmillan, 1998).
64 *Hegan v Carolan* [1916] 2 IR 27.
65 *Petrie v Owners of SS Rostrevor* [1898] 2 IR 556.
66 *Allan v Liverpool Overseers* (1874) LR 9 QB 180 at pp. 191–2, in respect of lodgers; *Larkin v Porter* (1828) 1 Hud & Br 524, in respect of hotel guests. Licensees would not have sufficient possession to maintain an action either, see McMahon & Binchy, *op. cit.* at p. 442; Salmond & Heuston, *op. cit.* at pp. 51–2.
67 *Cosgrave v National Telephone Co.* [1901] 2 IR 611, landlord entitled to sue in trespass in respect of physical damage to the building and the loss of rents when tenants left due to the damage. The case is primarily concerned with a procedural issue, but supports the plaintiff's entitlement to use trespass. *Cronin v Connor* [1913] 2 IR 119 holder of a turbary right (extracting turf) succeeded against the owner of the land for damage caused to his interest by grazing cattle. Street,

mean that there will be actual damage, though not necessarily (blocking a right of way would interfere with an easement without causing damage).

What Constitutes Sufficient Interference?

We have already identified some general features of a trespass action – the interference must involve direct and intentional or negligent impact on real property, resulting from voluntary conduct for which the defendant is responsible. The impact can take a variety of forms, falling into three main categories – entering, remaining on or bringing one's person or an object into contact with, the property.

Entering Property

Any passing of the boundary to real property will constitute trespass unless it is authorised by some form of lawful permission. It should be noted that dwellings are afforded special protection under Article 40.5 of the Constitution and, thus, may be more extensively protected than other property. It is possible, however, that the common law and constitutional provisions are coextensive.[68]

Property includes the air above and the soil below the land itself. In respect of the air, trespass would appear to be available only where the encroachment is such as to interfere with the possession of the property, while trespass below the soil depends on the plaintiff having a sufficient interest in the subsoil.[69] There are a number of enactments permitting interference above and below land, such as the state's mineral rights and statutory regulation of air transport and public utilities. These will be considered later in this chapter, when we examine defences.

The abuse of a right of entry can constitute a trespass; thus an entry which appears to be lawful may be a trespass because the entrant had a purpose outside the scope of the authority for entry. The leading Irish authority is the Supreme Court decision in *DPP v McMahon*.[70] Police officers entered licensed premises, without a search warrant, in order to investigate possible breaches of the

---

op. cit. suggests that such actions should be regarded as actions on the case for damage to the proprietary interest, at pp. 77–8; see also Trindade & Cane, *op. cit.* at p. 126.

68 For a general discussion of the constitutional position see Kelly, *op. cit.* at pp. 914 *et seq.*

69 For more detailed consideration of these matters see Fridman, *op. cit.* vol. 1 at pp. 16 *et seq.*; Salmond & Heuston, *op. cit.* at §4.3; Fleming, *op. cit.* at pp. 44 *et seq.*; in respect of air space see *Kelsen v Imperial Tobacco Company of Great Britain & Ireland Ltd* [1957] 2 QB 334; [1957] 2 WLR 1007; [1957] 2 All ER 343; see also *Bernstein v Skyviews & General Ltd* [1978] QB 479; [1977] 3 WLR 136; [1977] 2 All ER 902, where it was held that the right to air space is confined to such a height as is necessary for the ordinary use and enjoyment of property.

70 [1987] ILRM 87, majority judgment delivered by Finlay CJ, Walsh, Henchy and Hederman JJ concurring. The matter reached the Supreme Court by way of a case stated from the Circuit Court.

Gaming and Lotteries Act 1956. Section 39 of the Act required a warrant for entry to such premises. Two alternative sources of authority were addressed in the case – the implied invitation of the owner, to members of the public, to enter the premises and the power of entry under the licensing laws.

The first was insufficient because the invitation only related to the purchase or consumption of food or drink[71] and the second only related to investigation of breaches of the licensing laws.[72] Due to a finding of fact that the police officers' sole purpose in entering the premises was to investigate possible breaches of the 1956 Act,[73] their entry was categorised as trespass. The fact that the improper purpose was the sole purpose of the officers was crucial and an entry will not amount to trespass if the entrant has a mixture of proper and improper purposes. Although this case was a criminal prosecution, rather than a civil trial, it is instructive on the limits applicable to rights of entry.

Areas where abuse of a right of entry may be particularly important include comparison shopping and secret recording. Comparison shopping involves representatives of one business entering the premises of a competitor, ostensibly as a customer, but with the intention of discovering information about the running of the business. This clearly gives rise to a significant possibility of being regarded as trespass.[74] Similarly, entry for the purpose of filming, taping or taking photographs may be a sufficient abuse of a right of entry to amount to trespass.[75]

Remaining on Property

An entry which is initially lawful may become a trespass either by continuing beyond the expiry of the authorisation or by the entrant engaging in conduct exceeding the authorisation. Exceeding the authority is similar to the abuse of the right of entry just considered, except that the improper purpose arises after lawful entry, rather than prior to entry. The precise manner in which the entry becomes trespass is significant, as some conduct makes the entrant a trespasser *ab initio*; in other words, the trespass runs from the time of entry, rather than the time of abuse. The result is that conduct in the interim, which was initially lawful, becomes unlawful. The precise extent of this doctrine is uncertain, but has traditionally been considered to apply to misfeasance, rather than nonfeasance and does not apply to abuse of a private right of entry (i.e. an express or implied consent).[76] Misfeasance requires a wrongful act, whereas

---

71 *Ibid.* at p. 89.

72 *Ibid.* at pp. 90–1.

73 *Ibid.* at p. 89.

74 *A & B Sound Ltd v Future Shop Ltd* (1995) 62 CPR 3d 319.

75 *Savoy Hotel v BBC* (1983) 133 NLJ 105; *Barker v The Queen* (1983) 153 CLR 338.

76 See McMahon & Binchy, *op. cit.* at pp. 434–5; Salmond & Heuston, *op. cit.* at §4.5; Fridman, *op. cit.* vol. 1 at pp. 15–16 for more detailed discussion.

nonfeasance involves a culpable omission and the common law traditionally treats the former as being the more serious form of wrong.

Webb v Ireland[77] presents one of the few modern examples of trespass *ab initio*. In this case the plaintiffs entered onto the land of a third party, under a public right of entry to a national monument. They employed metal detectors to locate metal objects beneath the soil and dug up what transpired to be valuable treasure. The Supreme Court held that the digging made the plaintiffs trespassers *ab initio* and, in consequence, they could not have a superior claim than the landowners.[78] It would be arguable that the original entry was a sufficient abuse of the right of entry, due to the bringing of metal detectors and digging tools, but the purpose of entry may not have been exclusively concerned with the unauthorised activity and so the facts might not be sufficiently comparable with *DPP v McMahon*.

Contact with Property

The defendant's presence on the property is not essential, as one can commit trespass by coming into contact with the property or by bringing an object into contact with the property, while remaining outside. In *Whelan v Madigan*, Kenny J held that striking a door, with intent to break it down, and the removal of a door were sufficient acts of trespass to support an action.[79] Putting things onto property will also suffice,[80] as will instructing a third party to do so.[81] Even chasing animals onto the property of another may suffice, provided the likelihood of entry by the animals is known to the defendant.[82]

Continuing Trespass

Trespass to land can amount to a continuing wrong in some circumstances. This means that the interference by the defendant is an ongoing series of torts, capable of supporting several independent causes of action, rather than a single wrong, with one cause of action. If a trespass is sufficient to amount to

---

77 [1988] ILRM 565.
78 *Ibid.* at p. 589 per Finlay CJ (Henchy and Griffin JJ concurring); but note the dissent of Walsh and McCarthy JJ on the extent of the landowners' rights, at p. 601 and p. 607, respectively.
79 [1978] ILRM 136, at p. 142.
80 *Brannigan v Dublin Corporation* [1927] IR 513, dumping of rubbish; there was also physical damage involved, consisting of breaking down a wall and pillars and removing a gate; *Woodhouse v Newry Navigation Co.* [1898] 1 IR 161, dumping of dredged waste onto an oyster bed.
81 *Gibbings v Hungerford and Cork Corporation* [1904] 1 IR 211, the second defendant instructed the first to connect a sewage pipe to one flowing onto the plaintiff's property and was held liable for trespass.
82 *League Against Cruel Sports Ltd v Scott* [1986] QB 240; [1985] 3 WLR 400; [1985] 2 All ER 489.

a continuing wrong, then the obtaining of a judgment, by the plaintiff against the defendant, does not bring finality to the dispute between the parties. Trespass by wrongful entry or remaining on land is a continuing wrong for as long as the defendant is on the land. Thus if squatters fail to leave the property after judgment has been obtained against them, then a fresh cause of action may be pursued against them. The rationale for this is that the payment of damages following the judgment does not amount to a purchase of the right to occupy the land.

The fact that a trespass leads to several separate instances of damage and carries the potential to do further harm will not, of itself, suffice to treat the trespass as a continuing wrong. Thus, where a trespasser digs a hole on the land there is a single wrong and not a continuing wrong, even though the hole carries the potential to cause further harm. Continuing trespass would usually arise where the defendant places something on the land, whether goods or a structure,[83] though it has been held that disrupting the flow of a stream in order to extract water constitutes a continuing wrong.[84]

Trespass to Chattels

This tort protects against interference with possession of personal property, vindicating both economic and privacy interests. Like trespass to land, a person in possession, without lawful authority, can maintain an action against persons with no better claim to possession. In *Jennings v Quinn*,[85] the Supreme Court held that the plaintiff was entitled to recover possession of goods, which had been seized in the belief that they were stolen, without having to establish ownership of them. The decision in *Webb v Ireland*, discussed above, demonstrates the ability of a person with authority from a superior title holder to defeat a plaintiff's right based solely on possession. The defendants, having an entitlement to the goods derived in part from that of the landowners, were able to defeat the plaintiffs' claim for a return of the goods or payment of their full value.

A person with lawful possession can maintain an action for trespass against the owner of the goods if the owner exceeds any lawful right to interfere with possession. A *dictum* of Budd J in *Keenan Brothers Ltd v CIÉ*[86] indicated that

---

83 See Fridman, *op. cit.* vol. 1 at pp. 13–15; Salmond & Heuston, *op. cit.* at §4.2; Winfield & Jolowicz, *op. cit.* at pp. 389–90; *Restatement, Second, Torts* §160 and §161.

84 *Clarke v Midland Great Western Railway Co.* [1895] 2 IR 294. The defendants were using the water to supply their station. Although the entry to the plaintiff's land was on a once-off basis, the defendants were making a continuing use of the disruption caused. The case contains a detailed review of the case law and rationale behind the concept of a continuing wrong in both trespass and nuisance.

85 [1968] IR 305, at p. 310.

86 (1962) 97 ILTR 54, at p. 59.

it would be trespass if the owner of goods were to remove them from the railway wagons of the carrier, to whom they had been entrusted, unless the contract between the parties permitted such removal. In the case of goods which are leased or obtained on hire purchase, there are legislative restrictions on the parties' freedom of contract, designed for the protection of consumers, in respect of recovery of possession.[87]

Possession has a somewhat extended meaning from its everyday usage. In *Webb* it was held that an owner of land, in possession of that land, would also be regarded as being in possession of chattels attached to, or contained within, that land.[88] In *ESB v Hastings & Co. Ltd*,[89] it was held that the plaintiffs retained sufficient dominion over electric cables, buried four feet underground, to have possession for the purposes of maintaining a trespass action. Thus, a right to possession may constitute a sufficient basis on which to ground an action.

The nature of the interference which will be sufficient to constitute the tort is somewhat uncertain. If the tort is actionable *per se*, then touching another's personal property may be sufficient. Certainly taking possession of or damaging[90] the chattels will suffice; even a transient interference, such as moving the chattels, will suffice.[91] In the absence of extensive Irish case law on the issue, assistance may be derived from consideration of the matter in other jurisdictions.[92]

Further protection of interests in goods is provided by the torts of detinue and conversion, which are considered in chapter 7.

Special Defences

There are a variety of special defences which serve to justify conduct which would otherwise constitute trespass. These defences are central to an understanding of the scope of the trespass torts and differ in nature from more general defences to tort actions, such as contributory negligence or waiver. In the case of the general defences the defendant's conduct is tortious, but is wholly or partly excused by the defence, whereas the defences considered here have the effect of denying that the conduct is of tortious character at all. These

---

87 Consumer Credit Act 1995, s. 64 (hire purchase) and s. 85 (leasing).
88 [1988] ILRM 565, per Finlay CJ at pp. 588–9 (Henchy and Griffin JJ concurring); see also *Parker v British Airways Board* [1982] QB 1004; [1982] 2 WLR 503; [1982] 1 All ER 834.
89 [1965] Ir Jur Rep 51.
90 In *ESB v Hastings & Co. Ltd* [1965] Ir Jur Rep 51 the operator of a mechanical digger negligently struck and damaged the plaintiff's underground cable. Where the plaintiff has possessory rights only, the damaging of the goods may still cause a loss, for example by depriving the plaintiff of profiting from the use of the goods.
91 In *Whelan v Madigan* [1978] ILRM 136 the moving of a tenant's chairs by the landlord was treated as trespass.
92 See, particularly, Fridman, *op. cit.* vol. 1 at pp. 81 *et seq.*

defences are more akin to the denial of the existence of a substantive element in the plaintiff's claim. The difference between the two types of defence is of no practical significance once the defendant escapes liability, but some defendants may have a psychological preference for having their conduct adjudged to be lawful, rather than unlawful but excused. The real distinction between trespass and other torts is that the elements are structured to give the plaintiff a slight advantage by using a format requiring the defendant to establish lawfulness, as opposed to the more usual format of requiring the plaintiff to establish a wrong. In practice very few cases are likely to have their outcome affected by this distinction, though one should not underestimate the importance of the manner in which a legal dispute is framed.

Consent

If the plaintiff has expressly or implicitly consented to the defendant's conduct, or consent has been given by some other person with authority to provide consent, then that conduct is not a trespass. There is some doubt as to the burden of proof in respect of consent. In England, the plaintiff must prove the absence of consent.[93] Commentators have suggested that it is more appropriate to place the burden of establishing consent on the defendant.[94] Apart from this issue, there are three main grey areas which create fertile ground for legal dispute. The first is the determination of what constitutes a valid consent, the second is whether such consent was given, and the third is whether the conduct in question falls within the parameters of the consent. The first issue is a matter of law, while the latter two are primarily factual issues. Our principal concern is with a variety of matters affecting the first issue.

Who May Give Consent?

The plaintiff is the most obvious source for a valid legal consent and the plaintiff's consent to the defendant's conduct will provide a complete defence, unless the consent was improperly obtained or the defendant exceeded the parameters of the consent. There are also instances when persons other than the plaintiff are capable of giving consent. Parents may, for example, be able to give consent in respect of medical treatment for their children; the owner of land may authorise entry against the wishes of the occupier;[95] or the owner of a chattel may authorise its removal from a bailee.[96] The law in respect of

---

93 *Freeman v Home Office (No. 2)* [1984] QB 524; [1984] 2 WLR 802; [1984] 1 All ER 1036.
94 Fleming, *op. cit.* at p. 72; Trindade & Cane, *op. cit.* at pp. 41–2.
95 Provided the tenancy includes a right of entry for the landlord (e.g. to inspect or repair the premises).
96 Provided the terms of the bailment allow the owner to interfere with the bailee's possession.

consent to personal contact is unclear, due to the lack of authorities, while the law relating to property ownership is complex, though more settled. The result is that it is difficult to predict the outcome of disputes arising out of third party consents. In each instance the respective rights of the plaintiff and the consenting party must be carefully considered in order to determine the validity of the defendant's conduct. This can cause significant practical dilemmas when a person is faced with two persons, both of whom claim to have authority to consent to the proposed course of conduct, one of whom is giving and the other of whom is refusing consent. Declining to act may not pose a viable solution for the person faced by the dilemma in many instances because it may expose that person to financial loss or to liability for a culpable omission, or may be ethically or morally unpalatable. A typical example would be a doctor with a teenage patient where the parents and child disagree on the issue of consent. If the doctor proceeds with the treatment, an action in battery may result if the consent is insufficient, while refusal of treatment may, in exceptional cases, result in a negligence action against the doctor. Ethical or moral objections to refusal may be of greater concern to the doctor and legal uncertainty is distinctly unhelpful.

Minors and Incompetent Persons

People generally assume that parents have complete authority over their children, provided no criminal conduct is involved, while the children are minors or if they are adult but incompetent. Thus, parents are seen as having the authority to decide what their children are permitted to do and what may be done to their children. The constitutional provisions in respect of the family appear to provide legal support for this view, most notably in Article 41.1:

> 1º The State recognises the Family as the natural primary and fundamental unit group of Society, and as a moral institution possessing inalienable and imprescriptible rights, antecedent and superior to all positive law.
>
> 2º The State, therefore, guarantees to protect the Family in its constitution and authority, as the necessary basis of social order and as indispensable to the welfare of the Nation and the State.

Despite the impressive, albeit vague, language employed, detailed consideration by the courts of this and related provisions shows that it is difficult to give precise meaning to the text in concrete situations.[97] There is some judicial recognition of the reality that the interests of parents and children do not coincide in some situations and that sometimes preference should be given to

---

97 See Kelly, *op. cit.* at pp. 989 *et seq.*; Casey, *Constitutional Law in Ireland*, 2nd ed. (Dublin: Sweet & Maxwell, 1992) at chapter 17.

the child's interests, despite the intrusion on family authority.[98] Additionally, there is some judicial authority to suggest that Article 41.1 is concerned with the collective interests of the family and not with individual interests within the family.[99] The result is that there is no clear guidance as to the scope of parental capacity to consent to behaviour directly impacting on their children.

The issue of parental entitlement to give consent to medical care has arisen in England on a few occasions in recent years. In *Gillick v West Norfolk and Wisbech Area Health Authority*,[100] the Court of Appeal held that children can give consent to medical treatment provided they are capable of understanding what they are doing. In such cases there would be no battery even though the parents object to the treatment. The Court of Appeal has also held that parental power to give consent continues, even though the child has obtained the capacity to consent.[101] This means that parental consent will justify treatment against the child's wishes. The result is that there is no battery if either the child or a parent has consented to the medical treatment. The consent of only one parent may prove sufficient under the reasoning behind these cases. There is a lack of Irish authority on this issue, bar a *dictum* of Maguire J in *Holmes v Heatley*[102] in 1936 which indicated that the issue was unsettled.

In extreme cases the wardship jurisdiction of the High Court may be used to circumvent difficulties with respect to consent.[103] If the child is made a ward of court, then judicial consent may be obtained for the proposed treatment. Once the child is made a ward of court it would appear that judicial consent is necessary, save in emergency situations, and that parental consent is neither necessary nor sufficient to authorise treatment, though significant weight is

---

98 Kelly, *op. cit.* at pp. 1046 *et seq.*; Casey, *op. cit.* at pp. 505 *et seq.* This issue has primarily arisen in the context of custody disputes and intervention for child care purposes.

99 *Murray v Ireland* [1985] IR 532; [1985] ILRM 542, per Costello J at pp. 537–8; p. 547; *L v L* [1992] 2 IR 77; [1992] ILRM 115, per Finlay CJ at p. 108; p. 121.

100 [1986] AC 112; [1985] 3 WLR 830; [1985] 3 All ER 402; see also Eekelaar (1986) 102 LQR 4; Cretney (1989) 105 LQR 356.

101 *Re W (a minor) (medical treatment)* [1992] 4 All ER 627; noted by Lowe & Juss (1993) 56 MLR 865; see also the *dictum* of Lord Donaldson MR in *Re R (a minor) (Wardship: medical treatment)* [1992] Fam 11; [1991] 3 WLR 592; [1991] 4 All ER 177, at pp. 23–5; pp. 600–2; pp. 185–6; noted by Douglas (1992) 55 MLR 569; for a detailed analysis of these cases see Brazier & Bridge, 'Coercion or Caring: Analysing Adolescent Autonomy' (1996) 16 LS 84.

102 [1937] Ir Jur Rep 74, at p. 76; see also Tomkin & Hanafin, *Irish Medical Law* (Dublin: Round Hall Press, 1995), at pp. 37 *et seq.*

103 See Shatter, *Family Law in the Republic of Ireland*, 4th ed. (Dublin: Butterworths, 1997) at §§13.139–13.149; Cretney & Masson, *Principles of Family Law*, 5th ed. (London: Sweet & Maxwell, 1990) at pp. 569 *et seq.*; Dewar, *Law and the Family*, 2nd ed. (London: Butterworths, 1992) at chapter 12; see also *Re M, S and W (infants)* [1996] 1 ILRM 370.

given to the wishes of the family.[104] The legal principle applicable to making a decision on consent or refusal is 'the best interests of the ward', which must include the constitutional rights of the ward.[105] The Supreme Court has held that the right of the courts to exercise this jurisdiction does not amount to a violation of the family's rights under Article 41.1 of the Constitution.[106]

A decision in the Court of Appeal in England has indicated that the next of kin do not have authority to give or refuse consent to treatment in the case of an adult suffering a temporary incapacity (such as an unconscious patient).[107] However, the family may be consulted for the purposes of assisting the doctor in exercising clinical judgment as to what is in the patient's best interests.[108] The effect of this is that there is no consent and the conduct is really justified on the basis of necessity, i.e. that it is essential for the protection of the person. The test applied to the exercise of the doctor's judgment is similar to the test applied to the court's judgment in wardship cases, which may help to commend it to an Irish court should the need arise. Conversely, a person suffering from a psychiatric disorder may retain partial capacity to give or refuse consent. Such capacity is similar to that of children under the *Gillick* principle and depends on the person's ability to comprehend the ramifications of his decision.[109] In the case of adults, however, the initial presumption is that they are competent to give or refuse consent, and the party disputing that competence carries the burden of proving the absence of the necessary level of comprehension.[110]

In the absence of Irish authorities on many aspects of consent, the arguments raised in the English courts provide valuable guidance on the range of options available. The complexity of the issues and the sensitive nature of the rights in question make it impossible to predict the course that the Irish courts would take. One significant difference between Irish and English law is almost certain to make its presence felt – the fundamental rights provisions of the Constitution. It is almost inconceivable that any litigation on this topic in Ireland would

---

104 *In Re a Ward of Court* [1996] 2 IR 79; [1995] 2 ILRM 401, in particular see Hamilton CJ at p. 106; p. 411 and p. 127; p. 429 and Denham J at p. 156; p. 454 and p. 164; p. 461; *Re B (a minor) (Wardship: sterilisation)* [1988] AC 199; [1987] 2 WLR 1213; [1987] 2 All ER 206; *Re J (a minor) (Wardship: medical treatment)* [1991] Fam 33; [1991] 2 WLR 140; [1990] 3 All ER 930.
105 *In Re a Ward of Court* [1996] 2 IR 79; [1995] 2 ILRM 401; analysed by Byrne & Binchy, *Annual Review of Irish Law 1995* at pp. 156 *et seq.*
106 *Ibid.* at p. 118; p. 421 (per Hamilton CJ) and pp. 164–5; pp. 461–2 (per Denham J).
107 *Re T (adult: refusal of medical treatment)* [1993] Fam 95; [1992] 3 WLR 782; [1992] 4 All ER 649; Lord Donaldson MR, at pp. 102–3; p. 787; p. 653, was the only member of the court to make the point directly, but the other two judgments provide implicit support, by treating the case as one of justifiable intervention without consent.
108 *Ibid.*
109 *Re C* [1994] 1 WLR 290; [1994] 1 All ER 819.
110 *Ibid.*; for a general discussion of consent in respect of mentally incompetent persons see Tomkin & Hanafin, *op. cit.* at pp. 45 *et seq.*

proceed without resort to constitutional arguments. This alone will make such litigation more complex, though it offers little prospect of making the solutions any easier for the court to find (or for the rest of us to predict).

Judicial Limits on Consent

A number of cases in England in recent years have placed limits on the capacity of a person to consent to certain risks. In *R. v Brown*,[111] for example, it was held that sado-masochist sexual activity could amount to criminal conduct, despite the presence of voluntary consent from the 'victim'. The public policy aspects of criminal law may justify the imposition of such liability, but it should not necessarily follow that the injured party could seek to have his own consent set aside and recover damages.

The decision of Brown P, in *Re S*,[112] is of much greater significance, as it authorised the performance of a Caesarean operation on a woman who had expressly refused, on the grounds of religious belief, to undergo the procedure. This clearly involves the placing of a judicial limit on the scope of individual autonomy, by allowing a judicial consent to operate in direct opposition to the express wishes of the woman, who was fully competent at the time. The justification for the decision was the imminent risk that the foetus would die if the procedure was not undertaken. Were this situation to arise in Ireland, it would necessitate careful examination of Article 40.3.3º, which guarantees the right to life of 'the unborn', in order to determine the extent of the woman's autonomy. The provision expressly refers to 'the right to life of the mother' as a counterbalancing factor and it is doubtful that the woman's religious beliefs would be permitted to override the foetal right to life. A more difficult issue is whether the risk to the woman's health posed by the operation would be sufficient to preclude judicial interference with her decision.

Consent in Respect of Property

In cases of trespass to land or chattels, the consent of a plaintiff in possession of the property completely exonerates the defendant. In the absence of such consent, the defendant cannot normally avoid liability by asserting that a third party had a better legal claim to the property than the plaintiff.[113] If, however, the defendant has been given consent by the third party, then there is no trespass if the third party has the power to authorise the defendant's contact with the property. The power of the third party to give consent depends on the nature of his interest in the property. In some cases the plaintiff will have fettered

---

111 [1994] 1 AC 212; [1993] 2 WLR 556; [1993] 2 All ER 75.
112 [1993] Fam 123; [1992] 3 WLR 806; [1992] 4 All ER 671; noted by Stern (1993) 56 MLR 238. Brown P cited an American case, *In re AC* (1990) 573 A 2d 1235, in support of the overriding of the woman's decision.
113 The usual legal expression of this is that the defendant cannot plead a *jus tertii*.

his right to refuse consent, leaving a third party with power over the property, as in the case of a debenture issued by a company, authorising the creditor to appoint a receiver to take over the affairs of the company if the debt is not repaid.[114] The immediate source of consent in such cases is the debenture holder, though this ultimately rests on the prior consent of the company.

Significant areas involving specialised rules are rented land, goods obtained on credit (hire purchase and leasing goods) and the sale of goods. In the first two situations, and often also in the third, the possessor of the property is not the legal owner, but is afforded special protection. The owner's rights may be restricted by statute or contract and, consequently, the ability to authorise interference with possession is often limited or entirely absent. Readers should refer to specialised works in these areas for further consideration of the matter.[115]

Legal Nature of a Valid Consent

Consent must be given under circumstances that can be considered as voluntary in order to be legally valid. Absolute autonomy is not a feasible prospect in modern society; thus the legal conception of what is voluntary is inevitably a matter of some debate. Clearly extreme forms of deception or coercion will not be accepted and consent obtained by such means will not protect against liability for trespass, but where is the line to be drawn? Also, a person may be misled by a failure to provide information, just as easily as by the supply of misinformation. A voluntary consent, therefore, requires that the person giving the consent should have some awareness of what he is consenting to, but how much information must a person have before his consent to a proposed course of conduct can be regarded as genuine or satisfactory?

Consent Vitiated by Coercion

The common law, from its earliest stages of development, has regarded the use or threatened use of immediate personal violence to obtain the consent of another as invalid.[116] Modern developments in criminal and contract law have

---

114 For detailed consideration of the law in respect of receivers see Keane, *Company Law in Ireland*, 2nd ed. (Dublin: Butterworths, 1991) at chapter 24; *Gower's Principles of Modern Company Law*, 5th ed. (London: Sweet & Maxwell, 1992) at pp. 434 *et seq.*; *Poignand v NZI Securities Australia Ltd* (1994) 120 ALR 237 provides an example of an attempt, albeit unsuccessful, to use trespass to question the validity of a receiver's appointment.

115 Wylie, *Irish Landlord and Tenant Law* (Dublin: Butterworths, Loose-leaf) (in respect of rented land); Atiyah, *The Sale of Goods*, 9th ed. (London: Pitman, 1995) (in respect of the sale of goods); Bell, *The Modern Law of Personal Property in England and Ireland* (London: Butterworths, 1989) (for a general consideration of rights in respect of chattels).

116 McMahon & Binchy, *op. cit.* suggest that confining duress within these parameters is unlikely to continue with changing judicial attitudes, at p. 418.

produced a more sophisticated view of what amounts to improper coercion or persuasion, through judicial expansion of the concepts of duress and undue influence. Until recently there was little evidence of an equivalent development in tort law, but the beginning of such development can be found in cases such as *Norberg v Wynrib*[117] and *Re T (adult: refusal of medical treatment)*.[118] In *Norberg* an elderly doctor obtained sexual favours from a female patient in exchange for prescribing drugs for her, to which she was addicted. The dominant view in the Canadian Supreme Court was that the imbalance of power between the parties, coupled with the exploitation of that imbalance by the doctor, was sufficient to vitiate the patient's consent on grounds of undue influence.[119] In *Re T* the Court of Appeal in England held undue influence to be a valid basis for disregarding a patient's refusal of consent to treatment, with the primary factors in determining the issue being the patient's strength of will and the relationship between the patient and the influencing party.[120] The case concerned a pregnant patient, who had been involved in an accident. She refused consent to a blood transfusion, following a conversation with her mother. The mother, a Jehovah's Witness, had religious objections to the procedure, though the daughter was not a member of that faith. The Court of Appeal held that the medical staff were entitled to disregard the refusal, once the patient's life was endangered. Although the case was concerned with refusal, rather than granting, of consent, the court did acknowledge the similarity of the issues and regarded the law on both as substantially the same.[121]

Deception and Informed Consent

The traditional common law position was that a consent was valid provided the plaintiff was aware of the general nature of the act consented to; deception as to the quality of the act was not sufficient to vitiate the consent. Thus, in *Hegarty v Shine*,[122] the Court of Appeal rejected a claim for battery by a woman whose partner had infected her with a venereal disease, which he had

---

117 (1992) 92 DLR 4th 449; [1993] 2 LRC 408.

118 [1993] Fam 95; [1992] 3 WLR 782; [1992] 4 All ER 649; see also Balkin & Davis, *op. cit.* at pp. 145–6.

119 Per La Forest, Gonthier and Cory JJ; the second approach was that recovery should be based on breach of fiduciary duty, rather than trespass, per McLachlin and L'Heureux-Dubé JJ; the third view was that there was a breach of professional duty, without categorising the duty as 'fiduciary', per Sopinka J. For more general consideration of the relevant issues see Allen, 'Civil Liability for Sexual Exploitation in Professional Relationships' (1996) 59 MLR 56.

120 Per Lord Donaldson at pp. 113–14; p. 797; p. 662; Butler-Sloss LJ at p. 120; p. 803; p. 667; Staughton LJ at p. 121; p. 804; p. 669.

121 Per Lord Donaldson at p. 115; p. 797; p. 663; Butler-Sloss LJ at p. 120; p. 803; p. 668; see also Harrington, 'Privileging the Medical Norm: Liberalism, Self-Determination and Refusal of Treatment' (1996) 16 LS 348.

122 (1878) 4 LR Ir 288.

not disclosed. This decision has been criticised by some commentators,[123] and the modern trend is to regard the health aspect of sexual conduct as sufficiently central to the nature of the act as to affect the validity of the consent.[124] Certainly deliberate misrepresentation in respect of one's state of health would generally be regarded as a basis for vitiating consent,[125] but there is less agreement on whether mere non-disclosure would have the same effect.[126]

There is a considerable amount of case law and academic commentary, but little agreement, on the question of the necessary degree of disclosure in respect of a patient's consent to medical procedures. The English courts have refused to use trespass in cases of negligent non-disclosure of risks, confining the plaintiff to an action in negligence in such cases. Once the plaintiff is aware of the general nature of the procedure, the consent is valid, unless the patient has been wilfully deceived, such as being told a falsehood in response to a specific query in relation to the risk in question.[127] In America it is well established that a consent will only be regarded as genuine where there has been adequate disclosure of information to the patient and negligent non-disclosure will vitiate an apparent consent.[128] The standard by which the degree of disclosure is measured is that of the reasonable patient; in other words, the question of whether a risk should be disclosed should be decided on a standard operating from patients', rather than doctors', perspective.[129] However, Prosser & Keeton suggest that negligence, rather than battery, predominates in medical mal-practice cases.[130] In consequence, the differences between the American and English approaches may not be as great as the theoretical underpinnings would suggest. That theoretical difference is that the American approach gives greater weight to the patient's autonomy, while the English approach favours medical

---

123 McMahon & Binchy, *op. cit.* at pp. 416 *et seq.*; Street, *op. cit.* at p. 81 and p. 106.

124 *Restatement, Second, Torts* §892B presents a useful perspective on this issue. In determining whether consent is vitiated, it includes the plaintiff's error as to the extent of the harm likely to result from the contact, in addition to an error as to the nature of the invasion of his interests.

125 Though Winfield & Jolowicz, *op. cit.* suggest that deceit, rather than trespass, would be the appropriate tort to use, at p. 727.

126 Support for non-disclosure as a sufficient fraud includes McMahon & Binchy, *op. cit.* at p. 416; *Restatement, Second, Torts* §892B, comment d. The contrary view is expressed in Winfield & Jolowicz, *op. cit.* at p. 727.

127 *Chatterton v Gerson* [1981] QB 432; [1980] 3 WLR 1003; [1981] 1 All ER 257; *Hills v Potter* [1984] 1 WLR 641; [1983] 3 All ER 716; *Sidaway v Board of Governors of the Bethlem Royal Hospital* [1985] AC 871; [1985] 2 WLR 480; [1985] 1 All ER 643.

128 Prosser & Keeton, *op. cit.* at p. 120; *Salgo v Leland Stanford, Jr. University Board of Trustees* (1957) 154 Cal App 2d 560; 317 P 2d 170 was the case where the term 'informed consent' was, apparently, first employed.

129 *Canterbury v Spence* (1972) 464 F 2d 772.

130 Prosser & Keeton, *op. cit.* at p. 121.

paternalism.[131] Negligence is also regarded as the more appropriate tort to use in respect of negligent non-disclosure in Canada[132] and Australia.[133]

The majority in the Supreme Court in *Walsh v Family Planning Services Ltd*[134] stated, *obiter*, that trespass actions should be confined to cases where there was no consent at all and negligence should be used in cases where consent was given on foot of inadequate information.[135] McCarthy J, dissenting, felt that trespass should be available where there was a lack of informed consent.[136] The availability of trespass in such cases should not be regarded as definitively resolved. The views on the subject were *obiter*, since it had been held that adequate information had been given to the plaintiff in this case. There are two arguments in favour of the availability of trespass in such cases. The first relates to the availability of negligent trespass; it has already been shown that in England trespass is confined to intentional wrongdoing, whereas in Ireland negligent trespass remains part of our law. The removal of negligent trespass in England supports the exclusion of a trespass action in respect of negligence in the obtaining of consent, in order to maintain consistency. Conversely, consistency in Irish law would suggest the availability of trespass in respect of negligently obtained consent. Secondly, and perhaps more importantly, trespass is actionable *per se*, whereas negligence requires proof of damage; consequently, an action in trespass could serve to vindicate patient autonomy in circumstances where a negligence action would not do so. A patient that is inadequately informed as to the risks attached to a medical procedure may be unable to succeed in a negligence action, either because no injury was suffered or because a sufficient causal connection cannot be shown between the doctor's negligence and the harm suffered.[137] Such a patient could be awarded a small to moderate amount of damages in a trespass action, in recognition of the improper fashion in which the consent was obtained.

Outside of the issues of sexual contact and medical procedures, there is little case law on the subject of the degree of information a person should have before consent can be regarded as voluntary. There is ample scope for development in this area, based on reasoned argument relating to the competing social values involved in any given situation, and the law should not be regarded as settled.

---

131 See, generally, Robertson, 'Informed Consent to Medical Treatment' (1981) 97 LQR 102; Teff, 'Consent to Medical Procedures: Paternalism, Self-Determination or Therapeutic Alliance' (1985) 101 LQR 432; Tomkin & Hanafin, *op. cit.* at pp. 27 *et seq.*
132 *Reibl v Hughes* (1980) 114 DLR (3d) 1; Fridman, *op. cit.* vol. 1 at pp. 66 *et seq.*
133 *F v R* (1983) 33 SASR 189; Balkin & Davis, *op. cit.* at pp. 146–7.
134 [1992] 1 IR 496.
135 *Ibid.* at p. 513 per Finlay CJ; at p. 531 per O'Flaherty J (Hederman J concurring).
136 *Ibid.* at p. 522 (Egan J concurring).
137 Causal problems with respect to informed consent are considered in chapter 11 *infra*.

Implied Consent

There are many situations in which a person's consent to contact with his person or property may be said to exist in the absence of any formal expression. This will primarily be a question of fact based on the surrounding circumstances and carries so many permutations of fact as to be impossible to comprehensively articulate. The primary considerations will be matters such as the conduct of the plaintiff at the time, previous conduct of the parties and the nature of the relationship between the parties. The plaintiff's participation in a contact sport, for example, will indicate sufficient assent to routine contact within the nature of the sport; a history of practical jokes between the parties or a plaintiff's previous tolerance of passage over land may indicate consent to a further episode of a similar nature; a friendly relationship between neighbours may suffice to justify the borrowing of gardening equipment or a bucket of coal etc. from an unlocked shed. A sensible and rational approach to circumstances should yield a satisfactory result, though borderline cases clearly will arise from time to time.

There is one final point worth noting on consent. Where a person has consented to conduct which would otherwise be a trespass, may the performance of the task be delegated? In general the answer is probably yes; in the absence of express inclusion of a right to delegate, such an inference may be implicit in the circumstances. Thus, if one consents to a person entering land to conduct work or to a person taking possession of goods, the fact that the actual work or collection is carried out by an employee or agent should make no difference. In exceptional cases, where the plaintiff has placed particular emphasis on the identity of the specific individual to whom consent is given, consent to delegate should not be implied.[138]

Defence of Persons or Property

Reasonable force may be used in defence of one's person or property, or the person or property of another. Such force may involve contact with persons or property and so is not confined to any particular form of trespass, but may be relevant to all the types of action. The common law provisions on defence of persons or property have not been altered by the introduction of the Occupiers' Liability Act 1995; rather, they are expressly preserved by section 8(a) of the Act.

The extent of the force permitted will depend on the circumstances of each individual case and so it is impossible to provide a complete picture of the myriad permutations of fact which may arise in practice. All that can be done at this point is to highlight some examples of what has been held to be reasonable or unreasonable in a few representative cases.

---

138 See, particularly, *Walsh v Family Planning Services Ltd* [1992] 1 IR 496, consent to medical procedure treated as consent to medical team, rather than the specific doctor to whom it was given.

Physical violence is not generally countenanced by courts as a means of resolving private disputes. Judge Carroll in *MacKnight v Xtravision*[139] succinctly stated the position as follows:

> ... it is of the essence in a civilised state regulated by law that its citizens in very many – indeed in all but a very small minority of – cases, forego the right to redress their grievances by private violence and instead look to the courts for their remedy.[140]

The exceptional situations, which permit the use of force, require the force used to be proportionate to the risk against which it is employed and the surrounding circumstances will be crucial in determining the level of force permitted. Judge Carroll's judgment is instructive:

> What is reasonable force? Is it merely the amount of energy which is required to move a man out of a room, a house, or, as here, to loosen his grip on a door and move him away from it, no matter what may be the other consequences? I think not. It is necessary to take into account the occasion upon which the force is used.[141]

In general, the courts will regard force which exacerbates a situation as excessive, but will permit robust action in situations of serious danger. Let us first deal with some examples of the former situation. In *MacKnight v Xtravision*, the plaintiff was preventing access to the defendants' premises; this entitled them 'to lay hands lightly on the plaintiff to move him aside'[142] and, on failure of that, 'they should have desisted'.[143] Engaging the assistance of a light middleweight boxer to forcefully remove the plaintiff, leading to significant bruising and leaving the plaintiff unable to work for a number of weeks, was excessive. In *Little v Monarch Properties Ltd*,[144] security guards, employed by the defendants, were held to have used excessive force when they forcefully led the plaintiff through a shopping centre to an office, following a dispute in the car park. It would have been more appropriate to ask the plaintiff to leave the property after his licence to enter was revoked and, if he refused, he could then have been escorted away from the property. Reasonable force may also be used

---

139 Circuit Court, 5 July 1991, extracts in McMahon & Binchy, *A Casebook on the Irish Law of Torts*, 2nd ed. (Dublin: Butterworths, 1992), at pp. 407 *et seq.*; Byrne & Binchy, *Annual Review of Irish Law 1991* at pp. 417 *et seq.*
140 *Ibid.* at p. 410; p. 419.
141 *Ibid.* at p. 409; p. 418.
142 *Ibid.* at p. 410; p. 418.
143 *Ibid.*
144 Circuit Court, noted by Skeffington (1996) 14 ILT 22; see also *McAllister v Dunnes Stores* unrep. HC, 5 February 1987; *McEntee and McEntee v Quinnsworth* unrep. SC, 7 December 1993; Irish Times Law Report, 21 February 1994; Bolger, 'Who Will Protect the Security Guards?' (1994) 12 ILT 265.

to resist an unlawful arrest; thus, customers would be entitled to use moderate force to prevent themselves being wrongfully detained.[145]

Ross v Curtis[146] provides an example of the more indulgent approach taken in respect of defence against more serious risks. The defendant was disturbed, in the early hours of the morning, when the alarm in his premises was set off by intruders, including the plaintiff. He attempted to frighten the intruders off by firing a warning shot from a legally held rifle, but inadvertently hit the plaintiff in the skull. The judicial view of cases of serious risk is epitomised by a closing statement by Barr J:

> I am satisfied that the Defendant acquitted himself reasonably in all the circumstances of the case and that he was not guilty of reckless disregard for the safety of the Plaintiff which is the test appropriate to the circumstances of this case.[147]

This statement of principle is substantially in accord with the provisions of section 4 of the Occupiers' Liability Act 1995 and so remains a valuable guide to the scope of this particular defence in comparable situations, even though the case itself predates the Act. The case also serves as a guide to cases of serious risk outside of the scope of the 1995 Act, such as where the incident occurs in a public place.

It is unlikely that general threats to society at large would be accepted as justifying entry onto property. Consequently, activists in respect of environmental[148] or peace[149] issues probably would not be able to use defence of persons against an action for trespass where they have entered property in protest at activities conducted by the occupiers. The defence should, however, be available if a sufficiently immediate risk to identifiable persons can be shown to exist.[150]

---

145 *R. v Self* [1992] 1 WLR 657; [1992] 3 All ER 476; see also *Collins v Wilcock* [1984] 1 WLR 1172; [1984] 3 All ER 374; *R. v Wilson* [1955] 1 WLR 493; [1955] 1 All ER 744. Although these cases involve criminal prosecutions they also carry implications for the use of force as a defence in civil actions.

146 Unrep. HC, 3 February 1989.

147 *Ibid.* at p. 4 of the transcript; contrast *Revill v Newbery* [1996] QB 567; [1996] 2 WLR 239; [1996] 1 All ER 291, where the defendant was found not to have acted reasonably when he fired through a hole in a door, at body level, without making any attempt to ascertain the position of the intruder.

148 *Greenpeace Canada et al. v MacMillan Bloedel Ltd* (1994) 93 CCC 3d 289; 118 DLR 4th 1, interlocutory application to prevent environmental protesters trespassing.

149 *Limbo v Little* (1989) 65 NTR 19, criminal prosecution of peace protester entering a military installation, reasonable suspicion that crimes against peace or humanity were being committed provides no defence, per Martin J at p. 45 (Kearny and Rice JJ concurring). The same result would be likely in a civil suit.

150 In *Police v O'Neill* [1993] 3 NZLR 712, it was held that protesting in respect of legal abortions did not involve a sufficient risk to support a similar defence under the Trespass Act 1980.

It is clear that this defence will protect the defendant where the plaintiff or the plaintiff's property is the source of danger, but what if the danger emanates from a third party? Is a person who flees from an assailant protected against liability where he crosses the land, uses the chattels or makes contact with the person of another in self-defence? It is submitted that the primary source of the wrong is the person generating the risk and that the person at risk should not be liable, provided the interference with property was proportionate to the risk, or, at least, liability should be confined to cases of actual damage.[151]

Lawful Authority

Arrest, Entry, Search and Seizure

The criminal process entails a variety of powers which permit interference with persons and property. The main issues, for the purposes of trespass, are powers of arrest, entry, search and seizure. Powers of arrest provide a defence against false imprisonment and battery (in respect of necessary conduct in effecting an arrest). Powers of entry provide a defence in respect of trespass to land for persons who do not have the occupier's consent to enter. Powers of search and seizure legitimate conduct that would otherwise involve a number of types of trespass: trespass to chattels is the most obvious tort against which a defence is provided; the power to search also permits conduct that would otherwise be an abuse of a right of entry on land; furthermore, some powers of search permit body searches, thereby legitimating personal contact that would otherwise constitute a battery.

Arrest

The common law provisions governing arrest without a warrant have largely been replaced by the arrest provisions in section 4 of the Criminal Law Act 1997.[152] The general powers of arrest only apply to a defined category of offences (arrestable offences), the principal element of which is that the offence is punishable by five years' imprisonment or a more serious penalty.[153] Private persons have the right to arrest for such an offence in two categories of case:

---

151 See Fleming, *op. cit.* at p. 85; Street, *op. cit.* at p. 92; Prosser & Keeton, *op. cit.* at p. 129 and p. 140.
152 For treatment of the pre 1997 law see Kelly, *op. cit.* at pp. 830 *et seq.*; Casey, *op. cit.* at pp. 390 *et seq.*; Byrne et al., *Innocent Till Proven Guilty?* (Dublin: Irish Council for Civil Liberties, 1993) at pp. 20 *et seq.*
153 S. 2(1) of the Act provides a detailed definition of an arrestable offence; for a general consideration of powers of arrest and related matters see Walsh, *Recent Developments in Criminal Procedure 1996 and 1997* (Limerick Papers in Criminal Justice No. 2, Centre for Criminal Justice, University of Limerick, 1998).

(i) where they have reasonable cause to believe the person is in the act of committing an arrestable offence (i.e. where they have sufficient grounds to believe that they have caught a person red-handed during the commission of the offence);[154]

(ii) where an arrestable offence has been committed and they have reasonable grounds to suspect the guilt of the arrested person.[155]

Both of these powers of arrest are further qualified by the fact that the person effecting an arrest must also suspect, on reasonable grounds, that the person to be arrested is avoiding, or would attempt to avoid, arrest by the police. The person who makes such an arrest must then transfer the arrested person into police custody as soon as possible.

Police officers have more extensive powers of arrest without a warrant. They can arrest in either of the two situations where a private person can do so, but without the qualification that the arrested person is avoiding or attempting to avoid arrest. They also have a power of arrest, which is not available to private persons, where they have reasonable cause to suspect that an arrestable offence has been committed. Where a police officer has such a suspicion, he may arrest any person that he reasonably believes to be guilty.[156] The difference between this power and the second of the two powers set out above is that the police officer need only have a reasonable suspicion that an offence has been committed; in respect of arrest under section 4(2), which is available to private persons, an actual offence must have occurred.

These general powers of arrest are supplemented by additional statutory provisions which permit arrest without a warrant in respect of particular offences.[157] Statutory provisions also authorise arrest in a wider range of circumstances, provided a warrant has been issued by a court. The details of such powers greatly exceed the space available in a general text on tort, but readers should note that careful consideration needs to be given to both the governing legislation and the constitutional restraints resulting from the protection of liberty expressed in Article 40.4.1º of the Constitution.

Ancillary questions also arise in respect of arrest, such as the existence of accompanying rights to use force, search persons, enter property and seize goods.

---

154 S. 4(1); the power does not apply to arrest away from the scene, after the crime has been completed. Arrest of a person engaged in preparatory acts, which are not, in themselves, unlawful, probably falls outside the provision also.

155 S. 4(2); an actual offence must have occurred – reasonable suspicion that an offence has occurred will not suffice.

156 S. 4(3).

157 For example, s. 16 of the Criminal Assets Bureau Act 1996; s. 18 of the Domestic Violence Act 1996; see also Walsh, *loc. cit.* at p. 9; such powers tend only to be conferred on police officers, not on private citizens.

As with defence of persons or property, reasonable force may be used in effecting an arrest and the level of force will depend on individual circumstances.[158]

Entry

Entry into a dwelling, without a warrant, to effect an arrest requires express statutory authorisation and until 1997 the position was less clear with regard to other property.[159] Section 6 of the Criminal Law Act 1997 provides the police with extensive powers of entry to effect arrests, both with and without a warrant. Where an arrest warrant or a committal order has been issued, a police officer may enter any premises where the person is or where the officer reasonably suspects the person to be.[160] Entry without a warrant is permitted in respect of arrestable offences, where the person is on the premises or the police officer reasonably suspects the person to be on the premises.[161] In the case of dwellings there are additional criteria for entry without a warrant; one of the following must be satisfied before a police officer may enter a dwelling:

(i) the officer or another officer has observed the person within or entering the dwelling; or

(ii) the officer has reasonable grounds to suspect the person will obstruct the course of justice or abscond before an arrest warrant can be obtained; or

(iii) the officer has reasonable grounds to suspect that the person will commit an arrestable offence before a warrant can be obtained; or

(iv) the person ordinarily resides in the dwelling.

Various statutory provisions govern rights of entry to search for evidence and for miscellaneous other purposes, such as checking the identity of persons or examining records. Each provision must be carefully considered in light of the circumstances of the particular case. Entry without a warrant is authorised in a number of circumstances where a police officer has reasonable grounds to believe an offence is being committed.[162] In other circumstances a warrant

---

158 *Dowman v Ireland* [1986] ILRM 111.

159 See *DPP v McCreesh* [1992] 2 IR 239; *Freeman v DPP* [1996] 3 IR 565, in respect of dwellings; Art. 40. 5 of the Constitution provides special protection for dwellings; with respect to other property *The People (AG) v Hogan* (1972) 1 Frewen 360 suggests a power of entry is available in respect of arrest for serious offences; McCarthy J, in *McCreesh*, suggested that express authority would be required in respect of entry to any private place, at pp. 255–6.

160 S. 6(1); reasonable force may be used, if necessary; see Walsh, *loc. cit.* at pp. 20–1.

161 S. 6(2); again, reasonable force may be used, if necessary; see Walsh, *loc. cit.* at pp. 21–2.

162 See Kelly, *op. cit.* at pp. 914 *et seq.*; although the discussion is primarily concerned with Art. 40.5, on the inviolability of the dwelling, consideration is also

may be obtained to permit entry onto property. The criteria for obtaining a warrant vary and, once again, there are many statutory provisions related to particular offences.[163]

Search and Seizure

The leading Irish authority on the seizure of chattels, without a warrant, is *Jennings v Quinn*,[164] where O'Keeffe J, delivering the judgment of the Supreme Court, stated that:

> . . . the public interest requires that the police, when effecting a lawful arrest, may seize, without a warrant, property in the possession or custody of the person arrested when they believe it necessary to do so to avoid the abstraction or destruction of that property and when that property is:
>
> (a) evidence in support of the criminal charge upon which the arrest is made, or
> (b) evidence in support of any other criminal charge against that person then in contemplation, or
> (c) reasonably believed to be stolen property or to be property not in the lawful possession of that person;
>
> and that they may retain such property . . . as evidence . . .[165]

It is clear from this passage that the justification for the seizure of chattels is the public interest in the trial of the individual arrested, measured by the evidential status of the property seized. The failure of the police in this case to convince the court that the property was to be used for such a purpose led to the granting of an injunction to the plaintiff against the police requiring them to return the goods seized. This power of seizure does not extend to a general right to interfere with possession in the event of a civil dispute; it is expressly confined to cases involving the lawful arrest of the person in possession.

---

given to common law and statutory provisions relating to other property also; Walsh, *loc. cit.* at pp. 23–4; see, for example, s. 34 of the Control of Horses Act 1996; s. 14 of the Licensing (Combating Drug Abuse) Act 1997.

163 For example, s. 26 of the Misuse of Drugs Act 1977 as amended; s. 14 of the Criminal Assets Bureau Act 1996; s. 10 of the Criminal Justice (Miscellaneous Provisions) Act 1997 contains a more general power for granting search warrants; see Walsh, *loc. cit.* at pp. 22–3.

164 [1968] IR 305.

165 *Ibid.* at p. 309, Ó Dálaigh CJ and Walsh J concurring. O'Keeffe J went on to hold that such property could also be retained in respect of the extradition and trial abroad of the person arrested. Cited in support of the decision were *Dillon v O'Brien & Davis* (1887) 20 LR Ir 300 (seizure in respect of the charge on which the suspect was arrested, see particularly p. 317 on the public interest justification) and *Elias v Pasmore* [1934] 2 KB 164 (seizure in respect of other charges).

Judicial or statutory authority must be invoked in order to seize property in circumstances outside of the situations embraced by *Jennings v Quinn*. As with arrest and entry, there are miscellaneous statutory provisions regulating rights of seizure.[166] Many of the provisions governing entry also permit searches of the property and the seizure of evidence. If the relevant powers are not exceeded, then police officers will have a defence against a claim of trespass to chattels.

Statutory provisions may also permit police officers to stop and search persons.[167] Once the power is validly exercised, no claim for battery or false imprisonment will be available.

Other Authorisation

There are various other forms of authorisation available in respect of trespasses. A representative selection follows as a general guide to the range of such authorisations.

Necessity

It is generally accepted that necessity provides a defence to an action in trespass, though few practical examples exist. There is considerable overlap between this defence and the defence of persons or property. Street suggests that necessity should be employed in respect of interference with an innocent plaintiff, while defence of persons or property should be used where the plaintiff or the plaintiff's property is a source of risk.[168] It is primarily a matter of style as to which term is used to describe the justification for the invasion of the rights in question in most cases.[169] Nonetheless, necessity also has a role independent of defence of persons or property, such as medical emergencies and, perhaps, cases where a person touches another to gain that other's attention. In the case of medical emergencies personal protection is clearly at the core of the matter, but it hardly seems appropriate to describe it as 'defence'; consequently, necessity would seem to be the appropriate description of the justification.

---

166 For example, s. 15 of the Proceeds of Crime Act 1996; s. 37 of the Control of Horses Act 1996.

167 For example, s. 8 of the Criminal Law Act 1976 as amended permits police officers to stop vehicles and search the vehicle and the occupants on suspicion of particular offences; s. 23 of the Litter Pollution Act 1997 permits a police officer in limited instances to require a person to accompany the officer to a police station.

168 *Op. cit.* at p. 90; see also Salmond & Heuston, *op. cit.* at §22.1.

169 See, for example, *Police v O'Neill* [1993] 3 NZLR 712 and *Dehn v AG* [1988] 2 NZLR 564, where concerns for the well-being of a third party were considered under necessity.

Judicial Authority

The power of the courts, properly exercised, will provide sufficient authority for interference with persons or property. There are many situations where judicial authority must be sought; we have already come across some of these, such as consent in respect of wards of court, situations requiring warrants for arrest, or searches; others would include the appointment of an examiner or a liquidator over the affairs of a company in difficulties, or the trial of suspects in criminal cases. Apart from such cases, judicial decisions often impinge on the possession of property and conduct pursuant to the proper execution of a judgment would be lawful.

Discipline

The reasonable disciplining of children by parents, guardians or other persons *in loco parentis* (such as a teacher) provides a defence to trespass. Physical punishment is not now tolerated to the same degree that it was in earlier generations, so older authorities on the level of corporal punishment that may be regarded as acceptable would be out of step with modern values. Corporal punishment is no longer used in schools, but lesser punishments, such as detaining children for a limited period or temporarily confiscating items of personal property, would be permissible. As with other defences to trespass, the interference with the child's rights must be reasonable; consequently, the disciplinary measure employed would need to be proportionate to the objective.[170]

Statutory Authority

Apart from the investigation of crime, there are miscellaneous statutory provisions authorising conduct that would otherwise constitute trespass. These provisions relate to a variety of public functions, such as health, occupational safety, transport and public utilities. Detailed consideration of these issues exceeds the scope of a general text, but some brief examples will be considered to give some idea of the range of provisions in existence. It should also be noted that the judiciary will require strict compliance with the relevant statutory provisions for the defence to succeed and will only allow interference with private rights where the authority to do so is clear.[171]

---

170 See McMahon & Binchy, *op. cit.* at p. 423; Street, *op. cit.* at pp. 93–4; Salmond & Heuston, *op. cit.* at pp. 134–5; Fridman, *op. cit.* vol. 1 at pp. 76–7; Fleming, *op. cit.* at pp. 98–100; Prosser & Keeton, *op. cit.* at §27; Balkin & Davis, *op. cit.* at pp. 169 *et seq.*

171 See particularly *Woodhouse v Newry Navigation Co.* [1898] 1 IR 161 per Lord Ashbourne C at pp. 166–7 and Fitzgibbon LJ at p. 170, both of whom cite the House of Lords decision in *Herron v Rathmines Improvement Commissioners* [1892] AC 498.

There are a number of legislative provisions which justify conduct, which would otherwise constitute trespass, on the basis of health considerations. Section 38 of the Health Act 1947, for example, permits the detention and isolation of persons where a chief medical officer believes the person to be a probable source of infectious disease. Regulations under the Act also provide for compulsory examination and testing of people in respect of certain infectious diseases.[172] In respect of mental health, the Mental Treatment Act 1945 authorises the involuntary detention of persons under certain, fairly rudimentary, prerequisite conditions.[173] Section 260 of the Act restricts the ability of persons to sue in respect of conduct purported to be in pursuance of the Act. The section requires a claimant to seek the consent of the High Court for the initiation of proceedings and such consent may only be granted where 'there are substantial grounds for contending that the person against whom proceedings are to be brought acted in bad faith or without reasonable care'. The case law on this subject has provided an interpretation of the Act that strongly favours protection of the medical profession and others engaged in implementing the provisions of the Act, by setting a high standard for an applicant to attain in order to get the necessary consent to initiate proceedings.[174]

In the field of occupational safety, inspectors appointed by the National Authority for Occupational Safety and Health or an enforcing agency[175] have a wide range of powers to enter premises, examine records, take samples and so forth under section 34 of the Safety, Health and Welfare at Work Act 1989. While a warrant is required to forcibly enter premises, many of the powers are

---

172 The Infectious Diseases Regulations 1981 (SI 390/1981); Infectious Diseases (Amendment) Regulations 1985 (SI 268/1985).

173 See Tomkin & Hanafin, *op. cit.* at pp. 120 *et seq.*; Kelly, *op. cit.* at pp. 867–9; Casey, *op. cit.* at pp. 407 *et seq.*

174 *O'Dowd v North Western Health Board* [1983] ILRM 186; *Murphy v Greene* [1990] 2 IR 566; *O'Reilly v Moroney* unrep. SC, 16 November 1993; Irish Times Law Report, 28 February 1994; noted by O'Neill (1994) 12 ILT 211; *Kiernan v Harris* unrep. HC, 12 May 1998; *Melly v Moran* unrep. SC, 28 May 1998; see also Tomkin & Hanafin, *op. cit.* at pp. 121–3. The dissenting judgment of Blayney J in *O'Reilly v Moroney* provides a useful critical perspective on the law in this area. In *Croke v Smith and Others* unrep. HC, 8 April 1994 the applicant used the *habeas corpus* procedure, under Art. 40.4 of the Constitution, to challenge his detention under the 1945 Act. Although the attempt was unsuccessful on the facts, Flood J was somewhat critical of the level of safeguards in respect of the deprivation of liberty provided in the Act. See also *Croke v Smith (no. 2)* [1998] 1 IR 101 (SC). In *Bailey v Gallagher* [1996] 2 ILRM 433 the Supreme Court held that doctors should have at least a general awareness of the criteria governing detention; in the instant case the defendant failed to take account of the fact that the initial authorisation for detaining the plaintiff had expired.

175 Established under Part III of the Safety, Health and Welfare at Work Act 1989. Under s. 32 other bodies may be empowered as enforcing agencies by ministerial authority.

exercisable without a warrant. Public interest in accident prevention justifies this curtailment of autonomy over property. Notably, there is only a power to 'invite' persons to submit biological samples under section 34, thus preserving the need for consent in respect of personal contact.

Statutory authority permits aircraft to travel over property without liability for trespass, but the authority is confined to reasonable flight paths.[176]

Public utilities also have statutory powers of limited interference with property. The Electricity Supply Board, for example, may traverse property with power lines and may install fixtures to support those lines.[177] Once again, public interest considerations outweigh private rights, but the obligation to compensate for overriding the rights ensures that some protection is still afforded to those rights. Thus, it is effectively a right to purchase an intrusion, rather than an unfettered right to interfere with property.

Duress

A final question in respect of trespass relates to duress as a defence.[178] We have already seen that if the defendant forces the plaintiff to consent to conduct, the consent is invalid and trespass will lie. But what if the defendant's conduct results from pressure applied by a third party? Consider the following scenarios:

Example

X holds D's family at gun point and instructs D to take a substantial sum of money from P, D's employer, and bring it to X. D complies with the request and X absconds with the money.

D1, a builder, is engaged by Y on a substantial development. In the course of the work P1 informs D1 that a small portion of the land he is building on belongs to him (P1). Y insists that D1 should ignore P1; otherwise he will not get paid for any of the work he has done. D1 has cash flow problems and cannot afford to wait for payment; believing that legal remedies will be too slow in coming, he builds on P1's land.

---

176 S. 55 of the Air Navigation and Transport Act 1936, as amended by s. 47(1) of the Air Navigation and Transport Act 1988.

177 S. 53 of the Electricity (Supply) Act 1927, as amended by s. 46 of the Electricity (Supply) (Amendment) Act 1945 and s. 1 of the Electricity (Supply) (Amendment) Act 1985. The board's power to proceed in the absence of consent carries a corresponding duty to compensate, introduced after the original provision was regarded as an unconstitutional violation of property rights in *ESB v Gormley* [1985] IR 129; [1985] ILRM 494.

178 Duress was rejected in *Gilbert v Stone* (1647) Aleyn 35, defendant entered plaintiff's house, under threat of violence; actual compulsion, rather than a threat, was held to be sufficient to permit the defence in *Smith v Stone* (1647) Style 65; see also Winfield & Jolowicz, *op. cit.* at pp. 754–5.

Z wishes to beat up P2, but because his dislike of P2 is well known, he wants to appear to be dissociated from the beating. Z threatens to inflict a severe beating on D2, someone with whom neither Z nor P2 has any association, if he (D2) does not inflict a beating on P2. In fear of his own safety, D2 beats up P2.

Clearly the instigators in all three scenarios, X, Y and Z, are responsible for the interferences with P, P1 and P2, respectively. If it is impractical to proceed against them, would D, D1 and D2 also be liable for trespass? D appears to have a strong case for being relieved of responsibility, because of the extent of the pressure compared to the level of interference; D1 is under less pressure, but the level of interference with P1 is less drastic than the interference with P, so the position is open to argument either way; D2 has the weakest case, because his conduct involves an arbitrary, albeit understandable, preference for self-interest over an innocent party. In D2's case, police assistance may have been a viable alternative solution; consequently, the decision to beat up P2 is more voluntary than the other two. These situations overlap to an extent with defence of persons and property, though they do differ from the typical defence case. Of the three, D1's case, involving economic pressure, presents the greatest difference from defence cases.

These issues remain unresolved in Irish law and do not offer easy solutions. Should such cases arise, a balance will have to be struck between the competing interests, and while criminal and contract cases may provide some guidance, the differences with the functions of tort law will militate against wholesale adoption of principles from these other branches of law.

CHAPTER FIVE

Nuisance

Introduction

Nuisance, in colloquial speech, connotes annoyance or irritation and may refer to a person, a thing or a set of circumstances. Similarly, the legal concept of nuisance is somewhat ill-defined, but has been described as 'an act or omission which amounts to an unreasonable interference with, disturbance of, or annoyance to another person in the exercise of his rights'.[1] The subject is composed of two distinct causes of action, private nuisance and public nuisance. These torts straddle the boundaries between strict and fault based liability, so that some instances of interference will be actionable despite the exercise of reasonable care by the defendant, while in other instances the taking of reasonable precautions will protect a defendant.[2] The reason for this is twofold: first, it is a result of the historical origins of the subject; and, secondly, it is because the modern use of the concept focuses more on the impact on the plaintiff than on assessing the merits of the defendant's conduct. There is still a balancing of interests, but the balancing process often gives greater weight to the plaintiff's interests than that which would be given in negligence.

Civil liability for nuisance developed from two distinct actions – the assize of nuisance and the action on the case. The former primarily protected incorporeal property rights and could only be maintained between holders of freehold property. The latter protected a mixture of proprietary and personal rights related to the ownership of land. The action on the case gradually came to dominate the field of civil liability, but in doing so it borrowed elements of the assize of nuisance and also from the criminal misdemeanour of public nuisance. The modern torts are the product of this mixture and lack a unifying conceptual base.[3]

The generality and imprecision of the scope of nuisance are admirably captured by Fleming, when he suggests that:

---

1   Per O'Higgins CJ in *Connolly v South of Ireland Asphalt Co.* [1977] IR 99, at p. 103; for extensive treatment of nuisance see Buckley, *The Law of Nuisance*, 2nd ed. (London: Butterworths, 1996).

2   For further discussion see Eekelaar, 'Nuisance and Strict Liability' (1973) 8 Ir Jur (ns) 191, based on the view that truly strict liability involves the absence of knowledge of risk on the defendant's part. This chapter uses a different version of strict liability, which will include liability in the absence of negligence within the concept. The provisions in relation to remoteness of damage, considered in chapter 11 *infra*, suggest that some level of fault is always required.

3   See Vennell, 'The Essentials of Nuisance: A Discussion of Recent New Zealand Developments in the Tort of Nuisance' (1977) 4 Otago L Rev 56; Baker, *An Introduction to English Legal History*, 3rd ed. (London: Butterworths, 1990) at chapter 23.

Far from susceptible of exact definition, it has become a catch-all for a multitude of ill-assorted sins, linking offensive smells, crowing roosters, obstructions of rights of way, defective cellar flaps, street queues, lotteries, houses of ill-fame and a host of other rag-ends of the law.[4]

This broad range of coverage and imprecision of scope create scope for adaptation and development. A notable example of this potential arises in respect of environmental damage. Most, if not all, sources of pollution are capable of giving rise to actionable nuisance; thus, enforcement of private rights can have the convenient side-effect of protecting others in the neighbourhood of the successful plaintiff. These torts are by no means the only tool available for environmental protection, but they do expand the range of legal processes available to combat environmental damage.[5]

Private Nuisance

The tort of private nuisance protects persons from unreasonable invasion of rights related to the ownership or occupation of land. Historically, the action was only available for the protection of persons with proprietary interests, but in recent years it has been extended, in some jurisdictions, including Ireland, to include personal interests connected with land. The consideration of what is unreasonable differs between nuisance and negligence, a point which will be considered at more length later in this chapter. A further distinction between nuisance and negligence is that the latter is only remedied by compensation, after injury has occurred, whereas nuisance actions provide the plaintiff with a wider range of remedies. The primary reason for this is that negligence developed exclusively for the protection of personal interests, whereas private nuisance originated in proprietary interests. As a result, nuisance includes some practical remedies, so that the defendant may be required to abate the nuisance, or, at least, allow the plaintiff to enter his property to do so.[6] In its modern format, nuisance is often remedied by injunction, which may be either negative (requiring the defendant to cease the impugned conduct) or positive (requiring the defendant to undo the nuisance).

---

4 Fleming, *The Law of Torts*, 8th ed. (London: Law Book Co., 1993), at p. 409.
5 See Scannell, *Environmental and Planning Law* (Dublin: Round Hall Press, 1995) for extensive consideration of environmental protection law, particularly pp. 42 *et seq.* for consideration of the role of tort law as an environmental weapon (note a variety of other torts, such as trespass to land and *Rylands v Fletcher* liability, may also be used in a similar fashion); see also Steele, 'Private Law and the Environment: Nuisance in Context' (1995) 15 LS 236.
6 Baker, *op. cit.* at pp. 478–9.

Requisite elements:

1. Conduct for which the defendant is responsible
2. Damage or interference with rights
3. Unreasonableness
4. Causation
5. Absence of defence

Conduct for which the Defendant is Responsible

Liability in nuisance may arise from the defendant's own conduct or that of another for which the defendant is deemed to be responsible. The range of behaviour which can give rise to nuisance is as broad ranging and diverse as the range of interferences referred to earlier. The main issues to be considered are: first, responsibility for omissions; secondly, responsibility for the creation or authorisation of a nuisance; and thirdly, special provisions on the nature of the conduct, which distinguish nuisance from other torts.

Omissions

As indicated at the outset, nuisance can arise by way of either an act or an omission, though positive conduct is more likely to give rise to an actionable nuisance than an omission. There are few situations where inaction can lead to interference with neighbours, in the absence of some prior positive conduct by the defendant. The principal situations giving rise to actionable omissions involve failure to alleviate the effects of natural hazards, risks created by third parties, or deteriorating property. One of the few cases on a risk resulting from the natural condition of land is *Leakey v National Trust*.[7] The defendant held property at the rear of the plaintiff's house. The topsoil began to slip onto the plaintiff's property due to an unusual combination of climatic factors, thereby causing damage and creating a significant risk of further damage. The plaintiff took an action, based on private nuisance, claiming compensation for damage already caused and seeking mandatory injunctions to compel the defendant to remove soil and debris from his property and to take measures to prevent further encroachment.

The plaintiff succeeded, both at first instance and in the Court of Appeal. The majority held that persons in control of property will be liable in nuisance if they do not do all that is reasonable in the circumstances to prevent or minimise the risk of foreseeable damage where they know or ought to know that something on the land has encroached or threatens to encroach on neighbouring land. Furthermore, the financial capacity of both parties to protect the plaintiff's interests was held to be relevant to determining liability. Clearly this form of liability is almost

---

7 [1980] QB 485; [1980] 2 WLR 65; [1980] 1 All ER 17.

identical to negligence; indeed the decision was strongly influenced by an opinion of the Privy Council in a negligence case dealing with failure to control a natural hazard.[8] The dissenting judgment of Shaw LJ in *Leakey* was on the basis that nuisance was not the appropriate tort on which to base the complaint. The principal significance of treating the culpable omission as a nuisance, rather than negligence, is that it broadens the range of remedies available. The American *Restatement* adopts a different position, confining liability for failure to abate a natural hazard to cases of public nuisance near a highway.[9] Canadian[10] and Australian[11] authorities on natural hazards are consistent with the decision in *Leakey* and it was followed by Judge Buckley in *Daly v McMullan*.[12]

The decisions in *Leakey* and *Daly* were also influenced by the House of Lords decision in *Sedleigh-Denfield v O'Callaghan*,[13] which dealt with liability for the failure to alleviate a risk created by a third party. A local authority inserted a drainage pipe in a ditch which was partially on the defendants' property, without their consent or knowledge. The pipe was subsequently noticed by an employee of the defendants, who wrongly assumed that consent had been obtained for its installation. Due to defective installation of a protective grid, the opening to the pipe was susceptible to blockage by debris carried along the ditch by rainwater. Some years after its installation, the pipe became blocked, causing flooding on the plaintiff's property.

The House of Lords held the defendants liable, having continued the nuisance by failing to remove the risk, of which they were deemed to be aware. As with the later decision in *Leakey*, the rationale behind the imposition of liability was the failure to take reasonable steps where they knew or could reasonably have known of a foreseeable risk to the plaintiff's property. The American *Restatement* adopts a similar stance, basing liability on actual or constructive knowledge of the conduct and the unreasonable risk of nuisance, coupled with consent to the conduct or a failure to exercise reasonable care to offset the risk.[14]

Similarly, where the occupier takes the property with the nuisance already in place, perhaps by the conduct of the previous occupant, failure to take reasonable steps to reduce the interference with the plaintiff's rights will result

---

8 *Goldman v Hargrave* [1967] 1 AC 645; [1966] 3 WLR 513; [1966] 2 All ER 989.
9 *Restatement, Second, Torts* §840.
10 See Fridman, *The Law of Torts in Canada* (Toronto: Carswell, 1989), vol. 1, at p. 141, footnote 111, for case references.
11 See Balkin & Davis, *Law of Torts* (Sydney: Butterworths, 1991) at p. 481 for case references.
12 [1997] 2 ILRM 232; it is unusual for a Circuit Court judgment to be reported, but the issue is one of considerable importance and reviews a number of authorities in some detail; see also *Neill v Department of the Environment for Northern Ireland* [1990] NI 84.
13 [1940] AC 880; [1940] 3 All ER 349; approved by Judge Buckley in *Daly v McMullan* [1997] 2 ILRM 232, at p. 237.
14 *Restatement, Second, Torts* §838.

in liability.[15] The American *Restatement* also takes this approach, justifying the imposition of a positive duty by the occupier's control over the source of risk.[16]

Failure to repair one's property will generate responsibility, at least where reasonable care is not taken to ensure that the property is not a nuisance. Some English cases[17] have held that liability is strict in the cases of premises adjacent to the highway, so that the defendant is liable even where the nuisance could not reasonably have been discovered. Canadian authorities[18] have rejected this approach, preferring to base liability on the same footing as other omissions, while Irish authorities are divided on the issue.[19] The issue was considered in *Lynch v Hetherton*,[20] where the plaintiff's car was damaged in a collision with a tree, which fell from the defendant's land into the roadway. Following a number of English authorities on the question of falling trees, O'Hanlon J held the relevant legal principle to be as follows:

> . . . that a landowner having on his lands a tree or trees adjoining a highway or his neighbour's land is bound to take such care as a reasonable and prudent landowner would take to guard against the danger of damage being done by a falling tree.[21]

The formulation is specifically focused on the particular hazard in question and it remains to be seen whether this principle will be applied to other cases of failure to repair. In principle, it would seem fairer to require some level of culpability on the defendant's part in the case of omissions; strict liability is suited only to situations where one has voluntarily participated in the generation of risk. The decision in *Daly v McMullan*[22] supports this, as it suggests a single principle of fault based liability for all instances of nuisance by omission.

Where occupation and ownership are split, the plaintiff is faced with some uncertainty as to who is the correct defendant.[23] Where the development of the

---

15 *Penruddock's Case* (1597) 5 Co Rep 1006.
16 *Restatement, Second, Torts* §839.
17 See, for example, *Wringe v Cohen* [1940] 1 KB 229; [1939] 4 All ER 241; *Heap v Ind Coope & Allsopp Ltd* [1940] 2 KB 476; [1940] 3 All ER 634; *Mint v Good* [1951] 1 KB 517; [1950] 2 All ER 1159.
18 See, for example, *Schoeni v King* [1944] OR 38; *O'Leary v Melitides* (1959) 20 DLR (2d) 258; *Brewer v Kayes* [1973] 2 OR 284; *Wayen Diners Ltd v Hong Yick Tong Ltd* (1987) 35 DLR (4th) 722.
19 See McMahon & Binchy, *The Irish Law of Torts*, 2nd ed. (Dublin: Butterworths, 1989), at pp. 470 *et seq.*; contrast *Palmer v Bateman* [1908] 2 IR 393 and *Mullan v Forrester* [1921] 2 IR 412.
20 [1991] 2 IR 405; [1990] ILRM 857.
21 *Ibid.* at p. 408; p. 860; no reference is made to Irish decisions, such as *Palmer v Bateman* or *Mullan v Forrester*.
22 [1997] 2 ILRM 232.
23 Suing both occupier and owner circumvents the problem, leaving the court to determine responsibility. However, if one of the defendants is cleared of responsi-

nuisance predates the letting of the property, the landlord's liability is dependent on actual or constructive knowledge of the nuisance.[24] Where the nuisance arises after letting, older authorities suggest that the party that has undertaken to repair should be liable.[25] This proposition seems to have survived where the landlord covenants to repair, but not where the tenant does so.[26] It appears a little incongruous that the private arrangements between the landlord and tenant should affect the duty owed to a third party and, furthermore, the principle makes no provision for cases where the parties have made no provision for the responsibility to repair. It is submitted that the actual level of control that a party has over the property should be the key factor in determining responsibility and this would be consistent with the other cases of liability for failure to alleviate a nuisance.

There is only limited Irish authority on any of the issues raised here, but the dominant view in the authorities considered is that defendants should be responsible for a nuisance that they have not actively helped to create only where they were in a position to alleviate the risk and failed to take reasonable measures to do so.

Active Conduct

The creator of a nuisance will usually be liable for it, even where some other party, such as an occupier or landlord, is also responsible. In a case like *Sedleigh-Denfield*, for example, the local authority that laid the pipe on the defendants' property may be sued for compensation.[27] Where the creator of the nuisance has no control over the property from which the nuisance emanates, the plaintiff may be confined to seeking damages from that person in some cases. This would occur if the owner or occupier did not authorise the creation of the nuisance and was not negligent in failing to remove it. If the plaintiff is seeking abatement of the nuisance, this will require proceedings against the owner or occupier of the property. There are differing views on whether the conduct complained of may originate on the plaintiff's own property. In New Zealand nuisance is available where the conduct took place on the plaintiff's property, provided the defendant

---

bility, the plaintiff may be required to bear that party's legal costs. It is, therefore, preferable if the correct defendant can be identified at the outset.

24 *St Anne's Well Brewery Co. v Roberts* [1928] All ER Rep 28; 140 LT 1.
25 *Payne v Rogers* (1794) 2 H Bl 350 (landlord's covenant to repair); *Pretty v Bickmore* (1873) LR 8 CP 401 (tenant's covenant to repair).
26 See McMahon & Binchy, *op. cit.* at p. 469; Heuston & Buckley, *Salmond and Heuston on the Law of Torts*, 21st ed. (London: Sweet & Maxwell, 1996), at p. 69; Rogers, *Winfield & Jolowicz on Tort*, 14th ed. (London: Sweet & Maxwell, 1994), at p. 427.
27 Though in Australia a trespasser, who creates a nuisance, may not be liable to the plaintiff in nuisance; see *Beaudesert Shire Council v Smith* (1966) 120 CLR 145; 40 ALJR 211. Although the main principle established in *Beaudesert* was overruled in *Northern Territory of Australia v Mengel* (1995) 69 ALJR 527, the latter decision did not address the issue of liability of trespassers in nuisance.

had permission to be there.[28] In England nuisance is only available if the plaintiff and defendant are co-occupiers, not if the plaintiff has sole occupation.[29]

A defendant may be responsible for the conduct of others in a number of ways. Ordinary principles of vicarious liability will make a defendant responsible for the conduct of employees or other persons sufficiently under the defendant's control. In the case of nuisances created by independent contractors, the person engaging them will only be liable where there is a non-delegable duty owed to the plaintiff.[30] Liability in such circumstances is strict, as it does not require any wrongful conduct on the defendant's part. An owner or occupier, who is not initially answerable for an independent contractor's conduct, may become liable for the nuisance at a later stage, on the basis of a culpable omission, having continued or adopted it.

Where the creation or continuance of a nuisance was authorised or permitted by the defendant, liability will be more extensive than any of the foregoing forms of responsibility. Here the authorisation or permission serves to identify the defendant with the conduct, even though the defendant may take no further part in the objectionable activity. *Goldfarb v Williams & Co.*[31] provides a graphic example. The plaintiffs occupied the first and third floors of a building and the landlord let the second floor to a sports and social club. The club had expressly disclosed, to the landlord, an intention to run dances on the premises. Due to the nature of the building's construction, a significant level of noise emanated from the second floor, causing a nuisance to the plaintiffs, even though the dances were conducted with reasonable care.

There could be no question of the landlord being vicariously liable or owing a non-delegable duty, as the dance was not being conducted on the landlord's behalf. Liability was, however, imposed on the basis that the landlord had authorised the creation of the nuisance. The crucial factor leading to this finding was that the nuisance was an inevitable consequence of using the premises for the purpose for which it was let.[32] Had the interference resulted from negligence on the club's part, and had the construction of the building been such that it was possible to run dances without interference to neighbours, the landlord probably would not have been held responsible. Some Canadian decisions have gone a step further, imposing liability on the basis that the nuisance was a likely consequence of authorised conduct, rather than an inevitable one.[33] This extension was rejected

---

28 *Paxhaven Holdings Ltd v AG* [1974] 2 NZLR 185; *Clearlite Holdings Ltd v Auckland City Corporation* [1976] 2 NZLR 729.
29 *Hooper v Rogers* [1975] Ch 43; [1974] 3 WLR 329; [1974] 3 All ER 417.
30 Vicarious liability and non-delegable duties are considered in detail in chapter 14 *infra*.
31 [1945] IR 433; see also *Harris v James* (1876) 45 LJ QB 545; *Ross & Glendining Ltd v Hancock & Co.* [1929] NZLR 204; *Grierson v Osborne Stadium Ltd* [1933] 3 DLR 598; *Tetley v Chitty* [1986] 1 All ER 663.
32 [1945] IR 433 at p. 445.
33 *Aldridge v Van Patter* [1952] OR 595; *Banfai v Formula Fun Centre Inc.* (1984) 51 OR (2d) 361.

in England in *Smith v Scott*.[34] Fridman is highly critical of the principle, in either form, as it treats knowledge, coupled with permission, as an equivalent involvement to that of the actual creator of the nuisance.[35] The advantage of imposing liability, if there is one, is that it may encourage landlords to take greater account of the effect that prospective tenants may have on neighbours, at a point in time when the landlord still has a significant level of control over the property.

Furthermore, the owner of a business will be responsible for the conduct of third parties where such conduct is a natural or inevitable incident or side-effect of the defendant's business. In *O'Kane v Campbell*,[36] for example, the plaintiff was granted an injunction against a shopkeeper on the basis of disruption to sleep, resulting from noise generated by customers of the shop in the early hours of the morning. Lynch J stated that the defendant would be responsible for 'at least the ordinary and natural conduct of people whom he attracts to the neighbourhood'.[37] The responsibility appears to be strict, as the injunction was not qualified in terms of exercising reasonable care. Presumably, a similar situation would apply to disruption generated by suppliers delivering goods to the defendant.

One further point of note is that conduct which would not amount to nuisance when considered by itself may be regarded as a nuisance when combined with conduct of a third party. Thus, where the cumulative effect of the activities of several persons involves an unreasonable interference with the plaintiff, each such person will be responsible to the plaintiff, at least where they are aware of the conduct of the other contributors.[38]

Nature of the Conduct

Nuisance often involves objection, not only to past harm, but to the maintenance of a state of affairs which is disruptive of the plaintiff. So, where noxious substances are emitted from the defendant's factory, for example, the plaintiff's concern may be for more than the initial disruption and may extend to concern over the risk of further disruption if the defendant does not alter the manner in which the factory is operated. The conduct which is impugned, in many cases, is

---

34 [1973] Ch 314; [1972] 3 WLR 783; [1972] 3 All ER 645.

35 Fridman, *op. cit.* vol. 1 at p. 150.

36 [1985] IR 115; the defendant was operating a twenty-four hour shop on a corner at the intersection of a busy thoroughfare and a quiet residential street.

37 *Ibid.* at p. 117; see also *New Imperial & Windsor Hotel Co. Ltd v Johnson* [1912] 1 IR 327.

38 *Lambton v Mellish* [1894] 3 Ch 163, per Chitty J, *obiter*, at p. 165; see also *Pride of Derby v British Celanese Ltd* [1953] Ch 149; [1953] 2 WLR 58; [1953] 1 All ER 179; s. 12(3) of the Civil Liability Act 1961; this issue is considered further in the context of causation in chapter 11 *infra*. The *Restatement, Second, Torts* §840E makes similar provision in respect of liability for contribution to a nuisance. In such cases the defendant is only liable for his portion of the nuisance, unless the parties can be regarded as concurrent wrongdoers, see chapter 13 *infra*.

not merely an isolated act leading to a single incidence of harm, but the creation or maintenance of conditions that pose an ongoing threat to the plaintiff. The law recognises this concern by treating nuisance as a continuing wrong in such cases. This allows for a broader approach to the remedial aspect of the subject, such as coupling damages for past harm with an injunction to prevent future harm or allowing the plaintiff institute second and subsequent proceedings for further incidents of harm.

Damage or Interference with Rights

Injury to some interest of the plaintiff's is usually essential for a nuisance action to succeed. Ordinarily the plaintiff must prove the existence of the injury, but there are three exceptions, where the action can succeed in the absence of any harm having occurred:

(i) where damage can be presumed;
(ii) where there is interference with a servitude (such as an easement or profit *à prendre*);
(iii) where a *quia timet* injunction is sought.

Damage may be presumed only in exceptional cases, where it would be inevitable on the facts. Early authorities suggest that, where the defendant's building projects over the plaintiff's land, damage by dripping rainwater may be presumed.[39] No presumption will be made if there is any doubt as to the likelihood of damage.[40]

The main justification for making interference with servitudes actionable *per se* is that a plaintiff's difficulty in proving harm could lead to the defendant acquiring a prescriptive right to commit the offending conduct, thereby denying the plaintiff adequate protection in respect of the rights in question.[41] Prescriptive rights are proprietary interests, acquired by usage; in other words, a person that commits a nuisance for an extended period of time, without objection, can acquire a legal right to continue to do so.

A *quia timet* injunction may be granted where damage is imminent, but has not yet occurred.[42] Damages may be awarded in lieu of such an injunction under

---

39 *Baten's Case* (1610) 9 Co Rep 53b; *Fay v Prentice* (1845) 1 CB 828.
40 See, for example, *Meara v Daly* (1914) 48 ILTR 223, where an action for interference with grazing, by the erection of a barbed wire fence, failed because the plaintiff's fears might prove unfounded.
41 See Brazier, *Street on Torts*, 9th ed. (London: Butterworths, 1993) at p. 349; Winfield & Jolowicz, *op. cit.* at p. 429; prescription as a defence is discussed later in this chapter. A second justification for making these cases actionable *per se* is that they are more akin to trespass than other nuisance actions, see *Nicholls v Ely Beet Sugar Factory Ltd* [1936] Ch 343, per Lord Wright at p. 349.
42 Injunctions are considered in chapter 15 *infra*.

section 2 of Lord Cairns' Act 1858. The degree of care taken by the defendant to minimise the risk of nuisance will be a relevant factor in determining the likelihood of harm to the plaintiff. In *McGrane v Louth County Council*,[43] a *quia timet* injunction was refused in respect of the location of a dump. O'Hanlon J held that, as the council had engaged consultants to provide expert advice on the location and management of the dump, the activity was unlikely to become a nuisance.[44]

Private nuisance protects against three broad categories of harm – material damage, interference with use and enjoyment, and interference with servitudes. The first two are far more frequently litigated than the third and will be the main focus of attention here. A preliminary word of caution is necessary in respect of the two principal categories of harm; the two are not entirely separate and distinct, but rather reflect different points on a continuous spectrum. As a result, there will be cases that are not easy to classify, which may lead to some difficulty in determining the appropriate legal principles for those cases. Take gaseous emissions from a factory, for example. Over a period of time factors such as the toxicity, intensity and odour may vary; as a result, the emissions may initially be harmless, at a later point they will become disruptive to use and enjoyment (where the odour and intensity increase), and, later still, they will cause material harm (by driving down property prices or poisoning plants and animals). There will be points in time where the emissions are at a degree which represents a borderline between different levels of intrusion and disputes arising at such a time may prove particularly difficult to resolve if the law of private nuisance is employed to provide a solution.

Material Damage

Physical damage to land, which reduces its value and is not of a trivial nature, is actionable at the suit of the owner, whose proprietary interest is thereby infringed.[45] In *St Helen's Smelting Co. v Tipping*,[46] for example, damage to shrubs and trees, caused by fumes from the defendants' copper smelting plant,

---

43 Unrep. HC, 9 December 1993.
44 *Ibid.* at pp. 11–13; the refusal of the injunction would not preclude the plaintiff from making further complaint in the future if the operation of the dump gave rise to actual damage or disruption, *ibid.* at p. 14; see also *Halpin v Tara Mines Ltd* [1976–7] ILRM 28, at pp. 38–40, Gannon J refused an injunction where the defendants established that steps were being taken to remove the likelihood of further disruption to the plaintiffs.
45 There may be some difficulties in respect of owners out of possession but Trindade & Cane, *The Law of Torts in Australia*, 2nd ed. (Melbourne: Oxford University Press, 1993) at p. 605, justifiably argue that the proper plaintiff should be the person obliged to repair property, which would often be the owner, rather than the occupier. By analogy, a reversioner, whose interest in property is devalued by long term physical harm, such as high toxicity in soil, ought to have a legitimate claim for redress.
46 (1865) 11 HL Cas 642.

was held to be sufficient material damage.[47] In *Halpin v Tara Mines Ltd*,[48] it was held that cracks in a building due to vibrations would suffice, though the plaintiffs failed to prove the requisite causal link with the defendants' activities. Gannon J held that a 'party asserting that he has sustained material damage to his property by reason of an alleged nuisance must establish the fact of such damage and that it was caused by the nuisance as alleged'.[49]

Personal injury also constitutes a sufficient material damage to ground a claim in private nuisance in Ireland, though the point is less certain in other jurisdictions.[50] Early Irish authorities suggested that risks to the health of an occupier would be a sufficient ground for complaint[51] and the Supreme Court decision in *Hanrahan v Merck Sharp & Dohme*[52] puts the issue beyond doubt. In *Hanrahan* one of the plaintiffs succeeded in establishing a claim for personal injuries, while two others failed due to a lack of supporting evidence to substantiate the claims, rather than on any principled objection to such claims.[53] Furthermore, occupation of the property, rather than a proprietary interest, seems to provide a sufficient connection to give the injured party a sufficient basis on which to complain.[54] The plaintiffs in this case were all permanently resident on

---

47 A similar claim in *Hanrahan v Merck Sharp & Dohme* [1988] ILRM 629 failed due to a lack of evidence to substantiate the allegation of damage to plants caused by the defendants (p. 643), though the plaintiffs succeeded on other grounds.

48 [1976–7] ILRM 28.

49 *Ibid.* at p. 30; see also *Patterson v Murphy* [1978] ILRM 85, at p. 93, where the plaintiffs succeeded in establishing that the defendants' blasting operations had broken a window and a boundary wall and had caused minor cracks in walls in their house; *Stafford v Roadstone Ltd* [1980] ILRM 1, where one of the plaintiffs obtained an interlocutory injunction, having established a fair case to be tried as to the causing of physical damage.

50 In *Cunard v Antifyre Ltd* [1933] 1 KB 551 at p. 557; [1932] All ER Rep 558 at p. 560 Talbot J stated, *obiter*, that nuisance was only available for property damage and that negligence was the appropriate tort in respect of personal injuries caused by neighbours' activities.

51 *Hull v Mairs* unrep. HC, 21 December 1908 (cited in *New Imperial & Windsor Hotel Co. Ltd v Johnson* [1912] 1 IR 327 at p. 335) treated traffic vibrations as a nuisance where the 'nerves and health' of the occupier were affected. In *Gibbings v Hungerford* [1904] 1 IR 211 the discharge of sewage was described by Lord Ashbourne C as a nuisance as well as a trespass, although the claim was for trespass only, and the risk to the health of the plaintiff and his family was cited as one of the reasons for finding in favour of the plaintiff. More recently, in *Patterson v Murphy* [1978] ILRM 85, at p. 94, nervous strain resulting from blasting operations was treated as an interference with use and enjoyment, rather than as material damage. This may, however, be explained by the fact that there was no evidence of medically recognised injury associated with the strain.

52 [1988] ILRM 629.

53 *Ibid.* at pp. 640–3.

54 *Ibid.* at p. 633; Irish and English law differ in this respect, see *Hunter v Canary Wharf Ltd* [1997] AC 655; [1997] 2 WLR 684; [1997] 2 All ER 426, considered below in the discussion of interference with use and enjoyment.

the farm, so the question as to whether a more transient occupation of property, such as a guest, would suffice to ground a claim remains open.

Damage to chattels may also amount to sufficient material damage. In *Halsey v Esso Petroleum Co. Ltd*,[55] for example, Veale J held that damage to the plaintiffs' laundry, while hanging out to dry, amounted to sufficient harm. In *Hanrahan* injury to farm animals was held to be sufficient[56] and the Supreme Court did not make any attempt to find a correlation between any proprietary interest in the farm and ownership of the animals. Thus, it would appear that ownership of chattels and occupation of the property on which they are kept will be sufficient to ground a claim in respect of damage to those chattels. Once again a question remains as to whether ownership of the chattels alone would suffice.[57]

Interference with Use and Enjoyment

Private nuisance also affords protection to the personal interest in comfortable occupation, free from undue invasion from neighbouring activities. The level of protection afforded to an occupier in respect of the use and enjoyment of the occupied property is succinctly set out by Gannon J in *Halpin v Tara Mines Ltd*:

> In so far as the nuisance alleged consists of interference with comfort and enjoyment of the property of the plaintiff, his evidence must show sensible personal discomfort, including injurious affection of the nerves or senses of such a nature as would materially diminish the comfort and enjoyment of, or cause annoyance to, a reasonable man accustomed to living in the same locality.[58]

A similar formulation is given by Henchy J in *Hanrahan*:

> It is clear from the authorities on the law of nuisance that what an occupier of land is entitled to as against his neighbour is the comfortable and healthy enjoyment of the land to the degree that would be expected by an ordinary person whose requirements are objectively reasonable in all the particular circumstances.[59]

Clearly occupiers with a proprietary interest in the occupied property will be protected, but the modern law also offers protection to persons residing on

---

55 [1961] 1 WLR 683; [1961] 2 All ER 145; see also *Howard Electric Ltd v A.J. Mooney Ltd* [1974] NZLR 762 where it was held that persons with a sufficient interest in land could also recover for damage to chattels on the land.
56 [1988] ILRM 629, at pp. 643–6.
57 Such a claim was rejected in *Vaughn v Halifax-Dartmouth Bridge Commission* (1961) 29 DLR (2d) 523; for further discussion see Fridman, *op. cit.* vol. 1 at pp. 146–8.
58 [1976–7] ILRM 28, at p. 30.
59 [1988] ILRM 629, at p. 634, citing Gannon J from *Halpin* with approval.

property, even though they have no proprietary interest. In *Motherwell v Motherwell*,[60] the Alberta Supreme Court held that the wife of the owner of property, who resided on the property, was entitled to maintain an action in nuisance in respect of harassment by way of telephone calls. The Court of Appeal in England followed the reasoning from *Motherwell* in *Khorasandjian v Bush*[61] and extended the right to maintain an action to children of the owner in occupation.[62] More recently Pill J, delivering the judgment of the Court of Appeal in *Hunter v Canary Wharf Ltd*,[63] stated that 'occupation of a property, as a home' created a sufficiently 'substantial link' between the person and the property to maintain a nuisance action in respect of interference with use and enjoyment. The Irish courts had, effectively, reached this point somewhat earlier in *Hanrahan*. The House of Lords, however, overturned this aspect of the Court of Appeal decision, returning to the traditional requirement of a proprietary interest.[64]

As to what types of disruption will be regarded as sufficiently objectionable, much depends on whether the disruption is unreasonable, which we will consider below. At this point it will suffice to say that matters such as noise,[65] smells,[66] dust[67] and vibrations[68] have all been held to be capable of supporting an action; while disruption of television reception,[69] impeding of the plaintiff's view[70] or observing the plaintiff's property (without encroaching on privacy)[71] have been

---

60 (1976) 73 DLR (3d) 62.
61 [1993] QB 727; [1993] 3 WLR 476; [1993] 3 All ER 669; noted by Stanton (1993) 1 Tort L Rev 179; analysed by Manchester et al., *Exploring the Law* (London: Sweet & Maxwell, 1996) at chapter 6; Bridgeman & Jones, 'Harassing Conduct and Outrageous Acts: A Cause of Action for Intentionally Inflicted Mental Distress' (1994) 14 LS 180, at pp. 183 *et seq.*
62 This case, like *Motherwell*, involved harassment by telephone calls. The New Brunswick Court of Appeal also accepted the right of children to sue, based on occupation of the property, in *Devons Lumber Co. Ltd v MacNeill* (1987) 45 DLR (4th) 300.
63 [1997] AC 655; [1996] 2 WLR 348; [1996] 1 All ER 482; noted by English (1996) 59 MLR 726.
64 [1997] AC 655; [1997] 2 WLR 684; [1997] 2 All ER 426; noted by Oliphant (1998) 6 Tort L Rev 21.
65 *Mullin v Hynes* unrep. SC, 13 November 1972; *O'Kane v Campbell* [1985] IR 115.
66 *Hanrahan v Merck Sharp & Dohme* [1988] ILRM 629.
67 *Hunter v Canary Wharf Ltd* [1997] AC 655; [1996] 2 WLR 348; [1996] 1 All ER 482.
68 *Patterson v Murphy* [1978] ILRM 85.
69 *Hunter v Canary Wharf Ltd* [1997] AC 655; [1996] 2 WLR 348; [1996] 1 All ER 482; a contrary view was taken in *Nor-Video Services Ltd v Ontario Hydro* (1978) 84 DLR (3d) 221.
70 *Phipps v Pears* [1965] 1 QB 76; [1964] 2 WLR 996; [1964] 2 All ER 35; *Gartner v Kidman* (1962) 108 CLR 12, per Windeyer J at p. 46; *Restatement, Second, Torts* §829 comment c, however, suggests that disruption of view will be actionable if done maliciously.
71 *Victoria Park Racing & Recreation Grounds Co. Ltd v Taylor* (1937) 58 CLR 479.

held not to be so capable. Trindade & Cane observe that matters deemed capable or incapable of constituting a sufficient interference are not 'based on any set principles', but are 'the result of *ad hoc* value judgments'.[72] Certainly the precise parameters of the protection provided against disruption to comfortable occupation are imprecise and it is probably better if one does not regard precedent too rigidly. The law attempts to reflect contemporary notions of fair levels of protection, balancing the competing interests of the parties, and such notions will vary over time. Therefore, the fact that a particular type of interference has been deemed to be incapable of being a nuisance at one point in time should not preclude a future court from drawing a different conclusion, based on changing social perceptions of the respective interests of the parties.

Interference with Servitudes

Servitudes, as a form of limited interest in the property of another person, have been protected by the law of nuisance since the early stages of development of the torts. As a form of proprietary interest, the servitude falls naturally into the realm of private nuisance. The range of interests covered is far too large to be covered extensively here and is generally regarded as being within the realm of property law. Readers should refer to texts on property or land law for more detailed consideration of servitudes.[73] The interests which tend to give rise to disputes in tort are ones such as rights of way and rights in respect of water.

As an abstract form of property, a servitude cannot be physically damaged, but the property over which the servitude exists can be physically interfered with in a manner which disrupts the exercise of the rights in question. Such interference is actionable, even in the absence of any real injury or loss to the plaintiff, for reasons already outlined earlier.[74] Actual harm or interference with use and enjoyment is actionable on the basis of the same principles as other protected interests.

Unreasonableness

Nuisance differs from negligence in the treatment of reasonableness as a concept. Whereas negligence focuses on the defendant's conduct, in order to determine if it was lawful, nuisance focuses on the impact of the conduct on the plaintiff, in order to determine if it is objectionable.[75] In many cases the

---

72 Trindade & Cane, *op. cit.* at p. 604.
73 See Wylie, *Irish Land Law*, 3rd ed. (Dublin: Butterworths, 1997); Lyall, *Land Law in Ireland* (Dublin: Oak Tree Press, 1994); Coughlan, *Property Law*, 2nd ed. (Dublin: Gill & Macmillan, 1997).
74 At the beginning of the discussion of damage or interference.
75 There are a number of English authorities that have attempted to bring nuisance closer to negligence by introducing 'reasonable use' of the defendant's property as the criterion for establishing nuisance; these are critically reviewed by Cross, 'Does Only the Careless Polluter Pay? A Re-Examination of the Tort of Nuisance' (1995) 111 LQR 445.

outcome will be the same, as a certain balancing of interests is inevitable when there are conflicting claims being made by the parties, neither of whom wishes to have his freedom of action curtailed by the other. Thus, in a negligence action, the impact on the plaintiff will usually be a relevant factor in assessing the defendant's behaviour and, in a nuisance action, the nature of the defendant's conduct will sometimes be relevant to assessing the validity of the plaintiff's complaint. There are, nonetheless, cases where the shift in perspective will lead to different results, so that conduct may be regarded as reasonable for the purposes of negligence, but its effect may be regarded as unreasonable for the purposes of nuisance.

Consider the following scenario:

Example

D owns a factory and uses the best available filtration system to detoxify the emissions produced there. Despite the fact that D employs specialists to monitor and maintain the filtration equipment, it occasionally fails to function properly. Because of the regular monitoring, D is able to shut down the production process shortly after any failure in the system, in order to minimise the harmful output. Despite D's efforts, the toxic emissions which do occur from time to time kill much of the plant life on the neighbouring property, belonging to P.

If P were to take a negligence action against D, the action would be likely to fail, because D has probably discharged the standard of reasonable care (considering factors such as the magnitude of risk and the benefit–burden balance). A nuisance action, on the other hand, would be likely to succeed, as the disturbance to P is not merely fleeting or trivial. The interference may put P to significant expense and effort in restoring the plants or, alternatively, consign the property to an arid state; furthermore, the value of the property may be reduced as a result of the impact of the emissions. The absence of fault on D's part does not diminish the legitimacy of P's claim to redress for the harm suffered, though it may affect the selection of an appropriate remedy. It would be fair to require D to compensate P and the compensation may be regarded as part of the cost of D's entitlement to conduct business; to restrain D from operating at all may be excessive in light of the nature of the harm, thus a permanent injunction would be inappropriate.

A further point of distinction between the two torts is that negligence focuses on the circumstances prevailing at the time the defendant engaged in the impugned conduct, whereas nuisance usually focuses on the circumstances after impact on the plaintiff. Thus, in negligence the reasonableness of the activity is assessed prior to injury, while nuisance considers reasonableness in light of the injury. Clearly differences will arise between assessing the validity of a course of conduct in light of actual harm done and considering that same conduct in light of the potential for damage, before any actual harm has arisen.

These differences between the reasonableness concept in the two torts is not as objectionable or inconsistent as it may first appear. If one bears in mind that the purpose and scope of the two torts are different, then the fact that conduct which is lawful under one is unlawful under the other should not be surprising. In fact, nuisance would serve no useful purpose if it did not impose liability in circumstances where negligence did not.

It is well established that the relevant factors for determining nuisance are different in cases of material damage than for interference with use and enjoyment. A seminal statement on this issue was made by Lord Westbury LC in *St Helen's Smelting Co. v Tipping*.[76]

> My Lords . . . it appears to me that it is a very desirable thing to mark the difference between an action brought for a nuisance upon the ground that the alleged nuisance produces material injury to the property, and an action brought for a nuisance on the ground that the thing alleged to be a nuisance is productive of sensible personal discomfort.

He went on to add that 'the submission which is required from persons living in society to that amount of discomfort which may be necessary for the legitimate and free exercise of the trade of their neighbours, would not apply to circumstances the immediate result of which is sensible injury to the value of the property'.[77]

In the case of material damage, the judgment of Gannon J in *Halpin v Tara Mines Ltd* shows liability to be strict, as the plaintiff must establish damage and causation only.

> A party asserting that he has sustained material damage to his property by reason of an alleged nuisance must establish the fact of such damage and that it was caused by the nuisance as alleged. It is no defence to such a claim, if established, that the activities complained of were carried out with the highest standards of care, skill and supervision and equipment or that such activities are of great public importance and cannot conveniently be carried out in any other way.[78]

Street argues that even in cases of material damage the interference must be unreasonable.[79] The strict formulation in *Halpin* may simply reflect the fact that material damage will almost invariably be unreasonable, as it is difficult to envisage cases where significant material damage could be regarded as a

---

76 (1865) 11 HL Cas 642, at p. 650.

77 *Ibid.*

78 [1976–7] ILRM 28, at p. 30; cited with approval by Henchy J in *Hanrahan v Merck Sharp & Dohme* [1988] ILRM 629, at p. 634.

79 Street, *op. cit.* at p. 350.

reasonable intrusion. Alternatively it may indicate that reasonableness is not a relevant consideration in cases of material harm. Given that the shift from interference with use and enjoyment to material harm is gradual, rather than a sharp distinction, it may be that Gannon J's strict formulation is applicable to clear cases of material harm, while borderline cases may avail of the criteria applicable to cases of interference with use and enjoyment.[80]

In cases other than clear cases of material harm a number of relevant factors have been identified by the judiciary as being relevant to determining the question as to whether the intrusion on the plaintiff was unreasonable.

Magnitude of Harm

The most significant factor in determining a nuisance action is the level of intrusion caused to the plaintiff. The courts will not permit an action in respect of trivial inconvenience or irritation to succeed, but the division between what may and may not be complained of is not easily drawn. The intensity, duration and frequency of intrusion will be the main factors to consider in drawing this distinction. There are infinite factual permutations of these factors, but in general an abnormal level in respect of any one factor is likely to lead to a finding that the interference is unreasonable. *Patterson v Murphy*,[81] involving, *inter alia*, interference to enjoyment by means of nervous strain caused by blasting operations, demonstrates that infrequent and brief intrusions may, nonetheless, be actionable due to the high intensity of the disruption. Less intense disruptions may be unreasonable by virtue of greater frequency or duration and, as Gannon J insightfully observed in *Halpin*, irregular and unusual intrusions can be particularly discomfiting:

> Intermittent noises of their nature unusual to a locality which come at irregular or unpredictable intervals are likely to be more disagreeable than such noises which form part of the norm for the locality, such as passing traffic. Where these unusual noises are of such a nature that they instil apprehension and anxiety into the mind of the listener the sensitivity of the ear is likely to be more acutely perceptive of such noises, despite the amplitude of other more familiar and more acceptable noises simultaneously heard but instinctively disregarded.[82]

This point is equally pertinent for other forms of intrusion, such as odours and vibrations; people generally become impervious to regular or commonplace intrusions, unless they are particularly intense, but are more likely to be

---

80 Physical harm may, of course, be too trivial to ground an action, so the intrusion would not be unreasonable; see *Stormer v Ingram* (1978) 21 SASR 93 (bee stings not ordinarily sufficient to be a nuisance).
81 [1978] ILRM 85.
82 [1976–7] ILRM 28, at p. 37.

disrupted by aberrant occurrences. This will be so despite a lack of measurable scientific difference between the two sources of intrusion.

The magnitude of harm must be assessed according to an objective standard, so the plaintiff is expected to demonstrate the fortitude generally pertaining in society.[83] As with other areas of the law, a purely objective approach yields to a limited amount of consideration of subjective aspects of the plaintiff's circumstances. In *O'Kane v Campbell*,[84] for example, Lynch J considered the plaintiff's age to be relevant in respect of disturbance to her sleep: 'Young people can sleep in spartan conditions . . . Elderly people perhaps sleep more lightly but they are not abnormal for that and they are entitled to their night's sleep.'[85] If the defendant has caused an unduly high level of sensitivity in the plaintiff, through an earlier and more serious nuisance of the type complained of, then the plaintiff's subjective tolerance may be taken into account.[86]

Nature of Locality

Local conditions are often taken into consideration in determining whether the intrusion on the plaintiff was reasonable. Private nuisance requires a balancing of the competing interests of the plaintiff and defendant as to the use of their respective properties and the character of the neighbourhood in which they are located may be significant. For example, the level of noise or the quality of air that one can reasonably expect will differ between rural and urban locations. Greater crowding in large towns and cities, compared to smaller towns and villages, reduces the level of freedom from disturbance that one can expect in respect of a variety of activities;[87] conversely, there are other activities, the exercise of which will be precluded by the close proximity of neighbours,[88] a

---

83 *Robinson v Kilvert* (1889) 41 Ch D 88; see also Fridman, *op. cit.* vol. 1 at pp. 144–6. Gannon J in *Halpin* provides a detailed description of the reasonable plaintiff: 'a person whose notions and standards of behaviour and responsibility correspond with those generally pertaining among ordinary people in our society at the present time, who seldom allows his emotions to overbear his reason, whose habits are moderate and whose disposition is equable'. [1976–7] ILRM 28, at p. 30.

84 [1985] IR 115.

85 *Ibid.* at p. 118.

86 *Mullin v Hynes* unrep. SC, 13 November 1972. The fact that the plaintiff's sensitivity to noise from the defendant's ballroom was posing a risk to her health, rather than simply inconveniencing her, was also a relevant factor in the decision.

87 For example, a certain amount of noise resulting from public entertainment can be expected in a city, but would be less tolerable in a quiet rural area; contrast *New Imperial & Windsor Hotel Co. Ltd v Johnson* [1912] 1 IR 327 with *Mullin v Hynes* unrep. SC, 13 November 1972.

88 The odour generated by farm animals may be tolerable in an agricultural region in which such animals are regularly kept, but would not be acceptable in a residential suburb of a city; see *Ball v Ray* (1873) 8 Ch App 467 (stables in a residential area unreasonable).

point made by Erle CJ back in 1863: 'It seems to me that the affairs of life in a dense neighbourhood cannot be carried on without mutual sacrifices of comfort; and that, in all actions for discomfort, the law must regard the principle of mutual adjustment . . .'[89] The emphasis on mutuality is an important reminder that the law must reflect a balance between different interests and no one interest should receive undue preference or disadvantage.

The judicial consideration of locality is far more sophisticated than the broad urban–rural divide and takes account of details of the specific location where the dispute occurs. In *O'Kane v Campbell*,[90] concerning noise emanating from a twenty-four hour shop and disturbing the plaintiff's sleep, Lynch J gave detailed consideration to the location of the shop. As it was at the junction of a busy thoroughfare and a quiet, residential street, the residential aspect of the neighbourhood was held to be a relevant factor; had the shop been further away from the residential street and located exclusively on the busy street, the residential aspect would not have been considered.[91]

The English courts have held that the decisions of planning authorities may legitimately change the character of a neighbourhood and, if locality is an issue, then it is the character of the neighbourhood subsequent to the planning decision that will be taken into account.[92] The character of a neighbourhood will not be changed by every planning decision; only strategic decisions, taking account of public policy considerations, will have such an effect.[93] The Court of Appeal also held that a disturbance which inevitably results from such change of character will not be an actionable nuisance.[94] The granting of planning permission does not necessarily afford a defence in nuisance actions, but it can affect the assessment of what is reasonable.

Defendant's Purpose

Many nuisance cases involve a balancing of the competing interests of plaintiff and defendant and this often requires the court to take account of the objective of

---

89 *Cavey v Ledbitter* (1863) 13 CBNS 470, at p. 476.
90 [1985] IR 115; see also *Dewar v City and Suburban Racecourse Co.* [1899] 1 IR 345; *Sturges v Bridgeman* (1879) 11 Ch D 852; *Hourston v Brown-Holder Biscuits Ltd* [1937] 2 DLR 53.
91 *Ibid.* at p. 118.
92 *Gillingham Borough Council v Medway (Chatham) Dock Co. Ltd* [1993] QB 343; [1992] 3 WLR 449; [1992] 3 All ER 923; noted by Steel & Jewell (1993) 56 MLR 568; *Wheeler v J.J. Saunders Ltd* [1996] Ch 19; [1995] 3 WLR 466; [1995] 2 All ER 697.
93 *Wheeler v J.J. Saunders Ltd* [1996] Ch 19; [1995] 3 WLR 466; [1995] 2 All ER 697, per Staughton LJ at pp. 29–30; pp. 473–5; pp. 706–7; and Peter Gibson LJ at pp. 35–6; p. 480; p. 712. On the facts of the case a decision to permit an increase in the intensity of use of a pig farm was held to be insufficient to change the character of the neighbourhood.
94 *Ibid.*

the defendant's conduct. Improper motivations may result in the court being more inclined to characterise the conduct as a nuisance than innocent engagement in the same conduct. *Christie v Davey* [95] provides a classic example. The plaintiff was a music teacher, with a musical family, and the sound generated in her house could be heard in the defendant's house, the two houses being a semi-detached pair. The defendant took offence to the sound and wrote a letter of complaint to the plaintiff. When this brought no respite, he resorted to making a share of noise by banging on a variety of implements about his house, in order to annoy the plaintiff. The intent to annoy was the crucial factor in North J's decision to grant an injunction against the defendant; the noise would not have amounted to a nuisance if it had been generated innocently. [96]

The defendant's malice will be irrelevant, however, if the plaintiff lacks a sufficient interest to protect. In *Bradford Corporation v Pickles*, [97] for example, it was held that a property owner had no right to the receipt of water percolating from neighbouring property, rights to receipt of water being confined to that flowing in defined channels. Thus, deliberate disruption of the flow of percolating water could not amount to nuisance, as it did not interfere with any right the plaintiffs had in their property.

Cases involving the defendant's response to an earlier nuisance by the plaintiff may give rise to borderline cases between these two principles. The plaintiff has no legal right to protection in order to continue the nuisance and, in accordance with *Bradford*, cannot complain if the defendant takes lawful measures to abate the nuisance, even if the defendant has ulterior motives for such conduct. The plaintiff may complain, however, if the defendant engages in spiteful retaliation which disrupts some legitimate interest of the plaintiff. In practice it may be difficult to draw the line between lawful abatement and unlawful retaliation. Thus, while the principles underlying *Bradford* and

---

95 [1893] 1 Ch 316.

96 *Ibid.* at pp. 326–7; see also *Boyle v Holcroft* [1905] 1 IR 245 (erection of fences to obstruct the exercise of fishing rights); *Hollywood Silver Fox Farm Ltd v Emmett* [1936] 2 KB 468; [1936] 1 All ER 825 (shooting to disturb breeding foxes); *Rattay v Daniels* (1959) 17 DLR (2d) 134 (bulldozer disturbing breeding minks held not to be a nuisance where there was no intent to harm and the defendant had a legitimate purpose of levelling his land; furthermore, the timing of the activity was driven by factors beyond the defendant's control); an early precursor was *Keeble v Hickeringill* (1706) 11 East 573; [1558–1774] All ER Rep 286 (shooting to scare away wild ducks); analysed by Simpson, *Leading Cases in the Common Law* (Oxford: Clarendon Press, 1996) at chapter 3.

97 [1895] AC 587; [1896–9] All ER Rep 984. It has been held in England that in the reverse situation, where the recipient of the percolating water blocks the flow, liability will be imposed unless the blockage involves reasonable use of the defendant's land – *Home Brewery Co. Ltd v Davis & Co. Ltd* [1987] QB 339; [1987] 2 WLR 117; [1987] 1 All ER 637; the decision contains a useful review of cases relating to the flow of water.

Christie each have a legitimate role to play, there will be cases where it will not be clear which of the two is the appropriate one to determine the dispute.[98]

Just as improper purpose on a defendant's part may generate disfavour in the courts, worthy objectives may justify the granting of greater latitude to a defendant. The decision of the former Supreme Court in *Bellew v Cement Ltd*[99] indicates that questions of public utility may not be used to override the private rights of the plaintiff. This should not be taken to mean, however, that the defendant's purpose is of no relevance in private nuisance; in fact, such a suggestion would be at odds with a number of cases.[100] The core of the decision in *Bellew* is that the social utility of the defendant's conduct will not relieve the defendant of liability once the conduct amounts to a nuisance. Social utility may, however, be relevant in determining whether the interference with the plaintiff is sufficiently unreasonable to amount to a nuisance. This latter possibility is evident in the judgment of O'Byrne J, who suggests a threshold of interference up to which the defendant's purpose is a relevant consideration, but beyond which nuisance clearly occurs no matter how laudable the defendant's purpose.[101] Unfortunately this threshold cannot be located precisely, but involves a value judgment on the seriousness of the intrusion.[102]

Black J, dissenting in *Bellew*, suggested that public benefit, deriving from the defendant's conduct, was relevant to determining the appropriate remedy.[103] In a similar vein, Lynch J, in *O'Kane v Campbell*, held the defendant's interests to be a relevant factor in considering the appropriate duration of an injunction, stating that 'the defendant is to be disturbed in the use and enjoyment of his property to the minimum extent consistent with giving reasonable relief to the

---

98 There are surprisingly few superior court cases of this type, though it is unlikely that this dearth of cases results from widespread harmony and tranquillity in social relations between neighbours. Two useful decisions from Australia are *Fraser v Booth* (1950) 50 SR (NSW) 113 (frightening off pigeons with fire-crackers and water held not to be a nuisance); *Stoakes v Brydges* [1958] QWN 5 (phoning an employer during the night as retaliation for disruption caused by an employee held to be a nuisance).

99 [1948] IR 61, the court refused an appeal against an injunction restraining the defendants from blasting in their quarry, at a time when the defendants' products were needed for construction work throughout the country.

100 The balancing of interests in cases of interference with use and enjoyment, in particular, involves a consideration of the defendant's purpose. See *St Helen's Smelting Co. v Tipping* (1865) 11 HL Cas 642; *Mullin v Hynes* unrep. SC, 13 November 1972.

101 [1948] IR 61, at p. 66, dissenting on the facts, but agreeing with the majority as to the appropriate legal principles.

102 See Fleming, *op. cit.* at pp. 422 *et seq.*; Winfield & Jolowicz, *op. cit.* at pp. 408–9; *Restatement, Second, Torts* §828, which includes locality as one of the factors in determining the utility of the defendant's conduct, demonstrating the close connection between the two factors.

103 [1948] IR 61, at p. 70.

plaintiff'.[104] Thus, even where there is a nuisance, the defendant's purpose should not be regarded as entirely irrelevant.

Causation

The plaintiff must be able to demonstrate a causal connection between the conduct for which the defendant is responsible and the damage or interference suffered, in order to obtain a remedy. Causation is dealt with in detail in chapter 11, below. It should be noted, however, that causation can be particularly difficult to prove in practice in nuisance cases. One of the main reasons for this is the physical nature of many types of nuisance – noxious substances borne by air or water are often difficult to trace back to their source.[105]

Even where causation can be established, liability will not necessarily follow. Modern authorities have established that a defendant will only be responsible for causing harm of a type that could have been reasonably foreseen.[106] Unforeseen interference will not generate liability and this partially reduces the strict element in nuisance liability, bridging the gap between nuisance and fault based torts.

Public Nuisance

Public nuisance is not tied to property rights, but rather is concerned with interference with rights enjoyed by the public as a whole or a considerable class of the public. Public nuisance is a crime at common law, but civil action is also available in some cases. The Attorney General, as the representative of the public, may seek the private law remedy of an injunction to restrain the continuance of the nuisance.[107] Members of the public, who are affected by the nuisance, may employ the relator action, through the Attorney General, to enjoin the nuisance.[108]

---

104 [1985] IR 115, at p. 119; the injunction granted by the High Court required the defendant to close between midnight and 6 a.m. The Circuit Court had granted an injunction requiring closure between midnight and 8 a.m. See also *Kennaway v Thompson* [1981] QB 88; [1980] 3 WLR 361; [1980] 3 All ER 329.
105 *Hanrahan v Merck Sharp & Dohme* [1988] ILRM 629 provides a graphic example of the difficulties of proving causation in nuisance cases. For further illumination on the complexity of the problem in that case see O'Callaghan, *The Red Book* (Dublin: Poolbeg, 1992).
106 This issue has not been definitively resolved in respect of private nuisance in Ireland. For further consideration see chapter 11 *infra*, under 'remoteness'.
107 In Canada it has been suggested that the discretion to grant an injunction may be exercised against the Attorney General if the object of the action is the enforcement of the criminal law through a civil action, rather than a genuine attempt to remove the nuisance – *AG of Nova Scotia v Beaver* (1985) 32 CCLT 170; see Fridman, *op. cit.* vol. 1 at p. 170 for further discussion.
108 For further consideration of the relator action see Hogan & Morgan, *Administrative Law in Ireland*, 3rd ed. (Dublin: Round Hall Sweet & Maxwell, 1998) at pp. 758 *et seq.*; Casey, *The Irish Law Officers* (Dublin: Round Hall Sweet & Maxwell, 1996) at pp. 151–67. The action permits private individuals to institute proceedings

A private action by an individual will be available where the plaintiff suffers particular damage, other than the mere disruption of a public right, as a result of a public nuisance for which the defendant is responsible. The distinguishing feature of the action is the requirement of particular damage. The other elements largely overlap with private nuisance and so will only briefly be considered here.

The rules as to conduct for which the defendant is liable are not subject to any special variations for public nuisance. The conduct will amount to a public nuisance when it leads to unreasonable interference with the exercise of public rights.[109] The rights covered are as varied as the range of lawful public acts, but most of the case law tends to focus on rights of way and rights of access in respect of public roads, paths and waterways.[110] Whether a disruption is unreasonable will depend on the same factors as those already considered in respect of private nuisance. The threshold of disruption and the balance between competing interests may, however, be different, as one can hardly expect the same degree of freedom from disturbance in a public place as in one's own home or private land. The public utility of the defendant's conduct, in particular, may be a more significant factor, as it is being weighed against other public interests, rather than private rights.

Particular Damage

The plaintiff in a civil action for public nuisance must establish that he has suffered damage which differs from that suffered by other members of the public.[111] Some authorities suggest that the damage suffered must be different in kind than that suffered by the public. In other words the plaintiff must have suffered interference with a right other than the public right, such as suffering a personal injury in a traffic accident which resulted from an obstruction on the road.[112] The

---

for the enforcement of public rights where they would otherwise lack *locus standi*. The Attorney General, not the private individual, is the plaintiff and retains control over the action.

109 See the quotation from O'Higgins CJ in *Connolly v South of Ireland Asphalt Co.* at the beginning of this chapter.

110 For an extensive list of references see McMahon & Binchy, *op. cit.* at pp. 450 *et seq.* As there is no requirement that the conduct be independently unlawful, it is difficult to predict in advance whether conduct will constitute a nuisance. As with private nuisance, unlawfulness is primarily determined by the impact of the conduct.

111 This damage is usually referred to as special damage or particular damage; the latter phrase is preferred here, because the former has a technical meaning in respect of compensation which will be considered in chapter 15. For detailed discussion of the particular damage requirement in respect of public nuisance see Kodilinye, 'Public Nuisance and Particular Damage in the Modern Law' (1986) 6 LS 182; Jones, 'Public Rights, Private Rights and Particular Damage' (1983) 34 NILQ 341.

112 In *Hickey v Electric Reduction Company of Canada* (1970) 21 DLR (3d) 368 commercial fishermen failed in an action arising out of a fish kill, caused by the

approach taken in the Irish courts is that a difference in the degree of harm suffered will suffice.[113] The difference between the two approaches is largely semantic[114] and it is more useful to look at the circumstances that the courts have regarded as sufficient.

Personal injury is a sufficient harm,[115] as is damage to property.[116] In cases of fatal consequences, dependants will have a right of action.[117] Economic loss is more problematic, but has been held to be sufficient in a variety of circumstances, such as delay on the highway, causing significant delay or rerouting,[118] and nui-

---

defendants. The right interfered with was the right to fish, which is a public right, and the plaintiffs were held not to have suffered particular damage, even though they were more seriously affected than other members of the public (by having their income reduced). Similarly, in *Stein v Gonzales* (1984) 14 DLR (4th) 263, the plaintiffs, owners of a hotel and an apartment building, failed in an action against prostitutes, whose activities were driving customers away, as the right to conduct business was regarded as a public right. The *Restatement, Second, Torts* §821C also requires damage of a different kind, but provides a broader interpretation of the concept.

113 In *Boyd v Great Northern Railway* [1895] 2 IR 555 and *Smith v Wilson* [1902] 2 IR 45 financial losses as a result of the obstruction of roads were held recoverable; these losses would not qualify as different in kind under the approach in the Canadian cases, though they would under the approach in the *Restatement*. The position in England would appear to be the same as in Ireland, see *Tate & Lyle v Greater London Council* [1983] 2 AC 509; [1983] 2 WLR 649; [1983] 1 All ER 1159, economic loss resulting from disruption of the right to navigate a waterway held recoverable.

114 See the difference between the Canadian courts and the Irish and English courts in the previous footnotes. Another example of the difficulty in differentiating the two concepts is the right of access over public land of the occupier of adjoining land, which is actionable in tort, see *Coppinger v Sheehan* [1906] 1 IR 519 (right of access over foreshore, citing earlier authority on access over public land). This appears to be a difference in degree, but is classified as a difference in kind in the *Restatement, Second, Torts* §821C, comment f, as a proprietary right.

115 See, for example, *Mullan v Forrester* [1921] 2 IR 412 (wall falling on pedestrian); *Lynch v Dawson* [1946] IR 504 (truck driver injured when a high load hit an overhanging tree); *Cunningham v McGrath Bros* [1964] IR 209 (ladder falling on plaintiff); *Restatement, Second, Torts* §821C, comment d.

116 *Lynch v Dawson* [1946] IR 504 (damage to the truck also treated as particular damage); *Overseas Tankship (UK) Ltd v Miller Steamship Co. Pty Ltd (The Wagon Mound No. 2)* [1967] 1 AC 617; [1966] 3 WLR 498; [1966] 2 All ER 709 (ship damaged by fire, resulting from ignition of discharged furnace oil); *Halsey v Esso Petroleum Co. Ltd* [1961] 1 WLR 683; [1961] 2 All ER 145 (paintwork on car damaged by acidic smut from the defendants' boilerhouse).

117 *Connolly v South of Ireland Asphalt Co.* [1977] IR 99.

118 *Boyd v Great Northern Railway* [1895] 2 IR 555 (delay causing loss of business); *Smith v Wilson* [1902] 2 IR 45 (rerouting, with increased expense). Changing conditions may well mean that delays to traffic which would have been regarded as considerable at the beginning of the century would be treated as normal today. The extent of disruption would probably have to be greater now, in order to be actionable.

sance resulting in disruption to customer access to a business.[119] Intimidation or harassment, caused by public protest and leading to economic loss, has also been held to be sufficient in England.[120]

Special Defences

The general defences considered in chapter 12 are available, where applicable, in nuisance actions. Furthermore, the intervention of natural forces is sometimes described as the defence of 'act of God', but is dealt with as an aspect of causation in this text. The defences of necessity and defence of persons or property, considered in the previous chapter on trespass, may also be available in some nuisance cases. Nuisance actions are subject to two special defences – legislative authority and prescription. The former may also apply to some other torts, such as trespass and defamation, but each tort has, by its nature, different issues to consider in respect of legislative intervention.

Statutory Authority

The principles governing civil liability for nuisance tend to favour the maintenance of existing conditions and militate against development.[121] In addition, the moderate level of recognition given to the legitimacy of development favours gradual, rather than radical, change. One of the key features in producing this effect is the reduced role given to public policy considerations in private nuisance, compared to negligence. Legislative and administrative power is used to redress the imbalance. Legislative measures restricting private rights in favour of broader public policy objectives are quite common in modern democracies and the rights protected by nuisance, like many other rights, are often curbed by such provisions. The main areas of focus for nuisance are the powers and duties of local authorities (such as road construction and maintenance, water supply,

---

119 *Tate & Lyle v Greater London Council* [1983] 2 AC 509; [1983] 2 WLR 649; [1983] 1 All ER 1159 (ships unable to reach the plaintiffs' premises, due to reduction in the depth of the river, caused by deposits from the defendant's construction of ferry terminals).

120 *Bird v O'Neal* [1960] AC 907; [1960] 3 WLR 584; [1960] 3 All ER 254 (intimidating customers from entering business premises); *Thomas v NUM* [1986] Ch 20; [1985] 2 WLR 1081; [1985] 2 All ER 1 (intimidating workers from entering the workplace). The relationship between nuisance and freedom of expression, assembly and religion is considered in *AG of Ontario v Dieleman* (1994) 117 DLR (4th) 449 (anti-abortion protests; protesters' constitutional rights could be validly restricted on the basis of competing rights, particularly the right to privacy).

121 Though *Simpson, op. cit.* at chapter 7 notes that there was no long term inhibition of development by landowners through the use of nuisance and cases such as *St Helen's Smelting Co. v Tipping* (1865) 11 HL Cas 642 tended to be isolated instances, rather than regular occurrences. Despite this the inhibiting potential of nuisance is significant.

sanitary services and planning functions) and semi-state bodies (such as the ESB, CIÉ, Aer Rianta, Bord na Móna).

It is open to the legislature to make specific provision permitting or precluding the creation of a nuisance in furtherance of some statutory objective, such as the running of an airport[122] or a ferry terminal. However, the opportunity is not always taken to do so. The judiciary have provided some guidance, in cases where explicit legislative provision is absent. If a nuisance is the inevitable result of the proper performance of a task or activity authorised by statute, then the defence is available.[123] If the nuisance is not inevitable, but results from negligence in the performance of the activity,[124] or a deliberate choice of one method over a less intrusive method of performance,[125] then the defence will fail. Furthermore, statutory provisions are likely to be strictly construed, so as to minimise the degree to which individual rights are invaded. Thus, if the statute is capable of an interpretation that only permits the activity so long as no nuisance is generated, the defence will not be available.[126]

As we have already seen, a decision of a planning authority has been held not to have the same status as legislative authority, but policy based decisions can change the character of a locality and inevitable disruptions will not be characterised as nuisances.[127] Thus, major planning decisions produce a similar effect to statutory authority, though the availability of judicial review helps to ensure that individuals have some legal recourse where they believe that planning authorities have exceeded their powers.

---

122 Air Navigation and Transport Acts 1936–88.
123 *Smith v Wexford County Council* (1953) 87 ILTR 98 (deposit of debris on land during cleaning of a stream); *Superquinn Ltd v Bray Urban District Council and Others* unrep. HC, 18 February 1998 (drainage works carried out in the only reasonable manner available, no liability for flooding due to storm); *Allen v Gulf Oil Refining Co. Ltd* [1981] AC 1001; [1981] 2 WLR 188; [1981] 1 All ER 353 (noise, smells and vibrations from the construction and operation of an oil refinery). The onus is on the defendant to establish that the disturbance is inevitable.
124 *Wallace v McCartan* [1917] 1 IR 377 (discharging unsuitable material into a drain); *Manchester Corporation v Farnworth* [1930] AC 171; [1929] All ER Rep 90 (noxious emissions from an electricity generating station).
125 *Tate & Lyle v Greater London Council* [1983] 2 AC 509; [1983] 2 WLR 649; [1983] 1 All ER 1159.
126 *Woodhouse v Newry Navigation Co.* [1898] 1 IR 161; *Guardians of Armagh Union v Bell* [1900] 2 IR 371 (use of traction engine in statutorily prescribed fashion did not confer an entitlement to cause damage to pipes under the road); *Kelly v Dublin County Council* unrep. HC, 21 February 1986 (authority for carrying out road works held not to include authority to set up a depot for vehicles and materials).
127 *Gillingham Borough Council v Medway (Chatham) Dock Co. Ltd* [1993] QB 343; [1992] 3 WLR 449; [1992] 3 All ER 923; *Wheeler v J.J. Saunders Ltd* [1996] Ch 19; [1995] 3 WLR 466; [1995] 2 All ER 697. Note, the grant of planning permission does not make, in itself, the planning authority responsible for authorising the creation of a nuisance, see *Convery v Dublin County Council* [1996] 3 IR 156.

Prescription

The right to engage in conduct, which could otherwise be objected to as a private nuisance, may be acquired by prescription. The prescriptive right is a form of servitude governed by specialised principles of property law, based on presumed acquiescence, and is acquired by lengthy exercise without objection.[128] In cases where such a right has not been acquired by the defendant, it is not open to the defendant to claim a defence on the basis that the plaintiff 'came to the nuisance'; in other words, the fact that the defendant was engaged in the offending conduct prior to the plaintiff's acquisition of a sufficient interest in the affected property affords no defence.[129] Therefore, the plaintiff's assent to the intrusion can only afford a complete defence if it has continued for a sufficient duration to give rise to prescription[130] or if it amounts to a waiver under section 34(1)(b) of the Civil Liability Act 1961; otherwise it may provide a partial defence by way of contributory negligence.[131]

---

128 See Wylie, *op. cit.*; Lyall, *op. cit.*; Coughlan, *op. cit.*
129 *Bliss v Hall* (1838) 4 Bing NC 183; 132 ER 758; *Sturgess v Bridgman* (1879) 11 Ch D 852; *Belisle v Canadian Cottons Ltd* [1952] OWN 114; *Miller v Jackson* [1977] QB 966; [1977] 3 WLR 20; [1977] 3 All ER 338.
130 Assent is not directly relevant to prescription, but a prescriptive right may result from the lack of objection.
131 Waiver and contributory negligence are considered in chapter 12 *infra*.

CHAPTER SIX

Strict Duties

Introduction

Strict liability may be roughly considered to involve situations where the defendant is held legally answerable for harm to the plaintiff in the absence of any intent or neglect on the defendant's part in respect of that harm. This type of liability arises in a number of situations; for example, the concepts of vicarious liability and non-delegable duty impose liability, not on the basis of the defendant's own conduct, but as a form of imputed responsibility for the conduct of another.[1] In trespass we saw that the defendant's intent or negligence need only extend to the initial impact on the plaintiff and not the harm resulting from that impact, so liability may be strict in some cases.

In chapter 1 it was noted that liability and duty are not synonymous and, while the existence of a duty is a prerequisite for liability, other factors must also exist before liability can be imposed on a defendant. Many of the examples of strict liability in tort are grounded in fault based torts; looking back at the example of trespass, the initial duty not to impact on a protected interest is based on intent or negligence. Vicarious liability imposed on a defendant will usually be based on the negligent behaviour of a person under the defendant's control; so, while the defendant need not personally have been at fault, there will usually need to be fault on the part of someone for whom the defendant is answerable. Thus, strict liability often originates in a fault based duty, but there are duties which are truly strict in nature which are not fulfilled by the attainment of an objectively reasonable standard of care. Certain types of defamation and some statutory duties are of this type, as are common law duties relating to fire and certain instances in respect of control of animals. All of these duties are subject to specialised considerations of their own and are, therefore, considered separately in various parts of this text. This chapter is concerned with the strict duties attaching to unusual dangers or high risk activities. It is an area of law which lacks cohesiveness and, unlike negligence, has no unifying general principle or widespread application. Strict duties apply to a few limited areas of activity, forming a minor sub-set of tort law as a whole. Nonetheless, this minor sub-set is an important one, as it presents a different conception of responsibility from the fault based torts.

Strict duties are difficult to state in terms of the level of behaviour expected of the defendant, unlike negligence or intentional wrongs. The duties are not absolute, so not every failure to prevent harm constitutes a breach of the duty.

---

1   See chapter 14 *infra*.

The duties, therefore, involve a level of obligation that lies somewhere between the exercise of reasonable care and guaranteeing freedom from harm. The precise extent of the duty depends on the defences that are available, as these will determine the extent to which the duty falls short of being absolute.[2]

Rylands v Fletcher Liability

Most common law jurisdictions recognise a separate tort based on the principle in *Rylands v Fletcher*.[3] The judges in the case itself seemed to regard the matter as one of nuisance and several of the authorities relied on were nuisance cases. Indeed, the authorities following the principle regarded it as a specialised form of nuisance for a considerable period afterwards.[4] In modern discussions it is generally accepted that the development of criteria particular to actions under the principle are sufficient to make it a distinct tort;[5] however, it has never developed an appropriate name and continues to be referred to by the title of the seminal decision, which seems to add an aura of mystique to the tort.

The dispute in *Rylands v Fletcher* arose in the following circumstances. The defendants, Rylands and Horrocks, engaged independent contractors to construct a reservoir to supply water to their mill. Through the negligence of the contractors, but unknown to the defendants, the reservoir was constructed over some disused mine shafts and when it was partially filled the water broke through to one of the disused shafts, through the disused mines underneath and into the plaintiff's coal mine. The plaintiff suffered considerable loss as a result of the flooding of the mine, which he sought to recover from the mill owners.

---

2 England, *The Philosophy of Tort Law* (Brookfield: Dartmouth, 1993), at chapter 3, points out that fault and strict liability reflect differing points on a continuum and that in practice the rules under each category may be very close to each other; see also Honoré, 'Responsibility and Luck: The Moral Basis of Strict Liability' (1988) 104 LQR 530 on the blurred distinction between strict and fault based liability.

3 (1868) LR 3 HL 330; affirming (1866) LR 1 Exch 265; both decisions are reprinted in [1861–73] All ER Rep 1; for an interesting analysis of the decision and its social context see Simpson, *Leading Cases in the Common Law*, (Oxford: Clarendon Press, 1995), at chapter 8

4 See, for example, the judgment of Porter LJ in *Shell-Mex & BP Ltd v Belfast Corporation* [1952] NI 72; it is also interesting to note that the *Rylands v Fletcher* principle was the central focus of the case, but it is listed under nuisance in Harrison, *The Irish Digest 1949–58* (Dublin: The Incorporated Council for Law Reporting). The first separate listing for *Rylands v Fletcher* liability in the Irish Digest is in the subsequent volume, Ryan, *The Irish Digest 1959–70* (Dublin: The Incorporated Council for Law Reporting); see also Newark, 'The Boundaries of Nuisance' (1949) 65 LQR 480, at pp. 487–8.

5 It has become standard for textbooks to provide separate coverage of nuisance and *Rylands v Fletcher* liability. The judgment of Henchy J, for the Supreme Court, in *Hanrahan v Merck Sharp & Dohme* [1988] ILRM 629, at p. 633, accepts that *Rylands v Fletcher* liability and nuisance are separate torts and, although there is some overlap between them, each has areas of application that the other does not.

The plaintiff was successful in the courts and this, in itself, is not surprising and may be explained by the principles of private nuisance already considered.[6] The distinctiveness of this case comes from the manner in which the defendants' liability was explained in the superior courts. In the Exchequer Chamber, Blackburn J enunciated the following principle:

> ... the person who for his own purposes brings on his lands and collects and keeps there anything likely to do mischief if it escapes, must keep it in at his peril, and if he does not do so, is *prima facie* answerable for all the damage which is the natural consequence of its escape.[7]

This principle was justified on the following basis:

> ... it seems but reasonable and just that the neighbour, who has brought something on his own property which was not naturally there, harmless to others so long as it is confined to his own property, but which he knows to be mischievous if it gets on his neighbour's, should be obliged to make good the damage which ensues if he does not succeed in confining it to his own property. But for his act of bringing it there no mischief could have accrued, and it seems but just that he should at his peril keep it there, so that no mischief may accrue, or answer for the natural and anticipated consequences.[8]

In the House of Lords, Lord Cairns LC expressed the principle in slightly different terms:

> ... if the defendants, not stopping at the natural use of their close, had desired to use it for any purpose which I may term a non-natural use for the purpose of introducing into the close that which in its natural condition was not in or upon it, for the purpose of introducing water either above or below ground in quantities and in a manner not the result of any work or operation on or under the land; and if in consequence of their doing so, or in consequence of any imperfection in the mode of their doing so, the water came to escape and to pass off into the close of the plaintiff, then it appears to me that that which the defendants were doing they were doing at their own peril; and if in the course of their doing it the evil arose to which I have referred ... then for the consequence of that, in my opinion, the defendants would be liable.[9]

Lord Cairns' formulation is narrower than Blackburn J's, as it does not embrace all hazards brought by the defendant to the property, but only those

---

6 See chapter 5 *supra*. Modern authorities, requiring reasonable foreseeability of harm, might impair recovery. For detailed consideration, see the discussion of remoteness of damage in chapter 11 *infra*.
7 (1866) LR 1 Exch 265; [1861–73] All ER Rep 1, at pp. 279–80; p. 7.
8 *Ibid.*
9 (1868) LR 3 HL 330; [1861–73] All ER Rep 1, at p. 338; p. 13.

which amount to a non-natural use of the property.[10] Blackburn J's formulation includes restrictions not apparent in Lord Cairns' approach – that the defendant has knowledge of the dangerous nature of the accumulation and that limited defences would be available in suitable cases – but, as Lord Cairns cites Blackburn J's view with approval, he may be taken to have concurred with these requirements.[11] Both views share some common elements – the danger must be brought to the property by the defendant, the dangerous item must escape, and the harm must be within the class of risks which make the item a danger. The development of the principle has included both the common elements and those peculiar to each formulation.

Requisite elements:

1. Accumulation of a dangerous item
2. Non-natural use of property
3. Escape
4. Damage
5. Causation
6. Lack of defence

Accumulation of a Dangerous Item

The requirement that the defendant has accumulated a dangerous thing raises three distinct issues. First, what amounts to a sufficient accumulation? Secondly, what constitutes a sufficiently dangerous item to attract the operation of the principle? Thirdly, is there a need for a relationship between the defendant and the property on which the accumulation occurs?

Accumulation

It is clear from the judgments in *Rylands v Fletcher* that the principle was only intended to apply to things brought on to property by the defendant and did not extend to things already on the property or things coming naturally to the property. Thus, in *Healy v Bray Urban District Council*[12] rocks, forming part of a hillside, were held to fall outside the rule as they had not been brought there by the defendant council. So, exaggerating the flow of water naturally arising on the defendant's land should not attract the application of the

---

10 It may be argued that the non-natural use aspect of the principle is implicit in Blackburn J's approach, see Newark, 'Non-Natural User and *Rylands v Fletcher*' (1961) 24 MLR 557.

11 (1868) LR 3 HL 330; [1861–73] All ER Rep 1, at pp. 339–40; p. 13; the other member of the House of Lords in this case, Lord Cranworth, also concurred with Blackburn J's judgment at p. 340; p. 14.

12 [1963–4] Ir Jur Rep 9.

principle. However, in *McDonnell v Turf Development Board*[13] water drained from a bog was held to come within the principle.[14] Unlike *Rylands v Fletcher*, this did not involve the unintentional escape of water brought to the defendant's land, but the deliberate expulsion of water naturally occurring on the land. This extension of the principle is of dubious merit, as it serves to further blur the line between private nuisance and *Rylands v Fletcher*. Perhaps the *McDonnell* decision could be explained on the basis that the equipment used for drainage constituted the accumulation, but this is a rather strained interpretation. An alternative view is put forward by the High Court of Australia in *Burnie Port Authority v General Jones Pty Ltd*[15] – that the exclusion of things 'naturally there' only applies to things that are naturally in a 'mischievous' state and that things naturally arising in a safe condition, but made 'mischievous' by accumulation, would be covered. In fact, it is suggested that this is precisely what had occurred in *Rylands v Fletcher*.

The accumulation must be intentional, but the legal scope of intent is not merely a subjective one, as we have already seen in trespass. So, the defendant may be responsible for accumulations that were not deliberate, such as where storage of food attracts rats.[16]

Both of the extracts from *Rylands v Fletcher*, quoted above, indicate that the accumulation must be for the benefit of the defendant. Thus, a landlord would not ordinarily be liable for an accumulation by a tenant for the tenant's benefit, unless the landlord authorised the accumulation.[17] It has been held in a number of cases that public utilities, providing gas, water, electricity etc., derive a sufficient benefit from the activity to attract the operation of the *Rylands v*

---

13 (1944) 78 ILTR 94, the case may be explained on the basis of private nuisance; Murnaghan J did not expressly cite *Rylands v Fletcher*, but did regard the defendants' conduct as a non-natural user of land. At the time the phrase would have been as much associated with nuisance as with *Rylands v Fletcher* (which was, in any case, seen as a particular variety of nuisance).

14 See also *Carstairs v Taylor* (1871) LR 6 Ex 217; *Kiddle v City Business Properties Ltd* [1942] 1 KB 269; [1942] 2 All ER 216, accumulation of rainfall held capable of coming within the *Rylands v Fletcher* principle.

15 (1994) 120 ALR 42, at p. 52 per Mason CJ, Deane, Dawson Toohey and Gaudron JJ.

16 *Chu v District of North Vancouver* (1983) 139 DLR (3d) 201, per Meredith J, *obiter*, at p. 206; see also *Giles v Walker* (1890) 24 QBD 656; 62 LT 933, defendant not responsible for natural growth of thistles, which spread to plaintiff's land; a *dictum* of Lord Esher MR suggested that if the defendant's conduct in ploughing his land had caused the thistles to grow there, then he would have been responsible for their accumulation, see Brazier, *Street on Torts*, 8th ed. (London: Butterworths, 1993), at pp. 383–4

17 Liability based on authorising the accumulation appears to be similar to liability for authorising a nuisance, considered in chapter 5 *supra*; see *dicta* in *Rainham Chemical Works Ltd v Belvedere Fish Guano Co. Ltd* [1921] 2 AC 465; [1921] All ER Rep 48, per Lord Buckmaster at p. 476; pp. 53–4; Lord Sumner at p. 480; p. 54; Lord Parmoor at p. 489; pp. 58–9; Street, *op. cit.* at pp. 384–5.

Fletcher principle; the fact that public benefit is an integral part of the activity is not sufficient to draw the conclusion that the utility is not engaging in the activity 'for its own purposes'.[18] There are also decisions going the other way, holding the public utility aspect to be the dominant factor, thereby excluding utilities from the ambit of the principle.[19] It would, perhaps, be better to let the legislature decide whether public utilities should be immune from such liability and, in the absence of statutory exemption, regard them as sufficiently acting in their own interests to come within the principle.[20] Safety systems also pose some difficulty; are they to be regarded as being for public protection or merely the defendant's own protection? It is possibly a question of fact for each individual case, but measures such as fire extinguishers and sprinkler systems have been held to fall outside the principle.[21]

Dangerous Item

Blackburn J indicated that the strict duty under consideration would apply to 'anything likely to do mischief if it escapes'. Not every danger will satisfy this requirement and, in practice, it is only satisfied by things which involve a non-natural use of land, under Lord Cairns' formulation of the principle. The result is that items covered by the principle cannot be determined merely by examining their inherent nature and the general types of risk that they naturally present, but also require an examination of the context in which the items are employed.[22] A

---

18 *Northwestern Utilities Ltd v London Guarantee & Accident Co. Ltd* [1936] AC 108; [1935] All ER Rep 196 and *Shell-Mex & BP Ltd v Belfast Corporation* [1952] NI 72 re gas authorities; *Smeaton v Ilford Corporation* [1954] Ch 450; [1954] 2 WLR 668; [1954] 1 All ER 923 and *Lawrysyn v Town of Kipling* (1966) 55 WWR 108 re local authority sewers; in the leading Australian case on the subject, *Benning v Wong* (1969) 122 CLR 249, Windeyer J preferred the application of the principle in such cases at p. 301; Menzies and Owen JJ were against the principle at p. 283 and p. 324; the other two members of the court, Barwick CJ and McTiernan J, gave judgments without reference to the issue.

19 *Boxes Ltd v British Waterways Board* [1972] 2 Lloyd's Rep 183; *Danku v Town of Fort Frances* (1976) 37 DLR (3d) 377 (sewage).

20 *Dunne v North Western Gas Board* [1964] 2 QB 806; [1964] 2 WLR 164; [1963] 3 All ER 916 (gas and water authorities removed from the ambit of the principle by statute); *Smeaton v Ilford Corporation* [1954] Ch 450; 2 WLR 668; [1954] 1 ALL ER 923 (statutory immunity re sewers).

21 *Village of Kelliher v Smith* [1931] SCR 672 (fire extinguisher, which exploded during an attempt to put out a fire); *Elfassy v Syblen Investments Ltd* (1978) 21 OR (2d) 609 (sprinkler system flooding an office after a fire started on a part of the property occupied by another tenant); in *Peters v Prince of Wales Theatre (Birmingham) Ltd* [1943] KB 73; [1942] 2 All ER 533, a sprinkler system was treated as being outside the scope of the principle on the basis of the plaintiff's implied consent to the accumulation.

22 For further discussion of the link between dangerous items and non-natural use see Carroll, 'The Rule in *Rylands v Fletcher*: A Re-Assessment' (1973) 8 Ir Jur (ns)

wide range of things have been held to come within the rule at various times, but trying to produce a list of such items is pointless in the absence of consideration of the context of their use. There are, nonetheless, some general observations to be made about items within or beyond the ambit of the principle. First, there are some items which give rise to special problems, such as animals, fire and even people, as 'things' to which the principle may apply. Secondly, there is an important question as to whether knowledge of the risk is necessary for the item to come within the principle.

Animals[23] and fire (or flammable materials)[24] are capable of being regarded as dangerous items within the principle, but are generally treated separately due to the existence of specialised rules for the particular risks they pose. In some cases these rules will result in strict liability where the *Rylands v Fletcher* principle would not apply, while in other cases they will remove liability which would have arisen under the *Rylands v Fletcher* principle. In consequence, they will be considered separately.[25]

The possibility that people could be regarded as a dangerous item was considered in two English cases, *AG v Corke*[26] and *Smith v Scott*.[27] In the former case Bennett J held the owner of a field responsible for interference with neighbours caused by caravan-dwellers, whom he had permitted on his land; while in the latter a local authority was held not to be responsible for the conduct of tenants, to whom it provided housing. The principal distinction between the two situations was that the occupants of the field in *AG v Corke* were licensees, with the defendant retaining control over the land and possibly the occupants, while in *Smith v Scott* the occupants were tenants, to whom control of the property passed and who were not subject to the defendant's control.[28] This distinction is

---

208, at pp. 217 *et seq.*; see Brazier (ed.), *Clerk and Lindsell on Torts*, 17th ed., (London: Sweet & Maxwell, 1989), at chapter 19 for extensive coverage of the range of circumstances in which the principle has been either applied or rejected.

23 Johnson J, in *Brady v Warren* [1900] 2 IR 632, at p. 651, suggested, *obiter*, that foxes would be covered by the *Rylands v Fletcher* principle; Maguire P, in *Gibb v Comerford* [1942] IR 295, at p. 304, considered that wild animals would come under the principle, but not domestic animals. The distinction between wild and domestic animals is, perhaps, too crude, since dangerousness is the criterion for attracting the principle. Taylor J, in *Rigby v Chief Constable of Northamptonshire* [1985] 1 WLR 1242; [1985] 2 All ER 985, stated, *obiter* at p. 1255; p. 996, that a tiger would be a dangerous thing within the principle.

24 See Trindade & Cane, *The Law of Torts in Australia*, 2nd ed. (Melbourne: Oxford University Press, 1993), at p. 636; Clerk & Lindsell, *op. cit.* at §§19.44–19.63 for consideration of fire and combustible materials as items within the principle, both citing a useful selection of cases from various jurisdictions.

25 Chapter 10 *infra*.

26 [1933] Ch 89; [1932] All ER Rep 711.

27 [1973] Ch 314; [1972] 3 WLR 783; [1972] 3 All ER 645.

28 See Carroll, *loc. cit.* at pp. 215–16 for further consideration of control over the dangerous item as a basis for responsibility. A further distinction was that the

unsatisfactory, however, as the degree of control in *AG v Corke* can hardly have differed greatly from *Smith v Scott*. At a more fundamental level it is doubtful whether people are a suitable hazard at all for the purposes of the principle.[29]

Blackburn J's justification of the principle was based on the defendant's knowledge of the mischievous propensity and the liability was to cover the natural and anticipated consequences of the risk generated. There are differing views on the level of awareness of risk that must be present to satisfy this requirement. In *West v Bristol Tramways Co.*,[30] the plaintiff complained that fumes from creosoted wood used by the defendants to support their tram rails killed his plants and shrubs. The Court of Appeal held that the appropriate standard of knowledge was the 'common knowledge of mankind'. As to the specific hazard in question, creosote fumes, Farwell LJ simply indicated that, while chemists may be aware that they were not generally dangerous, this did not equate with a general awareness and so the use of creosote constituted a sufficient danger to come within the principle.[31] Lord Alverstone CJ held that the onus was on the defendants to show that the substance was generally known not to be dangerous, a matter on which the defendants had failed to adduce any evidence.[32]

More recently, the House of Lords in *Cambridge Water Co. Ltd v Eastern Counties Leather plc*[33] held that the appropriate standard was that of reasonable foreseeability, as used in negligence and private nuisance to determine the extent of consequences for which a defendant is liable. This standard, while itself less than certain, is far more demanding of a plaintiff, requiring him to establish that the defendant could, by reasonable means, have anticipated the harm to the plaintiff. This means that not only the general nature of the risk must be objectively capable of being known to the defendant, but the means by which it might escape and give rise to harm should also be capable of such anticipation.[34] Although the House of Lords treated the *Rylands v Fletcher* principle as a particular sub-set of nuisance,[35] the rule used in relation to foreseeability of

defendant in *AG v Corke* was operating for private profit, while the local authority in *Smith v Scott* was engaged in a public function, with broader policy goals.

29 See *Matheson v Board of Governors of Northcote College* [1975] 2 NZLR 106, at p. 117 per McMullin J; nuisance may be available, however, so the plaintiff is not left without a remedy against the landowner.

30 [1908] 2 KB 14; [1908–10] All ER Rep 215.

31 *Ibid.* at p. 25; p. 219.

32 *Ibid.* at p. 21; p. 218.

33 [1994] 2 AC 264; [1994] 2 WLR 53; [1994] 1 All ER 53, at pp. 301 *et seq.*; pp. 76 *et seq.*; pp. 72 *et seq.* per Lord Goff, with whom the other members of the House agreed; see also the case note by Heuston (1994) 110 LQR 185 for a general discussion of the ramifications of the case.

34 See chapter 11 *infra*, under remoteness, for further discussion of reasonable foresight.

35 [1994] 2 AC 264; [1994] 2 WLR 53; [1994] 1 All ER 53, at pp. 297–9; pp. 72–4; pp. 69–70, citing Newark, 'The Boundaries of Nuisance' (1949) 65 LQR 480, at pp. 487–8.

damage in nuisance is identical to that used in negligence. On the facts of the case the House of Lords held that the particular harm caused to the plaintiff was not reasonably foreseeable;[36] chemicals spilt on the floor of the defendant's factory and seeped down into the soil below, eventually contaminating percolating water, which ultimately reached the plaintiff's bore hole, 1.3 miles away, which was used to extract water for public supply. The latter approach was preferred in Ireland in *Superquinn Ltd v Bray Urban District Council and Others*.[37] In this case one of the defendants, Coillte (the national forestry company), was the owner of an artificial lake, which burst its dam, leading to flooding of the plaintiff's premises downstream. This was held to be foreseeable, but the defendant was relieved of liability on other grounds.[38]

The more exacting burden placed on the plaintiff by the *Cambridge Water* approach would drastically reduce the strictness of the obligation owed, bringing it closer to nuisance and negligence. Some element of strictness would remain, since a defendant would be liable for a foreseeable escape, despite the exercise of reasonable care in attempting to prevent it. However, the reasonable foreseeability requirement would further hamper plaintiffs attempting to rely on the *Rylands v Fletcher* principle. If this approach gains general acceptance then the value of the *Rylands v Fletcher* principle as a separate tort would be virtually wiped out. Even without such a restraint the tort is already of marginal impact, with only a small number of successful claims in reported cases.

Place of Accumulation

Blackburn J spoke of the accumulation on the defendants' land and, similarly, Lord Cairns spoke of the defendants' use of 'their close' (land) and its impact on the plaintiff's 'close'. Given that the case was probably regarded as one of nuisance, this was not unusual since, as we have already seen, at that time private nuisance was intimately concerned with relations between neighbouring landowners. Early authorities following *Rylands v Fletcher* regarded it as essential that the parties be owners or occupiers of land for the principle to apply.[39] The requirements have since eased somewhat and it has been held that a person who has permission or authority to use the land of another may be liable under the principle. In *Shell-Mex and BP Ltd v Belfast Corporation*[40] the defendant

---

36 *Ibid.*, at p. 306; pp. 80–1; p. 77.
37 Unrep. HC, 18 February 1998.
38 *Ibid.*, at p. 70 per Laffoy J; the point was *obiter*, since she held that the defence of *vis major* was applicable to the facts.
39 See, for example, Martin B in *Carstairs v Taylor* (1871) LR 6 Ex 217, at p. 223.
40 [1952] NI 72; see also *Charing Cross, West End and City Electricity Supply Co. v Hydraulic Power Co.* [1914] 3 KB 772; [1914–15] All ER Rep 85 (water escaping from mains of the Hydraulic Power Company, which were located under a public road and had been placed there under statutory authority).

corporation, acting under statutory authority, placed gas pipes under a road vested in the Harbour Commissioners and the Court of Appeal held the corporation liable under the *Rylands v Fletcher* principle for damage caused to the plaintiffs when leaking gas exploded. The defendant's control over the hazardous accumulation seems to be the justification for the extension of the principle to such cases.

There is little authority in respect of situations where someone has accumulated a dangerous item on the property of another without permission, but a Canadian decision, *Bridges Bros v Forest Protection Ltd*,[41] suggests that this would fall outside the scope of the principle, even though the defendant retains control over the item.

Non-natural Use of Property

The interpretation of the non-natural use requirement is not based on a colloquial distinction between natural and artificial activities or processes. The legal meaning attached to the term requires that the activity of the defendant is in some way unusual or out of the ordinary according to social standards. In *Rylands v Fletcher* the gathering of water in a reservoir for a mill was held to be a non-natural use,[42] but Lord Cairns indicated that had the defendants been engaged in mining activities, thereby causing an increase in the flow of water percolating through their property to the plaintiff's mines, this would have been a natural use. The distinction between natural and non-natural use appears to be a matter of value judgment, based on policy reasons in light of the surrounding circumstances. In fact Lord Macmillan, in *Read v J. Lyons & Co. Ltd*,[43] went so far as to say that decisions as to non-natural use are decisions of fact and so do not generate binding authority for future courts in respect of the activity in question. The veracity of this point is evidenced by the fact that three members of the House expressed doubt as to whether the use of a factory in an industrial area to make munitions during wartime could amount to a non-natural use,[44] despite the fact that the *Rylands v Fletcher* principle was successfully invoked before the House of Lords previously in *Rainham Chemical Works Ltd v Belvedere Fish Guano Co. Ltd*[45] in similar circumstances.

---

41 (1976) 72 DLR (3d) 335 (aerial spraying of insecticide without authority to fly over the land in question; liability was, however, imposed on the basis of negligence and nuisance).

42 See also *Superquinn Ltd v Bray Urban District Council and Others* unrep. HC, 18 February 1998, at p. 70, where an artificial lake was held to amount to a non-natural use.

43 [1947] AC 156; [1946] 2 All ER 471, at 174; p. 478; see also Lord Porter at p. 176; p. 479.

44 Lord Macmillan and Lord Porter *ibid.* and Viscount Simon LC at pp. 169–70; p. 475.

45 [1921] 2 AC 465; [1921] All ER Rep 48.

Another example of the difficulty in classifying an activity can be seen in *Cambridge Water Co. Ltd v Eastern Counties Leather plc.*[46] The defendant had been using a chemical solvent in its tanning process, which occasionally spilled on the floor of the plant. The solvent seeped through the ground, eventually reaching a supply of water used by the plaintiff to provide domestic water. On the issue of non-natural use, the trial judge held the use of the solvent to be natural, as it was ordinarily used in the tanning process and the defendant was acting in the ordinary course of business in an industrial area. The Court of Appeal and the House of Lords, however, regarded the use of the chemical as non-natural, with Lord Goff describing it as 'an almost classic case of non-natural use'.[47]

It is unsatisfactory to regard the concept of non-natural use as entirely factual; some thread of consistency must be given to the interpretation of the requirement or it will be impossible to determine the parameters of the law. The only real general guide is the statement by Lord Moulton, in *Rickards v Lothian*,[48] that there must be 'some special use bringing with it increased danger to others'. Use which is regarded as commonplace or ordinary tends to be regarded as natural, while activities generating an abnormally high risk tend to be classified as non-natural. Thus, the accumulation of water[49] or gas[50] for domestic purposes is likely to be treated as natural, while accumulation of the same items in large quantities for commercial purposes is likely to be treated as non-natural.[51] A distinction between domestic and commercial use is, however, too crude to serve as a reliable guide. Where a commercial concern, such as a hotel, accumulates water for sanitary facilities or gas for cooking, this is likely to be treated as a natural use, despite the fact that the size of the accumulation is much greater than in a private household.[52]

Social standards as to what is to be regarded as a high risk activity will change over time and this may be relevant to determining the question of whether a particular activity is non-natural. So, it may have been acceptable in the early decades of this century to regard petrol in the tank of a motor vehicle kept by the

---

46 [1994] 2 AC 264; [1994] 2 WLR 53; [1994] 1 All ER 53.
47 *Ibid.*, at p. 309; p. 83; p. 79.
48 [1913] AC 263; [1911–13] All ER Rep 71, at p. 280; p. 80.
49 *Ibid.* in *Victor Weston Ltd v Kenny* [1954] IR 191, at p. 197, Davitt P suggested, *obiter*, that any accumulation of water would come within the principle in *Rylands v Fletcher*. Lord Wright suggested, *obiter* in *Collingwood v Home & Colonial Stores Ltd* [1936] 3 All ER 200, at p. 208, that domestic use of utilities, such as gas, water and electricity, would constitute natural use, but bulk handling of the same items would be non-natural use.
50 *Miller v Addie & Sons (Collieries) Ltd* [1934] SC 150.
51 See the section on accumulation, *supra*, for a selection of cases in point.
52 *O'Neill v Esquire Hotels Ltd* (1973) 30 DLR (3d) 589 (gas for cooking in a hotel held to be natural use); *Collingwood v Home & Colonial Stores Ltd* [1936] 3 All ER 200 (electrical wiring in a grocery store held to be natural use).

defendant as non-natural,[53] but it is unlikely to be so now, given the increase in the use of such vehicles.[54] The result is that, even if abnormal risk can be accepted as the basis of non-natural use, over time the value of precedents on particular hazards may diminish as social perceptions of those hazards change.

It is difficult, due to the uncertain state of the law, to determine what factors to take into account and how to balance them in assessing the danger to see if it amounts to a non-natural user. If the analysis of risk is very detailed and includes factors such as the magnitude of the risk, the utility of the defendant's conduct and the balance between benefit and burden in the elimination of the risk, there is a significant possibility that such analysis will become indistinguishable from negligence.[55] If such detailed factors are used, rather than a rough division based on a contrast between ordinary and high risk activities, then non-natural user begins to mirror the concept of unreasonable risk generation in negligence. It may be argued that the two torts would still differ because of the different levels of obligation – strict duty and the duty of reasonable care. This difference is not all that great, however, in cases of serious risk. We have already seen that increasing levels of risk bring equivalent increases in responsibility in negligence and, in practice, the imposition of liability in negligence is closer to strict liability than the theory suggests in many cases. In fact, the gap between negligence and the *Rylands v Fletcher* principle has been bridged by the High Court of Australia in *Burnie Port Authority v General Jones Pty Ltd*,[56] where the obligation under *Rylands v Fletcher* was held to arise under the tort of negligence, though it was also held to be non-delegable, thereby preserving the defendant's responsibility for the conduct of independent contractors.

In this case the plaintiff, General Jones Pty, had a large quantity of frozen vegetables stored in cold rooms in a building it partly occupied. The remainder of the building was occupied by Burnie Port Authority, who were also the owners of

---

53 *Musgrove v Pandelis* [1919] 2 KB 43.

54 *Maron v Baert* (1981) 126 DLR (3d) 9; in *Perry v Kendricks Transport Ltd* [1956] 1 WLR 85; [1956] 1 All ER 154, however, the Court of Appeal held, *obiter*, that a coach which had its tank emptied still came within the *Rylands v Fletcher* principle, at p. 87; p. 157 per Singleton LJ; p. 90; p. 159 per Jenkins LJ; p. 92; p. 160 per Parker LJ; the court may have felt bound by the earlier decision in *Musgrove v Pandelis*, though Parker LJ was the only one to expressly say so. Romer LJ, in the Court of Appeal in *Collingwood v Home & Colonial Stores Ltd* [1936] 3 All ER 200, at pp. 208–9, expressed doubt as to the propriety of the decision in *Musgrove v Pandelis* and suggested that the House of Lords should overrule it when the opportunity arose.

55 See McMahon & Binchy, *The Irish Law of Torts*, 2nd ed. (Dublin: Butterworths, 1989), at p. 482; Fridman, *The Law of Torts in Canada* (Toronto: Carswell, 1989), vol. 1, at pp. 186–7; Heuston & Buckley, *Salmond & Heuston on the Law of Torts*, 21st ed. (London: Sweet & Maxwell, 1996) at §13.5; Rogers, *Winfield & Jolowicz on Tort*, 14th ed. (London: Sweet & Maxwell, 1994), at p. 453; Carroll, *loc. cit.* at pp. 211 *et seq.*

56 (1994) 120 ALR 42.

the building. Independent contractors, engaged by the authority, negligently caused a fire in a portion of the building occupied by the authority. The fire spread and destroyed General's goods. The Supreme Court of Tasmania had imposed liability on the authority on the basis of the *Rylands v Fletcher* principle. On appeal, the absence of clear guidance on the question of what constitutes a non-natural use and the related difficulty in identifying dangerous items for the purpose of the principle led the High Court of Australia to conclude that:

> . . . there is quite unacceptable uncertainty about the circumstances which give rise to its so-called 'strict liability'. The result is that the practical application of the rule in a case involving damage caused by the escape of a substance is likely to degenerate into an essentially unprincipled and *ad hoc* subjective determination of whether the particular facts of the case fall within undefined notions of what is 'special' or 'not ordinary'.[57]

The gradual development and adaptation of the various elements of the *Rylands v Fletcher* principle, through subsequent cases, was held by the majority to have led, not only to the confusion highlighted in the extract quoted, but to uncertainty in respect of all the elements of the action. Furthermore, the available defences had become increasingly similar to those available in negligence actions. The conclusion reached by the majority was that in almost any case in which recovery was possible under the *Rylands v Fletcher* principle, a negligence action would also succeed. The remaining situations could be embraced through the use of the concept of a non-delegable duty (and in rare instances, by using nuisance). On the facts of the case it was held that the magnitude of the risk, embracing the likelihood of foreseeable damage and the potential severity of that damage, was such that the duty of care should be treated as non-delegable. One significant problem with this decision is that the difficulties identified in ascertaining whether the *Rylands v Fletcher* principle is applicable to any given situation now arise in deciding whether or not a duty of care in negligence is non-delegable. In other words, the problems of interpreting the scope of the principle have been relocated, rather than resolved.

Escape

The foregoing requirements, accumulation of a dangerous item amounting to a non-natural use of property, give rise to the strict obligation under this tort; in other words, they are the equivalent, for the *Rylands v Fletcher* principle, of the duty of care requirement in the tort of negligence. Likewise, the requirement of escape is the equivalent of breach of duty. The level of obligation is, at least in theory, higher in the case of the *Rylands v Fletcher* principle, as it is not

---

57 *Ibid.*, at p. 54 per Mason CJ, Deane, Dawson Toohey and Gaudron JJ; Brennan and McHugh JJ dissenting.

discharged by the exercise of reasonable care by the defendant, but requires the defendant to accept responsibility for damage caused by the escape of the hazard, irrespective of the degree of precautions taken to prevent that escape. This apparently absolute duty is, however, reduced by the availability of defences against some types of escape and also by the fact that the damage must be within the scope of the foreseeable risk.

Escape is also a concept with a specialised meaning for the purposes of this tort and, as with the other elements, its precise ambit is uncertain. It appears that the tort is confined to the unintentional release of the accumulated hazard, with other torts, such as trespass, being employed to deal with intentional release. The point does not appear to have formed the *ratio* of any decision on the subject, but *dicta* from Canada[58] and England[59] suggest that intentional discharge falls outside the principle.

The escape requirement is satisfied if either the accumulated item or its dangerous effects escape. In *Rylands v Fletcher* the accumulated water flowed out of the reservoir and into the plaintiff's mines and it will often be the case that it is the actual accumulation that gets out and does the damage. In other cases the hazard is not so much that the accumulation itself will get out, but will cause something else to get out and do damage. So, in *Miles v Forest Rock Granite Co. (Leicestershire) Ltd*,[60] the defendants were held liable for damage caused by rocks thrown from their property by an explosion during blasting operations. The rocks were not the accumulated item – the explosives were – but the flying rock was a foreseeable consequence of the use of explosives. Furthermore the application of the principle here does not necessarily conflict with the *dicta* on intentional discharge because, although the detonation of the explosives was deliberate, the escape of flying rock was not; thus, the escape may be regarded as unintended.

One major aspect of the escape requirement remains unresolved and that is the precise meaning of the term 'escape'. We have already seen that in the early cases the principle applied only to hazards generated on the defendant's land getting onto the plaintiff's land and doing damage there. Expansion of the principle extended coverage to hazards generated on the land of another, where the defendant had authority to accumulate the dangerous item there. Furthermore, the plaintiff is no longer required to have an interest in land to

---

58   Krever J in the Ontario High Court in *North York v Kert Chemical Industries Ltd* (1985) 33 CCLT 184, at p. 200 (pumping of waste water into a sewer).

59   Taylor J in *Rigby v Chief Constable of Northamptonshire* [1985] 1 WLR 1242; [1985] 2 All ER 985, at p. 1255; p. 996 (firing of CS gas by the police to flush out a criminal).

60   (1918) 34 TLR 500, although the jury found negligence on the defendants' behalf, the Court of Appeal based responsibility under the *Rylands v Fletcher* principle. There are also Canadian authorities to the same effect, see Fridman, *op. cit.* vol. 1 at pp. 194–5, who is critical of their inclusion under the principle.

come within the protection of the principle.[61] This raises a question as to whether the hazard must leave the land on which it was accumulated and move to somewhere else in order to constitute an escape, or is loss of containment of the hazard sufficient? The English courts prefer the former interpretation, stemming from the House of Lords decision in *Read v J. Lyons & Co. Ltd*,[62] which sought to curb the earlier expansion of the principle and bring it closer to its original parameters.

The plaintiff was an inspector for the Ministry of Supply during the Second World War. While carrying out her duties at the defendants' munitions factory, she was injured in an explosion which occurred during the filling of shell cases with explosives. One of the central issues in the case was whether there was an escape for the purposes of the *Rylands v Fletcher* principle where the damage occurred on the defendants' property. The House of Lords unanimously held that the failure to contain the hazard did not amount to a sufficient escape and that the requirement of escape would only be satisfied where the hazard went from a place within the defendants' control to a place outside such control.[63]

Earlier cases had, however, considered failure to contain the hazard to be sufficient (usually expressed as a loss of 'control'). For example, in *Charing Cross, West End and City Electricity Supply Co. v Hydraulic Power Co.*[64] it was held that an escape of water from a hydraulic main under a street to an adjacent electric main under the same street was a sufficient escape. Lord Simonds, in *Read v Lyons*, suggested that highway cases were an exception to the general principle for escape and that loss of containment would suffice for such cases.[65] Viscount Simon LC and Lord Porter did not confine their acceptance of the correctness of such cases to incidents on the highway, but expressed them in terms of escape from a container under the defendants' control to property outside their control.[66] Either view would be capable of accommodating later judicial pronouncements in favour of loss of containment, such as the decision of the Northern Ireland Court of Appeal in *Shell-Mex and BP Ltd v Belfast Corporation* and Taylor J's *dictum* in *Rigby v Chief Constable of Northamptonshire*,[67] but the judges in question made no reference to constraints imposed by *Read v Lyons*. The approach by Viscount Simon and Lord Porter could extend to situations such as the escape of a

---

61 See the earlier discussion of 'place of accumulation' for the relevant authorities on the points recapitulated here.
62 [1947] AC 156; [1946] 2 All ER 471.
63 *Ibid.*, at p. 168; p. 474 per Viscount Simon LC; p. 174; p. 477 per Lord Macmillan; p. 177; p. 479 per Lord Porter; p. 183; p. 482 per Lord Simonds; p. 186; p. 484 per Lord Uthwatt.
64 [1914] 3 KB 772; [1914–15] All ER Rep 85.
65 [1947] AC 156; [1946] 2 All ER 471, at p. 183; p. 482.
66 *Ibid.*, at p. 168; p. 474 and p. 177; p. 497.
67 [1985] 1 WLR 1242; [1985] 2 All ER 985, at p. 1255; p. 996.

hazardous item from one container, owned by D, to another, owned by P, both of which were stored on the property of a third party, such as a warehouse.

The position in Canada corresponds with English law on this issue,[68] leaving some residual uncertainty to the precise parameters of the escape requirement. The Australian approach in *Burnie Port Authority v General Jones Pty Ltd* removes the need for a specialised principle on escape, by subsuming the entire *Rylands v Fletcher* principle within the tort of negligence.

Damage and Causation

Damage is an essential requirement under this tort, except where a *quia timet* injunction is sought in respect of impending harm. The decision in *Rylands v Fletcher* itself indicates that the occupier of neighbouring land can recover for physical damage to land and the attendant economic loss. It seems that an occupier can also recover in respect of damage to chattels or personal injury,[69] but the position is less clear in respect of such damage or injury suffered by a person with no right of occupation, such as a visitor or other person whose presence is transient.[70] The law on this subject, to a large extent, mirrors that of private nuisance on the issue of who is entitled to sue. Arguably, once the damage falls within the risk generated by the activity, the injured party should be allowed to recover independently of any interest in the property on which the incident took place; otherwise two persons suffering similar damage in the

---

68 See Fridman, *op. cit.* vol. 1 at pp. 193–4, citing a number of authorities on the point.

69 *Jones v Festiniog Railway Co.* (1868) LR 3 QB 733 (haystack set alight by sparks from a train); *Hale v Jennings Bros* [1938] 1 All ER 579 (personal injury to a tenant of a stall at a fair by the escape of a chair-o-plane); in Australia an occupier could recover for personal injuries prior to the absorption of the principle under negligence – *Benning v Wong* (1969) 122 CLR 249, at p. 255 per Barwick CJ; p. 318 per Windeyer J; the reference to *Rylands v Fletcher* in *Hanrahan v Merck Sharp & Dohme* [1988] ILRM 629, at p. 633 seems to confirm that an occupier could recover for personal injuries under this tort in Ireland.

70 *Miles v Forest Rock Granite Co. (Leicestershire) Ltd* (1918) 34 TLR 500; *Perry v Kendricks Transport Ltd* [1956] 1 WLR 85; [1956] 1 All ER 154 (personal injury recoverable); doubts as to whether personal injury came within the ambit of the principle were expressed by the House of Lords in *Read v J. Lyons & Co. Ltd* [1947] AC 156; [1946] 2 All ER 471, most notably by Lord Macmillan at p. 173; p. 477; Australian authorities prior to *Burnie Port Authority* favoured the availability of damages for personal injury independent of any occupation of property – *Fullarton v North Melbourne Electric Tramway & Lighting Co. Ltd* (1916) 21 CLR 181; *Benning v Wong* (1969) 122 CLR 249, at pp. 319–20 per Windeyer J, *obiter*; the majority in *Vaughn v Halifax-Dartmouth Bridge Commission* (1961) 29 DLR (2d) 523 indicated that recovery for damage to chattels would not be available to a transient visitor (in this case damage to a car parked on the property of another); Ilsey CJ dissenting at pp. 525–6; Fridman, *op. cit.* vol. 1 at pp. 180–1 argues that the dissent of the Chief Justice is a better reflection of the proper ambit of the principle.

one incident would be treated differently, based on a factor which is not significantly relevant to the incident, as where a property owner and his guest have their cars parked side by side and both are damaged by flying debris from an explosion on neighbouring property.

The economic cost of averting what would otherwise be damage within the scope of the principle also appears to be recoverable; thus, the plaintiff may recover expense incurred in preventing the escape causing damage.[71] Pure economic loss, such as a hazard deterring customers of a neighbouring business, would not appear to be recoverable, but may constitute an actionable nuisance. There is, however, no direct authority on this latter point and it is open to argument that such losses ought to be recoverable.

To recover compensation for loss the plaintiff must establish that the escape of the dangerous accumulation caused the loss and that the loss was not too remote a consequence of the accumulation and escape. Causation and remoteness are considered separately in chapter 11.

Defences

As with other torts, the general defences, considered in chapter 12, will be available. Furthermore, due to the uncertain parameters of the constituent elements of the tort, actions based on the *Rylands v Fletcher* principle present fertile ground for defendants to dispute that the facts fit the substantive requirements of the tort. There are also special defences which have particular relevance to this tort and these will be considered here.

Act of a Stranger

Where the escape results from the intervention of an unauthorised person, the defendant is not strictly liable, but is only liable for negligent failure to prevent the escape. *Box v Jubb*[72] is generally regarded as providing authority for this defence, but can actually be explained on other grounds.

The defendants had a reservoir for supplying water to their mill, which was in turn supplied by a watercourse to which they had access. The plaintiff's premises were flooded by an overflow of water from the defendants' reservoir. The overflow resulted from the discharge of another reservoir, belonging to a third party, above the defendants' mill and the blockage of the watercourse downstream of the defendants by another person.

Kelly CB and Pollock B held that the defendants were not liable, which is no surprise in itself, as the water which escaped through the defendants' reservoir was not actually that which they had accumulated at all. This

---

71 *New Zealand Forest Products Ltd v O'Sullivan* [1974] 2 NZLR 80.
72 (1879) 4 Ex D 76; [1874–80] All ER Rep 741.

decision was subsequently used by Lord Moulton in *Rickards v Lothian*[73] to support the broader proposition that where a stranger causes the release of the hazard generated by the defendant, the defendant will not be liable in the absence of negligence.

Other examples of this defence include *Perry v Kendricks Transport Ltd*[74] and *Beutler v Beutler*.[75] In *Perry* trespassing children threw a lighted match into the empty petrol tank of a coach, igniting fumes and causing an explosion which injured the plaintiff; the defendants were held not to be liable, as they were not negligent in respect of the children's interference. In *Beutler* a drunken driver rammed a wall, damaging a gas meter, causing an escape of gas and its explosion; the gas company were relieved of liability for the damage caused to the plaintiff. In *Shell-Mex and BP Ltd v Belfast Corporation*[76] the Northern Ireland Court of Appeal accepted the validity of the defence in principle, but found the defendants to have been negligent on the basis that the high level of risk demanded an equally high standard of vigilance and precautions. In this case their gas main became damaged and leaked after the owners of the road under which it had been laid excavated the area to install a sewer; the damage to the main resulted from pressure generated by subsidence after completion of the work.

A stranger, for the purposes of this defence, appears to be any person without authority to interfere with the accumulated item. The cases on the subject generally speak in terms of persons outside the defendant's control, but this can be misleading. Independent contractors are not really under the control of the person employing them, but they are not strangers under this defence and the defendant is responsible for their conduct, except, possibly, in cases of deliberate release by the independent contractor.

One of the effects of this defence is that it puts the defendant's responsibility for the conduct of others on a par with the position under nuisance, imposing strict liability for the conduct of persons whose involvement with the hazard is authorised, but requiring negligence on the defendant's part when the conduct is that of a stranger.

Vis Major

Where the accumulation results from a *vis major* (an irresistible force), sometimes described as an act of God, again the defendant will not be liable in the absence of negligence. This defence was one of those which Blackburn J

---

73 [1913] AC 263; [1911–13] All ER Rep 71, at p. 280; pp. 79–80 (unknown person blocked a sink and left a tap turned on in the defendant's premises, leading to flooding in the plaintiff's premises on a lower floor of the same building).
74 [1956] 1 WLR 85; [1956] 1 All ER 154.
75 (1983) 26 CCLT 229.
76 [1952] NI 72.

acknowledged as being relevant to the principle in his seminal judgment, though it was not applicable on the facts of the case. *Nichols v Marsland*[77] is a rare example where the defence has been successfully invoked. The defendant had a number of artificial lakes created on her property, by placing dams so as to disrupt the flow of a stream. Due to an unusually heavy rainfall the lakes burst their dams and the ensuing flood destroyed the plaintiff's bridges. The Court of Appeal held that the defendant was not liable on the basis of the jury's findings that the rainfall could not reasonably have been anticipated and the defendant was not negligent. In very similar circumstances the House of Lords in *Greenock Corporation v Caledonian Rail Co.*,[78] on appeal from the Court of Session in Scotland, held that unusually heavy rainfall did not constitute an act of God. Two factors contributed to this difference of opinion. First, *Greenock* was concerned with Scottish law, which, while similar to English law on the issue in question, had earlier precedents of greater weight than *Nichols*; and secondly, the Court of Appeal in *Nichols* was constrained by the jury's findings of fact. Both of these cases were recently considered in *Superquinn Ltd v Bray Urban District Council and Others*[79] and Laffoy J preferred *Nichols*, at least where the level of rain is vastly greater than anything previously experienced in the region. On the facts the defence succeeded, as the flooding was brought on by hurricane 'Charlie' (in August 1986), which was held to be 'within the category of the most extreme natural phenomena' capable of supporting the defence and 'could not reasonably have been anticipated or guarded against'.[80]

Canadian courts have been reluctant to treat heavy rain as a sufficient *vis major*, but do accept that unforeseeably severe rain could qualify as such.[81] The same reluctance is also evident in respect of other natural forces, with the defence confined not so much to the exceptional but to the unprecedented.[82]

The defence of *vis major* is not confined to natural disasters, but would include man made disasters, such as war. In doing so it overlaps with the defence of 'act of a stranger' and both are predicated on the same conceptual base. The combined effect of these defences is that the strictness of the liability generated by this tort is less than it first appears to be. The actual level of liability is less extensive than the general statements of Blackburn J and Lord Cairns LC would initially suggest. Liability, despite the exercise of reasonable care by the defendant, is confined to the conduct of the defendant;

---

77 (1876) 2 Ex D 1; [1874–80] All ER Rep 40.
78 [1917] AC 556; [1916–17] All ER Rep 426.
79 Unrep. HC, 18 February 1998, at pp. 76–7.
80 The evidence on the magnitude of the storm is detailed at pp. 15–34 of the judgment; contrast this with *Dockeray v Manor Park Homebuilders Ltd* unrep. HC, 10 April 1995, where O'Hanlon J rejected the defence.
81 *Nashwaak Pulp & Paper Co. v Wade* (1918) 43 DLR 141; *Kelley v Canadian Northern Railway Co.* [1950] 1 WWR 744.
82 *Gogo v Eureka Sawmills Ltd* [1945] 3 WWR 446 (high winds insufficient).

that of his employees or agents; and that of his independent contractors. In practice there will be very few circumstances where liability will be imposed where the conduct of the defendant, or his employees or agents, would not be classed as negligent, nor amount to a nuisance; thus, the main effect of the tort is the generation of liability for the conduct of independent contractors, as a specialised species of nuisance. Sifting through the complex requirements of the principle hardly seems worth the effort when any case that does produce a match is, in any event, probably explicable in terms of negligence or nuisance also. To be a true principle of strict liability the tort would need to extend responsibility to the consequences of unanticipated escape, rather than being confined to the predictable, though undesired release of the hazard. This would not lead to absolute liability, because defences such as waiver, consent to accumulation and statutory authority would still be available in appropriate circumstances.

Statutory Authority

This tort, like nuisance, tends to protect the position of existing property holders against new developments in neighbouring property, at least in respect of unusual hazards. It was also conceived at a time when planning control and environmental protection laws were not well developed.[83] Statutory authority will provide a defence to this tort on the same basis as its availability in nuisance. It remains to be seen whether the Irish courts would apply the same strict approach to interpretation that has been employed in trespass and nuisance;[84] the English courts have been willing to accept this defence, at least in the context of public utilities, on the basis of a more flexible interpretation of statutory provisions.[85]

Consent to Accumulation

If the plaintiff accepts the risk associated with the hazard, then a complete defence will be available, provided the requirements for waiver under section 34 of the Civil Liability Act 1961[86] are complied with. A partial defence based on consent is also available where the plaintiff has not accepted the full risk, but has consented to the accumulation. Here the defendant would remain responsible for negligence, but not for accidental escape. The leading Irish

---

83 See Carroll, *loc. cit.* at p. 210 for a discussion of the possibility that the policy basis behind the decision in *Rylands v Fletcher* was the protection of property owners against industrial development.

84 See chapters 4 and 5 *supra*.

85 *Smeaton v Ilford Corporation* [1954] Ch 450; [1954] 2 WLR 668; [1954] 1 All ER 923; *Dunne v North Western Gas Board* [1964] 2 QB 806; [1964] 2 WLR 164; [1963] 3 All ER 916.

86 Considered in chapter 12 *infra*.

authority is *Victor Weston (Eire) Ltd v Kenny*,[87] the facts of which were similar to *Rickards v Lothian*.

Both parties were occupants of the same building, with the plaintiff, a tenant, occupying a floor below the part of the building retained by the defendant landlord. The floor occupied by the plaintiff was flooded by an escape of water from the defendant's portion of the building, the water being part of the ordinary supply to the building. Davitt P held that the defendant was not liable on the basis that the plaintiff had implicitly consented to the accumulation of water for supply to the building as a whole and there was no negligence on the defendant's part.[88] The outcome could also be explained by other means – the water supply could constitute a natural use of property, or it could be argued that the supply was not accumulated for the defendant's own purposes – but Davitt P made no attempt to do so.

This defence reduces the strictness of the tort, by requiring proof of negligence. The defendant should, in principle, still be responsible where the negligence is that of an independent contractor, but there is a lack of authority on the point.

Non-delegable Duty in Respect of Ultra Hazardous Activities

There are miscellaneous examples of liability for the conduct of independent contractors, outside of those falling under the *Rylands v Fletcher* principle. While a general discussion of these is deferred until later,[89] one group of cases is worth considering at this point – those involving ultra hazardous activities. The reason for their inclusion at this point is that they are based on a generic concept similar to the *Rylands v Fletcher* principle, thus presenting an opportunity for the development of a general principle, producing a more stringent duty than that provided by the tort of negligence.

Bower v Peate[90] provides a useful starting point. The plaintiff and defendant owned adjoining houses. The defendant decided to demolish his house and build a new one, requiring deeper foundations, which would require excavating to a level below the foundations of the plaintiff's house. A builder was engaged to do the work, but failed to provide alternative support for the plaintiff's house during the conduct of the work, resulting in damage to the house.

The divisional court unanimously held the defendant liable for the damage caused by the builder. This, in itself, is not exceptional, as the harm could be

---

87 [1954] IR 191.
88 *Ibid.*, at p. 197, citing, *inter alia, Rickards v Lothian*.
89 Chapter 14 *infra*.
90 (1876) 1 QBD 321; [1874–80] All ER Rep 905, Cockburn CJ providing the judgment of the court; the principle was cited with approval by the House of Lords in *Public Works Commissioners v Angus & Co.* (1881) 6 App Cas 740; [1881–5] All ER Rep 1 on similar facts.

classified as a nuisance committed in the course of an authorised act, for which an owner-occupier is liable. But the judgment based liability on a broader general proposition that, where damage was virtually inevitable unless precautions were taken, the person instigating the work (the defendant) could not avoid liability by engaging an independent contractor to do the work. In other words, where injury or damage was probable, rather than possible, the defendant's duty to avoid harm could not be passed on to someone else. While the physical performance of the task could be entrusted to a third party, the legal obligation on the defendant would remain. The independent contractor would also be under a duty towards the plaintiff, but this would not relieve the defendant of all responsibility.

The authorities cited in support involved personal injuries in respect of public nuisances.[91] One possible interpretation of this is that the case merely expresses the circumstances in which liability in nuisance arises where the nuisance is generated by an independent contractor, rather than the defendant. On the other hand, the case may be an expression of a more general proposition, not confined to nuisance. The focus of the judgment was on the fact that in all the cases under consideration the activity was necessarily attended with serious risk; in other words, the activity would generate risk, even if carefully carried out. This aspect of the principle was also highlighted by Lord Watson in *Public Works Commissioners v Angus & Co.*,[92] in the House of Lords. It may be that, in any situation where there is a very high level of risk attached to the activity, the instigator of the activity must accept responsibility for the conduct of independent contractors in the performance of the task.

The existence of a general duty in respect of what may be described as ultra hazardous activities is supported by modern authorities, though there are few instances where the duty has actually been held to arise. The leading Irish authority on the issue is *Boylan v Northern Bank Ltd*,[93] a case also involving

---

91 *Pickard v Smith* (1861) 10 CBNS 470 (plaintiff falling into an open coal cellar belonging to the defendant, which had been opened by a coal merchant delivering coal at the defendant's instruction); *Gray v Pullen* (1864) 5 B & S 970 (plaintiff injured by falling into a trench on the highway, which the defendants had instructed independent contractors to dig); *Tarry v Aston* (1876) 1 QBD 314; [1874–80] All ER Rep 738 (plaintiff injured by falling lamp, which had been overhanging the highway from the defendant's premises; the defendant had engaged an independent contractor to secure the lamp).

92 (1881) 6 App Cas 740; [1881–5] All ER Rep 1; see also *Honeywill & Stein Ltd v Larkin Bros Ltd* [1934] 1 KB 191; [1933] All ER Rep 77, where 'inherent risk' was the justification for the invocation of the principle in respect of flash photography, leading to a fire (at the time the flash was produced by means of a minor explosion in a metal tray); *Holliday v National Telephone Co.* [1899] 2 QB 392; [1895–9] All ER Rep 359, benzoline flare lamp and molten solder being used for welding tubes carrying telephone cables; the lamp exploded, dispersing molten material, which injured a passing pedestrian.

93 [1976–7] ILRM 287.

damage to a building during demolition of a neighbouring building. Costello J, relying on a *dictum* of Atkin LJ[94] and the decision of the Court of Appeal in *Salsbury v Woodland*,[95] held that there was a non-delegable duty of reasonable care in respect of inherently dangerous operations. This differs from the principle in *Bower v Peate*, in that the duty is not strict in the sense outlined at the beginning of this chapter, as it requires negligence on the part of some person engaged in the operation. The duty is, however, more extensive than ordinary negligence and may be expressed as a duty to see that all reasonable care is taken, rather than to exercise reasonable care. The effect of this principle is to increase the defendant's level of responsibility to include the negligence of independent contractors as well as personal negligence or that of employees.

It may be that the two cases involve two separate rules relating to ultra hazardous activities, one based on nuisance and one on negligence. If this is the case, then the question of whether a breach of the duty requires proof of negligence will depend on which of the two principles the facts of a given case are classified under. On this interpretation the non-delegable aspect of the duty is a secondary aspect of the obligation and the originating obligation must arise under an existing tort.

Whether the cases give rise to one or two rules, one essential element is the level of risk required to make the obligation non-delegable. The duty embraces only risks which are inherent or inevitable and does not include collateral risks, though the distinction between the two is essentially a question of fact.[96] It might appear safe to conclude from the cases already considered that damaging a building during the demolition of a neighbouring one will be a sufficiently inherent danger, but this is too general a proposition. In fact, close attention is paid to detail in determining whether the risk is inherent or collateral. In *Bower v Peate* the danger was inherent because the buildings relied on each other for support and the work involved excavation to a level beneath the foundations of the plaintiff's premises; the loss of support would almost certainly lead to damage if no alternative support was provided. In *Boylan v Northern Bank Ltd* Costello J paid particular attention to the size of the gable wall of the premises being demolished, its physical proximity to the plaintiff's building and the manner by which the operation could cause damage (both collisions and vibrations caused by falling masonry) in determining that it constituted an inherent danger. In *Power v Crowley and Reddy Enterprises Ltd*[97] Blayney J

---

94 *Belvedere Fish Guano Co. Ltd v Rainham Chemical Works Ltd* [1920] 2 KB 487, at p. 504.
95 [1970] 1 QB 324; [1969] 3 WLR 29; [1969] 3 All ER 863.
96 There are clear parallels between the concept of inherent risk and dangerous accumulations amounting to non-natural user under the *Rylands v Fletcher* principle and similar difficulties may arise in classifying cases in practice.
97 Unrep. HC, 29 October 1992, at pp. 11–12; liability was, however, imposed on the company that engaged the independent contractor on the basis of occupier's

held that the demolition of an internal wall, approximately 10 feet high, was not an inherently dangerous operation. The fact that the work was carried out without scaffolding, which had been used earlier in knocking a similar wall on the same premises, was treated as a collateral risk.

The distinction between inherent and collateral risks is well demonstrated by the facts of *Salsbury v Woodland*. The occupier of a house engaged an independent contractor to fell a tree in the front garden. The tree was approximately 25 feet high and was positioned at a point some $12^1/_2$ feet from the house and 28 feet from the public footpath in front of the garden. Due to a lack of care in respect of the direction in which the tree fell, telephone wires strung across the garden were knocked and lay snaked on the road. The plaintiff was injured when jumping clear of the wires, which were thrown into a somewhat unpredictable movement by a passing vehicle.

The knocking of the tree could have been conducted in a manner which presented no danger to users of the highway in front of the house; the risk resulted from a lack of care in the manner in which the work was undertaken. If, on the other hand, the tree had been considerably bigger, or the garden considerably smaller, then the danger posed could have been regarded as inherent. This is because the felling of the tree would necessarily involve a high probability of some of it falling on the highway or on neighbouring property.

There are some similarities between the non-delegable duty in respect of ultra hazardous activities (under the *Boylan* formulation) and the *Rylands v Fletcher* principle. Both principles make the defendant responsible for the conduct of independent contractors; the level of responsibility under both is confined to conduct intimately connected with the hazard and does not include collateral activities or unauthorised activities. There are some differences between the two also. While the *Rylands v Fletcher* principle is confined to accumulations amounting to non-natural use of land, the non-delegable duty is capable of applying to any high risk activity; thus, natural items such as trees are capable of constituting sufficient hazards for the purposes of the non-delegable duty principle, where they would not satisfy the requirements of *Rylands v Fletcher*. The level of obligation may also differ between the two principles, with the *Rylands v Fletcher* principle being strict and the non-delegable duty involving a negligence based formulation. However, as we have already seen, judicial interpretation of the *Rylands v Fletcher* principle in other jurisdictions has brought it much closer to negligence in practice and the effect of the rule is little more than a non-delegable duty based on negligence, though the High Court of Australia is the only court to have expressly made such a ruling so far.

The present position would seem to be, therefore, that while there is some theoretical acknowledgment of strict obligations in relation to some types of

---

liability, a decision criticised, with some justification, by Byrne & Binchy, *Annual Review of Irish Law 1992* at pp. 591 *et seq.*

high risk activities, the strictness of the obligation rarely manifests itself in practice and the judiciary in many jurisdictions are pushing the basis of the obligation closer to negligence principles.

Further Development

The future of the principles discussed in this chapter is somewhat uncertain: they may remain as isolated and unconnected principles, each with its own area of application; alternatively, the *Rylands v Fletcher* principle may retract to a form of non-delegable duty in negligence, as it has in Australia, thereby merging with the *Boylan* principle; the third possibility is that they may develop into a general strict obligation. The second option seems more likely, given the growth of negligence to its present position of dominance, but it would be unwise to assume that present trends are permanent and inevitable. We have already noted that negligence in practice has moved closer to strict liability in some situations and a theoretical rationalisation of such moves can be expected to follow, unless the courts retract the expanded impact that negligence has attained. Thus, it is worth briefly considering how a general strict obligation might be forged from existing principles.

The *Restatement, Second, Torts* provides the following formulation of a general principle for a strict duty:

> §519
> (1) One who carries on an abnormally dangerous activity is subject to liability for harm to the person, land or chattels of another resulting from the activity, although he has exercised the utmost care to prevent the harm.
> (2) This strict liability is limited to the kind of harm, the possibility of which makes the activity abnormally dangerous.

It goes on to identify relevant factors in determining which activities should qualify as abnormally dangerous:

> §520
> In determining whether an activity is abnormally dangerous, the following factors are to be considered:
> (a) the existence of a high degree of risk of some harm to the person, land or chattels of others;
> (b) likelihood that the harm that results from it will be great;
> (c) inability to eliminate the risk by the exercise of reasonable care;
> (d) extent to which the activity is not a matter of common usage;
> (e) inappropriateness of the activity to the place where it is carried on; and
> (f) extent to which its value to the community is outweighed by its dangerous attributes.

The *Restatement* also recommends a more limited range of defences in respect of the strict obligation under §519, leaving a defendant liable for release of the hazard by a *vis major* or a non-deliberate intervention of a stranger.[98] The provisions of the *Restatement* have not, however, led the judiciary to greatly extend the ambit of strict liability. American cases on liability for ultra hazardous activities are largely consistent with the *Rylands v Fletcher* principle, with two principal exceptions: first, escape is based on the loss of containment, rather than the *Read v Lyons* approach, at least in respect of lawful visitors; secondly, contributory negligence has only a limited application as a defence and is not as extensively available under this tort as it is in negligence.[99] The exclusion of matters of 'common usage' by §520(d) also inhibits development to activities which have not traditionally fallen within the ambit of the *Rylands v Fletcher* principle.

There is a growing body of academic opinion on the development of strict obligations, ranging from calls for a radical revision of tort law under a general conception of responsibility for causing harm, to more modest calls for the extension of strict obligations to include particular types of activities.[100]

A general reconceptualisation of tort seems unlikely, as it would exceed the bounds of judicial authority for the courts to overturn an entire branch of law and replace it with new principles, while the political will is not there to introduce such a change by legislative means, since there is no public pressure for such reform. Popular opinion is more likely to favour retraction, rather than expansion of liability, as many people see themselves as potential defend-

---

98 *Restatement, Second, Torts* §522; the American Law Institute offers no view on deliberate acts of a stranger, intending to cause harm.

99 Prosser et al., *Prosser & Keeton on Torts*, 5th ed. (St Paul, Minn.: West, 1984), at §§78 and 79; the *Restatement* includes similar provisions in respect of lawful entrants (§520C) and contributory negligence (§524).

100 Epstein, 'A Theory of Strict Liability' (1973) 2 J Leg Stud 151 presents one of the leading examples of a general theory of strict liability; this and other leading theories are critically reviewed by Posner, 'Strict Liability: A Comment' (1973) 2 J Leg Stud 205; under Epstein's approach the outcome of most cases would not differ from the present state of the law, but the focus of argument would shift from questions of duty and reasonableness to causation; Kress, 'The Seriousness of Harm Thesis for Abnormally Dangerous Activities' in Owen (ed.), *Philosophical Foundations of Tort Law* (Oxford: Clarendon Press, 1995) proposes a general principle of strict obligation for abnormally dangerous activities, but with the level of injury as the guiding criterion, rather than the probability of occurrence; *Report of the Royal Commission on Civil Liability and Compensation for Personal Injury, 1978* (Pearson Commission) Cmnd 7054, chapter 31, recommending strict liability in respect of all inherently dangerous things and things, though ordinarily safe, capable of causing extensive personal injury; also recommending strict liability for specific activities such as motoring (vol. I para. 1086) and railway accidents involving personal injury caused by rolling stock (vol. I para. 1186); a number of the Pearson Commission's recommendations are criticised in Cane, *Atiyah's Accidents, Compensation and the Law*, 5th ed. (London: Butterworths, 1993), at pp. 90 *et seq.*; see also Pardy, 'Fault and Cause: Rethinking the Role of Negligent Conduct' (1995) 3 Tort L Rev 143.

ants, rather than potential plaintiffs (or at least see themselves as having to foot the bill for compensation payments, through higher insurance premiums and prices for goods and services). Any principled change is likely to come from judicial reform, which would be at a moderate level, within the established parameters of judicial authority. Any legislative measures are likely to be *ad hoc* provisions in respect of particular activities (like the product liability provisions considered in chapter 3).

One method of reform could be the development of a general principle of strict obligation for ultra hazardous activities. Just as the House of Lords in *Donoghue v Stevenson*[101] used isolated examples of duties to exercise reasonable care to establish a general obligation, based on proximity and foreseeability, by treating the examples as representative of an ulterior generic principle, so too could the cases of strict obligation be forged into a general principle. Such a generic principle would be of narrower application, being confined to high risk activities. The precise parameters of such an obligation would take time to evolve, as has the tort of negligence, but it is a feasible option, given the judicial will to develop in this direction. Some hint at such a possibility was given by McCarthy J in *Mullen v Quinnsworth (No. 1)*,[102] where he raised the possibility that personal injury to customers in supermarkets could come within the scope of such a duty, but declined to express a definite view as the matter had not been argued in the case. This option was partially raised in subsequent litigation between the parties, but did not form a significant element of the case, which was ultimately decided on the basis of negligence.[103] Lord Goff, in the House of Lords, has voiced opposition to such development, suggesting that increased levels of responsibility should be a matter for parliament.[104] Given that the Irish courts are not tied to the specific limitations imposed on the *Rylands v Fletcher* principle in other jurisdictions, such as the narrow interpretation of escape, the reasonable foreseeability rule of remoteness and the availability of the defence of act of a stranger, they have a better opportunity than their counterparts abroad to develop a general principle of strict obligation.

An alternative line of reasoning through which greater responsibility for ultra hazardous activities could be generated involves an expansion in the interpretation of reasonableness. Modern tort law in common law jurisdictions has been heavily dominated by imposing the perspective of the mythical, but

---

101 [1932] AC 562; [1932] All ER Rep 1; see chapter 1 *supra*.
102 [1990] 1 IR 59, at pp. 68–9.
103 *Mullen v Quinnsworth Ltd (No. 2)* [1991] ILRM 439, at p. 448 where McCarthy J makes brief reference to the issue, once again leaving it open for a more suitable occasion. The untimely death of McCarthy J has prevented any further elucidation of his views on the matter and the issue still awaits a proper airing in the courts.
104 *Cambridge Water Co. Ltd v Eastern Counties Leather plc* [1994] 2 AC 264; [1994] 2 WLR 53; [1994] 1 All ER 53, at pp. 304 *et seq.*; pp. 79 *et seq.*; pp. 75 *et seq.*

charismatic, icon – the reasonable man – on a multitude of situations. Defendants are relieved of liability where they have taken those precautions to avoid risk that the reasonable man would have taken and should the risk, nonetheless, manifest itself, the plaintiff is left to suffer the loss, as the defendant bore no 'fault'. Where an activity bears a particularly high degree of risk to others, might the 'reasonable man' not feel obliged to compensate victims of the activity, even in the absence of neglect in the conduct of the activity? A reasonable person might well recognise that certain types of activity are such that, while they may lawfully be carried on, they carry both a primary duty to be careful in the conduct of the activity and a secondary duty to accept responsibility for the accidental occurrence of injury within the known class of risks generated by the activity. Such an extension of responsibility may be justified in a limited class of cases, without awaiting legislative intervention and may be as consonant with social values as the present law of negligence.

The advancement of society through economic, scientific and technological development carries an inevitable element of risk and the law, rightly, tries not to unduly inhibit such development. But as society advances and more knowledge is gained in respect of the risks posed by particular activities, so too must responsibility for the consequences of one's activities grow. The acceptance of responsibility for adverse consequences is a greater measure of maturity than the acceptance of glory for success. Thus, the development of strict obligations should not be considered as an inhibition to social development, but rather as a measure of our understanding of our limitations, though, if we are to develop such obligations, the choice of suitable activities must be carefully made.

CHAPTER SEVEN

Economic Torts

Introduction

We have already seen that economic interests are protected to some extent by some of the torts that have been examined, particularly negligence and private nuisance. In many of the instances where such torts provide redress for economic damage, it is as an adjunct to the protection of other interests, where the loss is consequential to interference with personal or property rights. The protection provided against pure economic loss in negligence is still rather limited, even if a broad view is taken of the duty of care owed in respect of economic damage. Furthermore, the use of negligence is inappropriate in respect of intentional harm. It is, consequently, necessary to consider other causes of action which may be invoked for the protection of economic interests.

The torts considered here are not all exclusively concerned with the protection of economic interests; some of them may also be used to protect personal or proprietary interests, but their principal usage in practice is for the protection of economic interests. The first three torts considered – deceit, injurious falsehood and passing off – are based on loss suffered through various forms of deception. Deceit deals with cases where the defendant misleads the plaintiff by means of fraud; injurious falsehood deals with cases where the defendant misleads third parties by providing untruthful information concerning the plaintiff; passing off deals with cases where the defendant misleads third parties by falsely adopting an important aspect of the plaintiff's commercial reputation. The main emphasis will be on passing off, with an outline of the main aspects of deceit and injurious falsehood. The next tort considered is interference with economic relations, which is an embryonic tort of potential general application to intentional infliction of economic loss. The discussion will then move on to briefly consider a number of torts that are generally associated with economic protection, though not exclusively concerned with economic rights. This discussion will cover those torts which gave rise to the generic tort of interference with economic relations. Then there is an outline of detinue and conversion, two torts concerned with interference with chattels. In principle these two torts are concerned with possession and proprietary interests in personal property (and complement the tort of trespass to chattels), but their main use in practice is concerned with the economic value of the rights, hence their inclusion in this chapter. Finally, breach of confidence will be briefly outlined.

Deceit

The tort of deceit has a significant overlap with fraudulent misrepresentation in the vitiation of contract. While contract principles are primarily concerned with disentangling transactions affected by the fraud, and carry important implications for rights of ownership of property transferred under fraud, the tort of deceit is concerned with the right of the deceived party to recover damages from the fraudulent person, who instigated the deception. In practice there will be many cases where the fraudulent person either cannot be found or does not have the means to compensate the injured party, but where an action is feasible, it does enhance the range of remedial mechanisms available. This tort can be particularly useful where restitutionary measures to undo the effects of transactions resulting from the fraud are not available, as occurred in *Northern Bank Finance Corp. Ltd v Charlton*.[1]

The three defendants were investors in a commercial transaction, in receipt of financial advice and support from the plaintiff bank. The plaintiff's representative fraudulently provided misleading information relating to the financial affairs of a fourth investor, which materially affected their decision to enter into the transaction. The defendants ultimately entered into the transaction, the take-over of a public company, with the assistance of loans provided by the bank. The transaction was a financial disaster, causing considerable loss to the defendants, who in turn failed to repay some of the loans provided by the bank. In an action by the bank to recover the amounts due under the loans, the defendants successfully counterclaimed in respect of the fraud. The Supreme Court held that, as the transactions for the purchase of the shares from third parties were valid and the bank was not a party to those transactions, it was not possible to restore the defendants to their original position; consequently, damages for deceit was the appropriate remedy.

The elements of the tort action are only briefly considered here; readers should refer to works on contract law for more detailed consideration of the law relating to fraudulent misrepresentation.[2] It should be noted that the primary means of defence in respect of deceit is to dispute the existence of one or more of the elements of the action; the general defences, discussed in chapter 12, are unlikely to have any real impact on actions for deceit.

---

1 [1979] IR 149.
2 Friel, *The Law of Contract* (Dublin: Round Hall, 1995) at chapter 17; Cheshire, Fifoot & Furmston, *Law of Contract*, 13th ed. (London: Butterworths, 1996) at chapter 9; Treitel, *The Law of Contract*, 9th ed. (London: Sweet & Maxwell, 1995) at chapter 9; Clark, *Contract Law in Ireland*, 3rd ed. (London: Sweet & Maxwell, 1992) at chapter 11.

Requisite elements:

1. An untrue representation of fact
2. Fraud of the representor
3. Intent to induce reliance
4. Actual reliance by the recipient
5. Damage caused by reliance

Untrue Representation

The first matter that the plaintiff must establish in an action for deceit is that the defendant made a representation of fact which was untrue. Most representations are made in the form of statements, either written or oral, but there is no legal requirement that a representation must take the form of an express statement. An inference implicit in a statement or inferred from conduct may suffice.[3] In *Gill v McDowell*,[4] for example, the placing of a hermaphrodite bovine animal alongside bullocks and heifers was considered by Lord O'Brien LCJ to amount to a representation that the animal was either one or the other. The Lord Chief Justice indicated that the object of the exercise was abundantly clear: 'It is perfectly notorious that a bad animal is often placed among good, so that the defects of the bad animal may, by association with the good lot, escape detection.'[5]

To be actionable, the representation must be of a factual nature and, while the ambit of what constitutes fact is not precisely defined, there are some well established guidelines on the subject. An indication of one's opinion or intention does not ordinarily constitute a representation as to its substance, but does constitute a representation of the fact that one possesses the opinion or intention. Thus, if it can be proved that the defendant did not hold the view expressed, an action may lie.[6] The expression of expert opinion may constitute

---

3 '. . . there must be a representation of fact made by words, or, it may be, by conduct. The phrase will include a case where the defendant has manifestly approved and adopted a representation made by some third person.' *per* Viscount Maugham in *Bradford Third Equitable Benefit Building Society v Borders* [1941] 2 All ER 205, at p. 211; see also Lord Wright at p. 220. *Delany v Keogh* [1905] 2 IR 267 provides a useful example of a misrepresentation inferred by an express statement (see *infra*, in the discussion of fraud). Detailed consideration of what constitutes a misrepresentation can be found in the comment accompanying §525 of the *Restatement, Second, Torts*.

4 [1903] 2 IR 463, the action was for recission of the contract of sale.

5 *Ibid.* at p. 467.

6 See, for example, *Edgington v Fitzmaurice* 29 Ch D 459 (1884) per Denman J at pp. 474–5, confirmed on appeal (1885), in particular Cotton LJ at pp. 479–80 and Bowen LJ at p. 483. The representation involved a statement by the directors of a company to potential investors concerning the purposes to which their money would be applied. An intention was expressed that it would be spent on developing the trade of the company, through the purchase of goods and improvement of buildings, whereas the money was applied primarily to the repayment of a loan and

a representation as to its substance and usually will be regarded as a representation of fact where the recipient is not an expert.[7]

Failure to disclose information will not normally amount to a representation, even though the party in possession of the knowledge is aware of the fact that the other party is labouring under a mistaken belief on the matter. There are two exceptions to this principle. The first arises where the non-disclosure distorts the significance of a positive representation, thereby causing deception;[8] the second is where the relationship between the parties is one in which the law requires disclosure (such as fiduciary relationships or transactions *uberrimae fidei*).

A more difficult question arises in respect of indications as to the effect of the law on particular factual circumstances. Such a representation involves a mixture of fact and law, and so, is capable of being classified as either. The case law on the matter is divided, but since the representation is at least partially factual it would be better to treat it as capable of supporting an action in deceit, particularly where the representation is one of expert opinion.[9]

One particular type of representation worthy of special mention involves references as to the creditworthiness of another person, as these are subject to an additional statutory requirement. Section 6 of the Statute of Frauds Amendment Act 1828 states:

> No action shall be brought whereby to charge any person upon or by reason of any representation or assurance made or given concerning or relating to the character, conduct, credit, ability, trade or dealings of any other person, to the intent or purpose that such other person may obtain credit, money, or goods upon, unless such representation or assurance be made in writing signed by the party to be charged therewith.

The effect of this provision is that misrepresentations, fraudulently given to enable another person to obtain credit, are only enforceable where they have been given in writing and signed by the person against whom the action is brought. The object of the statutory provision was to ensure that the formal requirements were the same as those applicable to contracts of guarantee under section 2 of the Statute of Frauds (Ireland) 1695, since the action in deceit would essentially make the representor a guarantor in respect of the amount of credit given. The House of Lords, in *Banbury v Bank of*

---

this was what the directors had intended to do from the outset. See also *Ennis v Butterly* [1997] 1 ILRM 28.

7   *Brown v Raphael* [1958] Ch 636; [1958] 2 All ER 79; *Esso Petroleum Co. Ltd v Mardon* [1976] QB 801; [1976] 2 WLR 583; [1976] 2 All ER 5. Both actions were in contract, but the principle ought to apply in tort also.

8   *Restatement, Second, Torts* §529 provides a useful discussion of the deceptive nature of half truths.

9   For more detailed discussion and reference to English case law see *Halsbury's Laws of England*, 4th ed. vol. 31 para. 1013.

Montreal,[10] held that the provision applies only to actions for deceit and not to other actions involving misrepresentation, such as negligence. The basis for this interpretation is that the action in deceit is founded exclusively on the representation, while an action in negligence or contract is founded on a duty in which the representation is only one of several relevant circumstances; thus, only the action for deceit is 'upon or by reason of' the representation.[11]

Older authorities indicated some difficulty in suing legal persons, as the signature of an agent was not sufficient for the purposes of section 6.[12] The English Court of Appeal has, more recently, rejected this proposition, holding that the point did not form the *rationes decidendi* of those cases and that the signature of an authorised agent, officer or employee of a company, acting on behalf of the company and within the scope of authority, is to be treated as the signature of the company itself.[13] This latter view seems preferable; otherwise corporations could not be sued at all in cases covered by the section.

At first sight it appears peculiar that the victim of the more serious wrong (fraud) has a more difficult task to recover than the victim of the less serious wrong (negligence). The position may be defended, however, on the basis that the allegation of fraud casts a greater aspersion on the defendant than one of negligence and the plaintiff may rightly be required to produce a higher level of proof in such a case. In truth, the distinction drawn may have as much to do with a lack of judicial enthusiasm for the statutory provision as with any principled distinction between the wrongs involved. In any case, as a matter of sound business practice, it would be unwise to extend any serious level of credit on foot of a reference unless the representor is willing to commit to a signed documentary reference. The statutory requirement should not expose businesses to any serious lack of protection, once care is taken in respect of the degree of reliance placed on credit references.

Fraud

Fraud, for the purposes of deceit, was defined by Lord Herschell in *Derry v Peek*,[14] where he stated that 'fraud is proved when it is shown that a false representation has been made (i) knowingly, or (ii) without belief in its truth, or (iii) recklessly, careless whether it be true or false'.[15] The third proposition

---

10 [1918] AC 626; [1918–19] All ER Rep 1; see also *W.B. Anderson & Sons Ltd v Rhodes (Liverpool) Ltd* [1967] 2 All ER 850, at pp. 862–5.
11 *Ibid.*, per Lord Finlay LC and Lord Parker, at pp. 639–40; pp. 5–6 and p. 707; pp. 26–7 respectively.
12 *Swift v Jewsbury & Goddard* (1874) LR 9 QB 301; *Hirst v West Riding Union Banking Ltd* [1901] 2 KB 560; [1900–3] All ER Rep 782.
13 *UBAF v European American Banking Corp.* [1984] QB 713; [1984] 2 WLR 508; [1984] 2 All ER 226.
14 (1889) 14 App Cas 337; [1886–90] All ER Rep 1.
15 *Ibid.*, at p. 374; p. 22.

was considered to be a sub-category of the second, on the basis that reck-lessness would show a lack of genuine belief. An honest belief in the truth of the representation would relieve a defendant of responsibility[16] and a lack of reasonable grounds for the belief would not necessarily defeat the defendant, although it could cast doubt as to whether the belief was honestly held.

An exact correlation needs to be drawn between the representation and the fraudulent knowledge or belief if the action is to succeed. Likewise, a precise correlation between the representation and an honest belief will be necessary if the defendant is to show a lack of fraud. So, if the representation is one inferred from statements or conduct, the belief or lack thereof must relate to the inference. As a result, care needs to be taken in framing the facts of a case in order to identify the precise ambit of representations made and the extent of the repre-sentor's knowledge or belief. A contrast between *Derry v Peek* and *Delany v Keogh*[17] will serve to demonstrate the point.

In the former case, Peek sued the directors of a company on foot of a repre-sentation that the company had authority to use steam or mechanical power to run its trams, whereas it only had a conditional right to do so, requiring the sanction of the Board of Trade and two other bodies. The representation of the conditional right as an absolute one was clearly untrue, but the directors' honest, but misguided, belief that the consent would be forthcoming was sufficient to preclude a finding of fraud. In the latter case an auctioneer advertising the sale of a leasehold interest in property stated that the landlord had accepted a rent of £18 per annum over a number of years, although the lease stated the rent to be £25 per annum. Prior to the sale, the landlord had informed the auctioneer of his intention to seek the full rent from the purchaser; the auctioneer sought legal advice from the vendor's solicitor, who informed him that the landlord would be estopped from claiming the full rent, so the auctioneer let the advertisement stand. The landlord subsequently sued the purchaser and succeeded in recovering the full rent, and the purchaser, in turn, sued the auctioneer. If the misrepresentation was simply one as to the amount of rent payable, it is probable that the auctioneer would have had a sufficiently honest belief in its truth, but the Court of Appeal took a different view of the statement. The effective misrepre-sentation was held to be the inference that the auctioneer had no reason to believe that the reduced rent would no longer be accepted by the landlord. This materially reduced the extent to which the legal advice could support a claim of honest belief; as Holmes LJ observed: '. . . the defendant must have understood

---

16 See *Barber v Houston* (1885) LR Ir 475, at p. 477 per Porter MR, representation by an executor as to the sheep carrying power of land being sold, where the executor had no personal expertise on such matters, but had received an expert opinion; held to be an honest belief in the truth of the statement and, consequently, there was no fraud.

17 [1905] 2 IR 267.

the difference between a landlord accepting voluntarily an abated rent, and a tenant being forced to fight for the abatement in a doubtful lawsuit.'[18]

The use of a similar extension of the representation in *Derry v Peek* would not change the result, as the directors had no grounds for suspicion that the Board of Trade would withhold its consent. Nonetheless, the precision of formulation of the representation in *Delany v Keogh* seems particularly harsh on the defendant, though the damages came to less than 10 per cent of the purchase price and so should not have generated undue hardship for the auctioneer.

The defendant need not gain personally from the fraud to commit deceit; a deception which benefits a third party will suffice.[19] Furthermore, the motive of the defendant in committing the deception need not, as a matter of law, be proved by the plaintiff, but it may be relevant to the credibility of the allegation of fraud. The issue was addressed concisely by Finlay P in the High Court in *Northern Bank Finance Corp. v Charlton*:

> It is not necessary, as a matter of law, for the defendants to establish a motive for the fraud if they establish the fraud itself. However, in my view, the complete absence of any plausible motive would create, in any case of fraud, a doubt as to its proof.[20]

Intent to Induce Reliance

The representor must intend the plaintiff to rely on the representation in the manner in which the plaintiff does so.[21] Once again, intent is not confined to the subjective intentions of the defendant, but extends to intentions objectively inferred from the circumstances. It is not sufficient that there be an intent for some person, other than the plaintiff, to rely on the representation; the intent must include the plaintiff. As with negligent misstatement, the plaintiff need not be the immediate recipient of the representation; provided the defendant's intent includes transmission of the representation from the initial recipient to a wider class of persons, of which the plaintiff is a member, then the requirement is satisfied. If the plaintiff is outside the class of persons covered by the intent, then no action in deceit can be pursued.[22] Furthermore, the intended manner of reliance must correspond with the actual form of reliance placed in

---

18 *Ibid.*, at p. 290.
19 *Pasley v Freeman* (1789) 3 TR 51; [1775–1802] All ER Rep 31.
20 [1979] IR 149, at p. 168; the reference to proof by the defendants, rather than by the plaintiffs, arises from the fact that fraud was raised in a counterclaim.
21 *Edgington v Fitzmaurice* 29 Ch D 459 (1884) per Denman J at p. 467; (1885) (CA) per Cotton LJ at p. 479; Bowen LJ at p. 482; *Bradford Third Equitable Benefit Building Society v Borders* [1941] 2 All ER 205, per Viscount Maugham at p. 211.
22 *Peek v Gurney* (1873) LR 6 HL 377.

the representation by the plaintiff.[23] Thus, if the defendant provided the plaintiff with a fraudulent credit reference for a business, in respect of the provision of a loan, but the plaintiff bought out the business instead, then an action in deceit would not lie, because the transaction entered into in reliance on the reference was fundamentally different from the transaction that the defendant intended to induce.

The defendant need not intend any damage to flow from the reliance, though such an intent will usually be present in practice. If D encourages P to enter into a contract to buy goods from X, by deliberately lying about X's ability to complete the transaction, D will be liable to P for any loss that results, even though D was genuinely optimistic about X acquiring the ability to comply with the contract at some point between the date of contract and the time for performance. An honest aspiration that everything would turn out all right for P will not excuse D for deliberately supplying false information.

Actual Reliance

Actual reliance by the plaintiff provides the causal link between the defendant's wrongful conduct, in providing a fraudulent representation, and the harm ultimately suffered. By its nature, reliance is something that is not normally susceptible to proof by direct evidence – it is not a physical thing that can be produced and people often act on foot of representations without expressly acknowledging the connection between the representation and their conduct. Thus, it will often have to be inferred from the circumstances. Reliance will be readily inferred if the representation was one that would ordinarily induce conduct such as the plaintiff's.[24]

The representation need not be the sole inducement for the defendant's conduct, as the courts accept that a person may have several reasons for entering into a course of conduct and, if any significant factor amongst those reasons is based on fraud, then the plaintiff has good grounds for complaint. The requirement is that the representation must materially influence the plaintiff.[25]

If the plaintiff was not deceived by the representation, through reasons such as knowledge of its falsity or not having received the representation until after

---

23 *Bradford Third Equitable Benefit Building Society v Borders* [1941] 2 All ER 205, per Viscount Maugham at p. 211; see also *Smith v Chadwick* (1884) 9 App Cas 187; [1881–5] All ER Rep 242.

24 *Edgington v Fitzmaurice* 29 Ch D 459 (1885) where Fry LJ, at p. 485, described the finding of inducement as a 'natural inference from the facts'; see also *Gould v Vaggelas* [1985] LRC Comm 497, per Wilson J at pp. 514–18; Brennan J at pp. 526–9.

25 *Edgington v Fitzmaurice* 29 Ch D 459 (1884) per Denman J at p. 466; (1885) per Cotton LJ at p. 481; Bowen LJ at p. 483; *Leyden v Malone* unrep. SC, 13 May 1968, per Walsh J.

engaging in the harmful conduct, then there can clearly be no reliance. Some uncertainty remains, however, where the plaintiff is in fact deceived, but ought not to have been. In *Horsfall v Thomas*[26] it was held that the purchaser of goods could not claim reliance on a representation where a patent defect was in contradiction to the representation. Madden J, dissenting in *Gill v McDowell*,[27] stated that the purchaser of the hermaphrodite animal should have discovered the defect on examination of the animal and, consequently, could not claim reliance on any misrepresentation as to the gender of the animal. Palles CB, in *Phelps v White*,[28] however, stated that the fact that the plaintiff had reasonable means of discovering the untruth of the representation would not defeat his claim for compensation. These apparently conflicting views may be reconciled on the basis that mere negligence on the plaintiff's part, in failing to discover the untruth, should not defeat the cause of action, but recklessness or wilful disregard of the truth should. In the case of negligence on the plaintiff's part, the partial defence of contributory negligence would probably be available to the defendant, though the courts would be unlikely to attribute a significant portion of responsibility to the plaintiff in such a case.[29]

Damage

If no damage results from the plaintiff's reliance on the fraudulent misrepresentation, then no action in deceit will be available. Any affront to the plaintiff's dignity caused by the deception, or embarrassment caused by the exposure of his gullibility, is an insufficient harm to base an action on. There must be some material harm to the plaintiff to ground an action for damages and this damage will usually, though not necessarily, involve economic loss. Most cases of deceit involve the inducement of commercial transactions on the basis that they will be economically viable when, in fact, they are known to be at least doubtful.

Personal injury or property damage, resulting from a deception, will also be actionable. *Wilkinson v Downton*[30] and *Janvier v Sweeney*[31] both involved psychological damage, resulting from false statements made to the plaintiffs. The plaintiff in *Wilkinson* was deceived by a practical joke in which she was informed that her husband was seriously injured in an incident some distance away. In *Janvier*, the plaintiff was deceived by a private investigator, who misrepresented

---

26 (1862) 1 H & C 90; 158 ER 813.

27 [1903] 2 IR 463, at p. 471.

28 (1881) 7 LR Ir 160, at p. 164; see also *Dobell v Stevens* (1825) 3 B & C 623 and *S. Pearson & Son Ltd v Dublin Corporation* [1907] AC 351; [1904–7] All ER Rep 255.

29 McMahon & Binchy, *The Irish Law of Torts*, 2nd ed. (Dublin: Butterworths, 1989), at p. 670, suggest that the courts might even refuse to allow the defence at all, on public policy grounds.

30 [1897] 2 QB 57; [1895–9] All ER Rep 267.

31 [1919] 2 KB 316; [1918–19] All ER Rep 1056, both of these cases are considered further in chapter 10 *infra*.

himself as a policeman and threatened criminal proceedings against her if she did not supply him with information on another matter. These cases may be explained as examples of deceit leading to personal injury, though Wright J doubted this in *Wilkinson*, as the psychological harm did not result from reliance on the misrepresentation.[32] Street also argues that the cases are not examples of deceit, as the harm resulted directly from the misrepresentations and not as a result of any reliance on them by the plaintiffs.[33] However, since the purpose of reliance is to establish a causal link between the deception and the damage, and the plaintiffs' belief in the truth of the representations would serve the same purpose, the cases could be considered as unusual examples of deceit. Clearer examples of personal injury and property damage sounding in deceit include *Langridge v Levy*,[34] where the defendant had misrepresented the safety of a gun which exploded and injured the plaintiff, and *Mullett v Mason*,[35] where a misrepresentation as to the health of a cow resulted in five other cows contracting disease.

In America, deceit has been employed in a number of cases involving sexual intercourse, where consent to intercourse was obtained by fraudulent misrepresentation as to the representor's health or physical condition.[36]

Injurious Falsehood

This tort emerged from actions for slander of title and slander of goods, which involved losses caused by misstatements doubting the plaintiff's rights over land and goods respectively. The tort has grown to cover a much broader class of misrepresentations to third parties, concerning the plaintiff, causing pecuniary loss to the plaintiff. The tort is distinct from defamation, in that the misrepresentation need not reflect on the plaintiff's character. Thus, for example, an allegation that a person has ceased trading in a particular line of business may carry no adverse implications in respect of that person's character, but could cause potential customers to go elsewhere to conduct business. Such an allegation could form the basis of an action for injurious falsehood, though defamation

---

32 [1897] 2 QB 57; [1895–9] All ER Rep 267, at p. 58; p. 269.
33 Brazier, *Street on Torts*, 9th ed. (London: Butterworths, 1993), at p. 120.
34 (1838) 4 M & W 337; an analogous statutory provision is s. 17(3) of the Consumer Information Act 1978 which authorises a court, after convicting a person for an offence under the Act, to order compensation to be paid to a witness for personal injury, loss or damage resulting from the offence.
35 (1866) LR 1 CP 559.
36 *Barbara A v John G* (1983) 145 Cal App 3d 369; 198 Cal Rptr 422, false representation as to the defendant's sterility, resulting in an ectopic pregnancy, leading to sterility in the plaintiff; *Maharam v Maharam* (1986) 123 AD 2d 165; 510 NYS 2d 104, transmission of genital herpes; *Doe v Doe* (1987) 136 Misc 2d 1015; 519 NYS 2d 595, action for exposure to HIV failed, but only because the plaintiff had not contracted the virus and, therefore, suffered no damage. It was accepted, in principle, that an action would lie if the virus had been contracted.

would be unavailable.[37] There may, of course, be cases where a misrepresentation will give rise to both defamation and injurious falsehood, but the two torts have been recognised as distinct in this jurisdiction since the middle of the nineteenth century.[38] The seminal statement of the nature of the tort is that of the English Court of Appeal in *Ratcliffe v Evans*,[39] delivered by Bowen LJ:

> That an action will lie for written or oral falsehoods, not actionable per se nor even defamatory, where they are maliciously published, where they are calculated in the ordinary course of things to produce, and where they do produce, actual damage, is established law. Such an action is not one of libel or of slander, but an action on the case for damage wilfully and intentionally done without just occasion or excuse, analogous to an action for slander of title.

The *Restatement, Second, Torts* describes the tort in different terms, but to much the same effect:

> §623A. Liability for Publication of Injurious Falsehood
>
> General Principle
> One who publishes a false statement harmful to the interests of another is subject to liability for pecuniary loss resulting to the other if
> (a) he intends for publication of the statement to result in harm to the interests of the other having a pecuniary value, or either recognizes or should recognize that it is likely to do so, and
> (b) he knows that the statement is false or acts in reckless disregard of its truth or falsity.

Requisite elements:

1. Publication of an untrue representation
2. Malicious intent
3. Pecuniary damage

Publication

As with defamation, the representation made by the defendant must be to a person other than the plaintiff and not under the protection of privilege.[40] The

---

37 *Ratcliffe v Evans* [1892] 2 QB 524; [1891–4] All ER Rep 699; *Irish Toys & Utilities Ltd v The Irish Times Ltd* [1937] IR 298. In the latter case the action failed on the facts, as other essential ingredients had not been proved. See the illustrations in the *Restatement, Second, Torts* §623A for further examples of injurious falsehood.

38 *M'Nally v Oldham* (1863) 16 Ir CLR 298, per Lefroy CJ at p. 310, *obiter*; applied in *Jones v McGovern* (1867) IR 1 CL 100; see also *Joyce v Sengupta* [1993] 1 WLR 337; [1993] 1 All ER 897, per Sir Donald Nicholls VC at p. 341; p. 901 for further discussion of the distinction between the two torts.

39 [1892] 2 QB 524; [1891–4] All ER Rep 699, at pp. 527–8; p. 702.

40 The principles discussed in chapter 8 *infra*, as to what constitutes publication, are applicable here; see also *Restatement, Second, Torts* §§630 and 631. There is a lack

previous discussion of what constitutes a representation for the purposes of deceit is instructive as to the type of statements or other indications that are actionable.

Distinguishing between legitimate competitive practices and unlawful misleading of others can be difficult. In the law of contract this issue is addressed in the distinction between offers and invitations to treat; in deceit the intent to induce reliance is the crucial factor in determining whether the defendant was engaged in commercial bluster or unlawful deception; in injurious falsehood the likelihood of reliance is also the crucial feature in drawing the line. The decision in *De Beers Abrasive Products Ltd v International General Electric Company of New York Ltd*[41] is instructive.

The two companies were rival manufacturers of abrasive products, used for cutting concrete. The plaintiff's abrasive incorporated a natural diamond dust to provide its cutting edge, while the defendant used a synthetic diamond dust. The defendant company produced a pamphlet for potential customers, claiming that scientific tests proved that their product was superior to the plaintiff's. Walton J acknowledged that advertising puffs used by traders necessarily denigrate competitors to an extent, but that this was not actionable in itself, as traders have a right to promote their own business. However, specific claims or serious statements that customers can be expected to believe would qualify as representations on which an action could be based. The appropriate test is 'whether a reasonable man would take the claim being made as being a serious claim or not'.[42] This uses the reasonable recipient as the gauge of competitors' claims about the relative merits of their goods or services. Walton J was satisfied that the claim of scientific evidence was sufficiently specific and serious to form the basis of an action.[43]

Malice

The mere fact that a representation is untrue is not sufficient to establish any breach of obligation by the defendant. There must be fraud, in the sense used in deceit, with respect to the falsehood of the statement; mere carelessness will not suffice.[44] In *Ratcliffe* the Court of Appeal indicated a further requirement, that the defendant's conduct must be 'calculated' to produce harm or 'wilfully

---

of case law on the issue of privilege, but a useful discussion can be found in the *Restatement, Second, Torts* §635 and §§646A–650A.

41 [1975] 2 All ER 599.
42 *Ibid.*, at pp. 604–5.
43 *Ibid.*, at p. 608.
44 *Balden v Shorter* [1933] Ch 427; [1933] All ER Rep 249, per Maugham J at p. 430; p. 250; *Loudon v Ryder (No. 2)* [1953] Ch 423; [1953] 2 WLR 863; [1953] 1 All ER 1005, per Harman J at pp. 427–8; pp. 866–7; pp. 1007–8; *Irish Toys & Utilities Ltd v The Irish Times Ltd* [1937] IR 298, per Maguire P, citing *Ratcliffe* and *Balden*; *Joyce v Sengupta* [1993] 1 WLR 337; [1993] 1 All ER 897, per Sir Donald Nicholls VC at p. 345; p. 905.

... done without just occasion or excuse'. Thus, in addition to fraud with respect to the truth of the statement, *Ratcliffe* seems to require an intention to cause harm to the plaintiff through the falsehood. §623A of the *Restatement, Second, Torts* indicates that negligence with respect to the injurious consequences will suffice, but the authorities, and the authors of the leading textbooks, in other jurisdictions indicate that 'malice' is required.[45] An element of bad faith is required in order to show malice, at least where the representation is made for the protection of the defendant's own rights.[46]

There is no doubt that in many cases there will be difficulty in drawing the line between legitimate competition and unlawful interference with competitors' interests and in determining the extent of proprietary interests in land and goods. Thus, in cases where falsehoods are employed to provide a competitive edge or to bolster a claim to property, it seems fair that a defendant should only be in breach of the obligation imposed by injurious falsehood where there is bad faith. Minor untruths, used to provide oneself with some personal advantage, are a part of everyday life and, while one may raise moral objections to such practices, the case for legal proscription is unconvincing. Carelessness with respect to harmful consequences is probably best considered as a breach of obligation only in cases of special relationships giving rise to a duty of care in the tort of negligence.

Pecuniary Damage

The tort of injurious falsehood is designed to protect against interference with economic, rather than personal or proprietary interests. At common law the plaintiff had to plead and prove special damage in order to succeed, though a general loss of business was sufficiently specific in circumstances where identification of specific customers or transactions would not be possible, as in the case of auctions, pubs, restaurants, shops etc.[47] Section 20 of the Defamation Act 1961 provides that this is no longer necessary where the representation is 'calculated to cause pecuniary damage to the plaintiff' and is contained in permanent form, or relates to 'any office, profession, calling, trade or business' of the plaintiff's at the time of publication. The level of damages awarded will

---

45 *Loudon v Ryder (No. 2)* [1953] Ch 423; [1953] 2 WLR 863; [1953] 1 All ER 1005; *Spring v Guardian Assurance* [1995] 2 AC 296; [1994] 3 WLR 354; [1994] 3 All ER 129; *Manitoba Free Press Co. v Nagy* (1907) 39 SCR 340; Street, *op. cit.* at pp. 138–9; Brazier (ed.), *Clerk & Lindsell on Torts*, 17th ed. (London: Sweet & Maxwell, 1989) at §§22.13–22.16; Fridman, *The Law of Torts in Canada*, (Toronto: Carswell, 1989), vol. 2, at pp. 215–7.

46 *Halsey v Brotherhood* (1881) 19 Ch D 386, per Lord Coleridge LCJ at p. 388.

47 *Ratcliffe v Evans* [1892] 2 QB 524; [1891–4] All ER Rep 699, at p. 533; *Roche v Meyler* [1896] 2 IR 35, where the plaintiff was only required to furnish 'the best particulars she could give' with respect to interference with a sale by auction, where absent bidders could not be specifically identified; see also Clark & Smyth, *Intellectual Property Law in Ireland* (Dublin: Butterworths, 1997), at §24.50.

still depend, to some extent, on an ability to establish a loss flowing from the wrong, but the absence of such proof will not entirely preclude an action.

Cases not covered by the section are likely to be few, but would include representations in transient form, relating to a business that the plaintiff had not yet started; or relating to an activity, other than a business, of some financial value, such as selling an exclusive story to a newspaper, or perhaps even a person's marital prospects.

Where the plaintiff does seek to prove damage, causation will have to be shown through reliance and the prior discussion of this issue in respect of deceit will also be relevant to injurious falsehood. Finally, it seems that other types of loss, such as injured feelings or anxiety, cannot be claimed, even in a parasitic fashion (as an adjunct to pecuniary harm).

Passing Off

The tort of passing off is a specialised variation of injurious falsehood, whereby the customer is misled as to the origin of goods or services, causing damage to the plaintiff's business.[48] The significant difference is that passing off does not now require fraud on the defendant's part. In its original form it was concerned with the misappropriation of trade names and marks – i.e. blatant imitation, cashing in on the success of another trader by deceiving customers and pilfering a portion of the other trader's place in the market. It has developed to include a wide range of deceptive activities involving 'the adoption by the defendant of some element in the manner in which the plaintiff's goods [or services] are marketed',[49] where that element carries, in customers' minds, an important association with the plaintiff's business.

The core aspects of the tort are threefold: first, the plaintiff must have a commercial reputation associated with the particular aspect of marketing in question; secondly, the defendant must make a misrepresentation to customers through use of the plaintiff's reputation; and, thirdly, the misleading of customers must cause an adverse impact on the plaintiff's business.[50] Where the plaintiff seeks to preempt harm, by way of a *quia timet* injunction, then a likelihood of damage will suffice. Each element has a range of interpretations, linked to the variety of factual situations embraced by the tort, and a more detailed description is provided by Lord Diplock in *Erven Warnink BV v J. Townend & Sons (Hull) Ltd:*[51]

---

48 Heuston & Buckley, *Salmond & Heuston on the Law of Torts*, 21st ed. (London: Sweet & Maxwell, 1996) still include passing off as a sub-set of injurious falsehood, §§18.10 *et seq.*

49 *Player & Wills (Ireland) Ltd v Gallaher (Dublin) Ltd* unrep. HC, 26 September 1983, per Barron J at p. 1 of his judgment.

50 This threefold division is adopted by Drysdale & Silverleaf, *Passing Off: Law and Practice*, 2nd ed. (London: Butterworths, 1995); see also Healy, 'The Tort of Passing Off Part I'(1997) 15 ILT 196; Clark & Smyth, *op. cit.* at §§24.01–24.48.

51 [1979] AC 731; [1979] 3 WLR 68; [1979] 2 All ER 927.

[The] cases make it possible to identify five characteristics which must be present in order to create a valid cause of action for passing off: (1) a misrepresentation (2) made by a trader in the course of trade, (3) to prospective customers of his or ultimate consumers of goods or services supplied by him, (4) which is calculated to injure the business or goodwill of another trader (in the sense that this is a reasonably foreseeable consequence) and (5) which causes actual damage to a business or goodwill of the trader by whom the action is brought or (in a quia timet action) will probably do so.[52]

Lord Diplock qualified this outline of the tort by adding: 'It does not follow that because all passing off actions can be shown to present these characteristics, all factual situations which present these characteristics give rise to a cause of action for passing off.'[53] 'Puffing' in advertising was cited as an example of conduct that might fit the characteristics, but not be actionable. More generally, Lord Diplock indicated that general policy considerations, such as competition and honesty in commercial dealings, would be relevant in determining the parameters of the tort.

This outline of the tort, including the qualification, was adopted by McCracken J in *B & S Ltd v Irish Auto Trader Ltd.*[54] Given that this description of elements is more reflective of the full range of cases covered by the tort than the threefold division into reputation, misrepresentation and damage, it will be followed here to chart the landscape of passing off.

A necessary note of caution needs to be sounded at this point, before embarking on a detailed consideration of the elements. Many cases of alleged passing off are initiated by way of an application for an interlocutory injunction, requiring the applicant to show an arguable case that the elements of the tort exist and that the balance of convenience favours the granting of the injunction, as a temporary measure until full trial of the dispute.[55] In practice, the granting or refusal of the interlocutory injunction will often put an end to the matter, with the parties declining to pursue the dispute. There are a number of reasons for this. If an interlocutory injunction is granted, the defendant will be forced to find an alternative marketing strategy to the one that the plaintiff has objected to, or withdraw from the market; if the defendant incurs expense and effort in embarking on an alternative strategy, a return to the disputed strategy, via an uncertain legal battle, may not be a desirable commercial strategy. If, on the other hand, the interlocutory injunction is denied, the intervening period of time before the trial date may serve to demonstrate an absence of any detrimental effect on the plaintiff's business. Another possibility is that the interlocutory stage may serve to clarify some aspects of the case, giving the parties a better

---

52 *Ibid.*, at p. 742; pp. 74–5; pp. 932–3.
53 *Ibid.*, at p. 742; p. 75; p. 933.
54 [1995] 2 ILRM 152, at p. 155.
55 Injunctions are considered in more detail in chapter 15 *infra*.

idea of the likely outcome of a trial. Whatever the reason, the result is that many of the cases of alleged passing off do not get past the interlocutory stage and, in consequence, the decisions in such cases must be treated with caution. They may provide some guidance as to the scope of the tort, but they do not necessarily provide definitive answers to the disputed issues.

Requisite elements:

1. Misrepresentation
2. By a trader in the course of trade
3. To customers or ultimate consumers
4. Calculated to injure
5. Damage/likelihood of damage
6. Policy considerations

Misrepresentation

The general thrust of the misrepresentation requirement is that the defendant uses some aspect of the plaintiff's business in a manner which confuses the public into thinking that the defendant's goods or services are the plaintiff's or are associated in some way with the plaintiff. This involves three issues – the adoption of an element; the plaintiff's reputation with respect to that element; and the confusion generated by the adoption. Much of the ground originally embraced by passing off has been enveloped in the statutory provisions governing intellectual property, such as copyright, patents and trade marks. The tort of passing off, nonetheless, retains an important place in providing protection to business interests against the luring away of customers by deception.

There are a wide variety of ways in which the misrepresentation can occur in the tort of passing off; those listed below are not intended to provide a comprehensive list, but rather to show the principal ways in which attributes of one business can be used so as to generate confusion in the minds of customers.[56] The focus here is on the adoption of an element of the plaintiff's business; reputation and deception will be considered in further detail when the other elements of the tort are considered.

Names

The name of a business, product or service will usually serve as a point of distinction between it and its competitors. The law on registration of trade marks (which may include product names) provides extensive protection to

---

56 See McDonald, *Hotel, Restaurant and Public House Law* (Dublin: Butterworths, 1992) at §§19.17–19.66 for consideration of the range of ways in which distinctiveness can be established and interfered with in the field of business indicated in the title. The implications for the full panorama of commercial activity are that the possibilities are virtually infinite.

the registered owner.[57] Names not constituting registered trade marks can also develop a specific association with the plaintiff and may be protected against passing off.[58]

Business names may easily be used to misrepresent the defendant's business as the plaintiff's, as occurred in *C & A Modes v C & A (Waterford) Ltd*[59] and *Muckross Park Hotel Ltd v Randles*[60] (where the defendant was using the name 'Muckross Court Hotel'). The absence of any legitimate reason for the similarity in name will be highly influential. In the *C & A* case the letters bore no connection to the names of the individuals involved in the defendant company, while in the *Muckross* case the defendant's hotel was outside of the area known by that place name.[61] Similarly, the name of a product or service may generate a public association with the plaintiff, even where it is essentially a generic description of the product or service. In *An Post v Irish Permanent plc*[62] the plaintiffs were granted an interlocutory injunction, precluding the defendants from using the term 'savings certificates' to describe a financial product, as the evidence produced established a sufficient public association between the name and the plaintiffs' state guaranteed product. However, it is not easy to establish distinctiveness in respect of descriptive names and the plaintiff will have to produce some convincing evidence of a particular association in the mind of the buying public between the name and the plaintiff's business.[63] Conversely, esoteric names are more easily associated with a specific business, though the passage of time may transform an esoteric name into a generic description.[64]

A misrepresentation as to the origin of goods need not involve an allegation that the plaintiff was the producer of the goods, although such allegations form

---

57 See Clark & Smyth, *op. cit.* and Forde, *Commercial Law*, 2nd ed. (Dublin: Butterworths, 1997) at chapter 7, for detailed consideration of statutory measures for the protection of intellectual property.

58 See Drysdale & Silverleaf, *op. cit.* at §§3.17–3.40 for detailed consideration of names and words as distinctive features of a business, product or service.

59 [1976] IR 198.

60 [1995] 1 IR 130, the name 'Muckross' was held to have acquired a secondary meaning, referring to the plaintiff hotel, at p. 138 per Barron J, though this was not essential for the action to succeed, at p. 139; see also *Falcon Travel Ltd v Owners Abroad Group plc t/a Falcon Leisure Group* [1991] 1 IR 175.

61 Even where the name is the actual name of a director of the defendant company, it may be actionable if the name is deliberately employed in order to feign an association with the plaintiff; see *O'Neills Irish International Sports Co. Ltd v O'Neills Footwear Dryer Co. Ltd* unrep. HC, 30 April 1997; *Jameson v Dublin Distillers Co. Ltd* [1900] 1 IR 43.

62 [1995] 1 IR 140; [1995] 1 ILRM 336.

63 *Office Cleaning Services Ltd v Westminster Office Cleaning Association* (1946) 63 RPC 39, where the House of Lords refused to find a secondary significance in the words 'office cleaning' linking it to the plaintiff company.

64 There is a lack of case law directly in point, but the proposition is generally supported in the leading textbooks, see Street, *op. cit.* at p. 128 in particular.

the traditional core of the tort. In *J. Bollinger v Costa Brava Wine Co. Ltd (No. 2)*[65] the use of the term 'champagne' in respect of sparkling wine from Spain was held to constitute a misrepresentation relating to the place of origin, actionable at the suit of a number of producers from the Champagne region of France. The defendants, not having any connection with the region, were held to be falsely representing themselves as having an association with the area.

Misrepresentation as to the quality or significance attached to a name may be actionable, even though customers may not be deceived as to the source of the product in question. The *Warnink* decision provides a classic example. The plaintiffs were Dutch manufacturers of a drink, composed of a mixture of egg, spirits and wine, known as 'advocaat'. The defendants were English manufacturers of a drink composed of egg and fortified wine, originally marketed as 'egg flip', but subsequently marketed as 'Keeling's Old English Advocaat'.

The House of Lords held that, although there was no likelihood of deception as to the source of the goods, consumers could be misled as to the nature of the species of drink connoted by the term 'advocaat' and that such a misrepresentation could be a sufficient basis for an action in passing off. Similarly, in *Tattinger v Allbev Ltd*[66] the use of the name 'Elderflower Champagne' for a non-alcoholic sparkling wine was held to misrepresent the degree of quality associated with the term 'champagne'.

Packaging

The manner in which goods and services are presented can be as much a part of their identity as their names. Thus, a defendant's product may be deceptively similar to the plaintiff's, despite having an entirely different name. Similarities in matters such as the colour, dimensions, design and materials used in packaging a product may mislead customers into thinking that the defendant's product is, in fact, the plaintiff's product.[67] Again, there is a degree of overlap between statutory trade mark protection (and copyright) and passing off, but each also has applications that the other does not.[68]

---

65 [1961] 1 WLR 277; [1961] 1 All ER 561; see also the preliminary ruling [1960] Ch 262; [1959] 3 WLR 966; [1959] 3 All ER 800; *John Walker & Sons Ltd v Henry Ost & Co. Ltd* [1970] 1 WLR 917; [1970] 2 All ER 106 (Scotch whisky).

66 [1994] 4 All ER 75.

67 *Polycell Products Ltd v O'Carroll* [1959] Ir Jur Rep 34; *Michelstown Co-operative Agricultural Society Ltd v Golden Vale Food Products Ltd* unrep. HC, 12 December 1985, interlocutory injunctions were granted in both instances; see also Drysdale & Silverleaf, *op. cit.* at §§3.43–3.49.

68 For example, in *Coca-Cola v A.G. Barr & Co.* [1961] RPC 387 the shape of the plaintiff's bottle was held entitled to protection in passing off against use by another trader, while in *Re Coca-Cola* [1986] 1 WLR 695; [1986] 1 All ER 274; [1986] RPC 421, the shape of the bottle was refused registration as a trade mark.

Reckitt & Colman Products Ltd v Borden Inc.[69] provides a graphic example. The plaintiff company marketed 'Jif' lemon juice in a lemon shaped container for a number of years and an attempt by the defendant to market lemon juice in a similar container was held, by the House of Lords, to constitute a sufficient misrepresentation to ground an action for passing off. This was so despite the fact that the container was not an exact copy and the labelling of the defendant's product was quite distinctive.

As with names, a misrepresentation of an association with the plaintiff will suffice; it is not necessary to establish a misrepresentation as to the source of the product. Thus, in *Coca-Cola Co. v Gemini Rising Inc.*[70] the use of the plaintiff's distinctive script on T-shirts bearing the legend 'enjoy cocaine', mimicking the plaintiff's 'enjoy Coca-Cola' advertisements, was held to involve a sufficient misrepresentation. Similarly, in *Dallas Cowboys Cheerleaders Inc. v Pussycat Cinema Ltd*[71] the use of the plaintiff's uniform in a pornographic film was held to involve a sufficient misrepresentation.

Design

Some goods, particularly clothing, are sold without packaging. In relation to such goods, the design or appearance of the item itself may be adopted in a manner which amounts to a misrepresentation. As with packaging and descriptive names, the courts will not be easily convinced of the existence of a misrepresentation. In *Adidas Sportschuhfabriken Adi Dassler KA v Charles O'Neill & Co. Ltd*[72] both the High Court and the Supreme Court held that the use of three stripes on sports gear by the defendants amounted to no more than the adoption of a fashion trend. This conclusion was, however, based on the fact that the plaintiff did not have a significant reputation in Ireland at the time, while the defendant was a well established business in the sports gear market and there was little likelihood of confusion. A significant likelihood of confusion will increase the likelihood that a court will regard the similarity of design as a misrepresentation.[73]

Advertising

Even advertising techniques may be capable of giving rise to a sufficient misrepresentation on which an action may be based, provided the advertisements generate a sufficient association with the plaintiff to make them distinc-

---

69 [1990] 1 All ER 873; [1990] RPC 341.
70 (1972) 346 F Supp 1183.
71 (1979) 604 F 2d 200; 46 F Supp 366.
72 [1983] ILRM 112.
73 See *Gabicci plc v Dunnes Stores Ltd* unrep. HC, 31 July 1991, discussed in Byrne & Binchy, *Annual Review of Irish Law 1992* at pp. 39–40, where an interlocutory injunction was granted in respect of the sale of sweaters identical to the plaintiff's design.

tive of the plaintiff's products or services. The point was made, *obiter*, in *Cadbury-Schweppes Pty Ltd v Pub Squash Co. Pty Ltd*,[74] a case concerning the cultivation of a macho image for soft drinks on the Australian market. The action failed, however, on the grounds that the products were clearly distinguishable; thus there was no likelihood of confusion, so there could be no effective misrepresentation as to the source of the goods.

Associated Newspapers plc v Insert Media Ltd[75] provides an unusual example of how advertising can be used to mislead the public. Here the defendant produced a regional advertising leaflet and inserted copies in the plaintiff's newspapers prior to sale in the region, without the plaintiff's consent. The implication that the leaflet had the imprimatur of the plaintiff would affect the success of the advertising, which would, in turn, affect the defendant's ability to sell advertising space profitably. This implication was held to constitute a sufficient misrepresentation.

Merchandising

Modern commercial practice now widely engages the use of famous images in the sale of products; famous personalities, such as sports stars, actors and actresses, are used to advertise products; spin-off products are regularly sold on foot of the fame of recording artists and films, such as T-shirts emblazoned with tour dates and pictures from album covers, toy models of characters from films and so forth. English authorities in the 1970s generally resisted allegations that the exploitation of the fame of characters (real or fictional) and use of images implied that the defendant was authorised to do so.[76] Recent cases around the world show a greater judicial recognition of the fact that unauthorised use of another person's famous character, or other image, may involve a misrepresentation as to a connection.[77]

In the Course of Trade

Passing off is concerned with particular types of unfair trading; consequently, the misrepresentation must occur within a commercial context, in order to come within the scope of the tort. The interpretation of what constitutes a

---

74 [1981] 1 WLR 193; [1981] 1 All ER 213, at p. 200; p. 218 per Lord Scarman (delivering the advice of the Privy Council); see also *Masson Seely & Co. Ltd v Embossotype Manufacturing Co.* (1924) 41 RPC 160 (copying of sales catalogue was restrained).
75 [1991] 1 WLR 571; [1991] 3 All ER 535.
76 *Tavener Rutledge Ltd v Trexapalm* [1975] FSR 479; [1977] RPC 275; *Wombles Ltd v Wombles Skips Ltd* [1975] FSR 488; *Lyngstad v Anabas Products Ltd* [1977] FSR 62.
77 See Carty, 'Character Merchandising and the Limits of Passing Off' (1993) 13 LS 289; Drysdale & Silverleaf, *op. cit.* at §§3.53–3.55.

'trader' and what is to be regarded as being 'in the course of trade', for the purposes of Lord Diplock's definition, is reasonably broad. Retailers, for example, may be liable, where they are the source of the misrepresentation. In *Gillette Safety Razor Co. v Franks*[78] an injunction was granted against the defendant, precluding the sale of used Gillette razor blades under an inference that they were new. The tort also extends, however, to activities that might not appear, at first sight, to involve traders. A trade association, representing the interests of its members, but not itself engaged in trade, may be entitled to maintain an action against a trader who falsely represents a link with the association.[79] Similarly, the High Court in England has accepted that the fund raising activities of charitable organisations are sufficiently akin to trade to come within the scope of the tort.[80] Political parties have been refused protection in England[81] and Canada,[82] showing that there are limits to the degree of judicial latitude that will be given to the interpretation of the trade requirement.

To Customers or Ultimate Consumers

The misrepresentation must be made to some class of persons in the chain of purchase and consumption of the goods or services in question. It may be the immediate purchaser that is misled, such as a distributor or retailer purchasing goods from a manufacturer, but in most cases it will be a subsequent purchaser that is misled. Thus, a manufacturer producing goods deceptively similar to the plaintiff's will be held responsible for losses resulting to the plaintiff through the deception of the buying public, even though the goods were not sold directly by the manufacturer to the public, but were sold through an intermediate trader.

The essence of the complaint is that potential trade is lost to the plaintiff because the defendant's customers, or ultimate consumers of the defendant's product or service, were potential customers or consumers of the plaintiff's product or service. Difficulties can arise when the defendant and plaintiff are not engaged in the same line of business. In such cases an action is not necessarily precluded, but it is more difficult for the plaintiff to show how a representation to the defendant's customers or consumers can mislead them in a manner detrimental to the plaintiff. This issue will be considered in more detail below. Furthermore, it may be difficult to establish a claim where the

---

78 (1924) 40 TLR 606; see also McDonald, *op. cit.* at § 19.3.
79 *An Bord Tráchtála v Waterford Foods plc* unrep. HC, 25 November 1992, the plaintiff trade board failed to prove the necessary facts in order to succeed, but Keane J accepted, in principle, that such an organisation could maintain an action; see also *ILSI v Carroll* [1995] 3 IR 145; [1996] 2 ILRM 95.
80 *British Diabetic Association v Diabetic Society Ltd* [1995] 4 All ER 812.
81 *Kean v McGivan* [1982] FSR 119 in respect of the title 'Social Democrat Party'.
82 *Polsinelli v Marzilli* (1987) 61 OR (2d) 799 in respect of the term 'liberal' by a person who was not a member of the Liberal Party of Canada.

goods or services are supplied in a non-commercial context, such as a charitable donation by a commercial entity.[83]

Calculated to Injure

The term 'calculated' in Lord Diplock's formulation is somewhat misleading, as it may give the impression that fraud or intent must be shown. The meaning of the phrase, as elaborated by Lord Diplock, shows that the requirement is somewhat less, involving a reasonably foreseeable prospect of adverse impact on the plaintiff. The way in which this is ordinarily measured is the likelihood of confusion or deception of customers or consumers. This is, in turn, dependent on the plaintiff having a commercial reputation to which the confusion will attach. If the plaintiff has no commercial reputation, there is nothing to confuse the customer in respect of, and nothing to be damaged.

Reputation

Passing off is concerned with misappropriation of some attribute of another business to unfairly gain a commercial advantage. In order to succeed the plaintiff must establish that the attribute in question is publicly associated with the plaintiff; the tort does not extend to misconduct which precludes a plaintiff from gaining a reputation. Thus, in *Serville v Constance*[84] the plaintiff failed in a passing off action in respect of the defendant's false use of the title 'welter-weight champion of Trinidad', because the plaintiff had no reputation in Britain under that title, having just arrived. Even though the plaintiff was the legitimate title holder, since the defendant had been using the title in Britain for some time prior to the plaintiff's arrival, any public association with the title would have been with the defendant. The result was that the loss of business caused to the plaintiff by the inability to commercially exploit his title was not covered by passing off; injurious falsehood might have been more appropriate, but was apparently not pleaded.

Problems may arise where the plaintiff's reputation is in a different field of activity from the defendant. There is no principled exclusion of actions where the parties are engaged in disparate fields of activity, but it does become more difficult for the plaintiff to establish a likelihood of confusion and consequent

---

83 *Charles O'Neill & Co. Ltd v Adidas Sportschuhfabriken* unrep. SC, 25 March 1992 (*ex tempore*); Irish Times Law Report, 17 August 1992; the case was actually concerned with unlawful interference with economic relations, rather than passing off, but it seems doubtful that a passing off action would have been any more successful.

84 [1954] 1 WLR 487; [1954] 1 All ER 662; see also *Taverner Rutledge v Trexapalm Ltd* [1977] RPC 275, where the plaintiff was engaged in unlicensed merchandising of the TV character 'Kojak' in the sale of lollipops (the TV detective was noted for sucking lollipops) and succeeded in restraining a licensed trader from marketing a rival lollipop; see also *Anheuser-Busch Inc. v Budejovicky Budvar Narodni Podnik* [1984] FSR 413.

adverse impact on business or goodwill. The issue is primarily an evidential one and the plaintiff's task is certainly more difficult where the defendant's activities are different from the plaintiff's. This has been particularly evident in relation to character merchandising.[85] Where the plaintiff is already engaged in some forms of merchandising, it will be easier to establish a claim, even if the precise type of merchandising is different in the particular instance.[86] The Australian courts have been more generous to plaintiffs seeking to restrain unlicensed merchandising and have allowed claims where the plaintiff had not yet engaged in any commercial exploitation of characters.[87] Where the plaintiff is unlikely to engage in any activity related to the defendant, successful action is highly unlikely.[88]

The plaintiff's reputation must be within the state, so a plaintiff with a significant international reputation, which has not yet extended to Ireland, will not be able to maintain an action here.[89] However, one does not have to trade within the state to have a commercial reputation here, as may occur in the case of cross-border trade.[90]

Likelihood of Confusion

Proof of actual deception is not essential in passing off; the likelihood of deception will be sufficient to maintain a claim.[91] Even in an action for damages at common law, it is not essential for the plaintiff to produce specific evidence of confusion (for example, by calling as witnesses customers who were misled by

---

85 See Drysdale & Silverleaf, *op. cit.* at §3.55; Carty, 'Character Merchandising', *loc. cit.* at pp. 295–7.

86 *Mirage Studios v Counter Feat Clothing Co. Ltd* [1991] FSR 145 ('Teenage Mutant Ninja Turtles'), the plaintiffs were not directly engaged in merchandising, but were engaged in licensing others to exploit the success of their screen characters and succeeded in restraining the merchandising of a similar character by the defendant.

87 *Henderson v Radio Corp. Pty Ltd* [1969] RPC 218; *Hogan v Koala Dundee Pty Ltd* (1988) 83 ALR 187; *Pacific Dunlop v Hogan* (1989) 87 ALR 14.

88 *Granada Group Ltd v Ford Motor Co. Ltd* [1973] RPC 49, the plaintiff television company failed to obtain an injunction to restrain the use of the name 'Granada' by the defendant for a model of its motor cars.

89 *Adidas v O'Neill* [1983] ILRM 112, the plaintiff had only a small portion of the Irish sporting goods market at the time, which proved influential in the decision to refuse an injunction.

90 *C & A Modes v C & A (Waterford) Ltd* [1976] IR 198, the plaintiff was trading in the UK, but had a considerable reputation in the Republic of Ireland, due to extensive cross-border shopping by Southern residents in the plaintiff's Belfast store; held to be sufficient to support an action in the Republic. See Martin, 'The Dividing Line Between Goodwill and International Reputation' (1995) JBL 70; Carty, 'Passing Off and the Concept of Goodwill' (1995) JBL 139.

91 *An Post v Irish Permanent plc* [1995] 1 IR 140; [1995] 1 ILRM 336, per Kinlen J at p. 150; p. 343; *Muckross Park Hotel v Randles* [1995] 1 IR 130, per Barron J at p. 135.

the defendant). The causal role of confusion, in linking a plaintiff's loss to the defendant's misrepresentation, can be inferred, as a matter of probability, if it can be shown that the defendant's conduct was likely to mislead. Where an injunction is sought, the necessary degree of likelihood will vary, depending on whether the injunction sought is interlocutory or permanent.

The legal test of this likelihood is normally whether a casual customer is likely to be misled; the courts are cognisant of the fact that most consumers do not examine products in meticulous detail before purchasing, so passing off may occur even though careful scrutiny would enable the consumer to discover the distinction. The point is neatly summed up by Peter Gibson LJ in *Tattinger v Allbev Ltd*:[92] 'It is right not to base any test on whether a moron in a hurry would be confused, but it is proper to take into account the ignorant and unwary . . .'

Isolated instances of confusion may be insufficient to ground an action; the level of confusion should be reasonably widespread and should probably have a general tendency to occur.[93] In *Private Research v Brosnan*,[94] McCracken J held that there was insufficient proof of misrepresentation where the plaintiff had shown only some general similarity between the two businesses and that a few customers had erroneously contacted the defendant instead of the plaintiff.

Where the customer or consumer has a degree of expertise, the plaintiff will have to produce stronger evidence of confusion than the test outlined above. It will be necessary to show that even those with expertise would be likely to be confused. This is not really a different legal standard, but merely a recognition of the factual difference in circumstances, arising out of the actual customer profile for the goods or services in question.[95]

Damage

Damage is, ostensibly, an essential ingredient in passing off; however, recent cases have suggested that the threshold of proof is rather low. Actual damage must be shown if the claim is for damages at common law, while a likelihood of

---

92 [1994] 4 All ER 75, at p. 85; see also *Symonds Cider & English Wine Co. Ltd v Showerings (Ireland) Ltd* [1997] 1 ILRM 481, where Laffoy J preferred her own experience as a shopper, rather than market research, in assessing the likelihood of confusion.

93 There is a lack of clear authority on the issue, given the tendency to resolve disputes through the use of interlocutory proceedings.

94 [1996] 1 ILRM 27; see also *B & S Ltd v Irish Auto Trader Ltd* [1995] 2 ILRM 152, slight level of confusion not strong enough grounds for an interlocutory injunction, as the plaintiff would not be significantly prejudiced by refusal of the injunction, at p. 155 per McCracken J.

95 See, for example, *Hodgkinson & Corby Ltd v Wards Mobility Services Ltd* [1994] 1 WLR 1564, health care professionals as purchasers of wheelchair cushions held unlikely to be deceived, as they are particularly careful in making purchasing decisions.

damage is required in applications for injunctions. Traditionally the damage in question is interference with the plaintiff's goodwill; it is the reduction in the attractive force of the plaintiff's business that the law seeks to protect. Thus, misrepresentations that do not have any commercial impact, such as copying the name of another person's house,[96] are not actionable under passing off. It has been held, in the High Court, that damage to goodwill does not necessitate proof of adverse economic consequences; impact on goodwill alone is sufficient. The case in question, *Falcon Travel Ltd v Owners Abroad Group plc*,[97] was a somewhat unusual one.

The plaintiff company was a retail travel agent, operating in Dublin and Wicklow; the defendants were wholesale tour operators, operating in Britain for a number of years under the name 'Falcon Leisure group'. The defendants began to operate in Ireland, by opening an office and launching a special brochure. The plaintiff did not appear to lose any business as a result and, in fact, may have actually gained some customers by being associated with the defendants. The plaintiff, however, sought an injunction to restrain the defendants from using the name 'Falcon'. Murphy J held that there was sufficient damage to the plaintiff's goodwill in that the company's reputation was becoming 'submerged in that of the defendants' and that proof of adverse consequences flowing from that submerging was not necessary.[98] Damages were awarded in lieu of an injunction, as the effect of an injunction would be disproportionately severe on the defendants, who had not acted in bad faith. The measure of damages was based on the cost of advertising the difference between the two businesses.

Cases in other jurisdictions also display a low threshold in respect of damage. In *Tattinger v Allbev*, for example, the likely erosion of the distinctive and exclusive aspect of 'champagne', if used on an inferior product, was held to be sufficient for the granting of an injunction. This goes somewhat further than the earlier drinks cases, such as *Warnink v Townend* and *Bollinger v Costa Brava*, as the defendant's product was not even a competitor with the plaintiff's products, since it was non-alcoholic. The Australian decisions on character merchandising also extend the tort, by allowing claims of interference with prospective business, where the plaintiff has not yet begun exploiting the merchandising potential of his

---

96 *Day v Brownrigg* (1878) 10 Ch D 294.
97 [1991] 1 IR 175.
98 *Ibid.*, at p. 182; the decision is critically analysed by Coughlan, 'The Requirement of Damage in Passing Off' (1991) 9 ILT (ns) 138; see also *O'Neills Irish International Sports Co. Ltd v O'Neills Footwear Dryer Co. Ltd* unrep. HC, 30 April 1997, where the misappropriation of the plaintiff's goodwill was allowing the defendant to make unfair gains, rather than actually harming the plaintiff; *Bristol Conservatories Ltd v Conservatories Custom Built Ltd* [1989] RPC 455; noted by Holyoak (1990) 106 LQR 564, defendant using the plaintiff's brochures to sell the defendant's products.

reputation.[99] Carty has described the effect of these Australian cases as changing the tort to one of 'misappropriation of a trade value'.[100]

Defining the scope of damage will be critical in determining the future direction that this tort will take. A low threshold will greatly expand the role of the tort as a means of protecting commercial repute. Whether the tort should expand or remain within its traditional boundaries is a matter of policy, rather than purely legal principle.

Policy Considerations

Lord Diplock, in *Warnink v Townend*, indicated that the existence of the above elements would not be conclusive in determining whether a particular course of action amounted to passing off; policy considerations would also have to be considered. This would indicate that the role of policy is as an adjunct to be used in cases where all the elements exist, but doubt remains as to the appropriateness of the action. This masks the fact that the very decision as to whether the elements exist may, itself, be influenced by policy considerations. Decisions, such as those in the *Falcon Travel* and *Tattinger* cases, as to the extent of the damage requirement, or the *Bollinger* decision on the ability of a group of producers to protect a collective interest, surely represent policy choices on the scope of the tort. Those decisions all involve extensions of the ambit of the tort, raising fundamental questions as to the scope of protection that should be afforded to commercial entities. Extensions provided by these and other cases have stretched the conceptual boundaries of the tort and make it difficult to state its scope with precision.

There are also cases showing that there are limits to the level of extension that the courts are willing to permit. Cases on the necessity for customer or consumer confusion are the most obvious examples. In *Cadbury-Schweppes*,[101] for example, the plaintiff had expended a considerable amount of money on developing a market for its soft drink, but the defendant was able to exploit this market and obtain the benefit of the plaintiff's marketing, without incurring liability, because the two products were clearly distinguishable. The plaintiff's argument that this form of competitive practice was unfair and, therefore, improper failed to convince the Privy Council. Likewise, cases on lack of confusion, due to disparate fields of activity, show that taking advantage of other peoples' ideas and efforts is not always actionable. One objection to this limitation of passing off is that it discourages investment in the creation of markets or high profile reputation, because the market can be exploited by others and reputation can be

---

99 *Henderson v Radio Corp. Pty Ltd* [1969] RPC 218; *Hogan v Koala Dundee Pty Ltd* (1988) 83 ALR 187; *Pacific Dunlop v Hogan* (1989) 87 ALR 14.

100 'Character Merchandising', *loc. cit.* at p. 303; for further critical appraisal of the expanding conception of damage see Carty, 'Dilution and Passing Off: Cause for Concern' (1996) 112 LQR 632.

101 [1981] 1 WLR 193; [1981] 1 All ER 213.

diluted by use in unconnected fields of activity. Taking the contrary position, it may be argued that the protection of investment is not in itself a sufficient objective to be protected in all circumstances; investment can be as easily ploughed into activities which are dangerous (such as smoking) or frivolous as ones which are beneficial, and so is not necessarily deserving of wide ranging protection. Furthermore, the risk of exploitation by others may simply be regarded as a normal commercial risk, in the absence of legal protection.

There is considerable room for debate on the proper scope of passing off, with a wealth of competing arguments as to the degree of protection that the law should afford to commercial entities in respect of their activities.[102] Important choices remain open to the courts and the legislature, which will determine the extent of protection that is to be provided.

Interference with Economic Relations

Historically, a number of torts, such as intimidation, conspiracy and interference with contractual relations, were employed for the purpose of protecting economic interests. A *dictum* of the House of Lords in 1983, in *Merkur Island Shipping Corp. v Laughton*,[103] stated that these were particular species of a broader generic tort of interference with trade by unlawful means. The case for such a development had been made on a number of occasions, by Lord Denning in particular,[104] and has now been accepted by the Irish Supreme Court also, in *Charles O'Neill & Co. Ltd v Adidas Sportschuhfabriken*.[105] It is too early yet to

---

102 See Terry, 'Unfair Competition and the Misappropriation of a Competitor's Trade Values' (1988) 51 MLR 296, arguing for the development of a more extensive tort, based on misappropriation; Dworkin, 'Passing Off and Unfair Competition: An Opportunity Missed' (1981) 44 MLR 564, a case note on the *Cadbury-Schweppes* decision; Carty, 'Character Merchandising', *loc. cit.* at pp. 302 *et seq.*, outlining options for shaping the future scope of protection; Spence, 'Passing Off and the Misappropriation of Valuable Intangibles' (1996) 112 LQR 472 on the difficulties in determining the scope of a broader tort of misappropriation; Martino, *Trademark Dilution* (Oxford: Clarendon Press, 1996), offers a useful analysis of American developments and their potential influence on this side of the Atlantic; Healy, 'The Tort of Passing Off, Part II' (1997) 15 ILT 218 considers the implications of misappropriation in an Irish and EU context.

103 [1983] 2 AC 570; [1983] 2 WLR 778; [1983] 2 All ER 189, per Lord Diplock at p. 609; p. 788; p. 196.

104 Particularly in *Torquay Hotel Co. Ltd v Cousins* [1969] 2 Ch 106; [1969] 2 WLR 289; [1969] 1 All ER 522; *Hadmor Productions Ltd v Hamilton* [1981] ICR 690; [1981] 3 WLR 139; [1981] 2 All ER 724; for detailed analysis of the development and future potential of the tort, see Carty, 'Intentional Violation of Economic Interests: The Limits of Common Law Liability' (1988) 104 LQR 250; Fridman, 'Interference with Trade or Business' (1993) 1 Tort L Rev 19.

105 Unrep. SC, 25 March 1992 (*ex tempore*); Irish Times Law Report, 17 August 1992; the principle has also been accepted in New Zealand, in *Van Camp Chocolates Ltd v Aulsebrooks Ltd* [1984] 1 NZLR 1.

determine whether this generic tort will replace the specific causes of action previously used in respect of intentional interference or whether its role will be confined to instances falling outside of the ambit of the traditional causes of action. The experience with negligence as a generic tort shows, on the one hand, how rapidly and widely a tort can spread; while the principle in *Rylands v Fletcher*, on the other, demonstrates how a tort may stagnate and remain of marginal use. The outcome depends on the degree of enthusiasm with which this tort is greeted by practitioners arguing cases and the judiciary deciding them.

The precise ambit of this emergent tort is uncertain; the content of the constituent elements is ill-defined, as is the range of defences that may be available. At this point, we can do no more than look at some of the options for resolving these uncertainties.

Requisite elements:

1. Unlawful interference with economic activities
2. Intent to harm
3. Damage[106]

Unlawful Interference

There are two major areas of uncertainty within this first requirement. First, what type of conduct is 'unlawful' for the purposes of this tort? And, secondly, what type of 'economic activities' are to be protected? The answers to these questions will largely determine the range and flexibility of the tort, which will directly impact on its usefulness in practice.

Unlawful

This element encompasses conduct falling within the traditional torts used in this area – intimidation, conspiracy and interference with contractual relations. Other forms of unlawful conduct must also be included; otherwise the generic tort would be redundant, amounting to no more than the sum of the traditional torts. Carty asserts that there are three options open to define the concept of unlawfulness in respect of this tort:

> Policy one – unlawful means are any acts which the defendant is not at liberty to commit;
> Policy two – unlawful means are constituted by any legal wrongs;
> Policy three – unlawful means are only constituted by civil wrongs.[107]

---

106 These elements were laid down in *O'Neill v Adidas*, citing Clerk & Lindsell, 15th ed. at p. 747.

107 'Intentional Violation of Economic Interests', *loc. cit.* at p. 266; see also Clerk & Lindsell, *op. cit.* at §§23.59–23.75 for extensive discussion, highlighting the inconsistency of judicial pronouncements on the meaning of the 'unlawful'

The first offers the greatest degree of latitude to the judiciary, as it would permit them to treat acts, which are not otherwise unlawful, as tortious, on the basis of the intentional adverse impact. This would provide scope for the development of unfair competition, without having to distort the tort of passing off. The negative side of this approach is that it would generate an extremely high level of judicial discretion, leading to continuing uncertainty about the scope of the law.

The second option reduces the level of discretion, but is still very broad. The cases on breach of statutory duty, however, demonstrate that there are a considerable number of legal wrongs which the courts regard as unsuited to the generation of civil liability. The third option is, perhaps, unduly narrow, as there may be some criminal activities which are suitable for consideration as unlawful means of injuring a competitor and do not amount to a civil wrong. Illegal conduct, such as non-payment of tax or social welfare contributions, might be sufficient means, where the object is to gain unfair trade advantage and force a competitor out of the market. The conduct would not be actionable as a breach of statutory duty, as other traders are not within a class of persons intended to benefit from the obligation of others to make such payments; thus, it would not be a civil wrong, but it would present a plausible case for recovery under this emergent tort. This would produce a hybrid between policy two and policy three. The decision in *O'Neill v Adidas*[108] provides no clear guidance on this issue. The defendant company was sponsoring a charity rugby match, but had no suitable jerseys to provide. They purchased forty jerseys, manufactured by the plaintiff, from a retailer and removed the plaintiff's logos, replacing them with the defendant's logo. These were then used for the match.

In the High Court, Blayney J held that this conduct constituted unlawful means, as the conduct was a criminal act in contravention of section 2 of the Merchandise Marks Act 1887 and sections 2 and 4 of the Consumer Information Act 1978. As the other elements of the tort were absent, the action failed, so the finding in respect of unlawful means was *obiter*. The Supreme Court decision accepted Blayney J's statement of the requisite elements of the tort and his findings of fact on the absence of intent; thus, it was not necessary to determine the correctness of his finding of unlawful means of interference.

The Acts were designed for the protection of consumers and so a breach of the provisions could constitute the civil wrong of breach of statutory duty. This action would not be available to competitors, as they fall outside the protected class, but Carty's third policy option only requires that the impugned conduct constitute a civil wrong against someone; it need not be a civil wrong against

---

requirement. Balkin & Davis, *Law of Torts* (Sydney: Butterworths, 1991), argue that the general tort would be better if the focus changed from intentional use of 'unlawful' conduct to 'intentionally and unjustifiably causing loss', at pp. 664 *et seq.*
108 Unrep. HC, 22 June 1988.

the plaintiff. Thus, Blayney J's finding could be embraced by the third option, but he made no attempt to do so in his judgment.

The difficulty with the hybrid basis for defining 'unlawful' would lie in finding an appropriate mechanism for distinguishing between illegal conduct amounting to unlawful means and illegal conduct not constituting sufficiently unlawful means. Clearly the criteria used in respect of breach of statutory duty would not suffice, as it would only cover civil wrongs and it does not address the issue of non-statutory criminal conduct. Perhaps a suitable criterion would be that the illegal conduct should have a substantial connection with economic activities. This would allow for the inclusion of commercially relevant aspects of purely criminal conduct, while excluding others. Similarly, it could serve to exclude minor civil wrongs, tangential to the defendant's interference with the plaintiff.

Economic Interests

The interests protected would clearly include established business activities. The extent to which it will apply to potential economic activities, where expectations or opportunities are disrupted, or economically valuable activities of non-commercial bodies, such as those of charitable organisations or private persons (not acting in the course of a business), is uncertain. Given the broad approach taken to the definition of trading in passing off, it seems reasonable to expect some equivalent latitude in respect of interference with economic relations.

Intent

The defendant must intend to injure the plaintiff's economic interests for the tort to be established,[109] but is intent to be determined objectively or subjectively? Salmond & Heuston suggest that the requirement of intent should be interpreted in a manner similar to that used in trespass – if the unlawful act is intended and the injury is foreseeable, the requirement is satisfied.[110] Carty prefers a more subjective basis, suggesting that it must be shown that the plaintiff was intended as the target of the defendant's conduct.[111] The Supreme Court, in *O'Neill v Adidas*, held that the requirement would not be fulfilled where the defendant's sole intention was to further its own economic interests. This would seem to favour a somewhat subjective interpretation of intention to injure.

---

109 The Supreme Court, in *O'Neill v Adidas*, rejected the plaintiff's argument that reckless or negligent injury to business interests would suffice; see also *Copyright Agency Ltd v Haines* (1982) 40 ALR 264, per McLelland J at p. 275; *McLaren v British Columbia Institute of Technology* (1979) 94 DLR (3d) 411, per Taylor J at p. 416.

110 *Op. cit.* at §16.2; see also Clerk & Lindsell, *op. cit.* at §§23.57–23.58.

111 'Intentional Violation of Economic Interests', *loc. cit.* at pp. 274–7 and p. 280; this approach was also favoured by the High Court of Australia in *Northern Territory of Australia v Mengel* (1995) 69 ALJR 527.

Damage

For this tort to be complete, there must be actual damage. The precise parameters of the requirement are uncertain, as the seminal statements are from *dicta* in cases that did not require a definite answer on the degree of harm the plaintiff would have to show. By its nature, the tort must be confined to economic damage and exclude personal injury and property damage. It may be that the courts will be willing to recognise an abstract form of damage, such as interference with goodwill, as is the case in passing off after the decision in *Falcon Travel*, for the purposes of injunctive relief, at least. Actions for damages will probably require some demonstration of adverse consequences flowing from the interference.

Other Torts

A number of other causes of action are worthy of a brief mention at this point. The traditional nominate economic torts, falling within the genus of intentional interference with economic relations, need to be outlined, to show some of the established forms of unlawful interference.[112] These torts often arise in the context of industrial relations disputes, where their use is subject to significant statutory restrictions, contained in the Industrial Relations Act 1990, detailed consideration of which is beyond the scope of this text.[113] The torts of detinue and conversion, which protect certain interests in chattels, will also be outlined. Finally, breach of confidence will also be outlined; although it is not necessarily a tort, it does display characteristics akin to a tort in some circumstances.

Conspiracy

This tort is concerned with persons deliberately using their combined power to harm the plaintiff. The common law has, historically, been averse to collective conduct as a means of strengthening the position of the individual members. Consequently, the mere existence of a combination is unlawful in some situations, and the line between lawful and unlawful conduct is, perhaps, harder to draw here than in any other area of the law of torts. The law has been clarified and improved by statute in the context of industrial relations, but cases reliant on the common law for their resolution face a considerable degree of uncertainty.

---

112 The action by an employer for loss of services, resulting from injury to employees, is omitted, as it is of marginal significance; for consideration of this tort see McMahon & Binchy, *op. cit.* at pp. 556 *et seq.*; Balkin & Davis, *op. cit.* at pp. 673 *et seq.*; Fridman, *op. cit.* vol. 2 at chapter 5.

113 For detailed consideration see Forde, *Industrial Relations Law* (Dublin: Round Hall Press, 1991) at chapter 6; Kerr, *Trade Union and Industrial Relations Acts of Ireland* (London: Sweet and Maxwell, 1991); *Irish Current Law Statutes Annotated, 1989–1990*; some outline consideration is given to the statutory protection of unions and their officials and members in chapter 13 *infra*.

Combination

Conspiracy requires at least two people to combine deliberately for an agreed purpose. Historically, husband and wife were considered as one person in law and, therefore, incapable of conspiring. McMahon & Binchy express doubts on the propriety of this principle,[114] but the issue is unsettled, as there are still valid public policy considerations for exempting agreements by married couples from this tort, even if husband and wife are treated as separate persons. Where one of the parties is a legal, rather than a natural, person, a conspiracy is still possible, though difficulties may arise if the natural person is the 'controlling mind' of the company.[115] Thus, in the case of a private company under the control of a single individual it may be unrealistic to argue that there was a conspiracy between the company and the controlling individual.

There must be an agreement between the parties[116] and it must be implemented.[117] The parties need not act together or at the same time. The tort is probably complete even if only one party is to actually implement the agreement and the other party has only been involved in planning.

Unlawful Object or Means

To be actionable, a conspiracy must either have an unlawful purpose or involve the use of unlawful means to attain an otherwise lawful objective.[118] Where the object of the conspiracy is itself unlawful, such as an agreement to commit a tort, crime or breach of contract, the availability of the action is relatively uncontentious. The only plausible objection is that a plea of conspiracy may be superfluous where the agreement involved the commission of a tort against the plaintiff and all the conspirators are being sued as concurrent wrongdoers for that tort and for conspiracy.[119]

The fact that it is a tort to use unlawful means to attain a purpose that is not in itself unlawful is also unobjectionable where the conspiracy involves a subjective intention to cause harm, such as a deliberate violation of the plaintiff's constitutional rights.[120] The scope of the tort is, however, ill-defined and

---

114 *Op. cit.* at p. 575; see also *Midland Bank Trust Co. Ltd v Green (No. 3)* [1982] Ch 529; [1981] 2 WLR 1; [1981] 3 All ER 744.
115 See *R. v McDonnell* [1966] 1 QB 233; [1965] 3 WLR 1138; [1966] 1 All ER 193.
116 Conspiracy is defined in terms of agreement between two or more persons; see, for example, *Connolly v Loughney* (1952) 87 ILTR 49; the existence of an agreement may have to be inferred from circumstantial evidence, as direct evidence may be lacking.
117 *Molloy v Gallagher* [1933] IR 1; see also Balkin & Davis, *op. cit.* at p. 657, citing a number of authorities.
118 *Crofter Hand Woven Harris Tweed Co. Ltd v Veitch* [1942] AC 435; *Connolly v Loughney* (1952) 87 ILTR 49.
119 See Balkin & Davis, *op. cit.* at pp. 658–9.
120 *Meskell v CIÉ* [1973] IR 121; *Cotter v Ahern* [1976–7] ILRM 248; *Crowley v Ireland* [1980] IR 102; *Conway v INTO* [1991] 2 IR 305; [1991] ILRM 497; it is

some of the wider possibilities carry a plausible, but less than compelling, argument to support their inclusion. Two problem areas, in particular, arise. First, is the mere fact of combination 'unlawful' (is it unlawful for a group to do something that each member individually would be entitled to do)? And, secondly, is objective intention sufficient (are the parties to be held responsible for inevitable injury to the plaintiff, resulting from their unlawful conduct)?

It has been held that the mere combination of persons will be an actionable conspiracy, provided there is a subjective intention to harm and that this is the predominant purpose of the combination.[121] Thus, collective action is not necessarily unlawful, but when group strength is combined with a malicious purpose, the law treats it as improper. The House of Lords, in *Lonrho v Shell*,[122] held that the same limitation on intent should apply to all cases of conspiracy by unlawful means. This point has not been considered in Ireland yet and, should it arise, there are strong arguments against its acceptance. First, it seems desirable that mere combination should not be regarded as unlawful, so some additional requirement is needed to single out undesirable conduct and improper motivation may be regarded as a satisfactory means of doing so; however, independently unlawful methods are, in themselves, undesirable and should not require further qualification to be actionable, save perhaps a distinction between different degrees of unlawfulness (some unlawful acts being more serious and more reprehensible than others); thus, a different approach to intent for the two situations is justifiable. Secondly, intent in other areas of tort is ordinarily based on an objective interpretation and often need not even extend to the harmful consequences of the conduct, so a consistent approach would demand the same standard for conspiracy as for other intentional torts, with the subjective standard applied to mere combination standing as an exception.

Damage

Conspiracy is not actionable *per se*; proof of actual damage is required,[123] although a *quia timet* injunction may be available in cases where damage has not yet occurred, but is imminently likely.[124] The cases have traditionally involved economic harm, but an action might also be available in respect of personal injury or property damage.[125] There may be cases where such an action might be

---

worth noting that the statutory protection of trade union activities will not protect against deliberate invasion of constitutional rights.
121 *McGowan v Murphy* unrep. SC, 10 April 1967; *McKernan v Fraser* (1931) 46 CLR 343; *Crofter v Veitch* [1942] AC 435; *Canada Cement La Farge Ltd v Lightweight Aggregate Ltd* (1983) 145 DLR (3d) 385.
122 [1982] AC 173; [1980] 1 WLR 627; [1981] 2 All ER 456.
123 *Molloy v Gallagher* [1933] IR 1; *PTY Homes Ltd v Shand* [1968] NZLR 105; *Valley Salvage Ltd v Molson Brewery Ltd* (1976) 64 DLR (3d) 734.
124 See Fridman, *op. cit.* vol. 2 at p. 266.
125 *Ibid.*, at p. 274.

necessary, in order to allow the plaintiff to sue all persons involved in causing the harm suffered. In the case of a battery or false imprisonment, a person could be involved in planning the wrongdoing and facilitating its performance (e.g. supplying a weapon, a vehicle or premises for the commission of the wrong). Such involvement could fall short of producing liability for trespass, but it surely would be actionable, at least in cases involving actual harm. It is, however, possible that such a situation would be treated as giving rise to an action on the case for intentional infliction of harm, rather than conspiracy.

Intimidation

The object of this tort is to provide the plaintiff with redress either for being forced into engaging in detrimental conduct by the use of threats or for being the victim of conduct that a third party has been forced to engage in by the same means. It differs from assault, as the threat need not be one of immediate harm and the threatened harm need not be a battery.

Threat and Demand

In order to commit this tort, the defendant must issue a threat to engage in unlawful conduct against the recipient, unless the recipient acts or refrains from acting in a manner specified by the defendant. The threat may be expressly stated or implied from the defendant's conduct; the essential aspects are that there is some form of coercive pressure generated by the defendant and understood by the recipient. A threat alone is not sufficient to ground an action, even if it leads to damage to the plaintiff; it must be coupled with a demand for a particular type of response.[126] In other words, the recipient's reaction must be something that the defendant actively sought, and not merely be a reasonable response to the pressure exerted. As with the threat, the demand may be inferred from circumstances and need not be expressly stated.

A threat to commit a lawful act, however unpleasant it may be for the recipient of the threat, will not amount to actionable intimidation. The threat must be of an unlawful act,[127] and 'unlawful' has been held to include a breach of contract.[128]

---

126 *J.T. Stratford. & Son Ltd v Lindley* [1965] AC 269; [1964] 2 WLR 1002; [1964] 2 All ER 209, per Lord Denning MR at p. 283; p. 1015; p. 216; *Ansett Transport Industries (Operations) Pty Ltd v Australian Federation of Air Pilots* (1989) Aust Torts Reports 80; *Huljich v Hall* [1973] 2 NZLR 279.

127 *McKernan v Fraser* (1931) 46 CLR 343; *Morgan v Fry* [1968] 2 QB 710; [1968] 3 WLR 506; [1968] 3 All ER 452; *Mintuck v Valley River Band No. 63A* (1977) 75 DLR (3d) 589; see also McMahon & Binchy, *op. cit.* at pp. 571 *et seq.*; Balkin & Davis, *op. cit.* at pp. 649 *et seq.*

128 *Cooper v Millea* [1938] IR 749; *Riordan v Butler* [1940] IR 347; *Rookes v Barnard* [1964] AC 1129; [1964] 2 WLR 269; [1964] 1 All ER 367; *Latham v*

Detrimental Act or Restraint

The defendant's demand must require the recipient to engage in conduct, detrimental to the plaintiff. The conduct may involve positive action or restraint from action; the essential aspect is that a detrimental effect on the plaintiff must be intended. In cases of two party intimidation, where the plaintiff receives the threat and demand directly, the plaintiff will be required either to engage in some activity adverse to his interests or to refrain from engaging in a beneficial activity. In cases of three party intimidation, the recipient of the threat and demand will be required to engage in an activity harmful to the plaintiff or to refrain from activity beneficial to the plaintiff. The act or restraint itself need not be unlawful; thus, if the defendant uses a threat of unlawful behaviour to induce a third party to lawfully terminate a contract between the third party and the plaintiff, an action will lie.[129]

Intimidation is not actionable *per se*; it only arises where the recipient has succumbed to the threat and fulfilled the demand, leading to damage to the plaintiff.[130] The cases have principally concerned economic harm, but interference with personal or property rights may also be actionable.[131]

Justification

As with conspiracy, it is not entirely clear whether intimidation requires a subjective or objective intention on the defendant's part. There is some authority for the proposition that a defence of justification may lie where the defendant's primary purpose was the pursuit of some legitimate interest of his own.[132] The extent to which the courts will tolerate the use of unlawful methods in the pursuit of legitimate interests is questionable. Perhaps where the threats are of

---

Singleton [1981] 2 NSWLR 843; see also Fridman, *op. cit.* vol. 2 at pp. 281–2, where the relationship between intimidation and the doctrine of privity of contract is considered.

129 In *Rookes v Barnard* [1964] AC 1129; [1964] 2 WLR 269; [1964] 1 All ER 367, for example, the plaintiff's contract of employment was lawfully terminated by his employer, following threats by the defendants to institute a strike by other employees, in breach of their contracts of employment. The House of Lords upheld a jury finding that the tort of intimidation had been committed (though a retrial was ordered in respect of the amount of damages).

130 *Whelan v Madigan* [1978] ILRM 136, at p. 143 per Kenny J, citing from the 17th ed. of Salmond; *J.T. Stratford & Son Ltd v Lindley* [1965] AC 269; [1964] 2 WLR 1002; [1964] 2 All ER 209, per Lord Denning MR at p. 283; p. 1015; p. 215.

131 In *Whelan v Madigan* [1978] ILRM 136, for example, the landlord was attempting to force tenants out of their homes and, from the tone of the judgment, it seems likely that the claim of intimidation would have been sustained if the tenants had yielded to the threats.

132 *Latham v Singleton* [1981] 2 NSWLR 843; see also Fridman, *op. cit.* vol. 2 at pp. 288–9; Balkin & Davis, *op. cit.* at p. 652; in these passages a number of *dicta* from various jurisdictions are cited in support of the defence.

minor illegalities or where the illegal aspect is inadvertent the courts may be persuaded that there is no actionable wrong, if the defendant was pursuing an important and legitimate interest.

Interference with Contractual Relations

This tort originated with the wrong of enticing a servant away from his master, but over the centuries has grown and now covers various types of conduct which intentionally interfere with subsisting contracts.

Direct and Indirect Interference

The means which may be used to disrupt contractual relations, so as to give rise to an action in tort, are much broader than the types of behaviour covered by conspiracy and intimidation. A variety of forms of direct and indirect disruption of the performance of contracts can give rise to the tort. Direct interference would include persuading or inducing a party to a contract to break the contract, or actively preventing performance; while indirect interference may take the form of entering into dealings with a party to a contract, which are inconsistent with the performance of the prior contract, or employing unlawful means, which necessarily cause disruption as a side-effect.

Problems have arisen in a number of cases in determining the dividing line between innocently giving advice or information to a contracting party and persuading or inducing a contracting party to breach the contract or refuse performance in an improper manner. Essentially the problem is one of causation; in the case of advice or information being provided, the defendant's conduct is not the central or root cause of the disruption to the contract (though it may have played some part in the recipient's decision not to comply with the contract), whereas procurement signifies that the defendant's involvement was the decisive factor in the disruption.[133] In practice, the outcome will depend on whether the court is satisfied that the defendant's communications with the contract breaker were sufficiently influential in reaching the decision to withdraw from the contractual obligations in question.[134]

Direct prevention of performance can arise in a number of ways, such as physically restraining a contracting party or removing essential equipment from him.[135] In *GWK Co. Ltd v Dunlop Rubber Co. Ltd*[136] the plaintiff company had

---

133 See Balkin & Davis, *op. cit.* at pp. 635–6; Fridman, *op. cit.* vol. 2 at pp. 297 *et seq.; Restatement, Second, Torts* §766 comment h.

134 See McMahon & Binchy, *op. cit.* at pp. 560 *et seq.* for consideration of a number of cases demonstrating the practical difficulty in distinguishing improper interference from legitimate measures; see also *Restatement, Second, Torts* §766 comment o.

135 *D.C. Thomson & Co. Ltd v Deakin* [1952] Ch 646; [1952] 2 All ER 361, per Evershed MR at p. 678; p. 368; per Jenkins LJ at pp. 694–5; p. 378; per Morris LJ at p. 702; p. 385; *Restatement, Second, Torts* §766A comment g.

136 (1926) 42 TLR 593.

contracted to have their tyres placed on the cars of a particular manufacturer at a motor show, but the defendant company removed the tyres and replaced them with their own. This was held to be an actionable interference with the contract between the plaintiff and the car manufacturer.

Inconsistent dealings can amount to an indirect interference with contract; thus, if the defendant offers a third party a very high price for goods or services, knowing that the provision of those goods or services will preclude the third party from fulfilling a less profitable contract with the plaintiff, an action may lie.[137] Furthermore, a defendant may induce a breach of contract without having any direct dealings with either of the contracting parties. Thus, if the defendant invokes the aid of another party to do the actual persuading or disrupting, an action may lie. Where the defendant is not vicariously liable for the acts of the person involved in the actual persuasion or disruption, indirect interference of the contract is only actionable if the defendant induces the use of unlawful means to produce the disruption.[138]

Intention to Interfere

This tort is only available where there is an intention to interfere with the plaintiff's contract. The requirement of intention will be satisfied where the defendant has actual or constructive knowledge of the existence of the contract[139] and the interference is an 'ordinary and probable' consequence of the defendant's conduct.[140] This is clearly an objective assessment of intent.

Nature of Interference

Originally this tort required that there be a breach of a valid contract, but it has expanded to embrace disruptions to performance that would not amount to

---

137 *De Francesco v Barnum* (1890) 63 LT 514; *British Motor Trade Association v Salvadori* [1949] Ch 556; [1949] 1 All ER 208; *D.C. Thomson & Co. Ltd v Deakin* [1952] Ch 646; [1952] 2 All ER 361; *Restatement, Second, Torts* §766 comments m and n.

138 See McMahon & Binchy, *op. cit.* at pp. 566 *et seq.*; Balkin & Davis, *op. cit.* at pp. 638 *et seq.*; Fridman, *op. cit.* vol. 2 at pp. 300 *et seq.*; note that a servant or agent, who is merely performing his work, is not answerable to the plaintiff for the tort of interference with contractual relations, see *Montgomery v Shepperton Investment Co. Ltd* unrep. HC, 11 July 1995 (the employer would be liable).

139 *Cotter v Ahern* [1976–7] ILRM 248, per Finlay P at p. 261; *James McMahon Ltd v Dunne* (1964) 99 ILTR 45, per Budd J at p. 54; *White v Riley* [1920] All ER Rep 371; [1921] Ch 1; *Emerald Construction Co. Ltd v Lowthian* [1966] 1 WLR 691; [1966] 1 All ER 1013.

140 *James McMahon Ltd v Dunne* (1964) 99 ILTR 45, per Budd J at p. 56; *Exchange Telegraph Co. v Gregory & Co.* [1896] 1 QB 147; [1895–9] All ER Rep 1116; there is some support for the view that subjective intention should be required; the issue is discussed at some length by Fridman, *op. cit.* vol. 2 at pp. 294 *et seq.*; see also *Restatement, Second, Torts* §766 comment j.

actionable breaches of contract. The dominant view is that where the defendant induces a disruption to the performance of the contract an action may lie, even though the party that fails to perform may not be liable for the breach of contract.[141] The plaintiff must have a valid contract, however. Inducing a breach of a 'contract' which is void is not actionable under this tort.[142] The generic tort of interference with economic relations will have to be employed if the interference is with prospective contractual relations.

The interference must occasion some damage to the plaintiff, so no action will be available if the disruption causes no material loss to the plaintiff. Once again, an injunction may be available where damage is likely to result from continued interference with the plaintiff's contract by the defendant.[143]

Justification

In its original form this tort was based on malice, so a defendant could defeat a claim by showing some legitimate purpose as an overriding motivation for the conduct complained of.[144] Although malice is no longer required, justification has survived as a defence. Where the defendant's conduct is designed to further some important personal or public interest, it may be excused.[145] The defence leaves the courts with the unenviable task of balancing the merits of the defendant's objectives against the disruption to the plaintiff caused by the means that have been employed. Such balancing exercises are, however, a frequent part of the judicial function in other tort cases and in the law generally.

Detinue

This tort protects one's entitlement to possession of chattels. Thus, ownership is not essential to maintain an action. The tort is committed by a wrongful failure of a person in, or formerly in, possession of a chattel to deliver up possession to the person entitled to immediate possession.[146] The thrust of the tort is economic in most cases, as the usual form of remedy will be the value of the item and damages for its detention. Return of the item may be ordered,

---

141 Examples would include failures of performance excused by an exclusion clause or by invoking the doctrine of frustration.

142 For more detailed consideration of the nature of the interference required see McMahon & Binchy, *op. cit.* at pp. 562–3; Balkin & Davis, *op. cit.* at pp. 632–3; Fridman, *op. cit.* vol. 2 at pp. 306 *et seq.*

143 See Fridman, *op. cit.* vol. 2 at pp. 301–2.

144 *Lumley v Gye* (1853) 2 El & Bl 216; [1843–60] All ER Rep 208.

145 See McMahon & Binchy, *op. cit.* at pp. 568–9; Balkin & Davis, *op. cit.* at pp. 642 *et seq.*; Fridman, *op. cit.* vol. 2 at pp. 302 *et seq.*; *Restatement, Second, Torts* §§767–770.

146 See generally McMahon & Binchy, *op. cit.* at chapter 29; Balkin & Davis, *op. cit.* at pp. 107 *et seq.*; Fridman, *op. cit.* vol. 1 at pp. 115–16. This tort has been abolished in England and replaced by statutory provisions, see the Torts (Interference with Goods) Act 1977.

but this is usually only available in the case of unique items of 'special value or interest'[147] to the plaintiff.

Plaintiff's Right to Possession

The plaintiff's entitlement to possession is essentially a matter to be determined by other branches of the law, such as contract, property and bailment, and will not be considered here, except to note one area of particular difficulty – the finding of valuables. Where the owner cannot be found (as would be the case with ancient treasures, where evidence of ownership may have dissipated through the passage of time), the law must determine rights of possession and ownership. The contenders for rights in the find are the finder, the owner of the property on which the find occurred and the state. The leading decision in Ireland is that of the Supreme Court in *Webb v Ireland*.[148] In the case of chattels attached to or under land the owner of the land has a better claim to them than the finder, unless the owner was never in possession of the land, as possession of the land is legally deemed to include possession of things attached to it.[149] In the case of chattels on land, but not attached to it, the owner will only have a superior right to the finder if the owner has previously manifested an intention to exert control over such chattels (for example, by regularly searching the property for lost items).[150] The state has a right of ownership over antiquities of importance with no known owner, which is at least as extensive as the royal prerogative of treasure trove at common law; though the right is based on constitutional grounds other than prerogative.[151]

Wrongful Failure to Surrender Possession

The vital issue in detinue is determining what constitutes a 'wrongful' failure to surrender possession to the plaintiff. The mere fact that the plaintiff is not in

---

147 *William Whiteley Ltd v Hilt* [1918] 2 KB 808; [1918–19] All ER Rep 1005, per Swinfen Eady MR at p. 819; p.1010.

148 [1988] IR 353; [1988] ILRM 565.

149 The majority view was that the owner of the land would have a right of ownership over the find (except against the true owner), per Finlay CJ at p. 378; pp. 588–9, relying on principles set out by Donaldson LJ in *Parker v British Airways Board* [1982] QB 1004; [1982] 2 WLR 503; [1982] 1 All ER 834, at pp. 1017–18; pp. 514–15; p. 843. The minority view was that the owner of the land would have a right to possession only, per Walsh J at p. 390; p. 60; see McMahon & Binchy, *op. cit.* at pp. 539 *et seq.* In *Waverly Borough Council v Fletcher* unrep. QBD, 17 February 1994; noted by MacMillan (1995) 58 MLR 101, the English High Court held that a local authority was not in sufficient occupation of a public park to assert rights against the finder of an antique brooch.

150 *Parker v British Airways Board* [1982] QB 1004; [1982] 2 WLR 503; [1982] 1 All ER 834, in the passage cited *supra*.

151 *Webb v Ireland* [1988] IR 353; [1988] ILRM 565; the majority view relies on Article 10, per Finlay CJ at p. 383; pp. 593–4; the minority view is that Article 5 is the appropriate source of the right, per Walsh J at p. 393; p. 604; McCarthy J at p. 398; p. 609.

possession of the chattel and the defendant is or has been in possession of it is not sufficient. The defendant's failure to deliver up the chattel must be adverse to the plaintiff's right to possession. This is usually established by the plaintiff making a demand for the possession of the chattel, followed by a refusal or failure by the defendant to comply. The plaintiff need not issue a demand for possession where this would be clearly futile, such as where the chattels have been destroyed while in the defendant's possession, or where the defendant has allowed the goods to come into the possession of a third party.

The defendant's failure to provide the plaintiff with possession will be excused where it is reasonable. Examples of reasonable failure would include situations where there is a fair dispute as to the plaintiff's entitlement to possession[152] or where the chattel has been destroyed, through no fault of the defendant. The onus lays on the defendant to prove the absence of fault, not on the plaintiff to establish its existence.[153]

Conversion

The central thrust of conversion is to protect the owner of chattels against conduct which improperly denies his title to them. The tort also serves to protect rights of possession in circumstances not covered by detinue, such as the wrongful taking of possession or the sale of goods by a person with neither possession nor title to the goods. The essential complaint is that the defendant has intentionally interfered with the plaintiff's right to dominion over chattels.[154]

Plaintiff's Title or Right to Possession

As with detinue, the plaintiff's entitlement to chattels is to be determined by reference to a variety of disparate branches of law.[155] The extent of the plaintiff's interest is mainly relevant to the ability of the defendant to rely on the superior claim of a third party to the property, referred to as *jus tertii*. If the

---

152 *Clayton v Le Roy* [1911] 2 KB 1031; [1911–13] All ER Rep 284; *McCurdy v PMG* [1959] NZLR 553; *Poole v Burns* [1944] Ir Jur Rep 20, where a heavy onus was placed on the defendant to actively encourage a speedy resolution of the issue; criticised by McMahon & Binchy, *op. cit.* at p. 531.

153 *Sheehy v Faughnan* [1991] 1 IR 424; *Houghland v RR Low (Luxury Coaches) Ltd* [1962] 1 QB 694; [1962] 2 WLR 1015; [1962] 2 All ER 159.

154 The defendant need not intend any harm, so an innocent purchaser of stolen goods will be answerable in conversion, as the mistaken assumption of ownership is a denial of the true owner's title. Similarly where goods have been obtained by fraud and the original owner has rescinded the contract, a subsequent purchaser will be answerable in conversion, see *Hollins v Fowler* (1875) LR 7 HL 757; [1874–80] All ER Rep 118; Fridman, *op. cit.* vol. 1 at pp. 101 *et seq.*; see also *Marfani v Midland Bank* [1968] 1 WLR 956; [1968] 2 All ER 573; *Shield Life Insurance Co. Ltd v Ulster Bank Ltd* unrep. HC, 5 December 1995.

155 See Balkin & Davis, *op. cit.* at pp. 64 *et seq.*; Fridman, *op. cit.* vol. 1 at pp. 104 *et seq.*

plaintiff had actual possession then the defendant cannot defeat the claim merely by showing that some third party had a superior entitlement than the plaintiff; the defendant will succeed, however, if it can be shown that he has authority from the third party. If the plaintiff did not have actual possession, but is claiming merely a right to possession (and not ownership), then the defendant will be able to defeat the claim on the basis that a third party holds a superior entitlement to possession.[156]

Intentional Interference with Dominion

The tort embraces a wide range of conduct, making it difficult to describe with precision. The core feature is that the defendant's conduct not only must disrupt the plaintiff's rights, but must be inconsistent with those rights.[157] Take the following scenario:

Example

D owns a large warehouse, in which he stores a variety of goods for third parties. The warehouse is nearly full and a large consignment of goods is due to arrive. D reorganises the goods stored in the warehouse, in order to make more space available, and decides to store some containers of goods in a public car park adjacent to the warehouse. D moves P1's car with a crane, without her consent, in order to make room in the car park and the car is slightly damaged in the process. P2 comes to collect his goods from D, but the goods cannot be located for several days, as D lost track of them during the reorganisation. D sells a consignment of goods belonging to P3, and informs P3 that the goods were stolen.

The interference with P1's car is trespass, but not conversion; the failure to return P2's goods on time amounts to detinue, but not conversion; the sale of P3's goods is conversion. Conversion may arise from lesser acts inconsistent with the plaintiff's rights, such as a defendant using goods as though they were his own. Thus, joy riding in a car[158] or wearing jewellery may suffice, even though the defendant is asserting transient, rather than permanent, dominion over the goods.[159]

---

156 See McMahon & Binchy, *op. cit.* at p. 539; Balkin & Davis, *op. cit.* at pp. 71 *et seq.*; in England the common law rules have been changed by s. 8(1) of the Torts (Interference with Goods) Act 1977, which permits the defendant to avail of third party rights in all cases.

157 For a useful explanation of the general nature of the tort see Fridman, *op. cit.* vol. 1 at pp. 95 *et seq.*; *Restatement, Second, Torts* §222A.

158 *Aitken Agencies Ltd v Richardson* [1967] NZLR 65, per McGregor J at p. 66; McMahon & Binchy, *op. cit.* at p. 535.

159 See Balkin & Davis, *op. cit.* at pp. 77 *et seq.*; Fridman, *op. cit.* vol. 1 at pp. 98 *et seq.*; *Restatement, Second, Torts* §223 for detailed consideration of the variety of acts that may give rise to conversion.

Breach of Confidence

The action for breach of confidence is concerned with the defendant's disclosure or misuse of confidential information received from the plaintiff. It is an equitable wrong, straddling the borders between contract, tort and restitution. Since its origins are in equity, and the origins of torts are in common law, it is not, strictly speaking, a tort at all; but, since equitable remedies have crept into use in respect of torts and have introduced variations in the criteria applicable to some torts (such as nuisance and passing off), the distinction between torts and purely equitable obligations has become somewhat blurred.[160]

An obligation to treat information as confidential arises in a number of circumstances: it may be specified in a contract between the parties, such as a licensing agreement for the exploitation of a patent; it may arise out of a special relationship, independent of contract, such as that of professional and client; or it may arise in the context of negotiation of a transaction, even though the negotiations may ultimately fail.[161] The information must have some characteristic of secrecy or privacy in order to be protected against disclosure, though the dividing line between confidential and non-confidential information is not easy to draw.[162]

Where the relationship is contractual, an action for breach of contract may be employed to redress the harm suffered as a result of misuse or disclosure. In the absence of a contract, a restitutionary claim may be used to recover any profit or reward that the defendant has made from the breach of confidence. A claim for damages may be made where the plaintiff has suffered a loss as a result of the breach, independent of the question of benefit to the defendant.[163] The third type of action is substantially similar to a tort action for interference with the plaintiff's rights. The rights covered may be either personal or economic in nature, as may be seen from the range of circumstances in which the obligation of confidence arises.

---

160 For a discussion of the classification of breach of confidence, see Fridman, *op. cit.* vol. 2 at pp. 204 *et seq.*; Lavery, *Commercial Secrets: The Action for Breach of Confidence in Ireland* (Dublin: Round Hall Sweet & Maxwell, 1996) at chapter 2. For detailed consideration of the action, see Lavery, *op. cit.*; Clark & Smyth, *op. cit.* at chapter 23; McDonagh, 'Developments in the Action for Breach of Confidence' (1996) 14 ILT 98.

161 See Clerk & Lindsell, *op. cit.* at chapter 26; Goff & Jones, *The Law of Restitution*, 4th ed. (London: Sweet & Maxwell, 1993) at chapter 36.

162 The Court of Appeal decision in *Faccenda Chicken v Fowler* [1987] Ch 117; [1986] 3 WLR 288; [1986] 1 All ER 617 provides a useful discussion on the type of information protected; Costello J's judgment in the High Court in *House of Spring Gardens Ltd v Point Blank* [1984] IR 611 provides a guide to the scope of breach of confidence, at pp. 658 *et seq.*

163 *Dowson & Mason Ltd v Potter* [1986] 1 WLR 1419; [1986] 2 All ER 418; see Capper, 'Damages for Breach of the Equitable Duty of Confidence' (1994) 14 LS 313.

CHAPTER EIGHT

Defamation

Introduction

Defamation concerns the protection of a person's right to his reputation against false allegations.[1] This involves the imposition of restraints on freedom of expression and also raises questions in respect of other civil rights, such as privacy and interests in communication. The balance struck between these various interests by the common law is heavily weighted towards the right to reputation. Despite the fact that the rights concerned are subject to constitutional provisions,[2] there has been no significant constitutional influence on this branch of law yet. In fact, the most significant change to the common law in Ireland to date has come from the legislature, through the Defamation Act 1961. Since the 1980s, defamation has been the subject of intense debate and the academic treatment of the subject has been transformed from a position where there was little published material on the subject in Ireland to a position where there is a greater abundance of published material in Ireland on defamation than on any other single branch of the law of torts.[3]

Defamation comprises two constituent torts – libel and slander. The accepted criterion for distinguishing the two relates to the form that the defamatory

---

1 See the statement of Cave J in *Scott v Sampson* (1882) 8 QBD 91; [1881–5] All ER Rep 628, at p. 503; p. 634 indicating the general thrust of defamation to be the provision of redress against being discredited in the estimation of others.

2 The right to one's good name, Art. 40.3.2°; freedom of expression, Art. 40.6.1°; others include the right to communicate and the right to privacy, which have been held to be unenumerated rights under Art. 40.3, *AG v Paperlink* [1984] ILRM 343, McCormack (1984) 6 DULJ 144, Kelly, *The Irish Constitution*, 3rd ed. (Dublin: Butterworths, 1994) at pp. 782–3 (communication); *Kennedy and Arnold v Ireland* [1987] IR 587; [1988] ILRM 724, Kelly, *op. cit.* at pp. 767–70 (privacy).

3 Boyle & McGonagle, *A Report on Press Freedom and Libel* (Dublin: National Newspapers of Ireland, 1988); McDonald, *Defamation Law in Ireland*, 2nd ed. (Dublin: Round Hall Press, 1989); McMahon & Binchy, *The Irish Law of Torts*, 2nd ed. (Dublin: Butterworths, 1989), chapter 34; McGonagle, *A Textbook on Media Law* (Dublin: Gill & Macmillan, 1996) chapter 4; Boyle & McGonagle, 'Defamation – The Path to Law Reform' in McGonagle (ed.), *Law and the Media* (Dublin: Round Hall Sweet & Maxwell, 1997); Law Reform Commission, *Consultation Paper on the Civil Law of Defamation* (Dublin: Law Reform Commission, 1991); Law Reform Commission, *Report on the Civil Law of Defamation* (Dublin: Law Reform Commission, 1991) (LRC 38–91); McDonald, 'Towards a Constitutional Analysis of Non-Media Qualified Privilege' (1989) 11 DULJ 94; O'Dell, 'Does Defamation Value Free Expression?' (1990) 12 DULJ 50; O'Dell, 'Reflections on a Revolution in Libel' (1991) 9 ILT 181 and 214; Ní Raifeartaigh, 'Defences in Irish Defamation Law' (1991) 13 DULJ 76; Byrne & Binchy, *Annual Review of Irish Law 1991* at pp. 453–8; McDonald, 'A Response to LRC' (1992) 10 ILT 270.

allegation takes: libel is defamation by communication in permanent or lasting form; slander is defamation by communication in transient form.[4] Thus, an allegation contained in a book or a film would be a libel, while an unrecorded comment or gesture would give rise to slander. Some allegations give rise to problems with classification, such as live broadcasts of oral comments or reading to an audience from a prepared script. Radio and television broadcasts are treated as permanent forms of communication by section 15 of the 1961 Act and there is some judicial support for treating the reading of a written statement as a libel, even though the actual communication is transient.[5]

The principal difference between libel and slander is that all libels are actionable *per se*, while only some categories of slander are. Being actionable *per se* means that the plaintiff does not have to show that specific harm has occurred as a result of the defamatory allegation; harm to reputation is assumed once the defamatory nature of the defendant's communication is established. Those slanders which are not actionable *per se* require the plaintiff to prove special damage; this means that the plaintiff must show some adverse effect resulting from the slander.[6] There are four categories of slander which are actionable *per se*:

(i) an imputation of adultery or unchastity to a female;[7]
(ii) an imputation calculated to disparage a person's reputation in respect of any office, profession, trade or business;[8]

4　McDonald, *op. cit.* at pp. 78–81; McMahon & Binchy, *op. cit.* at pp. 612–13; LRC, *Consultation Paper, op. cit.* at pp. 4–6; *Gatley on Libel and Slander*, 8th ed. (London: Sweet & Maxwell, 1981) at §§141–142; it has been pointed out that the distinction between permanent and transient communication lacks definitive support in the cases as the criterion for determining the type of defamation, see Heuston, 'Recent Developments in the Law of Defamation' (1966) 1 Ir Jur 247, at p. 249; see also *Restatement, Second, Torts* §568 which classifies libel as defamatory material by print, writing, physical form or any communication with similar harmful qualities.

5　*Forrester v Tyrrell* (1893) 9 TLR 257; *Robinson v Chambers* [1946] NI 148; *Bander v Metropolitan Life Insurance Co.* (1943) 313 Mass 337; 47 NE 2d 595.

6　The second difference is that some libels also constitute a criminal offence, though this is not relevant for the purposes of this text; see Part II of the Defamation Act 1961; Law Reform Commission, *Consultation Paper on the Crime of Libel* (Dublin: Law Reform Commission, 1991) and Law Reform Commission, *Report on the Crime of Libel* (Dublin: Law Reform Commission, 1991) (LRC 41–91); for detailed consideration of what constitutes special damage in respect of slander see McDonald, *op. cit.* at pp. 91–3; Gatley, *op. cit.* at chapter 5, considering a wide variety of cases.

7　S. 16 of the 1961 Act; under the equivalent English provision it has been held that an imputation of lesbian acts comes within the provision, *Kerr v Kennedy* [1942] 1 KB 409; [1942] 1 All ER 412.

8　S. 19 of the 1961 Act; at common law the slander had to be about some essential element of the person's office or business etc. Now the slander may be about any aspect of the plaintiff's character, provided it is capable of having a knock-on effect

---

(iii) an imputation of the commission of a criminal offence punishable by imprisonment;[9]

(iv) an imputation that a person has a contagious disease.[10]

The constitutional validity of the first category is questionable, as there is a possible breach of the guarantee of equal treatment before the law, contained in Article 40.1.[11] The differing treatment of males and females might be justified on the basis of differing social perceptions of male and female chastity and fidelity, though this argument is tenuous and relies on an outmoded view of sexuality.

Slanders requiring proof of special damage are rarely seen in the reported cases, mostly dating from the nineteenth century, and have had little impact on the development of the modern law of defamation.[12]

Defamation law is particularly technical and mechanistic and is dogged by procedural rules to a greater extent than other aspects of the law of torts. The following treatment of the subject is intended as a general guide, rather than an exhaustive examination; it attempts to set out the principal characteristics of the law, along with an introduction to the potential for development that has gained momentum from recent intellectual debate.

Elements of a Cause of Action

Requisite elements:

1. Publication
2. Identification
3. Defamatory effect
4. Damage, for slanders not actionable *per se*
5. Absence of defence

---

on commercial reputation; see McMahon & Binchy, *op. cit.* at pp. 616–17; McDonald, *op. cit.* at pp. 87–9.

9 The imputation must involve a specific criminal offence – a vague indication of wrongdoing is insufficient; see, for example, *Corcoran v W. & R. Jacob Ltd* [1945] IR 446 (imputation of stealing); *Kirkwood-Hackett v Tierney* [1952] IR 158 (imputation of obtaining money by false pretences); see also McDonald, *op. cit.* at pp. 82–5; Gatley, *op. cit.* at §§149–165.

10 A *dictum* of Jackson J in *Barrett v Long* (1846) 8 ILR 331, at p. 335 seems to be the only Irish authority on the issue; see also McDonald, *op. cit.* at pp. 85–6; Gatley, *op. cit.* at §§166–167.

11 See Kelly, *op. cit.* at pp. 724 *et seq.* for detailed consideration of the scope of the guarantee of equality. It is notable that s. 16 predates the period of active judicial interpretation of the fundamental rights provisions of the Constitution, so the constitutional ramifications may simply not have been considered. See also *Restatement, Second, Torts* §574, comment c.

12 The Law Reform Commission has recommended the abolition of the distinction between libel and slander and the introduction of a single tort of defamation, LRC 38–91, *op. cit.* at §3.3.

Publication

Publication is any form of communication by which meaning can be signified to another person; it includes not only words, but other forms of communication, such as pictures, gestures, conduct and so forth.[13] The publication must be to a third party in order to be actionable. Communication to the plaintiff is insufficient because it cannot damage reputation, no matter how offensive or unpleasant it may be. Such a communication may be an actionable tort, other than defamation, if it causes harm to the plaintiff.[14]

Communication back to the original source is also an excluded form of communication, as it can have no effect on reputation. So, reading back a statement to its author, or returning documents or other material, will not involve a defamatory publication by the person sending the material back. Such communications are excluded because there is no potential for any adverse effect on reputation, as there is no independent person to be influenced by the communication.[15]

One category of communication to third parties, which can have an adverse effect on reputation, but is nonetheless regarded as exempt, is communication to the defendant's spouse; if a person communicates material to his own spouse, which is defamatory of a third person, no cause of action arises. This rule is grounded in public policy, favouring uninhibited marital discourse; spouses are free to affect each other's views, without extraneous interference.[16]

Apart from these general principles, there are also particular rules dealing with two areas involving special problems: responsibility for republishing and for unintended publication.

---

13 'An act of gesticulation, such as holding up an empty purse or the like' may be defamatory, *Cook v Cox* (1814) 3 M & S 110, at p. 114 per Lord Ellenborough; also the display of an effigy, portraying a person in such a way as to have an adverse effect on reputation, can be defamatory, *Edwards v Harding* (1787) Vern & Scriv 99; a security guard leading a customer forcefully through a store may be guilty of slander by conduct, even if no one else hears what is said; s. 14(2) of the Defamation Act 1961 states: 'Any reference in this Part to words shall be construed as including a reference to visual images, gestures and other methods of signifying meaning.'

14 Psychological harm could be actionable in negligence (see chapter 1 *supra*) or as an intentional wrong (see 'actions on the case' in chapter 10 *infra*), depending on the circumstances.

15 See LRC, *Consultation Paper, op. cit.* at §30 for further discussion.

16 *Wennhak v Morgan* (1888) 20 QBD 635; [1886–90] All ER Rep 572; the rule originated in the theory that husband and wife were one and that, therefore, there was no third party recipient. This theory could have had adverse consequences if applied to communication to the plaintiff's spouse, but was not so applied, *Wenman v Ash* (1853) 13 CB 836; 148 ER 1432; the shift in emphasis to treating inter-spousal communication as privileged on grounds of public policy helps to clarify the distinction between the two situations, as it can plainly be seen that the defendant should have a right to freely communicate with his own spouse, but

Republication

Each person that repeats or further distributes a publication is responsible for the additional publication. There are clearly some people in the distribution process whose level of responsibility ought to be different from others; thus, a blanket rule of responsibility for any dissemination, in any circumstances, would be unjust. The law draws a rough distinction between those actively involved in the process of publication, such as authors and editors, and those more passively involved, such as retailers. An exception to the general principle of liability for publication is available to distributors, other than the original publisher, who can show that:

(i) they had no knowledge of the defamatory content of the material;
(ii) nothing in the material or surrounding circumstances gave them grounds to suspect any defamatory content; and
(iii) they were not negligent in failing to discover the defamatory content.[17]

The onus is on the defendant to show that the exception is applicable, so the plaintiff is not required to prove knowledge or negligence on the defendant's part.[18] The exception has been held applicable to retailers[19] and libraries,[20] but is not available to media organisations[21] or printers.[22] Problems may arise with classification of persons involved in various forms of electronic communication,

---

need not have the same right to communicate with the plaintiff's spouse; see also McMahon & Binchy, *op. cit.* at p. 611 and p. 647; LRC, *Consultation Paper, op. cit.* at pp. 31–2; the Law Reform Commission recommended the abolition of the exception, LRC 38–91, *op. cit.* at §§4.23–4.25.

17 *Emmens v Pottle* (1885) 16 QBD 354; *Vizetelly v Mundie's Select Library* [1900] 2 QB 170; *Fitzgibbon v Eason & Son* (1910) 45 ILTR 91; see also McDonald, *op. cit.* at pp. 65 *et seq.*; LRC, *Consultation Paper, op. cit.* at §34; McGonagle, *op. cit.* at pp. 79–81.

18 *Ross v Eason & Son and The Winning Post* (1911) 45 ILTR 89, at p. 92 per Palles CB.

19 *Emmens v Pottle* (1885) 16 QBD 354; *Fitzgibbon v Eason & Son* (1910) 45 ILTR 91.

20 *Vizetelly v Mundie's Select Library* [1900] 2 QB 170.

21 McDonald, *op. cit.* at pp. 70–1, argues that the failure to allow broadcasters the exception in respect of live broadcasts may be unconstitutional; the argument based on unequal treatment is weak, as the courts have generally refused to apply the guarantee of equality to commercial activities, see Kelly, *op. cit.* at pp. 719 *et seq.*; the argument based on the reference to the role of the media in Art. 40.6.1° carries more force; the Law Reform Commission, however, recommended the retention of the broadcaster's liability, LRC 38–91, *op. cit.* at §12.33.

22 LRC, *Consultation Paper, op. cit.* at §35; *Newton v City of Vancouver* (1932) 46 BCR 67; though a printer was given the benefit of the exception in *Jensen v Clarke* [1982] 2 NZLR 268; the Law Reform Commission has recommended that printers and distributors be granted an immunity from suit where they are not the original publishers, though a defamed person would retain an entitlement to compel the disclosure of information in respect of the publisher and to prevent continued distribution, LRC 38–91, *op. cit.* at §12.32; in England s. 1 of the Defamation Act

such as telephone, e-mail and the internet, though these may well be resolved by analogy to participants in the more traditional forms of communication.[23]

Other innocent participants in the distribution of defamatory material are persons whose communication of the material is involuntary. A person compelled to forward material, such as a secretary posting a letter, should not be regarded as its publisher; the person that compels him to send it is the publisher. The position here is slightly different from persons such as retailers; it is not absence of knowledge that excuses the person, but the absence of choice over his involvement. A retailer chooses to sell a particular publication, but may not be in a position to ascertain its defamatory nature; an employee of the original publisher may be well aware of the defamatory content of the publication, but may have no choice but to send it out according to the employer's instructions.

Thus far we have considered the republisher's responsibility for further distribution of the defamatory material, but what of the original publisher? Is each publisher only liable for his own part in the process, or can one publisher be responsible for the republication by another person? A publisher is responsible for the republication if it was intended or is a natural and probable consequence of the original publication, e.g. a journalist submitting an article to an editor is responsible for the dissemination of the story to the general public through the eventual sale of the newspaper or magazine.[24] In fact, in such a case there will be several persons jointly liable for the eventual dissemination, such as the author, the editor, the newspaper or magazine proprietor and the printer.

One potential difficulty arising out of liability for republication is the possibility of multiple actions, where a defamed person may seek to take several actions against a defendant or several defendants, based on continued republishing of the original defamatory publication (such as the continuing sales of a book or broadcast of a film, which repeats the defamation to a new audience). In practice plaintiffs tend not to avail of this opportunity, but the imposition of a restricted time limit for subsequent actions has been recommended by the Law Reform Commission.[25]

1996 extends the defence of innocent dissemination to printers and to persons involved in the copying or distribution of films, sound recordings and electronic communications, and also to live broadcasters and any person in a comparable position to any of the above categories.

23 See Howarth, *Textbook on Tort*, 5th ed. (London: Blackstone, 1996), at pp. 563 *et seq.*; Tapper, *Computer Law*, 4th ed. (London: Longman, 1989) at pp. 258–60.

24 *Pierce v Ellis* (1856) 6 IR CLR 65, public representative giving a copy of a speech to a reporter held liable for its publication; *Ewins v Carlton UK Television Ltd* [1997] 2 ILRM 223, producer of a television programme liable for broadcast by another station; see also *Fitzsimmons v Duncan and Kemp & Co.* [1908] 2 IR 483; *Ross v Eason & Son and The Winning Post* [1911] 2 IR 459 at pp. 464–5; (1911) 45 ILTR 89, at p. 93 per Holmes LJ; *Speight v Gospay* (1891) 60 LJQB 231; McDonald, *op. cit.* at pp. 70 *et seq.*; Gatley, *op. cit.* at §§266–273.

25 LRC 38–91, *op. cit.* at §§14.57–14.58; see also McDonald, *op. cit.* at pp. 75 *et seq.*

Unintended Publication

Where publication was unintended, the publisher will only be liable if he could have reasonably foreseen the particular publication. So, if the defamatory communication is received by someone other than its intended recipient due to the defendant's negligence, then liability arises. In *Paul v Holt*[26] the defendant sent a letter to the plaintiff, in respect of arrears of rent, but the letter was addressed to 'Mr Paul', with no first name specified. The letter was opened by the plaintiff's brother, who lived at the same address. The Court of Appeal held that there was sufficient publication by the defendant, as there was evidence that he was aware of the brother's presence at that address. Liability will not arise in cases of deliberate and improper interception of a communication by a person other than the intended recipient, such as the unauthorised opening of mail by an employee of the addressee.[27] However, the opening of mail by authorised staff may be sufficiently foreseeable to make the sender responsible for publication.[28]

Identification

It is essential that the plaintiff is identified by the publication if an action is to be maintained. There must be some clear link between the defamatory publication and the plaintiff; otherwise the recipients of the publication could not think less of the plaintiff and no harm to reputation could occur.

As a preliminary matter, we must consider the question as to which persons may sue for defamation. The action is not confined to natural persons, but extends to artificial entities such as corporations,[29] partnerships,[30] friendly societies[31] and trade unions.[32] Unincorporated associations do not generally have a right to maintain an action, although individual members may do so if

---

26 (1935) 69 ILTR 157; see also Gatley, *op. cit.* at §§234–235.
27 *Huth v Huth* [1915] 3 KB 32; [1914–15] All ER Rep 242; see also *Pullman v Walter Hill & Co. Ltd* [1891] 1 QB 524, at p. 529 per Lopes J, *obiter*; McDonald, *op. cit.* at pp. 63 *et seq.*; likewise, there is no liability for unanticipated republication by a third party, in the absence of fault on the defendant's part, *Coates v Pope* (1863) 16 IR CLR 156; *Basse v Toronto Star Newspaper* (1984) 4 DLR (4d) 381.
28 Whether the publication could be foreseen will depend on surrounding circumstances; *Pullman v Walter Hill & Co. Ltd* [1891] 1 QB 524, opening of a letter by a clerk of a firm considered to be ordinary commercial practice and, therefore, sufficiently foreseeable; in *Keogh v Incorporated Dental Hospital* [1910] 2 IR 166 a letter was opened by an authorised clerk, but it was held that there was no publication; the plaintiff had requested the communication and had supplied the address to the defendant and there was no evidence of the defendant's having any knowledge that the plaintiff had a clerk; see LRC, *Consultation Paper, op. cit.* at §32.
29 Patfield, 'The Origins of a Company's Right to Sue for Defamation' (1994) 45 NILQ 233.
30 *LeFanu v Malcolmson* (1848) 1 HLC 637.
31 *Irish People's Assurance Society v City of Dublin Assurance Co. Ltd* [1929] IR 25.
32 *National Union of General & Municipal Workers v Gillian* [1946] KB 81.

they are sufficiently identified.[33] In the case of corporations, there is a difference of opinion as to whether the right is confined to cases involving trading character or extends to any aspect of corporate reputation. The narrower view would exclude actions by public authorities, various non-trading corporations and, perhaps, charitable institutions.[34]

The defamed person must exist at the time of publication; thus, a dead person cannot be defamed and the surviving family cannot bring a civil action to protect the dead person's reputation. They can, however, initiate a criminal prosecution, if leave to do so is obtained from the High Court.[35] Surviving relatives may bring a defamation action in their own right if the defamatory allegation against the deceased also reflects on their reputation.[36] Furthermore, if either party dies before the action is completed the action does not survive, either on behalf of or against that person.[37] McDonald suggests that the non-survival of actions against defendants who die before the action is complete

---

33 *London Association for the Protection of Trade v Greenlands Ltd* [1916] AC 15; [1916–17] All ER Rep 452, action against a trade association not permitted, due to lack of distinct legal personality; this lack of capacity would seem to preclude the taking of an action also; some unincorporated associations, such as trade unions and partnerships, are regarded as sufficiently analogous to corporations to have an independent legal personality for the purposes of suing and being sued, see *Williams v Beaumont* (1833) 10 Bing 260; 131 ER 904, unincorporated trading company entitled to maintain an action; the dividing line between those that do and those that do not have such rights is somewhat arbitrary, see McDonald, *op. cit.* at pp. 276 *et seq.*; Lloyd, 'Actions Instituted By or Against Unincorporated Bodies' (1946) 12 MLR 409.

34 *South Hetton Coal Co. Ltd v North-Eastern News Association Ltd* [1893] 1 QB 133; [1891–4] All ER Rep 548, identifies trading character as the basis for a corporation's right to sue for defamation; *Bognor Regis Urban District Council v Campion* [1972] 2 QB 169; [1972] 2 WLR 983; [1972] 2 All ER 61, local authority entitled to sue; overruled in *Derbyshire County Council v Times Newspapers plc* [1993] AC 534; [1993] 2 WLR 449; [1993] 1 All ER 1011; noted by Bix & Tomkins (1993) 56 MLR 738; Cumberbatch (1994) 45 NILQ 219; Geal (1994) 2 Tort L Rev 11; *Derbyshire* followed in *Ballina Shire Council v Ringland* (1994) 33 NSWLR 680, noted by Mullany (1995) 111 LQR 206; Tobin (1995) 3 Tort L Rev 9; *Saskatchewan College of Physicians & Surgeons v Co-operative Federation Publishing & Printing Co. Ltd* (1965) 51 DLR (2d) 442, council of a medical association entitled to sue; *Church of Scientology of Toronto v Globe & Mail Ltd* (1978) 19 OR (2d) 62, non-profit corporation may sue; *Goldsmith v Bhoyrul* [1998] 2 WLR 435; [1997] 4 All ER 268, political party not entitled to sue in respect of political reputation; see also Patfield, *loc. cit.* at pp. 248–50; Fridman, *The Law of Torts in Canada*, (Toronto: Carswell, 1989), vol. 2, at pp. 152–3; Loveland, 'Defamation of "Government": Taking Lessons from America?' (1994) 14 LS 206.

35 S. 8 of the Defamation Act 1961.

36 See McDonald, *op. cit.* at pp. 281 *et seq.*; LRC, *Consultation Paper, op. cit.* at §§498–501; LRC 38–91, *op. cit.* at §§12.7–12.13.

37 See chapter 13 *infra*, on the survival of actions.

may be an unconstitutional restraint on the plaintiff's right to a good name and the right to litigate.[38]

Indicia

Identification occurs if there is a sufficient indication that the publication refers to the plaintiff. The law will accept a wide variety of indicators in respect of identity; so, for example, a description from which identification can be inferred will suffice, even if there are some differences of detail.[39] Furthermore, the reference need not be wholly contained in the defamatory publication; evidence of extrinsic facts can be admitted to establish the link between the plaintiff and the publication. In *Campbell v Irish Press*,[40] for example, the impugned publication was an apology for untruths contained in an earlier article in the defendant's paper and identification was established by proving that the plaintiff was the author of the earlier article.

At common law the identification of the plaintiff could support an action, even if it was neither intended, nor the result of any negligence on the publisher's part. Section 21 of the Defamation Act 1961 now provides a defence in respect of unintentional identification, based on the exercise of reasonable care and an offer of amends.[41]

The appropriate test for determining if a publication is capable of fulfilling the identification requirement is whether the publication is reasonably capable of being understood to refer to the plaintiff. There is no difficulty satisfying this test if the plaintiff is named or a photograph is contained in the publication. In other cases, identification may prove problematic; the governing principle in such cases is set out in *Knupffer v London Express Newspaper Ltd*:[42]

---

38 *Op. cit.* at pp. 283–4.
39 *Sinclair v Gogarty* [1937] IR 377, where a reference in a book was held to identify the plaintiffs, despite the fact that the address of their business and the type of business were changed; for a general review of the various indicia accepted by the courts see McDonald, *op. cit.* at pp. 54 *et seq.*; McGonagle, *op. cit.* at pp. 72 *et seq.*
40 (1956) 90 ILTR 105; evidence of the reactions of third parties is also admissible for the purpose of establishing that the plaintiff was identified by the publication; see *Fulham v Associated Newspapers Ltd* [1955–6] Ir Jur Rep 45, evidence in respect of jeering crowds was admitted in order to establish that an article, which was critical of a former professional footballer, referred to the plaintiff.
41 The defence of 'offer of amends' is considered in more detail later in this chapter in the discussion of defences; examples of the common law rule can be found in *Newstead v London Express Newspaper Ltd* [1940] 1 KB 377; [1939] 4 All ER 319 (newspaper report of a bigamy trial held defamatory of another person with the same name and from the same district as the accused); *Cassidy v Daily Mirror Newspapers Ltd* [1929] 2 KB 331; [1929] All ER Rep 117 (photograph of a man and woman, coupled with an announcement of their engagement, held to be defamatory of the man's wife, who was not the woman in the picture); see also LRC, *Consultation Paper*, *op. cit.* at §§26–27.
42 [1944] AC 116; [1944] 1 All ER 495, at p. 119; p. 496 per Viscount Simon LC; approved in Ireland in *Duffy v News Group Newspapers Ltd (No. 2)* [1994] 3 IR

Where the plaintiff is not named, the test which decides whether the words used refer to him is the question whether the words are such as would reasonably lead persons acquainted with the plaintiff to believe that he was the person referred to.

It is ultimately a question of fact whether any of the recipients have understood the publication to refer to the plaintiff. If the case is conducted in the High Court, with a jury, then the identification question is twofold – first the judge must determine whether the statement is capable of referring to the plaintiff, then the jury must decide whether it actually does so. If the case is in the Circuit Court, it will be before a judge, without a jury, and both aspects of the issue will be decided by the judge alone.[43]

Groups

Where a group of persons is the subject of a publication, an action is only possible if the group is small enough to consider the individual members to be identifiable. If the group is large or its membership is not known, then there is no identification of any individuals within the group.[44] In *Duffy v News Group Newspapers Ltd*[45] the Supreme Court held that an allegation that terrorist activities were being planned at the clubhouse of a particular gaelic football club was capable of identifying the plaintiff, the chairman of that club. However, a statement that 'all lawyers were thieves' would be too vague a reference to be actionable.[46] The difference between these two situations is readily apparent, but as one moves across the spectrum it can be difficult to find a precise line of division.[47]

63; [1994] 1 ILRM 364, at p. 77; p. 371 per O'Flaherty J (with whom the other members of the Supreme Court agreed).

43 Civil juries were abolished in Circuit Court cases by s. 6 of the Courts Act 1971; on the respective roles of judge and jury see *Duffy v News Group Newspapers Ltd (No. 2)* [1994] 3 IR 63; [1994] 1 ILRM 364, at p. 73; p. 368 per O'Flaherty J (with whom the other members of the Supreme Court agreed); LRC, *Consultation Paper, op. cit.* at §25.

44 *Knupffer v London Express Newspaper Ltd* [1944] AC 116; [1944] 1 All ER 495; *Duffy v News Group Newspapers Ltd (No. 2)* [1994] 3 IR 63; [1994] 1 ILRM 364; see also McDonald, *op. cit.* at pp. 56 *et seq.*; LRC, *Consultation Paper, op. cit.* at §28; Prosser et al., *Prosser & Keeton on Torts*, 5th ed. (St Paul, Minn.: West, 1984), at pp. 784–5.

45 [1994] 3 IR 63; [1994] 1 ILRM 364; see also *Browne v D.C. Thomson & Co.* [1912] SC 359 (reference to religious authorities sufficiently identified the plaintiffs, as there were only seven people exercising such authority in the area).

46 *Eastwood v Holmes* (1858) 1 F & F 347, at p. 349 per Willes J, *obiter*, cited with approval in *Duffy v News Group Newspapers Ltd (No. 2)* [1994] 3 IR 63; [1994] 1 ILRM 364; see also *O'Brien v Eason & Son* (1913) 47 ILTR 266 (reference to the Ancient Order of Hibernians was held not to sufficiently identify the plaintiff, who was a member of the organisation).

47 In *Gallagher & Shatter v Independent Newspapers* Irish Times 10 May 1980 p. 10, for example, a letter referred to 'a handful of solicitors and judges' as being

McDonald is critical of the crude distinction between large and small groups, arguing that it is logically unsound and constitutionally questionable.[48]

Defamatory Effect

Defamatory effect is the capacity of a publication to have an adverse effect on the plaintiff's reputation. The cases have produced a variety of statements as to the type of adverse effect required, such as 'public hatred, contempt or ridicule',[49] vilification,[50] odium[51] or derision.[52] Mere abuse, such as foul language or common name calling, is not defamatory, as abuse does not generally have any real effect on reputation.[53] The *Restatement, Second, Torts* offers a definition which captures the essence of the case law on the subject:

> §559 A communication is defamatory if it tends so to harm the reputation of another as to lower him in the estimation of the community or to deter third persons from associating or dealing with him.

The definition of defamation provided by Winfield & Jolowicz is similar, but employs the same phraseology as that employed in judicial pronouncements in Ireland and England:

> Defamation is the publication of a statement which reflects on a person's reputation and tends to lower him in the estimation of right-thinking members of society generally or tends to make them shun or avoid him.[54]

There are a number of important issues raised by these definitions which require further elaboration. The use of the word 'tends' is, perhaps, the most

---

involved in undermining 'Catholic family life' and named particular cases; yet the plaintiff solicitors, who had acted in one of the cases, failed to convince a jury that they were identified by the publication.

48 *Op. cit.* at p. 58; there is considerable force in the argument, particularly as the general rule for identification is flexible enough to allow a rational distinction to be drawn between different situations in which allegations are made against groups, based on the individual circumstances of each case.

49 *Crotty v McMahon* (1835) 1 Jones 465, at p. 479 per Joy CB; see also *Mawe v Piggott* (1869) IR 4 CL 54, at p. 59 per Lawton J; *Parmiter v Coupland* (1840) 6 M & W 105.

50 *Ahearne v Maguire* (1840) Arm Mac Og 39, at p. 43 per Brady CB.

51 *Ibid.*

52 *Barrett v Long* (1846) 8 ILRC 331, at p. 373 per Burton J; ridicule or derision must be distinguished from simple humour or satire, but the division between legitimate jokes and defamatory aspersions is not always easy to draw; see McDonald, *op. cit.* at pp. 28–31; LRC, *Consultation Paper, op. cit.* at §13.

53 Again the dividing line between abuse and defamation is not always easily drawn, see McDonald, *op. cit.* at pp. 26–7.

54 Rogers, *Winfield & Jolowicz on Tort*, 14th ed. (London: Sweet & Maxwell, 1994) at p. 312; see, for example, *Quigley v Creation Ltd* [1971] IR 269; *Berry v Irish Times Ltd* [1973] IR 368.

significant feature of defamatory effect. The plaintiff is not required to establish that any particular individuals or categories of person developed an adverse view of him. What must be shown is that the publication has a propensity to have an adverse effect on the plaintiff's reputation. The *Restatement, Second, Torts* states that 'it is not necessary that the communication actually cause harm to another's reputation or deter third persons from associating or dealing with him. Its character depends upon its general tendency to have such an effect.'[55] This gives considerable weight to reputation, in that it allows a plaintiff to take an action, with the possibility of recovering a considerable amount in damages, on foot of a risk of harmful effect (except in cases of those slanders which are not actionable *per se*).[56] Harm is presumed, rather than proved, on the basis of the likely effect of the publication.[57]

The second important issue relates to the standard employed to determine the estimation of the 'community' or 'right-thinking members of society'. It must be said at the outset that the law will consider a negative impact in a respectable sub-section of society to be sufficient. It has been said that 'words are defamatory if they impute conduct which would tend to lower that person in the eyes of a considerable and respectable class of the community, though not in the eyes of the community as a whole'.[58] This still leaves open the question as to how the standard is set, to which we shall return shortly.

The third issue is establishing the meaning of the impugned publication. It is impossible to decide whether a publication can have an adverse impact on the plaintiff's reputation without first determining its meaning. Though the previous statement may seem rather obvious, it is no easy task to determine the meaning of a publication and a considerable amount of skill is required by a practising lawyer to convince a judge or jury to give a publication the meaning for which he is arguing. It is, therefore, important that some space should be devoted to an outline examination of how meaning is determined.

Standard of Measurement

An objective test is employed to determine whether a publication has a defamatory effect. To be defamatory, the impugned publication must be such as to lead

---

55 §559, comment d.
56 Other torts, such as nuisance and passing off, allow a plaintiff to obtain an injunction on foot of a risk of tortious interference, but defamation is exceptional in allowing the recovery of damages for such a risk. This only arises where the defamation is actionable *per se*. There are other torts, such as trespass, which are also actionable *per se*, but these require proof of some actual encroachment on the plaintiff's rights, though physical or material damage need not result.
57 The Law Reform Commission defends this approach, suggesting that to require proof of adverse impact would place too onerous a burden on the plaintiff, LRC 38–91, *op. cit.* at §3.5; McGonagle, *op. cit.* at p. 74, highlights the adverse impact the rule has on small publishers.
58 *Quigley v Creation Ltd* [1971] IR 269, at p. 272 per Walsh J.

a reasonable recipient to form an adverse view of the plaintiff's reputation. The law is not concerned with the defendant's intention, but with the impact the publication will generate in the minds of others,[59] as recipients will often derive a meaning different from that intended by the defendant. Likewise, the plaintiff's subjective perception of the statement is not relevant to determining its defamatory effect, since the protection is for reputation and not personal dignity. The result is that the personal perspective of both parties must yield to a more general societal measure of their respective interests. Defendants must sometimes accept responsibility for imputations which were unintended and plaintiffs must occasionally put up with assertions which they personally find distasteful. Determining the view of the reasonable recipient is easier said than done, but the law attempts to strike a balance between being too eager or too cautious to draw adverse inferences and to give them credence.[60]

In High Court cases the division of functions between judge and jury is the same as that applied to the question of identification. It is a question of law, for the judge to decide, whether the publication is capable of having a defamatory effect; it is a question of fact, for the jury to decide, whether a publication, which is capable of having a defamatory effect, actually does so or not.[61] The preliminary role of the judge in High Court cases, and the exclusive role of judges in Circuit Court cases, mean that the establishment of the appropriate standard of measurement is strongly influenced by judicial views of community opinion, rather than the ordinary perceptions of the general public.[62]

The determining of 'community' standards, or the perceptions of 'right-thinking members of society', is particularly problematic. The legal standard is not based exclusively on what people ought to think, but must take some account of how people actually respond. Thus, an allegation that a person was victimised might be defamatory, since people may react adversely despite the moral turpitude of doing so.[63] Likewise, the standard cannot simply be equated with majority views, but there also comes a point where a minority view may be socially unacceptable. Certainly, lowering a person's credibility

---

59 *White v Tyrrell* (1856) 5 IR CLR 477, at p. 487 per Monaghan CJ; *Bolton v O'Brien* (1885) 16 LR Ir 97, at p. 108 per May CJ.
60 See McDonald, *op. cit.* at pp. 13–16; LRC, *Consultation Paper, op. cit.* at §10.
61 *Barrett v Independent Newspapers* [1986] IR 13; *Duffy v News Group Newspapers Ltd (No. 2)* [1994] 3 IR 63; [1994] 1 ILRM 364.
62 See McDonald, *op. cit.* at pp. 14–15 and pp. 40 *et seq.* on the impact of the division of functions between judge and jury; the extension of the monetary limit on the jurisdiction of the Circuit Court to £30,000 means that only very serious cases will go before a jury in the High Court, thereby increasing the degree to which defamatory effect is determined by judicial opinion; see Byrne & McCutcheon, *The Irish Legal System*, 3rd ed. (Dublin: Butterworths, 1996) at chapter 5 on the jurisdiction of the courts.
63 *Youssoupoff v MGM* (1934) 50 TLR 581, an allegation that a woman was raped was held to be defamatory; cited with approval by Walsh J in *Quigley v Creation Ltd* [1971] IR 269, at p. 272.

within a criminal organisation will not be regarded as defamatory, but what of lowering a person in the eyes of a minority with radical, but lawful, beliefs?[64]

A further difficulty with determining defamatory effect is that previous cases do not always provide reliable guidance. Because the finding on defamatory effect is a finding of fact, based on the particular circumstances of the case, including the social values of the time, superficially similar allegations may be treated differently with changing circumstances. Nonetheless, some general guidance can be gleaned from cases, once the relevance of surrounding circumstances is kept in mind.[65] In *Berry v Irish Times*,[66] a false allegation that the plaintiff assisted British authorities in enforcing the law, by helping to have republicans imprisoned, was held by a jury not to be defamatory. However, if the allegation related to enforcing of the law in another country, with a government regarded by the Irish public as being corrupt or immoral, then a different result could be expected. An allegation that an amateur golfer profited from the commercial exploitation of his fame was held to be defamatory in *Tolley v J.S. Fry & Sons*,[67] more than half a century ago. It is possible that the result could differ now, given the subsequent growth in commercial advertising and character merchandising in amateur, as well as professional, sports. Such changes in result are by no means inevitable, but the crucial point is that the possibility for change, based on varying circumstances or changing values, exists and remains an important feature of the law.

Establishing Meaning

Communication is a complex process and, in many cases, a single communication may be open to multiple interpretations. The plaintiff in a defamation action must establish, by argument, a specific meaning for the impugned publication, from which the adverse impact on reputation tends to arise.[68] A simple example will serve to demonstrate the point:

Example

An article in a newspaper, reporting on crime in a particular city, names a specific public house as a haven for drug dealers and claims that various drugs are openly sold and consumed on the premises.

---

64 The difficulty is well demonstrated by the differing views in the Supreme Court in *Berry v Irish Times Ltd* [1973] IR 368, concerning a false allegation that the plaintiff assisted in having republican prisoners jailed in England; the majority refused to overturn the jury finding that the allegation was not defamatory while the minority felt that the allegation was necessarily defamatory and that the jury finding could not be supported; see also Prosser & Keeton, *op. cit.* at pp. 777–8; McDonald, *op. cit.* at pp. 16 *et seq.*; Howarth, *op. cit.* at pp. 547 *et seq.*

65 See McMahon & Binchy, *op. cit.* at pp. 620–1; McDonald, *op. cit.* at pp. 31 *et seq.*

66 [1973] IR 368.

67 [1931] AC 333; [1931] All ER Rep 131.

68 See McDonald, *op. cit.* at pp. 44 *et seq.*

It might seem simple enough to deduce that this would be likely to be regarded as defamatory of the proprietor of the pub, but even this situation gives rise to at least three potentially defamatory meanings, not all of which would necessarily be accepted. The first is that the proprietor is guilty of specific criminal offences, by permitting the premises to be used for drug dealing and consumption. The second is that, though the proprietor may not consent to or condone the drug related activities, the premises is being managed ineptly because those activities are taking place 'openly'. The third is that, although the proprietor may have done nothing wrong, respectable people may stay away from the premises simply because they wish to steer clear of the drugs scene. A further complication is that the first and third meanings involve factual allegations,[69] while the second is a critical comment and not a factual assertion. This difference is significant in that it affects the defences that may be employed to refute the plaintiff's claim. In less clear-cut situations, potential defamatory meanings will have to compete against non-defamatory interpretations of the communication in question and this will further complicate the matter for the parties.

Interpretation is primarily a practical skill, which requires careful use of the communication itself and the surrounding circumstances to convince a judge or jury that a particular meaning should be attached to a publication. This skill cannot be successfully conveyed by a brief sketch in the pages of a text, but requires extensive practice (though extensive reading of cases to glean information from the successes and failures of those who have already trod the path may prove a useful starting point).

There are, however, some general legal rules related to the problem of determining meaning. There are two ways in which meaning can be determined: one is by considering the natural meaning of the communication; the other is by considering a special meaning based on a combination of the communication itself and additional information. The plaintiff has the choice as to which approach to take, though there are special features to the second approach, to which we shall return later. Where the plaintiff relies on the natural meaning of the words, that meaning is found by applying the popular meaning to the words, signs or gestures used and not by reference to expert interpretation (though dictionaries are occasionally resorted to). The principle was set out by Lefroy B, in *Barrett v Long*,[70] as follows: 'The words of a libel are to be understood in the sense in which they would be understood by men in the ordinary intercourse of life.'

---

69 The third option is based simply on the likely effect of the assertion that drugs are being sold and consumed on the premises; the first option depends on how the article is written – there may be an inference drawn from the assertion about drug dealing and consumption being carried out openly or there may be some more explicit assertion of the proprietor's involvement.

70 (1846) 8 ILRC 331, at p. 343.

Furthermore, the plaintiff cannot take a portion of a publication out of context so as to artificially create a defamatory slant. So, if the plaintiff bases a claim on a segment of a book or newspaper article, for example, the segment is not considered in isolation. *Charleston v News Group Newspapers Ltd*[71] provides a good example. The plaintiffs were an actor and actress in a popular soap opera and pictures of their faces were superimposed on characters in some pornographic pictures, used in a computer game. The defendants ran a newspaper story on the matter, including one of the pornographic shots. The article itself made it clear that the plaintiffs had not consented to the use of their images.

The plaintiffs argued that the headline coupled with the picture was defamatory of them and that a significant portion of the public scanned the headlines and pictures, without reading all of the stories accompanying them. Thus, while many readers would read the whole piece and not draw the defamatory inference, many others would only consider the headline and picture and the plaintiffs' repute would be damaged in the view of these people. The House of Lords rejected this argument and held that the headline and picture could not be considered in isolation. Only one meaning could be ascribed to the article and this would have to be based on the entire article. In the absence of any innuendo, the meaning would be that which would be conveyed to 'an ordinary, reasonable, fair-minded reader'.[72]

This approach seems somewhat harsh on plaintiffs; even Lord Nicholls in *Charleston* described the rule as 'a crude yardstick'.[73] It is well established that a publication with a single meaning can have a defamatory effect on the plaintiff's reputation in the estimation of some people, but not others and that such a publication is actionable. It is a small step from this to accepting that a publication can have different meanings in the view of different groups of people. A similar proposition is already accepted in respect of the concept of a legal innuendo, which is considered below. Where such an innuendo arises, the law accepts that the publication creates a different effect on persons with access to additional information than on those who do not; furthermore, it is accepted in such cases that there may be multiple defamatory meanings, each of which gives rise to a distinct cause of action.

Innuendo

A publication may be defamatory by what can be inferred, rather than what is expressly stated. Where the inference is based on a combination of the publication and additional, extrinsic facts it is described in law as an

---

71 [1995] 2 AC 65; [1995] 2 WLR 450; [1995] 2 All ER 313; noted by Prescott (1995) 58 MLR 752; see also Prosser & Keeton, *op. cit.* at pp. 781–2, for further explanation of the view that a publication can have only one meaning.

72 *Ibid.*, at p. 71; p. 454; p. 317, per Lord Bridge, delivering the leading judgment in the case.

73 *Ibid.*, at p. 73; p. 457; p. 319.

innuendo.[74] This innuendo must be specifically pleaded by the plaintiff in bringing the action, and the extrinsic facts must be proved in order to support the special meaning which the plaintiff claims the publication bears. Where the inference arises from the ordinary meaning of the words, without any additional facts, there is no innuendo in law and, consequently, no need for any special pleading as to meaning.[75] It may be seen from this brief description that the legal meaning of the term 'innuendo' is a narrower one than that used in everyday speech and this gives rise to a certain potential for confusion.[76]

Some brief examples will help to demonstrate the general nature of the legal innuendo. In *Tolly v J.S. Fry & Sons*[77] the defendant, a chocolate manufacturer, used a caricature of the plaintiff to advertise one of its products. This in itself was not defamatory, but taken in conjunction with the additional fact that the plaintiff was a famous amateur golfer, it gave rise to the false implication that the plaintiff had used his reputation for profit (contrary to the spirit of amateurism). In *Cassidy v Daily Mirror Newspaper Ltd*[78] the defendant newspaper published a photograph of a man and a woman along with a caption announcing their engagement. The plaintiff, who was not in the picture, was already married to the man. The publication, considered in isolation, would not be defamatory, but coupled with knowledge that the plaintiff was known to many people to be living with the man in the picture, it carried the adverse inference that the plaintiff was behaving immorally. In *Braun v Armour & Co.*[79] a statement that a meat dealer was selling bacon was considered defamatory in light of the additional fact that the plaintiff was a kosher meat dealer. In all of these situations the plaintiffs are defamed in the view of persons who are aware of the additional information and, as we have already seen, this will be sufficient provided that those who are so aware represent a respectable sub-section of society.

Special Defences

Because of the ease with which defamation can be established in many instances, the defences play a crucial role in determining the precise scope of actionable wrongs. Apart from the general defences of waiver and contributory

---

74 See generally McDonald, *op. cit.* at pp. 44 *et seq.*; Gatley, *op. cit.* at §§94–95; LRC, *Consultation Paper, op. cit.* at §§15–19.

75 This is sometimes described by lawyers as 'popular innuendo' or 'false innuendo'.

76 Lawyers often err on the safe side and include inferences other than legal innuendoes in the pleadings. This caution is also seen in respect of the pleading of legal innuendoes, where the extrinsic facts are often included in the pleadings, though this may not be strictly necessary; see McDonald, *op. cit.* at pp. 47–8.

77 [1931] AC 333; [1931] All ER Rep 131.

78 [1929] 2 KB 331; [1929] All ER Rep 117.

79 (1939) 254 NY 514; 173 NE 845.

negligence, which apply to all torts, there are a number of special defences in respect of defamation.[80]

Justification

In earlier times the defence of justification applied to a range of circumstances which made the publication legally permissible, despite the potential for adverse effect on the plaintiff's reputation. Aspects of the original defence developed into separate defences, such as fair comment and privilege. The modern form of the defence of justification is used by defendants to establish the truth of factual allegations, which provides a complete defence.[81] The rationale of the defence is that, if the plaintiff's reputation is not based on truth, then it is not deserved; consequently, publication of truthful information cannot be unjust.[82] In theory, the law only seeks to protect the plaintiff against untruthful allegations, but falsity is assumed unless the defendant can prove truth. This presumption of falsity makes the law more favourable to plaintiffs in practice, since the publication of truthful information by a defendant who lacks the ability to prove the truth will amount to actionable defamation.[83]

The American Supreme Court has used the constitutional guarantee of free speech to radically reform the law, thereby reducing the need to rely on this defence, at least in the case of media defendants. Falsity is no longer assumed in American defamation law; the plaintiff has to establish the untruthfulness of the allegation.[84] Furthermore, strict liability no longer attaches to the defendant for the publication of false statements. The level of fault which the plaintiff must establish depends on whether the plaintiff is a public figure or a private figure. Private figure plaintiffs must establish that the defendant was negligent with respect to the falsity of the statement,[85] while public figure plaintiffs must satisfy the stricter standard of showing actual knowledge or reckless disregard of falsity by the defendant.[86]

---

80 See Ní Raifeartaigh, *loc. cit.*
81 The Law Reform Commission recommended renaming the defence as 'truth'; LRC 38–91, *op. cit.* at §7.2.
82 *McPherson v Daniels* (1829) 10 B & C 263; see also McDonald, *op. cit.* at p. 97; the publication of truthful information may give rise to liability under some other type of action, e.g. interference with privacy (see chapter 9 *infra*, on interference with constitutional rights), negligent infliction of psychological damage (see chapter 1 *supra*), or intentional infliction of psychological damage (see chapter 10 *infra*, on actions on the case).
83 See McGonagle, *op. cit.* at pp. 66 *et seq.* and pp. 85 *et seq.*; LRC, *Consultation Paper, op. cit.* at §57.
84 *Philadelphia Newspapers Inc. v Hepps* (1986) 106 S Ct 1558; 475 US 767.
85 *Gertz v Robert Welch Inc.* (1974) 418 US 323.
86 *New York Times Co. v Sullivan* (1964) 376 US 254; this decision applied the fault based approach (described as 'actual malice') to plaintiffs that were 'public officials'; the category of persons to whom this standard applied was later expanded to

The American approach has been rejected in Canada[87] and Australia.[88] The High Court of Australia has, however, introduced a defence based on the constitutional right to free communication. This defence is available if the defendant can establish that the defamatory publication concerned 'political discussion' and that the defendant was neither aware, nor reckless as to the falsity of the statement and that it was reasonable to publish in the circumstances. The Irish courts have yet to provide any detailed view on the interrelationship between the Constitution and the law of defamation. Commentators here have differed in their response to the American developments. O'Dell[89] and McDonald[90] are broadly in favour of the American approach, whereas the Law Reform Commission has taken a different approach. The commission divided over the presumption of falsity, the majority recommending its abolition.[91] On the issue of fault, it recommended the introduction of a defence of reasonable care, but rejected the distinction between public and private plaintiffs.[92] Despite the differences, there appears to be some consensus that the common law is unduly favourable to the protection of reputation and gives insufficient weight to freedom of expression.

Let us return now to consider the present extent of the defence of justification. In order to be effective, the justification must be as broad as the defamation. In other words, the facts that the defendant succeeds in proving must be enough to cover all of the barb of the defamatory publication. Partial truth or literal truth, which fails to prove the truth of significant aspects of the allegations made, will not suffice. Thus, in *Irish People's Assurance Society v*

'public figures' in the consolidated cases of *Curtis Publishing Co. v Butts* and *Associated Press v Walker* (1967) 388 US 130; see also *Gertz v Robert Welch Inc.* (1974) 418 US 323; for detailed consideration of these developments see Carlson, '*Philadelphia Newspapers Inc. v Hepps*: A Logical Product of the *New York Times* Revolution', 64 Denv UL Rev 65; Prosser & Keeton, *op. cit.* at §116; LRC, *Consultation Paper, op. cit.* at chapter 5.

87 *Hill v Church of Scientology of Toronto* (1995) 126 DLR (4th) 129, noted by Huscroft (1996) 112 LQR 46; the onus of proof in respect of falsity is placed on the plaintiff under the Nova Scotia Defamation Act; the constitutionality of the provision was upheld in *Coates v The Citizen* (1988) 44 CCLT 286.

88 *Theophanous v Herald & Weekly Times Ltd* (1994) 68 ALJR 713; 182 CLR 104; *Stephens v West Australian Newspapers Ltd* (1994) 68 ALJR 765, both noted by Trindade (1995) 111 LQR 199 and analysed more extensively by Cassimatis, 'Defamation – The Constitutional Public Officer Defence' (1996) 4 Tort L Rev 27.

89 'Does Defamation Value Free Expression?', *loc. cit.*; 'Reflections on a Revolution in Libel', *loc. cit.*

90 *Op. cit.* at pp. 113 *et seq.*; see also Boyle & McGonagle, *loc. cit.* at pp. 60–2.

91 LRC 38–91, *op. cit.* at §§7.28–7.35.

92 *Ibid.*, at §§7.17–7.27; though McGonagle, *op. cit.* at pp. 81–3, argues that such a distinction may yet find its way into Irish law, particularly through the influence of the European Court of Human Rights.

City of Dublin Assurance,[93] the defendant had published extracts from the plaintiff's balance sheet and, although the extracts were accurate, the defence failed because the defendant failed to prove the truth of the imputation that the plaintiff was in poor financial condition. The inference generated by taking the figures out of context could not be proved simply by relying on the literal accuracy of the figures extracted from the balance sheet. Similarly, in *Wakley v Cooke*,[94] the defence failed where the defendant, who had referred to the plaintiff as a 'libellous journalist', proved that one judgment for libel had previously been obtained against the plaintiff. The allegation was held to mean that the plaintiff habitually libelled people, so proof that he had once done so was not sufficient.[95]

The requirement of substantial, rather than literal, truth means that liability cannot be avoided simply by prefacing unfounded allegations with phrases such as 'it is rumoured', or 'it is alleged'. If a publication conveys the impression that the substance of a rumour is true, then proving the existence of the rumour will not suffice to establish justification. This does not preclude publications concerning unproved allegations, but it does require the publisher to exercise care in the presentation of the material, so that the uncertainty as to the substance of the allegation is apparent.[96] Likewise, the common practice of including a statement in a television programme or film that the events portrayed are fictional will not necessarily protect the makers or producers.[97]

Minor inaccuracies will be disregarded if the substance of an allegation is true. In *O'Connor v Wallen*[98] the plaintiff claimed that a number of allegations made against him by the defendant gave rise to the implication that he habitually engaged in misrepresentation. The defendant pleaded justification and the plea included one change in detail – in respect of an allegation that the plaintiff had claimed to be a captain of Dragoons, the defendant sought to show that the plaintiff had actually claimed to be a surgeon in the Navy. The Court of Common Pleas held that this change would not be sufficient to preclude the defence of justification. In *Alexander v North Eastern Railway*

---

93 [1929] IR 25.
94 (1849) 4 Exch 511; see also *Penton v Calwell* (1945) 70 CLR 219.
95 A further issue of contention in relation to allegations of this nature is the evidential status of previous decisions of courts and other tribunals; see McDonald, *op. cit.* at pp. 106–9; LRC, *Consultation Paper, op. cit.* at §§65–66; LRC 38–91, *op. cit.* at §§7.10–7.12.
96 See *Lewis v Daily Telegraph* [1964] AC 234; [1964] 2 WLR 736; [1963] 2 All ER 151, allegation that a person was being investigated by the fraud squad held not to infer guilt, as this would imply an inordinately high level of accuracy in police investigation. The case provides insightful discussion of the relationship between the defence of justification and the publication of stories about suspicions and unproved allegations.
97 See LRC 38–91, *op. cit.* at §§7.47–7.54.
98 (1856) 6 Ir CLR 378.

Co.[99] a minor inaccuracy in the defendant's statement about the sentence imposed on the plaintiff for travelling on a train without a ticket did not defeat the defence. The defendant had stated the sentence as a fine of £1 or three weeks' imprisonment in default, whereas the actual sentence was for £1 or two weeks' imprisonment in default.

The degree of inaccuracy permitted has been extended by section 22 of the Defamation Act 1961, which deals with cases of multiple allegations. Under the section the untruth of some allegations can be excused if the overall effect on reputation caused by the publication is merited. If the more serious allegations can be shown to be true, then the failure to establish the truth of other allegations will not prevent the defence from succeeding, provided that the unproved allegations 'do not materially injure the plaintiff's reputation having regard to the truth of the remaining charges'. McDonald is critical of the provision, as it suggests that 'minor defamations are of no account and can be ignored by the law'.[100]

If the truth of an allegation cannot be shown, a question arises as to whether the defendant can introduce evidence showing the plaintiff in a bad light and deserving of a poor reputation, by reference to other misconduct by the plaintiff, in circumstances not covered by section 22. Such a strategy will not amount to a complete defence, but may be employed for the purpose of minimising the damages payable, because evidence of bad character may establish that little real harm has been caused by the defamation. In *Plato Films v Speidel*,[101] the House of Lords held that general evidence of existing bad reputation in the relevant sector of the plaintiff's life was admissible in mitigation of damages. Evidence of specific misconduct, other than the allegations sued upon, was held to be inadmissible, as was evidence to show the reputation that the plaintiff ought to have. The dividing line between that which is admissible and that which is not would be difficult to draw in many instances. There is no Irish authority on the issue, though the Law Reform Commission recommended the rejection of the rule in *Plato Films*[102] and the rule has been changed in England by section 13 of the Defamation Act 1996, so that specific misconduct can be used to mitigate damages.

If the defendant fails in the attempt to prove the truth of the allegations or to show bad character on the plaintiff's part, then aggravated damages can be awarded to compensate the plaintiff for the further slight on his character caused by the conduct of the defence. A failed defence of justification will not necessarily lead to an increase in the damages awarded, since the defendant

---

99 (1865) 6 B & S 340; 122 ER 1221.
100 *Op. cit.* at p. 105.
101 [1961] AC 1090; [1961] 2 WLR 470; [1961] 1 All ER 876; see also *Dingle v Associated Newspapers Ltd* [1964] AC 371; [1962] 3 WLR 229; [1962] 2 All ER 737.
102 LRC 38–91, *op. cit.* at §§7.5–7.9.

may have done no more than exercise a legitimate right to mount a reasonable defence. But, if the defence strategy is unwarranted or amounts to mere sensationalism, which further injures the plaintiff, then such an award may be appropriate.[103] Raising bad character in mitigation of damages necessarily involves the raising of additional slurs on the plaintiff's character and so, is even more likely to lead to an award of aggravated damages.[104]

Privilege

The privilege defences are designed to protect the public interest in free speech in respect of special situations, which have been deemed to require a greater degree of latitude than others. Occasions of privilege involve various interests which are allowed to override the plaintiff's reputation, by permitting publication without regard to the truth of the content. This permits certain persons, such as public representatives, participants in legal proceedings and journalists reporting on such activities to speak freely, without being inhibited by the possibility of being sued over any inaccuracy in what they say. Privilege can be either absolute or qualified. The protection afforded by qualified privilege is dependent on the defendant having a proper purpose in publishing the defamatory material, whereas absolute privilege protects the defendant irrespective of the purpose or motivation behind the publication.

Absolute Privilege

Absolute privilege is confined to a limited range of communications, concerned with certain aspects of government or the administration of justice. These activities are regarded as sufficiently important to allow complete freedom of expression, irrespective of motivation. The exclusion of communications between husband and wife in the interpretation of 'publication' might also be viewed as a form of absolute privilege.

Article 13.8.1° of the Constitution provides the President with absolute privilege in respect of the exercise or purported exercise of any official functions or powers. The only way by which the President can be held to account for conduct in the exercise of official activities is through the impeachment pro-

---

103 For detailed consideration of the potential for aggravated damages see McDonald, *op. cit.* at pp. 111 *et seq.*

104 See *Kennedy v Hearne* [1988] ILRM 531; the plaintiff, a solicitor, had been defamed by the Revenue Commissioners when the process for recovery of unpaid taxes was continued after the plaintiff had paid the due amount; the defence sought to show that the plaintiff was, nonetheless, a cheat and deserving of a poor reputation in respect of the maintenance of his financial affairs. The Supreme Court held that aggravated damages of £10,000 should be paid to the plaintiff, since the original defamation had been to a small number of people, who were not acquainted with the plaintiff, but the failed attack on his reputation occurred in open court in front of many people familiar with the plaintiff and his business as a practising solicitor.

cedure, contained in Article 12.10. Members of the Oireachtas also have an absolute immunity from any court proceedings in respect of utterances in either House of the Oireachtas, under Article 15.13. Article 15.12 extends that privilege to reports of any utterance and this has been held to include unofficial reports;[105] thus, media coverage of parliamentary debates also benefits from the constitutional protection. These provisions are not, strictly speaking, defences which need to be pleaded and proved by the publisher of a protected statement; rather the Constitution ousts the jurisdiction of the courts.[106] The protection may be waived, however, but the precise circumstances in which waiver will be deemed to have occurred remain unclear. Mere repetition outside the Houses of the Oireachtas will not deprive a member of the protection, but where the repetition is 'voluntary, conscious and deliberate'[107] it may amount to waiver.

Statutory measures have extended the ambit of absolute privilege in respect of the governmental process. The Committees of the Houses of the Oireachtas Act 1976 extended the privilege of members to utterances in committees of either House.[108] Absolute privilege was also given to documents of the committee, documents of committee members connected with committee functions, utterances of persons such as advisers and agents, and reports of any of the privileged material.[109] More recently, further statutory measures have been introduced to provide protection for witnesses before such committees. Witnesses, other than members of either House, were not covered by the 1976 Act and even members may not have been protected in respect of documents, rather than oral statements. Section 2 of the Select Committee on Legislation and Security of Dáil Éireann (Privilege and Immunity) Act 1994 provides that witnesses before that committee shall have the same privileges and immunities as a witness in the High Court and documents are also privileged.[110] The same privilege applies in respect of other committees under section 11(1) of the Committees of the Houses of the Oireachtas (Compellability, Privileges and Immunities of Witnesses) Act 1997. The operation of this provision has some slight variations from the earlier Act. First, the Houses have a discretion in

---

105 *AG v Hamilton (No. 2)* [1993] 3 IR 227; the term 'utterance' appears to confine the protection to spoken words, excluding gestures and even written communications within the Oireachtas; this is particularly evident in the Irish text.

106 *Ibid.*, per Finlay CJ at p. 269; per Blayney J at p. 296.

107 *Ibid.*, per Blayney J at p. 296; in the instant case allegations made by members were used to formulate the terms of reference for the Tribunal of Inquiry into the Beef Processing Industry and were repeated in both written submissions and oral testimony before the tribunal; the majority view in the Supreme Court was that clarification of the allegations in this fashion was protected by Art. 15; for more detailed consideration of Art. 15 see Kelly, *op. cit.* at pp. 141–7; McDonald, *op. cit.* at pp. 119 *et seq.*

108 S. 2(1).

109 S. 2(2); see McDonald, *op. cit.* at pp. 124 *et seq.*

110 S. 4 authorises the establishment of sub-committees and provides that the protection in s. 2 extends to such sub-committees.

respect of the initiation or cessation of the applicability of the section to any particular committee;[111] and, secondly, if a witness is directed to cease giving evidence, any further statements by him before the committee are subject to qualified privilege.[112]

Communications by members of the executive and senior civil and public servants in the exercise of official functions also appear to be subject to absolute privilege at common law, though there is little modern authority on the subject.[113] Representatives and officials of foreign states and the European Union are also subject to immunity from suit.[114]

In chapter 1 we saw that advocates had an immunity from suit in respect of their advocacy and related preparatory work and that this was based on public policy, designed to ensure the fair and unfettered administration of justice. In the context of defamation, the need to ensure the attainment of public policy interests in the administration of justice is manifested by the provision of absolute privilege to participants in the legal process. Judges, lawyers, parties and witnesses all benefit from the privilege, in order to ensure full and uninhibited participation in the process.[115] The privilege includes ancillary aspects of the litigation process, such as pleadings.[116] The privilege does not apply to every aspect of a judge's activities; there are two situations where the privilege will not be available. The first is where the judge is acting without jurisdiction and without any reasonable grounds for believing he has jurisdiction.[117] The other is where the judge is acting 'ministerially' and not engaging in an administration of justice.[118] The distinction between ministerial acts and administration of justice is not easily drawn, but the key features of the latter are the exercise of discretion and decision making; thus, the performance of mandatory administrative acts would not provide an occasion of absolute privilege.

The privilege in respect of the administration of justice also applies to the limited exercise of judicial functions by bodies other than courts, but not to purely administrative bodies.[119]

---

111 S. 18.
112 S. 11(2).
113 See McDonald, *op. cit.* at pp. 139 *et seq.*; McMahon & Binchy, *op. cit.* at p. 647.
114 See chapter 13 *infra*.
115 *Ward v Freeman* (1852) 2 Ir CLR 450; *Kennedy v Hilliard* (1859) 10 Ir CLR 195; *Tughan v Craig* [1918] 1 IR 245; *Macauley & Co. v Wyse-Power* (1943) 77 ILTR 61 (judges); *Kennedy v Hilliard* (1859) 10 Ir CLR 195; *Looney v Bank of Ireland and Morey* [1996] 1 IR 157 (parties and witnesses); *Waple v Surrey County Council* [1997] 2 All ER 836 (solicitors); see McDonald, *op. cit.* at pp. 126 *et seq.*
116 *McCabe v Joynt* [1901] 2 IR 115; *Looney v Bank of Ireland and Morey* [1996] 1 IR 157.
117 *O'Keeffe v Cullen* (1873) IR 7 CL 319; *Sirros v Moore* [1975] QB 118; [1974] 3 WLR 459; [1974] 3 All ER 776.
118 *Ward v Freeman* (1852) 2 Ir CLR 450; *Ferguson v Kinnoull* (1842) 9 CL & Fin 251.
119 See McDonald, *op. cit.* at pp. 137 *et seq.*; McMahon & Binchy, *op. cit.* at p. 646; *Royal Aquarium and Summer and Winter Garden Society v Parkinson* [1892] 1

Qualified Privilege

The defence of qualified privilege is available in a variety of situations, governed by common law and statute, and it protects the publisher completely, provided the privileged occasion is not abused. The purpose of privilege is not merely to protect the defendant's interest on the particular occasion, but for the promotion of the common good by allowing uninhibited expression on certain types of occasion.[120]

Qualified privilege at common law protects communications where the publisher and recipient each have a duty or interest in the subject matter of the communication.[121] The duty or interest need not be one arising by law, but extends to social and moral obligations. The defence applies to publications 'fairly made by a person in the discharge of some public or private duty whether legal or moral, or in the conduct of his own affairs, in matters where his interest is concerned'.[122] The law has proven to be flexible in the application of the defence and there can be no complete or closed list of privileged occasions.[123]

The defence permits people to engage in reasonable protection of themselves and others. At one end of the scale we can see how the defence applies to suspicions of wrongdoing. The reporting of suspected wrongdoing to the proper authorities would be protected,[124] as would communications by those authorities to any person with an interest in the matter under investigation.[125] The investigation of wrongdoing would be seriously impaired if people involved in the process had no defence, should the suspicions ultimately prove to be incorrect or unprovable. Innocent suspects are not entirely unprotected, since they will have a right of action, if it can be shown that the privilege was exceeded or used for an improper purpose. At the other end of the scale,

---

QB 431; [1891–4] All ER Rep 429; *O'Connor v Waldron* [1935] AC 76; [1934] All ER Rep 281.

120 See Gatley, *op. cit.* at §§443–444 for detailed consideration of the underlying policy basis of the defence.

121 See McDonald, *loc. cit.* for detailed consideration of this branch of the defence.

122 *Toogood v Spyring* (1834) 1 CM & R 181, at p. 193 per Parke B; for an extensive account of the range of occasions subject to qualified privilege see Gatley, *op. cit.* at chapter 13; McDonald, *op. cit.* at pp. 144–70 and pp. 195–8; Fridman, *op cit.* vol. 2 at pp. 172–5.

123 *Hamerton v Green* (1863) 16 Ir CLR 77, at p. 97 per Hayes J; p. 106 per O'Brien J; *Hynes-O'Sullivan v O'Driscoll* [1988] IR 436, at p. 453 per McCarthy J; see also McMahon & Binchy, *op. cit.* at p. 648.

124 *Hartery v Welltrade (Middle East) Ltd and Hurley* [1978] ILRM 38 (complaint to the police of possible blackmail); *Denvir v Taylor* [1936] Ir Jur Rep 4 (report by supervisor to employer about the conduct of an employee).

125 *Kirkwood Hackett v Tierney* [1952] IR 185 (president of a university speaking to a student, in the presence of the bursar, during the investigation of an allegation that the student had wrongly obtained money, paid out through the university; bursar held to have a sufficient interest in the matter).

family members may communicate freely with each other in respect of matters such as the character of persons they associate with.[126]

There is no general privilege for matters of public interest.[127] Unless the publisher can establish a particular duty or interest of his own and one on the part of the recipients, the defence will not apply. The media do not have a sufficiently recognised general duty to communicate with the public at large on all matters of public interest to attract the benefit of qualified privilege and must rely on other defences, such as justification or fair comment, if a specific basis for the privilege cannot be found. The Court of Appeal, in *Reynolds v Times Newspapers Ltd*,[128] held that the reasons surrounding the fall of a government were of sufficient public interest to create a duty on the part of the defendants to publish and a reciprocal interest in the general public to receive the publication, but that the privilege did not extend to the inclusion of an unsubstantiated allegation, from an unnamed source, who turned out to be a member of staff of a political opponent of the plaintiff. The changes in American law, resulting from the decision in *New York Times v Sullivan*[129] and the subsequent line of cases on free speech, have resulted in the establishing of a more general qualified privilege for the media in discussing public figures there.

The use of a public forum may attract qualified privilege in limited instances. This would arise where the use of a public medium is considered an appropriate means of response to a public allegation. In *Nevin v Roddy and Carty*[130] the

---

126 *Todd v Hawkins* (1837) 8 C & P 88; 173 ER 411 (father warning his daughter about her fiancé); *Atkinson v Congreve* (1857) 7 Ir CLR 109 (first cousin writing to a woman about her fiancé); the protection may also extend to friends and associates, *Davis v Reeves* (1855) 5 Ir CLR 79 (solicitor warning a client about a debtor, outside the scope of the solicitor–client relationship); in the case of social or moral duty the case for qualified privilege is strengthened if the publisher was requested to provide the communication, rather than simply volunteering, see *Owens v Roberts* (1856) 6 Ir CLR 386 (requested communication privileged); *Gillis v M'Donnell* (1869) IR 4 CL 342 (volunteered communication between strangers not privileged); McDonald, *op. cit.* at pp. 150 *et seq.*

127 *Doyle v The Economist* [1980] NI 171 (magazine story that the plaintiff had been appointed to the County Court as a token Catholic not privileged); *London Artists Ltd v Littler* [1969] 2 QB 375; [1969] 2 WLR 409; [1969] 2 All ER 193 (letter published in a newspaper relating to the running of a theatre and the premature ending of a successful play not privileged); *Blackshaw v Lord* [1984] 1 QB 1; [1983] 3 WLR 283; [1983] 2 All ER 311 (newspaper report about a civil servant and the running of the government department in which he worked not privileged); see also *Truth (New Zealand) Ltd v Holloway* [1960] NZLR 69; *Brooks v Muldoon* [1973] NZLR 1; McDonald, *op. cit.* at pp. 161 *et seq.*; LRC, *Consultation Paper, op. cit.* at §111; McGonagle, *op. cit.* at pp. 97–8.

128 [1998] 3 All ER 961; [1998] 3 WLR 862.

129 (1964) 376 US 254.

130 [1935] IR 397; see also *O'Brien v The Freeman's Journal Ltd* (1907) 41 ILTR 35 (response in the defendants' paper to attacks made against them at public meetings and reported in the press); *Adam v Ward* [1917] AC 309; [1916–17] All ER

second defendant published a letter in the first defendant's newspaper, in response to allegations made by the plaintiff in the same paper. The Supreme Court upheld a jury verdict allowing the defendants the benefit of qualified privilege. The second defendant had a sufficient interest in the subject matter, as it related to his character, and the recipients had a corresponding interest in receiving the publication, as they had already received the plaintiff's allegations through the same medium.

It is essential that the recipients of a publication have a sufficient interest or duty in doing so. The duty or interest of the publisher and the recipient need not be identical; it is sufficient that each has some genuine duty or interest of his own. A mistaken belief by the publisher in the existence of a duty or interest, which does not in fact exist, will not suffice. The leading Irish decision is *Hynes-O'Sullivan v O'Driscoll*.[131] A dispute arose between the plaintiff, a psychiatrist, and defendant, a solicitor, over fees payable to the plaintiff in respect of her attendance in court as a witness. The plaintiff made a complaint to the Incorporated Law Society in respect of the defendant's behaviour. In responding to the society, the defendant made counter allegations against the plaintiff, which he repeated in letters of complaint to the Irish Medical Association (a trade union, of which the plaintiff was not a member) and the Medical Council (the governing body of the medical profession).

The central issue in the appeal to the Supreme Court was whether the letter to the Irish Medical Association could be regarded as privileged on the basis of an honest but mistaken belief that the association had an interest in the complaint. The court held that the defence was not available in those circumstances. Three members of the court went further and stated, *obiter*, that an honest and reasonable belief of a sufficient interest would not suffice (the defendant's belief was not reasonable in the circumstances).[132] Thus, an actual duty or interest on the part of the recipient must be shown by the defendant for the defence to succeed.

A limited amount of ancillary publication to persons without any interest or duty will, however, be tolerated. If it were otherwise, the law would be too rigid for practical purposes. It would be unreasonable, for example, for a defendant to have to show that the readership of different editions of a newspaper or

---

Rep 157 (letter in a newspaper by the secretary of the Army Council in response to allegations made in the House of Commons against a general).
131 [1989] ILRM 349.
132 *Ibid.*, at pp. 359–60 per Henchy J, Hederman J concurring; at p. 364 per McCarthy J; they felt that the constitutional right to the protection of one's good name required a degree of certainty in respect of the circumstances in which protection would be lost and that a test of honest and reasonable belief by the defendant in the existence of a sufficient interest or duty would be too vague to give adequate protection to the plaintiff's right; see also LRC, *Consultation Paper, op. cit.* at §§232–244; Gatley, *op. cit.* at §531.

magazine were identical, before allowing the defence in a case such as *Nevin v Roddy and Carty*, above. The presence of disinterested recipients may provide evidence of malice[133] or may raise a question as to whether the chosen method of publication was suited to the duty or interest, thereby raising a doubt as to whether the occasion was privileged at all.[134]

A wide range of media reports are granted qualified privilege under section 24 of the 1961 Act. The reports are set out in the second schedule and fall into two groups. Part 1 covers fair and accurate reports of the public proceedings of the following bodies – foreign legislatures; public inquiries established by foreign legislatures; international organisations of which the state or government is a member; international conferences at which the state or government is represented; international judicial or arbitral bodies; public registers. Part 1 also covers any notice or advertisement published with the authority of any court in the State or Northern Ireland. Part 2 covers fair and accurate reports of a variety of bodies, such as associations promoting art, science, religion, business, sports and so forth. It also extends to reports of public meetings and meetings of local authorities, statutory tribunals or inquiries; public companies; judges acting judicially outside of court; local inquiries by persons appointed by local authorities.[135]

Those set out in Part 2 of the second schedule of the Act are subject to explanation or contradiction.[136] This entitles the plaintiff to request that a reasonable statement, by way of explanation or contradiction, be published by the newspaper or broadcaster that published the report. Failure to comply with the request will remove the protection of the statutory privilege from the original report.[137]

Section 18(1) of the 1961 Act extends the privilege in respect of the administration of justice to media reports within the State or Northern Ireland, provided such reports are fair, accurate and contemporaneous. Section 18(2) excludes blasphemous or obscene matter from the scope of the privilege. There is disagreement as to whether the privilege under section 18 is absolute or qualified.[138]

---

133 *Keenan v Wallace* (1916) 51 ILTR 11, at p. 20 per Gibson J, *obiter*.

134 *Robinson v Jones* (1879) 4 LR Ir 391 (use of open postcard to demand payment of a debt); see also *Bell v Parke* (1860) 11 Ir CLR 413, at p. 429 per Pigot CB; McDonald, *op. cit.* at pp. 199–200.

135 For consideration of what is 'fair' and whether a document is public see *Tsikata v Newspaper Publishing plc* [1997] 1 All ER 655.

136 S. 24(2).

137 See generally McDonald, *op. cit.* at pp. 178 *et seq.*; McMahon & Binchy, *op. cit.* at pp. 653–5.

138 McDonald, *op. cit.* at pp. 171–2, argues that it is qualified; McMahon & Binchy, *op. cit.* at pp. 642–3, treat it as absolute; see also LRC 38–91, *op. cit.* at §5.11, recommending the introduction of a new provision granting absolute privilege and removing the need for the report to be contemporaneous.

In all cases of qualified privilege, common law or statutory, the protection will be lost if the publisher acts maliciously. Malice in this instance does not have its ordinary meaning of ill-will; all that is required is an improper purpose on the publisher's part. If the object of the communication is not genuinely connected to the duty or interest for which the privilege was granted, then the protection afforded for the privileged occasion is lost.[139] The onus is on the plaintiff to establish malice; it is not incumbent on the defendant to establish a bona fide exercise of the privileged occasion.[140] Direct evidence of motive will almost invariably be absent; thus, the plaintiff must seek to have malice inferred from evidence of surrounding circumstances.[141]

Liability may also attach to a defendant where there is an excess of publication. This would arise where the publisher, on a privileged occasion, includes allegations unrelated to the duty or interest which gave rise to the privilege. The inclusion of such matters can lead to two distinct results. First, the excess may be treated as unprotected, while leaving the protection for the material which is relevant to the privileged occasion; secondly, the excess may provide evidence of malice, destroying the protection for the entire communication.[142]

Fair Comment

This defence excludes liability for the expression of opinions, based on facts available to the public, provided that the opinion is honestly held and relates to a matter of public interest. This defence partially redresses the restriction on free speech created by the rejection of qualified privilege in respect of matters of general public interest. Each element of the defence – comment, factual basis, honesty of belief and public interest – must be carefully examined, in order to determine its boundaries.

The distinction between fact and opinion is the key to appreciating the nature of the defence. Fair comment protects the expression of opinion only; it does not extend to the making of factual statements. The publisher's belief in the facts is not sufficient to transform a factual statement into an opinion. If the

---

139 See *Clark v Molyneux* (1877) 3 QBD 237, at pp. 246–7 per Brett LJ; *Kirkwood-Hackett v Tierney* [1952] IR 185, at p. 199 and p. 203 per O'Byrne J; LRC, *Consultation Paper, op. cit.* at §114; McDonald, *op. cit.* at pp. 202 *et seq.*; McMahon & Binchy, *op. cit.* at p. 655 ; Gatley, *op. cit.* at §§772–786.

140 *McMullan v Mulhall* [1929] IR 470; *Kirkwood-Hackett v Tierney* [1952] IR 185; *Hennessy v K-TEL Ireland Ltd* unrep. SC, 12 June 1997; Irish Times Law Report 28 July 1997; see Gatley, *op. cit.* at §§790–798.

141 Proof of malice is considered in detail by McDonald, *op. cit.* at pp. 204 *et seq.*; see also Fridman, *op. cit.* vol. 2 at pp. 177–8; *Dawson v Irish Brokers Association*, unrep. SC, 27 February 1997.

142 *McKeogh v O'Brien-Moran* [1927] IR 348; *Horrocks v Lowe* [1975] AC 135; [1974] 2 WLR 282; [1974] 1 All ER 662; McDonald, *op. cit.* at pp. 200 *et seq.*; LRC, *Consultation Paper, op. cit.* at §115.

impugned allegation is of a factual nature, for example 'P murdered X' or 'P is a paedophile', then it cannot be defended as comment; justification or privilege would be the appropriate defence. To be regarded as an opinion, the impugned material must involve a considerable degree of value judgment. Thus, 'comment' describes matters incapable of definitive proof, such as 'P is despicable' or 'P is immoral'.[143] The distinction is aptly demonstrated in *London Artists Ltd v Littler*.[144] The defendant was the producer of a successful play, but the company which owned the theatre wished to cut its run short in order to use the theatre for other purposes. Much of the cast was represented by the plaintiff agency company, whose controlling shareholder was also a major shareholder in the company that owned the theatre. The play was cut short by the withdrawal of leading members of the cast, all represented by the plaintiff company, and the defendant wrote an article in which he suggested that a conspiracy had forced the premature curtailment of his play.

The Court of Appeal held the allegation of a conspiracy to be factual in nature and, therefore, incapable of being defended as a comment. This shows that even though a reasonable suspicion of a certain state of affairs might arise from facts available to a person, any publication asserting the truth of the inference cannot be treated as comment. A carefully worded publication, acknowledging the element of doubt as to the truth of the inference, would be permitted to raise the element of suspicion as a comment on the available facts.

The comment must be based on facts available to the public, though the relevant facts need not all be recited in the impugned publication. It will be sufficient if the publication refers to facts contained elsewhere, provided that such facts are sufficiently available to the public.[145] The facts must be substantially true,[146] except perhaps where stated on a privileged occasion. As

---

143 *Lingens v Austria* [1986] 8 EHRR 407, the European Court of Human Rights distinguished between fact and opinion on the basis that the former was susceptible to scientific proof, while the latter was not; the distinction is not easy to draw in practice, see McGonagle, *op. cit.* at pp. 88–92; LRC, *Consultation Paper, op. cit.* at §§319–337; Fridman, *op. cit.* vol. 2 at pp. 162–3.

144 [1969] 2 QB 375; [1969] 2 WLR 409; [1969] 2 All ER 193; the defendant may be required to clarify the pleadings, so that it is clear from the outset which aspects of the publication are sought to be treated as fact and which are sought to be treated as comment, see *Cooney v Browne* [1985] ILRM 673; the success or failure of the defence depends on the ability to convince the court of the appropriate division between fact and comment.

145 *Kemsley v Foot* [1952] AC 345; [1952] 1 All ER 501 (reference to tabloid journalism by a particular publisher; held that the broad circulation of the relevant newspapers made the general nature of their style and content matters of public knowledge).

146 See, for example, *Nolan Transport (Oaklands) Ltd v Halligan and Others* [1995] ELR 1, where one of a number of critical comments about the conduct of the plaintiff company's business was found not to have a factual basis; held that this comment could not be fair. The High Court decision was overturned on appeal on grounds unconnected to the defamation issue, unrep. SC, 15 May 1998; the

with the defence of justification, literal truth will not suffice if taken out of context. Geoghegan J, in *Foley v Independent Newspapers Ltd*,[147] held that a 'true statement of grounding facts is not necessarily constituted by a series of sentences which are literally accurate'.[148] Section 23 of the 1961 Act provides that partial truth of supporting facts will suffice if 'the expression of opinion is fair comment having regard to such of the facts alleged or referred to . . . as are proved'.[149] The possible exception of privileged statements of fact from the requirement of truth originates in *Mangena v Wright*.[150] It was held that facts stated on a privileged occasion, such as a parliamentary debate or a court judgment, could be reported and commented upon and that the defence of fair comment should be available despite any untruth in the facts. The status and extent of the rule is somewhat uncertain. The extent of the rule is unclear, as it may apply to all privileged statements of fact or only to certain types.[151] Its status is unclear, since it has not been considered in the Irish courts. The rule seems sensible, at least in its original context. If one can claim privilege in respect of a factual assertion, then it seems reasonable that one should be allowed to comment on its implications.[152] The case for allowing the repetition of privileged assertions outside of a privileged occasion, in order to support a comment, seems far less compelling.

'Fair' is a misnomer, since the law permits robust, vehement and unusual views to be expressed under this defence. A comment does not have to conform to a standard of reasonableness, but only has to be capable of being honestly held by a rational person in light of those facts which are either true or privileged.[153]

Supreme Court decision was grounded on the statutory immunities contained in the Industrial Relations Act 1990 (considered in chapter 13 *infra*).

147 [1994] 2 ILRM 61.

148 *Ibid.*, at pp. 64–5. The publication in question concerned the fees charged to the government by inspectors, appointed to investigate the affairs of a company. The stated facts failed to disclose that the fees were charged in accordance with a method and rate agreed earlier between the government and the inspectors, shortly after their appointment.

149 McDonald, *op. cit.* at p. 214 suggests that s. 23 applies only where the facts are contained in the statement and not where they are contained elsewhere; the wording of the section is somewhat ambiguous and the Law Reform Commission suggest the broader interpretation that the section applies to facts alluded to in the publication, but located elsewhere, LRC, *Consultation Paper, op. cit.* at §82.

150 [1909] 2 KB 958.

151 See McDonald, *op. cit.* at pp. 215–16; LRC, *Consultation Paper, op. cit.* at §83; LRC 38–91, *op. cit.* at §6.5.

152 In *Mangena* the reporting of facts was privileged under s. 3 of the Parliamentary Papers Act 1840; the broader principle asserted in the case, that a comment on facts stated by another person was not dependent on the truth of those facts, is questionable. See also *Foley v Independent Newspapers Ltd* [1994] 2 ILRM 61.

153 *Merivale v Carson* (1887) 20 QBD 275; *Stopes v Sutherland* [1925] AC 47; [1924] All ER Rep 19; *Telnikeff v Matusevitch* [1992] 2 AC 343; [1991] 3 WLR

There is some authority for the view that a comment must be objectively reasonable where it imputes base and dishonourable motives to the plaintiff,[154] but this approach has been heavily criticised by modern commentators and law reform bodies.[155] Despite the latitude generally afforded by the defence, proof that the defendant was actuated by malice may defeat the defence. As malice is a question of fact, it is difficult to predict when such a finding will be found and considered strong enough to displace the 'fairness' of the comment so as to defeat the defence.[156]

Public interest is given a wide interpretation. It covers matters of an inherently public nature, such as the conduct of government affairs or affairs of public bodies, and matters which have been submitted to the public, such as works of art, literature, commercial activities, sporting activities.[157] There are two main restrictions on what constitutes public interest. First, comment on the judicial process is limited by the law of contempt of court, which seeks to prevent the undermining of the process, while allowing latitude for legitimate criticism.[158] The second is that the private affairs of a public individual are not considered matters of public interest, unless they relate to the person's participation in such matters.[159]

952; [1991] 4 All ER 817; McDonald, *op. cit.* at pp. 217 *et seq.*; Gatley, *op. cit.* at §§707–709; LRC, *Consultation Paper, op. cit.* at §86; LRC 38–91, *op. cit.* at §6.2 recommends that the word 'fair' be dropped from the title of the defence.

154 *Campbell v Spottiswoode* (1863) 3 B & S 769; *Hunt v Star Newspaper Co. Ltd* [1908] 2 KB 309; [1908–10] All ER Rep 513.

155 See McDonald, *op. cit.* at pp. 219–220; LRC, *Consultation Paper, op. cit.* at §87; Heuston & Buckley, *Salmond & Heuston on the Law of Torts*, 21st ed. (London: Sweet & Maxwell, 1996) at p. 184.

156 *Stannus v Finlay* (1874) IR 8 CL 264; *Thomas v Bradbury Agnew & Co. Ltd* [1906] 2 KB 627; [1904–7] All ER Rep 220; *Adams v Sunday Pictorial Newspapers (1920) Ltd* [1951] 1 KB 354; [1951] 1 All ER 865; there are differing views on the precise relationship between malice and fairness (or honesty) in determining how the defence may be lost; see McMahon & Binchy, *op. cit.* at pp. 660–1; McDonald, *op. cit.* at pp. 223 *et seq.*; LRC, *Consultation Paper, op. cit.* at §93; Brazier, *Street on Torts*, 9th ed. (London: Butterworths, 1993) at pp. 465–6; Gatley, *op. cit.* at §§763–764; Fridman, *op. cit.* vol. 2 at pp. 165–7.

157 *Crawford and Frame v Vance* [1908] 2 IR 521 (voting activity in Dublin Corporation); *Black v Northern Whig* (1942) 77 ILTR 5 (voting activity in Belfast Corporation); *Kane v Mulvaney* (1866) IR 2 CL 402 (evidence of witness in judicial proceedings); *Campbell v Irish Press* (1955) 90 ILTR 105 (sports); *Kavanagh v The Leader* unrep. SC, 4 March 1955 (literary figure); McDonald, *op. cit.* at pp. 220 *et seq.*; McGonagle, *op. cit.* at p. 84; Gatley, *op. cit.* at §§731–746.

158 See LRC, *Consultation Paper on Contempt of Court* (Dublin: Law Reform Commission, 1991).

159 LRC 38–91, *op. cit.* at §90; Gatley, *op. cit.* at §742; *Loan v MacLean* (1975) 58 DLR (3d) 228.

Offer of Amends

The harshness of the common law rules in respect of identification and innuendo, which would make a publisher strictly liable for unintentional defamation, is offset by section 21 of the 1961 Act. This provides a defence, under certain conditions, where the publisher was unaware of the possibility that the plaintiff would be defamed, because there was no knowledge either of identification or of circumstances by which an innuendo would arise.[160] The publisher may make an offer of amends, which involves an offer to publish a correction and a suitable apology in a manner reasonably suited to reaching the recipients of the original publication.[161] If the offer is accepted and fulfilled, it operates as a bar to any further action against the person making the offer; if it is rejected, then it operates as a defence, provided the offer was made as soon as practicable after the defendant became aware of the potential defamation.[162] The defence is not available in respect of claims for special damage resulting from the publication.[163] In practice the defence is cumbersome, having a number of technical aspects which militate against its effectiveness and it does not appear to be widely invoked.[164]

Apology

The making or offering of an apology is not a complete defence, but may be used for the purposes of mitigating damage, under section 17 of the 1961 Act. The offer may be made before the action is commenced or as soon as possible after commencement, if there was no opportunity to do so prior to commencement. The provision does appear to have some limited practical effect, but may be hampered by the risk that the apology may be construed as an admission of liability.[165]

---

160 S. 21(5) provides a detailed definition of innocent publication; the publisher's innocence is dependent on having exercised reasonable care.

161 S. 21(3).

162 S. 21(1).

163 S. 21(6).

164 McGonagle, *op. cit.* at pp. 103 *et seq.*; McDonald, *op. cit.* at pp. 229 *et seq.*; LRC, *Consultation Paper, op. cit.* at §116 and §§395–410; Boyle & McGonagle, *op. cit.* at §614, Table H; see also LRC 38–91, *op. cit.* at §§7.36–7.42 for reform proposals.

165 McGonagle, *op. cit.* at pp. 102–3.

CHAPTER NINE

Emerging Causes of Action

Introduction

In recent years two new actions have been developed, which allow a person to recover damages for interference with certain rights not covered by established torts. These are the action for interference with constitutional rights and the action for breach of European Community law. It is open to question whether either of these actions can properly be regarded as a tort at all, since they both involve matters of a public law nature – the Constitution and the laws of the European Communities – which are concerned, to a significant degree, with matters of government, rather than private relations. The actions are, however, akin to torts. They give private citizens a right of action for damages in respect of interference with individual rights conferred by these laws and many of the concepts employed, such as breach of duty, causation and limitations, are borrowed from tort law.

Interference with Constitutional Rights

The law of torts seeks to delineate the scope of a wide range of civil rights and provide remedies for improper interference with those rights. This necessarily entails a degree of overlap with constitutional law, given that the rights governed by the law of torts are also either expressly or implicitly embraced by the Constitution, particularly by its fundamental rights provisions. Under the general principle of the supremacy of the Constitution over common law, it is open to litigants to challenge existing principles of common law on the grounds that they do not adequately protect or vindicate relevant constitutional rights. Such arguments, bringing constitutional considerations into play within traditional torts, are considered in the relevant chapters covering the various aspect of torts to which they relate.[1] However, a brief outline of the relationship between tort actions and constitutional rights is appropriate at this juncture.

The courts are not empowered to simply reformulate existing torts as they see fit, under the guise of the implementation of the constitutional obligations of the State. The cases show that the courts will generally consider established tort actions to be a sufficient form of protection for the constitutional rights

---

1 For example, chapter 8 in respect of the relationship between defamation and the right to one's reputation and the right to communicate; chapter 4 in respect of trespass and powers of arrest, entry, search and seizure, and also the constitutional dimension to the defence of consent; chapter 11 in respect of the causal requirement in private nuisance; chapter 12 in respect of the relationship between statutory limitation periods and the constitutional right of access to the courts.

affected by them, unless there is a significant and unjustified deficiency in the protection afforded to a particular right. Furthermore, where an established tort action is available, the courts will not impose a concurrent constitutional duty on the defendant. The cases from which this summary is derived are worth a brief examination, in order to elaborate on the issues raised.

In *Hanrahan v Merck Sharp & Dohme (Ireland) Ltd*[2] the plaintiffs in a nuisance action claimed that the existing law of nuisance did not adequately vindicate their personal rights under Article 40.3 of the Constitution, which reads:

> 1° The State guarantees in its laws to respect, and, as far as practicable, by its laws to defend and vindicate the personal rights of the citizen.

> 2° The State shall, in particular, by its laws protect as best it may from unjust attack and, in the case of injustice done, vindicate the life, person, good name and property rights of every citizen.

The specific allegation was that the requirement of proving causation was too onerous and that the common law, therefore, did not vindicate their rights to bodily integrity and their property rights in their land and livestock. The claim was rejected and Henchy J, delivering the judgment of the Supreme Court, explained the relationship between tort law and constitutional rights:

> The implementation of those constitutional rights is primarily a matter for the State and the courts are entitled to intervene only when there has been a failure to implement or, where the implementation relied on is plainly inadequate, to effectuate the constitutional guarantee in question.

He added that when a plaintiff

> . . . founds his action on an existing tort he is normally confined to the limitations of that tort. It might be different if it could be shown that the tort in question is basically ineffective to protect his constitutional right.[3]

Furthermore, Henchy J noted that the rights in question were qualified, not absolute. The particular qualifications here are the phrases 'as far as practicable' and 'in the case of injustice done'. The overall impression created is that the rules of tort will not be interfered with where they involve a reasonable balance between competing interests. Where a litigant's interest is defeated by the operation of a rule which is based on the protection of a legitimate countervailing interest (such as the rights of the opposing party or a public policy consideration), then judicial interference on constitutional grounds will not be warranted.

---

2 [1988] ILRM 629.
3 *Ibid.*, at p. 636.

The relationship between the two bodies of law was further considered by Costello P in *HMW v Ireland*.[4] The allegation in this instance was that the failure to speedily process an extradition request in respect of a person accused of sexual abuse crimes constituted an infringement of the right to bodily integrity of the plaintiff, a victim of some of those crimes. A duty of care in negligence was rejected on the grounds of public policy[5] and Costello P held that these grounds also precluded the imposition of any constitutional duty to the plaintiff. He noted, *obiter*, that constitutional rights are protected in two distinct classes of case:

> (a) those which, independently of the Constitution, are regulated and pro-
> tected by law (common law and/or statutory law) and
> (b) those that are not so regulated and protected.[6]

The particular right in question, the right to bodily integrity, is extensively regulated and protected by tort law and so, falls into the first category. Costello P felt that a distinct constitutional cause of action should not be available in such a case. He held that the State's obligations under Article 40.3 were fulfilled where common law or statutory provisions provided a cause of action in respect of an infringement of protected rights. He added, however, that the failure of a common law action does not, of itself, indicate that the relevant constitutional rights are not adequately protected.

> I am satisfied that the law of torts which is applicable in this case was not ineffective to protect the plaintiff's constitutionally guaranteed rights. It does not follow that because a plaintiff does not recover damages under the applicable law (in this case, the law of torts) that it must be ineffective in protecting guaranteed rights. It is necessary to consider why the plaintiff's claim has failed.[7]

In this particular instance the plaintiff's interests were outweighed by a specific public policy interest. This approach is consistent with, and derived from, Henchy J's statement of principle in *Hanrahan*. Furthermore, the rejection of a concurrent duty echoes a *dictum* of McCarthy J, in *Walsh v Family Planning Services*,[8] that a constitutional claim should not be 'used to elevate the status of a trifling cause of action'. Thus, in a claim in defamation, or trespass to the person, or trespass to land, a plaintiff may not seek to

---

4 [1997] 2 IR 142; see also Gaughran, 'Tort, Public Policy and the Protection of Constitutional Rights' (1998) 16 ILT 88 at pp. 89–90.
5 The advocate's immunity, considered in chapter 1 *supra*, and the potential conflict of interest in respect of the exercise of statutory powers, noted in chapter 2 *supra*.
6 [1997] 2 IR 142, at p. 164.
7 *Ibid.*, at p. 169.
8 [1992] 1 IR 496, at p. 522.

increase the damages payable for a minor, technical wrong by dressing the claim up in constitutional guise.

Constitutional rights may have a significant role to play in expanding the scope of the law of torts through the development of actions under the second limb of Costello P's classification, i.e. to protect rights not protected by existing common law or statutes. It is now well established that the courts may provide suitable redress for breaches of constitutional rights where other forms of action prove inadequate. This means that rights not falling within the ambit of traditional torts may, nonetheless, form the basis of an action for damages, where they have been improperly interfered with.[9] In *Kearney v Minister for Justice*,[10] Costello J stated that such an action was not a tort.[11] The action is, however, closely analogous to a tort, having to borrow tortious principles in respect of a number of issues. For example, in *Kearney* itself, Costello J had to consider questions of vicarious liability and the availability of exemplary damages, which he resolved by applying the principles used to determine these matters in tort actions. Similarly, Carroll J employed the limitation period applicable to tort actions in two cases involving alleged breaches of constitutional rights[12] and she described the action as being 'in the nature of a tort'.[13] Other issues which may require the application of tortious principles include causation and remoteness of damage.[14] This level of potential overlap indicates that the action may be sufficiently akin to tort to be included in this text and may require a re-evaluation of Costello J's statement, at least in respect of some of the situations where the action may be employed.

Not all constitutional rights are suited to enforcement by way of a civil action; those which are suitable must be designed to confer benefits to indivi-

---

9 See Kelly, *The Irish Constitution*, 3rd ed. (Dublin: Butterworths, 1994) at pp. 702 *et seq.*; Casey, *Constitutional Law in Ireland*, 2nd ed. (London: Sweet & Maxwell, 1992) at pp. 309–10; Cooney & Kerr, 'Constitutional Aspects of Irish Tort Law' (1981) 3 DULJ 1; Binchy, 'Constitutional Remedies and the Law of Torts' in O'Reilly (ed.), *Human Rights and Constitutional Law* (Dublin: Round Hall Press, 1992).

10 [1986] IR 116; [1987] ILRM 52.

11 *Ibid.*, at p. 122; p. 57.

12 *McDonnell v Ireland* [1998] 1 IR 134 (upheld on appeal by the Supreme Court); *Murphy v Ireland* [1996] 2 IR 307; [1996] 2 ILRM 461; both actions involved the dismissal of public sector employees under s. 34 of the Offences Against the State Act 1939, which was held to be unconstitutional in *Cox v Ireland* [1992] 2 IR 503; the plaintiffs had been dismissed sixteen years and twenty years prior to the initiation of their respective actions; notably, in *Hayes v Ireland* [1987] ILRM 651, at p. 655 the same judge held that an action in respect of a breach of constitutional rights was not a tort for the purposes of a trade union's immunity from suit under s. 4 of the Trade Disputes Act 1906.

13 *Murphy v Ireland* [1996] 2 IR 307; [1996] 2 ILRM 461, at p. 310; p. 465; see also *McDonnell v Ireland* [1998] 1 IR 134, at pp. 155–9 per Keane J.

14 Binchy, *loc. cit.* at pp. 210 *et seq.* argues that tortious principles will not necessarily be appropriate, as they often lack the necessary degree of sophistication for the elaboration of the parameters of constitutional rights.

duals and must involve a reciprocal obligation on the defendant not to interfere. Actions for breach of constitutional rights may lead to the development of a single nominate wrong, with a consistent set of principles used to determine the constituent elements; alternatively, each constitutional right may be considered separately, on its own merits, as a form of action on the case. The following discussion is confined to an outline of the development of the action for damages in respect of those rights where such claims have been made and is not an exhaustive review of the potential availability of civil actions for the enforcement of constitutional rights.

Privacy

Privacy is not so much a single right, as a bundle of rights with a common theme. It can embrace different facets of one's personal interest in being free from external scrutiny in a variety of contexts. Some aspects of privacy are afforded protection by the common law; for example, the trespass torts provide some protection against contact with one's person, land or chattels and breach of confidence protects certain categories of information against disclosure.[15] The protection of privacy is not, however, the central object of such actions, but is merely a collateral benefit for the plaintiff, arising as a side-effect to some applications of the actions. In America the law of torts has evolved to provide a significantly greater level of express protection for privacy interests,[16] but neither the courts nor the legislature in Ireland or England have followed the American lead in this respect.

The decision of the Court of Appeal in *Kaye v Robertson*[17] highlights the limitations of the common law protection of privacy in England. The plaintiff, a famous television and stage actor, suffered serious head injuries after being struck by a piece of advertising hoarding, when driving during a storm. While he was in hospital, a journalist and photographer from the *Sunday Sport*, a

---

15 For general consideration of the protection of privacy in the common law see McMahon & Binchy, *The Irish Law of Torts*, 2nd ed. (Dublin: Butterworths, 1989), at chapter 37; Wacks, *Privacy and Press Freedom* (London: Blackstone Press, 1995) at chapters 3 and 6; Warren & Brandeis, 'The Right to Privacy' (1890) 4 Harv L Rev 193; McGonagle, *A Textbook on Media Law* (Dublin: Gill & Macmillan, 1996) at chapter 5; Law Reform Commission, *Consultation Paper on Privacy* (Dublin: Law Reform Commission, 1996) at chapter 4. O'Dell, 'When Two Tribes Go to War', in McGonagle (ed.) *Law and the Media* (Dublin: Roundhall Sweet & Maxwell, 1997).

16 See Prosser et al., *Prosser & Keeton on Torts*, 5th ed. (St Paul, Minn.: West, 1984), at chapter 20, identifying five separate categories of protection – appropriation of name or likeness; unreasonable and offensive intrusion on seclusion; publicising a person's private life; placing someone in a false light in the public eye; and interference with autonomy in respect of personal decisions; the *Restatement, Second, Torts* at §§652B–D deals with the first four; the fifth results from constitutional developments.

17 [1991] FSR 62; noted by Markesinis (1990) 53 MLR 802 and Prescott (1991) 54 MLR 451.

weekly tabloid newspaper, gained access to his room, without authorisation. They proceeded to 'interview' the plaintiff and took photographs of him, though his medical condition at the time rendered him incapable of giving any real consent to these activities. The plaintiff sought an interlocutory injunction to restrain publication of the 'interview' and the photographs.

The injunction was ultimately granted, but only on the grounds that the story the defendants intended to publish alleged that the plaintiff had assented to the interview and photography. This allegation constituted a malicious falsehood, as it was known to be untrue and deprived the plaintiff of the full value of his right to sell his story. The publication of the pictures and words of the plaintiff would not have been inherently unlawful; it was the false allegation of consent that was objectionable. A number of other possible causes of action were also raised in this action. Libel was rejected as a sufficient ground for an interlocutory injunction, though it was possible that the allegation of consent could give rise to an action for damages for libel after publication, given that the defendant was a tabloid paper. Trespass to the person was also considered but, while the use of flash photography was capable of constituting a battery, there were no grounds for preventing the defendants from commercially exploiting the fruits of a trespass. The plaintiff's economic rights in his story were not sufficiently similar to a trader's interest to attract protection under passing off. From this it is plain that, by employing a degree of caution not to cause any physical harm and avoiding untrue inferences, a newspaper could engage in a considerable degree of invasion of privacy, with impunity.

In Ireland there has been some limited development in the protection of privacy as an unenumerated constitutional right, under Article 40.3. The right to marital privacy was recognised by the Supreme Court in *McGee v AG*,[18] in which legislation precluding the importation of contraceptives was held to violate that right. An attempt to expand this right into a more general right to sexual privacy failed before the national courts in *Norris v AG*,[19] but ultimately succeeded before the European Court of Human Rights.[20] These cases concerned constitutional challenges to restraints on privacy imposed by the criminal law and do not directly concern our present purpose. The most important development for present purposes was the High Court decision in *Kennedy and Arnold v Ireland*,[21] where it was held that damages were available for improper interference with privacy, in respect of telephone communications.

---

18 [1974] IR 284.
19 [1984] IR 36.
20 (1991) 13 EHRR 186.
21 [1987] IR 587; [1988] ILRM 472; the existence of either a general right to privacy or a specific right to telephonic communication, free from interception, was denied in England in *Malone v Metropolitan Police Commissioner* [1979] CH 344; [1979] 2 WLR 700; [1979] 2 All ER 620.

The state tapped the telephones of the first and second plaintiffs, without regard to the safeguards that had previously been employed by the Department of Justice. As a result, a number of conversations between the plaintiffs and third parties were recorded. While the first two plaintiffs were the intended targets of the tapping, conversations of the third plaintiff (the second plaintiff's wife) were also recorded.

Hamilton P indicated that the right to privacy was more general than the limited right identified in the earlier cases and held that its nature 'must be such as to ensure the dignity and freedom of an individual in . . . a sovereign, independent and democratic society'.[22] The right was stated to be qualified by the rights of others, the common good, public order and morality, but in the context of the case it included a right to have telephone conversations free of 'deliberate, conscious and unjustified interference'.[23] The interference with the third plaintiff was 'not done consciously or deliberately but incidentally',[24] yet £10,000 was awarded to her. The first two plaintiffs were awarded £20,000 each, as the interference with them was deliberate and conscious. This would indicate that unjustified interference is sufficient to give rise to grounds for action, while the degree of wilfulness relates to the measurement of compensation. It is clear from this that liability depends on some degree of fault on the part of the state and that some degree of justification must be allowed for, but the precise parameters are still uncertain.

In *Kane v Governor of Mountjoy Prison*,[25] the majority indicated that overt surveillance of an individual in a public place could constitute a sufficient invasion, if unjustified. However, the expectation that the police would have to execute an extradition warrant in respect of the plaintiff was considered to be a sufficient justification. The decision in *Devoy v Dublin Corporation and Others*[26] indicates that secret recording of an employee's conversations with his supervisor, in order to provide evidence of verbal abuse by the employee to be used in disciplinary proceedings, is a justified invasion of privacy. The recording was likened to taking a photograph of a person lifting concrete blocks when claiming to be suffering from a back injury, which, by implication, would also be justified.[27]

Education

Article 42 of the Constitution addresses the subject of education and has been the focus of a number of important decisions. Article 42.4, concerning the

---

22 *Ibid.*, at p. 593; p. 477.
23 *Ibid.*, at p. 592; p. 476.
24 *Ibid.*, at p. 595; p. 479.
25 [1988] IR 757; [1988] ILRM 724, considered in chapter 4 *supra*.
26 Unrep. HC, 18 October 1995; Irish Times Law Report, 22 January 1996.
27 *Ibid.*, at p. 11 of the judgment; the central issue in the case was whether the introduction of the tape at the disciplinary meeting constituted a breach of procedure; the privacy issue was not considered in detail.

state's obligation to provide for free primary education, is of particular relevance here. The two leading cases are *Crowley v Ireland*[28] and *O'Donoghue v Minister for Education*.[29] In *Crowley*, children attending national school in Drimoleague, County Cork, were temporarily deprived of primary education due to an industrial dispute. The dispute became protracted and eventually arrangements were made to provide transport to bring the children to other schools in the surrounding area. An injunction was sought against the state and the trade union in the dispute, to restore the provision of education to the children in their own school. In both the High Court and Supreme Court, it was held that the state's obligation was not to directly deliver education, but to ensure that sufficient arrangements were made for its provision to children.[30] In the event of a serious breakdown in the delivery, the state is obliged to make reasonable alternative arrangements and the onus is on the state to justify its actions in the event of such a breakdown.[31] In the High Court the alternative arrangements made by the state were found to be satisfactory, but McMahon J indicated that the state may have been liable to compensate the plaintiff for the deprivation of education prior to the making of such arrangements; the plaintiff, however, waived any claim to damages against the state.[32]

O'Donoghue involved a child suffering from a significant level of physical and mental disability, for whom the level of educational facilities available were considerably less than were available to children with lesser levels of disability. O'Hanlon J rejected the claim by the defence that the duty under Article 42.4 had been discharged by placing the plaintiff in a pilot scheme for the education of severely mentally disabled children. First, the provision of a place as a matter of grace would not necessarily discharge the state's obligation, since the plaintiff's entitlement amounted to a legal right.[33] Secondly, the level of provision (one teacher to twelve severely disabled children) was inadequate and did not sufficiently address important issues such as the age of commencement, and the duration and continuity of such education.[34] Thirdly, the plaintiff's inclusion in the scheme did not remedy the state's failure to make provision for such education in the years prior to his inclusion.[35] In consequence, the plaintiff was awarded a moderate sum, primarily to offset costs incurred in obtaining education from outside the state, during the period

---

28 [1980] IR 102.
29 [1996] 2 IR 20; analysed in depth in Byrne & Binchy, *Annual Review of Irish Law 1993* at pp. 150–7.
30 [1980] IR 102, at p. 111 per McMahon J (HC); p. 122 per O'Higgins CJ (Parke J concurring) and p. 126 per Kenny J (Henchy and Griffin JJ concurring) (SC).
31 *Ibid.*, at pp. 112–14 per McMahon J (HC); pp. 124–5 per O'Higgins CJ (Parke J concurring) and pp. 129–30 per Kenny J (Henchy and Griffin JJ concurring) (SC).
32 *Ibid.*, at p. 125.
33 [1996] 2 IR 20, at p. 68.
34 *Ibid.*, at pp. 69–70.
35 *Ibid.*, at p. 70.

prior to the placing of the plaintiff in the pilot scheme.[36] While the wider constitutional implications of the judgment are beyond the scope of this text, it is worth noting that the level of detailed consideration given by O'Hanlon J to the meaning of primary education, and the extent of the state's obligation to make provision for such education, goes considerably beyond that in previous cases.[37] The extensive analysis raises a number of issues that can no longer be easily avoided or overlooked in considering the obligations of the state and raises some potential for further actions against the state in respect of inadequacies in the primary education system.

A further problematic aspect of education is the question of action against private persons. The obligation on the state under Article 42.4, while less than clear as to its exact content, is at least an express duty. The right of children to receive an education carries no express obligation on private parties in the text of the Constitution, but such an obligation has been considered in a number of cases. In *Crowley*, McMahon J held that the actions of the Irish National Teachers' Organisation and its members, in depriving the children of their right to receive primary education, constituted unlawful means of pursuing a legitimate purpose, amounting to conspiracy.[38] In a subsequent case, arising out of the same dispute, *Hayes v Ireland*,[39] Carroll J held that the conduct of union members amounted to a breach of constitutional rights, as a separate action from a tort, which was not justified by the fact that the defendants were acting in pursuit of their own rights.[40] Both decisions clearly indicate that private persons may be subject to some level of obligation to respect the constitutional rights of others, but differ as to the nature of the obligation owed.

In *PH and Others v John Murphy & Sons Ltd*[41] the plaintiffs' father was killed at work, due to the defendant's negligence. Costello J held that the deprivation of the children's right to their father's influence in their education, due to the negligence of a private person, was not actionable.[42] This can be distinguished from *Crowley* and *Hayes* on the basis that the interference in those cases was intentional; furthermore, the fact that the defendants in *Crowley* and *Hayes* were employed in the delivery of education, whereas the defendant in *PH* was not involved in any way with the education process, may be an important point of distinction.

---

36 *Ibid.*, at p. 71, £7,645.71 was awarded to cover costs incurred in visiting the Peto Institute in Hungary and having a teacher sent over to Ireland from there.
37 *Ibid.*, at pp. 61–7, considered in Byrne & Binchy, *loc. cit.*; the earlier cases include *Ryan v AG* [1965] IR 294; *Crowley v Ireland* [1980] IR 102.
38 [1980] IR 102, at pp. 108–110, the union did not appeal to the Supreme Court; the appeal was exclusively concerned with issues relating to the state's obligation.
39 [1987] ILRM 651.
40 *Ibid.*, at pp. 654–5.
41 [1987] IR 621; [1988] ILRM 300.
42 *Ibid.*, at p. 627; p. 306.

As with privacy, rights in respect of education provide significant scope for litigation, but the boundaries of the applicable civil obligations are still uncertain.

Other Rights

Family Rights

Costello J, in *PH*, also held that the negligence of a private individual did not give rise to a cause of action for interference with family rights under Article 41, nor was there any duty of care under the tort of negligence in respect of the non-pecuniary aspects of the parent–child relationship.[43] He did indicate, *obiter*, that an action would lie against the state for a deliberate attack on family rights by a public official or through legislation.[44]

The Right to Vote

In *Graham v Ireland*[45] the plaintiff sought compensation for the deprivation of his right to vote. The returning officer had inadvertently permitted the plaintiff's father to vote, rather than the plaintiff (both having the same first name), and prevented the plaintiff from voting, as a vote had already been cast in respect of the single entry on the electoral register under their shared name. Morris J rejected the plaintiff's claim on the basis that there had been no negligence on the part of the returning officer, but the clear inference is that such an action could succeed if fault could be shown.

The Right to Communicate

Kearney v Minister for Justice[46] was concerned with interference with the postal communications of prisoners by prison authorities. The issue was dealt with under a separate and distinct right to communicate, rather than as a facet of the right to privacy. The principal complaint was against a provision in the prison regulations which permitted the governor to withhold post deemed to be 'objectionable' or to have the objectionable portion removed.[47] Costello J held that prison security constituted a valid constraint on the plaintiff's right to communicate[48] and, although the rule appeared to give complete discretion to the governor, its practical exercise was based on security considerations. The plaintiff did, however, succeed in respect of the unauthorised withholding of non-objectionable mail by prison staff, but only nominal damages of £75 were

---

43 *Ibid.*, at pp. 624–5; pp. 302–3 re negligence; pp. 626–7; pp. 303–5 re Art. 41.
44 *Ibid.*, at pp. 626–7; p. 305.
45 Unrep. HC, 1 May 1996.
46 [1986] IR 116; [1987] ILRM 52.
47 Rule 63 of the Rules for the Government of Prisons, SR & O No. 320/1947.
48 [1986] IR 116; [1987] ILRM 52, at p. 118; p. 54.

awarded, since there was no pecuniary loss and no evidence of vindictiveness on the part of prison officials.[49]

Residual Issues

A general problem, which remains only partially resolved in constitutional law as a whole, is whether private individuals may be sued for interference with the constitutional rights of another. State responsibility for breaching individual rights is well established (though there are some problematic aspects to state liability), but actions against private individuals have had mixed success. There is an absence of clear guidance as to which rights are amenable to enforcement against private individuals and which are only enforceable against the state, particularly in the context of personal rights under Article 40.3.[50] This problem stems in part from the fact that the development of unenumerated rights 'has not been based on a coherent theory of fundamental rights'.[51] The absence of coherence also makes it difficult to anticipate the precise rights that will develop and provide opportunities for civil actions.

Further difficulties arise in determining the extent of any duties owed; is there to be one standard, such as intention, or is each right to have its own standard? Is damage an essential requirement, or is interference actionable *per se*? These and other areas of doubt, such as remoteness, limitations and defences, await further examination by the courts to produce answers to the myriad questions that remain in delineating the obligations arising out of constitutional rights.

Breach of European Community Law

The Court of Justice has sought to ensure that European Community law is effective and that adequate enforcement procedures are available to ensure compliance. The rationale, like that of our national courts in the context of constitutional rights, is to ensure that rights are not deprived of their content due to a lack of remedial processes when infringements occur. In the early 1960s the Court of Justice established, for the first time, the supremacy of Community law over the national laws of the member states.[52] This was followed by the development of the principle that national courts were required to apply relevant Community law which was relied on by a litigant and, if necessary, they were required to refuse to apply any provision of national law which was

---

49 *Ibid.*, at p. 122; p. 58.
50 See *Report of the Constitution Review Group* (Dublin: Stationery Office, 1996) at pp. 266–71; Casey, *op. cit.* at pp. 379 *et seq.*
51 *Report of the Constitution Review Group, op. cit.* at p. 247.
52 Case 26/62 *Van Gend en Loos v Nederlandse Administratie der Belastingen* [1963] ECR 1; [1963] CMLR 105; Case 6/64 *Costa v ENEL* [1964] ECR 585; [1964] CMLR 425.

in conflict with the Community law.[53] Alongside the development of the concept of supremacy of Community law, the Court of Justice developed the concept of 'direct effect'.[54] The essence of this concept is that some Community laws are capable of being relied on by individuals, even in the absence of national laws implementing the Community provisions. The principle of direct effect was initially applied to Treaty provisions,[55] but was expanded to apply to secondary legislation, such as Regulations[56] and Directives.[57] The key feature required for a provision to be directly effective is that it must be clear, precise, unconditional and not subject to the exercise of discretion. The next significant development was the concept of 'indirect effect', which requires national courts to attempt, as far as possible, to interpret national laws in a manner which ensures that the objectives of Community law are achieved.[58]

Historically, enforcement of Community law, under these principles, has borne little relationship to the tort process, but the evolutionary development of enforcement mechanisms by the Court of Justice has recently generated a new tort.[59] The seminal decision marking the arrival of the new tort is that in the joined cases of *Francovich and Bonifaci v Italy*.[60] The plaintiffs in this case, Italian workers, were made redundant and their former employers were unable to pay their redundancy entitlements, due to insolvency. The Italian government had failed to implement a Directive (80/987), which required the establishment of a fund to guarantee redundancy payments. The Directive was specifically designed

---

53 Case 106/77 *Amministrazione delle Finanze dello Stato v Simmenthal SpA (No. 2)* [1978] ECR 629; [1978] 3 CMLR 263.
54 Case 26/62 *Van Gend en Loos v Nederlandse Administratie der Belastingen* [1963] ECR 1.
55 *Ibid.*
56 Case 43/71 *Politi v Italian Minister of Finance* [1971] ECR 1039. A Regulation is a general measure, like a statute, applicable throughout the Community.
57 Case 41/74 *Van Dutyn v Home Office* [1974] ECR 1337; [1975] 1 CMLR 1. A directive is a provision of Community law addressed to member states, requiring them to attain a specified legal objective. The Liability for Defective Products Act 1991, considered in chapter 3 *supra*, is an example of a national measure introduced to implement the terms of a Directive. Member states have a discretion as to the means by which the objectives of a Directive are achieved (e.g. by statute, statutory instrument or administrative action), but there is no discretion in respect of the objectives to be attained, unless such a discretion is expressly stated in the Directive.
58 Case 14/83 *Von Colson v Land Nordrhein-Westfalen* [1984] ECR 1891; [1986] 2 CMLR 430.
59 The evolution of enforcement procedures is neatly synopsised by Van Gerven, 'Bridging the Gap Between Community and National Laws: Towards a Principle of Homogeneity in the Field of Legal Remedies?' (1995) 32 CML Rev 679; see also Steiner, *Enforcing EC Law* (London: Blackstone Press, 1995).
60 Cases C–6 and 9/90; [1993] 2 CMLR 66; noted by Bebr (1992) 29 CML Rev 559; Parker (1992) 108 LQR 181; Ross (1993) 56 MLR 55; Steiner (1993) 18 EL Rev 3.

to avoid the type of situation faced by the plaintiffs, who found themselves with no remedy under national law. The Directive was not, however, directly effective, because it did not identify any particular body or agency as being responsible for the management of the fund. The Court of Justice held that an obligation contained in a Directive, which did not satisfy the criteria for taking direct effect, could be enforced by an action for damages against a member state for losses resulting from a failure to implement the Directive. Thus, a state's obligation to implement Community law would, in some instances, include an obligation to individuals not to cause loss by a failure to implement.

The Court of Justice set out three criteria which would have to be met in order for liability to arise in the case of failure to implement a Directive:

> The first of those conditions is that the result prescribed by the directive should entail the grant of rights to individuals. The second condition is that it should be possible to identify the content of those rights on the basis of the provisions of the directive. Finally, the third condition is the existence of a causal link between the breach of the State's obligation and the harm suffered by the injured parties.[61]

The first two criteria are concerned with examining the nature and scope of the Community law on which the plaintiff seeks to rely, in order to determine whether it is suitable for enforcement. To qualify the right must be both clearly defined and individual in nature. The third requirement encompasses three elements – breach, damage and causation. The scope of the action has been further clarified in a number of decisions and a more detailed view of the action is rapidly emerging. It is far too early yet to regard the parameters of liability as definitively settled, but a number of important landmarks have already been established.

Detailed procedural rules for the implementation of the right of action were left to be fulfilled by national law, within the general framework provided by the Court of Justice.[62] In Ireland the decision in *Tate v Minister for Social Welfare*[63] holds that this type of action is a distinct tort in its own right, akin to a breach of a constitutional duty, and not a form of breach of statutory duty.

---

61 *Ibid.*, at §40.
62 *Ibid.*, at §42; for consideration of the detailed issues left unresolved with respect to the parameters of liability and subsequent attempts to resolve them, see Flynn, 'State Liability in Damages for Failure to Observe EC Law' (1996) 14 ILT 170.
63 [1995] 1 IR 418; [1995] 1 ILRM 507, at p. 442; p. 525; followed in *Coppinger v Waterford County Council* unrep. HC, 22 March 1996 at p. 23 of the judgment; see also *Short and Others v British Nuclear Fuels plc* unrep. SC, 24 October 1996 involving a preliminary application for service of proceedings out of the jurisdiction; Barrington J, for the court, accepted that an application for injunctive relief for breach of Community law was akin to a tort action.

Appropriate Obligations

In *Francovich*, the right in question was contained in a directive, not having direct effect. The Court of Justice, however, indicated that the action for damages would not be confined to such measures, but would extend to other breaches of Community law, where it was necessary to ensure the effectiveness of individual rights.[64] This was subsequently confirmed in *Brasserie du Pêcheur SA v Germany; R. v Secretary of State for Transport, ex p. Factortame Ltd.*[65] The Court of Justice expressly rejected the argument that the action for damages does not apply to provisions which are directly effective; such argument being based on the premise that direct effect ensured adequate enforcement procedures, making an action for damages for breach of Community law superfluous.[66]

> [18] The German, Irish and Netherlands Governments contended that Member States are required to make good loss or damage caused to individuals only where the provisions breached are not directly effective: in *Francovich and Others* the Court simply sought to fill a lacuna in the system for safeguarding rights of individuals. In so far as national law affords individuals a right of action enabling them to assert their rights under directly effective provisions of Community law, it is unnecessary, where such provisions are breached, also to grant them a right to reparation founded directly on Community law.
> [19] That argument cannot be accepted.

The court added that, in the context of an action for damages in respect of a directly effective provision, 'the right to reparation is the necessary corollary of the direct effect of the Community provision whose breach caused the damage sustained'.[67] It also held that the right of action is not confined to secondary legislation, but also applies to breaches of Treaty provisions.[68] Thus, any aspect of Community law, designed to generate individual rights, is capable of forming the basis of an action for damages against a member state breaching the right. The state is the appropriate target, because the state carries

---

64 [1993] 2 CMLR 66, at §§31–37; for commentary on the potential application of the *Francovich* principle to a variety of aspects of Community law see Ross, *loc. cit.* at pp. 60 *et seq.*; Craig, 'Francovich, Remedies and the Scope of Damages Liability' (1993) 109 LQR 595.

65 Joined cases C–46 and 48/93; [1996] 1 CMLR 889; this case and two subsequent cases are analysed by Emiliou, 'State Liability Under Community Law: Shedding More Light on the *Francovich* Principle?' (1996) 21 EL Rev 399; Cahill, 'European Law – New Developments in Determining Criteria for Member State Liability' (1996) 18 DULJ 167.

66 *Ibid.*, at §§18–22; see also *Tate v Minister for Social Welfare* [1995] 1 IR 418, at p. 438; [1995] 1 ILRM 507, where a directly effective obligation under Directive 79/7/EEC, in respect of equal treatment of men and women in matters of social security, was held to be actionable.

67 *Ibid.*, at §22.

68 *Ibid.*, at §§23 and 27.

the responsibility for implementing Community law. The liability arises irrespective of which organ of the state is responsible for the breach.[69] It has been suggested, in academic commentary, that states may seek a contribution towards their liability from the European Commission in cases where the Commission has wrongly given the member state an assurance that the state has complied with its obligations under Community law.[70] This has not been attempted to date, but it does seem to be a plausible possibility.

The principal distinction between obligations which are suitable for this type of action and those which are incapable of supporting an action is whether the obligation is clearly defined and intended to benefit individuals. The cases to date provide some examples of appropriate obligations. The obligation in *Francovich* was to protect employees in the case of their employer's insolvency, so as to ensure that the employees would receive any outstanding payments due to them;[71] *Brasserie du Pêcheur* concerned the imposition of a measure equivalent to a quantitative restriction, precluding the export of beer from France to Germany;[72] *Factortame* involved unlawful conditions of registration for fishing vessels, impeding the right of establishment.[73]

In *Coppinger v Waterford County Council*[74] it was held that the mere fact that alternative interpretations of a provision were possible did not necessarily mean that it was too uncertain. The dispute concerned the obligation to fit trucks with underrun barriers, to prevent cars from going in under the rear of the truck in the event of a collision.[75] The defendant argued that the truck in question was within a class of exempt vehicles and further claimed that, as the classification of the vehicle was open to dispute, the obligation was too uncertain. Both arguments were rejected and Geoghegan J stated that the availability of arguments supporting different potential interpretations of the definition of vehicles did not amount to a discretion for the state in implementing the Directive; the obligation was definite, if somewhat imprecise.

Breach

The *Francovich* decision indicated that liability was strict, as the three conditions for liability did not include any need to show fault on the part of the

---

69 *Ibid.*, at §§32–36; in *Coppinger v Waterford County Council*, unrep. HC, 22 March 1996 the defendant's argument that a county council was not an emanation of the state for the purposes of civil liability was tersely rejected by Geoghegan J, at pp. 6–7, after a brief review of the authorities.
70 Parker, *loc. cit.* at pp. 185–6; the liability of Community institutions is considered further in chapter 13 *infra*.
71 Under Directive 80/987.
72 Contrary to Art. 30 of the EC Treaty.
73 Contrary to Art. 52 of the EC Treaty.
74 Unrep. HC, 22 March 1996 at p. 8 of the judgment.
75 The obligation arose under Directive 70/156/EEC, as amended by Directives 70/221/EEC and 79/490/EEC.

member state and the three conditions were stated to be 'sufficient to give rise to a right on the part of individuals to obtain compensation'.[76] Thus, any failure to implement Community law, from complete non-implementation to partial or inadequate implementation, could suffice. The concept of breach was not conditional on the state having any actual or constructive knowledge of the failure. Steiner, in a particularly prescient commentary on the case, noted that the broad implications of strict state liability for any breach of an appropriate obligation probably exceeded the limits to which the Court of Justice would, and ought to, go in ensuring the effectiveness of Community law. She opined that policy restraints would need to be introduced to curb the scope of the principle and that some degree of actual or constructive knowledge on the state's part would be required.[77]

The *Brasserie du Pêcheur* decision did introduce such limitations in respect of some categories of cases. A general distinction was drawn between obligations which required member states to produce a particular result, such as the implementation of a Directive within a specified time limit, and those which conferred a wide discretion, such as the implementation of a general policy objective. While the *Francovich* criteria would apply to the former, liability in the latter instance would be on a basis comparable to the liability of Community institutions under Article 215.[78] In the case of matters involving wide discretion, the following criteria were set out as necessary in order to maintain an action for damages:

> . . . the rule of law infringed must be intended to confer rights on individuals; the breach must be sufficiently serious; and there must be a direct causal link between the breach of the obligation resting on the State and the damage sustained by the injured parties.[79]

The significant change between this and *Francovich* is the qualification that the breach must be 'sufficiently serious'. Clearly not all breaches will suffice to ground an action. Some further indication was given as to the meaning of a 'sufficiently serious breach'; the dominant criterion is whether the state 'manifestly and gravely disregarded the limits on its discretion'[80] and relevant factors would include 'the clarity and precision of the rule', 'the measure of discretion', whether the breach and damage 'was intentional or involuntary', whether the error was 'excusable or inexcusable' and whether 'the position

---

76 [1993] 2 CMLR 66, at §41; see also Ross, *loc. cit.* at p. 57.

77 *Loc. cit.* at pp. 16 *et seq.*

78 [1996] 1 CMLR 889, at §§46–47; *Coppinger v Waterford County Council*, unrep. HC, 22 March 1996 provides an example of strict liability for non-implementation of a Directive, see p. 5 of the judgment.

79 *Ibid.*, at §51.

80 *Ibid.*, at §55.

taken by a Community institution may have contributed' to the error by the member state.[81]

The effect of this decision is that a form of fault based liability applies to obligations involving 'wide discretion', while strict liability applies to specific obligations with only limited discretion. This distinction may be difficult to draw, but the court held that the Treaty obligations breached in *Brasserie du Pêcheur* and *Factortame* fell into the category of wide discretion and indicated that the obligation in *Francovich* did not.[82] In *Brasserie du Pêcheur* the German legislature was regulating the quality of beer, a matter which it was legitimately entitled to do, provided it did not disregard Community law. Two aspects of the relevant legislation were under scrutiny: first the German legislature continued to preclude the sale of beer, lawfully produced in other member states, under different quality regulations; and, secondly, precluding the importation of beers containing additives. These matters clearly involve a significant degree of discretion, as there are no definitive Community law requirements expressly on the question of beer quality; the Community law infringed was a general prohibition on the use of quantitative restrictions on inter-state trade within the Community. On the question of the classification of the breach, the Court of Justice stated that, because of the rulings in earlier cases, which had indicated that certain aspects of the German beer law violated Community law by imposing a quantitative restriction, the first matter was likely to be a sufficiently serious breach.[83] The second restriction (in respect of additives) was not necessarily a sufficiently serious breach, since it was not apparent until a much later date that this violated Article 30.[84] The ultimate decision as to whether there was a sufficiently serious breach was left to the national court. *Francovich*, by contrast, imposed a very specific obligation (to establish a guarantee fund for redundant workers) and the Italian government simply failed to bring it into effect within the prescribed period.

The decision in *R. v HM Treasury, ex p. British Telecommunications plc*[85] has further reduced the scope of application of the strict liability principle, by holding that the discretion exercised by a state in implementing a directive may bring it within the narrower conditions of liability set out in *Brasserie du Pêcheur*. Where the state incorrectly implements Community law, as opposed

---

81 *Ibid.*, at §56; in *R. v Ministry of Agriculture, Fisheries and Food, ex p. Hedley Lomas (Ireland) Ltd* Case C–5/94; [1996] 2 CMLR 391 the Court of Justice held that if the specific state conduct in question involved little or no practical exercise of discretion, even though the general obligation did confer a wide discretion, then mere breach might amount to a 'sufficiently serious breach', at §28.
82 *Ibid.*, at §§46 re *Francovich*; §48 re *Brasserie du Pêcheur*; §49 re *Factortame*.
83 At §59; Case 120/78 *Rewe-Zentral v Bundesmonopolverwaltung für Branntwein (Cassis de Dijon)* [1979] ECR 649; [1979] 3 CMLR 494, in particular.
84 Case 178/84 *EC Commission v Germany* [1987] ECR 1227; [1988] 1 CMLR 780.
85 Case C–392/93; [1996] 2 CMLR 217.

to a complete failure to implement (which occurred in *Francovich*), liability will only arise if there is a sufficiently serious breach.[86] This confines the strict liability principle to a very narrow range of cases and it would appear that fault based liability is likely to dominate this form of action in the future. On the facts of the case the Court of Justice found that there had not been a sufficiently serious breach. The relevant provision, which had been breached by the UK government,[87] was ambiguous and so, although it was incorrectly interpreted and applied in the United Kingdom, the breach was not sufficiently serious.

> [43] In the present case, Article 8(1) is imprecisely worded and was reason-ably capable of bearing, as well as the construction applied to it by the Court in this judgment, the interpretation given to it by the United Kingdom in good faith and on the basis of arguments which were not entirely devoid of substance. That interpretation, which was also shared by other Member States, was not manifestly contrary to the wording of the directive or to the objective pursued by it.
> [44] Moreover, no guidance was available to the United Kingdom from case law of the Court as to the interpretation of the provision at issue, nor did the Commission raise the matter when the 1992 Regulations were adopted.

In light of the developments since the *Francovich* decision it may be argued that the case does not establish strict liability at all and that the factual circumstances – a failure to implement a clear and unequivocal directive, intended to grant specific rights to individuals – simply provide an example of a sufficiently serious breach. Such an approach, however, is open to criticism as being revisionist, since the concept of 'a sufficiently serious breach' did not emerge until after the *Francovich* decision.

Damage and Causation

The type of damage embraced by this type of action will depend on the nature of the obligation breached. Since the objective of much Community law is

---

86 *Ibid.*, at §40; while it would ordinarily be a matter for the national courts to determine whether the criteria have been satisfied, the Court of Justice, in this case, gave an express ruling, as all the necessary information was available to it (see §41); the decision is instructive on the application of the 'sufficiently serious breach' criterion; for detailed analysis of recent developments see Brown, 'State Liability to Individuals in Damages: An Emerging Doctrine of EU Law' (1996) 31 Ir Jur 7; Spink, 'Contravening EC Law: The Liability of the Member State' (1997) 48 NILQ 111. See also joined cases C–178, 179, 188, 189 and 190/94 *Dillenkoffer v Germany* [1996] ECR I–4845, which also involved a total failure to implement a Directive (90/314/EEC) creating clear, unconditional, individual rights. Like *Francovich*, the directive was not directly effective because it was unclear who these rights were to be enforceable against.

87 Art. 8(1) of Council Directive 90/531 on procurement procedures for entities involved in various activities, including telecommunications.

economic, financial loss is likely to be the dominant form of damage suffered and this has been the situation in the cases to date. A growing body of Community law is, however, concerned with safety and health, particularly in the fields of worker and consumer protection. Personal injury resulting from the failure to implement such laws may constitute a sufficient basis for an action, as occurred in *Coppinger*. It will ultimately depend on the proper construction of the relevant Community obligation as to whether the damage suffered falls within the ambit of protection.

The causal connection between breach and damage will fall to be considered under the same principles of national law used in other tort cases, the discussion of which is deferred to chapter 11 below.

CHAPTER TEN

Miscellaneous Torts

The law of torts deals with a variety of forms of interference with rights other than those covered in the preceding chapters. There are several torts which serve to fill in the gaps left by the principal causes of action and, while these may not be employed very often in practice, they serve to minimise the likelihood of a plaintiff being left without a remedy against unwarranted interference with his civil rights. These residual matters are presented here under several general themes, providing an overview of the principal issues, rather than by way of detailed explanation of the elements of all the nominate torts. Full elaboration of all the issues goes beyond the scope of an introductory text; this chapter is designed to provide some initial pointers to readers, from which they may embark on a more detailed exploration on their own.

Misuse of Process

A person that invokes the judicial process for an improper motive may be committing a tort against a person damaged by the proceedings. The essential objection is that the other person is put to expense or trauma (by either damage to reputation or psychological harm) for reasons other than those which the law regards as proper. The various torts concerned with misuse of process are rarely invoked in practice, but their mere existence may act as a deterrent to those tempted to misuse the legal system.

Malicious Prosecution

This tort is concerned with conduct causing unwarranted criminal proceedings to be maintained against another person, causing that person to suffer economic or personal harm. Not every failed prosecution will allow the accused person to pursue such an action; in fact the requirements of the tort are quite stringent, ensuring that it is only available in cases of serious abuse of the criminal process.

To succeed in an action for malicious prosecution, the plaintiff must prove
- (i) that the criminal proceedings terminated in his favour;
- (ii) that the defendant instituted and/or participated in the proceedings maliciously;
- (iii) that there was no reasonable or probable cause for such proceedings;
- (iv) that the plaintiff suffered damage.[1]

---

1 *McIntyre v Dolan and Lewis* [1991] 1 IR 121, at p. 132 per Hederman J, in the Supreme Court.

Failed Criminal Proceedings

There must have been criminal proceedings against the plaintiff, which were ultimately unsuccessful. Most cases involve criminal prosecutions that went to trial and led to an acquittal, but it appears that once a charge gets to the preliminary stage there is a sufficient prosecution, even if the charge is dropped prior to the commencement of the trial.[2]

The criminal proceedings must be unsuccessful to satisfy the requirement of terminating in favour of the plaintiff (in the malicious prosecution case). This is not confined to an acquittal, but would include the quashing of a conviction on appeal,[3] or the discontinuing of the prosecution.[4] Termination by way of a compromise agreement between the accused and the complainant will probably not suffice.[5]

Malicious Participation

For a malicious prosecution action to be available, the defendant must have played a key role in causing the prosecution to be brought against the plaintiff. In most cases the defendant will have been the person that proffered the charge against the plaintiff, but this need not necessarily be the case. What the plaintiff must prove is that 'the defendant was, in fact, active in advancing the prosecution'.[6]

Privileges, afforded because of public policy considerations in respect of the administration of justice, will not necessarily be available to protect a defendant from a malicious prosecution action. In *Murphy v Kirwan*[7] the Supreme Court held that, by analogy with cases of fraud, malicious prosecution and abuse of process cases provide an exception to the privilege in respect of communications between lawyer and client. Pre-trial discovery will be available in respect of such communications if the plaintiff can establish a 'viable and plausible' cause of

---

2 *Romegialli v Marceu* [1964] 1 OR 407 (plaintiff arrested on a charge of theft, proffered by the defendant, but the charges were dropped); *Casey v Automobiles Renault Canada Ltd* [1965] SCR 607 (information sworn before a magistrate, but no further action taken); Fridman, *The Law of Torts in Canada* (Toronto: Carswell, 1989) vol. 2 at pp. 237–8 is critical of the latter decision, arguing that it extends the concept of prosecution too far.

3 *Herniman v Smith* [1938] AC 305.

4 *Romegialli v Marceu* [1964] 1 OR 407; *Casey v Automobiles Renault Canada Ltd* [1965] SCR 607; Fridman, *op. cit.* vol. 2 at p. 239.

5 *Baxter v Gordon Ironsides & Fares Co. Ltd* (1907) 13 OLR 598; *Cockburn v Kettle* (1913) 28 OLR 407.

6 *Davidson v Smyth* (1887) 20 LR Ir 326, at p. 330 per Murphy J; the Court of Appeal in England held, in *Martin v Watson* [1994] QB 425; [1994] 2 WLR 500; [1994] 2 All ER 606, that merely making a false complaint to the police, on foot of which they instituted proceedings, was not a sufficiently instrumental role to base an action on.

7 [1994] 1 ILRM 293, at pp. 299–300 per Finlay CJ (O'Flaherty J concurring).

action.[8] Public prosecutors are not necessarily immune from action,[9] though judges probably retain their immunity.[10] These latter issues have not been considered in any Irish cases.

Malice requires an improper purpose on the defendant's behalf, in furthering the prosecution. The legitimate purpose of criminal prosecutions is to bring offenders to justice, so ulterior motives, such as initiating a prosecution in order to exert pressure in respect of a commercial transaction, would be improper. In practice, people often have mixed motives, but once there is a genuine desire to see justice done an action will probably not lie. If the ulterior motive is the dominant purpose of the defendant's participation in the prosecution, then the participation is malicious. In *Cruise v Bourke*,[11] Madden J held that malice could be inferred if it could be shown that the defendant had no reasonable or probable cause for advancing the prosecution and had no honest belief in the plaintiff's guilt. In cases of honest, but unfounded, belief in guilt, however, he stated that additional evidence of an improper motive would have to be adduced.

Absence of Reasonable or Probable Cause

If an action for malicious prosecution is to succeed, the plaintiff must establish that the prosecution was unfounded. The general principle is that the furtherance of the prosecution by the defendant is based on sufficient cause if the defendant had a bona fide belief in the plaintiff's guilt and that such a belief was based on reasonable grounds;[12] an 'eccentric or fantastic belief, even though honest' would not amount to reasonable or probable cause.[13] If the

---

8 *Ibid.*, at pp. 300–1.
9 *Nelles v R, in Right of Ontario* (1989) 60 DLR (4th) 609 (SCC); *Riches v DPP* [1973] 2 All ER 935, at p. 941 per Stephenson LJ; the judgment of Costello P, in *HMW v Ireland*, [1997] 2 IR 142 only considers the immunity in the context of a negligence action; it does not deal with malicious prosecution, though *Nelles* is cited.
10 *Sirros v Moore* [1974] 3 All ER 776, at p. 785 per Lord Denning MR; *Unterreiner v Wilson* (1982) 142 DLR (3d) 588, at p. 595 per Gray J; see Fridman, *op. cit.* vol. 2 at pp. 251 *et seq.*; judicial immunity was considered in *Deighan v Ireland* [1995] 2 IR 56; however, the judgment did not make any reference to malicious prosecution, though *Sirros* was cited.
11 [1919] 2 IR 182, at p. 186.
12 *Duane v Barry* (1879) 4 LR Ir 742, at p. 745 per Palles CB; *Hicks v Faulkner* (1878) 8 QBD 167, at p. 171 per Hawkins J; in *Kelly v Midland Great Western Railway of Ireland Co.* (1872) IR 7 CL 8 a complaint by a customer that the plaintiff, an employee of the railway company, had only given him a receipt for half of the amount of money he had paid was carefully considered by the company's solicitor and a prosecution ensued; this was held to amount to reasonable cause; see also Fridman, *op. cit.* vol. 2 at pp. 239 *et seq.*
13 *Cruise v Bourke* [1919] 2 IR 182, at p. 189 per Kenny J.

defendant changes his belief during the course of the proceedings, but has no new information in respect of the grounds for the belief, then there is no duty to disclose this change of belief. There may be a duty to disclose any additional information casting doubt on the grounds for belief.[14]

It is sometimes said that this requirement obliges the plaintiff to prove a negative, but this is not necessarily the case. A useful example is provided by *McIntyre v Dolan and Lewis*. The plaintiff was arrested by the defendants, both of whom were police officers, and charged with assaulting them. He was acquitted by a jury in the Circuit Court. In his action for malicious prosecution, the jury found that he was the victim of an attack by the defendants, rather than the other way around. This factual finding necessarily created an inference that the prosecution was unfounded, McCarthy J stating that the jury's finding created 'an overwhelming case of the absence of reasonable and probable cause'.[15]

The traditional view of the requirement to show an absence of reasonable or probable cause was that the judge would decide the issue, based on the facts found by the jury.[16] The Supreme Court in *McIntyre*, however, held that this is not always the case: 'While there may be cases where the trial judge should decide the issue of reasonable and probable cause, this is not one of them.'[17]

It would now appear to be the case that the trial judge need not make any express ruling where the issue can be inevitably inferred from the facts found by the jury.

Damage

This tort is not actionable without some proof of damage. The usual types of damage suffered are pecuniary loss, incurred in defending the unfounded proceedings, and damage to reputation, resulting from the public nature of the allegation. Personal harm, such as psychological damage, will also suffice. The extent of harm that the plaintiff will have to show is somewhat uncertain, due to the paucity of cases in the area.

Damage to reputation involves a degree of overlap with defamation; malicious prosecution may be seen as a means of overcoming the defence of privilege that would hinder a defamation action. Trifling charges will not give rise to such damage, as they would not have a sufficient implication of discreditable

---

14 *Fancourt v Heaven* (1909) 18 OLR 492; *Herniman v Smith* [1938] AC 305; [1938] 1 All ER 1.

15 [1991] 1 IR 121, at p. 136.

16 *Kelly v Midland Great Western Railway of Ireland Co.* (1872) IR 7 CL 8, at p. 16 per Whiteside J; *Cruise v Bourke* [1919] 2 IR 182, at p. 187 per Kenny J; *Herniman v Smith* [1938] AC 305; [1938] 1 All ER 1, at p. 308; p. 8 per Lord Atkin (for the House of Lords); the issue is regarded as a question of fact, rather than one of law, so it is somewhat unusual to remove the issue from the jury.

17 [1991] 1 IR 121, at p. 133 per Hederman J.

behaviour, but the precise line between trifling charges and ones which are sufficiently serious is not easily drawn.[18]

In *McIntyre*, the medical evidence adduced on the plaintiff's behalf indicated that the prosecution produced 'a mild reactive depression',[19] for which the Supreme Court awarded the plaintiff £5,000 in damages (in addition to an amount agreed between the parties in respect of expenses). This would suggest a relatively low threshold of psychological harm will be sufficient to satisfy the damage requirement.

Abuse of Process

An action for abuse of process is available in respect of situations where legal processes other than criminal prosecution have been unjustifiably invoked by the defendant against the plaintiff. Examples of such abuse would include proceedings to levy execution of a debt which has been paid;[20] or seeking an adjudication in bankruptcy to exert pressure on a debtor;[21] or obtaining a search warrant in respect of a person's property without reasonable cause.[22] It has even been stated, *obiter*, that an action will be available where the defendant has had disciplinary proceedings instituted against a fellow employee without cause.[23]

The High Court decision in *Dorene Ltd v Suedes (Ireland) Ltd*[24] has firmly established that an action will be available in respect of the institution of any civil proceedings which are wholly unfounded. Costello J outlined the nature of the action in terms substantially similar to the requirements for malicious prosecution:

> . . . a claim for damages at common law will lie for the institution or maintenance of a civil action if it can be shown that the action was instituted or maintained (a) without reasonable or probable cause, (b) maliciously, and

---

18 See generally *Savile v Roberts* (1698) 12 Mod Rep 208; 88 ER 1267; 91 ER 1147; 1 Ld Raym 374; [1558–1774] All ER Rep 456; *Rayson v South London Tramways Co.* [1893] 2 QB 304; *Berry v British Transport Commission* [1962] 1 QB 306; [1961] 3 WLR 450; [1961] 3 All ER 65; Fridman, *op. cit.* vol. 2 at p. 246.

19 [1991] 1 IR 121, at p. 134.

20 *Clissold v Cratchley* [1910] 2 KB 244 (the action failed, as the plaintiff could not establish malice on the defendant's part); *Harris v Bickerton* (1911) 24 OLR 41 (retrial ordered, as the issue of malice had not been put to the jury).

21 *Whitworth v Hall* (1831) 2 B & Ad 695; [1824–34] All ER Rep 484; *Metropolitan Bank v Pooley* (1885) App Cas 210; [1881–5] All ER Rep 949 (both actions failed, as the plaintiffs were unable to establish the necessary lack of reasonable cause).

22 *Everett v Ribbands* [1952] 2 QB 198; [1952] 1 All ER 823, at p. 205; p. 826 per Denning LJ, *obiter*; *Manning v Nicholson* [1927] 2 WWR 623.

23 *Molloy v Gallagher* [1933] IR 1, at p. 13 per Fitzgibbon J (for the Supreme Court); the plaintiff failed to establish the necessary facts to support the claim; for more detailed consideration of abuse of process see Prosser et al., *Prosser & Keeton on Torts*, 5th ed. (St Paul, Minn.: West, 1984) at §121.

24 [1981] IR 312.

(c) that the claimant has suffered actual damage or that the impugned action was one which the law presumes will have caused the claimant damage.[25]

The plaintiffs had applied for an order of specific performance in respect of a conditional agreement with the defendants for the lease of a premises and had registered a *lis pendens*. The conditions could not be satisfied, thus precluding the agreement from taking effect as a contract. The plaintiffs persisted with the proceedings, for the purpose of exerting pressure on the defendants to reach a new agreement, after receiving legal advice that the claim was unsustainable. The defendants had, in the meantime, been negotiating with a third party for the sale of the premises, but the plaintiffs' conduct caused the third party to withdraw from those negotiations. The defendants' counterclaim for abuse of process was upheld by Costello J.

The principles relating to malice and reasonable or probable cause would probably be the same as those used in respect of malicious prosecution. The only subsequent reported decision in Ireland on the subject is *Murphy v Kirwan*,[26] involving a pre-trial motion for discovery. The outline consideration given to the plaintiff's claim affirms the similarity in the substantive requirements for the two torts.[27]

Maintenance and Champerty

Maintenance involves the provision of assistance, without lawful justification, to a plaintiff or defendant in civil proceedings. There is no equivalent wrong in respect of criminal proceedings.[28] The essence of the tort is that there be 'officious intermeddling in . . . litigation in which the maintainer has no legitimate interest'.[29] There must be actual damage to the opposing party in the action before the tort is complete, and the costs and judgment of a successfully maintained action do not constitute such damage.[30] Loss of credit, resulting from allegations made against a person may constitute damage.[31] 'Legitimate interest' lacks precise definition, but charitable assistance does not amount to maintenance;[32] nor does assistance provided by persons related to the party that they assist.[33]

---

25 *Ibid.*, at p. 320.
26 [1994] 1 ILRM 293.
27 *Ibid.*, at pp. 300–1 per Finlay CJ (O'Flaherty J concurring).
28 *Grant v Thompson* (1895) 72 LT 264.
29 *Neville v London Express Newspaper Ltd* [1919] AC 368; [1918–19] All ER Rep 61, at p. 395; p. 74 per Lord Atkinson.
30 *Ibid.*; the costs of the defendant, incurred in a maintained or champertous action which failed, would be recoverable, *Alabaster v Harness* [1894] 2 QB 897; [1891–4] All ER Rep 817; *O'Keeffe v Scales* [1998] 1 ILRM 393.
31 *J.C. Scott Constructions v Mermaid Waters Tavern Pty Ltd* [1984] 2 Qd R 413; see also Balkin & Davis, *Law of Torts* (Sydney: Butterworths, 1991) at pp. 785–6.
32 *Harris v Brisco* (1886) 17 QBD 504; [1886–90] All ER Rep 564.
33 A variety of relationships may suffice, e.g. family relationships or master and servant – *Bradlaugh v Newdgate* (1883) 11 QBD 1, at p. 11 per Lord Coleridge CJ;

Champerty is a specialised form of maintenance under which the maintainer is to receive a share in the proceeds of a successful action. These torts are virtually unused in modern times and have been abolished by statute in some jurisdictions.[34] A rare example arose in a preliminary hearing in *O'Keeffe v Scales*,[35] where the defendant alleged that the plaintiff's solicitor was seeking to recover a debt owed by the solicitor's insolvent client to the solicitor and that the action against the defendant was being pursued as a means to generate funds with which to pay that debt. In other words, it was alleged that the solicitor had an interest in the action because any funds raised would go towards a debt owed to the solicitor by the plaintiff. The debt arose from matters entirely unconnected to the litigation between the plaintiff and defendant.

Interference with Domestic Relations

A number of actions existed at common law for the protection of certain aspects of the relations between family members. These torts are outdated in many respects, but little action has been taken by the legislature to respond to the detailed proposals for reform made by the Law Reform Commission.[36]

Loss of Consortium

Consortium has been described as 'living together as husband and wife with all the incidents that flow from that relationship'.[37] It has been more extensively defined as 'companionship, the rendering of services, sexual intercourse and affectionate relations between spouses'.[38] The wrongful deprivation of the right of a spouse to the consortium of the other spouse is a tort. The usual way in which the tort arises is that the defendant injures one spouse, leading to a lengthy period of hospitalisation, thereby depriving the other spouse of companionship and domestic services. Other forms of deprivation of consortium, such as false

---

Neville v London Express Newspaper Ltd [1919] AC 368; [1918–19] All ER Rep 61, at p. 389; p. 71 per Viscount Haldane; the relationship between a trade union and its members has also been held to be sufficient – *Hill v Archbold* [1968] 1 QB 686; [1967] 3 All ER 110.

34 S. 14 of the Criminal Law Act 1967 (England); s. 32 of the Wrongs Act 1958 (Victoria).

35 [1998] 1 ILRM 393; the High Court and the Supreme Court refused to dismiss the plaintiff's action at the preliminary stage, but accepted that the defendant might succeed after a plenary hearing.

36 Law Reform Commission, *The Law Relating to Seduction and the Enticement and Harbouring of a Child* (Working Paper No. 6, 1979); Law Reform Commission, *The Law Relating to Loss of Consortium and Loss of Services of a Child* (Working Paper No. 7, 1979); Law Reform Commission, *First Report on Family Law* (Law Reform Commission No. 1, 1981).

37 *McKinley v Minister for Defence* [1992] 2 IR 333, at p. 346 per Hederman J.

38 *Ibid.*, at p. 355 per O'Flaherty J.

imprisonment of a spouse, would also be actionable. Where the spouse is killed the action is not available, but a separate action under Part IV of the Civil Liability Act 1961 is available.[39]

Originally the tort was only available to the husband and not the wife, but the Supreme Court, in *McKinley v Minister for Defence*,[40] extended the action to allow a wife to recover. The defence argued that the inequality of the common law position made the action unconstitutional, violating the guarantee of equality in Article 40.1, and so the tort no longer existed in our legal system. The majority in the Supreme Court rejected this argument and held that equality should be achieved by extending the availability of the action. Hederman J relied on American authorities in support of the proposition that the courts should, where possible, equalise by positive rather than negative measures, thus favouring extension of the action over abolition.[41] McCarthy J held that abolition would involve legislating on an issue of social policy, as the husband's right to sue was well established and had been endorsed by the Supreme Court in previous cases.[42] The third member of the majority, O'Flaherty J, pointed out that it was in the nature of the judicial function to resolve anomalies in the law and that the proper means of doing so was to ensure that a just solution was achieved.[43]

Older authorities indicate that the loss of consortium must be total, i.e. all attributes of consortium must be removed, though it need not be permanent.[44] More recent authorities prefer the view that any substantial interference with consortium should be actionable.[45] Thus, where one spouse is rendered permanently impotent the action would be available, as a significant aspect of consortium has been removed, even though other attributes, such as communication or the performance of household duties, remain. Likewise, permanent brain damage would suffice, even though some limited aspects of communication remain.

---

39 Considered in chapter 13 *infra*.
40 [1992] 2 IR 333, noted by Hogan (1992) 14 DULJ 115, focusing on the constitutional aspects of the decision; see also *Coppinger v Waterford County Council* [1996] 2 ILRM 427.
41 *Ibid.*, at pp. 347–8, citing Cardozo, *The Nature of the Judicial Process* (Yale University Press, 1921); and Marshall CJ in *Marbury v Madison* (1803) 5 US 1.
42 *Ibid.*, at p. 354; the previous authorities are *Spaight v Dundon* [1961] IR 201 and *O'Haran v Divine* (1964) 100 ILTR 53.
43 *Ibid.*, at p. 357.
44 *Spaight v Dundon* [1961] IR 201.
45 *O'Haran v Divine* (1964) 100 ILTR 53; *McKinley v Minister for Defence* [1992] 2 IR 333, at pp. 354–5 per McCarthy J; O'Flaherty J, at p. 358, reserved his opinion, but suggested that it would be difficult to justify the denial of an action where a significant element of consortium was permanently removed.

Other Actions

There is no right for children to sue in respect of the loss of their domestic relationship with their parents,[46] though the Law Reform Commission has recommended the introduction of such an action.[47] Parents are entitled to sue in respect of the loss of a child's domestic services resulting from the commission of a tort against the child, but must be able to establish that the child performed such services.[48]

The other surviving actions are for the seduction, enticement or harbouring of a minor. Seduction allows for the recovery of loss to parents arising from persons having sexual relations with their children, such as the cost associated with a resulting pregnancy.[49] Enticement and harbouring are somewhat similar, but relate to a wider range of acts by which a parent may lose the child's services.[50] The difference between these actions and the action for loss of services is that seduction, enticement and harbouring need not involve any tort against the child.

Liability in Respect of Fire

The early common law imposed strict liability on occupiers for damage caused by fires started on their property, but in 1715 a statutory amendment was introduced excluding liability in respect of fires accidentally started in houses.[51] The Supreme Court, in *Richardson v Athlone Woollen Mills Co. Ltd*,[52] refused to apply the 1715 Act to a fire which began in a factory. Section 1(1) of the Accidental Fires Act 1943 now provides a more extensive exception to the

---

46 *PH and Others v John Murphy & Sons Ltd* [1987] IR 621; [1988] ILRM 300, at p. 625; p. 303.

47 Working Paper No. 7, *op. cit.* 1979 at pp. 37–9, 42; *First Report on Family Law, op. cit.* at p. 9; the proposal is for a more generalised family right of action for interference with domestic relations.

48 *Chapman v McDonald* [1969] IR 188; this action does not extend to other aspects of the relationship, but the Law Reform Commission proposals for reform would provide such an extension.

49 This tort derived from the law of master and servant, rather than from family rights. It is considered at some length in McMahon & Binchy, *The Irish Law of Torts*, 1st ed. (Abingdon: Professional Books, 1981) at pp. 415 *et seq.*; Law Reform Commission, Working Paper No. 6, *op. cit.* at chapter 1.

50 This action is also derived from the law of master and servant; McMahon & Binchy, *The Irish Law of Torts*, 2nd ed. (Dublin: Butterworths, 1989) at pp. 601–3; Law Reform Commission, Working Paper No. 6, *op. cit.* at chapter 2.

51 2 Geo. 1 c. 5, An Act for Preventing Mischief that may Happen by Fire; the preamble to the Act supports the proposition that common law liability was strict, though there is some doubt as to whether this was the case, see Heuston & Buckley, *Salmond & Heuston on the Law of Torts*, 21st ed. (London: Sweet & Maxwell, 1996) at p. 320.

52 [1942] IR 581.

common law rule, protecting the occupiers of all buildings or land from liability for damage caused by fires which occurred accidentally.[53]

Accidental

It appears that fires intentionally started under controlled circumstances, such as in a domestic fireplace, which accidentally go out of control, constitute accidental fires.[54] The protection of the 1943 Act does not extend to fires negligently started or negligently allowed to spread. The only case since the 1943 Act to expressly acknowledge this is *Kelly v McElligott*,[55] where the proprietors of a hotel were held liable for injuries suffered by a guest attempting to escape from a fire started by the negligence of a hotel employee. The decisions in *McKenzie v O'Neill & Roe Ltd*[56] and *Phillips v Durgan*[57] imposed liability for negligence without even mentioning the 1943 Act. In *McKenzie* a director of the defendant company burned a quantity of unwanted papers, but negligently failed to ensure that the fire was properly extinguished. The company was held liable for damage caused to neighbouring property when the wind caused the fire to spread.[58] In *Phillips* the defendant hired his sister to redecorate his house. The kitchen was extremely greasy and the only method for heating water was a poorly functioning gas cooker. Not surprisingly, a fire broke out during the sister's attempt to boil water for cleaning the place. The Supreme Court held that the defendant had been negligent, as he had neither warned his sister about the condition of the premises nor made any suitable arrangements for the safe provision of hot water. The duty owed also extended to her husband, who was injured in rescuing her from the fire.

It seems probable that an action under the principle in *Rylands v Fletcher* would be available against the occupier of property for fires negligently started by independent contractors, provided the fire arises out of a non-natural use of land.[59]

---

53 The Act is rigorously analysed by Osborough, 'Liability in Tort for Unintended Fire Damage' (1971) 6 Ir Jur (ns) 205; see also McMahon & Binchy, 2nd ed., *op. cit.* at chapter 26.
54 *Ruttledge v Land* [1930] IR 537 in respect of the 1715 Act; the opposite view was acknowledged by Asquith J in *Mulholland & Tedd v Baker* [1939] 3 All ER 253, at p. 255, but the issue was left undecided as negligence was found on the facts.
55 (1949) 85 ILTR 4.
56 Unrep. HC, 23 June 1977.
57 [1991] 1 IR 89; [1991] ILRM 321; noted by O'Dell (1992) 14 DULJ 65; Byrne & Binchy, *Annual Review of Irish Law 1990* at pp. 493–500.
58 The Privy Council in *Goldman v Hargrave* [1967] 1 AC 645; [1966] 3 WLR 513; [1966] 2 All ER 989 held that liability may also be imposed for negligent failure to contain a fire which began accidentally.
59 See Osborough, *loc. cit.* at pp. 214–15 on the relationship between the 1943 Act and the *Rylands v Fletcher* principle. He presents a persuasive argument that the

Miscellaneous Torts

Where the injured party is an entrant on the land where the fire occurs, the Occupiers' Liability Act 1995 may be applicable, but a number of premises are subject to additional legislative requirements. Section 18 of the Fire Services Act 1981 imposes a duty of reasonable care in respect of the prevention of fire and the safety of entrants in the event of fire. This duty applies to persons in control of a variety of premises in which large groups of people are likely to be, such as hotels, schools and places of entertainment.[60] It did not originally extend to industrial premises, but these were added to the premises covered in 1989.[61] Other workplaces are regulated by the Safety, Health and Welfare at Work Act 1989.

Additional Matters

Two further aspects of the protection afforded by the 1943 Act merit brief consideration – the onus of proof and the definition of damage. The Circuit Court decision in *Woods v O'Connor*[62] held that the plaintiff bears the responsibility of proving that the fire is not accidental. This is consistent with the general position of the law of torts on the onus of proof, as the plaintiff is usually required to prove intention or negligence when the behavioural standard is an essential ingredient. However, there are circumstances where the burden of proof is reversed and cases involving fire may be particularly suited to such a reversal, at least where the plaintiff would experience serious practical difficulty in establishing how the fire began.[63] The decision in *Woods* also indicates that the immunity under the 1943 Act extends to personal injury. Professor Osborough, however, has put forward a powerful argument for confining the immunity to property damage and this view merits serious consideration by the courts, should the issue arise.[64]

Non-occupiers

The immunity provided by the 1943 Act and the original common law liability both concern the occupier of the property on which the fire started. The responsibility of other persons, such as the person who started the fire, must be determined by ordinary tort principles, such as trespass, nuisance, negligence and the rule in *Rylands v Fletcher*. One further special provision must be noted in respect of liability for fire, however. Section 36 of the Fire Services Act 1981 precludes an action being taken against various public authorities for failure to

Act excludes a *Rylands v Fletcher* action where the fire is purely accidental (i.e. started through no fault of any person).
60 The places covered are defined in s. 18(1) of the Act.
61 Fire Services Act 1981 (Prescribed Premises) Order 1989 (SI 319/1989).
62 [1958] Ir Jur Rep 71.
63 Proof is considered in more detail in chapter 12 *infra*.
64 *Loc. cit.* at p. 211.

comply with functions allocated to them under the Act. This does not mean that such authorities can never be sued in respect of fire damage, but it means that the action cannot be based exclusively on the statutory role of the authority.[65]

Liability in Respect of Animals

Persons in control of animals may be liable under a number of torts, such as nuisance, negligence and trespass, for damage caused by the animals. In addition, there are special principles specifically dealing with responsibility for damage caused by animals. These special principles developed at common law prior to the emergence of the more general types of action, such as negligence, which dominate modern tort law.[66] They are anachronistic, but have survived, with only minor legislative changes, despite a reasoned call for their replacement by a single strict liability tort similar in scope to the *Rylands v Fletcher* principle.[67]

Cattle Trespass

Strict liability attaches in respect of damage caused by cattle which stray from land on which they are kept onto neighbouring land. This principle does not apply to cattle brought onto the highway, which stray onto property adjoining the highway; in such cases negligence must be shown on the part of the person in control of the cattle.[68] Neither does it apply to cases where animals stray onto the highway from land on which they are kept; at common law there was an immunity from liability in such cases,[69] but this has been removed by section 2 of the Animals Act 1985. This statutory provision requires any person placing an animal on land to take reasonable care to avoid damage being caused by the animal straying onto a public road and the Supreme Court has held that the onus is on that person to show that reasonable care has been exercised.[70]

---

65 For a more detailed analysis of the potential liability of public authorities, see McMahon & Binchy, 2nd ed., *op. cit.* at p. 502; see also Hogan & Morgan, *Administrative Law*, 3rd ed. (Dublin: Round Hall Sweet & Maxwell) at chapter 15.
66 The development of the law in respect of animals is usefully set out by the Law Reform Commission, *Civil Liability for Animals* (Working Paper No. 3, 1977).
67 *Ibid.* Osborough (1978) 13 Ir Jur (ns) 182 at pp. 184–5 expresses some sympathy for the position adopted, but argues that it was insufficiently argued; he also criticised the English legislation, the Animals Act 1971, for being unnecessarily complicated; see also Law Reform Commission, *Report on Civil Liability for Animals* (Law Reform Commission No. 2, 1982).
68 *Gibb v Comerford* [1942] IR 295, at p. 304.
69 *Howard v Bergin, O'Connor & Co.* [1925] 2 IR 110; *Searle v Wallbank* [1947] AC 341; [1947] 1 All ER 12.
70 *O'Shea v Tilman* unrep. SC, 23 October 1996; Irish Times Law Report, 16 December 1996; this confirms the interpretation provided by Johnson J in *O'Reilly v Lavelle* [1990] 2 IR 372.

It seems that the proper defendant in an action for cattle trespass is the person in possession or control of the animals, irrespective of ownership.[71] The term 'cattle' is generally understood to include all types of farm animals, including fowl, but does not include cats, dogs or wild animals.[72] In *Brady v Warren*,[73] for example, domesticated deer were treated as cattle for the purposes of liability, but rabbits were not. The damage requirement was traditionally confined to property damage, such as the destruction of crops, but some cases have suggested that personal injury would also be recoverable under this tort.[74]

Scienter

The scienter doctrine is based on the defendant's knowledge of the dangerous nature of an animal in his possession.[75] Such knowledge may be imputed by law in a number of instances. The action differs from cattle trespass in two principal respects – first, it can apply to any type of animal and, secondly, there is no requirement that the animal has escaped or strayed from the defendant's property.[76] Strict liability attaches to the defendant for physical damage to persons or property directly caused by the animal, once the requisite knowledge exists.

Animals are divided into two categories for the purposes of determining knowledge of their dangerous nature – naturally dangerous animals (*ferae naturae*) and naturally harmless animals (*mansuetae naturae*). The former are usually wild animals and the latter domestic. The defendant's knowledge of dangerousness is presumed by law in respect of animals classed as *ferae naturae*,[77] but must be proved in respect of animals classed as *mansuetae naturae*. The distinction between dangerous and harmless animals is not easy

---

71 *Dalton v O'Sullivan* [1947] Ir Jur Rep 25; *Winters v Owens* [1950] IR 225.

72 See Law Reform Commission, Working Paper No. 3, 1977 *op. cit.* at p. 49; McMahon & Binchy, 2nd ed., *op. cit.* at p. 516; Fridman *op. cit.* vol. 1 at p. 209; Balkin & Davis, *op. cit.* at p. 517.

73 [1900] 2 IR 632.

74 *Waugh v Montgomery* (1882) 8 VLR (L) 290; *Harrison v Armstrong* (1917) 51 ILTR 38; *Wormald v Cole* [1954] 1 QB 614; [1954] 1 All ER 683.

75 Liability is based on possession or control, rather than ownership; *Walker v Hall* (1876) 40 JP 456; *Breen v Slotkin* [1948] 4 DLR 46.

76 There has been some debate as to whether there must be an escape from the defendant's control for liability to arise; *Rands v McNeil* [1955] 1 QB 253; [1954] 3 All ER 593 favours such a requirement; *Higgins v William Inglis & Son Pty Ltd* [1978] 1 NSWR 649 rejects it; for detailed discussion see Fridman, *op. cit.* vol. 1 at pp. 219–21.

77 This presumption cannot be rebutted; thus in *Behrens v Bertram Mills Circus Ltd* [1957] 2 QB 1; [1957] 2 WLR 404; [1957] 1 All ER 583 the defendants were held liable for personal injury caused by a trained elephant chasing a dog that had barked and snapped at it; elephants were classed as *ferae naturae* and it was irrelevant that this particular elephant was tame.

to draw, but it is based on the traits of the species as a whole, rather than those of individual animals.[78]

In the case of animals of a harmless species, the plaintiff must establish that the defendant had knowledge of a tendency or propensity towards the type of mischief complained of.[79] There are some important issues to be borne in mind in respect of this requirement. First, an animal can display a dangerous propensity without causing any damage; so a tendency of a dog to bite, for example, may be established by the fact that he was growling and running at children, even though he had not yet bitten a child.[80] Secondly, knowledge held by family members or servants will be imputed to the defendant.[81] Thirdly, the tendency or propensity must be dangerous; mere friskiness will not suffice.[82]

Acts of a third party are not available as a defence in a scienter action and the position in respect of acts of God is uncertain.[83] Given the similarity between this action and the *Rylands v Fletcher* principle, it has been suggested that the defences for both should be the same.[84]

Statutory Liability for Dogs

The dangers posed by dogs have provoked legislative reaction in a number of jurisdictions, including Ireland. The current measures are contained in the Control of Dogs Acts 1986 and 1992. The bulk of the legislation is concerned with administrative matters, such as licensing and enforcement, and criminal liability for breach. Section 21 of the 1986 Act, however, does impose civil liability on dog owners.[85] Sub-section (1) imposes strict liability 'for damage caused in an

---

78 For consideration of the extensive case law on the distinction see McMahon & Binchy, 2nd ed., *op. cit.* at p. 511; Fridman, *op. cit.* vol. 1 at pp. 213–16; Balkin & Davis, *op. cit.* at pp. 521–3.
79 In *Glanville v Sutton & Co. Ltd* [1928] 1 KB 571, for example, it was held that proof that a horse had a tendency to bite other horses was not sufficient to show a vicious or mischievous tendency where the complaint was that the horse bit a person.
80 *Duggan v Armstrong* [1992] 2 IR 161; [1993] ILRM 222; noted in Byrne & Binchy, *Annual Review of Irish Law 1992* at pp. 588–91.
81 *Ibid.*; *Brennan v Walsh* (1936) 70 ILTR 252.
82 *Fitzgerald v Cooke Bourne (Farms) Ltd* [1964] 1 QB 249; [1963] 3 WLR 522; [1963] 3 All ER 36; though the dangerous propensity need not be permanent, *Howard v Bergin, O'Connor & Co.* [1925] 2 IR 110 at pp. 124–5 per Kennedy CJ.
83 *Baker v Snell* [1908] 2 KB 825; [1908–10] All ER Rep 398; *Behrens v Bertram Mills Circus Ltd* [1957] 2 QB 1; [1957] 2 WLR 404; [1957] 1 All ER 583; *Kavanagh v Centreline Ltd* [1987] ILRM 306; in England the position is now governed by the Animals Act 1971, which does not permit those defences. *Kavanagh* does not deal with acts of God, but precludes the defence of act of a stranger.
84 Law Reform Commission, Working Paper No. 3, 1977, *op. cit.* at p. 43; McMahon & Binchy, 2nd ed., *op. cit.* at p. 512.
85 Section 1 of the Act gives an extended definition of owner, so as to include occupiers of land where a dog is kept or permitted to remain, unless that person can prove that he is not the owner.

attack on any person by the dog and for injury done by it to any livestock'. This liability is independent of any knowledge of dangerousness, but is subject to some exceptions. Injury caused by a dog to a trespasser is dependent on proof of negligence,[86] while damage to livestock that stray onto land where a dog is lawfully present is only actionable if the defendant caused the dog to attack.[87]

Actions on the Case

We have already seen, in chapter 4, that much of the modern law of torts evolved from the action on the case. The central feature of the action on the case was that the plaintiff had to demonstrate the wrongfulness of the defendant's conduct by showing that the factual circumstances were sufficiently analogous to established wrongs. This type of action gradually led to the development of the various nominate torts, apart from trespass (which predates the action on the case). The action on the case still remains as a possible vehicle for providing a remedy to a plaintiff whose injury falls outside the scope of the nominate torts, but occurs in a manner closely analogous to established torts. There is a lack of Irish authorities on the issue, but other common law jurisdictions have produced a small collection of such cases, demonstrating the value of this residual type of action. Despite the lack of usage of this action in Ireland, its existence as a possible means of action must be accepted as part of the common law inheritance carried over by Article 50 of the Constitution.

Physical Damage

Not surprisingly, it is a tort to intentionally inflict physical injury on another without lawful excuse. Since the eighteenth century, trespass has been used in respect of the direct infliction of injury and actions on the case have been used to deal with indirect infliction of injury.[88] Most indirect, but intentional, injuries will now fall within the scope of one or other of the nominate torts already covered; for example, the setting of traps by an occupier of premises to harm trespassers will constitute a breach of section 4 of the Occupiers' Liability Act 1995;[89] deliberate injuring of a neighbouring occupier, by releasing a dangerous object, may constitute a private nuisance or a breach of the principle in *Rylands v Fletcher*. There may be residual cases that do not easily fall within the scope of existing torts and these would require the invocation of the action on the case in order to provide the injured party with a remedy. Suitable examples would include putting poison in another person's food or deliberately exposing someone to an infectious disease.

---

86 Sub-s. (3).
87 Sub-s. (2).
88 See chapter 4 *supra*.
89 At common law an action on the case would have been the appropriate cause of action; see *Deane v Clayton* (1817) 7 Taunt 489; *Bird v Holbrook* (1828) 4 Bing 628.

The most celebrated case of indirect, intentional physical harm is that of *Wilkinson v Downton*.[90] The defendant, a regular customer in the plaintiff's public house, informed the plaintiff that the plaintiff's husband had been seriously injured in a road accident some distance away and that he wished to be brought home. The plaintiff sent her son and a servant to do so, but it transpired that the story was false and intended as a practical joke. The incident traumatised the plaintiff to the extent that she suffered serious physical illness, with lasting effects on her.

Wright J doubted the appropriateness of deceit, but did uphold the plaintiff's claim on the basis that an action on the case was sufficiently made out where the defendant 'has . . . wilfully done an act calculated to cause physical harm to the plaintiff . . . and has in fact thereby caused physical harm to her'.[91] This proposition was subsequently endorsed by the Court of Appeal in *Janvier v Sweeney*,[92] also involving physical illness resulting from the psychological effect of untrue statements. The principle has been subjected to further consideration in a number of cases, in various common law jurisdictions.[93] From these some tentative observations may be made as to its scope and nature.

This action differs from trespass in two significant aspects, other than the indirectness of the physical impact. The first is that actual damage is required; the wrongful conduct is not actionable *per se*. Secondly, the defendant's intent must extend to the harm; an intent to have a harmless impact on the plaintiff will not suffice.[94] Intent is based on an objective evaluation, and an intention to produce harmful effects may be imputed to the defendant where they are substantially certain to occur or where the defendant has been reckless in respect of such effects.[95]

---

90 [1897] 2 QB 57; [1895–9] All ER Rep 267.
91 *Ibid.*, at pp. 58–9; p. 269; Wright J noted that the defendant had not offered any justification for his action, implying that some grounds of justification would be available in suitable cases; see chapter 7 *supra*, for consideration of the suitability of deceit.
92 [1919] 2 KB 316; [1918–19] All ER Rep 1056, per Bankes LJ at pp. 321–4; pp. 1059–60; per Duke LJ at p. 326; p. 1061; per Lawrence J at p. 328; p. 1062; the facts of this case are set out, briefly, in chapter 7 *supra*, in the discussion of deceit.
93 See Trindade & Cane, *The Law of Torts in Australia*, 2nd ed. (Melbourne: Oxford University Press, 1993) at pp. 62 *et seq.*; Mullany & Handford, *Tort Liability for Psychiatric Damage* (Sydney: Law Book Co., 1993) at chapter 14 for detailed consideration of the action.
94 The term 'calculated' by Wright J is generally understood to indicate intentional or reckless infliction of harm and does not extend to harm which is merely foreseeable; see *Stevenson v Basham* [1922] NZLR 225, at p. 229; *Abramzik v Brenner* (1967) 65 DLR (2d) 651, at p. 654 per Culliton CJS; *Restatement, Second, Torts*, §46 (but §312 makes provision for liability for foreseeable harm, as a separate wrong); Mullany & Handford, *op. cit.* at pp. 288–9; Rogers, *Winfield & Jolowicz on Tort*, 14th ed. (London: Sweet & Maxwell, 1994) at p. 75.
95 *Wilkinson* itself provides an example of imputed intent, [1897] 2 QB 57; [1895–9] All ER Rep 267, at p. 59; p. 269.

Examples of situations in which this action has been successfully invoked include a miscarriage resulting from the plaintiff hearing the defendant threaten her husband with burning the couple out of their home;[96] illness resulting from the plaintiff witnessing a battery on her husband;[97] and illness resulting from the plaintiff hearing a false rumour that her son had hanged himself, circulated by the defendant.[98]

Psychological Damage

Medical understanding and legal acceptance of mental illness were somewhat limited at the time of the decisions in *Wilkinson* and *Janvier*. The subsequent development of liability in respect of negligently inflicted psychological damage has brought the law to a position whereby medically recognised mental illness constitutes a recognised form of harm, without the need to establish additional physical illness. In the case of intentional infliction of psychiatric damage, an action on the case, similar to that in *Wilkinson*, is likely to be available. One of the few clear examples of such a case is *Timmermans v Buelow*,[99] where the plaintiff's landlord threatened to have him beaten up, knowing that he was prone to panic attacks, thereby causing a deterioration of his mental condition.

In America the law has developed beyond this point and an action is available for the intentional or reckless infliction of emotional distress, through extreme or outrageous conduct.[100] The emotional suffering must be severe, but is not confined to medically recognised psychiatric illness. The fact that the level of responsibility here is much greater than in negligence may be justified on the basis that the infliction of harm is intended, rather than inadvertent.

The decision in *Thomas v NUM*[101] is the closest that English law has come to invoking such a principle, indicating that harassment is actionable in circumstances falling outside the scope of the nominate torts and where no physical or economic damage occurs. This case concerned picketing by coal miners, involving a considerable degree of hostility towards those still working during the dispute. Scott J held that there was no assault of the working miners by those picketing, as the workers were in vehicles and the pickets were held

---

96 *Stevenson v Basham* [1922] NZLR 225.
97 *Johnson v Commonwealth* (1927) 27 SR (NSW) 133; *Purdy v Woznesensky* [1937] 2 WWR 116.
98 *Bielitski v Obadiak* (1922) 65 DLR 627; for a more extensive list of cases see Mullany & Handford, *op. cit.*
99 (1984) 38 CCLT 136; assault would not be available unless the threatened battery was imminent; the action on the case provides a useful extension to include threats which are more remote, though nonetheless real.
100 *Restatement, Second, Torts* §46; this principle has been employed extensively in the courts; references to this considerable body of case law may be found in Mullany & Handford, *op. cit.* at pp. 297 *et seq.* and Prosser & Keeton, *op. cit.* at pp. 60 *et seq.*
101 [1985] 2 All ER 1.

back by the police, so there was no imminent likelihood of battery; there was no actionable public nuisance, as the right of way of the workers was not blocked and there was no special damage, since they were able to get to work during the dispute; there was no interference with contractual relations, as the primary obligations of the National Coal Board to the workers were not impeded; and, finally, there was no intimidation in the traditional sense of the tort, as the pressure was unsuccessful.[102] The hostile protest was, however, held to constitute an unreasonable interference with rights, analogous to private nuisance (but without the connection to rights in land). The level of interference, in the circumstances, was held to be actionable: 'A daily congregation on average of 50 to 70 men hurling abuse and in circumstances that require a police presence and require the working miners to be conveyed in vehicles do not in my view leave any real room for argument.'[103] Scott J stated, *obiter*, that it would also be actionable harassment 'persistently to follow another on a public highway, making rude gestures or remarks in order to annoy or vex'.[104]

However, the Court of Appeal in *Burnett v George*[105] was only willing to hold that harassment would be actionable where there was impairment of the victim's health. This would confine the action to the parameters set by *Wilkinson*. In *Khorasandjian v Bush*,[106] the Court of Appeal granted a *quia timet* injunction in respect of harassing telephone calls, in the absence of any medical evidence on the extent of harm. One interpretation, offered by Jones, suggests that this has broadened the parameters of 'harm', bringing English law closer to the American position.[107] It may, alternatively, be no more than a generous interpretation of the likelihood of medically recognised illness occurring, unless the harassment was discontinued. The correctness of the *Khorasandjian* decision was cast into doubt by the subsequent House of Lords decision in *Hunter v Canary Wharf Ltd*.[108] The English legislature responded by introducing a statutory tort of harassment.[109]

The Irish superior courts have not yet had to resolve this issue, but have a range of options available to them. Given the advances in the understanding of mental illness, it would seem inappropriate to require physical injury in order to support an action on the case. Whether the action should be confined to

---

102 *Ibid.*, at pp. 20–1.
103 *Ibid.*, at p. 22.
104 *Ibid.*; see also Fricker (1992) 142 NLJ 247 suggesting a statutory tort of harassment, actionable *per se*.
105 [1992] 1 FLR 525.
106 [1993] QB 727; [1993] 3 WLR 476; [1993] 3 All ER 669.
107 (1994) 47 Current Legal Problems 177 at pp. 202 *et seq.*; see also Bridgeman & Jones, 'Harassing Conduct and Outrageous Acts: A Cause of Action for Intentionally Inflicted Mental Distress?' (1994) 14 LS 180.
108 [1997] AC 655; [1997] 2 WLR 684; [1997] 2 All ER 426.
109 S. 3 of the Protection from Harassment Act 1997.

cases of medically recognised illness or should extend to serious vexation is more problematic. Certainly the American approach has much to recommend it, at least for the purpose of establishing grounds for injunctive relief.

Property Damage and Economic Loss

There is considerably less support for the availability of an action on the case for property damage or economic loss which occurs in a manner that is not covered by the nominate torts. The principal authority supporting such an action is the decision of the High Court of Australia in *Beaudesert Shire Council v Smith*,[110] where it was held that:

> . . . independently of trespass, negligence or nuisance but by an action for damages upon the case, a person who suffers harm or loss as the inevitable consequence of the unlawful, intentional and positive acts of another is entitled to recover damages from that other.[111]

The council had removed gravel from the bed of a river, without authority, thereby committing a trespass against the owner of the property through which the stream was running. This interference with the stream destroyed a water-hole from which Smith, a neighbouring farmer, pumped water onto his farm, under a licence. The interference with Smith, resulting indirectly from a tort committed against a third party, was held to be an actionable wrong. Difficulties in determining the scope of the various criteria, particularly 'unlawful' and 'inevitable', have resulted in judicial reluctance to accept the general proposition suggested in the case and it has been rejected in New Zealand[112] and England.[113] The High Court of Australia has subsequently overruled the principle in a case concerning public officials inadvertently exceeding their authority, resulting in the imposition of restrictions on the sale of the plaintiffs' cattle causing significant economic loss.[114]

---

110 (1966) 120 CLR 145.
111 *Ibid.*, at p. 156.
112 *Takaro Properties Ltd v Rowling* [1978] 2 NZLR 314, at pp. 339–40 per Richardson J (with whom the other members of the Court of Appeal agreed); *Van Camp Chocolates Ltd v Aulsebrooks Ltd* [1984] 1 NZLR 354, at p. 359 per Cooke J (for the Court of Appeal).
113 *Lonrho Ltd v Shell Petroleum* [1982] AC 173; [1981] 3 WLR 33; [1981] 2 All ER 456, at pp. 187–8; pp. 40–1; p. 463 per Lord Diplock (for the House of Lords) rejecting the use of a breach of statutory duty as an unlawful act.
114 *Northern Territory of Australia v Mengel* (1995) 69 ALJR 527; noted by Mullany (1995) 111 LQR 583, providing useful critical analysis of the decision and suggesting that there may be a limited number of situations where the principle would be justified. In *Eurostock Meat Marketing Ltd v Ireland*, unrep. HC, 13 March 1998, the state conceded liability in respect of a ban improperly imposed on the export of oxheads to Northern Ireland, causing economic loss to the plaintiff.

The emergent tort of interference with economic relations may be regarded as a narrower form of the *Beaudesert* principle, confined to acts intended to affect the plaintiff. Oddly, the courts seem willing to work at resolving the uncertainties surrounding the elements of the generic economic tort, but not at the broader principle in *Beaudesert*. Surely the concept of 'inevitable consequence' is no more problematic than the concept of 'unlawfulness' in respect of interference with economic relations. Furthermore, we have already seen that many torts have areas of vagueness and uncertainty, but this has not generally inhibited the courts from attempting to develop and apply the law in novel and difficult situations.

The action on the case, though judicially unpopular, is not without merit in limited instances. Where the defendant's act is clearly wrongful (such as a serious criminal offence or an intentional tort against a third party) and causes significant harm to the plaintiff, it seems unjust to reject the plaintiff's claim merely because the facts do not present an exact match with established causes of action. Even if the general principle in *Beaudesert* is rejected, there may be a residual role for the action on the case in exceptional circumstances, for example as a vehicle for the protection of constitutional rights.

PART II

General Issues

CHAPTER ELEVEN

From Obligation to Liability I:
Causation and Remoteness

Introduction

The mere fact that a defendant has breached a duty owed to a plaintiff does not inevitably lead to the conclusion that a remedy is available to that plaintiff; the path from obligation to liability is often long and difficult. The establishment of the existence of an obligation is only the first step in the process of obtaining a remedy. The main obstacles impeding the path between obligation and liability are causation and remoteness of damage, proof, defences and the limitation of actions. Each of these aspects of the tort process present unique problems for plaintiffs, which must be considered in turn. Because of the central role played by the concepts of causation and remoteness they will be considered separately in this chapter, with the other issues being deferred until the following chapter.

Causation

Damage, in the sense of the infringement of a legally protected interest, is an essential ingredient of all tort actions. In most cases actual damage must be shown to have occurred before a remedy can be obtained, though in exceptional cases injunctions may be sought to prevent damage which is imminent, but has not yet occurred. Where a tort is actionable *per se*, such as libel or trespass to the person, a certain level of damage is presumed to have occurred by way of injury to reputation or dignity, without the plaintiff having to prove any physical harm to person, property or economic interests. Where the plaintiff is required to establish damage, there is an additional requirement of establishing a causal connection between the defendant's breach of obligation and the damage suffered. Without this causal connection the plaintiff's complaint cannot succeed against the defendant. Where an injunction is sought to prevent imminent damage the plaintiff must also establish a likely causal connection between the defendant's breach of obligation and the expected damage. In respect of torts which are actionable *per se*, the causal connection will be assumed in respect of the damage which is presumed to occur (such as injury to reputation or dignity). However, even in the case of such torts the plaintiff may wish to recover compensation for other actual losses over and above that which the law presumes to flow automatically from the breach. Such additional losses, and a causal connection to the defendant's breach, must be proved by the plaintiff if the claim is to succeed in respect of them.

The causal connection may be easily established in straightforward cases, such as a violent battery or a simple motor accident – defendant intentionally/ negligently strikes plaintiff with fist/cudgel/vehicle, breaking arm/leg/skull, requiring medical attention costing £X, and leading to a temporary loss of income (£Y) through the plaintiff's inability to work while suffering from the injury. Many tort cases fall into this category, but others are more complicated and involve the complex interaction of a wide variety of factors, not least of which are the limitations of human understanding of cause and effect in a variety of circumstances. In fact, the plaintiffs in *Hanrahan v Merck, Sharp & Dohme*[1] argued that the obligation on them to prove causation was sufficiently harsh as to amount to a failure by the state to fulfil the constitutional mandate, under Article 40.3, to vindicate the personal rights of the citizen. The case involved an allegation that toxic emissions from the defendant's chemical factory were causing a variety of illnesses suffered by the plaintiffs and had caused the death of plant and animal life on the plaintiffs' farm, which was neighbouring the factory. The scientific data on the emissions and their effects on humans, animals and plants was less than certain, to say the least, and the plaintiffs argued that the capacity of the defendant company to prove or disprove causation was much greater than that of the plaintiffs. Given the respective resources of the parties and the defendant's level of expertise in respect of the substances and processes under examination, the plaintiffs' argument as to the injustice of the causal requirement in the circumstances was not without merit, but was ultimately rejected by the Supreme Court, which held that the existing common law principles (the action was argued under the principles of the tort of private nuisance), including the requirement on the plaintiff to prove causation, constituted a sufficient vindication of the plaintiffs' personal rights. This decision confirms the role traditionally given to causation in tort actions and reiterates that it is the plaintiff who must establish the causal connection. The alternate approach, suggested by the plaintiffs, would have generated difficulties of its own, not least of which would be the potential injustice of requiring persons involved in novel or unusual activities to disprove their involvement in injuries sustained, which smacks of 'guilt by suspicion'.

Causal arguments are, to a large extent, unique to each individual case, but a number of general principles have developed over the years and these can help to give a general introduction to this area. At the initial stage a distinction must be drawn between factual and legal cause. Normally, in order for liability to be imposed on a defendant, it must first be shown that his conduct was a cause of the plaintiff's injury in a factual or scientific sense; secondly, it must be shown that the defendant's causal role was a sufficiently significant factor to attract or merit legal responsibility in respect of the injury. The first step in the process is the concept of factual cause, which is a necessary prerequisite to

---

1 [1989] ILRM 629.

the imposition of liability, but is not sufficient of itself to warrant the imposition of liability. The second step is the concept of legal cause, which involves the making of a value judgment as to whether legal responsibility is appropriate.

Factual Cause

The precision of scientific analysis is such that even simple occurrences can be seen to be the product of a multiplicity of factors, but it would be impractical to require litigants to explore the scientific significance of every possible factor involved in the sustaining of an injury; thus natural conditions and innocuous human conduct are often discounted as causes of injuries. The inquiry into factual cause in litigation tends to be focused on the examination of major rather than minor or background factors. Some American cases suggest that a defendant's behaviour should only be treated as a cause of an injury 'if it was a material element and a substantial factor in bringing it about'.[2] Minor causal elements are treated by the law as being no more than necessary background conditions; such an element is described as a *causa sine qua non* and is not regarded as a cause at all. A major factor may then be treated as 'the cause' of an injury and is described as the *causa causans*. Street observes that, in general, 'common sense and law unite in looking for the abnormal or the deliberate human act, and regarding that as "the cause"'.[3] Thus, in a motor accident a wet road is likely to be treated as a background condition, while the speed the driver chose to drive at will be treated as a cause. Abnormal natural conditions may be treated as causes, though they would probably have to be highly unusual and unforeseen.

A frequently used principle in determining factual cause is the 'but for' test. The gist of the test is to inquire whether but for the defendant's conduct the plaintiff would have suffered the injury complained of. If the answer is no, then the injury would not have occurred without the defendant's conduct and the conduct has, in a factual sense, been a cause. If the answer is yes, then the injury would have occurred irrespective of the defendant's conduct, so that the conduct was not a cause. This approach works quite well in many cases, particularly those where a single principal cause is responsible for the injury. The classic example of the principle in operation is the decision in *Barnett v*

---

2 See Prosser et al., *Prosser & Keeton on Torts*, 5th ed. (St Paul, Minn.: West, 1984) at p. 267; this approach was used by Laffoy J in *Superquinn Ltd v Bray Urban District Council and Others* unrep. HC, 18 February 1998, at p. 68, p. 81 and p. 82.

3 Brazier, *Street on Torts*, 9th ed. (London: Butterworths, 1993) at p. 250; for detailed consideration of the relationship between common sense and causal principles see Hart & Honoré, *Causation in the Law*, 2nd ed. (Oxford: Clarendon Press, 1985) at chapter 2; see also chapter 4 on the distinction between cause and background conditions; see also *Kenny v MIBI* unrep. SC, 3 April 1995; Irish Times Law Report, 5 June 1995.

Chelsea & Kensington Hospital Management Committee.[4] The plaintiff's husband was one of three workmen negligently sent away from the defendant's hospital, having been seen by a nurse who consulted with a doctor over the phone. It subsequently transpired that the plaintiff's husband had been suffering from arsenic poisoning and this led to his death shortly after being sent away. The plaintiff's case failed because the illness was so far advanced that, even if the doctor had not been negligent, her husband would probably have died. Similarly in *Kenny v O'Rourke*[5] the plaintiff was injured when he fell off a ladder, which was defective, but the fall was held to have occurred because the plaintiff leaned too far from the ladder; thus, the defect in the ladder was causally irrelevant to his injury. In upholding the High Court verdict Ó Dálaigh CJ in the Supreme Court stated that 'it was open to the jury to find, as they did, that the batten ladder was not the cause of the plaintiff's fall but that his fall was due to his having, unnecessarily, leaned over too far and thus overbalanced'.[6] It may be observed that the Chief Justice does not use the 'but for' formula at all, although the decision is consistent with the formula. The formula is one found more frequently in academic texts rather than in judgments but it does provide a useful explanation of relatively straightforward causation disputes, such as *Barnett* and *Kenny*.

The 'but for' test proves to be inadequate in dealing with more complex cases involving multiple causes. Examples of such cases fall into three basic classifications – simultaneous causes; successive causes; uncertain causes.[7] Let us consider each of these in turn, beginning with simultaneous causes, in order to identify the nature of the problems generated (we shall return to these cases in our consideration of legal cause to see the solutions offered).

Example

D1, D2 and P are owners of neighbouring properties. D1 and D2 each negligently cause fires to break out on their premises. Both fires spread to P's premises, which is located between those of D1 and D2. P's premises are totally destroyed.

Applying the 'but for' test, both D1 and D2 would be discounted as causes of the damage to P, which is plainly absurd. Would the damage to P have

---

4 [1969] 1 QB 428; [1968] 2 WLR 422; [1968] 1 All ER 1068; see also *Robinson v The Post Office* [1974] 1 WLR 1176; [1974] 2 All ER 737.

5 [1972] IR 339; see also *McWilliams v Sir William Arrol & Co. Ltd* [1962] 1 WLR 295; [1962] 1 All ER 623; for further examples see McMahon & Binchy, *The Irish Law of Torts*, 2nd ed. (Dublin: Butterworths, 1989) pp. 39–41.

6 [1972] IR 339, at p. 341.

7 For a more detailed classification of causal issues see Hart & Honoré, *op. cit.* at chapter 4; see also Waddams, 'Causation in Australia and Canada' (1993) 1 Tort L Rev 75.

occurred but for D1's negligence? Yes, because D2's fire would have caused it. Therefore, D1 is not a cause of the damage to P. Would the damage have occurred but for D2's negligence? Yes, because D1's fire would have caused it. Therefore, D2 is not a cause of the damage to P. In cases such as this, the 'but for' approach has to be disregarded and the conduct of both D1 and D2 should be treated as causes. The 'material element and a substantial factor' approach is more successful in addressing these types of case. There appear to be remarkably few reported decisions involving such simultaneous causes, but two noteworthy examples are *Lambton v Mellish*[8] and *Pride of Derby v British Celanese Ltd*.[9] In *Lambton* the two defendants operated fairground organs, independently of each other. The combined effect of their actions constituted a nuisance against the plaintiff, and the conduct of either defendant on its own would also have constituted a nuisance. It was held that both defendants were liable in respect of their contribution to the unlawful interference with the plaintiff's rights. *Pride of Derby* involved the pollution of a river by three separate sources which combined to damage the plaintiffs' rights and, once again, none of the defendants were allowed to escape liability on the basis that damage would have occurred without their participation.

Successive cause cases can also give rise to absurdity when subjected to the 'but for' test. In *Performance Cars Ltd v Abraham*[10] the plaintiff's Rolls Royce was damaged in a collision and a repainting of the lower section of the two tone car was required in order to match the colour of the repaired section. Prior to repair and repainting, the car was involved in a second collision, this time with the defendant. This caused further damage to the lower section of the car, at a different point from the first collision, which also required repainting to obtain a colour match. The 'but for' test would indicate neither accident to be a cause if applied after the two incidents, as with the simultaneous causes examined previously; again this result is unacceptable.

In cases of uncertain causes, the uncertainty may be such as to make it impossible to actually give an answer to the 'but for' inquiry, but this should not automatically lead to the failure of the plaintiff's case. There are a variety of instances where an injury has a number of possible causes and there is a lack of reliable evidence as to which has actually been the cause; typical examples can be found in *McGhee v National Coal Board;*[11] *Hotson v East Berkshire Area Health Authority;*[12] *Kay v Ayrshire & Arran Health Board*[13] and *Wilsher v Essex Area Health Authority*.[14] In *McGhee* the plaintiff complained that his

---

8   [1894] 3 Ch 163.
9   [1953] Ch 149; [1953] 2 WLR 58; [1953] 1 All ER 179; affirming [1952] 1 All ER 1326.
10 [1961] 3 All ER 413.
11 [1973] 1 WLR 1; [1972] 3 All ER 1008.
12 [1987] AC 750; [1987] 3 WLR 232; [1987] 2 All ER 909.
13 [1987] 2 Ali ER 417.
14 [1988] AC 1074; [1988] 2 WLR 557; [1988] 1 All ER 871.

employer's failure to provide adequate washing facilities led to his contracting dermatitis. Although the medical evidence adduced did not conclusively identify the defendant's breach of duty as the cause, the House of Lords did find that there was a significant increase in the danger to the plaintiff as a result of the defendant's conduct. *Hotson* involved a delay in diagnosis of a patient and it was found that the plaintiff would have had a 25 per cent chance of recovery if there had been prompt diagnosis and treatment, though this left a 75 per cent chance that the injury would have occurred in any event. In both *Kay* and *Wilsher* there was negligent treatment of the plaintiffs, but the injuries complained of were ones which might also have resulted from the original conditions for which the plaintiffs were being treated. In *Kay* a boy with meningitis was given an overdose of penicillin and later became deaf; there was a lack of evidence in respect of the effects of the overdose, but deafness is a possible effect of meningitis, even if properly treated. In *Wilsher* excess oxygen was administered to a premature baby, but was only one of six possible causes of the condition which led to the plaintiff's blindness. All of these cases involve causal questions which give no clear answer to the 'but for' inquiry, yet they all involve a real possibility that the defendants' conduct was a material factor in bringing about the injuries to the plaintiffs. Do such plaintiffs have a legitimate claim to some compensation? Would the imposition of liability on the defendants constitute examples of the adage 'hard cases make bad law'?

Uncertainty in respect of causation can also arise in the context of a defendant's failure to warn a plaintiff of a risk. If, for example, a doctor fails to warn a patient of a possible adverse consequence of a proposed course of treatment before obtaining the patient's consent to proceed and the risk materialises, can it be assumed that the failure to warn was the cause of the injury? The difficulty here is in ascertaining the impact the warning would have had on the patient's decision; if the patient would have declined the treatment because of the risk, then the failure to warn may be regarded as a cause of the injury; if, however, the patient would have proceeded, then the failure cannot have been a cause of the injury. The inquiry into this issue is necessarily a hypothetical one and a reliable 'factual' answer to the causal question is unlikely to be found; thus the issue is one to be decided as a matter of legal cause.

A more exotic form of the uncertain cause issue arose in two transatlantic cases, namely *Summers v Tice*[15] and *Cook v Lewis*.[16] The fact situation in both was that a plaintiff was injured by a gunshot fired by one of two defendants, who fired simultaneously. It could not be ascertained which gun the offending shot came from; thus one of the defendants clearly caused the injury and the other clearly did not, but it was impossible to discern which was which. The

15 (1948) 33 Cal 2d 80; 199 P 2d 1.
16 [1951] 1 DLR 1.

inability to establish, as a matter of probability, factual causation should logically lead to acquittal of both, but this would leave the innocent plaintiff to bear the consequences and many people would find this solution unpalatable. The solution to this, and the earlier causal problems, is to be found in the concept of legal causation, to which we now turn.

Legal Cause

The concept of legal cause involves the use of legal principles to attribute responsibility in respect of the factual causes of an injury and it is particularly helpful in resolving the complex types of cases identified earlier. The legal decision as to what is the cause (or causes) involves a value judgment as to where responsibility ought to rest as between the persons involved in the events which led to the injury in question. Thus the legal analysis of causation involves a truncated version of the issue as compared to that of philosophers.[17] Ordinarily factual cause is a prerequisite to establishing legal cause and approaches to factual cause, such as the 'but for' test or the 'material element and a substantial factor', simply help to weed out the irrelevant from the list of possible causes. Winfield & Jolowicz describe this role as a 'preliminary filter'.[18] However, in exceptional cases of uncertain cause, a plaintiff may succeed without clearly establishing that the defendant's conduct was a factual cause. Thus one can establish legal cause without being able to establish factual cause in certain instances.

Simultaneous Causes

The available decisions on simultaneous causes show that conduct which is not tortious in itself may be regarded as a cause of a tort when taken in conjunction with the conduct of others and that legal liability may attach to such a cause. A similar approach developed in the context of industrial relations disputes, with the use of the tort of conspiracy to restrain trade union activity, though statutory provisions have offset the common law developments to a large extent by providing unions and workers with immunity from suit in cases of legitimate trade disputes.[19] In *Lambton* Chitty J stated *obiter* that, even if the conduct of each defendant was independently insufficient to amount to a nuisance, both would be regarded as causes of a nuisance if the combined effect caused

---

17 See Hart & Honoré, *op. cit.* at chapter 3 on the relationship between causation and responsibility; see also chapters 6–10 on the application of general causal concepts to the law of torts.

18 Rogers, *Winfield & Jolowicz on Tort*, 14th ed. (London: Sweet & Maxwell, 1994) at p. 148.

19 Formerly the Trade Disputes Act 1906 governed the immunities from civil action, but this has now been replaced by Part II of the Industrial Relations Act 1990, considered in chapter 13 *infra*.

unreasonable interference to the plaintiff.[20] But such liability was stated to be contingent on the defendant's knowledge of the other acts, which, when combined with his own, created the interference with the plaintiff.[21] In the *Pride of Derby* case it was stressed that if one of the contributing acts was tortious and the others were innocent, the innocent actors would, nevertheless, bear legal responsibility proportionate to the impact of their conduct. It would seem, then, at common law that where the cumulative effect of several independent acts is a single species of injury to an innocent party, each of the acts may be regarded as a legal cause of the injury, even where that act would have been lawful if viewed in isolation. Both *Lambton* and *Pride of Derby* were nuisance cases and this tort has, historically, involved an element of strict liability; thus the imposition of liability in respect of apparently blameless conduct was not unusual.[22] In the case of fault based torts the blameless party would escape liability; not on the basis of a lack of causation, but because of the absence of any breach of duty. These cases also demonstrate the fact that the existence of a second cause of the injury will not necessarily excuse a defendant.

Successive Causes

In the case of successive causes the courts are faced with a choice as to which of the factual causes should be regarded as the legal cause and, consequently, who should bear responsibility for the injury. There are three options open to the courts in such cases. The first is to treat the initial incident as the primary cause; the second is to treat the second incident as breaking the causal link between the first incident and the injury, thereby making the second incident the legal cause; the final option is to treat both incidents as causes and divide the responsibility between them. *Performance Cars* provides a good example of the first option. In that case the first collision clearly caused a need for repainting of the car in order to match the colour of the repair to the damaged area with the rest of the car. Unfortunately for the plaintiff, the motorist who caused the first collision was unable to satisfy the judgment that the plaintiff obtained, leaving the plaintiff to attempt recovery from the motorist responsible for the second collision. The Court of Appeal held that the defendant (the motorist in the second collision) should only be liable for the additional damage which occurred in the second collision and not for the cost of repainting as 'the necessity for re-spraying was not a result of the defendant's wrongdoing because that necessity already existed'.[23] This suggests that where a particular item of damage already exists the defendant is not to be regarded as liable even though his tort would have

---

20 [1894] 3 Ch 163, at p. 165, citing James LJ in *Thorpe v Brumfitt* (1873) 8 Ch App 650.
21 *Ibid.*, at p. 166.
22 S. 12(3) of the Civil Liability Act 1961 incorporates this provision in respect of nuisance.
23 [1961] 3 All ER 413, per Lord Evershed at p. 416.

caused the same damage; thus, the defendant's liability is confined to the extent to which he has made the plaintiff's position worse, based on the actual circumstances at the time of the tort. A related question is whether the first wrongdoer's liability should be confined to damage suffered prior to the second incident or can include continuing effects after that time.

In *Baker v Willoughby*[24] the plaintiff's leg was damaged due to the defendants' negligence, but subsequently the plaintiff was shot in the same leg and had to have it amputated. The defendants contended that the subsequent injury superseded their wrongdoing and ended their responsibility for the consequences of their action. The House of Lords rejected this contention and held that, while the second wrongdoer would be liable for the additional loss caused by the second incident (based on *Performance Cars*), the defendants remained responsible for a portion of the plaintiff's loss after that second incident. Lord Reid explained the decision thus:

> A man is not compensated for the physical injury; he is compensated for the loss which he suffers as a result of that injury. His loss is not in having a stiff leg; it is in his inability to lead a full life, his inability to enjoy those amenities which depend on freedom of movement and his inability to earn as much as he used to or could have earned if there had been no accident. In this case the second injury did not diminish any of these.[25]

The defendants were held liable for damages based on what the plaintiff's loss would have been if he remained permanently lame, the additional loss being attributed exclusively to the second incident.

The subsequent House of Lords decision in *Jobling v Associated Dairies*[26] denied that the decision in *Baker* gave rise to any rule of continuing liability in such cases. In this case the plaintiff was injured at work and subsequently suffered a separate illness, unconnected to his work. The original injury caused partial incapacity to work, while the illness ended the plaintiff's capacity to work. It was held that his employers' liability for his incapacity terminated on the occurrence of the illness; consequently they were liable to the plaintiff for the difference between his initial earning capacity and his diminished earning capacity up to the time of the illness only. The facts are remarkably similar to those presented by *Baker* as both cases involved injuries giving rise to permanent incapacity followed by an exacerbation of the incapacity by a later event; yet in the earlier case the defendant was held liable for the difference in earning capacity which would have existed if the second incident did not occur, but in the later case the liability was confined to the period between the accidents. The rationale offered for the difference in outcome is unconvincing

---

24 [1970] AC 467; [1970] 2 WLR 50; [1969] 3 All ER 1528.
25 *Ibid.*, at p. 492; p. 55; p. 1533.
26 [1982] AC 794; [1981] 3 WLR 155; [1981] 2 All ER 752.

– Lords Russell and Keith based the distinction on the fact that the second incident in *Baker* was a tort, while the second incident in *Jobling* was an illness;[27] Lords Wilberforce and Edmund-Davies suggested that *Baker* was a correct decision on the facts of the case, but did not establish a general principle for all such cases;[28] while Lord Bridge agreed that *Baker* did not establish any general principle, but left open the question as to whether the decision was correct on the facts of the case.[29]

There does not appear to be any definitive Irish authority dealing with this type of case, involving a second injury causing separate damage, which submerges the original injury. The available alternatives are to provide a definite rule (or set of rules) for all such cases or to treat each case as unique. The latter option leaves a large level of discretion to the court, thereby risking inconsistency, while the former gives rise to a risk of injustice in a case where the rule operates unduly harshly against one of the parties. Given the rarity of such cases the risk of inconsistency would appear to be the lesser evil of the two and the better approach may be that of Lord Wilberforce in *Jobling*:

> Without any satisfaction I draw from this the conclusion that no general, logical or universally fair rules can be stated which will cover, in a manner consistent with justice, cases of supervening events whether due to tortious, partially tortious, non-culpable or wholly accidental events. The courts can only deal with each case as best they can in a manner so as to provide just and sufficient but not excessive compensation, taking all factors into account.[30]

A more common problem with successive causes is the case where the damage in question arises after the occurrence of both incidents (or all in the case of more than two possible causes). In such cases the first wrongdoer may argue that the second wrongdoer's conduct severs the causal connection between the first wrong and the plaintiff's injury. The legal term used to describe the severing of the causal connection is *novus actus interveniens*,[31] i.e. the second incident constitutes a new and intervening action, which is regarded as the legal cause of the injury. The leading Irish decision on this issue is that of the Supreme Court in *Conole v Redbank Oyster Co.*,[32] delivered by Henchy J. The defendants were testing a boat, built for them by Fairway Fabrics Ltd. It was discovered

---

27 *Ibid.*, at pp. 810–11; p. 165; p. 760, per Lord Russell; p. 815; p. 169; pp. 763–4, per Lord Keith.
28 *Ibid.*, at p. 804; p. 158; pp. 754–5, per Lord Wilberforce; pp. 806–9; p. 164; p. 759, per Lord Edmund-Davies.
29 *Ibid.*, at p. 821; pp. 174–5; pp. 767–8.
30 *Ibid.*, at p. 804; p. 159; p. 755.
31 Winfield & Jolowicz, *op. cit.* at pp. 169 *et seq.* use the more precise phrase *nova causa interveniens* – new and intervening cause – but this variant of the phrase is not frequently employed.
32 [1976] IR 191.

that the boat was taking on water faster than it could be pumped off and was, consequently, unsafe. Despite instructions to tie up the boat, one of the defendants' employees took the boat out with fifty children on board. The boat capsized and a number of children, including the plaintiff's daughter, were drowned. The issue that the Supreme Court was required to determine was whether the defendants could recover a contribution from Fairway as a concurrent wrongdoer.

It was held that the decision to use the boat subsequent to the discovery of the defect was the legal cause of the incident, breaking any causal connection between the alleged negligence of Fairway and the injury complained of. Henchy J stated that:

> If the defect becomes patent to the person ultimately injured and he chooses to ignore it, or to an intermediate handler who ignores it and subjects the person ultimately injured to that known risk, the person who originally put forth the article is not liable to the person injured. In such circumstances the nexus of cause and effect, in terms of the law of tort, has been sundered as far as the injured person is concerned.[33]

In *Cowan v Freaghaile*[34] O'Flaherty J interpreted 'patent' as meaning actual or, perhaps, constructive knowledge of the defect, but held that where the defect could only have been discovered by seeking professional assistance to examine the item which caused the injury (a wall), the defect was not 'patent' even though the defendants ought to have had such an examination conducted. Constructive knowledge would seem to be confined to what could have been discovered by personal examination, without expert assistance. It would seem

---

33 *Ibid.*, at p. 196; this statement was cited by Finlay CJ in delivering the Supreme Court decision in *Crowley v AIB* [1987] IR 282, at p. 287 again involving a contribution claim between the defendants and a third party. Here the third party, a firm of architects, successfully appealed a High Court decision requiring them to contribute to the damages payable by the defendant bank to the plaintiff, who was injured when he fell from a flat roof belonging to the defendants and designed by the third party. The Supreme Court held that although the third party was negligent in not providing for a protective rail or wall around a roof which was easily accessible, the defendants' failure to prevent youths, including the plaintiff, from playing on the roof broke the causal connection to the injury. The decision was relied on in *Quinn v Kennedy Brothers Ltd*, unrep. HC, 4 March 1994 where the plaintiff was injured in a collision when cycling around the defendants' parked van. The plaintiff and his friend cycled abreast around the van, while a third cyclist was approaching from the opposite direction with undue haste. It was held by Barron J (at p. 5 of the judgment) that the conduct of the three cyclists broke the causal connection between the bad parking and the injury. See also *Felloni v Dublin Corporation* [1998] 1 ILRM 133, at pp. 135–6, per Morris J, *obiter*; *Wright v Lodge* [1993] 4 All ER 299, noted by Jones (1994) 2 Tort L Rev 133.

34 Unrep. HC, 24 January 1991.

that the reasoning in *Conole* applies to dangers generally and is not confined specifically to defective items.[35]

The essence of the *Conole* decision is that there must be voluntary conduct disregarding a clear risk. If the intervening conduct is involuntary, such as a reflex reaction to the original act, then the original act will continue to be the operative cause of the injury. An early example of this is *Scott v Shepherd*,[36] where the defendant threw a lighted firework into a busy marketplace; two others threw it further afield when it landed near them and it exploded and injured the plaintiff following the second intervening throw. The defendant was held liable as the intervening conduct did not break the causal connection between his act and the injury. Gould J described the intervening conduct as 'the inevitable consequence of the defendant's unlawful act'.[37] De Grey CJ similarly held the conduct to be involuntary:

> It has been urged that the intervention of a free agent will make a difference; but I do not consider [the intervening parties] as free agents in the present case, but acting under a compulsive necessity for their own safety and self preservation.[38]

The case law also indicates that the conduct may be that of the plaintiff, a third party or a natural phenomenon.[39] In the event of a refusal to find a *novus actus interveniens* the court may apportion liability between the parties in the case of the first two, but this is not possible in the third case. Where the plaintiff's own conduct is at issue, a finding of contributory negligence will be possible; where the conduct is that of a third party, the original wrongdoer and the third party may be treated as concurrent wrongdoers.

The principal difficulty with this area of law is that, although voluntary conduct in disregard of the risk is a necessary ingredient, it is not always sufficient, as there are cases where even intentional wrongdoing by a third party is insufficient to break the casual link between the defendant's conduct and the plaintiff's injury. Cases such as *Home Office v Dorset Yacht Co.*,[40] involving a duty to control the third party, provide the clearest examples of this.[41] An easy

---

35 See *Crowley v AIB* [1987] IR 282, where the roof was not defective, but was dangerous due to the lack of any protective guard to prevent people falling over the edge; see also *Duffy v Rooney and Dunnes Stores (Dundalk) Ltd* unrep. HC, 23 June 1997; Irish Times Law Report, 8 September 1997; unrep. SC, 23 April 1998.
36 [1558–1774] All ER Rep 295; 2 Wm Bl 892; 3 Wils 403; 96 ER 525.
37 *Ibid.*, at p. 299.
38 *Ibid.*, at p. 300.
39 *Carslogie Steamship Co. Ltd v Royal Norwegian Government* [1952] AC 292; [1952] 1 All ER 20 is a rare example of extreme weather conditions being successfully invoked as a *novus actus interveniens*.
40 [1970] AC 1004; [1970] 2 WLR 1140; [1970] 2 All ER 294.
41 See chapter 14 *infra*, on responsibility for the conduct of others; see also *Stansbie v Troman* [1948] 2 KB 48; [1948] 1 All ER 599, where a decorator was held liable

method to separate these cases would be to say that the intervening act must be unforeseen in order to be a *novus actus interveniens* and that foreseeable acts do not break the causal link. This approach has, however, been rejected in England on the basis that there are some instances when the intervening act is foreseeable, but nevertheless should relieve the defendant of responsibility, because the intervening conduct was reckless or irresponsible.[42] McMahon & Binchy argue against the use of foreseeability in Ireland, based on the reasoning in the English cases.[43] Nonetheless, foreseeability is a useful indicator of the likely outcome. If the intervening conduct could not have been anticipated at the time of the original act then it is probable that it will be treated as a *novus actus interveniens*; if such conduct could have been anticipated there is a strong possibility that it will not be so treated. One should examine fact situations carefully in order to identify special considerations affecting the allocation of responsibility.

Uncertain Causes

Under traditional principles of proof, the courts must be satisfied that the defendant's conduct was a probable cause of the plaintiff's injury, i.e. the evidence must show that there is a better than 50 per cent chance that the impugned conduct was a relevant factor in bringing about the injury. Uncertainty in the sense that there is a possibility, even a significant possibility, that the conduct was not a relevant factor is disregarded. Similarly, the reverse proposition holds true where the plaintiff fails to attain the 50 per cent threshold. Where the evidential threshold is attained, factual cause is deemed to be established. There are, however, cases where legal certainty (i.e. probability) either cannot be established or gives rise to unsatisfactory outcomes. In such cases the inability to establish factual cause is not always fatal to a plaintiff's claim.

In *McGhee*, the facts of which were briefly outlined earlier, the evidence was only sufficient to establish that the defendant's breach of duty increased the risk of injury in a situation where there was a significant, though unquantifiable, chance that the injury would occur in any event. Strict applica-

---

for loss occasioned by theft after the defendant had left the plaintiff's house unlocked (though the case was decided on the basis of a contractual duty, the reasoning seems equally applicable to tort cases); *Emeh v Kensington, Chelsea and Westminster Area Health Authority* [1984] 3 All ER 1044; [1985] QB 1012, where the Court of Appeal held that a woman's refusal to have an abortion did not constitute a *novus actus interveniens* in an action for the cost of raising a child born after a failed sterilisation operation.

42 The leading decisions are those of the House of Lords in *McKew v Holland, Hannen & Cubbits (Scotland) Ltd* [1969] 3 All ER 1621 and *Home Office v Dorset Yacht Co.* [1970] AC 1004; [1970] 2 WLR 1140; [1970] 2 All ER 294.

43 See McMahon & Binchy, *The Irish Law of Torts*, 1st ed. (Abingdon: Professional Books, 1981) at pp. 40–2. The supporting argument is omitted from the 2nd edition, but the conclusion is maintained at p. 46.

tion of legal principle would dictate that the plaintiff should fail, as he established only a possibility, rather than a probability, that the defendant had caused the injury, but the House of Lords unanimously held for the plaintiff and refused to draw a distinction between conduct materially increasing risk and conduct materially contributing to the injury.[44] There are two possible interpretations of this decision. The first is that, as a matter of law, material increase in risk should legally be treated as a cause, where proof of factual cause is impossible; the second is that there was merely an inference that a factual link was more likely than not, using the ordinary standard of proof. The first interpretation would entail a special rule of law establishing legal cause without factual cause as a prerequisite; the latter would indicate nothing more than a generous interpretation of the evidence supporting the plaintiff's case.

The *McGhee* approach could not be used in *Hotson*, as the finding that there was a 75 per cent chance of injury occurring without any breach of duty by the defendants inevitably led to the conclusion that the breach probably was not the cause of the injury.[45] Unlike *McGhee*, the relative probability of the possible causes was ascertained by the evidence presented. The approach taken by the trial judge[46] and the Court of Appeal[47] merits consideration, however. In these courts the plaintiff was held entitled to recover 25 per cent of his loss, due to the fact that the defendants' breach of duty deprived him of a 25 per cent chance of recovery. Two of the three members of the House of Lords indicated that this approach should not be entirely disregarded, but felt it was not appropriate where a probable cause had been established.[48] This lost chance approach would also entail a special legal rule for legal cause in the absence of proof of factual cause. In fact, the approach taken by the trial judge and the Court of Appeal went further by establishing legal cause where factual cause was disproved (as opposed to uncertain) on the traditional rule of proof.

---

44 [1972] 3 All ER 1008, per Lord Reid at p. 1011; Lord Wilberforce at p. 1012; Lord Kilbrandon at p. 1015; Lord Salmon at p. 1017; Lord Simon at p. 1014. It is quite possible to envisage situations where conduct increases the risk that an injury will occur, but the injury is in fact caused by some other source; however in cases such as *McGhee*, where it is impossible to prove which of the possible causes led to the injury, it seems fair to equate risk with cause.
45 [1987] AC 750; [1987] 3 WLR 232; [1987] 2 All ER 909, per Lord Bridge at p. 782; p. 237; p. 913; Lord Mackay at pp. 789–90; p. 244; p. 919; Lord Ackner at p. 792; pp. 246–7; p. 921.
46 [1985] 1 WLR 1036; [1985] 3 All ER 167.
47 [1987] AC 750; [1987] 2 WLR 287; [1987] 1 All ER 210.
48 [1987] AC 750; [1987] 3 WLR 232; [1987] 2 All ER 909; Lord Mackay at p. 786; p. 240; p. 916; Lord Ackner at pp. 792–4; pp. 247–8; pp. 921–2; Lord Bridge at p. 783; p. 238; p. 914, however, prefers an all or nothing approach – if the defendants' conduct is a material cause then the entire loss is recoverable, if it is not then no damages can be recovered; see Reece, 'Losses of Chances in the Law' (1996) 59 MLR 188, who offers an interesting solution to the recovery of lost chances; see also Lunney, 'What Price a Chance?' (1995) 15 LS 1.

The decision in *Kay* failed to generate any significant progress in the legal debate on causation, as the inability to establish any increased risk due to the breach of duty brought the case outside the scope of the solutions postulated by the earlier cases. The decision in *Wilsher*, however, denied that *McGhee* had established any new principle of general application and indicated that it involved merely a liberal interpretation of the evidence in the plaintiff's favour, using the traditional rule for proof of causation:

> The conclusion which I draw . . . is that *McGhee v National Coal Board* laid down no new principle of law whatever. On the contrary, it affirmed the principle that the onus of proving causation lies on the pursuer or plaintiff. Adopting a robust and pragmatic approach to the undisputed primary facts of the case, the majority concluded that it was a legitimate inference of fact that the defenders' negligence had materially contributed to the pursuer's injury. The decision, in my opinion, is of no greater significance than that and the attempt to extract from it some esoteric principle which in some way modifies, as a matter of law, the nature of the burden of proof of causation which a plaintiff or pursuer must discharge once he has established a relevant breach of duty is a fruitless one.[49]

The House of Lords went further and indicated that any special rules modifying established causal requirements could not be introduced by the courts, but would have to be introduced by the legislature.[50] This decision indicates that in England there are no special principles circumventing the need for factual cause, despite earlier signs that such principles might be evolving in cases of uncertainty. This decision was cited with approval by O'Flaherty J in the Supreme Court in *Best v Wellcome Foundation Ltd.*[51] Having cited extensively from *McGhee* and *Wilsher* on the issue of the burden of proof in causation, he concluded:

> It seems to me that for the purposes of considering the issue in debate before us on this aspect of the matter the two cases are compatible. *McGhee* was concerned with negligence materially (though not, perhaps, exclusively or necessarily) contributing to the plaintiff's dermatitis; the case would, I venture to think, find a frequent resonance in our courts. *Wilsher*, on the other hand, simply reiterates that the burden of proving causation remains with the plaintiff when there are different *possibilities* as to what caused the injury.[52]

The conclusion to be drawn from these decisions is that the courts are reluctant to treat causes as uncertain and prefer to take a definite decision one

---

49 [1988] AC 1074; [1988] 2 WLR 557; [1988] 1 All ER 871, per Lord Bridge at p. 1090; p. 569; pp. 881–2 (the other four members of the court agreed with Lord Bridge's judgment at p. 1092; p. 571; p. 883).
50 *Ibid.*, at p. 1092; p. 571; p. 883.
51 [1993] 3 IR 421; [1992] ILRM 609.
52 *Ibid.*, at pp. 488–9; pp. 647–8.

way or the other as to whether a sufficient probability has been established, without displaying any great concern for mathematical precision. The inability to definitively establish factual causation is not fatal to this type of case; legal certainty, in the sense described earlier, is sufficient to determine such cases; the 'but for' rule is, consequently, side-stepped and the 'material element' approach preferred. The courts in Ireland and England appear unconvinced of the need for special causal rules in these cases.

Failure to warn cases raise a separate issue from the foregoing types of uncertainty because the court is concerned with the hypothetical impact that a non-existent event (the warning) would have had, rather than the examination of actual events and their probable effects. As a definite factual answer is impossible, the law must supply an answer based on some other ground. The available choice is between an objective and a subjective examination of the likely effect of a warning, or, thirdly, to disregard the hypothetical inquiry altogether and assume causation as a matter of law. The objective approach entails consideration of what a reasonable person in the plaintiff's position would do, if given the necessary warning, while the subjective approach entails consideration of what the particular plaintiff would probably have done. The Canadian Supreme Court adopted the objective 'prudent patient' test in *Reibl v Hughes*,[53] while the position in England is uncertain. Bristow J in *Chatterton v Gerson*[54] took account of the particular circumstances of the plaintiff, 'a lady desperate for pain relief', in a *dictum* indicating the absence of the necessary causal connection between the absence of a warning and the plaintiff's injury. Hirst J in *Hills v Potter*[55] was uncertain as to whether the test should be objective or subjective, but felt that in either case the plaintiff would fail. Egan J in *Walsh v Family Planning Services*[56] stated that he did not 'consider it necessary that there should be proof by the plaintiff that had a proper warning been given to him, he would not have submitted to the original operation'. This could be construed as supporting the third approach.

Each approach has its merits and flaws, which should be carefully considered before deciding which should be used. The subjective approach is concerned with what this actual plaintiff was likely to do and would be the best indicator of what would have happened, but proving a hypothetical scenario subjectively is likely to present great evidential difficulties for both parties, with the defendant being particularly prejudiced. The objective approach is the reverse, easing the difficulties of proof, while reducing the likelihood of an accurate answer to the hypothetical inquiry. The third approach takes an entirely different view of the situation, by not asking the hypothetical question. It imposes a presumption that

---

53 (1980) 114 DLR (3d) 1; see also *Arndt v Smith* (1997) 148 DLR (4th) 48, noted by Honoré (1998) 114 LQR 52.
54 [1981] 1 All ER 257, at p. 267.
55 [1983] 3 All ER 716, at p. 728.
56 [1992] 1 IR 486, at p. 537.

the failure to warn was a cause, thereby avoiding the difficulties of proof altogether, but this could be considered unjust to defendants in cases where reliable proof is available. There is one further point worth noting in respect of the medical cases involving failure to warn – they differ from other cases in that the factual cause is known, since the medical procedure has had an adverse outcome. The warning determines whether the procedure is lawful or tortious – once the warning is absent, the procedure constitutes a tort and that tort has caused damage. The fact that the same conduct could have been lawfully carried out by giving the warning, and the injury could have lawfully been inflicted, should be irrelevant in a causal inquiry. The separation of the warning from the procedure as distinct items of conduct, with separate causal roles, could be regarded as fallacious.

The third type of uncertainty identified previously differs from the other types of uncertainty, as it involves a perfectly balanced 50 per cent likelihood in respect of both possible causes. The solution offered in *Summers v Tice* and *Cook v Lewis* was to reverse the burden of proof and require the defendants to disprove the causal link.[57] In effect this means that both defendants must be held liable, as they will be subject to the same inability to establish what happened as the plaintiff. This clearly involves the imposition of liability on one party who definitely did not cause the damage, but the alternatives are even less palatable – either deny the plaintiff any compensation, which means the innocent victim bears the loss, or make one of the defendants fully liable, giving rise to a 50 per cent chance of the right defendant being selected, but an equal possibility that the wrong choice may be made. On the whole, the chosen solution minimises the level of injustice in a situation where a fully 'correct' decision is unattainable. It has been suggested that this line of reasoning is only applicable where the number of possible causes is small,[58] but if the object of the exercise is to minimise the injustice then, although large numbers will mean a greater number of innocent persons contributing to the cost of the accident, surely this is better than imposing the entire burden on the plaintiff by denying recovery.

Section 11(3) of the Civil Liability Act 1961 provides:

> Where two or more persons are at fault and one or more of them is or are responsible for damage while the other or others is or are free from causal responsibility, but it is not possible to establish which is the case, such two or more persons shall be deemed to be concurrent wrongdoers in respect of the damage.

---

57 See Christie & Meeks, *The Law of Torts*, 2nd ed. (St Paul, Minn.: West, 1990) at pp. 235–42 for a discussion of *Summers v Tice* and an extract from the judgment; see Fridman, *The Law of Torts in Canada* (Toronto: Carswell, 1989), vol. 1 at pp. 342–3 for a discussion of *Cook v Lewis*; see also Prosser & Keeton, *op. cit.* at pp. 270–2 and *Restatement, Second, Torts* §433B (3).

58 Christie & Meeks, *op. cit.*; Fridman, *op. cit.* vol. 1.

This means that in cases where it is impossible to separate the causal conduct from amongst a number of wrongdoers, all the wrongdoers are to be legally regarded as responsible for the injury suffered. Although the likelihood of such instances arising in practice may appear remote, there are a number of situations which could trigger the application of this provision; one such situation would be a defective product, such as a component part or a pharmaceutical, where there are a number of manufacturers of the dangerous item, but no way of determining which of them manufactured the particular item which injured the plaintiff; another would be a case of a road accident involving multiple collisions.

The difference between this provision and the problem presented by cases like *McGhee, Wilsher, Hotson* etc. is that section 11(3) is applicable only where the potential causes involve fault and not where there are innocent possibilities. Additionally, it only applies where a decision on probable cause cannot be reached and courts are generally reluctant to admit defeat in the search for a likely explanation for an injury.

Remoteness

The term remoteness is used to describe the legal principles concerned with the cut-off point for the defendant's responsibility for the consequences of tortious conduct. It is possible to include under this term much of the material we have just looked at under the term 'legal cause'; in fact, the material discussed in this section involves a particular sub-set of the legal cause concept. There is no precise dividing line between the use of 'legal cause' and 'remoteness' as a term to describe the phenomena covered and, in truth, either would be a satisfactory description of the entire area.[59] What is essential to keep in mind is that the object of the rules is to determine the extent of the defendant's legal responsibility for the consequences of the impugned conduct after duty, breach of duty and factual cause have been established (or are presumed to exist). In Ireland and England causal arguments tend to be used to determine whether a defendant bears any responsibility; remoteness arguments tend to be used for curtailing the amount of responsibility.

The specific problem that this section is concerned with is the attribution of responsibility for unforeseen consequences of the defendant's conduct. The common law has produced two basic approaches to this problem – 'direct consequences' and 'reasonable foresight'. Under the former, the fact that the damage resulting from tortious conduct was greater than could have been anticipated was irrelevant; once the damage flowed directly from the tort, the defendant was responsible. The latter only imposes liability for anticipated consequences, subject to certain exceptions. The debate between these two

---

59 In American works the term generally used for this area is 'proximate cause'; see Prosser & Keeton, *op. cit.* at chapter 7; Christie & Meeks, *op. cit.* at pp. 252–312; see also Hart & Honoré, *op. cit.* at preface pp. xlvii–lv.

approaches appears to have been initiated in the latter part of the nineteenth century. A *dictum* of Pollock CB in 1850 suggested that liability should only attach in respect of anticipated consequences,[60] while the Court of Exchequer Chamber suggested in 1870 that, once wrongdoing was established, it was irrelevant that the level of damage was greater than could be expected.[61]

The landmark decision of the Court of Appeal in *Re Polemis and Furness, Withy & Co. Ltd*[62] resolved this dispute in favour of the direct consequences approach. The case came to the court by way of a case stated by arbitrators to a dispute, who had found the facts to be as follows. Due to the negligence of the employees of the charterers of a ship, a plank was dropped into the hold during unloading. The impact of the plank caused a spark, which ignited petrol vapour, in turn causing an explosion which destroyed the ship.

The owners were held to be entitled to recover for the loss of the ship, even though such loss was unforeseeable, as was the manner in which it occurred. Bankes LJ stated that, once the defendants were responsible for negligence which led directly to the loss, 'it is immaterial that the causing of the spark by the falling of the plank could not have reasonably been anticipated'.[63] He went on to add that: 'given the breach of duty which constitutes negligence, and given the damage as a direct result of that negligence, the anticipations of the person whose negligent act has produced the damage appear to me to be irrelevant'.[64] The formulation used by Scrutton LJ is also worth noting:

> To determine whether an act is negligent, it is relevant to determine whether a reasonable person would foresee that the act would cause damage; if he would not, the act is not negligent. But if the act would or might probably cause damage, the fact that the damage it in fact causes is not the exact kind of damage one would expect is immaterial, so long as the damage is in fact directly traceable to the negligent act, and not due to the operation of independent causes having no connection with the negligent act, except that they could not avoid its results. Once the act is negligent, the fact that its exact operation was not foreseen is immaterial.[65]

Under this rule a defendant would be liable for all the consequences of his wrongdoing up to the occurrence of a *novus actus interveniens*. In the absence

---

60 *Rigby v Hewitt* (1850) 5 Ex 240, at p. 243 and repeated in *Greenland v Chaplin* (1850) 5 Ex 243, at p. 248; cited with approval by Vaughan Williams LJ in *Cory & Son Ltd v France, Fenwick & Co. Ltd* [1911] 1 KB 114, at p. 122.
61 *Smith v London and South Western Railway Co.* (1870) LR 6 CP 14; [1861–73] All ER Rep 167, particularly the judgment of Blackburn J. This approach was also applied in *Weld-Blundell v Stephens* [1920] AC 956; [1920] All ER Rep 32; see the judgment of Lord Sumner in particular.
62 [1921] 3 KB 560; [1921] All ER Rep 40.
63 *Ibid.*, at p. 571; p. 44.
64 *Ibid.*, at p. 572; p. 45.
65 *Ibid.*, at p. 577; p. 47.

of any intervening cause, the establishment of factual cause would be sufficient to impose liability.

The rule in *Re Polemis* survived in English law for four decades before
being rejected by the Privy Council in *Overseas Tankship (UK) Ltd v Morts
Dock & Engineering Co. (The Wagon Mound),*[66] which introduced reasonable
foreseeability as the criterion for determining whether liability should attach to
the consequences of the defendant's negligence. The principal reasoning
behind the decision was that as the obligation imposed in negligence is to
avoid foreseeable risks, liability should only attach in respect of such risks;
any injury of a different nature falls outside the parameters of the obligation.
Thus both the existence and the extent of the obligation are determined by the
same criterion – reasonable foreseeability. In the words of Viscount Simonds,
'It is vain to isolate liability from its context.'[67] Viscount Simonds also
provided a concise statement of the essence of the decision:

> Their Lordships . . . have been concerned primarily to displace the
> proposition that unforeseeability is irrelevant if damage is 'direct'. In doing
> so, they have inevitably insisted that the essential factor in determining
> liability is whether the damage is of such a kind as the reasonable man
> should have foreseen.[68]

The Irish Supreme Court had adopted a similar proposition a year earlier in
O'Mahony v Ford,[69] refusing to allow the plaintiff's claim for an injury of a
type which could not reasonably have been foreseen (cancer), where injury of
a different type (bruising) was reasonably foreseeable but did not occur. The
court did not deal with the situation where both a foreseeable and an unforeseeable injury occur, but it is submitted that the unforeseen injury should not
be compensated, under this rule, if it is of a different kind from that which
could have been anticipated.[70] The *Wagon Mound* decision has subsequently
been approved in a number of Irish decisions,[71] and should be regarded as
providing the proper approach to remoteness in negligence cases.

Kind of Damage

The use of reasonable foreseeability in respect of liability for negligence does
not mean that the plaintiff must be able to anticipate the exact manner in which

---

66 [1961] AC 388; [1961] 2 WLR 126; [1961] 1 All ER 404.
67 *Ibid.,* at p. 425; p. 141; p. 415.
68 *Ibid.,* at p. 426; p. 142; p. 415.
69 [1962] IR 146.
70 Unforeseen injuries may, however, be recoverable under the thin skull rule
   discussed later in this chapter.
71 Including *Irish Shipping v Dublin Port & Docks Board* 101 ILTR 182 (SC, 1965);
   Burke v John Paul & Co. Ltd [1967] IR 277.

an injury arises or its precise extent. What is required is that the injury suffered be of a general type which comes within the range of anticipated risks. We have already seen a rudimentary division of injuries into different categories when examining the duty of care in negligence.[72] We saw that physical, psychological and economic damage received different treatment by the courts. The division of injuries into types in relation to a remoteness inquiry is far more precise than this and carries its own particular difficulties.

In *Wagon Mound* the defendants had negligently spilled oil into a harbour during the loading of their vessel. The oil spread to the plaintiffs' wharf nearby, where they were carrying out repairs to a ship. The parties believed that the oil could not catch fire while floating on the water, but, contrary to their expectation, the oil was ignited as a result of the dropping of molten material from the plaintiffs' welding work (which apparently ignited floating debris, which in turn ignited the oil). The plaintiffs' wharf was extensively damaged by the ensuing fire and they sought to recover their loss from the defendants. It was found that, although damage by fouling was foreseeable, damage by fire was not and as the damage in fact caused was of the latter type the Privy Council held that the defendants were not liable. Thus, although both types of risk involved physical damage to property, this was not a sufficient similarity to regard the injury which occurred as being of the same kind as the risk which could be foreseen.

Kennedy v Hughes Dairy Ltd[73] provides an example of the difficulties facing courts and litigants in classifying damage. The plaintiff was employed by the defendants and his job included carrying crates of bottles and tidying up broken bottles. This posed a risk to the plaintiff that his hands or forearms might get cut. The provision of a gauntlet would have protected the plaintiff, but one was not provided. The plaintiff's forearm was injured by broken glass when he slipped and dropped the crate of bottles he was carrying.

The three judges in the Supreme Court classified the injury differently. Hederman J felt there was sufficient evidence for a jury to regard the injury as a cut to the arm, which was within the class of injury that was foreseeable and which a gauntlet would have protected against.[74] McCarthy J felt there was sufficient evidence on which a jury could regard injury by falling as reasonably foreseeable, declining to express any opinion on situations where the injury differed from that which the defendant was required to protect against.[75] Finlay CJ, dissenting, drew a distinction between injury by falling and injury by handling, finding the former was the one which occurred and was not reasonably foreseeable. He noted that the injury by falling could have affected any part of the plaintiff's body and that it was merely coincidence that the part affected

---

72 See chapter 1 *supra*.
73 [1989] ILRM 117; see also *Dunleavy v McDevitt* unrep. SC, 19 February 1992.
74 *Ibid.*, at p. 122.
75 *Ibid.*, at pp. 123–4.

would have been protected if precautions had been taken against a different type of injury.[76] This was exactly the point on which McCarthy J reserved his opinion, on the basis that such a situation did not exist in this case.

The judgments of Hederman J and Finlay CJ reflect fundamentally different views on whether the manner in which an injury occurs is relevant to the classification of the type of injury. The Chief Justice's analysis appears more consistent with the established principle, while Hederman J's view evidences a desire to bend the principle to accommodate a deserving plaintiff. Classification in cases like this is probably best regarded as unique to the specific case and it would be difficult, if not misleading, to try to draw any definitive rules for defining 'type' or 'kind' of damage. McMahon & Binchy observe that the courts 'have preferred to adopt a pragmatic, intuitive resolution of the problem, without any philosophical pretensions'.[77]

Once the court is satisfied that the injury suffered is of the same type as that to which the duty of care applied, the fact that the injury suffered is more extensive than could have been expected is irrelevant. The decision of Carroll J in *Egan v Sisk*[78] provides a useful example of the application of this principle. The defendants negligently flooded a warehouse in which the plaintiffs were storing catalogues for their mail order business. Due to the inability to get the magazines reprinted in time for the Christmas trade the plaintiffs failed to make the anticipated profit from sales.

Carroll J held that the defendants' inability to anticipate what was in the warehouse or the fact that the catalogues could not be replaced in time did not provide sufficient grounds to exclude liability for loss of anticipated profits. Once the defendants could anticipate that goods might be damaged, then their responsibility extended to the full economic worth of the goods, including the profit that would have been generated by them. The fact that the magnitude of the loss was unforeseeable was irrelevant once the type of loss (the economic value of the goods) was foreseeable.[79]

It is worth noting that the distinction between foreseeability of the 'type' rather than the 'extent' of damage was expressly rejected in *Re*

---

76 *Ibid.*, at p. 119.
77 2nd ed., *op. cit.* at p. 66. For further consideration of 'type' of damage and associated difficulties see the Supreme Court decision in *Dunleavy v McDevitt* unrep. SC, 19 February 1992, and critical comment on the decision in Byrne & Binchy, *Annual Review of Irish Law 1992* at pp. 556–7; see also *Doughty v Turner Manufacturing Co. Ltd* [1964] 1 QB 518; [1964] 2 WLR 240; [1964] 1 All ER 98. In this case an asbestos cover fell into a cauldron of molten material and erupted shortly afterwards, injuring the plaintiff. The defendant, his employer, was not liable, because injury by eruption was not reasonably foreseeable; injury by splashing was the only reasonably foreseeable injury in the circumstances.
78 [1986] ILRM 283.
79 *Ibid.*, at pp. 284–5; the plaintiff was awarded nearly £200,000, including approximately £140,000 for loss of profit, based on projected sales.

Polemis.[80] If applied to the facts of that case, the likely result is that the decision would be reversed, as a court would be unlikely to hold an explosion to be a reasonably foreseeable consequence of dropping a plank into a cargo hold.

The Thin Skull Rule

Prior to *Wagon Mound* there was a well established principle in English tort law that the defendant would be responsible for unforeseen consequences resulting from the combination of the tort and pre-existing weakness in the plaintiff. Thus, 'it is no answer to the sufferer's claim for damages that he would have suffered less injury or no injury at all if he had not had an unusually thin skull or an unusually weak heart'.[81] In *Smith v Leech, Brain & Co. Ltd*[82] it was held that the rule survived after the *Wagon Mound* decision. A workman suffered a burn to his lip from a piece of molten metal or flux, due to the negligence of the defendants, while he was working for them. His lip was in a pre-malignant condition due to previous work for a different employer. The combination of the burn and the pre-existing condition led to the workman developing cancer, ultimately leading to his death.

Lord Parker CJ, in the Queen's Bench Division, upheld the widow's claim against the defendants in respect of the death, holding that the 'thin skull' or 'egg shell skull' rule was not affected by the decision in *Wagon Mound*. On the question of foreseeability, he said:

> The test is not whether these employers could reasonably have foreseen that a burn would cause cancer and that he would die. The question is whether these employers could reasonably foresee the type of injury he suffered, namely the burn. What, in the particular case, is the amount of damage which he suffers as a result of that burn, depends on the characteristics and constitution of the victim. Accordingly, I find that the damages which the widow claims are damages for which the defendants are liable.[83]

Thus, only the initial injury need be foreseen by the defendant for liability to be imposed. If the plaintiff's suffering is unforeseeably increased by some pre-existing condition or weakness, then the defendant is also liable for the additional injury.

This decision was cited with approval in Ireland by the Supreme Court in *Burke v John Paul & Co. Ltd*,[84] Budd J stating that he would 'entirely adopt

---

80 [1921] 3 KB 560, at pp. 571–2; [1921] All ER Rep 40, at pp. 44–5, per Bankes LJ. The point appears to have been raised by junior counsel for the defendants.
81 *Dulieu v White & Sons* [1901] 2 KB 669; [1900–3] All ER Rep 353, at p. 679; p. 359 per Kennedy J.
82 [1962] 2 QB 405; [1962] 2 WLR 148; [1961] 3 All ER 1159.
83 *Ibid.*, at p. 415; p. 156; p. 1162.
84 [1967] IR 277.

the reasoning of Lord Parker'.[85] In this case the plaintiff alleged that he had been supplied with blunt cutting equipment by his employer and that, as a result of the additional effort required in using it, he suffered a hernia. The employers contended that the hernia resulted from a congenital weakness and so, could not have been anticipated by them. The High Court judge withdrew the case from the jury, accepting the employers' argument as to foreseeability, but the Supreme Court ordered a retrial. Budd J, delivering the only judgment, held that if the plaintiff's allegation could be established, then a straining or tearing of muscle was foreseeable, and the more extreme form of injury actually suffered due to the plaintiff's predisposition would be within the ambit of the defendants' responsibility.

There are two possible interpretations of these cases. One is that the injuries were of a foreseeable type, with the extent of injury being greater than could have been foreseen. This is clearly a reasonable interpretation of *Burke*, but in relation to *Smith* it requires a liberal interpretation of 'type' of damage. This interpretation would add nothing to the earlier discussion of the reasonable foreseeability principle, except to provide further examples of its operation. The second interpretation, however, is that where a reasonably foreseeable injury combines with an existing weakness in the plaintiff to cause a separate and unforeseeable kind of injury the defendant is liable for that latter injury. The facts of *Smith* would seem to involve an injury of a different kind from that which was foreseeable (cancer suffered, where a burn was foreseeable). The second approach differs from *Re Polemis*, as it would require the foreseeable damage to occur and trigger the additional damage before the defendant could be made liable for the unforeseeable consequences.

The broader interpretation gains considerable support from *dicta* in the later Supreme Court decision in *Reeves v Carthy & O'Kelly*.[86] Like *Burke*, the injury actually suffered by the plaintiff due to his pre-existing condition was held to be of the same type as that which could have reasonably been foreseen; however, the members of the court indicated that, had the injury not been of a foreseeable type, but a consequence of the interaction of a foreseeable injury and an inherent weakness in the plaintiff, then recovery would have been permitted on the basis of the thin skull rule discussed in *Burke* and *Smith*.[87] This approach has been applied by the High Court in *McCarthy v Murphy*.[88] The plaintiff suffered a minor physical injury in a traffic accident, which triggered depression and an irrational fear of pain, due to her frail personality.

---

85 *Ibid.*, at p. 285, having quoted extensively from Lord Parker's judgment in *Smith v Leech*.
86 [1984] IR 348.
87 *Ibid.*, at pp. 360–1, per O'Higgins CJ (Hederman J concurring at p. 367) and Griffin J at pp. 366–7.
88 Unrep. HC, 10 February 1998; Irish Times Law Report, 6 April 1998.

McCracken J allowed recovery for both the physical and the psychological damage. The psychological injury was unforeseeable and, if it had occurred without any physical injury, recovery for negligent infliction of psychological harm would not have been possible; however, since the psychological injury resulted from the combination of a foreseeable injury (the minor physical harm) and the plaintiff's predisposition to psychological injury, it was recoverable under the thin skull rule.

The Impecunious Plaintiff

The thin skull rule has not traditionally applied to losses resulting from the combination of the defendant's tort and the plaintiff's financial frailty. The seminal decision on this issue is that of the House of Lords in *Owners of Dredger Liesbosch v Owners of Steamship Edison*.[89] The respondents' steamship, *Edison*, caused the sinking of the appellants' dredger, *Liesbosch*, which was being used in work the appellants were carrying out for a third party. The appellants' financial position was such that they were unable to buy a replacement dredger. Almost six months after the sinking of the *Liesbosch*, they managed to hire a replacement at a high rate of hire. They ultimately purchased this vessel for a price considerably higher than that which a dredger similar to the *Liesbosch* would have cost at the time of the accident. The respondents admitted liability for the loss of the dredger, but disputed the amount of compensation due.

Lord Wright held that additional losses (i.e. the difference between market replacement cost and the amount actually paid in hiring and purchasing), due to the plaintiffs' lack of funds at the time of the sinking of the dredger, could not be recovered from the defendants.[90] He described the plaintiffs' impecuniosity as 'a separate and concurrent cause, extraneous and distinct in character from the tort',[91] even though 'its operative effect was conditioned by the loss of the dredger'.[92]

Conversely, a number of Irish decisions have held that costs reasonably incurred can be recovered, including interest on money borrowed.[93] McWilliam J in *Riordan's Travel Ltd v Acres & Co. Ltd*[94] found that in modern conditions it was reasonably foreseeable that a person would have to either expend interest bearing funds (thereby forgoing the interest) or borrow, in order to offset the

---

89 [1933] AC 449; [1933] All ER Rep 144.
90 *Ibid.*, at p. 460; p. 158; see also p. 468; p. 162 for the criteria for the assessment of the plaintiffs' loss. The other four Lords concurred at p. 456; p. 163.
91 *Ibid.*, at p. 460; p. 158.
92 *Ibid.*
93 Lord Wright expressly rejected a ruling from earlier hearings of the case that 'all their circumstances, in particular their want of means, must be taken into account and hence the damages must be based on their actual loss, provided only that . . . they acted reasonably in the unfortunate predicament in which they were placed . . .' *Ibid.*
94 [1979] ILRM 3.

effects of the destruction of their business premises and that the additional loss (the interest paid on the loan or loss of interest on savings or investments) should be recoverable.[95] The position in Ireland has been thrown into an uncertain state, however, by the decision of O'Hanlon J in *Rabbette v Mayo County Council*.[96] In relation to the decisions allowing recovery in cases of impecuniosity, he says that '[s]ome inroads have since been made on the full force and effect of [*Edison*] . . . but the principle underlying the decision is still accepted as valid'[97] and he later states that the decision has 'continuing relevance'.[98] The decision fails to give any clear indication as to the extent of *Edison*'s relevance and offers no statement of principle as to how claims for losses resulting from the combination of a tort and the plaintiff's financial position should be resolved. Geoghegan J, in *Doran v Delaney (No. 2)*[99] suggests that additional losses are recoverable if the plaintiff's impecuniosity is itself foreseeable.

Remoteness in Torts other than Negligence

The reasonable foreseeability test governs negligence cases and most remoteness disputes seem to arise in negligence cases, but there are occasional decisions in respect of other torts. In *Overseas Tankship (UK) Ltd v Miller Steamship Co. Pty Ltd (The Wagon Mound No. 2)*[100] the Privy Council indicated that the reasonable foreseeability test should apply to public nuisance actions also. The reasoning was that, although some nuisance actions involved strict liability and others required foreseeability to establish a cause of action, it was preferable to have a single rule for remoteness in all such actions than to use two different tests and, given the extensive overlap and similarities between nuisance and negligence, the

---

95 *Ibid.*, at p. 10; see also *Quinn v Quality Homes Ltd* [1976–7] ILRM 314, at pp. 324–5 per Finlay P; *Murphy v McGrath* [1981] ILRM 364, at p. 365 per O'Higgins CJ. It should be noted that a plaintiff is required to take reasonable steps to mitigate his loss, i.e. he must take reasonable measures to minimise the adverse effects of the tort. In *Riordan's Travel*, McWilliam J pointed out that reasonable foreseeability was not the essential test in respect of steps taken by a plaintiff in mitigating loss; rather it was a question of reasonableness in light of the circumstances at the time of mitigation, at p. 10; see also Carroll J in *Egan v Sisk* [1986] ILRM 283.
96 [1984] ILRM 156, the facts of which are set out under 'residual issues' below.
97 *Ibid.*, at p. 159, citing the House of Lords decision in *Raineri v Miles* [1980] 3 All ER 145 in support of the validity of the principle; the principle was distinguished in *Archer v Brown* [1985] QB 401; [1984] 3 WLR 350; [1984] 2 All ER 267, where the plaintiff's impecuniosity was caused by the defendant's deceit.
98 *Ibid.*, at p. 160.
99 [1999] 1 ILRM 225 (HC).
100 [1967] AC 617; [1966] 3 WLR 498; [1966] 2 All ER 709, this action was taken by the owners of the ship under repair at the Morts Docks' wharf in respect of damage suffered in the incident which led to the *Wagon Mound* case.

reasonable foreseeability test was to be preferred.[101] This reasoning was accepted in Ireland in *Wall v Morrissey*[102] and *Connolly v South of Ireland Asphalt Co. Ltd.*[103] The same argument may be extended to private nuisance, so that reasonable foreseeability should be regarded as the test for remoteness in such cases also.[104]

Rylands v Fletcher actions pose an interesting problem with respect to the choice of an appropriate remoteness rule. The *Wagon Mound* decision indicated that it did not intend to include such cases within the reasonable foreseeability test, but the relationship between *Rylands v Fletcher* and nuisance is such that the reasoning from *Wagon Mound No. 2* presents support for the contrary position. It would also seem consistent with *Rylands v Fletcher* that the damage suffered should be of the same type as the risk posed by the dangerous item in order to impose liability on the defendant.[105] Reasonable foreseeability, as interpreted by the House of Lords in *Cambridge Water Co. v East Counties Leather plc*,[106] may pose some difficulties in respect of the *Rylands v Fletcher* principle. In this case it was held that the defendant would have to be able to foresee the particular manner in which the hazard would cause harm to the plaintiff. The harm in question, the polluting of the water supply from a bore hole, resulted from the accumulation of chemicals in the soil from many small spillages on the floor of the defendant's factory; the chemicals seeped into the underground water over a lengthy period of time and the water eventually made its way to the bore hole, some 1.3 miles away from the defendant's factory. If one takes a broad view of the type of risk posed by the defendant's accumulation of chemicals, the risk of water being polluted by an escape could be regarded as an anticipated risk. However, the House of Lords took the view that the specific circumstances by which the damage occurred had to be foreseeable, which was not the case here. This decision was endorsed in Ireland in *Superquinn Ltd v Bray Urban District Council and Others.*[107] The point was *obiter*, but strong reliance was placed on the House of Lords decision in *Cambridge Water* and this approach is likely to prevail.

---

101 *Ibid.*, at p. 639; p. 509; p. 717 per Lord Reid.
102 [1969] IR 10, per Walsh J at p. 15, Budd J concurring at p. 16.
103 [1977] IR 99, per Kenny J at pp. 107–8 and p. 110.
104 In *Wagon Mound No. 2* Lord Reid uses the term 'nuisance' without distinguishing between public and private, but the discussion is clearly focused on public nuisance. Both *Wall* and *Connolly* involved public nuisance also. However, the House of Lords in *Cambridge Water Co. v East Counties Leather plc* [1994] 2 AC 264; [1994] 2 WLR 53; [1994] 1 All ER 53 interpreted the decision as covering private nuisance.
105 This was the approach adopted by the House of Lords in *Cambridge Water Co. v East Counties Leather plc* [1994] 2 AC 264; [1994] 2 WLR 53; [1994] 1 All ER 53.
106 *Ibid.*
107 Unrep. HC, 18 February 1998.

Trespass cases are probably subject to the direct consequences test, though there appears to be no definitive authority on the subject. The rationale in *Wagon Mound* was that the same test should apply to both the establishing of the duty of care and the extent of the defendant's responsibility. Applying this to trespass cases, the direct consequences test would be appropriate, given that trespass is based on direct interference. The *Wagon Mound* rationale is not beyond question, however, as the test for whether conduct is tortious and the test for the extent of responsibility need not be the same. This point is amply demonstrated by the reasoning in *Wagon Mound No. 2*, given its acknowledgment that the reasonable foreseeability test will apply to remoteness even in nuisance cases in which the same criterion is not an essential ingredient for establishing the tort. In a recent *dictum* in the Supreme Court, O'Flaherty J expressed a preference for the reasonable foreseeability test for trespass actions based on negligent, rather than intentional conduct: 'I would confine the notion that the plaintiff can recover all the damages that flow from an assault without having to prove that they are foreseeable to intentional assaults.'[108] This would give rise to two different tests for remoteness, depending on whether intention or negligence was applicable. This approach merits consideration, but would run counter to the argument for consistency within each cause of action.

The direct consequences test also survives in the tort of deceit[109] and probably in defamation. Given that defamation is actionable in circumstances where the defendant is unaware of the defamation, it would seem illogical to use foresight to delimit the extent of responsibility. Actions in respect of statutory duties give rise to special considerations based on the interpretation of the particular statutory provisions in each case. No uniform rule of remoteness applies to all such actions, given that some provisions protect specified interests, while others prohibit specified types of conduct; in the former case the injury should be within the class of risks covered, while in the latter any consequence of the wrongful conduct could arguably be covered. There is a dearth of authorities dealing with remoteness in other tort actions and if a dispute were to arise then it would probably be decided on the basis of its similarity to or distinction from the cases where a definite rule has already been established. There are likely areas for such a dispute to arise, such as an action for breach of constitutional rights.

---

108 *Walsh v Family Planning Services* [1992] 1 IR 486, at p. 533. The case was decided on negligence principles, not trespass. The decision also raises doubts about the availability of negligent trespass.
109 *Northern Bank Finance Corp. v Charlton* [1979] IR 149, per O'Higgins CJ at p. 187 (Butler J concurring at p. 213), citing Lord Atkin in *Clark v Urquhart* [1930] AC 28, at p. 68; Henchy J at p. 199 (Parke J concurring at p. 213), citing *Doyle v Olby (Ironmongers) Ltd* [1969] 2 QB 158; [1969] 2 WLR 673; [1969] 2 All ER 119; see also *Gould v Vaggelas* (1985) 56 ALR 31; [1985] LRC Comm 497 for an extensive discussion of the peculiarities of remoteness in deceit cases.

In practical terms the gap between the two approaches to remoteness is slight. The principal reasons for this are the survival of the thin skull rule, the reduced importance of the *Edison* decision and the fact that the type rather than the extent of damage must be foreseeable. These factors extend liability well beyond what could realistically be anticipated in many cases. A further factor may be the vagueness surrounding the interpretation of 'type' of damage, allowing courts to include losses that stretch the limits of 'reasonable' in relation to the foreseeability test.

Residual Issues in Remoteness

Having determined which test is applicable in a given case, there remains the difficulty of applying it to the circumstances of the case. With the direct consequences test one is left with the difficulty of determining which consequences are to be regarded as direct. In relation to contributing circumstances which existed at the time of the tortious action, a decision has to be taken as to whether the tortfeasor is to bear responsibility for these also, or should they be treated as extrinsic causes? If the circumstance is an inherent weakness in the plaintiff, then the thin skull rule will apply; if it is the plaintiff's financial frailty, then the difficulties discussed earlier in relation to impecuniosity arise; in other cases one may be thrown back to the general issue of factual and legal cause discussed previously. Where contributing circumstances arise after the tortious conduct, the principles governing *novus actus interveniens* (considered earlier in the discussion of causation) will have to be used to determine the extent of the defendant's liability.

The reasonable foreseeability test can also be difficult to apply and requires the making of a value judgment as to whether particular types of loss could have been anticipated. There is no precise measurement under the test and it often involves intuitive decision making by the courts. In *Wagon Mound*, for example, it was held that the fire could not have been foreseen because all the parties believed that the oil could not ignite while spread on the water, but in *Wagon Mound No. 2* the same fire was held to be reasonably foreseeable, principally due to having more detailed evidence and more specific findings of primary fact in relation to the likelihood of ignition and the defendants' knowledge thereof. *Rabbette v Mayo County Council* also serves to demonstrate the difficulties involved in applying the test. In this case the defendants' tortious conduct caused a disruption to the plaintiff's building business. Initially the sale of two houses was interfered with, but the disruption to the plaintiff's cash flow required him to borrow from a bank and also led to a loss of credit with his suppliers (including a loss of the discount on the price of materials). Additionally the plaintiff was unable to take up lucrative options on further sites, the profits from which would have allowed for the expansion and development of his business. O'Hanlon J held that the losses arising out of the interest payments to the bank, the loss of discount on materials and losses arising out of the immediate options were reasonably foreseeable, but that the failure of the business was not. No indication is given as to how the dividing line is drawn and clearly the loss of the first set of options is of a similar type to the further opportunities that would have arisen; thus the decision is difficult to explain, yet it appears to provide a fair solution to the dispute between the parties.[110]

---

110 See also *Meah v McCreamer (No. 2)* [1986] 1 All ER 943 for difficulties arising in the application of the reasonable foreseeability test. The value judgments involved in the cases demonstrate the fact that policy considerations are also an important feature of remoteness.

CHAPTER TWELVE

From Obligation to Liability II: Defences, Proof and Limitations

Defences

We have already seen that a defendant may defend a case by disputing the facts alleged by the plaintiff or by disputing whether those facts are sufficient to support the requisite elements of the tort in question. We have also met some special defences, peculiar to particular torts. However, there are also general defences which can protect a defendant, who has committed a tort, from liability for that tort. The protection available may be either partial or complete. At common law the defences of contributory negligence and voluntary assumption of risk, if established, provided the defendant with complete protection. Contributory negligence arose where the plaintiff's failure to exercise reasonable care was considered to have partly caused his own injury. The plaintiff's partial responsibility had the effect of leaving him without a remedy and the harshness of this rule led to a number of judicial ploys to circumvent it. The common law rules have been replaced by statutory provisions, contained in the Civil Liability Act 1961. Voluntary assumption of risk was a defence based on consent, arising where the plaintiff was deemed to have accepted the legal responsibility for the risk which led to the injury and such acceptance could be inferred from his words or conduct immediately prior to the injury. This defence has also been replaced by the provisions in the 1961 Act.

A further defence, based on the illegality of the defendant's conduct, was available at common law,[1] but this was abolished by section 57(1) of the 1961 Act. Section 4(3) of the Occupiers' Liability Act 1995 provides the courts with a discretion in respect of plaintiffs committing or attempting to commit a criminal offence. In such limited cases the illegality of the plaintiff's conduct may excuse the conduct of the defendant.[2] In other cases, the illegality of the plaintiff's conduct may be one of the considerations taken into account in determining whether there was contributory negligence on the plaintiff's part.

Contributory Negligence

Section 34(1) of the Civil Liability Act 1961 provides that damages must be apportioned between the parties where the damage suffered by the plaintiff

---

1 The defence was known as *ex turpi causa non oritur actio* (no action arises from a base cause).
2 The English legislation, the Occupiers' Liability Acts 1957 and 1984, has no such provision and the Court of Appeal refused to exclude an action where the plaintiff was acting illegally, *Revill v Newbury* [1996] QB 567; [1996] 2 WLR 239; [1996] 1 All ER 291.

results partly from the defendant's wrong and partly from the plaintiff's own negligence (or that of a person for whose conduct the plaintiff is responsible). The principle applies to actions in tort, breach of contract or breach of trust.[3] Apart from the plaintiff's own conduct, contributory negligence can stem from conduct for which the plaintiff is deemed to be responsible. Section 35(1) makes a plaintiff responsible for the conduct of others in a number of situations and thereby requires that conduct to be treated as contributory negligence for the purposes of the plaintiff's action. This may be described as 'imputed contributory negligence'.[4] There are, in all, eleven paragraphs detailing the circumstances in which responsibility for conduct is transferred to the plaintiff and these fall into three basic categories – persons for whom the plaintiff is vicariously liable; cases where the plaintiff is not the immediate victim of the wrong; and cases involving concurrent wrongdoers. The first category is relatively straightforward and does not require any detailed exposition.[5] The second category makes the plaintiff responsible for the conduct of the immediate victim where the plaintiff is suing for the dependants of a deceased person; as personal representative of a deceased person; on behalf of the victim as a nominal plaintiff; or as an assignee.[6] Where the plaintiff is acting as a personal representative he is also responsible for the conduct of persons who would benefit if the case were to succeed.[7] The third category relates to cases against a concurrent wrongdoer where another concurrent wrongdoer is left out of the action. The plaintiff is responsible for the conduct of the absent wrongdoer where that person benefited from a clause in a prior contract with the plaintiff, which excluded him from liability or limited his liability to less than his just share of responsibility; where that person's liability was discharged by subsequent agreement with the plaintiff (by way of release or accord); or where the plaintiff's case against the absent wrongdoer has become statute barred or was successfully defended.[8]

In order to establish the defence, the defendant must show that the plaintiff (or a person for whose conduct the plaintiff is responsible) was negligent and that this negligence caused some of the loss complained of. If the plaintiff succeeds in establishing the tort and the defendant succeeds in establishing

---

3 S. 2 provides this definition of 'wrong'.
4 See McMahon & Binchy, *The Irish Law of Torts*, 2nd ed. (Dublin: Butterworths, 1989) at p. 365.
5 *Ibid.*, at p. 366 for arguments on the merits of the inclusion of vicarious responsibility as a form of contributory negligence. See also s. 35(1)(a).
6 This does not apply to an action by a spouse for loss of consortium; the spouse's claim is independent of that of the primary victim; see s. 35(2) considered in *Coppinger v Waterford County Council* [1996] 2 ILRM 427.
7 S. 35(1)(b), (c), (d) and (e).
8 S. 35(1)(f), (g), (h), (i), (j). Strictly speaking, the absent party is not a wrongdoer where there is a contractual exclusion of responsibility.

contributory negligence, then the plaintiff's damages must be reduced and the defendant's liability is, consequently, curtailed.[9]

Negligence

There is no need to establish any duty of care owed by the plaintiff to the defendant for contributory negligence to apply. The essential issue is whether the plaintiff exercised reasonable care in respect of his own safety; thus it is really a case of having a duty to oneself, though the defendant is the beneficiary through the reduction in the damages that will be payable in the event of success in establishing the defence. Thus, for example, the failure of a car driver (or passenger) to wear a seatbelt or of a motor cyclist to wear a crash helmet may constitute contributory negligence, though it poses no danger to the defendant and is not even material to the occurrence of the collision between the parties.[10]

The principles applicable to the standard of care are the same as those in the tort of negligence.[11] The question is whether the plaintiff exercised reasonable care for his own safety in the circumstances, and the test is objective, though with modification for children and other special situations.[12]

Contributory negligence is concerned with the plaintiff's contribution to his injury, as distinct from his contribution to the accident which triggered the injury. Thus, behaviour after the initial incident, which exacerbates the injury, may lead to a reduction in the damages payable. The clearest example of this is failure to mitigate loss, which is to be regarded as contributory negligence, but only in respect of the additional loss caused.[13] The plaintiff is under a duty to take reasonable opportunities to reduce the loss resulting from a wrong and failure to do so will lead to an apportionment of the additional loss suffered, though it will not affect the defendant's liability for loss up to that point.

Contributory

The plaintiff's negligence must contribute to the injury suffered if the defence is to succeed. Thus there must be a causal connection between the negligence and the damage, and ordinary causal principles, discussed earlier, should apply. It has been suggested, however, that the approach taken by the Irish courts to

---

9 S. 36.
10 See *Hamill v Oliver* [1977] IR 73; *Sinnott v Quinnsworth* [1984] ILRM 523; *Ward v Walsh* unrep. SC, 31 July 1991; *Froom v Butcher* [1976] QB 286; [1975] 3 WLR 379; [1975] 3 All ER 520, in relation to seatbelts and *O'Connell v Jackson* [1972] 1 QB 270; [1971] 3 WLR 463; [1971] 3 All ER 129; *Capps v Miller* [1989] 1 WLR 839; [1989] 2 All ER 333 in relation to helmets.
11 Discussed in chapter 1 *supra*.
12 *McNamara v ESB* [1975] IR 1; *McComiskey v McDermott* [1974] IR 75.
13 S. 34(2)(b).

causation in contributory negligence cases is less rigorous than in other causal disputes.[14]

The damage suffered must stem from the particular risk in respect of which the plaintiff was negligent in order for the plaintiff's conduct to amount to contributory negligence;[15] it is not clear from the wording of the 1961 Act whether that requirement applies to cases of imputed contributory negligence, but a logical and consistent approach to the subject would seem to demand such a requirement. *Jones v Livox Quarries Ltd*[16] is instructive on deciding what 'particular risk' means. The plaintiff was travelling on the towbar of a work vehicle at a quarry, where he was employed by the defendants. He was injured when another vehicle collided with the back of the one he was on.

The Court of Appeal held that, while injury by falling was the most apparent danger, injury by collision was sufficiently within the range of risks that the plaintiff's negligence exposed himself to. Some other injury, such as being hit by a negligent gunshot, would not be.[17]

The impact of the change in contributory negligence from a complete to a partial defence has been to give the courts greater flexibility in relation to dealing with the causative force of a plaintiff's conduct. Prior to 1961 there was little distinction between *novus actus interveniens* and contributory negligence, since both had the same practical effect, though in theory they reflected a different evaluation of the plaintiff's conduct. Now practical substance can be given to this distinction by confining the use of *novus actus interveniens* to circumstances where the plaintiff's conduct is such that it is fair to treat it as the sole cause of injury, while using contributory negligence to apportion liability where the plaintiff's conduct was culpable, but not sufficiently so to deny any redress in respect of the resulting injury. A final point to note on the issue of causation is that cases, in practice, may involve multiple injuries and the same principle need not be applied in respect of each; just because a plaintiff has been the sole cause of one of his injuries should not affect his ability to recover for different injuries. Therefore, it is possible to have a situation where a plaintiff may recover in full for one type of injury, have the damages for another injury reduced due to contributory negligence, while being denied any redress for a third injury on the basis that his own conduct constituted a *novus actus interveniens*, where all three injuries arose out of a single accident.

Apportionment

Section 34(1) of the 1961 Act provides that apportionment is to be determined 'as the court thinks just and equitable having regard to the degrees of fault of

---

14 McMahon & Binchy, *op. cit.* at p. 361.
15 S. 34(2)(c).
16 [1952] 2 QB 608.
17 *Ibid.*, per Denning LJ at p. 615.

the plaintiff and defendant'. If the court is unable to determine the relative fault of the parties, liability is to be apportioned equally. 'Fault' has been interpreted as equivalent to blameworthiness, based on an objective evaluation of the parties' conduct.[18] It is important to note that the causative force is not relevant to blameworthiness. Two forces may have equal causative effect, but different levels of fault or blame attached to them, such as where the defendant's negligence puts others at risk and the plaintiff's negligence only poses a risk to himself (e.g. the seatbelt or crash helmet cases). Here, the defendant's conduct is surely more reprehensible than the plaintiff's and so the defendant should carry a greater degree of responsibility.[19] Conversely, two forces may be equally blameworthy, but have different causative effects, such as two motorists driving with equal degrees of carelessness, where one can be shown to have been the cause of a greater share of the damage.

Section 43 provides that where one person was in breach of a strict duty the court may take account of the fact that there was no actual fault on his part and can refuse to apportion any liability to that person. It would seem to be equally applicable to either the plaintiff or the defendant. This is consistent with the use of fault as a basis of apportionment and further indicates the separation between blameworthiness and causation as the criterion.

Section 40 deals with the calculation of the apportionment. The fact finding entity, whether it be judge, jury or arbitrator, must find and record the total amount of damages that would be payable, the percentage by which the plaintiff's award is to be reduced and the percentage for which the defendant is to be responsible (or, in the case of multiple defendants, the percentage that each is to pay). The use of percentages based on the total damages helps provide clarity in respect of the calculation process and helps to avoid some of the difficulties encountered elsewhere. For example, in England in *Fitzgerald v Lane*[20] the trial judge found the plaintiff and the two defendants to be equally culpable and so reduced the total damages by one-third. On appeal it was held by the Court of Appeal, and upheld by the House of Lords that contributory negligence and liability as between defendants had to be separated and that if there was equal responsibility between the plaintiff and defendants then the plaintiff's damages had to be reduced by half.

---

18 See, for example, *O'Sullivan v O'Dwyer* [1971] IR 275; *Carroll v Clare County Council* [1975] IR 211; Byrne & Binchy, *Annual Review of Irish Law 1991* at p. 442.

19 See Cane, *Atiyah's Accidents, Compensation and the Law*, 5th ed. (London: Butterworths, 1993) at p. 46 for a discussion of the distinction between these two categories of fault. *Shields v Boyle* unrep. HC, 6 November 1992 involved a collision between a pedestrian and a motorist. O'Hanlon J apportioned one-third responsibility to the plaintiff, though the causative effect of each party's conduct was considered to be roughly equal; see also *Sinnott v Quinnsworth* [1984] ILRM 523.

20 [1989] AC 328; [1988] 3 WLR 356; [1988] 2 All ER 961.

Consent or Waiver

A plaintiff's consent to tortious conduct can be used by the defendant to preclude liability for resultant injuries. We have already seen how consent operates in respect of torts such as trespass to the person[21] and *Rylands v Fletcher*.[22] A plaintiff may consent either to the invasion of an interest or to the risk of such invasion.[23] In negligence cases the defence of consent was of the latter type and was generally referred to as *volenti non fit injuria* (voluntary assumption of risk).[24]

Section 34(1)(b) of the Civil Liability Act 1961 provides that apportionment for contributory negligence 'shall apply notwithstanding that the defendant might, apart from this sub-section, have the defence of voluntary assumption of risk'. This effectively abolished the traditional defence of voluntary assumption of risk by requiring the use of contributory negligence in circumstances where the former defence would have applied. The sub-section does, however, also provide that it 'shall not operate to defeat any defence arising under a contract or the defence that the plaintiff before the act complained of agreed to waive his legal rights in respect of it'. This means that a complete defence is available in certain cases, based on the prior consent of the plaintiff, thereby preserving some aspects of the voluntary assumption of risk defence. Section 34(1)(c) also preserves the effect of contractual clauses restricting the financial level of the defendant's liability (as opposed to clauses excluding any liability for a particular loss).

It is clear from the wording of the 1961 Act that waiver and exclusion clauses provide separate grounds for defending an action; furthermore, section 34(1)(b) provides that waiver need not be for value. Consequently, agreements which would not amount to a binding contract may, nonetheless, provide a complete defence to a defendant in a tort action. In *O'Hanlon v ESB*[25] it was held that the provision required 'some sort of intercourse or communication' between the parties before the plaintiff could be regarded as having agreed to waive his rights. It is not clear what degree of communication is required to establish waiver, but the courts are generally unwilling to treat a plaintiff's conduct in undertaking a known risk as being sufficient in itself; consequently, patients, employees, rescuers, sports participants etc. are not deemed to have waived their right to take action despite willingly engaging in, or consenting to, conduct with a known risk of injury. It would seem desirable that the parties communicate with respect to responsibility for the risk, rather than its mere existence.

---

21 See chapter 4 *supra*.
22 See chapter 6 *supra*.
23 Brazier, *Street on Torts*, 9th ed. (London: Butterworths, 1993), at p. 276.
24 See, in particular, Fridman, *The Law of Torts in Canada* (Toronto: Carswell, 1989) vol. 1, at p. 352; McMahon & Binchy, *op. cit.* at p. 367.
25 [1969] IR 75, per Walsh J at p. 90.

The section was considered by the Supreme Court in *McComiskey v McDermott*.[26] The plaintiff and defendant were participating together in a rally; the plaintiff was the navigator and the defendant was the driver. During the course of the rally they crashed and the plaintiff was injured. The issue of waiver was raised because there was a notice on the dashboard of the car to the effect that passengers travelled at their own risk. The notice was already on the car when the defendant purchased it second-hand, a fact of which the plaintiff was aware since he was with the defendant when the car was purchased. The evidence showed that the parties had joked about the notice and did not take it seriously. It was held, applying *O'Hanlon v ESB*, that there was no communication between the parties on the issue of waiver in these circumstances and that the defence was not applicable.[27] In the case of a notice deliberately placed in the car by the driver, the mere presence of the notice coupled with the fact that the passenger remains in the car may not be sufficient, though the precise position is not clear from the judgments. It may be that the insertion of the notice amounts to communication to the passenger of the driver's wish to exclude liability and that the passenger by remaining in the car communicates implicit acceptance. The point is not directly addressed in the judgments, but their treatment of the case suggests that the defence should not arise in such a case.[28] It would be safer for the driver to expressly point out the notice to the passenger and seek a response on the matter.

The relationship between this statutory provision and the defence of consent in torts other than negligence is unclear. Consent in the form of a contractual provision or a waiver, based on sufficient communication, will provide a defence under section 34; the outstanding issue is the survival of implicit consent, falling short of waiver, in torts such as trespass to the person and *Rylands v Fletcher*, where 'voluntary assumption of risk' was not used to describe the defence. The lack of case law on the effect of the statutory provision precludes drawing any definitive conclusions on the issue, but it is submitted that traditional principles in respect of consent to torts which did not use 'voluntary assumption of risk' should be regarded as having survived the change in the law. With respect to cases traditionally within the ambit of voluntary assumption of risk, those based on express consent would clearly fall within the waiver principle under section 34, but those involving implied consent are in an uncertain position. The picture may be further clouded in respect of actions for interference with constitutional rights, since some rights may not be capable of waiver.[29] If waiver were raised in respect of a claim for breach of constitutional rights, then the constitutional validity of section 34(1)(b) could be called into question.

---

26 [1974] IR 75.
27 *Ibid.*, at p. 80, per Walsh J; p. 87 per Henchy J; pp. 94–5 per Griffin J.
28 *Ibid.*; see the judgment of Griffin J in particular.
29 A *dictum* of Walsh J in *Murphy v Stewart* [1973] IR 97 indicated that some constitutional rights might be incapable of waiver, but no right has ever actually been held to be so.

The law of contract controls the availability of protection through exclusion clauses and it is not proposed to cover the applicable rules in any detail.[30] A valid exclusion clause will bind the parties to the contract, but the privity of contract rule will generally preclude third parties from relying on the clause. Well established exceptions to the privity rule arise in respect of agency and assignment, whereby the principal or assignee is entitled to enforce the clause, despite not being an original party to the contract. The Privy Council decisions in *The Eurymedon*[31] and *The New York Star*[32] helped to expand the ability of a contracting party to protect sub-contractors, enabling them to benefit from exclusion clauses, by extending the law of agency. *Dicta* from the House of Lords[33] and one Court of Appeal[34] decision in England suggest that sub-contractors may claim the benefit of exclusion clauses contained in the main contract (between the employer and the main contractor), despite being beyond the parameters of the privity doctrine and its exceptions, in order to defend a tort action. The decisions in question do not set out definitive criteria, but the influential factors appear to have been that the employer could foresee that the work would be sub-contracted and that the contents of the main contract were at least a partial inducement to the sub-contractor in deciding to enter into the sub-contract. Given that section 34(1)(b) does not expressly require privity of contract, it is possible that this principle could be adopted in Ireland.[35]

Proof

The ability to succeed in a legal action does not so much depend on the *existence* of facts satisfying the necessary criteria as the ability to *prove* them. The discussion which follows is intended as a general overview of how the elements of a tort action (or defence) are proved; for more detailed consideration of the rules of evidence readers should consult specialised texts on the subject.[36]

---

30 See Friel, *The Law of Contract* (Dublin: Roundhall Press, 1995), at chapter 14; Clark, *Contract Law in Ireland*, 3rd ed. (London: Sweet & Maxwell, 1992) at chapter 7; Treitel, *The Law of Contract*, 9th ed. (London: Sweet & Maxwell, 1995, at chapter 7; Furnston, *Cheshire, Fifoot & Furmston's Law of Contract*, 12th ed. (London: Butterworths, 1991) at pp. 155 *et seq*; *Regan v RIAC* [1990] 1 IR 278.
31 [1975] AC 154; [1974] 2 WLR 865; [1974] 1 All ER 1015.
32 [1981] 1 WLR 138; [1980] 3 All ER 257.
33 Lord Roskill in *Junior Books v Veitchi Co. Ltd* [1983] AC 520; [1982] 3 WLR 477; [1982] 3 All ER 201, at p. 538 and p. 546; p. 487 and p. 495; p. 208 and p. 214; Lord Keith in *Scottish Special Housing Association v Wimpey Construction Ltd* [1986] 1 WLR 995; [1986] 2 All ER 957, at p. 999; pp. 959–60.
34 *Norwich City Council v Harvey* [1989] 1 All ER 1180.
35 For further discussion see Quill, 'Sub-Contractors, Exclusion Clauses and Privity' (1991) 9 ILT 211.
36 See generally Fennell, *The Law of Evidence in Ireland* (Dublin: Butterworths, 1992); Tapper, *Cross on Evidence*, 7th ed. (London: Butterworths, 1990); Strong, *McCormick on Evidence*, 4th ed. (St Paul, Minn.: West, 1992).

Burden and Standard of Proof

The concept of 'burden of proof' (or 'onus of proof') determines which of the parties is required to prove an issue in dispute. If the party carrying the burden of proof fails to discharge that burden, he fails to establish the point at issue. Ordinarily the plaintiff carries the burden of proving sufficient facts to establish the substantive elements of the cause of action. Thus, in a negligence action the plaintiff would have to establish facts from which a duty of care, breach of duty and damage (with causal connection to the breach) could be found to exist, or in a defamation action he would have to establish publication, identification and defamatory effect.

There are a number of ways in which the defendant may dispute the existence of any of these elements. One would be to argue that even if all the facts alleged were true, they fail to fulfil the necessary legal requirements. Another would be to argue that, although the alleged facts would constitute a tort, the plaintiff has not adduced sufficient evidence to support the allegations. It is more common, however, for the defendant to introduce contrary evidence in order to undermine the plaintiff's allegations. Once the plaintiff has introduced evidence which could support his allegations it is prudent for the defence to introduce contrary evidence, though not a legal necessity. There are exceptional cases where the defendant may have to disprove the existence of a substantive element. Rare examples in tort are the requirement on the defendant in actions for trespass to the person (other than on or near the highway) to disprove intention or negligence once the plaintiff has established direct injury, and in the cases where the principle *res ipsa loquitur* applies the defendant must disprove negligence.[37] The rationale behind these exceptional cases, which shift the burden of proof, was explained by Henchy J in *Hanrahan v Merck, Sharp & Dohme*[38] as follows:

> The ordinary rule is that a person who alleges a particular tort must, in order to succeed, prove (save where there are admissions) all the necessary ingredients of that tort and it is not for the defendant to disprove anything.

---

37 In respect of trespass to the person see McMahon & Binchy, *op. cit.* at pp. 399–400. *Res ipsa loquitur* is discussed at length *infra*; see also *Sheehy v Faughnan* [1991] 1 IR 424, which held that in detinue claims, once the plaintiff has established delivery of goods to the defendant in good condition and their return in damaged condition, the burden shifts to the defendant to show that there was no negligence. See Prosser et al., *Prosser & Keeton on Torts*, 5th ed. (St Paul, Minn.: West, 1984) at §38 in respect of actions against carriers. They also present a different interpretation of the effect of these situations, suggesting that they do not involve a true shift in the burden of proof; rather the defendant is required to introduce evidence, while the ultimate risk remains with the plaintiff and the plaintiff, not the defendant, will lose if the issue cannot clearly be determined.

38 [1988] ILRM 629, at pp. 634–5.

Such exceptions as have been allowed to that general rule seem to be confined to cases where a particular element of the tort lies or is deemed to lie, pre-eminently within the defendant's knowledge, in which case the onus of proof as to that matter passes to the defendant.

. . . The onus of disproof rests on the defendant only when the act or default complained of is such that it would be fundamentally unjust to require the plaintiff to prove a positive averment when the particular circumstances show that fairness and justice call for disproof by the defendant.

If the defendant wishes to raise a specific defence, as opposed to disputing the existence of a case to answer, then the burden of establishing the ingredients of that defence will fall on him.[39] Looking back on the earlier chapters, notice how the 'requisite elements' include the issues related to both sides of the case; thus, they not only embrace the elements which the plaintiff must prove, but include those elements in respect of which the defendant carries the burden of proof. The reason for that approach is because a successful case requires both the presence of the ingredients that the plaintiff must prove and the absence of those which the defendant must prove.

The standard or degree of proof required to discharge the burden of proof in civil cases is referred to as 'the balance of probabilities'. This means that the evidence must show that the version of events put forward by the party carrying the burden of proof is more likely to be true than not. If the person carrying the burden cannot establish his claim to be more probable than not, then he must lose on the issue in question. The test is succinctly stated by Lord Diplock in *Mallett v McMonagle*:[40] 'In determining what did happen in the past a court decides on the balance of probabilities. Anything that is more probable than not it treats as certain.'

In most cases the courts are able to reach a decision as to which party's view is more probable than not, but in exceptional cases the evidence may be evenly balanced; then the burden of proof becomes the deciding factor, as the party carrying the burden has failed to discharge it. A rare example of such a case is *O'Reilly Brothers (Quarries) Ltd v Irish Industrial Explosives Ltd*,[41] where the plaintiffs had alleged, *inter alia*, negligence by the defendants in the conduct of blasting that they were carrying out for the plaintiffs. The trial judge found that it was 'at least equally probable' that abnormalities in the rock that was being blasted had caused the damage; consequently, the plaintiffs had

---

39 *Wilson v McGrath* unrep. HC, 17 January 1996; Irish Times Law Report, 6 May 1996; see also *Wrenn v Dublin Bus* unrep. SC, 31 March 1995, the Supreme Court held that, where contributory negligence had not been pleaded and no evidence was adduced on the issue, it was not open to the trial judge to make a finding of contributory negligence and reduce the damages payable.
40 [1970] AC 166; [1969] 2 WLR 767; [1969] 2 All ER 178, at p. 176; p. 772; p. 191.
41 Unrep. SC, 27 February 1995.

failed to discharge the burden of proof.[42] Hamilton CJ, in the Supreme Court, held that the trial judge was correct as 'no adequate explanation had been put before him as to the cause of the [incident]'.[43]

In deciding a disputed issue the trier of fact must ultimately reach a decision based on the evidence and a useful description of that function may be found in Finlay CJ's judgment in *Best v Wellcome Foundation Ltd.*[44]

> The function which a court can and must perform in the trial of a case in order to acquire a just result, is to apply common sense and a careful understanding of the logic and likelihood of events to conflicting opinions and conflicting theories concerning a matter of this kind.

Although this statement was specifically concerned with causation, it may also be usefully applied to any issue on which there is conflicting evidence in order to determine whether the burden of proof has been discharged.

An unusual instance of proof of a disputed issue arose in the context of the army hearing cases. Conflicting evidence was produced before the High Court, in a number of cases,[45] in respect of the measurement of hearing loss. The state failed in its argument on this issue and, in light of the volume of impending cases, the Civil Liability (Assessment of Hearing Injury) Act 1998 was introduced. The Act requires the courts to take account of matters set out in the schedule of the Act in determining cases involving claims of injury arising from hearing loss.[46] This statutory intervention was considered by Lavan J in *Greene v Minister for Defence.*[47] He held that, although the statute requires the court to take account of the method of assessment set out in the legislation, the court retains a discretion as to the weight to be attached to the statutory formula in light of all the evidence presented. The effect of the Act was outlined as follows:

> ... while the Court must consider the approach adopted in the Green Book, it reserves the right to consider alternative approaches. The Court may then determine which is the most appropriate solution in each individual case. In the absence of a more appropriate alternative solution has been [*sic*] established to the satisfaction of the Court, the statutory formula should be applied.[48]

---

42 *Ibid.*, trial judge's comments are quoted by Hamilton CJ at p. 6 and p. 15 of his judgment.
43 *Ibid.*, at p. 16.
44 [1993] 3 IR 462; [1993] ILRM 609, at p. 462; p. 626; see also *O'Leary v Cork Corporation* unrep. SC, 4 July 1997.
45 See, for example, *Bastick v Minister for Defence* unrep. HC, 24 November 1995; *Gardiner v Minister for Defence* unrep. HC, 13 March 1998.
46 Ss. 3 and 4. The schedule contains the *Report to the Minister for Health and Children by an Expert Hearing Group, 1998.*
47 Unrep. HC, 3 June 1998.
48 *Ibid.*, at p. 38; the 'Green Book' is the report of the expert hearing group.

Res Ipsa Loquitur

The phrase *res ipsa loquitur* apparently originated from a comment by Pollock CB in *Byrne v Boadle*[49] and literally means 'the thing speaks for itself'. It originated as a form of circumstantial evidence which would permit the occurrence of an incident to be used as evidence of a defendant's negligence, in certain instances. Where the principle applied it would give rise to an inference or presumption of negligence on the defendant's part and this inference or presumption could be rebutted by contrary evidence. The two principal issues in relation to the principle are, first, determining when it applies and, secondly, determining its evidential effect. Both of these issues have proved extremely problematic and a clear statement of the law on the subject is difficult, if not impossible.

Pre-requisite Criteria

One of the earliest statements of the criteria required for the application of the principle is that of Erle CJ in *Scott v London & St Katherine Docks Co.*[50]

> There must be reasonable evidence of negligence. But where the thing [which caused the injury] is shown to be under the management of the defendant or his servants, and the accident is such as, in the ordinary course of things, does not happen if those who have the management . . . use proper care, it affords reasonable evidence, in the absence of explanation by the defendants, that the accident arose from want of care.

This would confine the principle to cases where the instrument causing the injury was known; the defendant was responsible for the control of that instrument; and the injury was one which would not usually happen unless there was negligence in the management or control of the instrument.

A more recent statement of the principle can be found in *Hanrahan v Merck, Sharp & Dohme:*[51]

> . . . where damage has been caused to the plaintiff in circumstances in which such damage would not usually be caused without negligence on the part of the defendant, the rule of *res ipsa loquitur* will allow the act relied on to be evidence of negligence . . .

This reflects a broader view of the principle, in that it does not require the instrument which caused the injury to be known, but it does require the

---

49 (1863) 2 H & C 722; 159 ER 299, at p. 726; p. 300.
50 (1865) 3 H & C 596; 159 ER 665; [1861–73] All ER Rep 246, at p. 601; p. 667; p. 248, cited with approval by Griffin J in the Supreme Court in *Mullen v Quinnsworth (No. 1)* [1990] 1 IR 59, at pp. 62–3, Finlay CJ concurring at p. 61.
51 [1988] ILRM 629, per Henchy J at p. 635; for critical analysis see Byrne & Binchy, *Annual Review of Irish Law 1995* at pp. 525 *et seq.*

circumstances surrounding the cause of the injury to be known. The causal element is often subsumed within one of the other principles, thereby presenting two criteria, rather than three. Morris J in *Lindsay v Mid-Western Health Board*,[52] for example, includes the causal requirement in the control criterion, while Maguire CJ and Black J in *Neill v Minister for Finance*[53] deal with cause in respect of the criterion that the injury must be one that would not usually occur.

In cases where the principle has been applied, the plaintiff has usually been able to show what caused the injury, but not how it came to do so. For example, in *Byrne v Boadle* a barrel of flour fell from a window and struck the plaintiff; in *Collen Brothers (Dublin) Ltd v Scaffolding Ltd*[54] scaffolding collapsed and a workman, who was on the scaffolding, fell and was injured. In these cases the instrument causing the injury is clearly identifiable, while the manner of its coming to do so is unclear. Thus a factual connection between the instrument and injury could be shown, while the negligent behaviour and its causal link to the factual cause could then be inferred. The Supreme Court decisions in *Hanrahan v Merck, Sharp & Dohme* and *Lindsay v Mid-Western Health Board*[55] have, however, cast doubt on the need to know the causal instrument. In *Lindsay* a child went into hospital to have her appendix removed, but failed to recover consciousness after the operation. There was uncertainty as to what led to the failure to return to consciousness, but *res ipsa loquitur* was, nonetheless, applied. The Supreme Court adopted a passage from Fleming which included the following statement:

> *Res ipsa loquitur* is no more than a convenient label to describe situations where, notwithstanding the plaintiff's inability to establish the exact cause of the accident, the fact of the accident by itself is sufficient in the absence of an explanation to justify the conclusion that most probably the defendant was negligent and that this negligence caused the injury.[56]

This statement is consistent with established principle, provided the causal presumption is related only to the connection between the inferred negligence and a known factual cause. If, however, the principle is to apply in the absence of establishing factual cause, then *Lindsay* must be regarded as having created a significant extension to its scope. It should be noted that the elements of control and that the injury was one not likely to occur if due care was exercised were both present, and factual cause could be regarded as having been partially established as there was an adverse outcome to a routine procedure under the defendant's control.

---

52 [1993] 2 IR 147 (HC).
53 [1948] IR 88, at p. 92 and p. 93 respectively.
54 [1959] IR 245.
55 [1993] 2 IR 147; [1993] ILRM 550.
56 *Ibid.*, at pp. 183–4; p. 555, per O'Flaherty J (Finlay CJ and Egan J concurring) quoting from Fleming, *The Law of Torts*, 7th ed. (Sydney: Law Book Co., 1987) at p. 291.

The control requirement is generally given a broad interpretation and includes situations where the defendant formerly had control, provided there was no interference with or change in the thing which caused the injury in the interim. Thus, manufacturers or repairers may have sufficient control over a product for the principle to apply in the event of an injury arising during ordinary use of the product and a tradesman may have sufficient control over materials installed by him.[57]

The requirement that the injury be of a type that would not ordinarily occur if the defendant exercised due care involves the application of common sense and experience to the established facts. A complete list of types of incidents which will give rise to the application of the principle cannot be given, but some examples will serve to demonstrate the variety of accidents covered. A barrel of flour falling out a window[58] or sacks of sugar falling from a hoist[59] have been regarded as capable of satisfying the requirement, as has the collapse of scaffolding.[60] Adverse outcomes to medical procedures have proved problematic and it appears that, while an adverse outcome to a 'straightforward procedure carrying no inherent risks' may satisfy the requirement, in most cases an unsatisfactory outcome will not be sufficient because medical science has not developed to the point where a patient may always expect to be improved by treatment.[61]

The decision in *Hanrahan v Merck, Sharp & Dohme* has produced two new criteria for the application of the principle. Henchy J treated *res ipsa loquitur* as an example of a more general rule on the shifting of the burden of proof, the criteria for that rule being that the defendant is in a superior position to provide proof of the issue and that it would be unjust to require the plaintiff to prove that issue. It is not clear whether the criteria set out by Henchy J operate in addition to, instead of, or as an alternative to the traditional criteria.

If they are to replace the existing criteria then the principle will have been dramatically cut back. On the traditional understanding of the principle, it could be invoked where neither party was in a position to prove what happened, but under the Henchy test it would not apply to such a situation because the defendant would not have any superior capacity of proof. Examples of such a situation would be where the defendant is vicariously responsible for the conduct of a person who caused injury to the plaintiff, but that person is unavailable as a witness due to death, or an absence of memory, or departure from the jurisdiction. Conflicting decisions have emanated from the High Court on this issue. Johnson J applied *res ipsa loquitur* in *O'Reilly v*

---

57 See McMahon & Binchy, *op. cit.* at pp. 135–6.
58 *Byrne v Boadle* (1863) 2 H & C 722; 159 ER 299.
59 *Scott v London & St Katherine Docks Co.* (1865) 3 H & C 596; 159 ER 665; [1861–73] All ER Rep 246.
60 *Collen Brothers (Dublin) Ltd v Scaffolding Ltd* [1959] IR 245.
61 *Lindsay v Mid-Western Health Board* [1993] 2 IR 147, at p. 169 per Morris J citing *Girard v Royal Colombian Hospital* (1976) 66 DLR (3d) 676.

Lavelle[62] and held the defendant liable where he was unable to explain how the injury to the plaintiff came about, while Barr J refused to apply the principle in *Maitland v Swan*[63] because the defendant had no recollection of the incident and, consequently, lacked a superior capacity to establish what had occurred.

If the criteria are alternatives, and a plaintiff need only satisfy one set or the other, then the scope of the principle has been expanded to cover cases that do not easily fit within the traditional criteria. This would remove much of the confusion arising from the *Lindsay* case, as the facts of that case clearly satisfy Henchy J's criteria. As pointed out earlier, the causal aspects of the case were problematic, but since Henchy J's test was framed so as to apply to any of the constituent elements of a cause of action, its application to causation would be satisfactory.

If the criteria are additional then the plaintiff is faced with additional obstacles when invoking the principle. The decision in *Hanrahan v Merck, Sharp & Dohme*, itself, provides support for this interpretation, as the *res ipsa loquitur* principle is treated as a particular variant of the general principle. Consequently, the principle would be subject to the criteria applicable to all cases within the general class and to the criteria which distinguish *res ipsa loquitur* from the other cases within the general class. The Supreme Court decision in *Lindsay* also gives some support to this interpretation because the difference in capacity of proof was regarded as essential,[64] while the traditional criteria were also invoked. Keane J, in *O'Shea v Tilman*,[65] suggested that the *Hanrahan* reformulation of the principle may need reconsideration and he based his decision on the *Scott* formulation. This opinion was a minority one and Hamilton CJ expressly reserved his opinion on the need for reconsideration.

Procedural Effect

There are a number of possible effects that the *res ipsa loquitur* principle can have. At its weakest, the principle merely provides some evidence of causal negligence on the defendant's part and it is open to the trier of fact to decide whether to draw the inference or not. If the circumstances leading to the application of the principle are particularly strong then the inference may be inevitable, unless contrary evidence is introduced. In those situations the weak

---

62 [1990] 2 IR 372 stating at pp. 375–6 that the case of straying animals was particularly suited to the application of the principle.
63 Unrep. HC, 6 April 1992; Irish Times Law Report, 6 July 1992.
64 [1993] 2 IR 147; [1993] ILRM 550, at p. 183 and p. 184; p. 554 and p. 555; see also *Merriman v Greenhills Foods Ltd* [1996] 3 IR 73; [1997] 1 ILRM 46, Blayney J, delivering the majority judgment in the Supreme Court, relied on *Scott*, at p. 77; p. 49 and on the defendant's better capacity to establish what had occurred, at p. 78; p. 50.
65 Unrep. SC, 23 October 1996; Irish Times Law Report, 16 December 1996. The reason given by Keane J was that the *Hanrahan* formulation had been subject to criticism; he cited McMahon & Binchy, *op. cit.* at pp. 142–4, as an example.

version of the principle would again allow a decision either way, once some contrary evidence was introduced. In both of these situations the burden of proof remains on the plaintiff and the action only succeeds if the trier of fact is satisfied that causal negligence on the defendant's part is the more probable explanation of the plaintiff's injury. The difference between the two is the weight attached to the inference, based on the supporting facts, rather than a distinction of legal principle. This view seems to have found favour in most US states.[66] A slightly stronger version of the principle applied in Canada until recently. The plaintiff would succeed once the principle applied, unless the defendant introduced some contrary evidence.[67] This allowed the plaintiff to establish a *prima facie* case, which the defendant had to answer, but the ultimate burden of proof remained with the plaintiff. However, in *Fontaine v Loewen Estate*,[68] the Supreme Court of Canada opted for the weaker version of the principle, favoured by the American judiciary, and denied that the principle has any distinct doctrinal status in the law of torts. A third interpretation involves a transfer of the burden of proof to the defendant, requiring the disproof of causal negligence. This third proposition is favoured by the Irish courts[69] and has also found favour in many English decisions, though there is considerable support in England for the second interpretation.[70] In Ireland the defendant can defeat the operation of the principle by showing either that he exercised reasonable care or the absence of a causal link between his conduct and the injury. In either case one of the vital elements of the plaintiff's case will be removed, thereby defeating the claim.[71]

It should also be noted that the principle need not be specifically pleaded by the plaintiff in the statement of claim in order to be relied on in the course of a case. Once 'the facts pleaded and the facts proved show that the doctrine is applicable to the case, that is sufficient'.[72]

---

66 Prosser & Keeton, *op. cit.* at §40.
67 Fridman, *op. cit.* vol. 1 at pp. 317–18.
68 (1997) 156 DLR (4th) 577; noted by McInnes (1998) 114 LQR 547. The Supreme Court upheld the trial judge's refusal to draw an inference of negligence on the part of the driver of a truck which crashed in a remote area, killing both the driver and passenger. The lack of any witnesses and the inconclusive nature of the physical evidence meant that the facts were consistent with a number of explanations.
69 See *Collen Brothers (Dublin) Ltd v Scaffolding Ltd* [1959] IR 245, per Davitt P at p. 248; *O'Reilly v Lavelle* [1990] 2 IR 372, per Johnson J at p. 375 and p. 376; *Mullen v Quinnsworth (No. 1)* [1990] 1 IR 59, per Griffin J (Finlay CJ concurring) at p. 63; *Merriman v Greenhills Foods Ltd* [1996] 3 IR 73; [1997] 1 ILRM 46, per Blayney J at pp. 78–9; pp. 51–2.
70 Heuston & Buckley, *Salmond & Heuston on the Law of Torts*, 21st ed. (London: Sweet & Maxwell, 1996) at p. 246; Rogers, *Winfield & Jolowicz*, 14th ed. (London: Sweet & Maxwell, 1994) at pp. 143–5.
71 *Lindsay v Mid-Western Health Board* [1993] 2 IR 147; [1993] ILRM 550, per O'Flaherty J (Finlay CJ and Egan J concurring) at pp. 184–5; pp. 555–6.
72 *Mullen v Quinnsworth (No. 1)* [1990] 1 IR 59, per Griffin J (Finlay CJ concurring) at p. 63, citing *Bennett v Chemical Construction (GB) Ltd* [1971] 1 WLR 1571;

Types of Evidence

There is a variety of types of evidence, some of which may be used to establish a cause of action or a defence and some of which may not.[73] Evidence is generally admissible once it is relevant and does not have an unduly prejudicial effect.[74] The common law is heavily reliant on the oral presentation of evidence by witnesses (testimony), though other types of evidence, such as documents and physical evidence, are also used.

Facts at issue may be proved by either direct or circumstantial evidence – direct evidence being that which tends to establish a disputed fact; circumstantial evidence being that which tends to establish facts from which a disputed fact may be inferred. There is a common misapprehension that direct evidence is better or more reliable than circumstantial evidence, but either type can vary widely in the force it lends to supporting the disputed facts.[75] *Basmajian v Haire and Others*[76] provides an example of circumstantial evidence being preferred to direct evidence. In this case expert interpretation of physical evidence, such as tyre marks, the location of glass fragments and the final position of the cars, was preferred to the testimony of the plaintiff in relation to the manner in which a collision came about and the speed of the vehicles immediately prior to impact. At a more general level, Finlay CJ in *Best v Wellcome* rejected the suggestion that there should be a prioritised scale for the weighting of evidence.[77] The reversal of the burden of proof on the application of the *res ipsa loquitur* principle represents an anomaly which is difficult to justify and the case law gives no clear explanation as to why this exception should exist, giving such force to one particular category of evidence.[78]

The different types of evidence which may be presented in support of facts and those which are to be excluded are each subject to special rules of their

---

[1971] 3 All ER 822; applied by Johnson J in *O'Reilly v Lavelle* [1990] 2 IR 372, at p. 373.

73 See Cross, *op. cit.* at chapter 1 section 3 for a useful introduction to the principal types of evidence; see also McCormick, *op. cit.* at chapter 1 on the preparation and presentation of evidence, as these matters can often be as important as the substance of the evidence.

74 See Cross, *op. cit.* at chapter 1 section 4 on relevance and admissibility of evidence.

75 *Ibid.*, at pp. 21–41 for examples of circumstantial evidence.

76 Unrep. HC, 2 April 1993. See also Prosser & Keeton, *op. cit.* at p. 243 for an example of circumstantial evidence (dog tracks on the ground) outweighing direct evidence (witnesses' denial of dog's presence).

77 [1993] 3 IR 421; [1992] ILRM 609, at p. 471; p. 633 (Egan J concurring).

78 Prosser & Keeton, *op. cit.* at p. 243, suggest that early decisions on reversal of the burden of proof resulted from two separate issues, namely the sufficiency of circumstantial evidence and exceptions in respect of the burden of proof, becoming 'confused and intermingled', thereby leading to an unwarranted elevation of *res ipsa loquitur* to doctrinal status.

own. Testimony offered by witnesses must be first-hand, based on their own observations through their senses, and should not include opinions or conclusions, but there are exceptions; for example, testimony may be reconstructed with the aid of notes or records and expert witnesses may give opinions related to their area of expertise.[79] Where documentary evidence is to be used litigants are ordinarily required to produce the originals, but where this is impossible secondary evidence establishing the accuracy of the copy is admissible and a copy may be used.[80] A variety of other forms of evidence are also available, such as physical objects, places, maps and diagrams, models and reconstructions. These are sometimes described as 'real' evidence, though the term 'demonstrative' evidence is probably more accurate.[81] Such evidence can often be more convincing than descriptive testimony due to its dramatic effect. While it is an essential aspect of a trial lawyer's armoury, courts must be careful not to allow the mesmeric effect of such evidence to distract them from the task at hand. Ultimately fact finders, be they judges or jurors, must bear in mind that all items of evidence, even strong evidence such as expert opinion or physical objects, are to be assessed for their tendency to support disputed facts and should not be accepted in an unquestioning fashion.

There are also instances where relevant evidence may be excluded because of overriding considerations. The main categories of exclusion are hearsay, privilege, public policy and estoppel. The rule against hearsay evidence provides that assertions other than by a witness giving testimony are inadmissible as proof of facts asserted. Thus, if A claims that he heard B say that he saw the defendant drive at 70 mph and collide with the plaintiff, A's evidence of B's assertion is inadmissible to prove that the defendant was driving at 70 mph. A's testimony would, however, be admissible as proof that the statement was made and could be used to question the credibility of B, if B gave evidence differing from the earlier statement. There are a number of exceptions to the rule, such as admissions by a party to the dispute, statements made contemporaneously with an act or statements in public documents (registers, certificates etc.). The operation of the rule and the exceptions is one of the more complex aspects of the law of evidence and requires careful and detailed consideration of the relevant principles.[82]

There are numerous situations where relevant evidence will be excluded from a trial because it is subject to a privilege or its admission would be contrary to public policy. Typical examples would be the privilege applicable to communica-

---

79 See Cross, *op. cit.* at chapter 13; McCormick, *op. cit.* at chapter 3; Fennell, *op. cit.* at chapter 6 on opinions; see Cross, *op. cit.* at pp. 271–80; McCormick, *op. cit.* at chapter 28; Fennell, *op. cit.* at p. 105 on reconstructed evidence.
80 Cross, *op. cit.* at chapter 19; McCormick, *op. cit.* at chapter 23; Fennell, *op. cit.* at chapter 13.
81 McCormick, *op. cit.* at chapter 21.
82 Cross, *op. cit.* at chapters 14–16; McCormick, *op. cit.* at chapter 24; Fennell, *op. cit.* at chapter 9.

tions between lawyers and their clients or the rules relating to illegally or unconstitutionally obtained evidence. While these issues generally have more bearing on criminal trials, they occasionally surface in civil actions, as where a government report on an accident may be withheld from a victim pursuing an action for compensation.[83]

There are two principal types of estoppel to be noted at this point. One is estoppel of a cause of action, which precludes the bringing of a cause of action which has already been determined between the parties. The finality of judicial proceedings cannot be destroyed by reissuing proceedings on issues already determined in respect of the parties. The second estoppel is issue estoppel, where a party to proceedings may not raise an issue which has already been determined against him in previous proceedings. This differs from the first in that it is concerned with a matter previously determined against one of the parties, not a decision affecting both parties. It does not preclude bringing the later action, but it does preclude parties reopening issues, which have already been decided against them in previous proceedings.[84]

Appealing Findings of Fact

Section 94 of the Courts of Justice Act 1924 gives parties to tort actions the right to have issues of fact tried by a jury. Section 1 of the Courts Act 1988 restricts this right by excluding High Court actions which are wholly or partly based on claims for personal injuries arising out of negligence, nuisance or breach of duty (including statutory duty); such actions are tried by a judge alone. The right to trial by jury is preserved for High Court personal injuries cases involving trespass to the person. (Section 6 of the Courts Act 1971 abolished the use of juries in civil cases in the Circuit Court.) While appeals from trial courts are mainly confined to issues of law, factual issues can also be appealed. The role of the appeal court in considering the evidence and the differing claims as to what that evidence proves is significantly different from that of the original trier of fact, whether judge or jury. Appeal courts generally consider transcripts of the original trial, rather than having a complete rehearing; thus they are not in as good a position as the original trier of fact to judge the veracity or credibility of witnesses. Once the findings of fact of the judge or jury are capable of being supported by the evidence presented at the trial, then they will not normally be interfered with, even if the appeal court would prefer a different interpretation. McCarthy J, in *Hay v O'Grady*,[85] made the point forcefully, when he stated:

> If the findings of fact . . . are supported by credible evidence, this Court is bound by those findings, however voluminous and, apparently, weighty the testimony against them. The truth is not the monopoly of any majority.

---

83 Cross, *op. cit.* at chapters 11–12; McCormick, *op. cit.* at chapters 8–15; Fennell, *op. cit.* at chapters 7–8.
84 Cross, *op. cit.* at pp. 76–85; Fennell, *op. cit.* at chapter 12.
85 [1992] 1 IR 210; [1992] ILRM 689, at p. 217, p. 694.

If, however, the finding is wholly unreasonable, then it will be overturned. A more extensive statement of the law may be seen in the judgment of Henchy J in *Northern Bank Finance Corp. v Charlton*:[86]

> In a civil case such as this where a tribunal of fact, be it a judge or jury, has decided a question of specific fact and the resolution of the question depended wholly or in substantial measure on the choice of one version of controverted oral testimony as against another, a court of appeal which is dependent on a written record of the oral evidence given at the trial will not normally reject that finding merely because an alternative version of the oral testimony seems more acceptable. The court of appeal will only set aside a finding of fact based on one version of the evidence when, on taking a conspectus of the evidence as a whole, oral and otherwise, it appears to the court that, notwithstanding the advantages which the tribunal of fact had in seeing and hearing the witnesses, the version of the evidence which was acted on could not reasonably be correct.

In a later decision,[87] Henchy J further clarified the law on this subject by drawing a distinction between primary and secondary findings of fact. Primary facts are those which are dependent on the trial court's assessment of 'the credibility and quality of the witnesses'.[88] Secondary facts are those which are inferred from primary facts proved (or admitted) and are essentially 'evaluative of the primary facts'.[89] Decisions in respect of primary facts will only be overturned when they are contrary to the weight of evidence, whereas secondary facts may be more readily overturned, as the appellate court is in as good a position as the trial court to determine the inferences to be drawn from the primary facts. The Supreme Court has further qualified this statement of principle by indicating that there may be occasions where inferences will also be dependent on the credibility of witnesses; this finding of fact, although inferential, is more akin to Henchy J's primary fact category than the secondary category. McCarthy J, speaking for a unanimous Supreme Court, stated:

> It may be that the demeanour of a witness in giving evidence will, itself, lead to an appropriate inference which an appellate court would not draw. In my judgment, an appellate court should be slow to substitute its own inference of fact where such depends upon oral evidence or recollection of fact and a different inference has been drawn by the trial judge. In the

---

86 [1979] IR 149, at p. 191, cited by Finlay CJ in *Dunne v National Maternity Hospital* [1989] IR 91; [1989] ILRM 735, at p. 107; pp. 743–4.
87 *JM and GM v An Bord Uchtála* [1988] ILRM 203, at p. 205 and repeated in *Hanrahan v Merck, Sharp & Dohme* [1988] ILRM 629, at p. 637.
88 *Ibid.*; see also *Nolan Transport (Oaklands) Ltd v Halligan and Others* unrep. SC, 15 May 1998, per Murphy J at p. 13 of his judgment.
89 *Ibid.*; see also O'Flaherty J in *Best v Wellcome Foundation Ltd* [1993] 3 IR 421; [1992] ILRM 609, at p. 482; p. 642.

drawing of inferences from circumstantial evidence, an appellate tribunal is in as good a position as the trial judge.[90]

In would appear that the same principles are applied to jury trials and non-jury trials,[91] but a practical difference arises between the two because a judge's findings of fact will usually be accompanied by a more detailed account of the evidence relied on, and the weight attached to it, than a jury's decision. This should assist an appeal court in analysing the judgment, by giving more information to facilitate the classification of the findings and to assess their validity.

Limitation of Actions

A cause of action may fail, without any consideration of the substantive merits of the plaintiff's claim, on the basis that there has been too great a delay in bringing the action. In most cases delays will impair the availability and accuracy of evidence, thus reducing the chances of reaching a just outcome. The law attempts to balance the plaintiff's right of access to the courts against the defendant's right not to be unduly prejudiced by the delay. The principal provisions governing this issue are contained in the Statutes of Limitation 1957 and 1991, though there are important additional principles contained in the Civil Liability Act 1961 and the discretionary powers of the courts. Other statutes occasionally include special limitation provisions also.[92]

General Time Limit

Section 11 of the Statute of Limitations 1957 provides that tort actions shall not be brought more than six years after the date on which the cause of action accrued[93] and, where the action includes a claim for damages for slander, a shorter period of three years is applicable.[94] The three year period applicable to damages for slander also applied to any action which included a claim for

---

90 *Hay v O'Grady* [1992] IR 210; [1992] ILRM 689, at p. 217; p. 694, cited by O'Flaherty in *Best v Wellcome Foundation Ltd* [1993] 3 IR 421; [1992] ILRM 609; see also the House of Lords decision in *Whitehouse v Jordan* [1981] 1 WLR 246; [1981] 1 All ER 267, which regards the issues of credibility and demeanour as central to determining what constitutes primary fact. Trial courts' decisions as to evidential weight are treated as secondary fact and, therefore, more prone to review. Notably factual findings are regarded as being on a sliding scale, rather than rigid classification.

91 See particularly *Northern Bank Finance Corp. v Charlton* [1979] IR 149; *Dunne v National Maternity Hospital* [1989] IR 91; [1989] ILRM 735; and *Hay v O'Grady*, [1992] IR 210; [1992] ILRM 689.

92 See generally Brady & Kerr, *The Limitation of Actions in the Republic of Ireland*, 2nd ed. (Dublin: Incorporated Law Society of Ireland, 1994).

93 S. 11(2)(a) of the 1957 Act.

94 S. 11(2)(c) of the 1957 Act.

personal injuries, but the provision has been modified by section 3 of the Statute of Limitations (Amendment) Act 1991.[95]

The central issue, in cases other than those involving personal injuries, is determining the date of accrual, as the calculation is based on this date. The leading authority is the Supreme Court decision in *Hegarty v O'Loughran*,[96] where it was held that a cause of action accrues once the tort is complete, i.e. once the constituent elements that the plaintiff is required to establish have come into existence.[97] In respect of torts which are actionable *per se*, such as libel or trespass, the date of the wrongful act will be the relevant date, but in the case of torts requiring proof of damage the date of accrual will be the date on which damage first occurred. Torts which are regarded as continuing wrongs, such as trespass to land and nuisance, give rise to a new cause of action on a daily basis and accrual will be calculated from the last date of interference, rather than the first.

The principal difficulty presented by the interpretation of accrual in *Hegarty v O'Loughran* is that it causes hardship to plaintiffs in a number of situations. Foremost among these are cases where there is latent damage, i.e. damage which cannot be discovered until some time after it has actually occurred. Here the cause of action may accrue before the plaintiff is even aware of the damage, thereby reducing the amount of time available to the plaintiff to take action. It is even possible that the limitation period will have entirely expired before the plaintiff discovers the damage. Such cases are compounded by the fact that the connection between the injury and the wrongful act may not be obvious at the time when the damage is first discovered. Thus, there is a significant possibility that a plaintiff's cause of action may be time barred before the plaintiff is aware of having a case against the defendant. Such a possibility is not merely gloomy speculation, but has arisen in a number of reported decisions. In *Cartledge v E.F. Jopling & Sons Ltd*[98] the plaintiff suffered lung damage, as a result of inhaling asbestos dust in the course of his employment, but the damage was not discovered until many years after it had actually occurred. The House of Lords held that the claim was statute barred, as there was no statutory provision delaying the running of the limitation period in cases where the damage was not discoverable. Similarly, in *Hegarty v O'Loughran*, the plaintiff suffered damage as a result of medical treatment she had received, but the injury could not be

---

95 The original provision was contained in s. 11(2)(b) of the 1957 Act. S. 2(c) of the 1957 Act defines 'personal injuries' as including 'any disease and any impairment of a person's physical or mental condition'.
96 [1990] 1 IR 148.
97 *Ibid.*, at p. 157 per Finlay CJ (Walsh and Hederman JJ concurring) and at p. 158 per Griffin J.
98 [1963] AC 758; [1963] 2 WLR 210; [1963] 1 All ER 341; see also *Pirelli General Cable Works Ltd v Oscar Faber & Partners* [1983] 2 AC 1; [1983] 2 WLR 6; [1983] 1 All ER 65, in respect of latent property damage.

diagnosed until some years after it had actually occurred. By this time the limitation period had elapsed and the plaintiff was unable to maintain an action.

In cases involving personal injuries caused by negligence, nuisance or breach of duty, the limitation period is three years from the date of accrual of the cause of action, except where certain information is not known to the injured person, in which cases the period runs from the date of knowledge.[99] The relevant information is set out in section 2(1) of the 1991 Act:

(a) that the person alleged to have been injured had been injured;
(b) that the injury in question was significant;
(c) that the injury was attributable in whole or in part to the act or omission which is alleged to constitute negligence, nuisance or breach of duty;
(d) the identity of the defendant; and
(e) if it is alleged that the act or omission was that of a person other than the defendant, the identity of that person and additional facts supporting the bringing of an action against the defendant.

Knowledge can be actual or that which the person 'might reasonably have been expected to acquire', including knowledge that could be discovered with the assistance of expert advice, provided that it is reasonable to expect such expert advice to be sought.[100] If a person takes reasonable steps to obtain and act upon expert advice, then there will be no imputation of knowledge of any fact which should have been discovered, but was not.[101] In *Boylan v Motor Distributors Ltd and Daimler Benz AG*[102] Lynch J held that to require plaintiffs to always seek expert reports before issuing proceedings would place too onerous a burden on them.[103] In this case the plaintiff had injured her fingers in the door of a van and, in the course of proceedings against the owners of the van, the plaintiff's solicitor was advised by senior counsel to obtain an engineer's report in respect of the door. The solicitor did so and when the report was eventually received it indicated a design defect, which indicated for the first time that the manufacturers might be responsible for the plaintiff's injuries. It was held that the plaintiff had not acted unreasonably in not seeking an engineer's report earlier, as the manner in which the injury occurred did not create any suspicion of such a defect.

---

99 S. 3(1) of the Statute of Limitations (Amendment) Act 1991. S. 7 applies the Act to actions accruing before or after its passing and to those pending at the time of passing.
100 S. 2(2) of the 1991 Act.
101 S. 2(3) of the 1991 Act.
102 [1994] 1 ILRM 115.
103 *Ibid.*, at pp. 125–6; contrast *Whitely v Minister for Defence* [1997] 2 ILRM 416, where the facts known to the plaintiff were sufficient to indicate that the injury was significant; Quirke J, at pp. 427–9, found the claim to be out of time as the plaintiff was aware of the injury for a considerable number of years.

Knowledge of injury has been interpreted to mean an awareness that the defendant's conduct was harmful. In *Maitland v Swan*[104] the defendant operated on the plaintiff in 1971, when she was thirteen years old, and removed her right ovary, on which there was a benign cyst. In 1983 she discovered that she did not have a normal left ovary and was, therefore, sterile as a result of the earlier operation. She instituted proceedings in 1985 for negligence in relation to the defendant's failure to properly consider the gynaecological implications of the surgery. Her claim was allowed to proceed on the grounds that, although she was aware of the removal of her ovary in 1971, she would have considered the surgery beneficial at the time and it was not until 1983 that she discovered that it amounted to a significant harm.

An action on behalf of the dependants of a victim in the case of fatal injuries was also subject to a limitation period of three years from the death of the victim,[105] but such cases also benefit from the extension of time relating to later discovery of vital knowledge.[106]

The failure to include an extension based on discoverability in respect of cases of property damage or economic loss could give rise to unfairness, but the constitutionality of the six year limitation period, without extension, was upheld by the Supreme Court in *Touhy v Courtney*.[107]

Extended Limitation Periods

There are a number of situations in which the limitation period may be varied from the usual three or six year period after accrual, due to special circumstances. We have already seen how the running of time in personal injuries cases is delayed until certain information related to the cause of action could reasonably be discovered by the injured party. The other major extensions relate to incapacity, fraud and contribution actions under the Civil Liability Act 1961.

Disability

In the case of persons under a disability on the date that the cause of action accrued, the limitation period does not begin to run until the end of the disability or the death of the person.[108] The categories of persons under a disability, for the purpose of this extension, are:

---

104 Unrep. HC, 6 April 1992; Irish Times Law Report, 6 July 1992; analysed in Byrne & Binchy, *Annual Review of Irish Law 1992* at pp. 432–3.
105 S. 48(6) of the Civil Liability Act 1961.
106 S. 6 of the 1991 Act.
107 [1994] 2 ILRM 503.
108 S. 49(1)(a) of the 1957 Act.

(i) minors
(ii) persons of unsound mind
(iii) convicts subject to the operation of the Forfeiture Act 1870, in whose case no administrator or curator has been appointed under the Act.[109]

It was held in *Rohan v Bord na Móna*[110] that a person suffering brain damage in an accident qualifies as a person of unsound mind, as the date of his disability and the date of accrual coincide, thus making the person subject to a disability on the date of accrual. The fact that the accident momentarily precedes the disability is irrelevant, as the Act merely requires that the disability be present on the date of accrual, which spans the entire day. The provision may not, however, extend to cases where the mental impairment occurs some time later, as with post traumatic stress disorder.

The extension for persons under a disability does not apply where the person under the disability is claiming in respect of a cause of action that originally accrued to someone else, where that other person was not under a disability.[111] In the case of a cause of action accruing to a person under a disability, and on that person's death under disability it accrues to a second person also under a disability, no extension applies in respect of the disability of the second person.[112]

The extension in respect of persons under a disability was originally confined to such persons not in the custody of a parent, but this provision was held to be unconstitutional in *O'Brien v Keogh*[113] as it unduly restricted the right of access to the courts of persons under a disability who were in the custody of a parent. The main reason for the decision was that there was a risk that some parents would be unwilling or unable to take action on their child's behalf, thereby depriving the child of the opportunity to obtain redress.

The scope of the disability extension has been increased by section 5 of the Statute of Limitations (Amendment) Act 1991. In claims for personal injuries, including fatal injuries, the disability extension also applies where the disability was present at the date of knowledge, where this is later than the date of accrual. Thus, a person who was not subject to a disability at the date of accrual, but had become subject to a disability prior to discovery of essential

---

109 S. 48(1) of the 1957 Act; the provision in relation to minors originally applied to persons under twenty-one years of age, but the age was reduced to eighteen years (or the date of marriage in the case of persons married prior to attaining the age of eighteen) by s. 2 of the Age of Majority Act 1985. In relation to persons of unsound mind, s. 48(2) of the 1957 Act creates a conclusive presumption that persons detained in any institution under an enactment authorising the detention of persons of unsound mind or criminal lunatics are of unsound mind for the purposes of the Statute of Limitations.
110 [1991] ILRM 123.
111 S. 49(1)(b) of the 1957 Act.
112 S. 49 (1)(c) of the 1957 Act.
113 [1972] IR 144; the relevant provision was s. 49(a)(ii) of the 1957 Act.

information in respect of the cause of action, would benefit from the extended limitation period.

Fraud

Fraud can give rise to extension of the limitation period in two distinct ways – the cause of action may be based on the fraud of the defendant or his agent, or of a person through whom he claims; alternatively, the right of action, though not itself based on fraud, may have been concealed by any such person. In either case time in respect of the limitation period does not begin to run until the plaintiff has, or could with reasonable diligence have, discovered the fraud.[114] Deceit would be the most obvious action in the first category, but the second category depends on the interpretation to be given to the phrase 'concealed by fraud'. Morris J, in *McDonald v McBain*,[115] expressed the opinion that if the defendant 'either by stealth or silence, succeeded in hiding [an essential fact] from the plaintiff, and she was left in complete and total ignorance of the identity of the wrongdoer' then the right of action would be concealed by fraud.[116] He added that if the plaintiff had sufficient evidence to give rise to a reasonable prospect of succeeding, then the concealing of an item of proof by the defendant, which would enhance the plaintiff's case, would not give rise to the operation of the extension. 'I know of no authority which allows the plaintiff to postpone bringing her case until she has available to her evidence which she believes will copperfasten the matter in her favour.'[117]

In *Heffernan v O'Herlihy*[118] Kinlen J held that a solicitor's failure to inform a client that no proceedings had been instituted on her behalf amounted to fraud for the purposes of section 71 of the 1957 Act. In this instance the defendant had taken instructions from the plaintiff in 1980, but did not institute any proceedings and did not inform the plaintiff of this fact. The earliest point at which the plaintiff could have discovered this fact for herself was in 1987; thus proceedings issued against the defendant in 1990 were not statute barred. Kinlen J, in determining the appropriate time at which the plaintiff could have discovered the relevant fact, rejected the defendant's argument that the plaintiff could have searched the Central Office of the High Court herself at an earlier point.

Section 46 of the 1957 Act precludes the use of the extension in actions against a personal representative of a wrongdoer where the personal representative was not party to the fraud.

---

114 S. 71(1) of the 1957 Act.
115 [1991] 1 IR 284.
116 *Ibid.*, at p. 286.
117 *Ibid.*, at p. 287.
118 Unrep. HC, 3 April 1998; Irish Times Law Report 13 July 1998; see also *Behan v Bank of Ireland* [1998] 2 ILRM 507.

Contribution Actions

A contribution action, taken by one wrongdoer against another, may be brought within the limitation period applicable to the injured person or within 'two years after the liability of the claimant is ascertained or the injured person's damages are paid, whichever is the greater'.[119] This means that the defendant in the contribution action is prone to action for a number of years beyond the initial limitation period applicable to the injured party. This is because the injured party may bring a claim against one wrongdoer towards the end of the appropriate limitation period; the litigation may take some years to be resolved and the wrongdoer then has two further years in which to initiate a contribution action.

Other Special Extensions

The case law on the limitation of actions has also thrown up some additional variants on the operation of the statutory provisions. In *Poole v O'Sullivan*[120] Morris J held that where the expiry date for the limitation period was one on which the court was closed then, where some action by the court was needed to complete the plaintiff's task in initiating the claim, the limitation period would extend to the end of the next day that the court was open. A more extensive extension is available in cases where the defendant is estopped from pleading the statute. The Supreme Court in *Doran v Thomas Thompson & Sons Ltd*[121] held that a representation by the defendant, which induced the plaintiff to reasonably believe that liability would be admitted and, in consequence, induced the plaintiff to refrain from initiating proceedings, would give rise to an estoppel, denying the defendant recourse to the protection of limitations provisions.[122] Such a representation would, however, have to be clear and unambiguous.[123] In this case the medical practitioner appointed by the defendants examined the plaintiff after the limitation period had expired, but this was held to be insufficient to give rise to an estoppel. In *Curran v Carolan & Boyle Ltd*[124] Johnson J held that two express requests by the defendant's solicitor to the plaintiff's solicitor not to issue proceedings were sufficient to give rise to an estoppel, where the plaintiff's solicitor had already expressed his concern about the expiry of the limitation period and had the statement of claim drafted.

---

119 S. 31 of the Civil Liability Act 1961.
120 [1993] ILRM 55.
121 [1978] IR 223.
122 The courts have generally considered that it is necessary to plead the limitation provisions in order to benefit from them, despite the apparently imperative wording of the provisions; see, for example, Henchy J in *O'Domhnaill v Merrick* [1984] IR 151; [1985] ILRM 40, at p. 158; p. 45; *Touhy v Courtney* [1994] 2 ILRM 503.
123 [1978] IR 223, at p. 225 per Henchy J; p. 230 per Griffin J; p. 237 per Kenny J.
124 Unrep. HC, 26 February 1993.

Reduced Limitation Periods

There are a number of situations where the operation of special limitation provisions can reduce the amount of time available to bring claims. These provisions do not reduce the period in every case, but can have that effect in some cases.

Admiralty

Section 46(2) of the Civil Liability Act 1961 prescribes a two year period in respect of damage or injury caused by the sole or concurrent fault of a vessel to another vessel or to persons or property on board a vessel, though the court has a discretion under section 46(3) to extend this time limit and must do so if there has not been a reasonable opportunity to arrest the offending vessel. The relevant factors in respect of the exercise of the discretion were set out by Barr J in *Carleton v O'Regan*[125] as the degree of blameworthiness of the parties; the length of the delay; whether the delay was due to circumstances beyond the plaintiff's control; and whether justice would be done between the parties if the extension were granted.

Actions Against the Estate of a Deceased Person

Section 9(2) of the Civil Liability Act 1961 provides a special limitation period in respect of actions surviving against the estate of deceased persons. As originally drafted, such an action could only be maintained if it was either:

(i) pending at the date of death, having been commenced within the ordinary limitation period, or
(ii) commenced within the lesser of the following:
    (a) the ordinary limitation period, or
    (b) two years after death.

The effect of this was that in certain cases the limitation period would be reduced. In the event of a tortfeasor being killed in the incident causing the damage to the plaintiff, the period would be reduced to the minimum period of two years. The reason for this reduction appears to be to provide certainty in respect of the administration of the estate of the deceased, by providing an outer limit of two years after death for the making of tort claims against it. The constitutionality of this provision was tested in *Moynihan v Greensmyth*,[126] where the Supreme Court

---

125 [1997] 1 ILRM 370, extension denied as the plaintiff had been aware that time was running out and the quantum of damages was still in dispute and agreement had not been reached on the question of an extension of the limitation period, though the matter had been discussed; *Lawless v Dublin Port & Docks Board* [1998] 1 ILRM 514, extension granted as the plaintiff had a reasonable, but mistaken, belief that the reduced period under s. 46(2) only applied to actions *in rem* and not actions *in personam*.
126 [1977] IR 55.

418

held that the provision was valid, reflecting a reasonable balance between the competing interests of the parties. The provision has now been slightly modified, in that it does not apply to claims under the Liability for Defective Products Act 1991;[127] otherwise it takes effect in the manner described.

Product Liability

Actions under the Liability for Defective Products Act 1991 are subject to a limitation period of three years and time runs from the accrual of the cause of action, or the date on which the plaintiff became (or should reasonably have become) aware of the damage, defect and producer's identity, whichever is later.[128] This is qualified by the provision that the right of action under the Act ceases ten years after the producer put the actual product which caused the damage into circulation, unless proceedings have already been instituted.[129] Under the first of these two provisions actions for damage to property are subject to a shorter than usual period of limitation. The second provision provides producers with a degree of certainty and finality with respect to the bringing of actions but it may reduce the limitation period for some plaintiffs. This provision is protected against any constitutional challenge by Article 29.4.5° of the Constitution. The constitutional provision precludes the use of the Constitution to invalidate laws 'necessitated by the obligations of membership of the European Union or of the Communities'. As the provision of the ten year time bar, contained in section 7(2) of the 1991 Act, was mandated by Article 11 of the Directive on Products Liability, it benefits from the protection of Article 29.4.5°.

Detinue and Conversion

In respect of detinue and conversion the limitation period begins to run from the time of the initial wrongdoing and subsequent acts of detinue or conversion do not give rise to separate periods of limitation.[130] Thus in the case of such subsequent wrongs there is a shortened period of limitation. The impact of the limitations provision is made more severe by the fact that expiry of the limitation period will lead to extinction of the plaintiff's title, unless action has been taken by the plaintiff.[131]

---

127 S. 7(3) of the Liability for Defective Products Act 1991 excludes the operation of s. 9 and s. 48(6) of the Civil Liability Act 1961 in respect of claims arising under the 1991 Act.
128 S. 7(1) of the Liability for Defective Products Act 1991.
129 S. 7(2) of the Liability for Defective Products Act 1991.
130 S. 12(1) of the 1957 Act; s. 26 provides exceptions in respect of chattels held on trust.
131 S. 12(2) of the 1957 Act.

Air Transport

A reduced limitation period of two years applies to accidents occurring in the course of air transport. This is provided for by section 17(1) of the Air Navigation and Transport Act 1936, which incorporates the provisions of the Warsaw Convention into Irish law. The reduced limitation period is contained in Article 29(1) of the Convention and runs from either the date of arrival, the date the plaintiff ought to have arrived, or the date on which the carriage actually stopped. Under Article 17 the provision applies to accidents occurring on board an aircraft, or during the course of embarking or disembarking operations. The High Court held, in *Burke v Aer Lingus*,[132] that travel in a shuttle bus from an aircraft to a passenger terminal constitutes an operation within the scope of the Convention.

Judicial Discretion

Section 5 of the Statute of Limitations 1957 provides that the equitable jurisdiction of the courts to refuse relief is not affected by the Act. Therefore, the fact that an action is commenced within the limitation period is no guarantee that it will be allowed to proceed. There are two principal areas of discretion to be considered – the first is the dismissal of 'stale' claims; the other is dismissal for want of prosecution. The first area concerns delay in bringing the claim; the second concerns delay in prosecuting the case after it has been initiated.[133] The central issue for the court was succinctly stated by Henchy J in *O'Domhnaill v Merrick*:[134]

> In all cases the problem of the court would seem to be to strike a balance between a plaintiff's need to carry on his or her delayed claim against a defendant and the defendant's basic right not to be subjected to a claim which he or she could not reasonably be expected to defend.

The bulk of cases are concerned with dismissal for want of prosecution and the leading statement of the applicable principles is that of Finlay P in *Rainsford v Corporation of Limerick*.[135] The requirements are:

---

132 [1997] 1 ILRM 148.
133 Delay in initiating a claim is dealt with by statute in England, s. 33 of the Limitation Act 1980; see Jones, *Limitation Periods in Personal Injury Actions* (London: Blackstone Press, 1995) at chapter 3.
134 [1984] IR 151; [1985] ILRM 40, at p. 157; p. 44.
135 Noted in the report of *O'Domhnaill v Merrick* [1984] IR 151, at pp. 152–4; [1995] 2 ILRM 561 (the actual date of the High Court decision was 31 July 1979); see also Jones, *op. cit.* at chapter 6.

(i) that the delay has been both inordinate and inexcusable, and

(ii) the court must also consider whether the 'balance of justice' favours dismissal or continuing with the action.[136]

The position was somewhat clouded by the Supreme Court decision in *Toal v Duignan (No. 1)*,[137] where, after citing *Rainsford*, Finlay CJ stated that:

> . . . where there is a clear and patent unfairness in asking a defendant to defend a case after a very long lapse of time between the acts complained of and the trial, then if that defendant has not himself contributed to the delay, irrespective of whether the plaintiff has contributed to it or not, the court may as a matter of justice have to dismiss the action.[138]

It is difficult to reconcile this statement with the requirement that delay be both inordinate and inexcusable, since it permits dismissal where there has been no contribution to the delay by the plaintiff. What is clear from the cases is that the respective interests of the parties must be balanced against each other, a point which was emphasised by Barron J in *Moroney v D'Allesandro*,[139] where he rejected the possibility of taking account of the deterrent effect a dismissal would have on others bringing stale claims.

The decision in *Toal v Duignan (No. 2)*[140] indicates that the onus is on the defendant to establish a probability of injustice if the case is allowed to continue, before the discretion will be exercised in his favour.[141] Both the *O'Domhnaill* and *Toal (No. 2)* decisions appear to support the application of the discretion to delays in bringing proceedings, as well as to cases of delay subsequent to initiating claims, but the point is unresolved.[142] Curiously, none of the cases on the question of discretion to dismiss make any reference to section 5 of the 1957 Act.

---

136 *Ibid.*, at p. 153; p. 567; see also *Kelly v Cullen & the Mid-Western Health Board*, unrep. SC, 27 July 1998.

137 [1991] ILRM 135.

138 *Ibid.*, at p. 139; for analysis of the decision see White, 'The Limitation of Personal Injuries and Death Actions' (1991) ILSI Gaz 37.

139 Unrep. HC, 4 February 1993, at p. 4 of the judgment.

140 [1991] ILRM 140.

141 *Ibid.*, at p. 145 per Finlay CJ (Griffin J concurring).

142 In *Hogan v Jones* [1994] 1 ILRM 512 the parties conceded that the discretion could not apply to a delay in bringing the action and Murphy J quoted a passage from *Birkett v James* [1977] 2 All ER 801 supporting that view.

CHAPTER THIRTEEN

Parties to Tort Actions

Introduction

The law of torts has a number of specialised rules related to the participation of certain categories of person as parties to a tort action. These rules are not subject to any single unifying principle or theory, but are merely *ad hoc* developments, designed to deal with particular sets of circumstances. One particular category of participant – persons responsible for the conduct of others – are of greater practical significance and are considered separately in the next chapter.

The State

The concept of royal prerogative at common law precluded the bringing of an action against central government for the actions of its officials. This principle was thought to have been carried over into Ireland after independence, so as to prevent the state being sued for damage inflicted by the conduct of state employees. It was common, in both Ireland and other common law jurisdictions, to mitigate the harshness of this principle by introducing legislative provisions allowing some actions against the state.[1] There was a dramatic reappraisal of the question of state immunity in tort in *Byrne v Ireland and the AG*.[2]

The plaintiff instituted proceedings against the state for injuries which she alleged to have occurred as a result of the negligence of persons employed by the Department of Posts and Telegraphs. She claimed that their negligent repair of a footpath, after the digging of a trench, caused the subsidence of the path, causing her to fall when she was lawfully walking on it. The defence claimed immunity from suit.

The Supreme Court held that the state was not immune from liability. The primary reason for this finding was that ultimate sovereignty lay with the people under the Constitution, not with the state as a distinct entity; thus the state must ultimately be answerable to the people and cannot, in any general sense, be above the law. This decision represents a strong and bold application

---

1 See the Crown Proceedings Act 1947 (England); the Federal Tort Claims Act 1945 (America); for a general discussion of the American position, including the immunity of state governments, see Prosser et al., *Prosser & Keeton on the Law of Torts*, 5th ed. (1984) at §131; see Balkin & Davis, *Law of Torts* (Sydney: Butterworths, 1991) at p. 877 for a list of relevant legislation in Australia, relating to states, territories and federal liability.

2 [1972] IR 241; for detailed analysis see Osborough, 'The Demise of the State's Immunity in Tort' (1973) 8 Ir Jur 275; Osborough, 'The State's Tortious Liability: Further Reflections on *Byrne v Ireland*' (1976) 11 Ir Jur 11 and 279.

of the concept of the rule of law. The general principle that those that govern should be answerable under the law on the same basis as those governed was applied so as to make the state subject to ordinary principles of tort law. On the facts the liability issue was one of vicarious liability, but it would seem that direct liability should also apply in suitable cases.[3]

There are numerous examples of actions against the state since this decision and it would be fair to say that, although the state is more likely than a private individual to be able to successfully invoke public policy arguments, the general principles on which state liability is founded are the same as those applicable to private individuals.[4] Furthermore, the courts have not been unduly deferential or lenient towards the state in the application of tortious principles. The application of the rule of law concept, as applied to state liability in tort, has been reinforced by the development of the action for breach of European Community law and the action for breach of constitutional rights, considered in chapter 9.

Injunctions, however, are normally directed towards the specific state agency engaged in the impugned activity, rather than against 'Ireland', though the state may be included as a party in the proceedings.[5] This does not preclude state responsibility, but does require precision in drafting the application, since the specific agency must be identified.

In light of this, the special principles applicable to local authorities may appear somewhat incongruous and require a brief comment.[6] Those special principles are the absence of liability for nonfeasance and for policy decisions. The nonfeasance issue, in particular, raises the question as to whether local authorities should be held liable for omissions on the same basis as private individuals. The immunity was clearly sensible in the context in which it was developed, where government generally was treated as immune from tortious liability. However, given the absence of any general principle of state immunity, the continuing validity of the nonfeasance rule is open to

---

3 Direct liability would include liability as an employer, strict liability in nuisance or under the *Rylands v Fletcher* principle. A number of torts, such as deceit, passing off or conspiracy, are, by their nature, unlikely to be committed by the state. State liability for defamation is unlikely, due to the scope of the privilege defences. See also *Webb v Ireland* [1988] IR 353; [1988] ILRM 565 where the Supreme Court rejected the view that the royal prerogative of treasure trove had carried over to the state.

4 See, for example, *Ryan v Ireland* [1989] IR 177; [1989] ILRM 544; *Rohan v Ireland* unrep. HC, 19 June 1992 (duty towards members of the defence forces, using ordinary negligence principles); *O'Brien v Ireland* [1995] ILRM 22 (privilege against discovery of certain documents on public policy grounds); *Deighan v Ireland* [1995] 2 IR 56; [1995] 1 ILRM 88 (judicial immunity from suit; the state could not be vicariously liable in the absence of any primary liability on the judge's part).

5 *Pesca Valentia Ltd v Minister for Fisheries and Forestry, Ireland and the AG* [1985] IR 193; [1986] ILRM 68; noted by Casey (1985) 7 DULJ 123; *Beara Fisheries & Shipping Ltd v Minister for the Marine, Ireland and the AG* [1987] IR 413; *Grange Developments Ltd v Dublin County Council* [1989] IR 377.

6 See chapter 2 *supra*, for consideration of local authorities' obligations.

question.[7] One significant aspect of this issue was raised in *The State (Sheehan) v The Government of Ireland*.[8] Section 60 of the Civil Liability Act 1961 removed the immunity of road authorities for nonfeasance, but was not to take effect until a later date, to be specified by the government. The government, however, never brought the section into effect and their failure was questioned in *Sheehan*. Costello J, in the High Court, granted an order of mandamus, compelling the government to implement the provision. The majority in the Supreme Court overturned this decision, adopting a literal approach to the wording of the section, which provided that the government *may* fix a date for its implementation. This case was focused on the relationship between the legislature and the government and, although nonfeasance was the subject of the section in question, the judgments do not directly address the more general question of the continuing validity of the immunity for nonfeasance.

Foreign States

Foreign states are immune from liability in respect of activities other than trading or commercial activities.[9] Officials of foreign states are also given a considerable degree of protection against civil actions under the Diplomatic Relations and Immunities Acts 1967 and 1976 in order to facilitate international relations. There are three categories of personnel for the purposes of the Acts – diplomats, technical and administrative staff and service staff – and these are subject to a descending scale of protection. The limits of the immunities in respect of the law of torts are that diplomats have no immunity in respect of professional or commercial activities outside their official functions; the other two categories have no immunity for any conduct outside their official duties. The immunities are, therefore, primarily confined to official activities, but some latitude is permitted to the more senior officials.[10]

---

7 In fact, the rule had been described as 'anomalous' by Murnaghan J in *O'Brien v Waterford County Council* [1926] IR 1, at p. 8, indicating that doubt on the issue is not new; for more recent doubts as to its validity see Kerr, *The Civil Liability Acts 1961 and 1964* (Dublin: Round Hall Press, 1993) at p. 120; the rule was, however, recently applied in *Convery v Dublin County Council* [1996] 3 IR 156.

8 [1987] IR 550; analysed by Hogan (1987) 9 DULJ 91.

9 *Zarine v Owners of SS Ramava* [1942] IR 148; *Saorstát and Continental Steamship Co. Ltd v De Las Morenas* [1945] IR 291; *Government of Canada v Employment Appeals Tribunal* [1992] 2 IR 484; [1992] ILRM 325; analysed by Byrne & Binchy, *Annual Review of Irish Law 1992* at pp. 90–2 and Heffernan (1992) 14 DULJ 160; *McElhinney v Williams* [1995] 3 IR 382; [1994] 2 ILRM 115; *Schmidt v Home Secretary of the Government of the United Kingdom* [1995] 1 ILRM 301, both of these decisions are analysed by Byrne & Binchy, *Annual Review of Irish Law 1994* at pp. 107–8; *Playa Largo v I. Congreso del Partido* [1983] AC 244; the immunity in English law has been reduced by the State Immunity Act 1978.

10 The detailed provisions are set out in the Vienna Convention on Diplomatic Relations, which is set out in the first schedule to the 1967 Act; s. 5 adopts the provisions into Irish law. A reduced level of immunity applies in respect of

It was held, in *Norton v General Accident, Fire & Life Assurance Co.*,[11] that diplomatic immunity is an exemption from the jurisdiction of the court, rather than from liability. While this makes no practical difference to the official, it does permit the plaintiff to take an action against the insurance company in cases of motor accidents.[12]

The 1967 Act also extends protection to a number of international organisations and their officials, such as the United Nations and its agencies,[13] the Council of Europe[14] and the Organisation for Economic Co-operation and Development.[15] Section 1 of the 1976 Amendment Act permits the extension of protection to other international organisations and their officials. This power has been exercised on a number of occasions for the benefit of organisations such as General Agreement on Tariffs and Trade[16] and the European Bank for Reconstruction and Development.[17]

The European Community/Union

Article 215(2) of the EC Treaty provides for tortious liability of the European Community and includes liability for the wrongs of the institutions and its servants:[18]

> In the case of non-contractual liability, the Community shall, in accordance with the general principles common to the laws of the Member States, make good any damage caused by its institutions or by its servants in the performance of their duties.

The jurisdiction over such claims against the Community is given to the Court of First Instance, with an appeal to the Court of Justice on a point of law.[19] Despite the rather broad statement of liability in principle, it is difficult to maintain a successful action against the Community in practice.

The liability is fault based in the case of individual acts, though the concept of fault does not correspond precisely with negligence at common law.[20]

---

consular relations, s. 6 and the second schedule to the Act (Vienna Convention on Consular Relations).

11 (1939) 74 ILTR 123.

12 S. 76(1)(d) of the Road Traffic Act 1961 allows a direct action against the insurance company in a number of instances. A similar provision under the Road Traffic Act 1933 was applicable in *Norton*.

13 Parts III and IV.

14 Part V.

15 Part VI.

16 SI 465/1994.

17 SI 65/1991; see also SI 144/1992 (re international assistance in cases of nuclear or radiological incidents); SI 186/1992 (re oil pollution).

18 See Steiner, *Enforcing EC Law* (London: Blackstone Press, 1995) at chapter 10 for detailed consideration of Community liability.

19 Art. 168a and Art. 178.

20 Cases 5, 7 and 13–24/66, *Firma E Kampffmeyer v Commission* [1967] ECR 245.

Where the conduct complained of concerns a more general legislative act, involving the exercise of discretion or the making of policy choices, then a serious breach of a rule designed for individual protection is required.[21] Initially a restrictive view was taken of the types of losses recoverable, with damages being confined to actual loss and not extending to lost profits.[22] The Court of Justice has now accepted that lost profits may be claimed, but such a claim is subject to the plaintiff's duty to take reasonable steps to mitigate the loss.[23] A restrictive approach has also been taken on the degree of causal connection required between the breach and the damage.[24]

Community officials and employees are granted immunity from liability for acts done or statements made in their official capacity.[25]

Associations

Some special consideration must be given to the application of tort law in cases involving various associations. Many activities are carried out by collective, rather than individual action. In each case the applicable principles will depend on the type of association involved.

Corporations

By their nature, corporate bodies are incapable of being the victim of a variety of torts, such as trespass to the person.[26] The liability of a corporation for the commission of a tort will usually be vicarious, as it must necessarily act through human agents, though there may be instances where the degree of support within the corporation for a course of action is so strong that the act can be regarded as that of the corporation itself. Apart from these limitations, related to the nature of corporate personality, there are no special rules pertaining to corporations as parties and they can sue or be sued as a distinct legal entity.[27]

---

21 Case 5/71, *Aktien-Zuckerfabrik Schöppenstedt v Council* [1971] ECR 975; Joined Cases C–104/89 and C–37/90, *Mulder v Council and Commission of the EC* [1992] ECR I–3061; noted by Heukels (1993) 30 CML Rev 368.
22 See, for example, Case 74/74, *Comptoire National Technique Agricole SA v Commission* [1975] ECR 533; [1976] ECR 797; [1977] 1 CMLR 171 and Cases 5, 7 and 13–24/66, *Firma E Kampffmeyer v Commission* [1967] ECR 245.
23 Joined Cases C–104/89 and C–37/90, *Mulder v Council and Commission of the EC* [1992] ECR I–3061.
24 Cases 64 and 113/76, *P Dumortier Frères SA v Council* [1979] ECR 3091.
25 The appropriate immunities are set out in the Protocol on Privileges and Immunities of the European Communities, as amended.
26 The capacity of corporations to maintain defamation proceedings has already been dealt with in chapter 8 *supra*.
27 Even where the conduct of a corporation's agent is *ultra vires*, it appears that liability will attach, see *National Telephone Co. Ltd v Constables of St Peter's Port*

Partnerships

A partnership does not have a separate legal personality, so the individual partners are responsible for the liabilities of the firm. It is possible for some partners in a firm to have limited liability, but there must be at least one partner with unlimited liability.[28] A partnership may sue and be sued in the name of the firm, rather than the names of the individual partners.[29]

The general position is that partners are jointly and severally liable for torts committed by any one of them, provided the tort was either authorised by the other partners or carried out in the course of the partnership's business.[30] Partners are also subject to the ordinary principles of vicarious liability, under which they are responsible for torts committed by employees in the course of their employment.

Unincorporated Associations

Unincorporated associations do not have the capacity to sue or be sued in the name of the association; rather the members (or trustees, if there are any) are the proper litigants in respect of the association's affairs. It is possible for one member to act in a representative capacity for all the members, provided there is a common interest in the litigation.[31] The liability of members for the affairs of the association is broadly similar to that of partners, based on principles of agency. Liability depends on the conduct being within the scope of the association's objects or being expressly authorised.[32]

One significant feature of the rules relating to unincorporated associations is that a member may not sue for a tort committed by the association, because the plaintiff would also be a defendant, due to the lack of separate personality for the association.[33] This is so even if trustees are named as defendants, rather than all the members.[34] The rule is harsh, as it precludes action by members, who may be far removed in practice from the administration of the association, in the event of injuries incurred while attending functions run by the association or participating in events on its behalf. The protection of members can be attained through insurance, however, so the harshness of the rule can be offset by the careful arrangement of the association's affairs.

[1900] AC 317; *Campbell v Paddington Corporation* [1911] 1 KB 869; Jenkins, 'Corporate Liability in Tort and the Doctrine of *Ultra Vires*' (1970) 5 Ir Jur 11.

28 Limited Partnerships Act 1907; Investment Limited Partnerships Act 1994.

29 Order 14 of the Rules of the Superior Courts 1986.

30 Ss. 10 and 12 of the Partnership Act 1890.

31 Order 15 of the Rules of the Superior Courts 1986.

32 *Murphy v Roche and Others (No. 2)* [1987] IR 656, at p. 661 per Gannon J; see also *Crean v Nolan and Others* (1963) 97 ILTR 125.

33 *Murphy v Roche and Others (No. 2)* [1987] IR 656; *Kirwan v Mackey and Others* unrep. HC, 18 January 1995.

34 *Nolan v Fagan and Others* unrep. HC, 1 May 1985.

It should be noted that the rule only operates to preclude actions by persons that have been properly appointed as members of the association. In *Walsh v Butler and Others*[35] it was held that a person playing for a rugby club was not a member, as the formal rules of the club for accepting a member were never employed in respect of him. The fact that he had played for the club over a number of years did not make him a member and did not give rise to an estoppel. No finding was reached on whether the payment of a membership subscription would disentitle the plaintiff to bring an action, as he had not paid a subscription for the season in which the injury occurred.

Trade Unions

The regulation of labour relations falls outside the scope of any general text on torts and forms a separate area of study in its own right. It is necessary, however, to outline the statutory protection against liability granted in respect of certain types of conduct in the course of 'trade disputes'. Extensive liability was imposed at common law on those engaged in trade union activities[36] and in *Taff Vale Railway Co. v Amalgamated Society of Railway Servants*[37] it was held that a union could be held liable for its members' actions.[38] The Trade Disputes Act 1906 granted an extensive immunity from civil liability to unions and their officials and also to individual workers. This Act was repealed and replaced by Part II of the Industrial Relations Act 1990.

Section 13 of the 1990 Act provides that a tort action may not be maintained against a trade union (including an employers' association), or its trustees, officials or members, for acts 'committed by or on behalf of the trade union in contemplation or furtherance of a trade dispute'. The Act also contains specific provisions related to particular aspects of labour disputes, which do not depend on the activity being carried out on behalf of a trade union. Collective action in connection with a trade dispute will only amount to a conspiracy if the conduct would also be considered unlawful if carried out by a lone individual.[39] Peaceful picketing at an employer's place of business, for the purpose of communicating information or persuasion of others to refrain from working, is permitted.[40]

---

35 [1997] 2 ILRM 81.

36 For example *Lumley v Gye* (1853) 2 E & B 216; [1843–60] All ER Rep 208 (inducing breach of contract); *Quinn v Leathem* [1901] AC 495; [1900–3] All ER Rep 1 (conspiracy); see chapter 7 *supra*, on the modern parameters of the 'industrial' based torts.

37 [1901] AC 426.

38 Unlike other unincorporated associations, a trade union may sue and be sued in its own name as the *Taff Vale* decision held that the Trade Union Act 1871 had conferred a form of legal personality on unions. In fact s. 9 of the Act had provided for actions to be brought in the name of trustees, but this appears to have been overlooked in the decision.

39 S. 10(2).

40 S. 11(1), this only permits picketing of one's own employer in connection with a trade dispute; s. 11(2) allows secondary picketing of an employer, other than one's own, if

Interference with contractual relations and interference with economic relations are permitted in connection with trade disputes, provided that the means used are not otherwise unlawful.[41]

Section 9 qualifies these provisions, specifying that sections 11, 12 and 13 only apply to unions holding a current negotiating licence under the Trade Union Act 1941[42] and sections 10, 11 and 12 are dependent on agreed procedures for dispute resolution being exhausted.[43] A trade dispute is confined to disputes between employers and workers relating to any aspect of employment, thereby excluding disputes between workers or inter-union disputes.[44]

Sections 10, 11 and 12 delimit the scope of lawful behaviour, making acts within the parameters of the sections lawful, whereas section 13 provides an immunity from suit in respect of torts committed. Sections 10, 11 and 12 apply to non-unionised workers and, probably, to members of unions without a negotiating licence. This is because the sections apply to any person acting on his own behalf in the course of a trade dispute. Thus, any worker who is a party to such a dispute is entitled to engage in any activity covered by the sections, irrespective of union membership. Officials of unions which do not hold a negotiating licence are entitled to the benefit of section 10, since this provision is not subject to the qualification contained in section 9. This means that those officials do not commit conspiracy simply by acting in combination with others. Such officials will not be protected by sections 11 (picketing) and 12 (interference with trade) if they are not acting on their own behalf. This conclusion results from the qualification in section 9. Section 13 (the immunity from suit for torts) applies exclusively to unions holding a negotiating licence. Section 9 precludes unlicensed unions from benefiting. In respect of individuals, the wording of section 13 plainly states that trustees, members and officials are immune from suit when they are sued 'on behalf of themselves *and all other members of the trade union*'.[45] This makes it clear that the section does not provide protection against tort actions for individuals acting on their own behalf and engaged in conduct outside the scope of sections 10, 11 and 12.

The Motor Insurers' Bureau of Ireland

The victims of uninsured or untraceable drivers may, in some instances, recover compensation through the Motor Insurers' Bureau of Ireland, under an agreement

---

that other has assisted one's employer for the purpose of frustrating industrial action. Trade union officials are also allowed to participate in peaceful picketing – s. 11(4).

41 S. 12.

42 S. 9(1).

43 S. 9(2); s. 17 further provides that these sections do not apply to actions in disregard of the outcome of a secret ballot; see *Nolan Transport (Oaklands) Ltd v Halligan and Others* unrep. SC, 15 May 1998 (Murphy J in particular) on the interpretation of s. 17.

44 S. 8.

45 Emphasis added.

between the government and the insurance companies. The action is clearly not one in tort, but makes up for a practical deficiency of the tort system. The general position is that full compensation is available for personal injuries caused by an uninsured or untraceable driver; property damage caused by an uninsured driver is recoverable up to the level of minimum compulsory insurance under the Road Traffic Act 1961, subject to a small threshold borne by the victim; property damage caused by an untraceable driver is not recoverable, to avoid the risk of fraudulent claims by people who had damaged their own property.[46] The problem of injuries caused by foreign motorists is dealt with under a similar scheme administered by the Irish Visiting Motorists' Bureau.[47]

Minors

We have already seen that special problems arise in respect of child plaintiffs and the defence of consent in trespass.[48] Further problems arise in respect of children's responsibility for their own conduct. As with many aspects of the law, the law of torts raises special questions with respect to children's responsibility. There are three distinct issues to be considered – the responsibility of minors for contributing to their own injuries; the liability of minors for damage caused to others; and parental responsibility for the conduct of a minor. Consideration of the third question is deferred until the next chapter, on responsibility for others, but it may be noted at this point that there is no general principle of parental responsibility in tort for the conduct of children. In relation to the other two issues, the general position is that the objective approach normally employed in tort law is tempered by subjective considerations when dealing with children.

Contributory Negligence

Most reported cases dealing with children's responsibility in tort concern contributory negligence. Very young children are incapable of contributory negligence, because it is not practicable to expect them to take precautions for their own safety.[49] There is, however, no precise age at which it can be said, as a matter of law, that a child is capable of contributory negligence. The reported cases do establish that children as young as six or seven have been found

---

46 For further consideration of the operation of the scheme see Madden, 'The Uninsured or Untraceable Driver: MIBI Litigation' (1995) 13 ILT 52; McMahon & Binchy, *The Irish Law of Torts*, 2nd ed. (Dublin: Butterworths, 1989) at pp. 29–31.
47 See Madden, *loc. cit.*
48 Chapter 4 *supra.*
49 *Cooke v Midland Great Western Railway of Ireland* [1908] IR 242, at p. 268 per Palles CB; *Fleming v Kerry County Council* [1955–6] Ir Jur Rep 71, at p. 72 per O'Byrne J.

capable of contributory negligence and there is a general reluctance to impose responsibility on children below this age bracket.[50]

Once it is determined that a child is capable, as a matter of law, of contributory negligence a further question arises as to the standard to be employed in measuring the child's behaviour.[51] The appropriate test is that set out by O'Byrne J in *Fleming v Kerry County Council*:[52] 'In the case of a child, the standard is what may reasonably be expected, having regard to the age and mental development of the child and the other circumstances of the case.' This appears to be a subjective test, based on the capacity of the particular child in the specific circumstances, but some subsequent *dicta* raised doubts, giving rise to the possibility that the appropriate test might be the reasonable child of the plaintiff's age.[53] The more subjective standard, taking account of age, mental development and personal experience, has, however, found favour in the Supreme Court subsequently.[54] The Law Reform Commission has described this standard as that of 'a reasonable child of the same age, mental development and experience as the plaintiff' and has recommended its retention in determining contributory negligence.[55] This approach uses an objective formulation, with considerable concessions to the subjective circumstances of the plaintiff.

The facts of *McNamara v ESB*[56] clearly demonstrate the nature of this standard in practice and show that its application is not free from doubt. The plaintiff was an eleven year old boy, living in Limerick city. He was seriously injured while playing in an ESB sub-station near his home, to which he had gained access by climbing over an inadequate fence. The plaintiff had previously played there and had been told to go away from there by passers-by and by his father, but the reasons for keeping away were not explained to him.

---

50 *O'Donovan v Landy's Ltd* [1963] IR 441, at p. 449 per Kingsmill-Moore J, *obiter*, in respect of a six and a half year old; *Brennan v Savage Smyth & Co.* [1982] ILRM 223, where a seven and a half year old was found guilty of contributory negligence; see Law Reform Commission, *Report on the Liability in Tort of Minors and the Liability of Parents for Damage Caused by Minors* (Dublin: Law Reform Commission, 1985) (LRC 17–1985) at pp. 5 *et seq.*

51 The distinction between the initial question of law as to the child's capacity for contributory negligence and the factual question as to whether the standard was breached was particularly important in the case of jury trials – see LRC 17–1985, *op. cit.* at pp. 5–7; the distinction is of reduced importance since the abolition of juries for most personal injuries actions by s. 1 of the Courts Act 1988 and s. 6 of the Courts Act 1971; see chapter 12 *supra*, for further discussion of this issue.

52 [1955–6] Ir Jur Rep 71, at p. 72.

53 *Duffy v Fahy* [1960] Ir Jur Rep 69, at p. 74 per Lavery J; *Kingston v Kingston* (1965) 102 ILTR 65, at p. 67 per Walsh J; see also McMahon & Binchy, *op. cit.* at p. 719 for further examples.

54 *McNamara v ESB* [1975] IR 1, at pp. 17–18 per Walsh J (Budd J concurring), p. 36 per Griffin J; a more ambivalent stance was adopted by Henchy J, at p. 27 and Fitzgerald CJ; *Brennan v Savage Smyth & Co.* [1982] ILRM 223.

55 LRC 17–1985, *op. cit.* at pp. 45–7.

56 [1975] IR 1.

He was able to read and had seen warning notices posted around the sub-station, but had not read them. Therefore, the plaintiff knew that he should not be in the sub-station, but was unaware of the danger which it posed to him.

The minority view in the Supreme Court was that these facts were sufficient to support the jury verdict that there was no contributory negligence on the plaintiff's part.[57] The majority view was that the verdict was not supported by the evidence. Henchy J provides the clearest application of the standard to the facts:

> The jury were, of course, entitled to accept the plaintiff's evidence that he was ignorant of the danger from electricity if he climbed over the fence. But they were not entitled to excuse that ignorance when it resulted from his culpable failure to read the warning notices, and when that failure contributed substantially to the happening of the accident . . . it was perversely indulgent of them to excuse his unaccountable failure to read notices which he admitted having seen . . .[58]

This statement demonstrates the limits of the level of subjectivity that ought to be permitted in assessing a child's responsibility. While a child's individual abilities and circumstances are relevant, an objective view must be taken on the question of whether the child has made sufficient use of his capabilities.

Liability as a Principal Wrongdoer

Actions against children, as principal wrongdoers, are rare, which is not surprising when one considers that children will rarely have the resources to compensate the victims of their actions and there is no general principle of parental responsibility for a child's torts. The result is that there is a lack of clear guidance from the courts on the extent of a minor's liability.

Strict liability torts may initially seem unproblematic – as no intent or neglect is required, minority status should afford no special protection. However, even strict liability torts require some initial voluntary conduct, such as the accumulation of a hazardous item under the *Rylands v Fletcher* principle or a voluntary communication in defamation. It may not be appropriate to consider the actions of very young children as voluntary at all; as the Law Reform Commission points out, 'voluntariness involves the direction and control over conduct by a conscious mind'.[59] The commission also cites the decision of the Ontario High Court in

---

57 *Ibid.*, per Walsh and Budd JJ; the Supreme Court decision produced a curious majority on this issue. The court held, by a 4:1 majority, that a duty was owed to the plaintiff. However, the four judges in the majority on the main issue were split evenly on the question of contributory negligence. The dissenting judge, Fitzgerald CJ, found it necessary to rule on contributory negligence, in light of the imposition of a duty by the majority; he held, at p. 8, that the plaintiff had been negligent.
58 *Ibid.*, at p. 27 and p. 28.
59 LRC 17–1985, *op. cit.* at p. 2.

Tillander v Gosselin,[60] where Grant J refused to treat the conduct of a three year old, dragging an infant on the ground causing a skull fracture, as voluntary.

In the case of the trespass torts, the voluntariness issue is compounded by the need to establish intention or negligence, with respect to the initial impact on the plaintiff. In the case of young children it may be that they are incapable of forming the necessary mental state, but there is uncertainty as to the precise age at which a child is capable of being held responsible. In *O'Brien v McNamee*[61] liability was imposed on a seven year old for trespass, where he left a lighted paper in a hay barn, causing the entire barn to burn down. Davitt P, however, suggested that the situation would be different if the tort required intent as to the consequences.[62] In such cases it could be difficult to establish the requisite mental state, even in a child somewhat older than the defendant in *O'Brien v McNamee.*[63] There is a lack of authority on the responsibility of children younger than seven, but one surely cannot go much further back in fixing a starting point for responsibility and, in practical terms, there would seem to be little point in doing so.

In the tort of negligence, where an objective measure of behaviour based on societal expectations has generally prevailed, the position is unclear. Leading commentators suggest that the principles of responsibility in negligence should be the same as those used in cases of contributory negligence,[64] and the Law Reform Commission has recommended this approach for children under sixteen.[65] Some jurisdictions have adopted a two tiered system in respect of minor defendants in negligence cases – where they are involved in 'adult activities' they are held to the ordinary standard of care, but in other situations a reduced standard is applied.[66] The Law Reform Commission recommendation, after detailed consideration, was against the adoption of such an approach in Ireland,[67] but did recommend the introduction of a special compensation fund for

---

60 [1967] 1 OR 203.

61 [1953] IR 86.

62 *Ibid.,* at p. 88. It should be recalled that trespass only requires intent or negligence with respect to the initial contact with the plaintiff's land; it does not require any such mental state in respect of the ensuing damage.

63 Many of the torts discussed in chapters 7 and 10 *supra* would prove problematic in cases involving minors as defendants; see also McMahon & Binchy, *op. cit.* at p. 714; LRC 17–1985, *op. cit.* at pp. 62 *et seq.*, recommending that the onus should be on the minor to establish a lack of responsibility in trespass, based on age, mental development and experience, and recommending no change in the law in respect of intentional torts.

64 McMahon & Binchy, *op. cit.* at p. 722; Heuston & Buckley, *Salmond & Heuston on the Law of Torts,* 21st ed. (London: Sweet & Maxwell, 1996) at pp. 411–12.

65 LRC 17–1985, *op. cit.* at p. 53.

66 See Prosser & Keeton, *op. cit.* at pp. 179 *et seq.; Restatement, Second, Torts* §283A (America), the same two tiered approach is taken to the contributory negligence of a minor; *Taurunga Electric Power Board v Karora* [1939] NZLR 1040 (New Zealand).

67 LRC 17–1985, *op. cit.* at pp. 14 *et seq.* and pp. 53 *et seq.*

injuries caused by drivers under sixteen, where no other source of compensation was available to the plaintiff.[68]

Mentally Disabled Persons

Mental disability can arise as a natural condition from birth, as a result of physical damage to the brain or as a result of mental illness. However it arises, it raises important questions as to how the law should apply in respect of such persons, an issue succinctly expressed by the Law Reform Commission in outlining its approach to proposals for reform:

> Our aim . . . is to accommodate in as sensitive a manner as possible the goals of establishing just and humane criteria of legal responsibility with those of protecting the legitimate interests and expectations of the members of society . . . [69]

There are several issues to be considered, falling into two general categories – the responsibility of mentally disabled persons for their own conduct and special provisions in actions alleging wrongdoing against a mentally disabled person.

Responsibility of Mentally Disabled Persons

There is an even greater paucity of case law in this area than in the case of the responsibility of minors, though in principle the main issues are much the same. Despite the similarity of issues, the solutions need not be identical, given the differences in the types of incapacity involved.

Trespass and Strict Liability

All torts require some initial voluntary conduct on the part of the tortfeasor, so a person lacking the mental capacity to be regarded as acting voluntarily will not be held responsible for his conduct. Unfortunately there is no clear guidance as to the degree of incapacity needed in order to relieve a person of responsibility.[70]

In *Morriss v Marsden*[71] the defendant, who 'knew the nature and quality of his act, but whose incapacity of reason arising from the disease of his mind was of so grave a character that he did not know that what he was doing was wrong',[72] was

---

68 *Ibid.*, at p. 59 *et seq.*
69 Law Reform Commission, *Report on the Liability in Tort of Mentally Disabled Persons* (Dublin: Law Reform Commission, 1985) (LRC 18–1985) at p. 1.
70 The law in a number of jurisdictions is extensively reviewed by the Law Reform Commission, LRC 18–1985, *op. cit.* at chapters 2 and 3 (dealing with common law and civil law jurisdictions respectively).
71 [1952] 1 All ER 925, noted by Todd (1952) 15 MLR 486; the defendant, suffering from schizophrenia, was a guest in a hotel and he struck the hotel manager on the head with a blunt instrument.
72 *Ibid.*, at pp. 926–7.

held liable for assault and battery. This was followed in Ireland in *Donoghue v Coyle*,[73] a decision of the Circuit Court. Since knowledge of wrongfulness is not ordinarily a requisite element of the trespass torts, it seems fair that the absence of such knowledge or understanding should not afford an excuse to a defendant. A different approach was taken in New Zealand in *Beals v Hayward*.[74] McGregor J held that a defendant's knowledge of the nature and quality of an act may not be sufficient to support a finding that the act was voluntary; furthermore, even if the act is treated as voluntary, it does not automatically follow that the defendant should be treated as intending the impact on the plaintiff. On the facts, the defendant was held not liable in trespass for firing a starting pistol, taking a child's eye out, despite a finding that he was capable of understanding the nature and quality of the act.

The Law Reform Commission recommended that a person should be relieved of responsibility on the basis that his conduct was involuntary when the following criteria are satisfied:

(a) that the defendant was so affected by mental disability as substantially to lack the capacity to act freely, and
(b) that as a result of this substantial lack of capacity the defendant did the act complained of . . .[75]

Intent, Negligence and Contributory Negligence

Some torts require a specific mental element, such as intent to harm or malice, in addition to the capacity for voluntary conduct. In such cases the liability of a mentally disabled person is probably dependent on having the capacity to form the necessary mental state, though there is a lack of clear authority on the issue.[76]

Negligence gives rise to greater difficulty, as the modern law treats negligence more as a standard of social expectation than as a particular mental state. In using an objective measure of the standard, the law disregards a variety of subjective aspects of ability and capacity. The question then arises as to whether this objective social standard should be applied to mentally deficient defendants, or should mental disability provide an excuse? Support can be found for either alternative and no clear view has emerged.

---

73 [1953–4] Ir Jur Rep 30.
74 [1960] NZLR 131.
75 LRC 18–1985, *op. cit.* at p. 58 in respect of trespass and p. 61 in respect of other torts. It also recommended, at pp. 60–1, that a mistake resulting from mental disability should only afford a defence if a defence of mistake would be available to a fully competent adult.
76 There is tentative support for such a rule in some *dicta*, see *Donaghy v Brennan* (1900) 19 NZLR 289, per Connolly J at p. 294; Stout CJ, for the Court of Appeal, at p. 299; *Emmens v Pottle* (1885) 16 QBD 354, per Lord Esher at p. 356. See LRC 18–1985, *op. cit.* at p. 61 recommending this approach.

The *Second Restatement of the Law of Torts* supports the view that the ordinary standard of care should be applicable to mentally disabled persons, unless they are children.[77] This is justified on a number of grounds, including, first, the difficulty in drawing a dividing line between disabilities for which allowance may be made and those for which no allowance should be made; and, secondly, the possibility of false claims of mental disability.[78] There are some judicial decisions, however, which suggest that a defendant should not be held responsible where he cannot appreciate the duty to take care.[79] This approach is justifiable on the grounds that negligence requires some appreciation of the distinction between prudent and dangerous behaviour. Against this, it may be argued that modern negligence law is so devoid of any question of moral blameworthiness that many mentally competent adults are incapable of appreciating the nature of the obligation imposed on them by law.

A further question arises as to whether a mentally disabled plaintiff should be held responsible for contributory negligence, thereby reducing the amount of compensation that he may recover. Because contributory negligence involves a lack of care for oneself, without necessarily exposing others to risk, the public policy argument for full responsibility, based on social expectations, is somewhat weaker than in negligence cases. Allowance is more likely to be made for mental disability in respect of contributory negligence.

The Law Reform Commission has recommended a single rule for both negligence and contributory negligence, under which the ordinary standard of care would apply to a person unless:

(a) at the time of the act in question, he or she was suffering from a serious mental disability which affected him or her in the performance of the act, and

(b) that disability was such as to have made him or her unable to behave according to the standard of care appropriate to the reasonable person.[80]

This differs from the approach taken to minors, in that it does not use a modified standard of care, but divides situations into ones of full responsibility and no responsibility.

Actions by Mentally Disabled Persons

Where a mentally disabled person is the plaintiff, the ordinary rules of tort normally apply. However, if the defendant's conduct was purported to be done

---

77 §283B; §283A provides that the standard for children is that of a reasonable child of the same age, intelligence and experience.
78 §283B, comment b.
79 *Buckley and Toronto Transport Commission v Smith Transport Ltd* [1946] OR 798; *Breunig v American Family Insurance Co.* (1970) 45 Wis 2d 536; 173 NW 2d 619.
80 LRC 18–1985, *op. cit.* at p. 70.

pursuant to the provisions of the Mental Treatment Acts 1945–61, then a preliminary application must be brought to the High Court for permission to institute proceedings and such permission can only be granted where the court is 'satisfied that there are substantial grounds for contending that the person against whom the proceedings are to be brought acted in bad faith or without reasonable care'.[81] It should be noted that this provision also applies to persons suspected to be suffering from mental illness, who have been detained under the powers provided in the Acts. The purpose of the restriction would seem to be to protect those invoking or implementing the Acts' provisions against spurious claims, by inserting a preliminary phase to the proceedings to weed out unfounded actions.

The case law has been predominantly concerned with actions arising out of involuntary detention under Part XIV of the 1945 Act. The prescribed procedure is that a person (usually a relative) makes an application to a registered medical practitioner (usually a GP) to have a person detained;[82] the practitioner must visit and examine the person within twenty-four hours of receiving the application and either make a recommendation to have the person removed to a mental hospital or refuse the application;[83] on being brought to a hospital the person must be examined by a psychiatrist, who must decide whether to receive or release the person.[84] Despite the deprivation of liberty involved, it has been held that this process is not an administration of justice requiring judicial sanction. The process is seen by the judiciary as a benign exercise of a paternalistic function, despite the potential adverse impact on a person who is detained but found not to be mentally ill.[85]

The case law to date has been particularly favourable to medical practitioners, leaving applicants under section 260 of the 1945 Act with a considerable threshold to surmount in order to obtain leave to institute proceedings. In order to convince the court that there are substantial grounds to support an action, it is not enough for the plaintiff to establish a *prima facie* case, but he does not have to prove that the substantive action will probably succeed.[86] This means that the plaintiff has to establish facts which do more than simply raise a case for the

---

81 S. 260 of the 1945 Act; sub-s. 2 provides that the proposed defendant must be notified of the application and is entitled to contest it.

82 S. 162 of the 1945 Act as amended by s. 6 of the 1961 Act. Where the application is not by or at the request of a relative, reasons must be given to explain why it is not so; s. 165 makes special provision for a police officer to take a person into custody, in the interests of public safety or that of the person detained, and then make an application.

83 S. 163, a recommendation must record a number of details, in particular a statement of facts supporting the opinion that detention is required; s. 167 provides that the person must be brought to the hospital within seven days or the recommendation lapses. See *Melly v Moran and the North Western Health Board*, unrep. SC, 28 May 1998.

84 S. 171; slight variations of this process apply in cases of private patients (ss. 177–183) and in cases of temporary reception (ss. 184 and 185).

85 *In Re Philip Clarke* [1950] IR 235, s. 165 survived a constitutional challenge; s. 172 survived a similar challenge in *Croke v Smith (No. 2)* [1998] 1 IR 101.

86 *Murphy v Greene* [1990] 2 IR 566.

defendant to answer, but may fall short of proving the commission of a tort. This makes the test difficult to pinpoint accurately. The plaintiff's case is further hampered by the possibility that the standard of care imposed on medical practitioners exercising functions under the Acts may be more lenient than in other situations.[87]

The interpretation of the procedural aspects of involuntary detention provide additional difficulties for a plaintiff. In *O'Reilly v Moroney*[88] a general practitioner signed a recommendation to have the plaintiff removed to a mental hospital based on information provided to him by her husband and father and on his own observation of her behaviour when he called to her home (at which point she was involved in a dispute with her husband). The majority in the Supreme Court held that he had conducted a sufficient examination of the plaintiff. Thus, persons can be temporarily deprived of their liberty, without even having an opportunity to respond to the allegation. Furthermore, in *O'Dowd v North Western Health Board*[89] the majority in the Supreme Court were satisfied that the plaintiff had been received in accordance with the requirements of section 171 of the 1945 Act, despite the fact that the psychiatrist who signed the reception order was not the doctor who examined the plaintiff on his arrival at the hospital and that the order was not signed until three hours after the plaintiff had been compulsorily detained at the hospital.

Concurrent Wrongdoers

There are many situations in which more than one person is responsible for the commission of a tort. Part III of the Civil Liability Act 1961, as amended, governs the allocation of responsibility between multiple wrongdoers. These provisions simplified the law greatly and removed a number of anomalies, which created unnecessary obstacles to the recovery of compensation. Complications remain in this area, but these result chiefly from the complex nature of the factual situations that the law must regulate, rather than the legal rules themselves. The rules in this area fall into two general categories – principles on the allocation of responsibility and procedural rules. The present discussion is confined to wrongdoers other than the injured person; the issue of the plaintiff's own responsibility, as a wrongdoer in respect of his own injury, has already been addressed.[90]

Concurrent Liability

Prior to 1961 the law in respect of multiple wrongdoers was governed by the principles on joint and several liability at common law, as amended by the Joint

---

87 *Ibid.*, at p. 566 per McCarthy J; *O'Reilly v Moroney* unrep. SC, 16 November 1993, per Egan J at p. 10 of his judgment; Blayney J, dissenting, suggested that the standard should be very high, due to the drastic consequences in respect of personal liberty, at p. 17 of his judgment; the case is analysed by O'Neill (1994) 12 ILT 211.
88 Unrep. SC, 16 November 1993.
89 [1982] ILRM 186; Henchy J recorded a trenchant dissent.
90 Chapter 12 *supra*, under the defence of contributory negligence.

Tortfeasors Act 1951. These provisions have now been replaced by those contained in Part III of the 1961 Act. The primary purpose of this Part of the Act is to maximise the plaintiff's ability to recover adequate compensation, by protecting against the possible inability of some wrongdoers to provide their just share.[91]

Concurrent Wrongdoers Defined

Concurrent wrongdoers are defined as any 'two or more persons . . . when both or all are wrongdoers and are responsible to a third person . . . for the same damage'.[92] The wrongs may involve any combination of tort, breach of contract or breach of trust.[93] The key feature in defining concurrent wrongdoers is that the wrong of each must lead to the one injury to the plaintiff;[94] this may arise where the wrongdoers have acted in concert to cause a single injury to the plaintiff or where the independent wrongs of separate wrongdoers have led to a single injury to the plaintiff.[95] In fact, it is not even necessary for all the wrongdoers to have actually participated in the injury of the plaintiff; for example, an employer may be vicariously liable for a tort committed by an employee – here the employer and employee are concurrent wrongdoers, though the employer was not involved, by act or omission, in the causing of harm. Likewise, a person subject to a non-delegable duty, such as the *Rylands v Fletcher* principle, may be a concurrent wrongdoer along with the independent contractor that caused the injury.

Independent wrongdoers, causing separate injuries to the plaintiff, are not concurrent wrongdoers and are not subject to the special provisions on concurrent liability. There are some special provisions governing these independent wrongdoers, but the general position is that separate actions lie against each wrongdoer and each action is confined to the harm actually caused by the particular defendant.[96]

Persons may be concurrent wrongdoers in respect of a portion of the injuries caused to a plaintiff and independent wrongdoers in respect of other injuries caused. Consider the following situation:

---

91 For a general overview of the legislative provisions see Byrne, 'Joint and Several Liability: A Need for Reform?' (1996) 14 ILT 46.
92 S. 11(1) of the 1961 Act.
93 S. 11(2)(b).
94 See *Lynch v Beale* unrep. HC, 23 November 1974 where it was argued that a building sub-contractor and an architect were not concurrent wrongdoers where one was responsible for subsidence in the foundations and the other for inadequate design in the first floor of the building. Hamilton J held that they were concurrent wrongdoers, as the collapse of the building was a single injury, not divisible into separate items attributable to the separate causes; see also Kerr, *op. cit.* at pp. 27–8.
95 These two factual situations were treated differently prior to the Act, see McMahon & Binchy, *op. cit.* at pp. 75–6; *Iarnród Éireann v Ireland* [1996] 3 IR 321; [1995] 2 ILRM 161, at pp. 356–7; pp. 193–4 per Keane J.
96 S. 12(2) provides for apportionment of responsibility between independent wrongdoers, causing damage of the same type; the Rules of the Superior Courts permit the consolidation of separate actions in limited instances.

Example

D1 and D2 both negligently collide with P's car. D1 causes extensive damage to the back of P's car, while D2 causes extensive damage to the driver's side of the car. The combined effect of the two collisions causes P serious physical injury, which keeps him out of work for six months.

D1 and D2 are concurrent wrongdoers in respect of the personal injury and the loss of income, but are independent wrongdoers in respect of the separate items of damage to the car. Causation plays a central role in classifying wrongdoers as either concurrent or independent and has been considered already in chapter 11.

Extent of Responsibility

Concurrent wrongdoers are each liable for all the damage in respect of which their wrongs are *concurrent*,[97] subject to the limitation that the plaintiff cannot recover more than the amount at which the damage has been measured. The 1961 Act provides three exceptions to this principle of full liability for each wrongdoer. The first is where the plaintiff agrees to accept an apportionment of liability amongst the defendants, based on their individual degrees of fault. In such a case each defendant is only liable for his own portion of the damage. However, if any of the wrongdoers fails to meet his portion, the plaintiff may apply to the court to distribute the deficiency among the other concurrent wrongdoers.[98] The second exception arises where there is a finding of contributory negligence against the plaintiff. In such a case the court must determine the respective degrees of fault of the parties to the action (i.e. excluding the fault of concurrent wrongdoers who were not involved in the action) and each defendant is only liable for his own portion of the damage. Again, a secondary judgment may be obtained to distribute a deficiency in the plaintiff's recovery of the damages due.[99] The third exception involves collisions at sea, where each wrongdoer is only liable for the portion of damage that is proportionate to his degree of fault.[100]

A concurrent wrongdoer can seek to reduce liability in one of two ways – by seeking to have other wrongdoers joined as co-defendants, where the plaintiff has not done so, or by taking a separate action for contribution from a concurrent wrongdoer after the action by the plaintiff has been resolved.[101] In either case, it is a practical matter as to the solvency of other concurrent wrongdoers that will

---

97 S. 12(1) and s. 14(2); the wrongdoers do not share liability for any additional damage in respect of which they are independent wrongdoers.
98 S. 14(3).
99 S. 38.
100 S. 46.
101 Contribution claims are governed by ss. 21–33 of the 1961 Act. The procedural provisions in s. 27 favour the resolution of the issues in one action, rather than in separate actions; s. 27(1)(b) gives the court discretion to refuse to order contribution, where there was an unreasonable failure to join the concurrent wrongdoer to the

determine the ability to reduce liability. Liability to the plaintiff is largely independent of the issue of the proportions of responsibility between the wrongdoers.

The principle of full responsibility for each concurrent wrongdoer was recently subjected to a challenge, on constitutional grounds, in *Iarnród Éireann v Ireland*,[102] but the challenge failed. The background to the case was as follows. A train was derailed as a result of a collision with a herd of cattle. A passenger injured in the accident succeeded in an action against the railway company and the owner of the cattle and the apportionment of liability in the High Court was 30 per cent against the railway company and 70 per cent against the owner of the cattle. The owner did not have any significant means and the successful claimant exercised his right to refuse the apportionment and recover the full amount from the railway company, as a concurrent wrongdoer.[103]

The railway company instituted proceedings claiming, *inter alia*, that sections 12 and 14 of the 1961 Act violated their property rights, by imposing an excessive level of liability. The state responded by arguing that allowing the effect of one wrongdoer's lack of funds to fall on the innocent injured party would be a failure to vindicate the injured person's constitutional right to adequate compensation.[104] Keane J held that the relevant provisions of the 1961 Act did not amount to an unjust level of interference with the rights of the railway company and this view was upheld by the Supreme Court on appeal.[105] Furthermore, he stated that reducing their liability to the injured party would 'have been to exonerate . . . the blameworthy at the expense of the blameless'.[106]

In cases where apportionment has been accepted, or where contribution is sought, relative fault is the basis of determining the levels of liability of the wrongdoers.[107] Fault is based on the relative blameworthiness, rather than the causal force, of each wrongdoer's conduct.[108] Where one wrongdoer is responsible for breach of a strict duty and the other is responsible for breach of

---

original action; see Kerr, *op. cit.* at pp. 53 *et seq.* for detailed consideration of s. 27. Furthermore s. 22 and s. 27(4) are designed to facilitate out of court settlements, by allowing contribution claims in respect of reasonable settlements and making provision for ensuring that the injured person is also bound by the arrangements made.

102 [1996] 3 IR 321 (HC and SC); [1995] 2 ILRM 161 (HC).
103 The plaintiff's right of election is contained in s. 14(3) and was expressly acknowledged by Keane J, *ibid.*, at p. 356; p. 193.
104 The arguments are set out in some detail in the judgment of Keane J, *ibid.*, at pp. 333 *et seq.*; pp. 173 *et seq.*
105 *Ibid.*, at p. 369; p. 204; the test of constitutional validity is considered at pp. 360 *et seq.*; pp. 197 *et seq.* and is one of proportionality between the legal principles and the rights affected by them (HC); p. 376 (SC).
106 *Ibid.*, at p. 368; p. 204.
107 S. 14(3) and s. 21(2).
108 *Iarnród Éireann v Ireland* [1996] 3 IR 321; [1995] 2 ILRM 161, at pp. 359–60; pp. 195–6; *Connolly v Dundalk Urban District Council and Mahon & McPhillips* unrep. SC, 18 November 1992; White, *Irish Law of Damages* (Dublin: Butterworths, 1998) at §§1.7.02–1.7.03.

a fault based duty, the court may take this into account. It is open to the court to refuse to place any responsibility on the party in breach of the strict duty.[109]

Procedure

A detailed consideration of procedural rules is beyond the scope of a general text,[110] but a few brief words should be said on the issue. The general purpose of the legislation is to encourage the parties to raise all relevant issues in a single action; this is done by imposing restrictions on any second or subsequent proceedings, unless there is some good reason why the issues could not have been raised in the original action.[111]

Section 13 of the 1961 Act gives the plaintiff the option of suing any one, or any combination of the concurrent wrongdoers and section 18(1)(a) provides that obtaining a judgment does not, in itself, preclude the institution of a separate action against another concurrent wrongdoer. However, section 18(1)(b) provides that the damages awarded in the subsequent action may not exceed the measure of damages for the concurrent wrong in the original action, so the plaintiff cannot use separate proceedings to increase the level of compensation for the wrong. Furthermore, the sub-section provides that the plaintiff may not recover the costs of the subsequent action, unless there were reasonable grounds for bringing separate proceedings. Section 16 precludes the taking of a separate action once full satisfaction has occurred, i.e. once the plaintiff has received the full amount of damages, all concurrent wrongdoers are discharged of their liability to the plaintiff, irrespective of whether they actually contributed to the payment. Section 17 deals with arrangements other than full satisfaction. A release or accord with one concurrent wrongdoer will only discharge the others if there is an indication of an intention to do so.[112] If there is no such intent, then the plaintiff may only recover a reduced amount from the other wrongdoers, which takes account of the arrangement.[113]

Joinder

Parties other than those selected by the plaintiff can be joined to the proceedings. Section 13(b) allows the court to require the joinder of all interested parties where

---

109 S. 43; a party in breach of a strict duty may, of course, be found to have behaved in a blameworthy fashion; this matter would not be relevant in determining that a breach of obligation had occurred, but would be central to the allocation of responsibility.
110 For detailed treatment of the subject see O'Floinn, *Practice and Procedure in the Superior Courts* (Dublin: Butterworths, 1996).
111 See, for example, *Gilmore v Windle* [1967] IR 323, at p. 329 per Lavery J; p. 332 per Walsh J; p. 334 and p. 336 per O'Keeffe P; *Board of Governors of St Laurence's Hospital v Staunton* [1990] 2 IR 31, at p. 37 per Finlay CJ.
112 S. 17(1).
113 S. 17(2); ss. 16 and 17 were considered in detail in *Murphy v J. Donoghue Ltd* [1993] 1 IR 527; [1992] ILRM 378; see also *Hussey v Dillon* [1995] 1 IR 111 re s. 16.

the action involves a question as to title (which may arise in cases of trespass, or nuisance in particular). A more frequent example of joinder is where a defendant seeks to have other concurrent wrongdoers included. Section 27(1)(b) requires that the defendant serve such parties with notice 'as soon as is reasonably possible'. The object of this provision, in addition to consolidation of all the issues in one action, is to give the third party as early an opportunity as possible to prepare and defend his position.[114]

This provision has been subjected to a considerable amount of judicial scrutiny, from which some general conclusions can be drawn. First, a defendant should institute third party proceedings as soon as he has a general awareness of the nature of the claim made against him and the potential for a claim for contribution from a third party; waiting for corroborating evidence to strengthen the case may involve an unnecessary delay.[115] Secondly, any delay in applying for or serving a third party notice will have to be justified by the defendant.[116] Thirdly, the courts have a considerable degree of discretion as to whether or not the third party may be joined to the proceedings[117] and the timing of the application, while important, is not the only relevant consideration. A central feature of the exercise of judicial discretion in this area is the degree of prejudice that will result from a decision; third party notice will be permitted or refused largely on the basis of which option will allow the issues to be resolved with the lesser degree of disruption to the parties.[118] It should also be noted that a person may be joined as a third party, despite an unreasonable delay by the defendant, if

---

114 *A & P (Ireland) Ltd v Golden Vale Products Ltd* unrep. HC, 7 December 1978, at pp. 6–7 per McMahon J.

115 *Board of Governors of St Laurence's Hospital v Staunton* [1990] 2 IR 31, at p. 36 per Finlay CJ; see also *Johnson v Fitzpatrick* [1992] ILRM 269; *Quirke v O'Shea and CRL Oil Ltd* [1992] ILRM 286; *Carroll v Fulflex International Co. Ltd and Combined Freight Services* unrep. HC, 18 October 1995.

116 In *Gilmore v Windle* [1967] IR 323 the Supreme Court accepted that the defendants were awaiting the outcome of separate litigation on the entitlement to make such applications and that this was a valid reason for delay; in *Neville v Margan Ltd (defendant) and Pullman Kellogg Ltd (third party)* unrep. HC, 1 December 1988 the defendant failed to explain a delay of over two years between being given leave to serve notice on a third party and the actual service of the notice, by which time the plaintiff's claim had been settled; Blayney J refused the claim for contribution; see also *Dillon v MacGabhann* unrep. HC, 24 July 1995; *Grogan v Ferrum Trading Co. Ltd* [1996] 2 ILRM 216; *Dowling v Armour Pharmaceutical Co. Inc.* [1996] 2 ILRM 417; *Connolly v Casey & Murphy and Fitzgibbon*, unrep. 12 June 1998.

117 *Gilmore v Windle* [1967] IR 323, at p. 335 per O'Keeffe P.

118 *Ibid.*, at p. 332 per Lavery J; pp. 336–7 per O'Keeffe P; see also *Johnson v Fitzpatrick* [1992] ILRM 269; *Quirke v O'Shea and CRL Oil Ltd* [1992] ILRM 286; *D'Arcy v Roscommon County Council* unrep. SC, 11 January 1991; these three decisions are noted in Byrne & Binchy, *Annual Review of Irish Law 1991* at pp. 352 *et seq.*

the third party has taken an active part in the proceedings and has delayed unreasonably in raising an objection to the third party procedure.[119]

Separate Action for Contribution

While there is a general preference for consolidating all issues in a single action, there are circumstances where this is either not possible or not desirable. In such cases a contribution action may be initiated separately, by plenary summons.[120] The court has a discretion as to whether such an action should be allowed to proceed and will have to be satisfied that there are valid reasons for using this procedure, rather than joining the third party to the original action. One such reason may be that joinder was refused on the grounds that it would have been prejudicial to one of the parties in the original action.[121] It has also been stated, *obiter*, that separate proceedings may be initiated where essential evidence is not discovered until after the original trial.[122] Another possible reason may be that joinder would have been pointless, perhaps due to insolvency or an inability to locate a third party who was out of the jurisdiction.

Personal Representatives

Death gives rise to two distinct issues, requiring special consideration. First, does the wrongful killing of a person amount to a tort, permitting an action either by the estate of the deceased or by dependants or relatives? Secondly, if a person commits a tort, or is the victim of a tort, and subsequently dies, does the cause of action survive against, or in favour of, the estate of the deceased? At common law the answer to both of these questions was no; causing death was not an actionable wrong,[123] and tort actions were seen as personal and so, incapable of surviving the death of either party.[124] The position in respect of

---

119 *Carroll v Fulflex International Co. Ltd and Combined Freight Services* unrep. HC, 18 October 1995; *Tierney v Fintan Sweeney Ltd and La Marazinni Ernestos SPA* unrep. HC, 18 October 1995.

120 Procedural aspects of contribution claims are governed by s. 27 of the 1961 Act.

121 *Johnson v Fitzpatrick* [1992] ILRM 269; *Quirke v O'Shea and CRL Oil Ltd* [1992] ILRM 286; *D'Arcy v Roscommon County Council* unrep. SC, 11 January 1991; in each case the defendant sought to have a parent of the plaintiff joined as a third party, but the application was refused on the grounds that the conduct of the plaintiff's case could be adversely affected.

122 *A & P (Ireland) Ltd v Golden Vale Producs Ltd* unrep. HC, 7 December 1978, at p. 7 per McMahon J.

123 *Baker v Bolton* (1808) 1 Camp 493; where the death occurred some time after the tort, the death itself was not actionable, though losses related to the intervening period could be – *Osborn v Gillett* (1873) LR 8 Ex 88; the principle in these cases is not beyond question, however, and a viable argument in support of a claim at common law could be made; see McMahon & Binchy, *op. cit.* at p. 734.

124 For detailed consideration of the history of this rule see Winfield, 'Death as Affecting Liability in Tort' (1929) Col L Rev 239; for a brief account see Rogers, *Winfield & Jolowicz on Tort*, 14th ed. (London: Sweet & Maxwell, 1994) at p. 683.

both issues has, however, been changed by statute. The current law on both fatal injuries and the survival of actions is contained in the Civil Liability Acts 1961–96. In the case of fatal injuries the action is taken for the benefit of the dependants of the deceased,[125] but the personal representative of the deceased may bring the proceedings on the dependants' behalf.[126] This action is considered in more detail below, under actions by relatives.

Survival of Actions

Survival of Actions Vested in the Deceased

The survival of actions for torts committed against the deceased is provided for by section 7 of the 1961 Act. All tort actions, except defamation or seduction, which were vested in the deceased survive and are transferred to the deceased's estate.[127] The action is for the benefit of the estate; thus the fruits of the action are not confined to dependants, but may include other beneficiaries of the estate. The personal representative is authorised by section 48 of the Succession Act 1965 to bring such an action.

The damages recoverable under this type of action are confined to economic losses and property damage and exclude any losses of a personal nature.[128] The estate can recover losses such as medical expenses and lost income. Where the tort is the cause of death, damages are calculated without regard to losses or gains to the estate associated with the death, with the express exception of funeral expenses.[129] This means that amounts paid under life insurance policies will not be deducted from the damages awarded, but neither will the award be increased by outgoings such as expenses incurred in taking out probate or in the administration of the estate; neither will losses such as the termination of a life interest in property be taken into account. Under equivalent legislation in England and Australia it has been held that the estate can recover lost income for the 'lost years'.[130] In other words, the income that the deceased would have

---

125 S. 48(1).
126 S. 48(3).
127 Defamation and seduction are excluded from the survival provisions by s. 6(a). The term 'vested' seems to indicate that the cause of action must be complete prior to death, though there is a lack of authority on the issue. Thus, if a person engaged in wrongful conduct against the deceased prior to death, but property damage or economic harm ensued after death, an action might not be available if the tort is one in which damage is a requisite element. Actions compromised prior to death do not survive – *Mahon v Bourke* [1991] 2 IR 495; [1991] ILRM 59.
128 S. 7(2) expressly excludes recovery of 'exemplary damages, or damages for any pain or suffering or personal injury or any loss or diminution of expectation of life or happiness'.
129 S. 7(3).
130 *Gammell v Wilson; Furness v B & S Massey Ltd* [1982] AC 27; [1981] 2 WLR 248; [1981] 1 All ER 578; *Fitch v Hyde-Cates* (1982) 150 CLR 482; 39 ALR 581; the effect of these cases has been overturned by subsequent legislation – s. 4 of

earned in a normal lifetime, had the tort not caused death, can be taken into account in assessing the damages payable. Academic commentators here are generally agreed that this interpretation would also apply to the Irish legislation.[131] Furthermore, the rights of the estate are in addition to the rights of dependants,[132] leaving open a possibility that a defendant might have to pay twice for certain elements of the losses incurred. This might happen where the dependants recover for loss of support and the estate recovers for loss of income. However, careful attention to the measurement of the loss of income should include the deduction of expenses that the deceased would have incurred in supporting himself and any dependants. Such double recovery is unlikely if the action for the dependants occurs after the action for the estate, as the calculation of the dependants' loss, under section 49 of the 1961 Act, allows the deduction of the dependants' entitlements out of the estate.

Survival of Actions Subsisting Against the Deceased

The survival of actions for torts committed by the deceased is provided for by section 8 of the 1961 Act, with defamation and seduction again excluded. Subsisting actions are defined so as to include torts in which the damage occurred at the time of or after death and so, are not confined to torts completed before death.[133] There are no special principles in respect of the calculation of damages in such an action. The only special provisions relating to such an action are the provision of a reduced time limit for bringing an action in certain circumstances[134] and a provision to allow such claims to be proven as a debt in the event of the estate being insolvent.[135]

Relatives

The relatives of the victim of a tort may suffer as a side-effect of the injury to the primary victim. This is recognised in the law of torts in a number of ways. In chapter 10 we saw that family members have limited rights to sue for interference with domestic relations, most notably the spouse's right to sue for loss of consortium. An action for negligently inflicted psychological damage will also be available, in some circumstances, to compensate relatives as secondary victims of a tort. Assistance provided by family members in caring for a relative who has been seriously injured may be included in the assessment of damages in an action

---

the Administration of Justice Act 1982 in England; see Balkin & Davis, *op. cit.* at p. 396 for a list of the Australian provisions; apparently Queensland was the only state to have made such provision prior to the cases in question.
131 White, 'Insurers at Bay – Repercussions of *Gammell v Wilson*' (1981) 75 ILSI Gaz 77; McMahon & Binchy, *op. cit.* at p. 731; Kerr, *op. cit.* at pp. 21–2.
132 S. 7(4).
133 S. 8(2).
134 S. 9, considered in chapter 12 *supra*.
135 S. 10.

by the injured party.[136] Apart from these situations, relatives of the victim of a fatal accident have a limited right to compensation under Part IV of the Civil Liability Act 1961.

Fatal Injuries

Availability of Action for Fatal Injuries

Section 48(1) of the 1961 Act provides that an action may be brought for the benefit of the dependants of a deceased person against the person responsible for wrongfully causing the death.[137] This action is only available if the impugned conduct would have been an actionable wrong against the deceased,[138] had it not been fatal. Thus, any tortious conduct which causes death can provide grounds for an action on behalf of the dependants, provided that an action would have been available to the deceased.[139]

The action under section 48 is not separately available to each individual dependant, but is a type of collective action for all the dependants, as a single group,[140] and only one action is permitted against a defendant.[141] The action may be initiated by the personal representative at any time within the limitation period applicable to the action or by any or all of the dependants after six months has elapsed since the death.[142] The benefit of placing the initial responsibility with the personal representative is that all aspects of the deceased's affairs can be dealt with together. The ability of the dependants to take direct action avoids the possibility of undue delay in providing compensation, which might occur

---

136 Considered in chapter 15 *infra*.
137 For persons killed while flying, the equivalent provision is s. 18 of the Air Navigation and Transport Act 1936, as amended, which is the same in substance as the provisions under the Civil Liability Acts.
138 'Wrong' is defined, in s. 2(1), as 'a tort, breach of contract or breach of trust' and includes wrongs attributable to the defendant, but carried out by other persons, for whom the defendant is responsible. Our interest is confined to torts against the deceased.
139 The right of action on behalf of the dependants will not survive if the deceased settled the action or if the limitation period had expired prior to death; see *Read v Great Eastern Railway Co.* (1868) LR 3 QB 555; *Williams v Mersey Docks & Harbour Board* [1905] 1 KB 804; *Nunan v Southern Railway Co.* [1924] 1 KB 223; [1923] All ER Rep 21; these three cases were concerned with the predecessor to s. 48 of the 1961 Act, s. 1 of the Fatal Accidents Act 1846; *Mahon v Burke* [1991] 2 IR 495; [1991] ILRM 59; White, *op. cit.* at §§8.3.02–8.3.06; Kerr, *op. cit.* at p. 99; an action will not be available against the deceased's insurers where the deceased was solely responsible for his own death.
140 S. 48(4); in making the award the courts may allocate separate amounts to each dependant, under s. 49(4), but it is not necessary that each dependant be a party to the action. In fact, if the action is brought by the personal representative, none of the dependants need actually be party to the action.
141 S. 48(2).
142 S. 48(3).

because a personal representative has not been appointed in the first six months after death or because a personal representative has simply failed to take an action for some reason.

One of the central features of the action is the definition of dependants. Section 47(1) defines a dependant as 'any member of the family of the deceased who suffers injury or mental distress'. The interpretation of family membership was originally confined to the following relationships to the deceased – spouse, parent, step-parent, child, step-child, grandparent, grandchild, or sibling[143] – with a provision to treat the relationship with adopted children or with persons *in loco parentis* in the same fashion as natural relationships.[144] More recently, provision has been made to include former spouses[145] or persons who cohabited with the deceased for three years prior to death.[146] Persons cohabiting for less than three years or whose cohabitation with the deceased was not continuous appear not to be covered. It is possible that such persons could base a claim on a *dictum* of O'Hanlon J in the High Court, giving an extended meaning to the term '*in loco parentis*'.[147] However, this *dictum* was made in the context of the earlier legislation, which had failed to address the issue of cohabitation. The courts may be less willing to engage in such manipulation of terminology in light of the express legislative provision on cohabitation. In order to qualify as a dependant, the family member must suffer either injury or mental distress. This provision gives some recognition to emotional dependency, independent of financial dependency.[148]

Damages for Fatal Injuries

Section 49 of the 1961 Act provides for three categories of damage, which are available to compensate dependants for their loss – injury, mental distress and expenses.

---

143 S. 47(1); the definition includes children born out of wedlock, s. 47(2).
144 S. 47(2); the relationship between a child and a person *in loco parentis* continues to be considered as a familial one after the child has ceased to be dependent on the other person, see *Waters v Cruickshank* [1967] IR 378, where the deceased had lived with his uncle for a number of years; the nephew was supporting the uncle, due to the latter's inability to work; the Supreme Court accepted that the uncle had been *in loco parentis* and could claim as a dependant in respect of the nephew's death.
145 S. 47(1)(b) inserted by s. 1(1) of the Civil Liability (Amendment) Act 1996, the divorce must be one which was either granted in the state or granted abroad and recognised in the state. The provision only applies to causes of action accruing after 25 December 1996 – s. 1(2) of the 1996 Act.
146 S. 47(1)(c) inserted by s. 1(1) of the Civil Liability (Amendment) Act 1996; this provision is also confined to actions accruing after the operative date of the 1996 Act.
147 *Hollywood v Cork Harbour Commissioners* [1992] 1 IR 457, at pp. 464–6; see Byrne & Binchy, *Annual Review of Irish Law 1992* at p. 612; Kerr, *op. cit.* at p. 97.
148 In *McCarthy v Walsh* [1965] IR 246 the Supreme Court allowed recovery by infant siblings, who had suffered emotionally, but not financially from the death of their sister.

Injury is interpreted as loss of financial support.[149] This restricts the ability of dependants to recover in respect of personal services. Services can be included in the award, in so far as they are capable of financial measurement,[150] but loss of society and other personal aspects of family relations appear to fall outside the ambit of 'injury'. White is critical of the exclusion of such losses from the calculation of the dependants' injury and presents a persuasive argument in favour of their inclusion, citing a number of American authorities in support of his position and also drawing an analogy with criminal injuries compensation in Ireland.[151] Despite the limited theoretical approach, the amount recoverable for services capable of financial valuation, such as housekeeping, may be quite significant. In *Cooper v Egan*,[152] for example, £90,000 was awarded to the deceased's widower and children in respect of the loss of her domestic services, while only £8,000 was awarded in respect of loss of her income.

The measurement of injury is largely consistent with the principles used for calculating financial loss in tort actions generally.[153] Fatal injuries claims are slightly more complicated by the need to assess the proportion of the deceased's resources which would have been provided to the dependants.[154] One special provision of note is section 50 of the 1961 Act, which precludes the deduction from the award of any benefit received under a contract of insurance, pension, gratuity or other similar benefit resulting from the death.[155] This does not, however, preclude a reduction based on other possible sources of income or support for the dependants, such as remarriage.[156] Furthermore, in the case of

---

149 *Gallagher v ESB* [1933] IR 558, at p. 566 per Kennedy CJ; *O'Sullivan v CIÉ* [1978] IR 407, at p. 421 per Griffin J; *Fitzsimons v Bord Telecom Éireann* [1991] 1 IR 536; [1991] ILRM 276, at p. 547; pp. 287–8 per Barron J; *McDonagh v McDonagh* [1992] 1 IR 119; [1992] ILRM 841, at p. 123; p. 844 per Costello J; as a matter of public policy a plaintiff may be precluded from recovering loss based on income of the deceased which was not declared to the tax authorities, see *Fitzpatrick v Furey* unrep. HC, 12 June 1998; Irish Times Law Report, 31 August 1998.
150 *Mehmet v Perry* [1977] 2 All ER 529; *Wycko v Gnodtke* (1960) 105 NW 2d 118; *Fussner v Andert* (1961) 113 NW 2d 355; White, *op. cit.* at §§11.4.04–11.4.06; *Cooper v Egan* unrep. HC, 20 December 1990; *McDonagh v McDonagh* [1992] 1 IR 119; [1992] ILRM 841, at p. 123; p. 844.
151 *Op. cit.* at §§11.4.07–11.4.13.
152 Unrep. HC, 20 December 1990.
153 See chapter 15 *infra*; see White, *op. cit.* at chapter 9 for a detailed analysis of the calculation in fatal injuries cases; also Kerr, *op. cit.* at pp. 101–4.
154 The issue was further complicated in *McDonagh v McDonagh* [1992] 1 IR 119; [1992] ILRM 841, where the defendant was the husband of the deceased. Here the court had to try to separate the value of the children's dependency from their father's, since the father, as the tortfeasor, could not recover; for further analysis see Byrne & Binchy, *Annual Review of Irish Law 1991* at pp. 445–6.
155 See Kerr, *op. cit.* at pp. 106–7; White, *op. cit.* at §§9.4.03–9.4.16.
156 See *Fitzsimons v Bord Telecom Éireann* [1991] 1 IR 536; [1991] ILRM 276, at pp. 547–52; pp. 288–93; *Cooper v Egan* unrep. HC, 20 December 1990; both cases are analysed in Byrne & Binchy, *Annual Review of Irish Law 1990* at pp. 568–74;

cohabitees, the court must take account of the fact that the person did not have an enforceable right to financial maintenance, if that is the case.[157] The provision for compensation for mental distress allows recovery for the emotional effects of the death on family members, as a solatium for injured feelings.[158] The total amount recoverable by all dependants is currently capped at £20,000,[159] with a provision for variation by ministerial order, in order to keep abreast of the changing value of money.[160] Former spouses are precluded from recovering under this head of damages.[161] The claim for mental distress should not be confused with an action for psychiatric harm, which may give rise to a distinct cause of action for a breach of duty owed to the relatives individually.[162]

The expenses recoverable include reasonable funeral expenses and other costs, such as medical expenses,[163] related to the death. Any grant of expenses under section 63 of the Social Welfare (Consolidation) Act 1993 may be deducted from the damages payable for expenses.[164]

---

for a general consideration of deduction see White, *op. cit.* at §§9.4.01–9.4.02 and §§9.4.17–9.4.27.

157 S. 49(5), inserted by s. 2(1)(c) of the 1996 Act.

158 See Veitch, 'Solatium – A Debt Repaid' (1972) 7 Ir Jur (ns) 77; White, *op. cit.* at chapter 10.

159 Originally the amount was £1,000, but this was increased by s. 28(1) of the Courts Act 1981 to £7,500, which was 'usually . . . a token' amount in comparison to the distress caused – *Cooper v Egan* unrep. HC, 20 December 1990, per Barr J at p. 6 of the judgment. The new figure was inserted by s. 2(1)(a) of the 1996 Act.

160 S. 2(1)(b) of the 1996 Act.

161 S. 49A, inserted by s. 3(1) of the 1996 Act.

162 See Byrne & Binchy, *Annual Review of Irish Law 1991* at pp. 446–7 on the distinction between mental distress and 'nervous shock'.

163 Funeral expenses are expressly mentioned in s. 49; medical expenses are not, but may be taken to be included – *Byrne v Houlihan & de Courcy* [1966] IR 274, at p. 283 per Kingsmill Moore J, *obiter*; for detailed consideration see White, *op. cit.* at chapter 12.

164 S. 75(3) of the Social Welfare (Consolidation) Act 1993.

CHAPTER FOURTEEN

Responsibility for Others

Introduction

There are many situations in which a person may be held responsible for an injury that has been caused by the conduct of another person. Employers, for example, will often have to bear the responsibility for injuries inflicted by their employees in the performance of their work; in other cases adults may be held responsible for injuries inflicted by children under their supervision. Such cases are divided into three different categories – vicarious liability, non-delegable duties and duties of control.

Vicarious liability is a form of imputed responsibility,[1] based on the relationship between the defendant and the person who inflicted the injury on the plaintiff. It is most frequently applied to employers in respect of their employees' conduct. Liability is strict, since liability is imposed on the basis of the relationship and not the employer's own conduct. Non-delegable duties are similar, but are based on the defendant's relationship to the activity being performed, rather than the person performing the activity.[2] The principle in *Rylands v Fletcher* is a prominent example of such a duty.

Duties of control are not forms of imputed responsibility, but involve direct responsibility for allowing a third party the opportunity to cause injury. Typical examples would be where an adult negligently fails to control a child, who runs into the street, causing an accident; or where an adult fails to exercise proper control over a dangerous implement, which a child then uses to cause an injury to someone.

Vicarious Liability

People regularly engage others to act on their behalf in respect of activities which pose risks to third parties. The liability of each of the parties for his own personal conduct is unexceptional, but the law has also developed the view that some relationships, by their nature, require the person who engages others

---

1 The responsibility is not simply transferred, as the employee's personal responsibility remains alongside the employer's vicarious responsibility and both are concurrent wrongdoers. In practice, the employee is rarely a suitable financial target as a defendant, so the responsibility does shift to the employer, rather than being shared between the employer and employee.

2 See Kidner, 'Vicarious Liability: For Whom Should the "Employer" be Liable?' (1995) 15 LS 47 highlighting the distinction between the two situations.

451

to accept responsibility for the conduct of those others. The most important such relationship for practical purposes is that of employer and employee, though the vicarious liability principle also has applications in respect of the relationship of principal and agent, the relationship between partners and even gratuitous services in some cases.

The employer's vicarious liability for employees' torts is derived from the law relating to the master–servant relationship, the predecessor to the modern employment relationship. The principle was based on the fiction that the servant's conduct in the performance of the duties of the relationship was effectively the conduct of the master.[3] While the relationship has changed considerably in modern times, the principle of vicarious liability has remained. Academic commentators have offered a number of justifications for the retention of the principle, though there is little judicial comment on the underlying rationale for its retention.[4] The reasons offered are based on a mixture of principles of justice and pragmatic considerations. One reason is that the employer is the principal beneficiary of the employees' endeavours and so, must bear the responsibility for any harm incidental to the generation of that benefit; another argument is that the employer is in a position to introduce protective measures and the imposition of liability encourages the development of safer practices; a third is that the employer is in a better position to distribute the loss, through either insurance or the pricing of goods or services; a fourth is simply that the employer is a better financial target, so the operation of the principle greatly increases the likelihood that the victim of the tort will receive adequate compensation.

The practical difficulty with applying the principle to the relationship between employer and employee is that one must determine first whether the necessary relationship exists between the wrongdoer and the person who engaged him and, secondly, whether the wrongdoing occurred within the context of that relationship. The difficulty with the first matter is that labour services can be supplied under two distinct legal relationships – a contract of service, giving rise

---

3 See, for example, *Bartonshill Coal Co. v McGuire* (1858) 3 Macq 300, at p. 306 per Lord Chelmsford LC; Baker, *An Introduction to English Legal History*, 3rd ed. (London: Butterworths, 1990) at p. 465.

4 Atiyah, *Vicarious Liability in the Law of Torts*. (London: Butterworths, 1967) at chapter 2; Jones, *Textbook on Torts*, 5th ed. (London: Blackstone, 1996) at §8.4.1; Landes & Posner, *The Economic Structure of Tort Law* (Cambridge, Mass.: Harvard University Press, 1987) at pp. 120–1; much of the justificatory theory is not new, but has a rather lengthy history, see Heuston & Buckley, *Salmond & Heuston on the Law of Torts*, 21st ed. (London: Sweet & Maxwell, 1996) at §21.1 and Cornish & Clark, *Law and Society in England 1750–1950* (London: Sweet & Maxwell, 1989) at pp. 489 –90; one of the more memorable judicial comments on the principle is that of Lord Pearce in *Imperial Chemical Industries Ltd v Shatwell* [1965] AC 656; [1964] 3 WLR 329; [1964] 2 All ER 999, at p. 686; p. 348; p. 1012, where he described its basis as 'social convenience and rough justice'.

to the relationship of employer and employee, or a contract for services, giving rise to the relationship of hirer and independent contractor. In the latter situation the worker is self-employed and selling his services as a business and the person engaging the services is not vicariously liable. The diversity of modern work practices makes it difficult to categorise the relationship in many cases.

Employees and Independent Contractors Distinguished

Employees and independent contractors need to be distinguished in law for a variety of reasons, the vicarious liability of the person engaging them being but one. Others include the calculation and administration of tax deductions, contributions and entitlements under the social welfare system, and the applicability of protective labour legislation. The two methods of providing labour cannot be distinguished on the basis of the type of work performed, as it is possible to do the same types of work under either structure. Take the following scenario:

Example

Two electricians, X and Y, are both carrying out work on the premises of a company, Z. X often works for Z and is paid a separate fee each time he does so, but he also works for others on a similar basis, though most of his income derives from working for Z. X supplies his own equipment and materials and is not supervised in the performance of his work. Y works only for Z and is paid a regular weekly salary; he works with equipment and material provided by Z and he is subject to supervision by a member of Z's managerial staff.

In this situation X is an independent contractor, while Y is an employee. There are several distinguishing features between their respective relationships with Z, such as the method of payment and the level of authority exercised over them. It is important to discern which features are regarded as important for the purposes of legal classification and which are irrelevant.

The traditional method of distinguishing the two categories is the 'control test'.[5] A person hiring an independent contractor only exercises control over what work is to be done, leaving the contractor with a considerable degree of discretion as to how the work should be performed, while an employer generally has control over the manner in which an employee performs the work, in addition to controlling the issue of what work is to be done. So, in the

---

5 *Performing Rights Society Ltd v Mitchell & Booker (Palais de Danse) Ltd* [1924] 1 KB 762; *Honeywill & Stein Ltd v Larkin Bros Ltd* [1934] 1 KB 191; [1933] All ER Rep 77; *Walshe v Bailieboro Co-op Agricultural & Dairy Society and Gargan* [1939] Ir Jur Rep 77; *Lynch v Palgrave Murphy Ltd* [1964] IR 150; *Roche v P. Kelly & Co. Ltd* [1969] IR 100.

above example, it is the degree of supervision exercised by Z which is the crucial feature determining the type of relationship between Z and the two electricians. Likewise, where a person hires a taxi or a coach, the hirer is not vicariously liable for the driver's conduct, but if one employs a chauffeur, vicarious liability will arise. The same approach can be seen in cases where equipment is hired out, along with a specialised operator, trained in its use. The owner of the equipment is treated as the employer of the operator rather than the hirer, for whom the operator is temporarily acting, unless the hirer has been given control over the manner in which the equipment is to be operated.[6]

The principal shortcoming of the control test is that it is inadequate when applied to specialist employees, such as hospital doctors, in-house lawyers and other professionals, who work as salaried employees. These employees usually have expertise beyond that of their superiors in the employer's organisation and so cannot be subjected to control over the manner in which they perform their work. It is generally accepted that vicarious liability attaches in such cases,[7] though the search for an explanation of the relationship in a manner which makes it distinctive from hiring an independent contractor is more difficult than in unskilled and semi-skilled work.[8]

An early attempt to provide a more incisive test was made in *Stevenson, Jordan & Harrison Ltd v Macdonald & Evans,*[9] where Denning J considered that the appropriate distinction was whether the worker was engaged in work integral to the employer's business or ancillary to the business. This integration test is rarely employed by the courts, due to the difficulty in distinguishing between integral and ancillary functions.[10]

---

6 *Lynch v Palgrave Murphy Ltd* [1964] IR 150; *McGowan v Wicklow County Council and O'Toole* unrep. HC, 27 May 1993, necessary co-operation between the operator and the hirer's supervisory staff was held not to amount to control over the operator; see also *Dunne v Honeywell Control Systems Ltd and Virginia Milk Products Ltd* [1991] ILRM 595 on the issue of temporary transfer of employees to do work for another company; Fridman, *The Law of Torts in Canada* (Toronto: Carswell, 1989) vol. 2, at pp. 325 *et seq.*

7 *Cassidy v Ministry of Health* [1951] 2 KB 343; [1951] 1 All ER 574, noted by Kahn-Freund (1951) 14 MLR 504; see also the cases considered in respect of professional negligence in chapter 2 *supra*, many of which involve vicarious liability (particularly those where health authorities are named as defendants); Fridman, *op. cit.* vol. 2 at pp. 319–21.

8 In the context of skilled or semi-skilled workers the courts have taken the view that a theoretical right of control, which is not exercised in practice, will suffice to establish the relationship of employer and employee, *Roche v P. Kelly & Co. Ltd* [1969] IR 100, at p. 108 per Walsh J; *Phelan v Coillte Teo.* [1993] 1 IR 20, at p. 23 per Barr J.

9 [1952] 1 TLR 101.

10 See, for example, *Stevens v Broadrib Sawmilling Pty Co. Ltd* (1986) 160 CLR 16, at p. 28 per Mason J; a rare example of the application of the integration test is *In re Sunday Tribune Ltd* [1984] IR 505 in respect of the status of a number of journalists engaged by the paper; the test has some support in Canada, see

A more influential approach is the 'mixed test' of MacKenna J in *Ready Mixed Concrete (South East) Ltd v Minister of Pensions and National Insurance*.[11] This test acknowledges control as a primary feature of the relationship, but also emphasises personal service as an important feature and suggests that additional features of the relationship must also be taken into consideration. The personal nature of the employment relationship means that the employee must do the work himself and may not generally delegate its performance to another person. An independent contractor is engaged to ensure that the work is done and may ordinarily delegate its performance, unless the contract specifies otherwise (as would often be the case with artists and performers, for example). Other relevant factors would be the remuneration involved (employees tend to be paid wages periodically; independent contractors participate in profits and run the risk of suffering losses) and the issue of investment in the business (employees are usually provided with equipment and materials; independent contractors usually provide their own). This approach looks at the totality of the arrangement between the parties and has proved influential in many cases.[12]

The mixed test allows the question of control to be outweighed by other factors in deciding the nature of the relationship between the parties.[13] However, the courts have taken a step further and are now of the view that the labour relations between two parties can be classified differently for different purposes, so that a worker may be an independent contractor for the purposes of tax and social welfare contributions and entitlements, but an employee for the purposes of vicarious liability. *Phelan v Coillte Teo*.[14] provides a graphic example. The plaintiff was an employee of the defendants, the state forestry company, and was injured due to the negligence of a welder/fitter with whom he was working. The negligent worker was engaged under different terms than forestry workers; he did not have entitlements such as holiday pay and pension rights and the tax and social welfare arrangements were those of a self-employed person; he provided his own equipment and negotiated an hourly

---

Armstrong v Mac's Milk Ltd (1975) 55 DLR (3d) 510; *Mayer v J. Conrad Lavigne Ltd* (1979) 105 DLR (3d) 734.

11 [1968] 2 QB 497; [1968] 2 WLR 775; [1968] 1 All ER 433.

12 See, for example, *Market Investigations v Minister of Social Security* [1969] 2 QB 173; [1969] 2 WLR 1; [1968] 3 All ER 732; *Lee Ting Sang v Chung & Shun Sing Construction & Engineering Co. Ltd* [1990] 2 AC 374; [1990] 2 WLR 1173; [1990] IRLR 236; *Lamb Brothers Dublin Ltd v Davidson* unrep. HC, 4 December 1978; *Ó Coindealbháin (Inspector of Taxes) v Mooney* [1990] 1 IR 422; *Zuijs v Wirth Bros Pty Ltd* (1955) 93 CLR 561.

13 The mixed test does, however, give considerable weight to control. There is some evidence that control is playing a lesser role in more recent cases in England; see, for example, *Hall (Inspector of Taxes) v Lorimer* [1994] 1 WLR 209; [1994] 1 All ER 250.

14 [1993] 1 IR 18; see also Byrne & Binchy, *Annual Review of Irish Law 1992* at pp. 606–8.

rate of pay each year, along with a mileage allowance for the use of his own vehicle. The negligent worker provided his own labour and did not delegate it to anyone else; 99 per cent of his work was for Coillte and he took general instructions from a Coillte engineer as to what work needed to be done.

If one was to opt for a single classification of the negligent worker's status, it would probably be an independent contractor. Barr J, however, held that the financial aspects of the relationship were separable from the conduct of the work, so the worker could be self-employed for tax and social welfare purposes without affecting vicarious liability arising out of the working arrangements.[15] The control test was held to be the predominant method for determining the issue of vicarious liability, though the personal service aspect of the relationship was also considered important.[16] By comparing the worker's position to a hypothetical tradesman under a contract of service (i.e. an employee), Barr J found sufficient comparability to conclude that the worker was an employee when engaged in carrying out his work.[17] He further indicated, *obiter*, that an employer could be vicariously liable for the torts of an independent contractor if the employer's degree of control was comparable to that over an employee.[18]

There are a number of unsatisfactory aspects to this decision. First, it acknowledges professional employment as an exception to the control test, without any explanation as to what distinguishes professional employment from other skilled employment. Secondly, the lack of practical control is side-stepped on the basis of a theoretical right of control, reached by comparison to a hypothetical employee.[19] Thirdly, the distinction between employees and independent contractors is further blurred, both by the acceptance of double classification for the one worker and by the suggestion of vicarious liability for independent contractors under the same degree of control as employees.[20] Perhaps most

---

15 *Ibid.*, at p. 24.
16 *Ibid.*, at pp. 22–4.
17 *Ibid.*
18 *Ibid.*, at p. 25; see also *Kelly v Michael McNamara & Co.* unrep. HC, 5 June 1996, per Budd J at p. 26.
19 The reasoning used was that a skilled employee would not be subject to any significant level of control in practice, thereby making the two situations comparable. This approach begs the question as to why control is the central factor at all. The degree of supervision actually exercised looks remarkably similar to that described as 'necessary co-operation' with an independent contractor in *McGowan v Wicklow County Council and O'Toole* unrep. HC, 27 May 1993.
20 The dual classification of a worker for different purposes has also been applied by the Court of Appeal in England – *Lane v Shire Roofing Co. Ltd* [1995] IRLR 493, where it was accepted that a worker could be self-employed for tax purposes, but an employee for the purpose of imposing a duty of care on the employer for his safety. See also *US v Silk* (1946) 331 US 704; Kidner, *loc. cit.* at p. 49 also argues in favour of a dual classification approach, on the basis that the objectives of tort differ from those of revenue, social security and employment law; he does, however, acknowledge that it would be better if the term 'employee' was no longer

importantly, the decision fails to indicate the basis on which one test is judged to be more appropriate than the others, leaving the suspicion that the choice of solution is instinctive, rather than the product of the application of reasoned principle.

Other cases have contributed to this vagueness and the *Phelan* decision is representative of a general trend, rather than an isolated instance.[21] The imposition of liability for gratuitous services, considered below, is another example. The result is that the law is in a confused state as to when vicarious liability arises, with the language of control being used to mask the reasons underlying the decisions of the courts.

Kidner suggests a new approach, departing from the use of the distinction between employees and independent contractors. Instead he suggests that vicarious liability should be based on the substance of the relationship between the employer and the worker, using three factors – control, organisational integration and entrepreneurship.[22] Although this is essentially a repackaging of the existing tests, it does have some novel features – control is based on actual control, measured principally in terms of managerial accountability for the performance of work, rather than on the theoretical right of control used by the courts; the integration issue is a revival of Denning's approach in *Stevenson, Jordan & Harrison Ltd v Macdonald & Evans*, but taken in combination with other factors, rather than as a stand alone test; the entrepreneurial aspect involves an examination of how the investment, risk and profits are divided between the parties and not matters such as tax and social security arrangements. Vicarious liability would not arise if the worker could genuinely be considered to be an entrepreneur, with a separate business, distinct from that of the employer. Vicarious liability would arise if the worker was, in reality, a part of the employer's business. The outcome would be independent of the classification of the worker as an employee or independent contractor. This combined approach is more coherent than the approach taken by the courts, but may be too complex to be adopted in practice.

Scope of Employment

Vicarious liability applies to conduct falling within the parameters of the employee's employment.[23] In many instances this will be easy enough to

---

employed in respect of vicarious liability, as it would be unsatisfactory for the term to have different meanings in different contexts. See also McKendrick, 'Vicarious Liability and Independent Contractors: A Re-Examination' (1990) 53 MLR 770.

21 See *Moynihan v Moynihan* [1975] IR 192, in particular.

22 *Loc. cit.* at pp. 58 *et seq.*

23 At common law an exception arose under the doctrine of common employment, which provided that the employer was not vicariously liable where the victim of the employee's tort was a fellow employee; the doctrine was abolished in respect of personal injuries actions by s. 1 of the Law Reform (Personal Injuries) Act

determine, as the employee will be operating a machine or carrying out a process at the employer's premises, during working hours with the employer's authorisation. Difficulties arise in dealing with a variety of situations, such as practical jokes, theft, embezzlement and employees with a wide degree of flexibility in respect of matters such as the time, place and manner of working.

The general principle is that an employee's tort is committed in the course of employment 'if it is either (1) a wrongful act authorised by the master, or (2) a wrongful and unauthorised mode of doing some act authorised by the master'.[24] It is clear, therefore, that the conduct must be linked to the performance of the employee's legitimate functions, but it is also clear that an employer cannot avoid vicarious liability simply by giving detailed instructions as to how employees may behave. Liability does not extend to every conceivable aspect of workers' behaviour, because there must be some appreciable link with their proper functions, and it is not unduly confined, since the employer must accept responsibility for some unauthorised behaviour. Practical implementation of the rule is not easy, however, since the general principle is slightly vague and factual situations can be manipulated to produce multiple interpretations. The cases provide some rough guidance.[25]

In *Poland v John Parr & Sons*[26] the defendant's employee hit the plaintiff on the back of the neck with his hand, as he reasonably believed the boy to be stealing his employer's property. The Court of Appeal held that the act, in defence of the employer's property, came within the range of acts which the worker was implicitly authorised to engage in, so the employer was held to be vicariously liable. It was acknowledged that excessive force could bring the conduct outside the class of authorised acts and that the difference between the authorised and unauthorised level of force 'is a question of degree'.[27] In *Reilly v Ryan*[28] the manager of a public house used a customer as a shield against an

---

1958; its application to other cases has probably been curtailed by s. 34(1)(b) of the Civil Liability Act 1961, as the doctrine was based on implied consent and was broadly similar to the defence of *volenti non fit injuria*, which was replaced by the statutory defence of waiver; see McMahon & Binchy, *The Irish Law of Torts*, 2nd ed. (Dublin: Butterworths, 1989) at p. 768.

24 Salmond & Heuston, *op. cit.* at p. 443; approved in England in *Poland v John Parr & Sons* [1927] 1 KB 236; [1926] All ER Rep 177, at p. 240; p. 178 per Bankes LJ; and in Ireland in *Reilly v Ryan* [1991] ILRM 449, at p. 451 per Blayney J, also citing Rogers, *Winfield & Jolowicz on Tort*, 14th ed. (London: Sweet & Maxwell, 1994) at pp. 568, 570 and 574 (13th ed.) (pp. 600–1 and 603 of the 14th ed.).

25 For an extensive review of the issue, see Winfield & Jolowicz, *op cit.* at p. 600 *et seq.*; McMahon & Binchy, *op. cit.* at pp. 755 *et seq.*; Brazier (ed.), *Clerk & Lindsell on Torts*, 17th ed. (London: Sweet & Maxwell, 1989) at §§5.20–5.43; Fridman, *op. cit.* vol. 2 at pp. 331–8; Balkin & Davis, *Law of Torts* (Sydney: Butterworths, 1991) at pp. 815–24.

26 [1927] 1 KB 236; [1926] All ER Rep 177.

27 *Ibid.*, at p. 243; p. 180 per Scrutton LJ; see also Atkin LJ at p. 245; p. 181.

28 [1991] ILRM 449.

intruder, wielding a knife and demanding the contents of the till (approximately £40). The intruder stabbed the customer in the arm. One of the defence arguments was that the manager was acting in self-defence and, consequently, was acting outside the scope of his employment, as it was his own, rather than his employer's, interests that were being advanced. Blayney J held that the self-defence aspect was not a sufficient basis to treat the conduct as outside the scope of employment, since the manager was also acting in defence of his employer's property. The manner of defence, though, was sufficiently excessive to amount to an unauthorised act. Byrne & Binchy are critical of the decision, describing the outcome as 'intuitively wrong'.[29] Both the decision in *Reilly* itself and the criticism highlight the fact that in the final analysis the solution is as much a matter of individual opinion as principled reasoning.

If the foregoing rule was consistently applied, one would expect that criminal conduct, such as theft or fraud, would almost invariably fall outside the scope of employment, but such is not the case. The leading Irish case is *Johnson & Johnson (Ireland) Ltd v C. P. Security Ltd*,[30] where a security guard, employed by the defendant to protect the plaintiff's premises, was assisting others in stealing van loads of goods from the premises. Egan J, while unwilling to articulate a general principle of liability for unlawful conduct arising out of opportunities presented in the course of employment, held that 'vicarious liability must apply in the present case where the employers were specifically engaged to safeguard the plaintiff's property'.[31] A number of English cases have imposed vicarious liability for fraud, where the employee had ostensible authority to engage in transactions of a broadly similar type to that used to perpetrate the fraud.[32]

The general thrust of the cases is that the type of responsibility given to the employee must be such as to facilitate the unlawful activity under the guise of the performance of duties. Mere opportunity, arising in the course of employment, is not enough. Thus, in *The Health Board v BC and the Labour Court*,[33] Costello J

---

29 *Annual Review of Irish Law 1990* at p. 559, citing a number of New Zealand and older Irish cases attempting to address the dividing line.

30 [1985] IR 362; [1986] ILRM 559.

31 *Ibid.*, at p. 366; p. 562, relying on the House of Lords decision in *Lloyd v Grace Smith & Co.* [1912] AC 716; [1911–13] All ER Rep 51 (vicarious liability of a firm of solicitors for the fraud of a clerk; in the course of selling a client's property, he had it conveyed to himself, sold it on and made off with the proceeds) and the Court of Appeal decision in *Morris v C.W. Martin & Sons Ltd* [1966] 1 QB 716; [1965] 3 WLR 276; [1965] 2 All ER 725 (employee of a dry cleaning business stole a fur coat which a customer had left in for cleaning; employer held vicariously liable).

32 *Lloyd v Grace Smith & Co.* [1912] AC 716; [1911–13] All ER Rep 51 is a classic example; see also *Armagas Ltd v Mundogas SA* [1986] 1 AC 717; [1986] 2 WLR 1063; [1986] 2 All ER 385.

33 [1994] ELR 27; see also Flynn, 'The Basis and Extent of Employers' Liability for Sexual Harassment in Irish Law' (1993–5) 28–30 Ir Jur 36.

refused to hold a health board vicariously liable for a violent sexual assault, committed by two employees against another employee, as it was not sufficiently connected with their duties.[34] The result would probably be different if the assault was against a patient under the care of the assailant.

Given the acceptance of vicarious liability for some criminal conduct, it is not surprising that the courts have also accepted that 'horseplay' by an employee can give rise to vicarious liability where it is closely connected with the authorised functions of the employee.[35] As with the other situations considered above, the courts draw the line at deliberate misconduct where the only connection to work is that the workplace provided the opportunity for the conduct in question.[36]

Other Situations

There are two statutory examples of vicarious liability – the liability of partners under the Partnership Act 1890 and the liability of vehicle owners for the conduct of a person driving the vehicle with their consent, under section 118 of the Road Traffic Act 1961. The liability of each partner for the conduct of other partners is broadly similar in scope to the employer's vicarious liability for employees, embracing authorised acts and acts in the course of the business, including fraud committed in the course of such acts.[37] The liability of an owner under section 118 of the 1961 Act embraces any acts 'in accordance with the terms of such consent'. In order to maintain an action against the owner it is necessary to establish the existence of the consent and that the conduct causing the injury fell within the terms of the consent. The courts have shown a degree of flexibility in the interpretation of the section, which has favoured claimants.

Consent has been implied by the courts in a number of circumstances where there was an absence of express consent. In *Guerin v Guerin and*

---

34 Direct liability for failure to take appropriate preventative measures, in breach of a duty of care, could arise, but was not considered in the High Court in this instance. It was proposed to introduce vicarious liability for unlawful discrimination by employees under s. 15 of the Employment Equality Bill 1996, but the bill was held to be unconstitutional by the Supreme Court, in an Art. 26 reference from the President; the imposition of vicarious liability in civil cases was described as 'unexceptional' (unrep. SC, 3 April 1997, at p. 76 of the judgment), but the manner in which vicarious criminal liability was imposed by the section was regarded as unconstitutional (pp. 76–85). See s. 15 of the Employment Equality Act 1998.

35 *Harrison v Michelin Tyre Co. Ltd* [1985] 1 All ER 918 (driver of machinery deliberately steered off course, colliding with a fellow employee).

36 *Hough v Irish Base Metals Ltd* unrep. SC, 8 December 1967 (gas fire placed in close proximity to a fellow employee who was injured escaping from the heat); *Aldred v Nacanco* [1987] IRLR 292 (shoving an unsteady washbasin against a colleague, causing her an injury).

37 See chapter 13 *supra*; liability extends to activities that a partner has ostensible authority to engage in, see *Allied Pharmaceutical Distributors Ltd and All-Phar Services Ltd v Walsh* unrep. HC, 14 December 1990, noted in Byrne & Binchy, *Annual Review of Irish Law 1990* at pp. 561–2.

McGrath,[38] for example, the owner of a car left the country to live in England and left the keys of his car with his father, having arranged for a neighbour to drive his family, since none of them were able to drive; the father gave the second defendant permission to drive the car on family business and the plaintiff was injured in the course of this journey. Costello J held that the consent granted by the owner implicitly extended to any person driving on behalf of the family with the father's permission and was not confined to the specific neighbour with whom the express arrangement had been made. In *Buckley v Johnson & Perrott Ltd and Woods*,[39] the hirer of a car failed to return it at the end of the rental period, thereby falling outside the express terms of the rental agreement, and subsequently caused an accident. The penalty under the contract for such a breach was the imposition of an extra charge, which led Lavan J to the conclusion that such extension of the period of hire was implicitly accepted by the first defendant and, therefore, that the driver had sufficient consent for the purpose of section 118. Despite the latitude afforded to plaintiffs in some instances, there are limits beyond which the interpretation of consent may not be taken and consent obtained by fraud will not suffice to give rise to vicarious liability on the owner's part.[40]

The courts have also shown some latitude towards plaintiffs where there was consent, but there was a dispute as to whether the use fell within the parameters of the consent. The Supreme Court in *Buckley v Musgrave Brook Bond Ltd*[41] held that the onus is on the owner to show that the use is outside the scope of the consent given, so it is not sufficient for the defendant to raise a doubt as to whether the use was authorised. It also appears that an inadvertent or unknowing excess of authority may not suffice to bring the use outside the scope of the consent.[42]

---

38 [1992] 2 IR 287; [1993] ILRM 243.
39 Unrep. HC, 29 July 1992.
40 *Kelly v Lombard Motor Co. Ltd* [1974] IR 142, car hired by a person using the name and driving licence of another person; held not to have the hirer's consent.
41 [1969] IR 440; the defendant company had given a van to a driver to return from Dublin to Cork on a Saturday and he was to return it on the Sunday or early on the Monday morning; he used the van for social purposes on the Sunday and caused an accident. The defendant argued that the use fell outside the parameters of the consent, because the permission was not for social purposes, but merely to allow the driver to get home and to return the van thereafter. The Supreme Court ordered a retrial on the basis that the defendant had failed to discharge the onus of proving that the use fell outside the scope of the consent.
42 *Ó Fiachain v Kiernan* unrep. HC, 1 November 1985, a vehicle was leased to a business and assigned to another business, then used without insurance, contrary to the terms of the lease. It was held that this use did not fall outside the scope of the owner's consent, as the assignee had no specific knowledge of the condition in the lease; followed in *Buckley v Johnson & Perrott Ltd* unrep. HC, 29 July 1992; driving without insurance falls outside of the scope of consent if the driver has

There are isolated examples of vicarious liability outside of the foregoing situations; a principal may be liable for tortious conduct of an agent (other than an employee), committed within the scope of actual or ostensible authority,[43] and a person receiving the benefit of gratuitous services will be liable for torts committed in the course of performance, if he has a sufficient degree of control over the provision of the services.[44]

A general thread running through all the examples of vicarious liability, except for that of vehicle owners under section 118 of the Road Traffic Act 1961, is that the person to whom responsibility is imputed is a beneficiary of the conduct in question and is usually the principal beneficiary. This may help to explain the imposition of vicarious liability in the established situations and the refusal in respect of other relationships, such as parent and child. In the case of parents and children, the nature of the relationship differs radically from employer and employee, as the child is being prepared for adulthood and independence and the parents' role is primarily to protect and guide the child. Thus, it is the child who is the principal beneficiary of the relationship and the child is ordinarily expected to develop his own independent sense of responsibility.[45] Parents will be vicariously liable where they employ their children as employees, agents or gratuitous servants on the same basis as any other employer would, but the parent and child relationship is not the basis of the imputed responsibility. Parents will also be responsible for their children in respect of non-delegable duties and they will be liable for their own breach of any duties of control.[46]

---

express knowledge of breach of condition as to insurance, *Fairbrother v MIBI* [1995] 1 IR 581.

43 See Clerk & Lindsell, *op. cit.* at §5.69, suggesting that, where there is only ostensible authority, such liability is confined to cases of fraud by the agent; see also Balkin & Davis, *op. cit.* at p. 799 and Fridman, *op. cit.* vol. 2 at p. 316, suggesting that there is little purpose in differentiating between agents and employees in respect of vicarious liability.

44 *Moynihan v Moynihan* [1975] IR 192; *Johnson v Lindsay* [1891] AC 371, at p. 377 per Lord Herschell, *obiter; Cunningham v Grand Trunk Railway Co.* (1871) 31 UCQB 350; *Poppe v Tuttle* (1980) 14 CCLT 115.

45 The independent responsibility of children and parents is of ancient lineage in Judaeo-Christian culture, being mentioned in the Bible – Deuteronomy 24.16; it is eloquently set out by the Jewish historian, Josephus, as follows: 'You are not to punish children for the faults of their parents, but on account of their own virtue rather to vouchsafe them commiseration, because they were born of wicked parents, than hatred, because they were born of bad ones: nor indeed ought we to impute the sin of children to their fathers, while young persons indulge themselves in many practices different from what they have been instructed in, and this by their proud refusal of such instruction.' *Antiquities of the Jews, translated by Whiston, The Works of Flavious Josephus* (Edinburgh: W.P. Nimmo, Hay & Mitchell) Book IV, Chapter VIII at §39.

46 In German law the general position on parental responsibility is similar, except that failure to control is assumed unless the parent can show that he exercised

Non-delegable Duties

Certain activities give rise to obligations which are legally regarded as incapable of being avoided. This is a relatively common phenomenon in a variety of situations in different branches of law. Non-delegable duties form a particular sub-set of such obligations, which have arisen on an *ad hoc* basis, rather than as a result of any consistent rationalised principle. Particular types of activity have been interpreted by the courts as giving rise to a duty, performance of which may be delegated to another, but for which responsibility for the manner of performance may not be delegated. In other words, the defendant can get someone else to do the work, but cannot avoid responsibility by engaging an independent contractor.

These duties may be seen as an extension of vicarious liability to include independent contractors in limited instances, though this is not strictly accurate. The theoretical basis is slightly different, being based on the defendant's relationship to the activity rather than to the person performing the activity. In practice the two are very similar, since a detailed examination of vicarious liability shows it to be as much concerned with the employer's relationship to the work as it is with the employer's relationship with the worker. The second difference is that vicarious liability is an imputed responsibility for the *torts of another*, whereas non-delegable duties create imputed responsibility for the *conduct of the activity*, so liability can arise even though the conduct of the other was not a tort, in some instances.

Hazardous Activities

Liability under the *Rylands v Fletcher* principle attaches to the defendant in respect of the escape of the accumulated hazard; the fact that the escape was caused by an independent contractor, who exercised reasonable care, is irrelevant. The strict obligation arises as a result of the defendant's accumulation of a dangerous item for his own benefit and not on the basis of any special relationship to the person actually conducting work in connection with the dangerous accumulation.

A non-delegable duty may also arise, outside of the *Rylands v Fletcher* principle, in other situations where there is an unusually high level of risk attached to the activity. The line of cases dealing with inherently dangerous operations, considered in chapter 6, imputes responsibility on an employer for the negligence of an independent contractor. The duty differs from *Rylands v Fletcher*, in that there must be negligence on the contractor's part. The duty may differ from vicarious liability, in that it might not extend to intentional wrongdoing by the

reasonable care; thus, the burden of proof is reversed from the common law position; the same rule applies to other situations involving a duty to control the conduct of others – §832 Bürgerliches Gesetzbuch; see Markesinis, *The German Law of Torts*, 3rd ed. (Oxford: Clarendon Press, 1994) at pp. 899–900.

contractor. The successful actions in this area involved contractors' negligence, so the question of the employer's liability for intentional wrongdoing has not been resolved. The duty is generally presented as an obligation to have reasonable care exercised in the performance of the work, irrespective of the identity of the person who does the work. This requires the employer to accept responsibility for a lack of reasonable care by an independent contractor, but it seems unlikely that it would be extended to wilful wrongdoing.

In Australia, the assimilation of *Rylands v Fletcher* liability into the tort of negligence gives rise to just such a general principle of non-delegable duty for hazardous activities. The decision in *Burnie Port Authority v General Jones Pty Ltd*[47] indicates that, where an activity is entrusted to an independent contractor, a non-delegable duty arises if the activity is one 'fraught with danger unless special precautions are taken against "collateral" negligence'. Because this duty is framed in negligence, there must be a lack of reasonable care on the part of either the employer or the independent contractor and liability cannot attach for 'pure' accidents (i.e. where injury has occurred despite the exercise of all reasonable precautions).

Employers' Duties to Employees

Some aspects of the duties owed by an employer in respect of the safety of employees at common law have been held to be non-delegable, thereby making the employer liable for the negligence of independent contractors engaged to fulfil the employer's responsibilities. In *McDermid v Nash Dredging & Reclamation Co. Ltd*[48] the House of Lords held that the employer's duty in respect of the provision and operation of a safe system of work was non-delegable. The defendants were held responsible for an injury caused to an employee by the negligent operation, by an independent contractor, of the procedure for unmooring a tug – the pilot started the tug before the plaintiff had signalled that he was clear of the ropes and the plaintiff was seriously injured when caught in the trailing ropes as the tug pulled away. In *Connolly v Dundalk Urban District Council and Mahon & McPhillips (Water Treatment) Ltd*[49] the Supreme Court held that the duty to provide a safe place of work was non-delegable. The first defendant was held jointly liable for the negligence of the second defendant in installing piping carrying chlorine gas, which leaked causing injury to the plaintiff.

---

47 (1994) 120 ALR 42, at pp. 68–9.
48 [1987] AC 906; [1987] 3 WLR 212; [1987] 2 All ER 878; noted by Barrett (1986) 49 MLR 781.
49 Unrep. SC, 18 November 1992; see Byrne & Binchy, *Annual Review of Irish Law 1990* at pp. 505–7 in respect of the High Court decision; *1992* at pp. 568–9 in respect of the Supreme Court decision; see also *Paine v Colne Valley Electricity Co.* [1938] 4 All ER 803.

The position with respect to the provision of safe equipment is less clear. Earlier authorities had held that the employer's duty was discharged once the equipment was obtained from a reputable supplier,[50] but the decision in *Connolly* includes 'safe plant' within the scope of the non-delegable duty.[51] Clearly there is some overlap between 'plant' and 'equipment', though the two terms may be regarded as referring to different things. One possible way of resolving the issue is to apply the non-delegable duty to equipment in the nature of a fixture, which may be regarded as part of the premises, and apply the lesser duty to portable equipment, such as tools. Even this does not provide a definitive solution, as some heavy equipment will be difficult to classify as it will bear some of the characteristics of each type.

The non-delegable duties arise via the primary duties on employers under the tort of negligence; thus a failure to exercise reasonable care is essential to establish liability. The non-delegable aspect imputes responsibility to the employer for the negligence of any person engaged to fulfil the employer's obligations, but does not generate strict liability in the true sense of liability in the absence of negligence on the part of anyone.

Statutory Duties

Several statutory duties have been held to be non-delegable, as the courts have been unwilling to allow a duty, imposed on the defendant by the legislature, to be avoided simply by the hiring of an independent contractor to carry out the task. Examples include employers' statutory obligations in respect of occupational safety,[52] a shipowner's duty in respect of the seaworthiness of a vessel[53] and the duty of a local authority as a roads authority.[54] Some of the obligations involved

---

50 *Keenan v Bergin* [1971] IR 192; *Davie v New Merton Board Mills Ltd* [1959] AC 604; [1959] 2 WLR 331; [1959] 1 All ER 346.

51 [1990] 2 IR 1, at p. 7 in the High Court, citing *Paine v Colne Valley Electricity Co.* [1938] 4 All ER 803, at p. 807; p. 2 of the judgment of O'Flaherty J in the Supreme Court.

52 *Smith v Cammell Laird & Co. Ltd* [1940] AC 242; [1939] 4 All ER 381; *Hosking v De Havilland Aircraft Co. Ltd* [1949] 1 All ER 540.

53 *Riverstone Meat Co. Pty Ltd v Lancashire Shipping Co. Ltd* [1961] AC 807; [1961] 2 WLR 269; [1961] 1 All ER 495.

54 *Weir v Dún Laoghaire Corporation* [1984] ILRM 113; the case is particularly unusual, in that the local authority did not engage the contractor in question, but had given planning permission for the development which included the construction of the road. The Supreme Court held that the obligation as a roads authority was, nonetheless, applicable. The Supreme Court decision in *Convery v Dublin County Council* [1996] 3 IR 156 indicates that the court in *Weir* erred in finding that the local authority had authorised the activity, as it did not consider s. 26(11) of the Local Government (Planning and Development) Act 1963. This section, as interpreted in *Convery*, indicates that a grant of planning permission does not amount to an authorisation to engage in unlawful activity. The *Convery* decision does not overturn the broader question of principle, i.e. the non-delegable nature of the local authority's duties.

in the cases were strict duties in the true sense of liability being independent of any want of care, while others involved imputed responsibility for failure to exercise due care.[55] The non-delegable nature of the first category is not unusual; the obligation is essentially to ensure a particular outcome, not merely to exercise a particular level of care, so the issue of who assists in producing the result is irrelevant to the question of ultimate responsibility for the outcome. In the latter instance the non-delegable aspect of the obligation is not inevitable and depends on a careful examination of the statutory provisions to see if it is necessary.

The decision in *Darling v AG*[56] goes a stage further in holding that a duty arising from the exercise of a statutory power was non-delegable. An independent contractor was appointed by a government department to examine the mining potential of private land, entry to which was based on a statutory power of entry, and the government was held liable for the contractor's negligence. This would represent a considerable extension of the field of non-delegable duties, if it was to be widely applied by the courts, particularly in light of the developing nature of duties in respect of statutory powers.[57]

Duties of Control

These duties are based on ordinary principles of tortious responsibility, founded on the defendant's own conduct, and are included here only for the purpose of highlighting the difference between direct and vicarious responsibility. The fact situations are ones which might be confused with vicarious liability by a person unversed in the law, particularly since control is a central aspect in both types of liability.

Control of Persons

In chapter 2 we saw that a motorist's duty to other road users included a duty to control passengers' behaviour in some instances, particularly where the passenger is a child.[58] There are many instances where similar duties arise, such as the duty of prison authorities to exercise reasonable control over prisoners to ensure that they do not cause injury to other prisoners, or to the general public in the course of an escape,[59] or the duty of a school to control pupils.[60] While a school, prison

---

55 *Smith v Cammell Laird* involved a strict duty; *Riverstone Meat Co. Pty Ltd v Lancashire Shipping* involved both types of obligation.
56 [1950] 2 All ER 793.
57 See chapter 2 *supra*, on duties in respect of statutory powers.
58 *Curley v Mannion* [1965] IR 543.
59 *Home Office v Dorset Yacht Co.* [1970] AC 1004; [1970] 2 WLR 1140; [1970] 2 All ER 294; *Muldoon v Ireland* [1988] ILRM 367; *Kavanagh v Governor of Arbour Hill Prison* unrep. HC, 22 April 1993; *Boyd & Boyd v Ireland* unrep. HC, 13 May 1993; *Byrne & Binchy, Annual Review of Irish Law 1987* at p. 326; *1993* at pp. 551–2.
60 *Carmarthenshire County Council v Lewis* [1955] AC 549; [1955] 2 WLR 517; [1955] 1 All ER 565; for a general consideration of the duty to control persons see

authority or other such institution will be vicariously liable for the conduct of its staff, it is not vicariously liable for the conduct of pupils or prisoners. However, where reasonable control is not exercised, the institution will be liable to the plaintiff for injuries inflicted by the child or prisoner.

The essential difference between these situations and vicarious liability is that the defendant's responsibility is dependent on the existence of a direct duty to the plaintiff and proof that the defendant was in breach of that duty. Furthermore, vicarious liability makes one liable for the *torts* of another, whereas breach of a duty of control gives rise to liability even where the conduct of the person under the defendant's control did not amount to a tort. This is most apparent in cases of failure to control young children; the child may be incapable of having a sufficient awareness of risk to commit a tort, but the supervising adult is liable for the failure to exercise reasonable control over the child's conduct.

Control of Objects

A person in control of a dangerous object, such as a gun, owes a duty of care to avoid foreseeable harm to others. This duty may include a duty to take reasonable care to prevent third party interference with the object.[61]

In England there has been a notable reluctance to impose a duty of control over chattels and real property in recent years. The most dramatic example is the decision in *Topp v London Country Buses (South West) Ltd.*[62] The driver of a minibus parked it, leaving it unlocked and with the key in the ignition. Another driver was supposed to take over the driving of the vehicle, but did not turn up, due to illness. The defendant company was aware of the situation, but failed to take any steps to secure or remove the minibus. It was subsequently stolen and the plaintiff's wife was killed as a result of being run over by the thieves.

The trial judge and the Court of Appeal held that it would be unjust to impose a duty on the defendant company and so rejected the plaintiff's claim, despite finding that there had been carelessness on the defendant's part. Howarth is strongly critical of the decision, arguing that it is based on a misinterpretation of the relevant legal principles.[63] The criticism appears to be well founded and it

---

Prosser et al., *Prosser & Keeton on Torts*, 5th ed. (St Paul, Minn.: West, 1984) at §56; Fridman, 'Non-Vicarious Liability for the Acts of Others' (1997) 5 Tort L Rev 102.

61 *Dixon v Bell* (1816) 5 M & S 198.
62 [1993] 1 WLR 977; [1993] 3 All ER 448; see also the cases considered in chapter 1 *supra*, in respect of omissions.
63 'My Brother's Keeper? Liability for Acts of Third Parties' (1994) 14 LS 88; the decision is curious in light of the general reasoning behind the imposition of duties of control, as the facts reveal no obvious reason why the bus company should be relieved of an obligation to innocent road users; see also *Haynes v G. Harwood & Son* [1935] 1 KB 146; [1934] All ER Rep 103, liability imposed for failure to properly secure horses and van (CA) and *Wright v Lodge* [1993] 4 All ER 299, liability for failure to move a vehicle off the road after it had broken down (CA).

seems unlikely that an Irish court would follow the decision;[64] however, it is not the correctness of the outcome that is of interest for our present purpose. The point to note is that the approach taken, both by the courts and by Howarth, seeks to determine whether there is a direct duty owed by the bus company to the victim, based on the company's control over the vehicle. It is the relationship to the object that is important here, not a relationship to the thieves.

Control of Situations

A further variation on the theme of direct responsibility for a failure to exercise sufficient control involves situations where the defendant has control over a set of circumstances or activity, rather than a person or thing. A prime example is the duty to exercise reasonable care in the selection of an employee or an independent contractor to perform a task which carries a reasonably foreseeable risk to third parties.[65] Another example is the duty of the police or private security firms to exercise reasonable care in controlling access to events.[66]

Like the other duties of control, any liability imposed on the defendant for the effects of the behaviour of third parties is based on the defendant's breach of a direct duty, independent of the question of whether the third party conduct amounted to a tort.

Comment

A more contentious example of a duty to control is the emerging responsibility of those serving liquor.[67] This embraces elements of the duties to control persons and objects, but is perhaps best viewed as control over a general situation. The principal argument in favour of imposing a duty to control is that the seller is engaged in a commercial enterprise for profit and should bear at least some of the known risks associated with the product being sold. The counterargument is that

---

64 See *Davoren v Fitzpatrick* [1935] Ir Jur Rep 23 and *Cahill v Kenneally* [1955–6] Ir Jur Rep 15, Circuit Court cases imposing liability for negligently facilitating the taking of vehicles.

65 See chapter 2 *supra*, in respect of an employer's duty to select competent staff; *Ward v McMaster* [1988] IR 337 (selection of an auctioneer rather than a surveyor to value a property amounted to a breach of duty towards the purchaser).

66 See, for example, the Hillsborough cases, considered in chapter 1 *supra*, in respect of psychological damage; see also *Adderly v Great Northern Railway Co.* [1905] 2 IR 378 (duty of railway company to exercise control over a drunk passenger).

67 *Hall & Kennedy v Routledge* unrep. HC, 20 December 1993; *Walsh v Ryan* unrep. HC, 12 February 1993, both cases deal with a publican's duty to protect a customer against a battery by another customer; see Byrne & Binchy, *Annual Review of Irish Law 1993* at pp. 558–9 for comment on the possible extension of the principle to persons injured by a customer after leaving the premises; the principle of liability of the vendor of alcohol is well established in some jurisdictions, such as Canada; for detailed consideration see Solomon & Payne, 'Alcohol Liability in Canada and Australia: Sell, Serve and be Sued' (1996) 4 Tort L Rev 188.

such liability will impinge on individual freedom, as publicans and other licensed sellers of alcohol will be the ones determining how much a patron may consume, rather than the patron deciding for himself. Both arguments have some force and there is no obvious point of balance between the two. The precise balance chosen will depend on factors such as social attitudes towards alcohol consumption and the degree of risk involved in particular cases.

While the issue of liability of vendors of alcohol may be particularly problematic, all the examples of duties of control raise fundamental questions of policy in respect of the imposition of affirmative duties. Apart from such issues, even if one accepts the current state of the law in respect of affirmative duties, the distinction between these duties and the present law of vicarious liability is logically difficult to maintain. An employer's vicarious liability arises because of the existence of a particular relationship, which is in turn based on control and this control may often be notional rather than real. The affirmative duties are based on real control, but do not generate any 'special' relationship between the person in control and those under that control. The result is that the employer may have less control, but is subject to a stricter type of liability. It may be that other facets of the employment relationship justify the retention of stricter liability for employers, but the continued reliance on the control test looks increasingly dubious in light of recent developments in the area of duties of control.

The legal distinction normally drawn between the two situations is that control is only a test of the state of the relationship in vicarious liability cases (i.e. it is a characteristic feature to identify the nature of the relationship), but in the case of affirmative duties control acts as a *justification* for the imposition of an obligation.[68] Even this distinction is blurred by the decision of Barr J in *Phelan v Coillte Teo.*,[69] which suggests that control is the justification for vicarious liability.

---

68 McMahon & Binchy, *op. cit.* at p. 750, citing the judgment of Walsh J in the Supreme Court in *Moynihan v Moynihan* [1975] IR 192, at p. 198 and the High Court decision in *Davey v CIÉ* (1968) 103 ILTSJ 164.
69 [1993] 1 IR 20, at p. 23.

CHAPTER FIFTEEN

Remedies

Introduction

The provision of effective remedies is an important means of measuring the real value of legal rights and obligations; some might even suggest that it is their only measure, though that is an overly cynical view. The investment of a considerable amount of time, effort and money by a plaintiff in pursuing a claim must be weighed against the nature and quality of the available remedy in order to determine the value of the interests involved in that claim. If the investment will produce a mild censure for the defendant and a moderate return, or even a loss, for the plaintiff, then the legal value of the defendant's obligation to the plaintiff will be perceived as small and litigation will be rare. If, on the other hand, the plaintiff has the potential for a significant return, with a serious impact on the defendant, then the obligation will be seen to be of greater importance.[1]

The law of remedies represents a substantial area of study in its own right. This chapter merely provides an overview of the general principles by which torts are remedied. The primary focus is on judicial remedies, i.e. solutions imposed by the courts in disputed cases, though a brief treatment of non-judicial remedies is also included. This balance does not reflect the relative importance of the different types of remedy. In practice only a minority of cases result in a full trial with a remedy imposed by the courts, but the judicial remedies represent the legal evaluation of the rights and obligations, whereas non-judicial remedies are influenced by extralegal considerations. The non-legal aspects of the non-judicial remedies exceed the scope of this work, but are an extremely important aspect of the practice of law. The treatment of judicial remedies concentrates on the substantive principles and does not extend to procedural aspects, such as pleading, or the enforcement mechanisms.

Damages

The remedy of damages at common law is the principal one used to redress tortious wrongs. The law seeks to provide the plaintiff with a monetary replacement for the harm caused by the wrongful interference with the plaintiff's rights. The primary purpose of the law is to try to put the plaintiff in

---

1 Practical circumstances can have a distorting effect on the value of claims. Battery claims, for example, may be hindered by the wrongdoer's lack of means, but this does not mean that the law places little value on the victim's right to bodily integrity. Nonetheless, the gap between the practical and theoretical value of the victim's right can lead to public dissatisfaction with the legal system.

the position he would have been in had the tort not occurred.[2] In many cases this is not possible, as an accurate monetary value cannot be placed on that which has been lost. This is particularly so in the case of personal injuries, where any monetary measure of physical and mental capacity is arbitrary. However, even cases of economic loss and property damage are often incapable of precise measurement – damages for economic loss usually involve speculation as to probable future impact on the plaintiff, while property damage sometimes involves items which are incapable of repair or replacement.

The inability to provide accurate measurement for losses, coupled with problems in establishing liability, contributes significantly to the public perception of tort litigation as a lottery. It would be harsh to criticise the law simply for inaccurate measurement, since any system of compensation will necessarily have problems with accuracy. It is, however, legitimate to level criticism at the way in which the legal rules cope with the difficulties that the cases present.

Damages may also be used for secondary purposes, such as the vindication of rights, deterrence and public censure of undesirable behaviour. Vindication is relevant to all awards; however, it comes to the fore particularly in respect of torts which are actionable *per se*, where there is no 'loss' as such to be replaced, but there is some significant intrusion which needs to be recognised and measured in order to give meaningful content to the rights which have been violated. These secondary objectives are governed by some distinct principles of their own, though many cases involve a mixture of compensating losses and the pursuit of secondary objectives, and the two areas become blurred.

Damages in equity arise in limited instances, most notably under section 2 of the Chancery Amendment Act 1858 (Lord Cairns' Act), in lieu of an injunction. This will be considered after the treatment of injunctions, because of the close relationship between the two remedies. Equitable damages are also available in actions for breach of confidence.[3]

Categories of Damages

Damages are divided into several categories, each with a different objective to address in the pursuit of the various goals of the tort system. The principal category is compensatory damages, which provides a monetary sum to approximate the harmful effects of a tort. The other categories are exemplary (or punitive),[4] nominal and contemptuous damages.

---

2 For an insightful analysis of the nature of compensation in tort see Stapleton, 'The Normal Expectancies Measure in Tort Damages' (1997) 113 LQR 257.

3 See Burrows, *Remedies for Torts and Breach of Contract*, 2nd ed. (London: Butterworths, 1994) at pp. 246–7; Lavery, *Commercial Secrets: The Action for Breach of Confidence in Ireland* (Dublin: Round Hall Sweet & Maxwell, 1996) at pp. 244 *et seq*.

4 At one time it was suggested that the terms 'punitive' and 'exemplary' referred to different categories of damages, but it is now clear that the terms are interchangeable

Compensatory Damages

This category was traditionally sub-divided into special, general and aggravated damages. The distinction between special and general compensatory damages has been a source of considerable confusion and has largely been abandoned by academic commentators.[5] The Irish courts tend to use the term 'special' in personal injury cases to refer to loss of income and expenses incurred. The term 'general damages' is used to refer to non-pecuniary losses, such as pain, suffering and loss of amenity. McCarthy J, in *Reddy v Bates*,[6] explained the function of general damages in personal injury cases as follows:

> Such damages are frequently stated to be for pain and suffering; they would be better described as compensation in money terms for the damage, past and future, sustained to the plaintiff's amenity in all its aspects, actual pain and suffering, both physical and mental, both private to the plaintiff and in the plaintiff's relationships with family, with friends, in working and social life and in lost opportunity.

O'Higgins CJ, in *Sinnott v Quinnsworth*,[7] adopted a similar approach:

> General damages are intended to represent fair and reasonable monetary compensation for the pain, suffering, inconvenience and loss of the pleasures of life which the injury has caused and will cause to the plaintiff.

The modern approach to compensatory damages distinguishes between pecuniary loss in personal injury cases; non-pecuniary loss in personal injury cases; and loss in cases of economic and property damage. Furthermore, pecuniary damages are sub-divided under various heads, representing different types of loss, such as income, medical expenses and domestic assistance.

Aggravated damages are awarded in exceptional cases to compensate for additional harm suffered by the plaintiff, beyond that which would normally flow from the type of tort in question, as a result of either the manner in which the harm was inflicted or the defendant's behaviour towards the plaintiff after the initial tort. Examples would include a failed attempt to justify or mitigate a

---

and refer to a single category – *Conway v INTO* [1991] ILRM 497, at pp. 504–5 per Finlay CJ; *McIntyre v Dolan & Lewis* [1991] 1 IR 121, at p. 138 per McCarthy J; p. 139 per O'Flaherty J.

5 See White, *Irish Law of Damages* (Dublin: Butterworths, 1989) at §3.2.01, chapters 4, 5 and 6 deal respectively with loss of benefits, expenses and non-pecuniary loss; McMahon & Binchy, *The Irish Law of Torts*, 2nd ed. (Dublin: Butterworths, 1989) at chapter 44; *McGregor on Damages*, 15th ed. (London: Sweet & Maxwell, 1988) at §§19–27; Burrows, *op. cit.* at chapter 3; Dobbs, *The Law of Remedies*, 2nd ed. (St Paul, Minn.: West, 1993) at §3.3(1) and chapter 8.

6 [1983] IR 141; [1984] ILRM 197, at p. 151; p. 205.

7 [1984] ILRM 523, at p. 531.

defamation, causing further harm to the plaintiff's character;[8] or an intimidating or demeaning manner in which a trespass was committed.[9] This is still a form of compensation, but is sometimes listed as a distinct item in order to emphasise that the compensatory award is higher than usual because of the additional injury, by way of anxiety or offence to dignity, caused by the defendant.

Compensatory damages address the primary aim of the tort process – reparation for the adverse effects, past and future, of the tort on the plaintiff.[10] The secondary aim of vindicating rights is also partially addressed, particularly in torts which are actionable *per se* or in cases where aggravated damages are awarded. This is because the plaintiff is provided with reassurance, through a public forum, that the rights violated are of significant value, independent of pecuniary effects.[11] The award may even satisfy a plaintiff's desire for retribution in some cases. It is often asserted that an element of deterrence results from the making of an award against the defendant, though this is doubtful in most cases.[12]

Exemplary Damages

Exemplary damages are not concerned with compensating the plaintiff for the effects of the wrong, but are awarded as a mark of censure for the manner in which the tort was committed and as a deterrent to further wrongful behaviour. They are intended as a punishment for the defendant and to serve as an example to others. Therefore, this category of damages is aimed exclusively at secondary aims of the tort process and, consequently, only arises in exceptional cases.

The distinction between this category and compensatory damages is amply demonstrated by judicial remarks in *Conway v INTO*.[13] Barron J, in the High

---

8   *Kennedy v Hearne* [1988] ILRM 531, considered in chapter 8 *supra*; see also Law Reform Commission, *Consultation Paper on the Civil Law of Defamation* (Dublin: Law Reform Commission, 1991) at §125; *Law Reform Commission, Report on the Civil Law of Defamation*, (Dublin: Law Reform Commission, 1991) (38–91) at §§7.13–7.16.

9   *Whelan v Madigan* [1978] ILRM 136; see also Howarth, *Textbook on Tort* (London: Butterworth, 1995) at pp. 593–5; Jones, *Textbook on Torts*, 5th ed. (London: Blackstone, 1996) at pp. 515–16; Balkin & Davis, *Law of Torts* (Sydney: Butterworths, 1991) at pp. 831–2; *Conway v INTO* [1991] ILRM 497, at p. 503 per Finlay CJ.

10 White, *op. cit.* at §1.2.01; McGregor, *op. cit.* at §§9–18; Burrows, *op. cit.* at pp. 21–6.

11 See Cane, *Tort Law and Economic Interests*, 2nd ed. (Oxford: Clarendon Press, 1996) at p. 468; Dobbs, *Remedies, op. cit.* at pp. 211–12.

12 See Cane, *op. cit.* at pp. 469–70 and p. 474, pointing out that the imposition of liability only causes potential defendants to develop preventive strategies in limited situations and that making a defendant compensate the plaintiff is not a particularly efficient device for preventing the infliction of harm.

13 Unrep. HC, 7 December 1988; [1991] ILRM 497 (SC); see also *Worthington v Tipperary County Council* [1920] 2 IR 233, at p. 245 per Maloney CJ. In *Conway*, the union could not avail of the statutory immunity, as it had been held in *Hayes v Ireland* [1987] ILRM 651 (an earlier action, arising out of the same employment

Court, stated that 'exemplary damages should be measured in an amount to meet the wrongdoing rather than to benefit the wronged'.[14] He awarded the plaintiff £1,500 exemplary damages, in addition to the amount assessed for proper compensation, on the basis that she was one of approximately seventy people with similar claims arising out of the defendant's wrongdoing and that this figure would generate a total level of exemplary damages in the region of £100,000 for the defendant union, which was an appropriate measure of censure.[15] It can be seen from this that the measure of damages is an estimate of wrongfulness of the defendant's behaviour, independent of the impact on the plaintiff. The plaintiff's receipt of any or all of the amount assessed is purely a matter of chance, dependent on the number of victims that will share in the distribution of the additional award. Finlay CJ, in the Supreme Court, gave a more expansive explanation of the role of this category:

> Punitive or exemplary damages arising from the nature of the wrong which has been committed and/or the manner of its commission . . . are intended to mark the court's particular disapproval of the defendant's conduct in all the circumstances of the case and its decision that it should publicly be seen to have punished the defendant for such conduct by awarding such damages, quite apart from its obligation, where it may exist in the same case, to compensate the plaintiff for the damage which he or she has suffered.[16]

Griffin J was equally clear in explaining the aim of the law:

> The object of awarding exemplary damages is to punish the wrong-doer for his outrageous conduct, to deter him and others from any such conduct in the future, and to mark the court's . . . detestation and disapproval of that conduct. Such damages are to be awarded even though the plaintiff who recovers them obtains the benefit of what has been described in the case law as a fortunate windfall.[17]

This gives a clear picture of the purpose of such damages, but leaves open the question as to when such an award may be made. One of the leading judgments

---

dispute) that the interference with constitutional rights was not a tort action for the purposes of s. 4 of the Trade Disputes Act 1906.

14 Unrep. HC, 7 December 1988 at p. 7 of the judgment.
15 But, in *McIntyre v Dolan & Lewis* [1991] 1 IR 121, it was suggested that the assessment of exemplary damages should be proportionate to compensatory damages, per Hederman J at p. 134 and O'Flaherty J at p. 141; this suggests a connection between the two categories, which is not warranted and only serves to disguise the difference between the two categories; see Byrne & Binchy, *Annual Review of Irish Law 1990* at pp. 582 *et seq.*; ratio rules are also used in some American jurisdictions, see Dobbs, *Torts and Compensation*, 2nd ed. (St Paul, Minn.: West, 1993) at pp. 814–15; Dobbs, *Remedies, op. cit.* at §3.11(11); for an alternative strategy for controlling the level of exemplary damages see *Thompson v Commissioner of Police of the Metropolis* [1997] 3 WLR 403; [1997] 2 All ER 762.
16 [1991] ILRM 497, at p. 503.
17 *Ibid.*, at p. 509.

in English law governing the circumstances in which such damages are available is that of the House of Lords in *Rookes v Barnard*,[18] where Lord Devlin proposed three categories in which an award could be made:

(i) oppressive, arbitrary or unconstitutional action by the servants of government;
(ii) conduct calculated to make a profit, exceeding the compensation payable; or
(iii) express statutory authorisation.

This rigid classification has met with a considerable amount of disapproval, both judicial and academic.[19] The main difficulty relates to the first category, where it is felt that the restriction of the principle to 'servants of government' is unduly narrow, since arbitrary or vindictive conduct by lesser public officials and private persons may equally warrant public censure. *Conway v INTO* has put beyond doubt the fact that the first category is not applicable in Ireland, as exemplary damages were awarded against a trade union for interfering with the right to primary education of a group of children, in the course of an industrial dispute.[20] A second difficulty with the first category is the use of the term 'unconstitutional'. Constitutionality raises different connotations in a legal system, such as

---

18 [1964] AC 1129; [1964] 2 WLR 269; [1964] 1 All ER 367; at pp. 1226–7; pp. 328–9; pp. 410–11.

19 The classification has been rejected by courts in Australia – *Uren v John Fairfax & Sons Pty Ltd* (1966) 117 CLR 118; *Australian Consolidated Press Ltd v Uren* [1969] 1 AC 590; [1967] 3 WLR 1338; [1967] 3 All ER 523 (PC); New Zealand – *Fogg v McKnight* [1968] NZLR 330; *Taylor v Beere* [1982] 1 NZLR 81; and Canada – *Paragon Properties Ltd v Magna Investments Ltd* (1972) 24 DLR (3d) 156; even the Court of Appeal in England held the classification to be *per incuriam*, but this was overturned on appeal – *Broome v Cassell & Co.* [1971] 2 QB 354; [1971] 2 WLR 853; [1971] 2 All ER 187 (CA); [1972] AC 1027; [1972] 2 WLR 645; [1972] 1 All ER 801; see also White, *op. cit.* at §§1.2.07–1.2.10; White, 'Exemplary Damages in Irish Tort Law' (1987) 5 ILT 60; American law has generally taken a broader perspective on punitive damages and has shown a greater willingness to make awards, see Dobbs, *Remedies, op. cit.* at §3.11; Dobbs, *Torts and Compensation, op. cit.* at pp. 810–16; Burrows, *op. cit.* at pp. 282–5 argues for the abolition of exemplary damages in tort; McGregor, *op. cit.* at §§414–415 argues that the classification is not based on a principled distinction between public and private defendants, but simply served as a means of allowing existing precedent to stand, while precluding the development of a general principle allowing exemplary damages for arbitrary or vindictive infliction of harm.

20 There was already a considerable body of authority to suggest that the categories in *Rookes* were not applicable in Ireland; see *Reeves v Penrose* (1890) 26 LR Ir 141 (exemplary damages in respect of trespass to land by a private individual); *McDonald v Galvin* unrep. HC, 23 February 1976 (*dictum* of McWilliam J that exemplary damages could be available in an action for assault and battery against a private individual); the full range of Irish authorities are considered in some detail in White, *op. cit.* at §§1.2.11–1.2.13; McMahon & Binchy, *op. cit.* at pp. 774–8; Law Reform Commission Consultation Paper on Aggravated, Exemplary and Restitutionary Damages (Dublin: 1998).

the Irish one, which employs a written constitution. Arguably any tort involves some form of violation of constitutional rights, but it would be inappropriate to regard this in itself as a sufficient basis for an award of exemplary damages. Barron J, in the High Court in *Conway*, felt that an award was justified on the facts, because 'There was a totally conscious and deliberate action on the part of the defendants to gain their own ends without any thought to those who could suffer as a result.'[21] Griffin J, in the Supreme Court, stated that 'Such damages may be awarded where there has been on the part of the defendant, wilful and conscious wrongdoing in contumelious disregard of another's rights.'[22] This makes it clear that there must be some seriously discreditable behaviour on the defendant's part, bringing the case beyond the parameters of 'ordinary' wrongdoing, before such an award will be made.

The second category proposed by Lord Devlin is designed to deter people from treating the law as a means to 'buy' the right to commit torts, by treating compensation as a cost to be incurred in pursuing one's own ends, without any real regard for the interests of others. This category may be unnecessary in Ireland, given the rejection of the narrow confines of the first category. The cases covered by this second category may simply be a sub-set of the cases covered by the broader rule on arbitrary or wanton disregard of the victims' rights.[23]

One aspect of Lord Devlin's judgment in *Rookes* which has been well received is the suggestion that, in cases where exemplary damages are appropriate, there are three considerations relevant to their assessment. These are:

(i)   the plaintiff must be a victim of the defendant's wrongdoing;
(ii) the power to award should be used with restraint; and
(iii) the means of the parties must be considered, as must any other aggravating, or mitigating, factor.[24]

The first consideration is designed to prevent the use of the civil process as a means of private prosecution of wrongdoing by unaffected parties, thereby undermining the criminal process. While the damages are for a non-compensatory purpose, the *locus standi* to bring a claim is confined to victims of the impugned behaviour, thereby confining claims to persons with a distinct and independent grievance to pursue.

---

21 Unrep. HC, 7 December 1988 at pp. 6–7.
22 [1991] ILRM 497, at p. 509; see also the views of Finlay CJ at pp. 505–7 and McCarthy J at p. 513.
23 Cane, *op. cit.* at p. 467 suggests that this element of taking the proceeds of the wrong from the defendant (disgorgement) is not really punitive in nature, but is more akin to unjust enrichment principles; he also points out, at p. 468, that exemplary damages also reflect an element of vindication for the plaintiff. The line between aggravated compensatory damages and exemplary damages is difficult to draw as a result of this overlap of aims; see also Howarth, *op. cit.* at pp. 594–5; *AB v South West Water Services* [1993] QB 507; [1993] 2 WLR 507; [1993] 1 All ER 609.
24 *Conway v INTO* [1991] ILRM 497, at pp. 511–12 per Griffin J; *McIntyre v Dolan & Lewis* [1991] 1 IR 121, at pp. 140–1 per O'Flaherty J.

The second consideration serves as a reminder that the defendant is being punished, by the imposition of a fine, without the usual procedural protections of the criminal process, so caution is advisable in the exercise of this anomalous power.[25] The English courts have exercised this caution to the extent that exemplary damages may now only be awarded in respect of a tort in relation to which the power to make an award existed prior to *Rookes*. The exceptional nature of the remedy is such that they are unwilling to extend its use to situations where it was not recognised as being applicable prior to the attempt in *Rookes* to confine its scope.[26] The approach adopted by the Irish courts does not reflect the same degree of constraint, as the wrong in *Conway* could not possibly fall within the restriction, since breach of constitutional rights was not a clearly recognised cause of action prior to 1964 (when *Rookes* was decided). Furthermore, McCarthy J, in *McIntyre v Dolan & Lewis*,[27] expressed a more robust approach to the circumstances in which an award could be made, insisting that 'it is inconsistent with the dynamism that characterises the common law to delimit in any restrictive way the nature of its development'.

The third consideration allows a degree of flexibility in fixing the extent of the punishment, since the punitive effect of a specific sum will clearly vary with the means of the defendant. The means of the plaintiff, while not obviously relevant, does appear to be accepted by the courts as a valid factor and may be connected to an element of vindication in the award.[28] Other factors which may be relevant would include any provocative conduct by the plaintiff or an apology by the defendant in open court, either of which may be considered in mitigation.[29]

There is no requirement that exemplary damages be specifically pleaded by the plaintiff, though it is preferable that the defendant should be given some prior warning as to the possibility of such damages being sought, in order that a defence may be mounted on the issue.[30]

Nominal Damages

Nominal damages is the award of a token amount, where the plaintiff has established a wrong but has suffered no harm. The recognition of the plaintiff's

---

25 McGregor, *op. cit.* at §426 notes that this consideration is employed to keep awards at a moderate level.

26 *AB v South West Water Services* [1993] QB 507; [1993] 2 WLR 507; [1993] 1 All ER 609; see Burrows, *op. cit.* at pp. 278–80 for the chequered history of the development of this constraint.

27 [1991] 1 IR 121, at p. 138; although this comment was directed towards Lord Devlin's categories, it is also clearly applicable to the follow-on restriction, which seeks to fossilise the award within its pre-1964 parameters.

28 McGregor, *op. cit.* at §427 asserts that it serves no useful purpose.

29 See McGregor, *op. cit.* at §§428–430; the level of the compensatory award may even be a relevant factor, as it will incorporate a deterrent element.

30 *Conway v INTO* [1991] ILRM 497, at pp. 507–8 per Finlay CJ; *McIntyre v Dolan & Lewis* [1991] 1 IR 121, at pp. 133–4 per Hederman J.

right by the court serves as sufficient vindication, without the need for significant compensation. An example of an appropriate case would be a boundary dispute, resolved by a trespass action, where there was no bad faith on the defendant's part. Although the plaintiff suffers no material harm, there is a valid interest to pursue and the action is not frivolous.[31] Another appropriate situation would be a minor defamation, with no likelihood of any serious adverse impact on reputation, but involving insult to the plaintiff's feelings or dignity. Here the award of nominal damages acts as a sort of declaratory relief, allowing the plaintiff the requisite vindication of good name, without imposing serious financial liability on the defendant.[32]

In theory the plaintiff should not lose out in the event of a nominal award, as costs would normally be awarded to the successful party. The defendant might not, however, have the resources to meet the costs involved. A plaintiff may, nonetheless, consider the vindication of rights to be worth the expense involved.

Contemptuous Damages

Contemptuous damages is the award of a token amount, where the plaintiff establishes a technical wrong, but is considered not to have a sufficient reason for bringing litigation. This category would be used where the plaintiff has suffered no material harm and has no significant interest to protect.[33] Furthermore, the plaintiff will not be awarded costs and may even have the defendant's costs imposed upon him.[34] A contemptuous award may not be made in cases of actual harm, so as to reduce the compensation payable, as there is no equivalent of a punitive award against a plaintiff who has acted improperly in the course of litigation.[35] In *Fagan v Wong*,[36] for example, the plaintiff feigned injury greater than that actually suffered and thereby sought an excessive level of compensation. It was held that the plaintiff should receive full compensation for the actual injury suffered. However, only that portion of the costs appropriate to the

---

31 See *Hanna v Pollock* [1898] 2 IR 532 (trespass to restore a supply of water to a tank, where the defendant had no enforceable right to the supply); McGregor, *op. cit.* at §§396–405.

32 The Law Reform Commission's proposals in respect of alternative remedies could supersede the role of nominal damages in defamation cases, if implemented; see LRC 38–91, *op. cit.* at §§9.4–9.11 in respect of declaratory relief and §§9.12–9.17 in respect of correction orders.

33 See Balkin & Davis, *op. cit.* at p. 829. Such an award was made in *Reynolds v Times Newspapers Ltd* [1998] 3 All ER 961; [1998] 3 WLR 862, but was overturned on appeal, at pp. 984–6; pp. 888–91, on the grounds that the judge had misdirected the jury to an extent which denied the plaintiff a fair trial of his case.

34 The principles applicable to the awarding of costs are set out in *Reynolds v Times Newspapers Ltd* [1998] 3 All ER 961; [1998] 3 WLR 862, at pp. 987–8; pp. 891–2.

35 *Deans v Sheridan* unrep. SC, 26 October 1993; Irish Times Law Report, 1 and 3 January 1994.

36 Unrep. HC, 6 July 1995; Irish Times Law Report, 16 October 1995; upheld on appeal unrep. SC, 7 May 1997.

proper pursuit of that claim were awarded; additional costs incurred by bringing the cases in the High Court, rather than the Circuit Court, and by unnecessarily increasing the length of the case were not awarded to the plaintiff.

Quantum

The quantification of the amount of compensatory damages is heavily dependent on the individual circumstances of each case, but the process is based on general principles which provide an outline view of how harm is measured. We must first consider the general features of an award and then consider issues peculiar to each head of loss under which the award is quantified.

Damages are awarded as a lump sum payment for all losses, past, present and future. The advantage of this approach is that it brings finality to the dispute between the parties, preventing the continuous reopening of issues. The drawback is that the award has to be based on a degree of guesswork as to what the future holds; matters such as the extent of the plaintiff's recovery from physical injury, the amount of the plaintiff's working life that has been impaired, the extent of alternative working opportunities, the impact of inflation, the impact other hazards (redundancy, illness and so forth) would have had, are all difficult to assess with any precision. Furthermore, a plaintiff accustomed to a periodic income has a significant adjustment to make, in order to manage the investment and spending of a once-off payment. In England there is a growing tendency to resort to structured settlements, to overcome the difficulties caused by the lump sum method of compensation. The plaintiff, under this type of arrangement, receives a periodic payment from an annuity purchased by the defendant and the arrangement can be varied to adapt to changing circumstances. The settlement must be by agreement and cannot, as yet, be imposed on the parties by the courts.[37] While the structured settlement approach allows for greater accuracy with respect to future uncertainties, it does require a certain amount of administration and makes compensation an ongoing process between the parties, rather than a final resolution.

The modern practice is to itemise the various heads of damage and award a specific amount for each item, so that the lump sum is determined by quantifying its various components.[38] After determining the itemised heads, the court must also review the global figure and take account of the interest bearing capacity of the award.[39] This is to ensure that there is no overcompensation

---

37 S. 2 of the Damages Act 1996 allows the courts to make an order for periodic payment of damages only where the parties have consented; for a comparison of lump sum awards and structured settlements see Burrows, *op. cit.* at pp. 100–4.

38 *Sexton v O'Keeffe* [1966] IR 204, at p. 210 per Kingsmill Moore J; *McArdle v McCaughey Bros Ltd* [1968] IR 47, at p. 53 per Walsh J; *O'Leary v O'Connell* [1968] IR 146, at p. 155 per Walsh J; *Carroll v Clare County Council* [1975] IR 221, at p. 230 per Kenny J; see also McGregor, *op. cit.* at §§1446–1449.

39 *Reddy v Bates* [1983] IR 141; [1984] ILRM 197, at p. 148; pp. 202–3 per Griffin J delivering the majority judgment in the Supreme Court (Hederman J concurring);

through duplication or overlap between the different items, but has been strongly criticised.[40]

In a typical case of serious personal injury, the type of heads of damage one would expect to find would be loss of income up to the date of trial, loss of future income, medical expenses incurred to the date of trial, medical expenses for the future, other itemised expenses up to the date of trial and for the future, general damages up to the date of trial and general damages for the future. This process assists in generating consistency in awards and facilitates the appeal process. It assists consistency in the following way – consider two plaintiffs having similar injuries, but radically different career prospects; one would expect a similar award for general damages for both of them, but a significantly different award for lost income. A single, non-itemised award would give no clear indication of how much was awarded for the different aspects of damage, whereas an itemised award clearly segregates the issues, which can provide better guidance for future cases. At a more complex level, itemised awards can allow courts to develop a consistent approach to matters such as inflation and the risk of unemployment that the plaintiff would have faced in a normal working life. The itemisation assists the appeals process, as it allows the appeal court to assess the correlation between the evidence on the various items of damage and the amounts awarded.

The once and for all nature of the award precludes the initiation of any further action between the parties in respect of the same tort.[41] Where the same incident leads to two or more distinct injuries, as where a negligent act causes personal injury and property damage, the better view is that there are two distinct causes of action and the conclusion of an action for one does not preclude the initiation of an action for the other.[42] Where there is a continuing wrong, as may occur in nuisance or trespass to land, there is no bar to further action on conclusion of the initial action; damages awarded in such cases are for the initial wrong and do not

---

affirmed in *Cooke v Walsh* [1984] ILRM 208, at pp. 219–20, per Griffin J (O'Higgins CJ, Henchy and Hederman JJ concurring) and *Sinnott v Quinnsworth* [1984] ILRM 523, at p. 531 per O'Higgins CJ (Henchy, Griffin and Hederman JJ concurring).

40 See White, *op. cit.* at §§3.3.01–3.3.06; McCarthy J dissenting on the use of global review and income bearing capacity in *Reddy v Bates* [1983] IR 141; [1984] ILRM 197, at p. 151 and p. 153; p. 205 and p. 206; McCarthy J reiterated his doubts in respect of the use of income generating capacity of the award in *Sinnott v Quinnsworth* [1984] ILRM 523, at p. 535; for less stringent criticism see McMahon & Binchy, *op. cit.* at p. 785.

41 *Fitter v Veal* (1701) 12 Mod Rep 542; McGregor, *op. cit.* at §§390–395.

42 *Brunsden v Humphrey* (1884) 14 QBD 141; [1881–1885] All ER Rep 357; *Darley Main Colliery Co. v Mitchell* (1886) 11 App Cas 127; [1886–90] All ER Rep 449; McGregor, *op. cit.* at §§371–372 and §378; however, in *Donohoe v Browne & McCabe* [1986] IR 90, Gannon J held that personal injury and property damage arising out of a road traffic accident arose from the same cause of action; White, *op. cit.* at p. 6 criticises the judgment for the failure to distinguish between duty and a complete cause of action; while the one duty of care may apply to both types

anticipate a continuation of the wrongdoing by the defendant.[43] The rule against further action for the same tort does not preclude an appeal court from ordering a retrial on foot of additional evidence, as litigation is not concluded prior to appellate process.[44] In such a case the original trial is inconclusive and the retrial is, effectively, part of the same litigation and not a new action.

Pecuniary Loss: Personal Injury Cases

Personal injury is usually accompanied by a variety of consequential financial losses, such as the cost of medical treatment and lost income. Serious injuries often generate additional financial burdens, such as the acquisition of special equipment necessitated by the plaintiff's condition or the cost of adapting the plaintiff's home (or even acquiring a more suitable home). Much of the detail in quantifying such losses is a factual matter, peculiar to each individual case, but even these losses raise some questions of legal principle.

Lost Earnings

Loss of income is usually the most significant element of lost financial benefits arising out of serious personal injuries.[45] The calculation of the loss of future earnings raises a variety of problems. Even cases involving a plaintiff with a stable occupation and a reasonably predictable career path can give rise to some difficulties – the long term prognosis of the injury may be uncertain, leaving open a question as to the plaintiff's residual capacity to work; or there may be uncertainty about the likelihood that the plaintiff's career might have been affected by illness in any event, which would have reduced earning capacity. For a child plaintiff, where one has no clear idea of the probable career path that would have been chosen, the problems are magnified by the fact that there is no baseline income to start from. These problems are primarily factual in nature and must be resolved according to the rules of evidence.[46]

There are some broad legal principles applicable to the quantification process. The calculation must take account of the hazards of disruption to earning power, such as the potential for periods of unemployment, redundancy, illness and so

---

of injury, there are, nonetheless, two distinct wrongs. While the criticism is well-founded, the actual decision could be justified on the narrower ground of issue estoppel, at least with respect to the plaintiff and the first defendant.

43 See McGregor, *op. cit.* at §§374–376.

44 *Danagher v Roscommon County Council* unrep. SC, 21 December 1973; the introduction of new evidence is considered in the discussion of appeals later in this chapter.

45 For detailed consideration of the entire process governing lost benefits see White, *op. cit.* at chapter 4; McGregor, *op. cit.* at §§1450–1513.

46 See chapter 12 *supra*; the balance of probabilities is not always an appropriate test for future uncertainties; in some cases chance valuation may be more appropriate, see White, *op. cit.* at §4.2; *Cooke v Walsh* [1984] ILRM 208 and *Conway v INTO* unrep. HC, 7 December 1988 provide good examples of quantifying lost income

forth.[47] The residual ability of the plaintiff to work at a reduced level must also be deducted.[48] The latter principle is theoretically sound, since the plaintiff only loses the difference between pre and post accident income, but its practical application can be difficult, since residual capacity can be as difficult to estimate as the plaintiff's original earning potential. The estimation of residual capacity is further complicated by the fact that the courts must recognise that a certain amount of prejudice against disabled persons may be present in the marketplace, so that a person with the physical capacity to do a job may not always be given the opportunity to do so.[49]

The plaintiff is also entitled to recover income for 'lost years'; this means that where life expectancy is shortened by the injuries sustained, the plaintiff can claim lost income on the basis of his pre-accident life expectancy, less living expenses for the 'lost' period. Living expenses are deducted here because the plaintiff is not expected to be alive to incur the expenses, but would have incurred them, if the injury had not shortened his life span.[50] This allows the plaintiff to recover the disposable portion of the income for the lost years, which may be helpful in making provision for dependants, for example.

The impact of income tax and other deductions, such as social insurance, must be taken into consideration in calculating lost income. If the award of damages is exempt from taxation, then it must be calculated on the basis of net, rather than gross income. If the award is not exempt, then no deduction should be made for tax, since the plaintiff will still have to pay it.[51] The capital sum,

---

for child plaintiffs; see also *Reddy v Bates* [1983] IR 141; [1984] ILRM 197; McMahon & Binchy, *op. cit.* at pp. 786–8 in respect of adult plaintiffs.

47 *Reddy v Bates* [1983] IR 141; [1984] ILRM 197, at pp. 146–7; pp. 201–2 per Griffin J (for the majority in the Supreme Court), although the actuarial figures had not taken account of these hazards the actuary's estimate for lost income was substituted for the jury's award; the failure to reduce for hazards was apparently offset by some evidence of the plaintiff's potential for increased income and the fact that she worked in a relatively stable and secure field of employment, at pp. 150–1 and p. 152; p. 205 and p. 206 per McCarthy J; *Cooke v Walsh* [1984] ILRM 208, at pp. 216–17 per Griffin J (for the majority in the Supreme Court) noting that, in the eight months intervening between the trial and the appeal, unemployment had risen significantly and that the long term forecast was for continued deterioration in the market; the award was set aside for failing to take this and other factors into account; note the dissent of McCarthy J, at pp. 220–2, who was unwilling to assume that employment prospects would remain in such a poor condition throughout the period for which income would be lost (1989–2022); see also White, *op. cit.* at §4.3.09; McGregor, *op. cit.* at §§1476–1476A.

48 *Ward v Walsh* unrep. SC, 31 July 1991.

49 *Ebbs v Forking & Co. Ltd* unrep. SC, 6 May 1961 (quoted in McMahon & Binchy, *op. cit.* at pp. 787–8); White, *op. cit.* at §§4.1.05–4.1.09; Burrows, *op. cit.* at p. 203.

50 *Doherty v Bowaters Irish Wallboard Mills Ltd* [1968] IR 267, at p. 285 per Walsh J; see White, 'Damages for the Lost Earnings of the Lost Years' (1985) 20 Ir Jur 295; White, *op. cit.* at §§4.9; Burrows, *op. cit.* at pp. 201–2; McGregor, *op. cit.* at §§1470–1474.

51 *British Transport Commission v Gourley* [1956] AC 185; [1956] 2 WLR 41; [1955] 3

awarded as compensation for lost income in personal injury cases, is exempt from taxation.[52] Income from an award of damages is exempt from tax if the plaintiff is 'permanently and totally incapacitated' and the award is the primary source of income.[53] While this arrangement eases the administrative burden for the plaintiff in the management of the award, it does complicate the calculation of the award, since the long term position on the level of taxation is as uncertain as the other aspects of future income. It appears that defendants are the primary beneficiaries of the tax arrangements, since the award is calculated on net, rather than gross income, once the award is tax free; thus the plaintiff derives no financial benefit, but the revenue is deprived of tax that would otherwise have been paid on the plaintiff's income.[54]

The other main issue with respect to lost income is whether compensating benefits, such as payments under an insurance policy, a pension or the social welfare system, should be deducted. The general position is that they are not deductible.[55] Some of the payments excluded from consideration are contractual in nature and the rationale behind their exclusion is that if the plaintiff has made contractual arrangements for a particular contingency, it should not fall as a benefit to the defendant by reducing the level of liability.[56] Where the benefit is gratuitous, the rule can be justified because the gratuity is based on sympathetic consideration for the injured person and should not be used to partially exculpate the tortfeasor. The main exception to the rule relates to social welfare payments, some of which are deductible from the lost earnings award. Deduction must be

---

All ER 796; *Glover v BLN* [1973] IR 432; *Cooke v Walsh* [1984] ILRM 208; *Allen v Mid-Western Health Board* unrep. SC, 11 March 1996; White, *op. cit.* at §§4.6.01–4.7.04; Burrows, *op. cit.* at pp. 132 *et seq.*; McGregor, *op. cit.* at chapter 13.

52 S. 24(1)(c) of the Capital Gains Tax Act 1975.

53 S. 5 of the Finance Act 1990; the section applies to all income from the award, not just that portion which represents lost earnings, *Allen v Mid-Western Health Board* unrep. SC, 11 March 1996, per Murphy J at pp. 18–19 of his judgment.

54 *Allen v Mid-Western Health Board* unrep. SC, 11 March 1996, per Murphy J at p. 18 of his judgment.

55 S. 2 of the Civil Liability (Amendment) Act 1964 is the primary provision governing this area; see Kerr, *The Civil Liability Acts 1961 and 1964* (Dublin: Round Hall Press, 1993) at pp. 133–4; *Greene v Hughes Haulage Ltd* [1998] 1 ILRM 34; Lewis, 'Deducting Collateral Benefits: Principle and Policy' (1998) 18 LS 15; some benefits still fall to be considered at common law, where the general rule is that collateral benefits are non-deductible; see White, *op. cit.* at §4.10; Burrows, *op. cit.* at pp. 119 *et seq.*; McGregor, *op. cit.* at §§1481–1513; it should be noted that sick pay is not regarded as a compensating benefit, but rather forms part of the plaintiff's residual earning capacity, so that portion of income is not actually lost by the plaintiff at all, see *Hussain v New Taplow Paper Mills Ltd* [1988] AC 514; [1988] 2 WLR 266; [1988] 1 All ER 541.

56 Payments under an insurance policy taken out by the plaintiff's employer are not deductible, even though the plaintiff is not privy to the contract under which the payment is made, see *Greene v Hughes Haulage Ltd* unrep. HC, 28 June 1997; Irish Times Law Report, 29 September 1997.

made for the value of rights accrued, or likely to accrue, in respect of injury benefits or disablement benefits, for a period of five years, dating from the accrual of the cause of action.[57] If the five years has not expired by the trial date, the onus is on the plaintiff to establish that the Department of Social Welfare intend to alter the level of benefits provided, in order to avoid the full deduction.[58]

If the plaintiff has been awarded compensation in the course of a criminal trial against the tortfeasor, in accordance with section 6 of the Criminal Justice Act 1993, then this must be deducted from any subsequent award in a civil trial.[59] If the civil award is less than the amount received under section 6, then the excess must be returned.

Medical Expenses

Reasonable medical expenses are recoverable, including the estimated cost of future care given the present prognosis of the plaintiff's position. Because of the existence of a reasonably extensive public health system, many aspects of medical care do not involve any cost to the patient, but the public system is not unlimited – some aspects of necessary treatment for tort victims may not be freely available and, in addition, many people fall outside the eligibility criteria for free services. Charges improperly imposed by a health board, or excessive charges by a private health care provider, are not recoverable,[60] so the plaintiff should consider the appropriateness of the costs sought by health care providers before paying and should not assume an automatic right to recover. What of the plaintiff who chooses private health care, where free or low cost public health care is available? It seems that the cost of such private care is recoverable where the plaintiff has evidenced a prior preference for private care, for example by subscribing to a private medical insurance scheme.[61] Byrne & Binchy are critical of this rule, as they suggest that the recovery of the cost should simply be based

---

57 S. 75(1) of the Social Welfare (Consolidation) Act 1993.
58 *O'Sullivan v Iarnród Éireann* unrep. HC, 14 March 1994, per Morris J at pp. 13–14 of the judgment.
59 S. 9 of the Criminal Justice Act 1993. S. 6 allows a court, on conviction of an accused person, to make a compensation order in favour of any person suffering personal injury or loss as a result of the offence (or any other offences taken into account in the sentencing of the accused). The order may be made in addition to any fine or term of imprisonment imposed.
60 Eligibility for free services was considered in some detail in *Cooke v Walsh* [1984] ILRM 208, at pp. 210–14 per O'Higgins CJ (Henchy, Griffin and Hederman JJ concurring); at pp. 214–15 per McCarthy J; here it was found that charges imposed by the health board on the plaintiff were *ultra vires* and the defendant had sufficient *locus standi* to question their validity; the plaintiff would have to look to the health board for the return of such expenditure. On the inability to recover excessive fees charged by a private hospital, see *Connolly v Bus Éireann and Others* unrep. HC, 29 January 1996, per Barr J at p. 31 of his judgment.
61 *Ward v Walsh* unrep. SC, 31 July 1991.

on whether it was reasonable to incur it in the circumstances and not on the prior expression of a preference by the plaintiff.[62]

Domestic Help

The plaintiff can recover the value of the provision of domestic services if the injury has impaired his self-sufficiency. There are differing views as to the nature of the loss in question. On one view it is an item of special damage, incurred only where the plaintiff expends money on the provision of such services and not available where services are provided gratuitously by the plaintiff's family. The courts modified the harshness of this approach by accepting that the gratuitous carer was entitled to reimbursement, at least where there was some moral or social obligation to provide assistance.[63] The alternative is that there is a loss to the plaintiff, because the plaintiff needs such services, independently of how they are provided. The latter view is the dominant one.[64] This raises the possibility that the loss should properly be regarded as part of lost amenity and, therefore, be considered as part of the general damages, but this does not appear to occur in practice.[65]

A difficulty may arise where the care is provided by the tortfeasor; the English approach is that no recovery is allowed, since it would benefit the wrongdoer. In *Hunt v Severs*[66] the House of Lords reverted to the view that the object of the award is to allow the plaintiff to pay the carer. On this approach the cost of services would still be available in respect of gratuitous provision, under a social or moral duty, except where the carer was the tortfeasor.

Financial Advice

The plaintiff may need professional assistance to invest the award properly, so as not to dissipate it prematurely, particularly if the plaintiff lacks the experience or capacity to handle his financial affairs. A moderate amount was allowed

---

62 *Annual Review of Irish Law 1991* at p. 444; see also White, *op. cit.* at §5.2.01.
63 *Cunningham v Harrison* [1973] QB 942; [1973] 3 WLR 97; [1973] 3 All ER 463; *Wattson v Port of London Authority* [1969] 1 Lloyd's Rep 95; Burrows, *op. cit.* at pp. 193–7.
64 *Donnelly v Joyce* [1974] QB 454; [1973] 3 WLR 514; [1973] 3 All ER 475; *Housecroft v Burnett* [1986] 1 All ER 332; *Doherty v Bowaters Irish Wallboard Mills Ltd* [1968] IR 277; *Cooke v Walsh* [1984] ILRM 208; White, *op. cit.* at §§5.6.02–5.6.05.
65 See, for example, *Hughes v O'Flaherty* unrep. HC, 19 January 1996, where significant sums were awarded in respect of family expenses, such as travel and subsistence incurred in visiting the plaintiff in hospital, and an award was made to the plaintiff's wife in respect of the provision of care; see also *Cooke v Walsh* [1984] ILRM 208, at pp. 218–19 per Griffin J.
66 [1994] 2 AC 350; [1994] 2 WLR 602; [1994] 2 All ER 385; noted by Lunz (1997) 113 LQR 201; see also Howarth, *op. cit.* at pp. 617–19.

under this head in *Ward v Walsh*,[67] giving some recognition to the fact that plaintiffs may need assistance in adapting to changed financial conditions, just as they need assistance adapting to changed physical conditions.

Actuarial Evidence

The courts often rely on actuarial evidence to assess pecuniary loss. The actuary is a specialist in calculating an appropriate capital amount to replace periodic payments over a given period of time. So, if there is evidence as to the plaintiff's weekly income and the number of working years left (based on the plaintiff's expected life span), and some estimation of the various hazards can be made, then the actuary can produce a figure by which the weekly wage is to be multiplied in order to produce a lump sum to replace the lost income.[68] The courts are not bound to follow the actuarial evidence and they should depart from the actuary's figures where it appears that the calculation process has failed to properly consider the relevant issues or where an irrelevant criterion has been included. Griffin J succinctly explained their role: 'Whilst the mathematical calculations made by the actuary are constant and correct, they should be applied in the particular circumstances of every case with due regard to reality and common sense.'[69]

Non-pecuniary Loss

The assessment of damages for matters such as pain, suffering, loss of amenity and so forth is, necessarily, an artificial exercise, as there can be no precise monetary measurement of the plaintiff's personal interest in that which has been lost. Cane describes these awards as 'essentially arbitrary and inadequate, in the sense that they are more in the nature of solace, than of recompense'.[70] The problem of assessment is most starkly evident in cases of serious, long term injury, as evidenced by the remarks of O'Higgins CJ in *Sinnott v Quinnsworth*,[71] where the plaintiff was rendered quadriplegic in a road traffic accident:

> To talk of compensating for such a terrible transformation is to talk of assaying the impossible. Nevertheless, it is this impossible task which the court must attempt in endeavouring to determine, in terms of money, compensation for such an injury. The danger is that in doing so all sense of reality may be lost.

---

67 Unrep. SC, 31 July 1991.
68 The process is considered in more detail in *Cooke v Walsh* [1984] ILRM 208, at p. 216 per O'Higgins CJ.
69 *Reddy v Bates* [1983] IR 141; [1984] ILRM 197, at p. 147; p. 201; see also *Ward v Walsh* unrep. SC, 31 July 1991; White, *op. cit.* at §§4.3.13–4.3.14; Burrows, *op. cit.* at pp. 197–8; McGregor, *op. cit.* at §§1453–1456.
70 *Op. cit.* at pp. 5–6; for detailed consideration of this head of damages see White, *op. cit.* at chapter 6; Burrows, *op. cit.* at pp. 186 *et seq.*; McGregor, *op. cit.* at §§81–82, §§1514–1529; see also Dobbs, *Remedies, op. cit.* at §8.1(4).
71 [1984] ILRM 523, at p. 532.

Since money cannot possibly compensate, [one] may question whether it matters what sum is awarded. It matters to the defendant, or his indemnifiers, and, would be a legitimate ground for complaint, if the sum awarded were so high as to constitute a punishment for the infliction of the injury rather than a reasonable, if imperfect, attempt to compensate the injured. It also matters to contemporary society if, by reason of the amount decided upon and the example which it sets for other determinations of damages . . . the operation of public policy would be thereby endangered.

This raises two distinct forms of constraint upon the assessment. One involves a balance between the interests of the parties themselves, aimed at preventing the imposition of exemplary damages in inappropriate cases; the other is a more generalised constraint, aimed at preventing a spiralling of awards and a consequential increase in insurance and other costs for a variety of activities. These are important matters in the fixing of compensation, but the latter issue raises a point of some concern – does the curbing of the quantum impair the deterrent effect of the tort process? It may be argued that the spiralling social cost of accident compensation, and the consequential rise in insurance and other costs, is a result of causing too many accidents, rather than of overcompensating individual plaintiffs. The public policy constraint, therefore, dilutes the principle of full compensation in the pursuit of a public policy objective which might be better addressed by other means.

The Chief Justice, in *Sinnott*, gave slightly more concrete form to the notion of 'realistic' levels of compensation by stating that the award should take account of the ordinary living standards in society and the things on which the plaintiff may be expected to spend the money awarded. On this basis the court set aside an award of £800,000 general damages, as it would give the plaintiff an income beyond 'even the most comfortable and best off in our community'.[72] It is open to argument whether 'ordinary living standards' is an appropriate form of measurement in respect of injuries which have placed the plaintiff in far from ordinary circumstances, but, more significantly, the judgment provides no empirical data in support of the conclusions drawn in respect of the relationship between the award and the policy issues identified.[73]

The plaintiff's lack of awareness of his injuries or loss of amenity is a factor which can be used to reduce the level of general damages awarded. In *Cooke v Walsh* the plaintiff's injuries were such as to leave him with a mental age of approximately one, with a long term prognosis of a possible rise to two. The Supreme Court found an award of £125,000 general damages to be excessive, as 'compensation should be moderate',[74] given that the plaintiff had been spared

---

72 *Ibid.*
73 For further analysis see McMahon & Binchy, *op. cit.* at pp. 800–1.
74 [1984] ILRM 208, at p. 219 per Griffin J for the majority; McCarthy J, at p. 223, expressed reservations about using lack of awareness as a reducing factor. The reduction suggests a subjective evaluation of the plaintiff's loss; subjective

much suffering because of his lack of appreciation of his condition. In *Hughes v O'Flaherty*[75] Carney J refused to make such a deduction where the plaintiff had demonstrated limited awareness of his plight. This suggests that the deduction will only be made in extreme cases, rather than being a deduction scaled in accordance with the severity of the reduced awareness.

An additional award may also be made for lost expectation of life, though the amounts awarded are usually moderate.[76] In England, awareness of lost life expectancy is considered as part of the pain and suffering award, rather than as a separate head of loss.[77]

Imposition of Tariffs

The courts have sought to impose an upper limit on the amount of general damages that may be awarded in the most serious cases.[78] In *Sinnott* the amount allowed by the Supreme Court was £150,000, which would have to be regarded as being close to that limit, given the extent of the plaintiff's injuries. Recent cases have increased the amount to £200,000 to keep pace with inflation.[79] The type of case to which this level of award is appropriate was described by Barr J, in *Connolly v Bus Éireann and Others*,[80] as 'catastrophic permanent disablement', which he went on to explain as:

> . . . major permanent personal injuries . . . which render the injured party dependent on others to maintain a viable way of life and where he/she has suffered a grievous permanent change in pre-accident capacity to lead a normal existence and to enjoy the normal range of pleasures in life which he/she might reasonably have expected to enjoy but for the injuries sustained.[81]

---

evaluation is an intrinsic part of the assessment of general damages, but there is also an objective element, based on the notion that one has a right akin to property in one's person, which is overlooked here; see White, *op. cit.* at §§6.3.01–6.3.03; Burrows, *op. cit.* at pp. 189–91. The tension between objective and subjective evaluation is also in evidence with respect to measuring damages for lost life expectancy, see White, *op. cit.* at §§6.3.09–6.3.10.

75 Unrep. HC, 19 January 1996.

76 See White, *op. cit.* at §§6.3.09–6.3.10.

77 It was abolished as a separate category by s. 1 of the Administration of Justice Act 1982; see McGregor, *op. cit.* at §83, §§1530–1531.

78 *Doherty v Bowaters Irish Wallboard Mills Ltd* [1968] IR 277; *McNamara v ESB* [1975] IR 1; *Sinnott v Quinnsworth* [1984] ILRM 523; Pierse, 'Recent Developments in General Damages' (1997) 15 ILT 58; approved by the Supreme Court in *Allen v O'Suilleabhain and the Mid-Western Health Board* unrep. SC, 11 March 1997.

79 *Connolly v Bus Éireann and Others* unrep. HC, 29 January 1996, per Barr J at p. 30 of his judgment; *Coppinger v Waterford County Council* unrep. HC, 22 March 1996; Irish Times Law Report, 15 July 1996, per Geoghegan J at p. 30 of his judgment.

80 Unrep. HC, 29 January 1996, at p. 27.

81 *Ibid.*, at p. 30.

This covers a broad range of injuries and leaves little scope for the possibility of a more serious injury. One such possibility can be seen in *Coppinger v Waterford County Council*, where Geoghegan J also allowed an additional £7,500 for loss of expectation of life, which indicates that the £200,000 tariff covers pain, suffering and loss of amenity without a diminution of life expectancy.[82] Another situation where an additional amount may possibly be awarded would be a case where aggravated compensatory damages were appropriate. Thus, the *Connolly* tariff appears to provide a maximum award for pain and suffering, but does not represent the maximum possible award of general damages; however, few cases would involve any greater amount. The recent decision in *Brady v Doherty & O'Leary*[83] is slightly out of line with the foregoing cases. The plaintiff suffered serious permanent injuries and, although he did not suffer the same loss of mobility as other plaintiffs in catastrophic cases, he suffered and will continue to suffer continuous pain 'from which in all probability he will never escape'.[84] Barr J awarded the plaintiff £280,000 in general damages, but offered no explanation as to why the award was greater than that which he himself had awarded in *Connolly*. He simply noted that he had 'taken into account the judgment of the Supreme Court in *Sinnott v Quinnsworth* and subsequent authorities which amplify the principle therein laid down'.[85]

Lesser injuries are subject to tariffs scaled back proportionately from the maximum.[86] The degree of proportion between different injuries is difficult to gauge, but rough guidance can be derived from the cases and some anomalies can also be identified by comparing different injuries. In *Griffiths v Van Raaj*[87] the Supreme Court awarded two-thirds of the *Sinnott* tariff (i.e. £100,000) in respect of 'severe and permanent intellectual and emotional impairment' and moderate physical disability. More recently, in *Sheriff v Dowling*,[88] the Supreme Court increased an award of general damages from £90,000 to £135,000, where the plaintiff suffered a back injury, which left her with permanent physical injuries, an inactive lifestyle and some psychiatric problems. Given the change in the maximum tariff, this award is comparable to that in *Griffith*.

---

82 Unrep. HC, 22 March 1996; Irish Times Law Report, 15 July 1996, at p. 31 of the judgment; see also *Hughes v O'Flaherty* unrep. HC, 19 January 1996, where an award of £225,000 general damages was made; in this case the plaintiff's loss of expectation of life was significant (assessed at 20 per cent).
83 Unrep. HC, 31 July 1998; Irish Times Law Report, 9 November 1998.
84 *Ibid.*, at p. 17 of the judgment.
85 *Ibid.*, at p. 18 of the judgment.
86 *McNamara v ESB* [1975] IR 1, at pp. 20–1 per Walsh J; pp. 28–9 per Henchy J; p. 38 per Griffin J; *Griffith v Van Raaj* [1985] ILRM 582, at p. 588 per Griffin J (Hederman J concurring); see McMahon & Binchy, *op. cit.* at p. 799; Pierse, *loc. cit.* at pp. 59–60; McGregor, *op. cit.* at §§1519–1521, §§1526–1529.
87 [1985] ILRM 582.
88 Unrep. SC, 26 May 1993; Irish Times Law Report, 13 September 1993.

Dunne v Honeywell Control Systems Ltd[89] and *Murphy v White Sands Hotel*[90] both involved foot injuries causing long term pain and permanent disability. In *Dunne* the plaintiff's position was exacerbated by the fact that he was likely to develop secondary arthritis in ten to fifteen years as a result of the original injury and the Supreme Court upheld a High Court award of £125,000 general damages. Blayney J suggested that this may have been slightly above the appropriate tariff, but not by so much as to warrant interference.[91] In *Murphy* Flood J awarded £98,600 in general damages. While the injuries in these cases were serious, it must be doubted whether they could realistically be considered to be so close to those in *Griffiths* and *Sheriff* as the awards suggest.[92] The implication is that the tariff for the more serious cases is too low or the awards in the later cases are too high.

More serious doubts are cast by examining the amounts awarded in respect of non-physical injuries. Libel cases have produced some very high awards of general damages. The Supreme Court upheld an award of £90,000 in *McDonagh v News Group*,[93] holding it to represent the upper end of the scale in respect of a libel falsely alleging that the plaintiff, a prominent barrister, was a terrorist sympathiser. The sum of £75,000 was considered the upper limit for a slander in respect of shoplifting in *McEntee and McEntee v Quinnsworth*.[94] More recently a High Court jury awarded a politician £300,000, in respect of allegations that he supported anti-Semitism and violent communist oppression and that he was involved in or tolerated serious crime.[95] Such awards demonstrate an extremely high value for reputation and a comparison between them and awards for physical injury defy rationalisation; plainly either reputation is overvalued or physical injury is undervalued. It may even be argued that both propositions are true and neither set of tariffs maintains a proper reflection of the injury involved. The relative balance between these awards has been the source of considerable academic debate, highlighting a

89 Unrep. SC, 1 July 1993; Irish Times Law Report, 15 November 1993.
90 Unrep. HC, 21 May 1993.
91 Unrep. SC, 1 July 1993 at pp. 8–9 of the judgment (Finlay CJ and O'Flaherty J concurring).
92 See also *Duffy v Rooney* unrep. HC, 23 June 1997; Irish Times Law Report, 8 September 1997, £150,000 awarded in respect of pain and suffering where a three year old had been burned, causing permanent scarring to her thigh and buttock. While the injury is serious, it does not seem to be comparable with *Griffith* and *Sheriff*, though the award is of similar magnitude.
93 Unrep. SC, 23 November 1993; Irish Times Law Report, 27 December 1993.
94 Unrep. SC, 7 December 1993; Irish Times Law Report, 21 February 1994 (the second plaintiff was awarded £60,000 by the Supreme Court).
95 *De Rossa v Independent Newspapers Ltd* Irish Times, 1 August 1997; Irish Independent, 1 August 1997; the reports do not indicate whether this includes an element of aggravated damages or exemplary damages. An award of £515,000 was held to be excessive in *Dawson v Irish Brokers Association*, unrep. SC, 27 February 1997.

similar imbalance in other jurisdictions.[96] The European Court of Human Rights has held that inordinately high damages awards violate the right to freedom of expression under Article 10 of the European Convention on Human Rights[97] and it has been suggested that the same argument should prevail in Ireland.[98]

Damages for psychological harm appear to be somewhat low, when compared to other injuries. In *Mullally v Bus Éireann*,[99] £75,000 was awarded, where the plaintiff suffered a severe change in personality, with a poor long term prognosis.[100] In *Kelly v Hennessy*[101] the Supreme Court reduced the award from £75,000 to £55,000, on the grounds that the plaintiff was expected to make a partial recovery. While these amounts are significant, they are considerably less than the awards for serious personal injury and are at a similar level to awards for moderate defamation. The type of suffering described in the reports appears to be comparable to that suffered in personal injuries cases such as *Dunne v Honeywell Control* and *Murphy v White Sands* (perhaps even *Griffiths* and *Sheriff*). It can hardly be doubted that the harm exceeds that suffered by victims of even the most serious defamations, but the awards do not compare favourably for the victims of psychological harm. Despite this, the awards in Ireland are high compared to other jurisdictions and it may be that the undervaluation of these claims is a further product of the cautious judicial attitude to them.[102]

Torts, such as trespass to the person, which are actionable *per se* tend to give rise to moderate, but significant, compensation. Compensatory awards for battery and false imprisonment can be in the region of £5,000 each, even though no significant injury results.[103] This ensures that some significant value

---

96 Tobin, 'Defamation and Personal Injury – Vindication Dethroned' (1994) 2 Tort L Rev 73; Skidmore, '"If this is Justice, I'm a Banana" (Again) or Libel Damages Revisited' (1996) 4 Tort L Rev 101; Halpin, 'Law, Libel and the English Court of Appeal' (1996) 4 Tort L Rev 139; Burrows, *op. cit.* at pp. 226–8; McDonald, *Defamation Law in Ireland*, 2nd ed. (Dublin: Round Hall Press, 1989) at pp. 240–57; LRC, *Consultation Paper, op. cit.* at §§108–128; LRC 38–91, *op. cit.* at §§63–68; see also the Law Reform Commission proposals on declaratory relief, for the purpose of vindication – LRC, *Consultation Paper, op. cit.* at §134; LRC 38–91, *op. cit.* at §§70–74.

97 *Tolstoy-Miloslavski v UK* (1995) EHRR 422; followed in *Elton John v Mirror Group Newspapers Ltd* [1997] QB 586; [1996] 3 WLR 593; [1996] 2 All ER 35.

98 Kennedy & Reed, 'A Delicate Balancing Act – Defamation, Damages and Freedom of Expression' (1996) 14 ILT 215.

99 [1992] ILRM 722.

100 *Ibid.*, at pp. 727–30.

101 [1995] 3 IR 253; [1995] 1 ILRM 321.

102 See Mullany & Handford, *Tort Liability for Psychiatric Damage* (Sydney: Law Book Co., 1993) at chapter 13, for comparison of the awards in various jurisdictions.

103 See *McIntyre v Dolan & Lewis* [1991] 1 IR 121 (£5,000 for battery and false imprisonment awarded in the High Court and upheld on appeal; £5,000 for

is seen to attach to the rights infringed and plaintiffs are given some sense of vindication in respect of the affront suffered. Reported cases are rare, so it is difficult to determine whether the figures in the cases represent an upper limit.[104] Any consequential harm, flowing from the tort, will necessarily increase the award, as the plaintiff will have to be compensated both for the actual harm and for the more abstract interference with rights.

There has been some considerable public debate on damages in recent years, fuelled mainly by concern over rising insurance costs. The possibility of introducing statutory controls to reduce the level of damages was considered. A report to the government in 1996 recommended that statutory measures should not be introduced to cap the level of damages in personal injuries cases, finding no significant support for the view that our courts overcompensate victims.[105] One significant suggestion in the report for reducing costs is that a personal injury tribunal should be introduced. It would fix the amount of compensation in cases where there is no dispute as to liability and injuries are moderate.

Property Damage and Economic Loss

The measurement of compensation for damage to property and economic loss is generally less complicated than personal injuries compensation. Nevertheless, there are occasional difficulties, which must be approached with some care.

---

malicious prosecution awarded by the Supreme Court); *McEntee and McEntee v Quinnsworth* unrep. SC, 7 December 1993; Irish Times Law Report, 21 February 1994 (£5,000 for assault [*sic*] and £5,000 for false imprisonment awarded to the first plaintiff; £5,000 for assault [*sic*] and £15,000 for false imprisonment awarded to the second plaintiff); *Thompson v Commissioner of Police of the Metropolis* [1997] 3 WLR 403; [1997] 2 All ER 762 (award of £1,500 arising from a wrongful detention and malicious prosecution; the Court of Appeal stated that £10,000 general damages and £10,000 aggravated damages would be more appropriate to the wrong); see also McGregor, *op. cit.* at chapters 35 (trespass to the person) and 36 (malicious prosecution and abuse of process).

104 The cases in the previous footnote all involved significant damages under other headings (exemplary damages, defamation). A moderate award for trespass or malicious prosecution as part of a larger award should not necessarily set the tariff for cases where the whole of the award is addressed to the trespass or malicious prosecution. In *Thompson v Commissioner of Police of the Metropolis* [1997] 3 WLR 403; [1997] 2 All ER 762, for example, the jury awarded £50,000 exemplary damages; the Court of Appeal felt that £25,000 was more appropriate; however, since the total jury award of £51,500 was not significantly disproportionate to the amount the Court of Appeal felt was appropriate (£45,000), the original award was allowed to stand. The Court of Appeal decision is more instructive on the appropriate tariff than the jury award.

105 Deloitte Touche, *Report on the Economic Evaluation of Insurance Costs* (Dublin: Department of Enterprise and Employment, 1996); 'Counting the Cost of Personal Injuries' (Editorial) (1996) 2 Bar Rev 48; Pierse, 'Irish Insurance Costs and Damages' (1997) 15 ILT 15; Kelleher, 'Cutting the Cost of Personal Injury Claims' (1995) 13 ILT 253.

Land and Goods

Where a plaintiff's existing property is damaged, as a result of the defendant's tort, then 'compensatory aims dictate that the plaintiff should be put into as good a position as if his property had not been damaged'.[106] The difficulty is that there are two methods of measuring loss and they do not always produce the same quantum for a given item of damage. One method of assessment is to measure the diminution in value of the particular item of property. This is found by subtracting the market value of the property in its damaged state from its market value in an undamaged state. The alternative method is to measure the cost of cure, i.e. the cost of repairing or replacing the damaged property. In some cases these two methods will coincide, but this will not always be the case. Repairing, in particular, can often exceed the diminished value, while replacement will sometimes require the plaintiff to buy a more expensive equivalent for the lost item.[107]

The law does not automatically opt for the lowest available valuation of the damage, but rather seeks to choose the valuation appropriate to the particular circumstances of the case. Courts look at the surrounding circumstances in order to determine which valuation is reasonable and the plaintiff must be able to demonstrate some good reason for selecting the more expensive route where the disparity is significant.[108] If the property has some esoteric value, which the law recognises as important, then the higher measurement will be regarded as reasonable and appropriate. Recognised value would include buildings of historical importance or with some long term family association;[109] goods with a sentimen-

---

106 Burrows, *op. cit.* at p. 156; see also *Murphy v Wexford County Council* [1921] 2 IR 230, at p. 240 per O'Connor J, cautioning against enriching, rather than compensating, the aggrieved party.

107 In the case of real property, it is often difficult to find a replacement property which exactly matches that which has been damaged. In the case of goods, the plaintiff will often have to buy a new item to replace one which was destroyed, as there may be no second-hand market to provide an exact replacement. It is worth noting that in defective buildings cases, although the loss may be categorised as pure economic loss, damages are calculated under the same principles as physical damage to land. See, for example, *Colgan v Connolly Construction* [1980] ILRM 33, where the cost of repair (assessed at £300) was awarded. See also *Junior Books Ltd v Veitchi Co. Ltd* [1983] AC 520; [1982] 3 WLR 477; [1982] 3 All ER 201; *Invercargill City Council v Hamlin* [1996] AC 624; [1996] 2 WLR 367; [1996] 1 All ER 756.

108 *Munelly v Calcon Ltd* [1978] IR 387, at p. 400 per Henchy J; pp. 405–7 per Kenny J; *Dodd Properties (Kent) Ltd v Canterbury City Council* [1980] 1 All ER 928; Burrows, *op. cit.* at pp. 156–65; Cane, *op. cit.* at pp. 92–5.

109 *Murphy v Wexford County Council* [1921] 2 IR 230, at p. 235 per Sir James Campbell C, *obiter*; see also *Hollebone v Midhurst & Fenhurst Builders Ltd* [1968] 1 Lloyd's Rep 38 (rebuilding cost of domestic residence allowed); *Dominion Mosaics & Tile Co. v Trafalgar Trucking Co. Ltd* [1990] 2 All ER 246 (relocation costs for an ongoing business allowed); in *Munelly v Calcon Ltd* [1978] IR 387, rebuilding costs of £65,000, for a building valued at £35,000, were rejected by the Supreme Court, as the plaintiff could have obtained a similar

tal value;[110] or any property with unique features, which defy accurate market valuation. This recognises that non-pecuniary aspects of property rights exist and merit vindication in appropriate cases. Furthermore, the courts do not ordinarily deduct from the award any beneficial effects of repair or replacement. Thus, a plaintiff may be left with a slightly more valuable item than that which was damaged. If the disparity is great, however, a deduction will probably be made.[111]

Torts involving interference with property, but without causing any physical damage, also raise problems with assessment. Torts such as trespass to land or chattels, detinue or conversion can involve misuse or misappropriation without any damage to the property. A common measure for such interference is the market cost for use or acquisition of property, i.e. the defendant will be obliged to pay a rental or purchase value for the interference.[112] This may be used as an economic measure of the value of the plaintiff's interest, even though the plaintiff would not have actually rented or sold the property.[113] In some cases, however, the plaintiff will seek a restitutionary remedy, rather than compensatory damages, claiming the gain made by the defendant out of the tort. This may exceed the compensatory damages, particularly where the plaintiff was unlikely to have exploited the profitable potential of the property.[114] This approach has a similar effect to the award of exemplary damages, where the defendant has calculated to make a profit from the tort – the award seeks to deprive the defendant of the unjust enrichment, even though the enrichment does not reflect any loss suffered by the plaintiff.

---

property elsewhere for £35,000, without any disruption to business; see also *C.R. Taylor (Wholesale) Ltd v Hepworths Ltd* [1977] 1 WLR 659; [1977] 2 All ER 784 (rebuilding costs rejected, as ownership of the property was always intended as an investment, rather than an ongoing business); *Sunderland v McGreavy* [1987] IR 372 (cost of rectifying property of £100,000 disproportionate to value of property, approximately £45,000; £22,500 diminution of value awarded).

110 *O'Grady v Westminster Scaffolding Ltd* [1962] 2 Lloyd's Rep 238, repair costs awarded in respect of a car, despite exceeding the cost of replacement; justified by the plaintiff's attachment to the car, evidenced by the fact that he had personally maintained the car, expending considerable time and effort, prior to the accident which damaged it; contrast *Darbishire v Warran* [1963] 1 WLR 1067; [1963] 3 All ER 310, where the car had no special significance and only the diminution in value was allowed (cost of replacement, less scrap value).

111 See Burrows, *op. cit.* at pp. 166–7; McMahon & Binchy, *op. cit.* at pp. 810–11.

112 See Burrows, *op. cit.* at pp. 167–71; an unusual variation can be seen in *Livingstone v Rawyards Coal Co.* [1879–80] 5 App Cas 25, the defendant company trespassed and mined the plaintiff's land; damages measured by reference to appropriate royalty payments, as the plaintiff was not in a position to exploit the mining potential himself; see also *Inverugie Investments Ltd v Hackett* [1995] 1 WLR 713; [1995] 3 All ER 841; noted by Trindade (1996) 112 LQR 39.

113 *Whitwham v Westminster, Brymbo, Coal & Coke Co.* [1896] 2 Ch 538; *Swordheath Properties Ltd v Tabet* [1979] 1 WLR 285; [1979] 1 All ER 240.

114 See Burrows, *op. cit.* at pp. 288–307.

Pure Economic Loss

Some torts do not involve any interference with the plaintiff's tangible property, but merely cause interference with intangible economic rights. Torts in respect of which pure economic loss is the more usual form of harm suffered include negligent misstatement, deceit, passing off and the various torts dealing with interference with economic relations. There are also various instances where a duty of care may be owed, under the tort of negligence, in respect of pure economic loss.[115] The appropriate measure of loss will vary for the different wrongs; for example, the negligent drafting of a will deprives the beneficiary of the intended legacy, while passing off deprives the plaintiff of profit from potential business with deceived customers and a misrepresentation can cause the recipient to invest in a worthless venture. The general principle is that the plaintiff can recover expenses incurred and gains forgone, provided they are not too remote.[116]

The most difficult area in practice is measuring loss for misrepresentation, whether in negligence or deceit. The objective is to put the plaintiff in the position he would have been in had the representation not been made (not the position he would have been in had the representation been true).[117] This is because the purpose of compensation in tort is to undo the wrong, rather than to fulfil false expectations. Misrepresentations are tortious only when they induce detrimental reliance, i.e. when the recipient acts on foot of the representation and suffers harm as a result, and it is this which the law seeks to undo. Many misrepresentations lead to the purchase of property and, in such cases, the normal measure of loss is the difference between the price paid on foot of the misrepresentation and the market value of the property at the time of purchase.[118]

Consequential Loss

Damage or interference with property or economic rights can give rise to secondary losses. For example, incidental expenses may be incurred in acquiring a replacement for property that has been destroyed;[119] profits from the use of

---

115 See chapters 1 and 2 *supra*.
116 See Burrows, *op. cit.* at pp. 176–86.
117 *Northern Bank Finance Corp. Ltd v Charlton* [1979] IR 149; *Doyle v Olby (Ironmongers) Ltd* [1969] 2 QB 158; [1969] 2 WLR 673; [1969] 2 All ER 119 (deceit); *Esso Petroleum Co. Ltd v Mardon* [1976] QB 801; [1976] 2 WLR 583; [1976] 2 All ER 5 (negligence); see Burrows, *op. cit.* at pp. 172–6; McGregor, *op. cit.* at §§1718–1721 for consideration of the general principle; §§1723–1733 on the measure for cases where a contract results from deceit; §1734 where deceit causes pecuniary loss, other than through a resultant contract; §§1740–1741 for losses in negligence cases.
118 *McAnarney v Hanrahan* [1994] 1 ILRM 210; *Gardner v Marsh & Parsons* [1997] 3 All ER 871.
119 The destruction of a dwelling will often force the owner to rent alternative accommodation, while seeking to rebuild or to purchase another dwelling; some damages for

property may be lost, while awaiting repair or replacement.[120] Subject to the rules on remoteness, these additional losses are ordinarily recoverable. Care must be taken, however, to ensure that the loss has actually occurred. If, for example, the plaintiff has been compensated for the destruction of a building, based on diminution of value (on the assumption that it was owned as an investment for resale), then he cannot also recover lost profit in respect of use. This is simply because one cannot simultaneously sell and use the same item of property.[121]

Appellate Courts

An appeal may be made by either party in respect of the quantum of damages. The traditional approach was that an appeal court could only overturn an award if it was grossly disproportionate to the injury suffered.[122] There has been a slight variation in the approach with the introduction of itemised awards. In the case of pecuniary loss, obvious calculation errors may be corrected, even if the adjustment is relatively small. In the case of general damages and, perhaps, damages for pecuniary loss involving a significant degree of discretion (where, for example, there is conflicting evidence with respect to the appropriate level of earnings or the likely impact of hazards), the traditional rule still applies. In respect of general damages, the difference between the amount awarded and the amount that the appeal court regards as appropriate 'must be a significant percentage of that item of the award, as a general rule not less than 25 per cent', in order to justify intervention.[123] A mere difference of opinion on the part of the

---

inconvenience may also be awarded, in recognition of non-pecuniary aspects of the plaintiff's property rights; see *Ward v McMaster* [1988] IR 337; [1989] ILRM 400; a more unusual example of expenses incurred in consequence of a tort can be seen in *Wall v Hegarty* [1980] ILRM 124, where the plaintiff, a beneficiary and the executor of a will, recovered legal expenses incurred in proceedings defending the validity of the will negligently drafted by the defendant (in addition to compensation for the failure to receive the benefit under the will), see chapter 2 *supra*.

120 *Rabbette v Mayo County Council* [1984] ILRM 156 provides an unusual example of lost profit; the defendant's nuisance caused a loss of profit on the sale of the plaintiff's property (not unusual in itself), but the interruption to the cash flow of the business caused, *inter alia*, a loss of profits on subsequent opportunities for development, some of which were recoverable; see chapter 11 *supra*, for further details of the consequential losses.

121 A limited amount of lost profit on use may be recoverable, if it can be shown that there would have been a delay in completing a sale and that profitable use was likely during the interim.

122 *McGrath v Bourne* (1876) IR 10 CL 160; *Foley v Thermocement Products Ltd* (1954) 90 ILTR 92.

123 *Reddy v Bates* [1983] IR 141; [1984] ILRM 197, at p. 151; p. 205 per McCarthy J, suggesting that the principle applied to general damages only. It may be argued, however, that where special damages involve significant discretion, the level of value judgment (as opposed to precise objective calculation) makes the decision making process sufficiently analogous to the intuitive process involved in assessing general damages and the same rule should apply to both in respect of appeals.

appeal court as to the appropriate amount is, therefore, not a sufficient ground to overturn an award; the award must exceed a relatively wide margin of error (approximately 25 per cent in either direction).

If the award is by a jury and the defendant appeals on the grounds that the award is excessive, then the appeal court must take the plaintiff's case in its strongest light on the evidence.[124] This approach means the appeal court will only set aside an award which exceeds the maximum possible award and will not attempt to second guess the jury on the appropriate weight to attach to the evidence. If the plaintiff appeals from a jury award on the grounds that it is too low, then the appeal court must take the weakest view of the plaintiff's case on the evidence, setting aside only those awards which fall below the minimum possible amount. Thus, juries are left with a relatively broad field of discretion, within which an appeal court will not interfere. If the award is by a judge, without a jury, the appeal court must base its decision on the facts found by the judge, unless they are wholly unsupported by the evidence.[125] There is no need for the appeal court to make any assumptions on the strength or weakness of the plaintiff's case, because the judge's decision will contain detailed findings and an indication of the weight attached to the various items of evidence. Jury trials have been abolished in the lower courts since 1971 and in most High Court personal injuries actions since 1988.[126] The rules with respect to appeals from juries, therefore, are confined to High Court trials for torts such as defamation and intentional trespass to the person.

When an award is set aside, the appeal court has a discretion as to whether to send the case back to the lower court to assess damages or to substitute its own award for that which has been appealed.[127] A substituted award will usually be made if a retrial on damages would involve unnecessary or disproportionate costs on the parties.[128] A retrial would usually be ordered where there was a lack of evidence on significant aspects of the award and a considerable level of damages was involved.[129] The consent of the parties is not required for the substitution of

---

124 *Foley v Thermocement Products Ltd* (1954) 90 ILTR 92, at p. 94 per Lavery J; *Holohan v Donoghue* [1986] ILRM 250, at p. 255 per Finlay CJ.

125 *Sheriff v Dowling* unrep. SC, 26 May 1993; Irish Times Law Report, 13 September 1993; *Dunne v Honeywell* unrep. SC, 1 July 1993; Irish Times Law Report, 15 November 1993.

126 S. 6 of the Courts Act 1971; s. 1 of the Courts Act 1988, considered briefly in chapter 4 *supra*; see also 'Restoration of the Jury Trial for Personal Injury Actions' (Editorial) (1995) 13 ILT 153.

127 Art. 34.4.3 of the Constitution; s. 96 of the Courts of Justice Act 1924, re-enacted by s. 48 of the Courts (Supplemental Provisions) Act 1961.

128 *Gahan v Engineering Products Ltd* [1971] IR 30, award of £2,000 substituted for £3,200 general damages; *Holohan v Donoghue* [1986] ILRM 250, award of £55,000 general damages for the future reduced to £30,000; almost eight years had already elapsed from the time of injury and detailed medical evidence of the plaintiff's prognosis had already been presented and was not in dispute.

129 See, for example, *Cooke v Walsh* [1984] ILRM 208.

an award and a retrial need not necessarily be granted even if the parties would prefer one.[130]

The appeal court has a discretion to admit new evidence in exceptional circumstances, where justice requires it. This discretion will be exercised where the new evidence shows that the original judgment was based on a fundamental assumption of fact which is false, but not where the new evidence simply relates to uncertainties within the trial court's realm of discretion.[131] Thus, new evidence relating to matters such as the likely effects of inflation, taxation and unemployment or the long term prognosis for the plaintiff's injury will not be admitted. If, however, the parties had proceeded on the assumption that the plaintiff would continue in employment, at a reduced rate of income, and it transpires shortly afterwards that he is unable to do so, then evidence of the further loss of income may be allowed by the appeal court.[132]

Injunctions

An injunction is a preventive, rather than a compensatory, remedy, which can be used 'to restrain the threatened infringement, or the continued or repeated infringement, of some legal right'.[133] The remedy is more explicitly protective than damages, which is primarily a form of restoration and vindication. Injunctions are sought because a plaintiff will often be more concerned with avoiding harm than with compensation after harm has been suffered. There are significant limits to the availability of injunctions to restrain the commission of torts, and damages remain the principal remedy.[134]

The law governing injunctions is extensive, as the remedy is available in respect of a wide variety of legal and equitable interests and the law of torts is but one of its many fields of application. This section will outline the general principles governing injunctions and examine specific aspects of their use in the law of torts. As an equitable relief, the injunction is discretionary and the principles outlined are guidelines, rather than definitive rules. The classification of injunctions is based on a number of overlapping distinctions, rather than discrete and

---

130 *Hosty v McDonagh* unrep. SC, 29 May 1973; *Holohan v Donoghue* [1986] ILRM 250, at p. 254 per Finlay CJ; at p. 261 per Henchy J.

131 *Murphy v Stone Wallwork (Charlton) Ltd* [1969] 1 WLR 1023; [1969] 2 All ER 949; *Mulholland v Mitchell* [1971] AC 666; [1971] 2 WLR 93; [1971] 1 All ER 307; *Lim Poh Choo v Camden & Islington Area Health Authority* [1980] AC 174; [1979] 3 WLR 44; [1979] 2 All ER 910; *Fitzgerald v Kenny & Fouhy* unrep. SC, 24 March 1994; Irish Times Law Report, 23 May 1994; Burrows, *op. cit.* at p. 106; McGregor, *op. cit.* at §§1437–1444.

132 As occurred in *Fitzgerald v Kenny & Fouhy* unrep. SC, 24 March 1994; Irish Times Law Report, 23 May 1994.

133 Meagher, Gummow & Lehane, *Equity, Doctrines and Remedies*, 3rd ed. (Sydney: Butterworths, 1992) at §2105.

134 For a discussion of the relative merits of injunctions and damages see Burrows, *op. cit.* at pp. 399–403.

exclusive divisions.[135] The law distinguishes, for example, between prohibitory and mandatory injunctions and also between temporary and permanent injunctions; but the temporary injunction may be either prohibitory or mandatory, as may the final injunction. It is simpler and more beneficial to set out the main distinctions than to set out an exhaustive list of the possible permutations.

Quia Timet *Injunctions and Injunctions After the Commission of a Wrong*

The *quia timet* injunction is used where the defendant has not yet committed any wrong, but the plaintiff can establish a strong probability that a wrong is about to occur.[136] The more usual type of injunction is one granted after the commission of a wrong, in order to prevent the continuation or repetition of the wrong. The *quia timet* injunction is pre-emptive and the courts are cautious about exercising their authority against a defendant who has, as yet, done no wrong to the plaintiff. Nonetheless, such injunctions are occasionally granted.

The types of tort most likely to give rise to applications for *quia timet* injunctions are nuisance, trespass to land and economic torts, such as passing off and interference with economic relations.[137] This is so because the fact situations involved in these torts often involve the plaintiff having knowledge of the defendant's activities prior to the completion of the tort. Negligence is particularly unsuited to the granting of injunctions, since advance knowledge of imminent risk either does not arise or arises too late to prevent it. There is, however, no principled objection to granting an injunction against anticipated harm from a breach of a duty of care.[138]

There are some situations where there are special principles, limiting the availability of *quia timet* injunctions. One is where the plaintiff seeks to restrain a media publication; another involves trade disputes. Prior restraint on the media is a significant interference with freedom of expression and the courts have shown a considerable reluctance to order 'gagging writs', as they

---

135 See Meagher, Gummow & Lehane, *op. cit.* at §2102; Keane, *Equity and the Law of Trusts in the Republic of Ireland* (London: Butterworths, 1988) at §15.02; Delany, *Equity and the Law of Trusts in Ireland* (Dublin: Round Hall Sweet & Maxwell, 1996) at pp. 370–2.

136 *AG (Boswell) v Rathmines & Pembroke Joint Hospital Board* [1904] 1 IR 161, at pp. 171–2 per Fitzgibbon LJ; at p. 188 per Walker LJ; at p. 198 per Holmes LJ; *Independent Newspapers Ltd v Irish Press Ltd* [1932] IR 615, at pp. 631–2 per Meredith J; see also *Redland Bricks Ltd v Morris* [1970] AC 652; [1969] 2 WLR 1437; [1969] 2 All ER 576; *Szabo and Others v Esat Digiphone Ltd* unrep. HC, 6 February 1998; Irish Times Law Report, 20 April 1998; Burrows, *op. cit.* at pp. 389–90 and pp. 420–2; Keane, *op. cit.* at §15.32; Delany, *op. cit.* at pp. 401–3.

137 See, for example, *Goodhart v Hyatt* (1883) 25 Ch D 182; *Dicker v Popham Radford & Co.* (1890) 63 LT 379 (nuisance); *C & A Modes v C & A (Waterford) Ltd* [1976] IR 198 (passing off); *Francombe v Mirror Group Newspapers Ltd* [1984] 1 WLR 892; [1984] 2 All ER 408 (breach of confidence; breach of statutory duty).

138 See Meagher, Gummow & Lehane, *op. cit.* at §2120.

are colloquially described.[139] The law does not preclude the granting of *quia timet* injunctions against the media, but the plaintiff would be expected to show a more pressing case than someone seeking to prevent a nuisance or passing off. In the area of trade disputes, the Industrial Relations Act 1990 has restricted the availability of injunctions, including *quia timet* injunctions. An injunction may not be granted to restrain industrial action resulting from the outcome of a secret ballot, provided notice has been given to the employer and the defendant can establish a fair case that the action is in contemplation or furtherance of a trade dispute.[140] This restriction applies to torts interfering with economic rights (like interference with contractual relations), but not to trespass to property or physical damage to property or persons.[141]

Prohibitory and Mandatory Injunctions

A prohibitory injunction is negative in substance, requiring the defendant to refrain from engaging in or continuing conduct which would constitute a wrong against the plaintiff. Examples would include injunctions requiring the defendant to withhold publication of defamatory material or to discontinue work which would give rise to a nuisance.[142] A mandatory injunction requires the defendant to actively engage in conduct to undo a wrong or to remove a source of risk. Examples would include injunctions to remove material which constitutes a trespass on the plaintiff's land or to restore support wrongly removed from the plaintiff's land.[143] Prohibitory injunctions are more common, but there is no principled distinction on the availability of the two types, though it is generally harder to satisfy the general criteria in the case of mandatory injunctions.[144]

---

139 See *Maguire v Drury* [1995] 1 ILRM 108, involving an unsuccessful attempt to restrain the publication of details of the plaintiff's marital breakdown; one of the grounds on which the application was based was the potential psychological harm to the children, see pp. 114–17 for consideration of freedom of expression; see also *X v RTÉ* unrep. SC, 27 March 1990; noted by Byrne & Binchy, *Annual Review of Irish Law 1990* at pp. 534 *et seq.*; *NIB Ltd v RTÉ* [1998] 2 ILRM 196 (on appeal from the order of Shanley J, unrep. HC, 6 March 1998); *R. v Central Independent Television plc* [1994] Fam 192; [1994] 3 WLR 20; [1994] 3 All ER 641; McGonagle, *A Textbook on Media Law* (Dublin: Gill & Macmillan, 1996) at pp. 169 *et seq.*; McDonald, *op. cit.* at p. 262. *Reynolds v Malocco & Others*, unrep. HC, 21 December 1998 is a rare example of a successful application.
140 S. 19(2); notice must be at least one week, the ballot must conform to the principles in s. 14 and the dispute must fall within the definition in s. 8.
141 The limits of the prohibition are set out in s. 19(4).
142 See Burrows, *op. cit.* at pp. 391–403; see also *Parsons v Kavanagh* [1990] ILRM 560; *Lovett v Gogan* [1995] 1 ILRM 12 (injunctions prohibiting further breaches of statutory duty).
143 *Kelsen v Imperial Tobacco Co.* [1957] 2 QB 335; [1957] 2 WLR 1007; [1957] 2 All ER 343 (respondent ordered to remove a sign trespassing on the applicant's air space); *Allen v Greenwood* [1980] Ch 119; [1979] 2 WLR 187; [1979] 1 All ER 819 (respondent ordered to remove a caravan and a fence, which were blocking light to the applicant's greenhouse); see Burrows, *op. cit.* at pp. 414–18 and pp. 440–3.
144 In the early development of injunctions the mandatory one was significantly more

Interim, Interlocutory and Perpetual Injunctions

Interim and interlocutory injunctions are temporary measures, employed prior to a full trial of the issues between the parties and usually based on affidavit evidence, whereas the perpetual injunction is a final remedy, granted after a full trial.

The interim injunction is an emergency measure, of short duration, usually obtained on an *ex parte* application.[145] Section 19(1) of the Industrial Relations Act 1990 precludes the use of *ex parte* applications against industrial action.[146] The types of case where it might be employed would be one where the plaintiff has just discovered a serious risk of harm and the delay caused by giving notice for an interlocutory injunction would allow the harm to occur; for example, the plaintiff may discover that a neighbouring business has begun to emit hazardous waste, which has a known link with certain illnesses, or is about to commence blasting operations, with a significant risk of physical damage to the plaintiff.[147]

The interlocutory injunction is designed to preserve the status quo until a full trial of the issues. It is usually granted where the plaintiff can show that there is a serious question to be tried and the 'balance of convenience' favours granting the injunction.[148] The 'serious question' requirement falls short of requiring the plaintiff to show a probability of success at trial, while the 'balance of convenience' comprises a number of factors, such as the adequacy of damages for each party; the likelihood that such damages will be recovered; the behaviour of the parties; or special circumstances, related to the particular facts of the case.[149]

---

difficult to obtain, but the judicial hostility waned at the end of the nineteenth century; see Meagher, Gummow & Lehane, *op. cit.* at §§2191–2197; Burrows, *op. cit.* at pp. 388–9; Keane, *op. cit.* at §15.02; Delany, *op. cit.* at pp. 386–9; Dobbs, *Remedies, op. cit.* at pp. 163–4.

145 The application is one made without giving prior notice to the other party and only lasts until the hearing of interlocutory proceedings; see Keane, *op. cit.* at §15.27; Delany, *op. cit.* at p. 371; see also Dobbs, *Remedies, op. cit.*, at §2.11(2) on temporary injunctions in general.

146 The action must be in compliance with secret ballot procedures and at least one week's notice must be given to the employer for the prohibition to take effect.

147 In cases of false imprisonment an *ex parte* application may be appropriate where the prisoner is imminently likely to be removed from the jurisdiction, *O'Boyle v AG* [1929] IR 558, at p. 566 per Meredith J, *obiter*; false imprisonment is ordinarily dealt with under the *habeas corpus* procedure in Art. 40.4 of the Constitution, rather than by injunction.

148 *American Cyanamid Co. v Ethicon Ltd* [1975] AC 396; [1975] 2 WLR 316; [1975] 1 All ER 504; *Campus Oil Ltd v Minister for Industry and Energy (No. 2)* [1983] IR 88; *Westman Holdings Ltd v McCormack* [1992] 1 IR 151; [1991] ILRM 833; *Symonds Cider & English Wine Co. Ltd v Showerings (Ireland) Ltd* [1997] 1 ILRM 481; Meagher, Gummow & Lehane, *op. cit.* at §§2167–2182; Burrows, *op. cit.* at pp. 423 *et seq.*; Keane, *op. cit.* at §§15.22–15.26; Delany, *op. cit.* at pp. 390 *et seq.*; Byrne & Binchy, *Annual Review of Irish Law 1991* at pp. 190 *et seq.*; *1992* at pp. 315 *et seq.*; *1993* at pp. 284 *et seq.*

149 *Moloney v Laurib Investments Ltd* unrep. HC, 20 July 1993, Lynch J refused an interlocutory injunction in a personal injuries action, where the plaintiff would have

There are certain situations where some modification is required. First, if the application is also *quia timet*, the plaintiff will have to show more than a serious question and will have to demonstrate the probability that a tort is imminent.[150] Secondly, in defamation cases the courts are particularly reluctant to grant injunctive relief, because of the restriction on freedom of expression and an injunction will almost invariably be refused if the defence of justification is pleaded.[151] Thirdly, section 19(2) of the Industrial Relations Act 1990 precludes the use of interlocutory injunctions on the same conditions as it prohibits *quia timet* injunctions.[152] Fourthly, in cases of trespass to land, where the plaintiff can clearly establish title, it may fall to the defendant to establish a serious question to be tried on the availability of a defence.[153] This reverses the usual burden of proof and provides valuable protection for the non-economic aspect of ownership, particularly where the plaintiff can show no risk of actual harm. Finally, if a full trial is unlikely and the interlocutory ruling is likely to end the matter, then the relative strength of the parties' prospects of success on a full trial may form the basis of the decision.[154]

Two specialised forms of interlocutory injunction are worthy of particular mention – the *Mareva* injunction and the *Anton Piller* order (both of which are named after the seminal cases in which they were developed). The *Mareva* injunction is used to prevent a defendant from removing assets from the jurisdiction or dissipating assets, in a manner designed to frustrate the plaintiff's claim.[155]

---

been unable to compensate the defendant for losses incurred; the injunction could also have prejudiced the interests of the defendant's creditors; in *Egan v Egan* [1975] Ch 218; [1975] 2 WLR 503; [1975] 2 All ER 167, the plaintiff obtained interlocutory injunctions against her son requiring him to vacate her home, not to attempt to re-enter and not to assault or harass her; while injunctive relief is rare in respect of trespass to the person and in family disputes, the established history of assaults and present threat of further assaults were sufficient to convince the court to grant the relief in this case; in *DSG Retail Ltd v PC World Ltd* unrep. HC, 13 January 1998; Irish Times Law Report, 16 March 1998, a large disparity of economic strength was held to be a relevant factor in declining an interlocutory injunction.

150 This results from the fact that *quia timet* injunctions require the plaintiff to show a strong probability that harm is likely; see footnote 136 *supra*.
151 *Sinclair v Gogarty* [1937] IR 377; *X v RTÉ* unrep. SC, 27 March 1990; *Connolly v RTÉ* [1991] 2 IR 446 (HC); LRC, *Consultation Paper, op. cit.* at §137; LRC 38–91, *op. cit.* at §§9.1–9.2.
152 See footnote 140 *supra*.
153 *Woolerton & Wilson Ltd v Richard Costain Ltd* [1970] 1 All ER 483; *Patel v W.H. Smith (Eziot) Ltd* [1987] 1 WLR 853; [1987] 2 All ER 569; this may be part of a more general exception where there is little or no dispute on the facts and the law is relatively straightforward, see Burrows, *op. cit.* at pp. 439–40.
154 *NWL Ltd v Woods* [1979] 1 WLR 1294; [1979] 3 All ER 614; *Lansing Linde Ltd v Kerr* [1991] 1 WLR 251; [1991] 1 All ER 418; see also Burrows, *op. cit.* at pp. 432–4.
155 *Mareva Compania Naviera SA v International Bulk Carriers SA* [1975] 2 Lloyd's Rep 509; *Nippon Yusen Kaisha v Karageorgis* [1975] 1 WLR 1093; [1975] 3 All ER 282; *Countyglen plc v Carway* [1995] 1 ILRM 481; see Meagher, Gummow &

The object of the relief is to preserve sufficient assets to meet the plaintiff's claim, should the action succeed at trial. There are no specific causes of action to which the *Mareva* injunction is particularly suited; it is particular factual circumstances which indicate its appropriateness. The most common factual element giving rise to its use is a lack of substantial connection between the defendant and the jurisdiction in which the assets are held (and in which the action is taken). The *Anton Piller* order is akin to a private search warrant, in that it requires the defendant to allow the plaintiff to enter premises and seize documents or property in cases where there is a serious risk that the defendant will destroy the evidence.[156] It is predominantly used in respect of suspected interference with intellectual property rights. Due to the invasive nature of both of these types of injunction, they are used sparingly and only in cases where the plaintiff is able to demonstrate a strong case for their necessity.[157]

Perpetual injunctions are granted after a full trial, where it would be unjust to confine the plaintiff to the remedy of damages. As the remedy is discretionary, the court will take account of other relevant considerations, particularly the conduct of the parties.[158] The main difference between the perpetual injunction and the temporary orders is the degree of proof required.

Damages in Lieu of Injunctions

If the plaintiff applies for an injunction, but the court exercises its discretion against granting the relief sought, the plaintiff will not necessarily be left without redress. The court may award damages instead, to compensate the plaintiff for the anticipated harm.[159] Without this power the courts would be faced with denying the plaintiff any remedy, despite the anticipated commission or continuance of a

---

Lehane, *op. cit.* at §§2185–2190 (particularly critical of this form of injunction); Keane, *op. cit.* at §§15.34–15.41; Delany, *op. cit.* at pp. 415 *et seq.*; Samuel & Rinkes, *Law of Obligations and Legal Remedies* (London: Cavendish, 1996) at p. 115 on the distorting effects that this type of injunction can have on substantive rights.

156 *Anton Piller KG v Manufacturing Processes Ltd* [1976] Ch 55; [1976] 2 WLR 162; [1976] 1 All ER 779; see Meagher, Gummow & Lehane, *op. cit.* at §§2198–2199 (particularly critical of this form of injunction); Keane, *op. cit.* at §15.42; Delany, *op. cit.* at pp. 427 *et seq.*; Samuel & Rinkes, *op. cit.* at pp. 115–16; two limiting factors curbing its use are (i) the remedy must be proportionate to the risk involved – *Lock International plc v Beswick* [1989] 1 WLR 1268; [1989] 3 All ER 373; and (ii) the defendant may be able to plead the privilege against self-incrimination – *Rank Film Distributors Ltd v Video Information Centre* [1982] AC 380; [1981] 2 WLR 668; [1981] 2 All ER 76.

157 The judgment of Girvan J in *Group 4 Securitas v McIldowney* unrep. HC of Justice (NI), 13 February 1997; Irish Times Law Report, 12 May 1997 warns against using such applications as a trawling exercise, in the vague hope of finding some evidence.

158 Keane, *op. cit.* at §§15.08–15.09; Delany, *op. cit.* at pp. 372–82; Burrows, *op. cit.* at pp. 391–9 and pp. 414–18.

159 S. 2 of the Chancery Amendment Act 1858; damages at common law would be confined to the consequences of a completed tort only, but damages in equity can be granted in respect of future wrongs, such as the continuation of a nuisance or trespass.

wrong; or alternatively, granting an unsuitable remedy, thereby prejudicing the defendant. Judicial guidelines indicate that damages may be awarded, allowing the tort to continue, in the following circumstances:

   (i) the injury to the plaintiff is slight;
  (ii) it is capable of estimation in monetary terms;
 (iii) the amount involved is small;
 (iv) the injunction would have an oppressive impact on the defendant;
  (v) the defendant has not acted in disregard of the plaintiff's rights.[160]

The application of these guidelines to a tort action is demonstrated in *Falcon Travel Ltd v Owners Abroad Group plc*.[161] The defendants were using the name 'Falcon' in their Irish operation, as they had traded under this name in the UK for a number of years. In a passing off action Murphy J awarded damages, assessed as the cost of advertising the fact that the two businesses were unconnected. Damages were appropriate because the confusion generated by the defendants was unintended, the plaintiff had suffered no trading losses and developing a new identity for their Irish sub-division, different from the UK parent company, would impose inordinate expense on the defendants.

Self-help

The law does not generally encourage victims to exact justice on wrongdoers personally, but there are limited instances where a person may be allowed to take unilateral steps to ameliorate the effects of wrongdoing. The two areas of the law of torts where self-help is permitted are the defence of persons and property and the abatement of a nuisance or trespass to land. The role of self-protection and the protection of third parties as a defence to a trespass action has already been considered and we have seen that it is an exceptional course of action, permitted only in limited instances.[162] We have also seen that malicious retaliation to a nuisance can itself be a nuisance, so that the initial victim becomes the wrongdoer.[163]

Abatement, however, differs from retaliation, as it involves the taking of steps to stop the nuisance or trespass, rather than simply reciprocating the disruption. In simple cases of nuisance or trespass, such as overhanging

---

160 *Shelfer v City of London Electric Lighting Co.* [1895] 1 Ch 287; [1891–4] All ER Rep 838; *Patterson v Murphy* [1976–7] ILRM 85, in both cases the guidelines were stated *obiter* and the injunctions sought were actually granted because there was significant material damage to property; see Meagher, Gummow & Lehane, *op. cit.* at §§2306–2321; Keane, *op. cit.* at §15.08 and §15.33; Delany, *op. cit.* at pp. 382–6.
161 [1991] 1 IR 175, considered in chapter 7 *supra*.
162 Chapter 4 *supra*.
163 Chapter 5 *supra*; but there will be no nuisance if the malicious behaviour does not infringe any legally protected right, as in *Bradford Corporation v Pickles* [1895] AC 587; [1896–9] All ER Rep 984.

branches or the once-off dumping of rubbish, the expense of legal proceedings may be unjustified and the plaintiff may resort to self-help. If the interference is significant or there are significant factual or legal issues in dispute, then self-help will not be justified. The proper limits of self-help are imprecise, but a reasonable picture can be gleaned by contrasting *Lemmon v Webb*[164] with *Burton v Winters*.[165] In *Lemmon* the defendant, while remaining on his own property, cut overhanging branches from the plaintiff's trees, without notice. This was held to be lawful and did not infringe any right of the plaintiff's. It was stated *obiter* that, if someone wished to enter a neighbour's property to abate a nuisance, then he could only do so in an emergency or if he had given the neighbour notice to abate which had not been complied with.[166] In *Burton* the plaintiff failed to obtain a mandatory injunction requiring the defendant to remove a garage wall, built by a predecessor in title, which encroached on the plaintiff's property by a few inches. The plaintiff was subsequently restrained from retaliating by deliberately attempting to build on the defendant's land and was found guilty of contempt after damaging the garage on a number of occasions. The attempt to abate by knocking the wall was held to exceed the parameters of lawful self-help and the case was one where the plaintiff was confined to a remedy in damages. Lloyd LJ stated that 'the courts have confined the remedy of self-redress to simple cases such as an overhanging branch, or an encroaching root, which would not justify the expense of legal proceedings, and urgent cases which require an immediate remedy'.[167]

Self-help may involve the incurring of expenditure, such as the hire of a truck for the disposal of refuse. Reasonably incurred expenses are recoverable as damages resulting from the initial tort, but in practice the amount may not be sufficient to justify litigation.

Alternative Dispute Resolution

Non-judicial remedies, other than self-help, may be employed to resolve tort disputes. Most cases are actually settled by negotiation before trial. This form of settlement is generally the result of negotiations between the parties' lawyers and is heavily influenced by the principles applicable to judicial remedies.[168] Such settlements are often completed just as the trial is about to

---

164 [1895] AC 1; [1891–4] All ER Rep 749.
165 [1993] 1 WLR 1077; [1993] 3 All ER 847.
166 [1895] AC 1; [1891–4] All ER Rep 749, per Lord Herschell LC at p. 5; pp. 750–1; see also Lord Davey at p. 8; p. 752.
167 [1993] 1 WLR 1077; [1993] 3 All ER 847, at p. 1081; p. 851.
168 See Cane, *Atiyah's Accidents, Compensation and the Law*, 5th ed. (London: Butterworths, 1993) at chapter 10; MacFarlane (ed.), *Rethinking Disputes: The Mediation Alternative* (London: Cavendish Publishing, 1997) at pp. 6–7; Noone, 'Mediating Personal Injuries Disputes' in MacFarlane (ed.), *op. cit.* at p. 28.

begin, so much of the time and expense associated with the litigation process is still incurred by the parties.

Disputes may also be resolved by arbitration, conciliation or mediation. Arbitration is a form of private adjudication, outside the formal court system. The arbitrator will not be a serving judge and will usually be an independent expert in the field of activity with which the dispute is concerned. This method of dispute resolution is not generally of relevance to tort disputes, but may have applications in respect of economic torts where the parties are in a continuing relationship.[169] Its main advantages are that it is less formal, faster and often cheaper than litigation.

Conciliation and mediation are non-adjudicative processes in which the parties are personally involved in the negotiations and an independent third party acts to facilitate them in reaching a solution. The principal difference between the two is that a mediator takes a more active role than a conciliator in bringing the parties to a negotiated solution. The main advantages of this type of approach are that the parties themselves are more actively involved, the process is not adversarial and interests other than legal rights recognised by the courts can be taken into consideration.[170] The combined effect is that the process is more inclusive and user friendly to the parties. It can also be faster and cheaper than resort to the courts. Mediation may be particularly useful in respect of nuisance cases and can even be of benefit in quantum disputes in personal injury cases, where liability is not in doubt.[171]

---

169 Industrial relations disputes, in particular, may be better dealt with by arbitration, rather than litigation.

170 See MacFarlane (ed.), *op. cit.* at chapter 1; Cane, *op. cit.* at pp. 372–7; Bevan, *Alternative Dispute Resolution* (London: Sweet & Maxwell, 1992) at chapters 2 and 3 on the role of mediation in general as an alternative to litigation, identifying several key factors in assessing the suitability of a dispute for this form of resolution; Cane, *op. cit.* at pp. 364–6 on the particular relevance of conciliation and mediation to tort disputes.

171 See Liebmann, 'Community and Neighbourhood Mediation: A UK Perspective' in MacFarlane (ed.), *op. cit.*; Marshall, 'Neighbour Disputes: Community Mediation Schemes as an Alternative to Litigation' in Mackie (ed.), *A Handbook of Dispute Resolution* (London: Routledge, Sweet & Maxwell, 1991) (nuisance); Noone, *loc. cit.* (personal injury); *First Report of Special Working Group on a Personal Injuries Tribunal* (Dublin: Department of Enterprise and Employment, 1997) recommending a mediation service, attached to the courts, in respect of quantum disputes.

The Role of Tort Law: Development and Appraisal

Introduction

The foregoing text has set out the fundamental rules upon which tort law is founded. Though it might have seemed long and detailed to the first time student, it barely scratches the surface of a vast subject. The aspects of the law covered in the text provide the raw materials, from which one can go on to develop a deeper understanding of the law. This afterword seeks to offer a few pointers on going further down the road of deeper understanding. Three areas of significance are highlighted. The first is alternative compensation systems; to evaluate the tort system effectively, one must have some knowledge of alternative means of attaining its goals, for comparative purposes.[1] Secondly, the relationship between torts and other aspects of law and society must be considered; like any other facet of life, tort does not stand alone in splendid isolation and self-sufficiency. Its interplay with other areas is a vital ingredient of its functioning in practice. The final issue is alternative views of the structure and nature of tort law; no one view of this subject can provide a complete picture and this text has merely provided one perspective; many other perspectives are available, each presenting its own unique insight. The consideration of as many views as possible provides one with the opportunity to form an informed opinion, thereby building one's own perspective.

Alternative Compensation Systems

There is a considerable amount of academic writing devoted to reform of tort law, a significant volume of which is devoted to alternative forms of compensation.[2]

---

1 For detailed treatment of the objectives of tort law, see England, *The Philosophy of Tort Law* (Aldershot: Dartmouth, 1993); Cane, *Atiyah's Accidents, Compensation and the Law*, 5th ed. (London: Butterworths, 1993) at chapter 18; Cane, *Tort Law and Economic Interests*, 2nd ed. (Oxford: Clarendon, 1996) at chapter 10; for critical appraisal of tort law see also Owen (ed.), *Philosophical Foundations of Tort Law* (Oxford; Clarendon Press, 1995) Bayles & Chapman, *Justice, Rights and Tort Law* (Dordrecht: Reidel, 1983).

2 An excellent outline of American reform proposals over the course of the twentieth century can be found in Nolan & Ursin, *Understanding Enterprise Liability: Rethinking Tort Reform for the Twenty-First Century* (Philadelphia: Temple University Press, 1995); for a comparison and evaluation of American tort law and alternative approaches to the aims of tort law, based on empirical data, see Dewees et al., *Exploring the Domain of Accident Law* (New York: Oxford University Press, 1996); see Atiyah, *op. cit.* at chapter 19 in respect of proposals for English law.

The primary focus of such writing is personal injuries compensation. There are two distinct types of alternative structure proposed – first party insurance and a state run administrative tribunal. The key feature of both is that they operate on a no fault basis, allowing an injured person to recover on proof of suffering injury within the scope of the scheme, without having to establish a failure of duty on the part of some person responsible for causing the harm. A key feature of such proposals is that they are focused predominantly on compensation, thus not corresponding precisely with the objectives of tort law and, consequently, making comparison difficult.[3] To fully consider the implications of such alternative systems one must either find other means to address the remaining objectives of tort law, to complement the compensation system, or alternatively make a conscious choice to change the objectives of the law.

First party insurance is where a person pays a premium to an insurance company, which in turn agrees to pay a prescribed level of compensation to that person, if a specified risk materialises during the period covered by the policy. This is a two party arrangement, involving a contract between the insured person and the insurance company, for the protection of the insured against particular losses; the contract specifies the risks covered and the rate of payment. Once a loss, covered by the contract, is suffered by the insured, a claim for payment can be made and there is no need to establish the liability of a third person and no need to establish that the loss was wrongly inflicted on the insured. This is quite distinct from third party insurance (liability insurance), under which the insurance company agrees to compensate any other person for harm tortiously inflicted on them by the insured. People obtain first party insurance to protect against loss to themselves, while third party insurance is obtained to cover losses inflicted on others for which the insured is legally liable.

First party insurance is commonly available on an optional basis for many risks. Most people insure their home and its contents; many also obtain comprehensive cover for their vehicles, protecting against damage to their own vehicles, in addition to damage inflicted on others (which is the third party element of such policies); protection against medical expenses and loss of income, resulting from serious illness, is also becoming widespread and many commercial risks can also be insured against (insurers can even obtain reinsurance, protecting them against loss of profits due to high levels of claims being made against them). As the legal system is presently structured, the insurance company has a right of subrogation, which allows it to pursue any legal rights the insured person had in respect of the loss. This means that, if the loss was tortiously inflicted on the insured, the insurance company has a right

---

3 Stapleton, 'Tort, Insurance and Ideology' (1995) 58 MLR 820 emphasises the ideological differences between first party insurance and tort law which make comparison difficult and potentially misleading; Dewees et al., *op. cit.* provides a rare exception to the focus on compensation – the work also focuses on penal and regulatory approaches to the objectives of tort law.

to pursue the tort claim and thereby recover some or all of the payment made to the insured.[4]

One method of reform would be to introduce compulsory first party insurance for specified risks and remove the availability of a tort action (and the insurer's right of subrogation) in respect of those risks. This approach would facilitate the compensatory aim of tort law and has the potential to be significantly faster in making awards at a lower administrative cost than the tort process. The primary reason for these potential benefits is that the need to establish liability issues such as breach of duty and proximate cause is removed and litigation against a tortfeasor does not have to be taken. Furthermore, insured persons unable to establish a tort claim would be entitled to compensation they would not otherwise receive. The disadvantage of this approach is that it does not fulfil functions such as vindication, corrective justice, deterrence and prevention; furthermore, the contributions to the system come from those at risk, which means that it is the potential victims that provide the financial pool for their own compensation.

There are areas of activity to which this approach may be suited however. If the activity is one where compensation is the primary goal, secondary aims of the tort system are not of any great practical significance and the pool of potential victims corresponds with the pool of potential risk creators, then first party insurance may be more effective and efficient than tort law. Road accidents are a potential candidate for this type of approach. The deterrent effect of tort law is likely to be slight (for reasons considered in the introduction to this text), corrective justice is already offset by the availability of liability insurance, and vindication, in the sense of gaining public recognition that the other driver was wrong, is not really necessary. If the system is confined to motorists, thereby leaving pedestrian injuries to another system, then the potential victims are also the risk creators and an element of both distributive and corrective justice can be attained.[5] Corrective justice is attained, not in the individualised sense of one to one pairings of wrongdoer and victim that the tort system uses, but a more collective correction, based on wrongdoers paying into the victims' compensation pool.

Medical injuries provide an example of cases unsuited to this type of approach; vindication and deterrence are more significant features of such cases and the pools of victims and risk creators are distinct. However, McCarthy J, in *Hegarty v O'Loughran*,[6] takes a different view: 'The case for a no fault system of compensation for those who suffer injury as a result of medical treatment seems so strong as to be virtually unanswerable.' Certainly, a no fault scheme would make compensation available to those suffering adverse effects of medical treatment where there has been no lack of care by their doctors. Perhaps, if

---

4   For a comparison of first party insurance and tort, see *Atiyah, op. cit.* at pp. 245 *et seq.*
5   See Dewees et al., *op. cit.* at chapter 2.
6   [1990] 1 IR 148, at p. 164.

such a scheme was accompanied by a scheme for complaints in respect of malpractice (for the purposes of vindication of patients and censure of errant practitioners), a satisfactory balance could be attained and significant improvements on the present law could be achieved.

The other main alternative is a state run administrative scheme, as a hybrid arrangement combining features of first party insurance and social security systems. Entitlement to compensation would arise as a result of suffering a loss covered by the scheme, without the need to establish the liability of a wrongdoer. The scheme would operate in place of the tort system, so no civil action against a wrongdoer would be available for recovery of compensation (though actions for punitive damages could still be permitted). Financing would come either from general taxation or through licence fees for risk generating activity.

This approach focuses primarily on compensation, but does so in a manner which is significantly different from tort law. Because the wrongdoing of a third party does not have to be established, the range of claimants would be wider than under the tort system, as persons unable to identify a defendant, or unable to establish one or other of the necessary ingredients of a tort action, would be permitted to recover. The increase in the number of persons protected is offset by excluding damages for pain and suffering; thus, proposals for such a scheme generally favour recovery of lesser amounts of compensation to a larger group of victims. The object is to produce a situation whereby the overall compensation bill is roughly the same under the scheme as that under the tort system, but the number of people sharing in the payout is greater.

The significant advantage of this approach is that it can make compensation available to those falling outside the tort system (because of an inability to establish some necessary ingredient) and who are unable to obtain or are otherwise unsuited to first party insurance. Distributive justice can be attained by spreading loss, either amongst society as a whole or amongst those engaging in risk generating activity. The choice as to which group the cost should be imposed on is primarily political, but the imposition of costs on risk generators would give the system a corrective element similar to first party insurance. Such a scheme would not address the other aims of tort law and, consequently, would need to be complemented by administrative, regulatory and penal measures, to aid deterrence and prevention of injury.

The only jurisdiction to go as far as implementing a comprehensive no fault liability scheme is New Zealand. The scheme was first introduced by the Accident Compensation Act 1972 (which came into effect from April 1974) and the present scheme is contained in the Accident Rehabilitation and Compensation Insurance Act 1992. This state run scheme covers accidentally inflicted personal injuries. Tort actions for such injuries have been abolished, though tort actions remain for damage to property and economic losses and for

wilfully inflicted personal injuries.[7] A number of American states have introduced first party insurance schemes for motor accidents, and administrative
schemes for workers' compensation for occupational injuries are also prevalent.[8]
The reports in Ireland and England on compensation reform have not favoured
abolition of tort and the introduction of a comprehensive alternative system, so
radical reform seems unlikely at present and the tort system will remain for the
immediate future.[9]

There have, however, been some *ad hoc* departures from tort principles in
limited instances. Occupational injuries were dealt with under a special scheme
until the introduction of the Social Welfare (Occupational Injuries) Act 1966
brought such cases within the general social welfare structure.[10] Some special
provisions still apply to occupational injuries suffered by police officers.[11]

There have been two particularly notable instances where the Irish legislature
has seen fit to respond to particular disasters by the setting up of compensation
tribunals, as an alternative to the tort process. The first was the Stardust Victims'
Compensation Tribunal, set up in response to a fire in a night club which killed
and injured a large number of young people and seriously traumatised survivors
and the families of the immediate victims. The tribunal was established by
resolution of both Houses of the Oireachtas on 22 October 1985 and made
payments, on an *ex gratia* basis, totalling almost £10.5 million, compensating 823
people.[12] The second was the Hepatitis C Compensation Tribunal, established by
statute to deal with victims who contracted Hepatitis C from infected blood
products.[13] Both of these tribunals were established as a result of public dissatis-

---

7 For a review of the general working of the scheme and the difficulties encountered
   in its implementation see New Zealand Law Commission Report No. 4 – *Personal
   Injury: Prevention and Recovery* (Wellington: New Zealand Law Commission,
   1988).
8 See Prosser et al., *Prosser & Keeton on Torts*, 5th ed. (St Paul, Minn.: West, 1984)
   at chapter 14.
9 Deloitte Touche, *Report on the Economic Evaluation of Insurance Costs*, (Dublin:
   Department of Enterprise and Employment, 1996); Pearson Commission Cmnd
   7054.
10 See also Part II, Chapter 5 of the Social Welfare (Consolidation) Act 1981 and
   Part II, Chapter 10 of the Social Welfare (Consolidation) Act 1993; the relationship between social welfare benefits and tort compensation has been considered
   already in chapter 15 *supra*.
11 Garda Síochána (Compensation) Acts 1941 and 1945.
12 *Report of the Stardust Victims' Compensation Tribunal* (Dublin: Stationery Office,
   1991).
13 Hepatitis C Compensation Tribunal Act 1997; the Act also permits claims by
   family members to whom infection was passed on, s. 4(c), and persons suffering
   financially in providing care for an infected person, s. 4(d); the Act also provides
   for action by dependants, where the infection has contributed to the death of the
   infected person, s. 4(e); there is also a ministerial power in s. 9 to extend the class
   of eligible persons.

faction with the normal legal process as a means of dealing with the injuries suffered. The major advantage of such tribunals is that the adversarial aspect of the legal process is removed and the victims can also be given a sense of vindication through having their suffering recognised as an exceptional situation, meriting special attention. The process can also avoid delays experienced in the legal system. Furthermore, the claims are less fragmented, as they are all considered by a single tribunal, rather than being dispersed among several courts throughout the country.

There is no provision in Irish law to deal with mass disasters by way of a class action, as occurs in American law. The class action is a useful device for dealing with large scale injuries, involving multiple victims and multiple tortfeasors. Typically this would arise in the case of a dangerous product, where many manufacturers would release similar products, all with the same defect, or a number of industries would emit similar toxins into the environment. Individual actions by all victims would be extremely difficult as it would often be impossible to trace a connection between a specific manufacturer and a specific victim. The class action allows a representative case to be taken and, if successful, this forms the basis of a scheme of compensation covering all victims and wrongdoers.[14] Unless such a process is adopted in Ireland, we will have to continue to operate on the basis of *ad hoc* responses to unusual situations which strain the effectiveness of the tort system in delivering a just solution.[15]

Relationship and Interaction with Other Subjects

The introduction to this text sketched some of the comparisons and contrasts between tort and other legal categories, such as contract and criminal law; further interaction was noted from time to time, during the treatment of the substantive rules of tort law (for example, the integrity of the rules of contract as a policy argument in negligence in chapter 1; concurrent liability in contract and tort in chapter 2; rules of criminal procedure in respect of entry, search and seizure as a defence to trespass in chapter 4). A practising lawyer needs an awareness of a variety of such interactions, in order to deal effectively with his clients' needs. The practitioner may find that the information presented by a client raises issues in a number of branches of law and must try to adopt an appropriate strategy to maximise the benefit to the client (without transgressing ethical barriers). Thus, an action in trespass, or even private nuisance, may be an appropriate vehicle to deal with a property dispute between neighbours, but the outcome will princi-

---

14 For a general description of the process see Fleming, *The American Tort Process* (New York: Oxford University Press, 1988) at chapter 7; for an extensive examination of the workings of the process in a specific instance see Schuck, *Agent Orange on Trial: Mass Toxic Disasters in the Courts* (Cambridge, Mass.: Belknap Press, 1986) (dealing with a chemical defoliant used during the Vietnam war).

15 The potential need for the development of a form of class action in Ireland is considered by Lennox, 'Toxic Torts now a Reality in Ireland' (1997) 15 ILT 236.

pally turn on rules of property law rather than tort. In a dispute between commercial rivals, a possible instance of passing off may also have to be examined in the light of other aspects of intellectual property law and even competition law, before determining the appropriate strategy to adopt. It is essential, therefore, for a lawyer to integrate his knowledge of tort with knowledge of other legal subjects.[16] It is vital that knowledge be integrated; a general awareness of different compartments of knowledge is inadequate, as it fails to consider the interplay between different fields of law – the policy arguments on the boundary between contract and tort provide a useful example (likewise, the policy issues raised by public authorities' liability, which raise important questions about the relationship between private and public law).

For the non-practitioner, knowledge of the relevance of other branches of law is also of vital importance. Whether one is merely an interested observer or an active critic promoting law reform, understanding and appraisal of tort law requires an awareness of its interaction with other legal spheres. If one is considering the protection afforded to consumers by the tort of negligence, one also has to have an awareness of protective legislation in criminal and contract law, designed to benefit consumers. An apparent shortfall in tortious protection may well be remedied by such a provision. Likewise, if one is assessing nuisance as a means for environmental protection, tort law cannot be considered in isolation. Statutory provisions must also be considered and public law remedies against relevant agencies may also be of central importance.

From this brief sketch we can see that tort law cannot be understood in isolation from other areas of law. To examine rules of tort on their own can give a distorted view of the law. Similarly, to consider only legal aspects of the subject can also have a distorting effect. The law does not operate in either an abstract or an ideal context; it operates in the real world and is influenced by both legal and non-legal forces. This text has only given some general indications of the values reflected in the law (such as the tension between individual autonomy and paternalism in trespass or the balance between self-responsibility and responsibility towards others in negligence, contributory negligence and causation). Critical appraisal of the law must embrace a variety of perspectives if it is to be thorough and effective.

Two major practical issues which impinge on the functioning of tort law are the legal process itself and liability insurance. The legal process involves both expense and delay, which must be taken into account when evaluating the effectiveness of the law and the strength of the values it protects. Both personal injuries cases and defamation have recently been subjected to considerable examination on the influence of the legal process on the rights

---

16 The relationship between tort and other legal subjects is considered extensively in Cane, *op. cit.* at chapter 6; see also Fridman, *The Law of Torts in Canada* (Toronto: Carswell, 1989) vol. 2, at chapter 17.

and values involved in those branches of tort law.[17] The influence of the legal process on defamation is particularly interesting; in theory one would think that interests in personal safety, bodily integrity, property and economic rights would be more important than reputation, yet in practice, defamation cases involve extremely high stakes for both sides. The costs and potential damages payable in defamation cases are high in comparison to personal injuries cases and belie their relative theoretical importance.

Liability insurance has a significant bearing on the extent and manner in which tort law attains its objectives. The widespread availability of insurance has greatly assisted the pursuit of the compensatory goal of tort law. Few plaintiffs are now faced with a defendant who is unable to pay, as an insured target can usually be found and the rules in relation to concurrent wrongdoers ensure that the insured defendant can make up for the insolvency or lack of insurance of other tort-feasors. In some instances one can see the courts straining the interpretation of legal rules in order to impose liability on an insured (or solvent) defendant, where rigid adherence to legal theory and a strict interpretation of principles would suggest that the plaintiff should fail.[18]

The widespread use of liability insurance has a distributive effect, spreading the cost of compensation amongst the risk creators. Commercial entities can, in turn, pass on their insurance costs to the general public, through pricing of goods and services. Private individuals, such as motorists, are not normally in a position to defray the cost of liability insurance, but there is, nonetheless, a significant distributive effect. Thus, despite the corrective format which the rules of tort take (defendant liable to compensate plaintiff for damage proximately caused by a breach of duty), the practical effect of the system is distributive. There is, consequently, a significant disparity between the theoretical conception of justice which has been central to the development of modern tort law (corrective justice) and the practical effect of the rules in society. Whether this disparity is a cause for concern is as much a matter of political choice as of legal principle. It is open to debate as to whether the distributive effect of insurance is just or unjust and readers must form their own views as to whether the present provision of compensation to victims and the distribution of the cost amongst society is fair.

The availability of liability insurance may also reduce the deterrent effect of tort law, but does not necessarily do so. In theory, the fact that the defendant

---

17 Deloitte Touche, *Report, op. cit.*; Atiyah, *op. cit.* at chapters 8–10 and 17 (personal injuries); McGonagle, *A Textbook on Media Law* (Dublin: Gill & Macmillan, 1996), see chapter 15, p. 135; McGonagle (ed.), *Law and the Media* (Dublin: Round Hall Sweet & Maxwell, 1997) (defamation).

18 *Moynihan v Moynihan* [1975] IR 192 and *Phelan v Coillte Teo.* [1993] 1 IR 20, considered in chapter 14 *supra*, are good examples; Stapleton, *loc. cit.* at pp. 823–9, argues that there is little evidence to suggest that the availability or non-availability of liability insurance has a significant effect on substantive rules of tort law.

does not have to actually pay the plaintiff's compensation should remove the deterrent effect of tort law. However, a successful action against a defendant may lead to an increase in his subsequent insurance premium; furthermore, any claim will involve some degree of inconvenience for the defendant, and involvement in litigation, even without the risk of financial penalty, can be a stressful experience. Consequently, the impact of insurance on deterrence may not be significant in practice.

Beyond these forces, which are intimately connected with the legal process, there are many jurisprudential perspectives which cover a broad range of non-legal forces relevant to understanding and critically assessing the law. General schools of legal thought, such as realist jurisprudence, and sociological analysis of law apply as much to tort law as they do to other branches of law.[19] More specific critiques of tort law can be found in schools of thought such as economic analysis of law,[20] feminist legal theory[21] and the critical legal studies movement,[22] all of which deal extensively with various political and social values reflected in the law.

Alternative Classification and Evaluation

The manner in which a subject is set out affects our understanding of it; there is a natural tendency to initially structure one's understanding of an area in the format in which it was learned. A more sophisticated understanding comes from considering different perspectives, which allows us to find links between areas that we initially conceived as being quite distinct. Such rearrangements can also highlight anomalies or expose facets of the law which had previously gone unnoticed. All of the various texts referred to throughout this work have their own unique structure, within which they present the law of torts and each has its own merits. Furthermore, many monographs and journal articles adopt different structural approaches as analytical tools in the examination of particular facets of the law. Students should consider as many different approaches as possible, in order to form their own picture of the subject, its role and its effectiveness.

---

19 For an introduction to realist jurisprudence see McCoubrey & White, *Textbook on Jurisprudence*, 2nd ed. (London: Blackstone, 1996) at chapters 9 and 10; for an introduction to sociological analysis see Cotterrell, *The Sociology of Law*, 2nd ed. (London: Butterworths, 1992).

20 Landes & Posner, *The Economic Structure of Tort Law* (Cambridge, Mass.: Harvard Univerity Press, 1987); Cane, *op. cit.* at pp. 473 *et seq.*

21 Bender, 'A Lawyer's Primer on Feminist Theory and Tort' (1988) 38 J of Legal Educ 3; Bender, 'Changing the Values in Tort Law' (1990) 25 Tulsa LJ; Bender, 'Feminist (Re)torts: Thoughts on the Liability Crisis, Mass Torts, Power and Responsibility' (1990) Duke LJ.

22 Abel, 'Torts'; Horwitz, 'The Doctrine of Objective Causation' both in Kairys (ed.), *The Politics of Law*, 2nd ed. (New York: Pantheon, 1990); Conaghan & Mansell, *The Wrongs of Torts* (London: Pluto, 1993).

515

This text has deliberately focused on the nominate causes of action themselves as a means of listing the various torts, in order to give students an idea of the fragmented nature of the subject. The grouping of some torts is based on common features of their constituent elements. Even within the structure offered in this text, one could make an argument for placing the strict duties (covered in chapter 6) and the generic tort of interference with economic relations (covered in chapter 7) in the first section on 'umbrella' torts, given their diverse contents. They were omitted from that section on the grounds that they are not sufficiently developed as general torts and are still confined to particular situations.

Other texts which deal with torts on the basis of setting out the constituent elements of the various actions and the general rules of the tort process use various ways of grouping issues. Street, for example, uses groupings including 'intentional invasion of interests in person and property' (covering the trespass torts and conversion and providing separate chapters on persons, goods and land);[23] 'intentional interference with economic interests' (covering torts such as deceit, passing off, injurious falsehood, unlawful interference with trade and so forth); 'negligent invasions of interests in person and property and economic interests' (negligence); 'invasions of interests in persons and property where intentional or negligent conduct need not always be proved' (covering torts such as product liability, nuisance, *Rylands v Fletcher*, breach of statutory duty). This structure focuses on the behavioural standards as a key feature of the law of torts and the primary means to classifying the nominate torts. This is a traditional approach to tort law, focusing on the wrongfulness of conduct as the central theme of the subject as a whole. It is also commonplace to provide separate chapters on matters such as product liability and employer's liability (including both negligence and statutory duty). Stanton departs from this approach and focuses on the interests protected by tort law, using divisions including 'personal injuries and death' (with separate chapters on intentionally inflicted injury, negligently inflicted injury and strict liability); 'economic interests' (again dealing separately with intentional infliction, negligence and strict liability); 'torts concerning land' (with chapters on trespass and nuisance and one with miscellaneous matters such as negligence, *Rylands v Fletcher* and fire). This shifts the emphasis from torts as a correction of wrongs to tort as a means of protection for various interests. This shift presents us with a symbolic shift of emphasis and a focus on a different range of issues for evaluating the law.

A more dramatic and far reaching restructuring can be found in works such as Cane, *The Anatomy of Tort Law*,[24] and *Atiyah's Accidents, Compensation*

---

23 Given the survival of negligent trespass in Ireland, this approach would be misleading in an Irish text.
24 (Oxford: Hart, 1997).

and the Law and in monographs on various aspects of tort law.[25] Atiyah focuses on accident compensation, rather than tort law as a whole, and offers an insightful critique of tort principles. The work focuses predominantly on the role of fault and on aspects of the tort process in practice, rather than on a theoretical statement of the rules of nominate torts. Cane eschews entirely the classification of torts by reference to nominate torts and instead focuses on the key features of tort law to present 'a system of ethical rules and principles of personal responsibility for conduct'.[26] The entirety of the subject is analysed on the basis of a threefold grouping of issues – conduct subject to sanction,[27] protected interests and sanctions. These works, and others which similarly adopt alternative approaches to the subject, offer different ways of viewing the subject. Atiyah and Cane both offer critical perspectives on the law, rather than a description of its rules, but the structures they adopt provide insights into the functioning of tort law which cannot be conveyed by the examination of distinct nominate torts. Their focus is on issues which cross the boundaries between different torts.

The net lesson to be learned from these various approaches to tort law is that no one view holds all the answers. Each approach to the subject and each method of classifying its contents brings its own insights into the subject and, to properly understand the subject and evaluate its strengths and weaknesses, one must consider as many views as possible.

---

25 Such as Cane, *Tort Law and Economic Interests, op. cit.*; Mullany & Handford, *Tort Liability for Psychiatric Damage* (Sydney: Law Book Co., 1993).
26 *The Anatomy of Tort Law, op. cit.* at p. 1.
27 'Sanction' in the sense of penalising, rather than authorising.

Index

Index

Index

Index

strict liability, 133
supplier's liability, 130–131
PROFESSIONAL DUTY, 84–91; *see also*
Professional negligence
PROFESSIONAL NEGLIGENCE, 83–98
advice, 85
advocate's immunity from suit, 41–2
concurrent liability in contract and tort,
83
contractual liability, 83, 84
duty of care, 84–91
scope of, 84–5
third party duties, 85–91
duty of care to third parties
auditors and accountants, 33–4, 90–91
doctors, 88–90
solicitors, 85–8
misstatements, 85
standard of care, 91–8
informed consent to medical
treatment, 95–8
standard practices within the
profession, 92–3
types of conduct, 94–5
statements, 85
PROFESSIONAL STANDARD OF CARE, 91–8
PROHIBITORY INJUNCTIONS, 499, 500
PROOF, 398–411
appealing findings of fact, 409–11
burden of proof, 50–51, 399–401
res ipsa loquitur, 51, 402–06
standard of proof, 400
criminal and civil law, distinction
between, 8
types of evidence, 407–09
PROPERTY
damage to, 51, 52–3. *see also* Economic
loss
actions on the case, 357–8
compensation for, 471, 492–6
consequential economic loss, 52,
53–7, 495–6
land and goods, 493–4
nuisance, 199–200; *see also* Private
nuisance
defence of
reasonable force, 178–81
interference with. *see also* Conversion;
Detinue; Trespass to chattels;
Trespass to land
compensation, 494
non–natural use of, 226–9; *see also*
Rylands v. Fletcher liability
trespass. *see* Trespass to land

PROSECUTION OF OFFENCES
malicious prosecution, 339–43
whether duty of care owed to victims,
110
PROXIMATE CAUSE, 378n
PROXIMITY, 19–21
psychological damage, and, 61, 64, 65
PSYCHOLOGICAL DAMAGE, 57–67, 355
actions on the case, 355–7
chain of causation, 61
damages for, 491
deceit, arising from, 253–4
fatal injuries actions, 450
fear of physical injury, 58–9
fraudulent claims, 58
grief, arising from, 58
intentional infliction of, 355–7
negligent infliction of, 355
non-consequential, 58
personal injury, consequential to, 57–8
post-traumatic stress disorder, 59, 64
criteria for, 64
practical jokes, resulting from, 253–4
recovery of, in negligence actions,
57–67
judicial reluctance, 58
scope of duty of care
bystanders, 59, 60, 61, 63, 65
foreseeability, 61, 63, 65, 66
'immediate aftermath' cases, 60–67
Kelly v. Hennessy principles, 64–6
legal test, 60
parents, 59, 60, 61–2, 63–64, 66
primary and secondary victims,
distinction between, 62–63, 67
proximity, 61, 64, 65
recognised psychiatric illness, 65
relatives, 60, 62, 65, 66
rescuers, 60, 63, 67
shock-induced injury, must be, 62,
65–6
spouses, 62, 66
witnesses, 59, 60, 61, 63
PUBLIC AUTHORITIES' DUTIES, 104–10
building authorities, 108
defective housing cases, 107–08
misfeasance, 105n, 109
nature of the function, 105–06
nonfeasance
absence of liability for, 423–4
planning authorities, 108
'policy' and 'operational' decisions,
105–06

539

Index